# COLONEL HOUSE
# IN PARIS

COLONEL HOUSE

*Edward M. House Papers, Yale University Library*

*Inga Floto*

# COLONEL HOUSE IN PARIS

*A Study of American Policy at the*
*Paris Peace Conference 1919*

»It is so all over the World. Peace
must be swift if it beats anarchy.
As the pressure intensifies, the
work centers in fewer and fewer
hands – smaller conferences, quieter
discussions – inside understandings
that the painful documentary historian
will never get – and never evaluate
properly«

*(Ray Stannard Baker notebook,*
*March 18, 1919).*

UNIVERSITETSFORLAGET I AARHUS
1973

Denne afhandling er af det humanistiske fakultetsråd
antaget til offentligt at forsvares for den
filosofiske doktorgrad.

*København,* den 23. maj 1972.

*Bjarne Nørretranders*
h. a. decanus

ISBN 87 504 0320 6

PRINTED IN DENMARK BY
AARHUUS STIFTSBOGTRYKKERIE A/S
4982.72

*To Heinz*

# Preface

This book would never have been written had it not been for the help and encouragement of colleagues at various institutions, and I should like to take this opportunity of extending my sincerest thanks to them all.

Professor Sven Henningsen inspired me to undertake the project and gave me his constant support throughout the work. My colleagues, Carsten Due-Nielsen, Karl Christian Lammers, Kay Lundgreen-Nielsen and Jørgen Sevaldsen assisted with constructive criticism of the manuscript, and I am especially grateful for the fruitful research atmosphere they created. At several critical moments, Professor Povl Bagge exercised a decisive influence on my professional development; and my colleagues, Torben Damsholt, Kaj Hørby and Erik Stig Jørgensen were generous with their encouragement and support.

*Københavns Universitet* provided me with the very best conditions for research; and *Danmark-Amerika Fonden, Statens almindelige Videnskabsfond* and *Statens samfundsvidenskabelige Forskningsråd* made grants that enabled me to make two study tours to the United States.

My examination of the House Collection at the *Yale University Library* was greatly facilitated by Judith A. Schiff and her staff; and I encountered the same courteous helpfulness at the *National Archives,* Washington D. C., and the *Manuscripts Divisions* of the *Library of Congress* and the *Princeton University Library. Det kongelige Bibliotek* at Copenhagen spared no effort to fulfil even the most difficult request for books.

Mrs. Pauline M. Katborg translated the manuscript, and Art Director Ole Knappe designed the cover. Mrs. Therese Henrichsen was of great assistance, both in the typing of the manuscript, and in the trying task of proof-reading.

*Jyllinge,* April 1971 and December 1972

*Inga Floto*

# Contents

# Introduction

Edward Mandell House, for many years the close friend and adviser of Woodrow Wilson, is the principal of the following pages. Yet another attempt is made here to investigate what can be called "the House myth", viz, the background for the "break" that occurred between the President and his adviser at the Paris Peace Conference in 1919. To this end I have chosen to study House's conduct in a number of situations leading up to and during the Peace Conference, and these situations have been selected primarily because they tell us something about House. Apart from this, I have, as far as possible, described the situation independently of House, in other words, the method is not really biographical, but an attempt at combining—or perhaps, rather, compromising between—an analysis of American policy at the Peace Conference and an account of House's part in its formulation.

With such a procedure there is, of course, a risk of falling between two stools, since there is the obvious danger that neither analysis will be satisfactory. The method also has certain drawbacks as far as the actual framework of the study is concerned, the principal objection being that important problems arise and disappear in step with their relevance to House's role in a given situation. This will become particularly clear during the critical phase of the Conference after Wilson's return in the middle of March, 1919, and I have tried to remedy the worst defects by providing a very full annotation. My main reason for deciding to follow this procedure despite its obvious weaknesses is that earlier writers have chosen one or the other method and have thereby, in my opinion, reached a misleading or at least a distorted result. The literature on the subject can be roughly classified into three main themes on the reasons for the break:

The first version, which can also be called the "contemporary" or "official" version, was presented by, inter alios, Cary Grayson, Wilson's personal physician and friend, and publicly recorded by Wilson's biographer, *Ray Stannard Baker,* in his three-volume work on the Conference: *Woodrow Wilson and World Settlement,* which was published in 1923[1]). According to this interpretation, which incidentally—although on quite different premises—received the support of *Henry Wickham Steed[2]),* editor of "The Times" and definitely not a member of the clique about Wilson, the reasons for the break are primarily to be sought in House's conduct during the President's absence from the Conference in February-March 1919, and the break itself is given as having occurred in the period immediately after Wilson's return to Paris in the middle of March. Especially House's policy on the problems relating to the Preliminary Peace Treaty and the League of Nations is advanced as decisive, together with his conciliatory attitude to the French demands for a Rhenish Republic.

This theory was strongly refuted by House's official biographer, *Charles Seymour,* in his edition of House's diary and letters: *The Intimate Papers of Colonel House,* the fourth volume of which was published in 1928[3]). Using excerpts from the then still unpublished minutes of meetings of the Council of Ten, Seymour repudiated the charge that House had acted illoyally to the President in February-March 1919. At the same time, however, he admitted that House had been more willing to compromise with the Allied Powers than even Wilson himself appears to have been. This was, in fact, a not unimportant admission on the part of Seymour, because another of Baker's lines of argument was that House, by his enthusiasm for compromise both during Wilson's absence and after his return, had contributed considerably towards undermining the position of the President.

Whereas Baker viewed the Peace Conference from the angle, "Old" versus "New Diplomacy", "a conflict between the evils of the old European diplomatic system and the virtues of the new world idealism", Seymour regarded this as a gross over-simplification[4]): "Such a picture is attractive to those who will not try to understand the complexities of historical truth. In reality the Peace Conference was not nearly so simple. It was not so much a duel as a general mêlée, in which the representatives of each nation struggled to secure endorsement for their particular methods of ensuring the peace." The methods may have differed, but their aim had been the same and, according to Seymour, the American programme too, had been "coloured by self-interest." "Our interest lay entirely in assuring a regime of world tranquillity; our geographical position was such that we could advocate disarmament and arbitration with complete safety. Wilson's idealism was in line with a healthy *Realpolitik*."

Seymour may have hoped in this way to lead the debate into new paths[5]); if so, he had cause for both satisfaction and disappointment. The former, because later research did in fact accept his refutation of Baker's thesis that the February-March period had been decisive for the break, and the latter, because the next large American work on the Peace Conference again made House not only the principal, but also the scapegoat.

*Poul Birdsall*'s book: *Versailles Twenty Years After[6]),* which was published in 1941, was a contemporary attack on a generation of disillusioned Liberals and "realistic" "appeasement"-politicians. The book constituted a defence of Wilson's firm attitude and an attack on all who had been willing to compromise, i. e., first and foremost, House. According to Birdsall, House was blameworthy not only for his eagerness to compromise, which had undermined Wilson's negotiating position in a number of critical situations, but also for his internal manipulations, which had split and thus weakened the American Delegation. The decisive phase as regards the break had, however, now shifted. No longer was it the events during Wilson's absence that were regarded as decisive, but House's conduct during the Italian crisis, by which Birdsall considered that he had both split the Delegation and undermined Wilson's policy. Even though Birdsall tried to avoid personal accusations and to keep the discussion on a theoretical plane, House could not help but appear as the scapegoat par excellence, especially as Birdsall's presentation, particularly of the Italian crisis, lacked all proportion.

Seymour, too, advanced a theory on the break between the two men: It was not a question of an event that could be clearly fixed in time, but of a gradual development. This point of view was later supported by *Thomas A. Bailey*[7]) and can now be regarded as generally accepted[8]). At the same time, the research on the question has partly taken new roads, although a psychological, or psychologistic, approach to the study of Colonel House's career can hardly be called new—on the contrary, it was the angle taken quite automatically by a number of contemporary "eye-witnesses"[9]). All the same, the latest contribution within this genre must be characterized as epoch-making. *Alexander and Juliette L. George's Woodrow Wilson and Colonel House. A Personality Study,* from 1956[10]), is not just the result of close cooperation between a political scientist and a psychologist[11]), but also the first attempt at a consistent utilization of House's voluminous diary in its full, chronological scope. However, before continuing to a detailed analysis of this latest, exhaustive contribution to the discussion, it might be wise to study in a little more detail the debate on House in general.

Seymour's edition of House's papers provides a comprehensive view of House and his work; a view which later research has disputed on a number of points, but which did not meet really serious opposition until the publication by George and George of their thorough analysis of House's diary. And in my opinion, even these authors have not taken the matter to its logical conclusion because they have still accepted Seymour's evaluation of House in certain respects. The first volume of Seymour's book included a preface by House himself, in which he stated that the book was in no way a conventional apology. However, Seymour, in his subsequent preface, accepted full scientific responsibility for the edition and at the same time thanked House for his invaluable comments and advice, adding, moreover, that "(w)hatever deletions appear in the published papers have been dictated by the exigencies of space or by a regard to the feelings of persons still alive, and in no case do they alter the historical meaning of the papers." In another context, Seymour expressed his own view of House as follows: " ... Counsellor and Idealist, Wise, Courageous, Unselfish"[12]).

As source material, the book is very poor. Even its form, "arranged as a narrative" makes it difficult—and sometimes even impossible—to discover when Seymour's comments are his own views, when they are paraphrasing omitted parts of the diary, and when they are just summarizing the subsequent text. Another serious defect is the fact that, for stylistic reasons, Seymour frequently omits the date from citations. However, the main point of controversy is the actual selection, or rather, the omissions. The question is whether the selection provided is really representative, and the answer is both a yes and a no. The selection is representative in so far as it illustrates the most important aspects of Wilsonian policy and House's part in this. But even contemporary commentators pointed to a tendency to over-estimate House's role here[13]), and in the light of more recent research it must be emphasized that the picture of House as the ever loyal and unselfish adviser drawn by Seymour has, to say the least, been given a number of new facets. There were certain aspects of House's activities that Seymour simply omitted or glossed over— aspects that he did not, or would not, see. And what is more, there is a definite trend in the omissions, the question that Seymour consistently avoided was the fundamental one—the problem of House's loyalty.

One of the points on which Seymour's book is not exhaustive concerns the conversation between House and the German Ambassador, Count Bernstorff in a number of critical situations during the period of neutrality. In 1958, *Karl E. Birnbaum,* working on the basis of a telegram from Bernstorff to Auswärtiges Amt of 21 November, 1916, proved, or at any rate showed it to be highly likely, that House had not at this time interpreted with complete loyalty Wilson's ideas for a peace-move—to which House himself had been opposed—[14]). Birnbaum's not altogether positive demonstration of illoyal behaviour on the part of House is only one of many produced by later historians. It is stressed here, however, because it prompted a reply, although only an indirect one, by Seymour. In the memorial volume for G. P. Gooch in 1961, he wrote an article on *The House-Bernstorff conversations in perspective,* which can hardly have been inspired by anyone but Birnbaum[15]). What is characteristic about the article is, however, the fact that Seymour did not take up the question of House's loyalty at all, but simply wrote roughly the same as he had always written, and with the same source references. There were still sides of House that he chose to ignore.

This is not the only time in recent years that Seymour has returned to the question of House. In 1957, on the occasion of the centenary of Wilson's birth, he wrote an article, *The role of Colonel House in Wilson's diplomacy,* for inclusion in the memorial volume, giving in just a few pages a brilliant presentation of his evaluation of House's role in Wilson's foreign policy[16]). Using as a basis the greatly varying degrees of importance attached over the years to

House's influence, Seymour presented his own conviction ". . . that the reaction emphasizing the political importance of House is likely to increase in strength", but that it would at the same time become "discriminatory in character." It would be shown that House's influence had been greatest "in policies relating to Western Europe and particularly to the issues raised by the war . . . but with certain shadings in emphasis. His service will tend to be interpreted as that of diplomatic tactician and executive agent rather than as a determining or decisive influence in the formation of policy. Wilson's basic principles were by no means inspired by the Colonel. . . . He was a political catalyst, an expert on method, a purveyor of facts, a stimulus and a corrective"[17]). "He was not qualified to originate policy, but he was supremely qualified to facilitate its execution". He possessed all the traits that characterize "the finished diplomatist"[18]).

Incidentally, the spheres advanced by Seymour as characteristic of House's influence were identical to those he had stressed 30 years earlier, with a single exception: the negotiations between the United States and the Allies prior to the Armistice with Germany. Seymour still regarded the result as "a diplomatic victory of distinction", although he stressed the fact that ". . . House's success was not as clear-cut as he imagined and it was not effectively capitalized"[19]). He blamed Wilson for the latter, but left the former, and most interesting, comment untouched. This remarkably clearly drawn portrait of House represented an important modification of the far cruder picture painted in Intimate Papers; but Seymour stuck to his guns on one point: for him, House was still the diplomat par excellence or, as *Harold Nicolson* has put it, ". . . the best diplomatic brain that America has yet produced . . ."[20]).

Intimate Papers constitutes the only attempt at a comprehensive, political biography of House, but Wilsonian research of recent years has naturally also touched upon his closest adviser. And practically every author has managed to unearth from the House papers etc. details that shake the picture established by Seymour in his Intimate Papers. One of the latest analyses of House as a diplomat has been provided by *Arthur S. Link* in the fourth volume of his biography of Wilson, in connection with his discussion of the so-called House-Grey memorandum, one of the most debated documents of the period of neutrality[21]). Link's evaluation is one of the hardest judgments ever made on House. In his negotiations with the European statesmen in February 1916, House "grossly misrepresented the President and misinformed him as well"; in other words, he had conducted an independent policy. However, in Link's opinion, not only had he behaved in an illoyal manner to Wilson, he had also failed as a negotiator[22]):

"House had heard what he wanted to hear in Paris and London. He had deluded himself into believing that the British and French wanted American mediation for a negotiated peace. It did not matter that this was not true, or that the British and French leaders had said nothing to indicate that it was either true or possible. House was out of touch with reality by the time of his conversations in Paris and his return to London. He consequently not only misinformed and misled President Wilson but also encouraged him to base fundamental foreign policy on the assumption that American mediation was possible in the immediate future."

There is thus not much left of House, the diplomat.

Nevertheless, a number of problems still remain, and these are problems that will stay with us throughout this entire book—because House possessed, to an unusual degree, the ability of being "all things to all men." Just as we think we have grasped the "essence" of the man, the image crumbles away, only to reappear in a new form, and this is really also the case with Link's portrait. As House appears in the above passages, he must be regarded as a man with an obsession, as the naive amateur in the hands of cynical professionals. However, there are other aspects of House's time in Europe that present him in quite a different light: as the man able to make a cool and realistic analysis of a political situation and draw the relevant conclusions. One example of this has been pointed out by Link himself[23]. House spent three days in Berlin and at once apprehended the entire situation: the fight between the civilian and the military leaders, and the increasingly precarious position of the former, which could be completely upset by too harsh American demands. He explained this situation in lucid detail in a letter to the President, and pointed out the consequences to the political constellation in Germany of a severe American course in the renewed Lusitania-negotiations. And this letter persuaded Wilson to withdraw forthwith the support he had hitherto given to the hard line followed by the Secretary of State, Robert Lansing[24]:

"It was as if Wilson had seen a great light. For the first time he understood what Gerard (the American Ambassador in Berlin) had failed to make clear, or even to mention—that severe demands might well tip the balance in Germany against the Chancellor and set engines in fatal motion under the seas."

The objection can be made that Link's approach is very narrow, being too closely tied to the direct statements of his sources, and it is therefore hardly surprising that other authors, who have approached the matter from different angles, have arrived at more finely shaded evaluations of House's behaviour during this same visit to Europe[25]. It is, for example, the wider political perspectives of House's negotiations that have interested *Edward H. Buehrig* in his book, *Woodrow Wilson and the Balance of Power*[26]. However, it should be noted that Buehrig used only published material in his assessment of House's peace mission, i. e. primarily Seymour's selection; had he had Link's material at his disposal, he might have arrived at a slightly less favourable conclusion. However, it is in any case quite different sides of the matter that he brings to light than Link. The important thing for Buehrig is not so much the actual events as their significance, and it is thus not really the negotiations themselves but the prelude to them, i. e. the preliminary correspondence between House and Sir Edward Grey, that interests him. In Buehrig's view, a negotiated peace between the contending parties was the solution that best accorded with America's interests[27]):

"A bold (American) diplomatic intervention thus held enticing prospects. Yet its execution required the United States to be more than an amiable intermediary. American power would have to be brought into play, incurring the danger of military involvement or, though a lesser evil, loss of prestige. ... Actually, considerably prior to the President's espousal of an interventionist diplomacy, Col. House had grasped its importance. First of all, therefore, we should note those moves initiated by House which were designed to hasten the end of the war. Although failing of their immediate objective, they had consequences of singular importance."

During his first peace mission in 1915, House advanced the idea that "a second convention" after the actual Peace Conference should discuss amendments to international law. Grey had desired American participation, also in the Conference itself, and was therefore not satisfied, but he used this as a premise for an argumentation that continued in the subsequent correspondence and, during the summer and autumn, led House and Wilson a long way along the road of collective security and the League of Nations. House's plans thus achieved a far wider perspective than he himself had at first envisaged. It was thanks to House's peace plans that the idea of a League of Nations made its entry in the diplomacy of the war years, even though it perhaps assumed a different guise than Grey had originally envisaged. The picture Buehrig draws of the negotiations themselves is also extremely favourable, but then, of course, it is only based on Seymour, and like Seymour, Buehrig takes House seriously, attempts to assess his extremely difficult negotiating position and, on this basis, is astonished that anything came out of it at all—and there perhaps he is right.

*Ernest R. May,* in his book, *The World War and American Isolation. 1914–1917*[28]), has also paid particular attention to the House-Grey memorandum, giving his chapter on the subject the very telling title, "Wilson's threats of mediation". May has used the House-diary and the House-Wilson correspondence, but unlike Link, he has concentrated not on whether House interpreted Wilson correctly on this or that occasion, but rather, on the situation itself. Whereas, to Link, it looked as though House had lost all touch with reality, May has a different conception of the situation: As soon as House came to England, he realized, through his talks with British politicians that "the likelihood of Britain's moderating her economic war had become remote, and future friction was almost certain. The Colonel, who had felt theretofore, that his plan might be developed slowly, changed his mind. He began to think it urgent that an agreement be reached whereby Wilson could safely demand peace"[29]). And it was this feeling of urgency that thereafter determined House's actions.

However, there can be no doubt that Link has made a very vital point in his clear establishment of House's complete over-estimation of the importance of the House-Grey memorandum. And his assessment of House is fully supported by one of the latest and most independent contributions to the discussion: *Victor S. Mamatey*'s brief but precise characterization in *The United States and East Central Europe. 1914–1918*[30]). Against the picture portrayed by both Seymour and, later, George and George, showing House as a man who worried himself about the smallest detail, the consummate technician, Mamatey sets "a happy extrovert", a man bored by detail, who is only interested in the grand design, the general picture; a man who prefers to gather his information from talks rather than from studies and who is therefore always well-informed on the very latest events, but whose information is, on the other hand, often one-sided; in fact, a superficial and intellectually indolent man[31]). To George and George, the break between House and Wilson at the Peace Conference was primarily psychologically conditioned, while Birdsall seems to have considered it mainly as the result of a fundamental difference in the two men's conception of the method—and partly also the aim—of the negotiations. Mamatey, on the other hand, takes a different view[32]):

"During the war when issues were of necessity broad and when technical questions could be postponed, House's counsels were generally wise and perspicacious. During the armistice negotiations and the Peace Conference, however, when questions inevitably became highly complex and technical, he found himself out of his depth and his effectiveness as a negotiator declined. The President then lost confidence in his judgment, and their relations cooled."

In other words, House had simply been inadequate.

We can thus in no way say that the debate on House is at an end, but simply ascertain that the varying assessments have depended not only on the different approaches of the authors to their subject, but also on the nature of the source material at their disposal. What has primarily made House a key figure in the historiography of the Wilson period is the simple fact that we have here not only a man who held a central position in the decision-making processes, but also one who kept an exceedingly voluminous diary. This diary is one of the most important sources of information on the political history of the period, but the question is how far we can permit ourselves to trust its testimony. This is really not a question to which there is a universal answer, but one to which each researcher must find the answer that is compatible with his own ego, his material and his conscience, from one situation to another. This, however, is not a unique state of affairs, but simply the common lot of the historian.

The first to be confronted with the problem was Charles Seymour, publisher of the diary, and he solved it in the simplest way imaginable. He called his version "The Intimate Papers . . .", and here is what he wrote about the diary[33]):

"Through Miss Denton (Francis B. Denton, House's secretary) was made possible the diary which forms the heart of the entire collection of papers. Every evening, with rare exceptions and during eight years, Col. House dictated to her his resumé of the day. *Definitely and objectively he related his conversations* with, often the very words of, his political associates, and he was associated with the men who made the history of the decade. The result is a journal of more than two thousand pages, a record drafted at the moment and *with a frankness which suggests that it was not designed for publication*. It was the Colonel's comments on men and events, opinions which he sometimes changed, prophecies which upon occasion were fulfilled, a personal document such as the biographer dreams of and seldom discovers."

Put in another way, Seymour took House at his word, indeed in some places he even went so far that, as he himself admits[34]), he came to see the events with House's eyes, or perhaps we should say, as House wished them to be seen.

In the passage quoted above, the first statement underlined is the most astonishing at first glance, not only because it discloses an exceedingly simple and unsophisticated attitude to the source material, but also because it follows immediately upon Seymour's explanation of the way in which the diary was written; a process that shows how easily unintentional inaccuracies could have crept in. The "intimate" character of the diary is, moreover, shown here in quite another light. The second underlining reveals Seymour's evaluation of the aim of the diary in a negative sense: he did not consider that it was intended for publication. Victor S. Mamatey takes quite a different view: " ... His diary, incidentally, is not an intimate, personal one, as is commonly supposed, but one written for future publication. He frequently addresses himself in it to the future reader ..."[35]). And this view is directly substantiated by House's own statements in the diary. It was, quite simply, written to ensure that posterity received what House considered to be the correct conception of his political importance. However, this was not its only purpose; it also functioned as a kind of safety valve for the frustrations inherent in such a delicate position as that held by House, and it undoubtedly had a salutary psychological function: the pleasure and satisfaction of dwelling upon his own achievements. On the other hand, there is one obvious function that the diary does not seem to have had: it did not apparently serve as an aide-memoire for House when he had to formulate his policy in any given situation. On the contrary, House was very careful to make it clear that when a suitable section of the diary had been written, it was locked away and not taken out again. Thus, as it was not intended as a tool, it does not contain analyses of situations or problems. Nor, incidentally, do House's other papers. That was apparently not the way he worked[36]).

A valuable contribution to the illumination of the problems surrounding the diary has been made by Alexander and Juliette L. George in their book on Woodrow Wilson and Colonel House[37]). This work is an attempt at a phychological motivation study of Wilson[38]), and House is discussed primarily because the authors consider that the relationship between the two men illustrates important aspects of Wilson's motives. The method adopted by the authors is that of applying a psychological conceptual apparatus to the course of events already established in the usual historical accounts; the book is ". . . largely a synthesis of facts assembled by previous writers . . ."[39]). It is thus not as a politico–historical but as a psychological study that the book can claim originality. As regards the House-diary, the authors have made an exception in that they have gone straight to the source and have thereby managed, on the basis of hitherto largely unpublished passages, to achieve their greatest "coup" from an historian's point of view.

House and Wilson met for the first time in November 1911. At that time, Wilson was Governor of New Jersey and was actively engaged in efforts to win the Democratic nomination for the Presidency. House, who was financially independent, had previously acted as adviser to various Texas Governors and had a certain standing in the Democratic party on a national level. He had always consistently refused all official posts, which gave him the reputation of being unselfish and disinterested. However, his pleasure in manipulating people and events was obvious[40]). The first meeting soon led to others, and the casual acquaintanceship gradually developed into a more intimate friendship, and for long periods of time, House was Wilson's only confidante[41]). The credit for elucidating the "mechanism" of this friendship is due to George and George[42]). They have succeeded in showing that the friendship was, to a high degree, deliberate on House's side and that he cultivated it by "handling" Wilson in a particular way. House had analysed Wilson's need for security, encouragement and flattery and was willing to fulfil it. On the other hand, however, House's admiration and enthusiasm for the President were genuine enough—at any rate in the beginning.

Nonetheless, it is of decisive importance that George and George have been able to prove by their analysis of the entries in House's diary that these indicated as early as 1913 that House felt a certain irritation over Wilson, an irritation that grew stronger as time went by[43]). This was accentuated after Wilson's wedding in December 1915[44]) and increased in step with the growing tension between House and the new Mrs. Wilson. This irritation on the part of House finds expression in a number of critical comments in the diary, both as regards Wilson himself and as regards his policies, accompanied by accounts of what House *himself* would have done in Wilson's place[45]):

"The frustrations of House's position were increased by the advent of the second Mrs. Wilson. Whether and to what extent this added tension accounts for it, the fact is that after the marriage the Colonel had much more to say in criticism of the President in his diary."

The question is whether House's increasing coolness towards the President was purely psychologically conditioned, or whether there were also real differences of a political nature. And, in the latter event, whether they were of a fundamental character—whether there was a consistent line or whether they were just ordinary disagreements from one case to another. The two authors have not provided a clearcut answer to these questions, simply noting from time to time that there was discord, without analysing its character in detail. However, we shall see later that it is in fact possible to prove that fundamental political differences did develop between the two men during the course of the war, but that the break cannot, on the other hand, be attributed to them[46]).

The new ground opened up by George and George's analysis is thus their explanation of the deterioration of the friendship and of its frail psychological foundation. And in my opinion, this result is unassailable. However, there may be good reason for discussing the two authors' assessment of House and thus also their use of the diary. The picture drawn of the friendship by George and George has been based on an analysis of the diary and the House-Wilson correspondence, and the obvious discrepancy between House's utterances in these is an important and indisputable link in the line of reasoning. But the picture otherwise portrayed by the authors is far too influenced by the diary and by Seymour's account. Like Seymour, they take House at his word, and they do not seem anywhere to have considered the motives behind the framing of this grandiose monument, but almost to have accepted Seymour's interpretation[47]), which is, as we have seen, one-sided to say the least of it.

That the authors have neglected these problems is naturally related to the fact that the 'hero' of the book is quite definitely Wilson, and that their interest is psychological. However, it also has something to do with the method of the book, primarily, that the interpretations are made on the basis of established facts, i. e. on an existing *selection,* the aim of which thus tends to determine the conclusions of the new synthesis. All the same, the decisive point is that the two authors have managed, through their studies of the diary, to raise fundamental doubt as to the representativeness of Seymour's selection. Other authors have, of course, also done this, both before and since, but whereas the doubts previously raised related to interpretations of individual instances, which could admittedly, have been pieced together to indicate a certain trend, George and George have illustrated a ruthlessly consistent omission of anything that might touch upon the question of loyalty. In fact, after this, the Seymour House-edition can no longer be used, either as a source material or as a biography, because his evaluation of House is based on a selection of material in which we can no longer have any faith. The authors themselves seem to be unaware of the problems of the source material that they have raised, or at any rate, they have not taken the obvious consequences of their findings. For them, Seymour is still the main source for their *political* assessment of House, but this means that their House-portrait disintegrates, which in turn affects their entire interpretation of the break between House and Wilson.

These weaknesses already make their appearance in the two authors' evaluation of House as a diplomat[48]). An introductory characterization places House among the so-called realists[49]), in line with the views held by a branch of the latest research. The authors themselves cite the works of Edward H. Buehrig and

Robert E. Osgood[50]), as well as the Seymour version of House, but it must be remembered that neither Buehrig nor Osgood used anything but published material in their evaluations of House—indeed, Buehrig used mainly Seymour. Later, the authors modify their views somewhat: ". . . House's own approach to international affairs, unusual in his day and since, was in many respects a synthesis of both realist and idealist views of world policies"[51]), and thereby leave the door open for a discussion of the evaluation of House. George and George are fully aware of the content of this discussion[42]), but they let it go at this, and their assessment of House's role in the formulation of Wilson's neutrality policy is thus[53]):

"It was all the more fortunate, therefore, that his (Wilson's) closest adviser—his alter ego, as he sometimes called him—was thoroughly at ease in the setting of the realist philosophy of international relations. It became Colonel House's task to interpret events from this standpoint and to initiate, and prepare the ground for, some of the most important foreign policy projects which Wilson undertook in response to the European conflict."

Perhaps this rather superficial interpretation also derives from the fact that Arthur S. Link, in his *Woodrow Wilson and the Progressive Era*[54]), could only in one instance prove that House had not provided Wilson with a completely loyal account of his negotiations[55]). However, this presents yet another example of the serious weakness in the method applied by the authors: they depend too much on the conclusions of others. What makes this particularly grave is the fact that Link has since had to revise his views considerably, so the authors' characterization of House's attempts to mediate must also be regarded as out-of-date[56]):

"If House's peace efforts failed, they did so perhaps more by reason of circumstances over which he had no control rather than because of any want of skill on his part. Indeed, he had displayed a distinguished talent for exploring passionate questions dispassionately and for bringing divergent views to their closest point of approximation. That there remained a gap which no diplomatic legerdemain could bridge is no reflection upon his ability as a negotiator."

The authors' analysis of House as a negotiator[57]) is based exclusively on the material furnished by Charles Seymour in the first and second volumes of his House-edition[58]). And the picture that appears is hardly surprising; it is a portrait of the eminent tactician and organizer, who carefully acquainted himself with even the slightest details, so that he completely mastered all the circumstances of a negotiation. The man who understood and foresaw every situation, and who analysed his opponent's assumptions and psyche in advance and marshalled his arguments accordingly. In short, the picture that presented itself to Seymour's admiring eye, and the picture House wished to paint of himself. Not until the next chapter and in another context, do the authors provide the following significant supplement to their characterization, on the basis of their own studies of the diary[59]):

"There can be no question that at the zenith of his career, House exercised tremendous influence upon the course of diplomatic negotiations. Making the fullest allowance for his actual (and extraordinary) power, however, one suspects that he had the capacity for exaggerating the importance of his own role in international affairs. A master of flattery himself, he seems to have been naively susceptible to the compliments of foreign diplomats, whose expressions of esteem, it seems safe to assume, were not always entirely artless. ... He recorded in his diary literally hundreds of such expressions of esteem, and it is interesting to note that he had the highest estimate of the abilities of the authors of some of the most glowing ones. Such intoxicating praise made it easy for House to forget that his power derived exclusively from his association with Wilson. House seems to have come to believe that the Allied statesmen sought him out for his own capabilities rather than as a spokesman for another and, in his view, less informed man."

We meet this same confused attitude to House again in the chapter on the break[60]). After reading this, we are left with a number of unanswered questions: What really happened? Who was to blame, House or Wilson? What was the reason, Wilson's jealousy or House's persistence, or perhaps something quite different?

In an earlier chapter, the authors have sketched House's state of mind at the end of the war and at the beginning of the Conference, as it appears from the entries in his diary: "coldly realistic about the President's short-comings"; "resentful of his own subordinate role in policy-making"; "thinking that European statesmen sought his advice for its own sake"; "prey to grandiose notions of his own importance and capacity to influence the foreign policy of the Allied nations". "To state the matter baldly, House considered that he could better negotiate the peace treaty than Wilson. ... House wanted, for once, to act directly, independently"[61]). The authors might therefore have been expected to base their account of the break on the question of House's loyalty, and, to a certain extent, they do this, introducing their thesis with a repudiation of all accusations (i. e., principally those of Mrs. Wilson and R. S. Baker) against House for disloyalty. Here, the authors do not base their arguments on independent source studies but on the scientific debate on the subject, and on this foundation, they draw their first conclusions[62]):

"Neither of the accusations against House, therefore, appears to be warranted. Both seem to be explanations contrived later for the President's undoubted change of attitude toward House during the second half of the Conference. How, then is Wilson's perceptible, gradual cooling toward House upon his return to Paris to be explained?"

I consider that the two authors have hereby precluded themselves from gaining the full benefit of their own analysis, because, as pointed out above, they overlook the fact that the rejection by later researchers of Baker's thesis is based on Seymour's account—precisely the account shown by the investigations of George and George to provide a not very credible picture of House. Therefore, the only thing the authors gain by neglecting the problem of loyalty is that their analysis gets on the wrong track right from the beginning. And it is led further astray because they, at the same time, and apparently without justification, accept the theory of the gradual break. They thereby deconcretize the motives of the two men, placing the whole matter on a psychological plane[63]):

"It was an unfortunate combination of circumstances—Wilson's increased sensitivity to House as a possible competitor and House's overpowering desire to "come into his own"—that contributed heavily to the gradual waning of the President's enthusiasm for his closest collaborator. No one incident marks the end of the friendship between Wilson and House. The relationship was never terminated in a clearcut fashion. Rather, Wilson gradually withdrew his affection and gradually ceased to consult House."

However, this approach also alters the dimensions of the entire affair, for if there had really been no conflict of loyalty, the matter would be reduced to simply a question of arrogance and jealousy. House wanted to be in the limelight; he was tired of playing second fiddle, tired of always just agreeing; and Wilson could therefore no longer find the satisfaction in the friendship that had previously been his—on the contrary, it now increased his anxieties. The assumptions thus fail, the whole things disintegrates, and House ends up as a scapegoat for Wilson's bad conscience. But where then is the drama that managed to inflame both contemporaries and posterity?

In the following I have tried to subject the break once more to a detailed analysis, and for this purpose I am deeply indebted to George and George. Through their analysis of the diary, new paths have been opened, and I have tried to continue from where I believe they went astray: The question of loyalty cannot be eliminated, and Baker's thesis must not simply be ignored. On the contrary, both must be taken up for renewed consideration in the light of the insight gained through the analysis of the diary. Only then will it be possible to expose the House-myth.

## Chapter 1

# Pre-Armistice Negotiations

When the United States entered the war on the side of the Allies in 1917, it did so on its own terms: The United States was not a member of the Alliance and was not bound by the promise not to conclude a separate peace or by the secret treaties. Wilson chose the designation "Associated" to describe America's position, thereby clearly stressing the fact that he intended to retain his full diplomatic freedom. This attitude was based on, among other things, a deep distrust of Allied aims and motives, and the President therefore wished to retain his right of independent decision with regard to the coming Peace Conference. "Indeed, the salient feature of American diplomacy from April 1917 to October 1918 was Wilson's attempt to impose a moratorium on political consultation with the Allies. It was as if he had announced to the Allies, as he did to domestic politicians, that politics was adjourned. There would be no alliance, and there would be no negotiations over objectives"[1]).

However, this suspicious attitude was not shared by Edward House. On the contrary, it was he, of all Wilson's advisers, who advocated most warmly close collaboration with the Allies, and he had taken this stand right from the beginning of the war. A salient feature of Wilson's policy of neutrality had been his policy of peace and mediation, and House had had a decisive influence on the formulation of this policy. He held the conviction that an understanding with Britain was an absolute prerequisite for an American peace mission, and it was this idea that lay behind the formulation of the so-called House-Grey memorandum[2]). Despite repeated invitations from the Americans —the most recent of which had been made in Wilson's "League of Nations speech" on 27 May 1916—the British could not be induced to make a move, and Wilson therefore began the change in American policy that was to culminate in the independent American peace drive of December 1916. This was a policy that ran completely counter to the principles House had regarded as fundamental, and it was implemented despite the protests of both House and Secretary of State Lansing. The new policy was characterized by, inter alia, a deep distrust, not only of the Central Powers, but also of the Entente. Wilson was never more neutral than when he was hovering on the brink of war[3]).

House thus had to see his policy disavowed, although only for a time. When the United States became an active belligerent, cooperation with the Allies became essential, and it was in this sphere that House came to make his most important contribution to wartime diplomacy. Not only did he lead two diplomatic missions to Europe; he also became liaison officer between the Entente, particularly the British Government, and the President. It is to House that a great deal of the credit is due for the fact that the wartime collaboration between the two countries functioned as well as it actually did, despite the mutual distrust that characterized relations between Wilson and Lloyd George[4]).

Entry into the war meant a number of new tasks for the American Government—and for House. The American economy and production apparatus had now to be switched over to wartime conditions, and it soon proved necessary also to bring its armed forces up to combat strength[5]). On the diplomatic front, the ideological offensive started by the President even before America entered the war, with his "Peace without Victory" speech of 22 January 1917, was continued with the presentation of "The Fourteen Points" and subsequent declarations. These constituted not only an appeal to the Liberal and Socialist forces in Germany and the other Central Powers, but also an attempt to provide an alternative to Lenin's ideological challenge, and were thus an appeal to the Liberal and Socialist forces in the Allied countries as well. Wilson became the principal advocate of the "Liberal Peace Programme"[6]). And this provides us with an indication of yet another dimension of Wilson's wartime diplomacy: the preparation of the coming peace, the problem that had, as we have seen, absorbed him during the period of neutrality.

But what was House's position in this new situation? The war brought both an enlargement and a reduction of his sphere of influence. In February 1917 he had followed his traditional course of refusing to choose any official post he liked. However, when, in June of that year, he proposed that the President let him organize the "war machine", he was rebuffed. Whether this meant, as suggested by Alexander and Juliette L. George, that there was now a tacit agreement between the two men that House should keep to foreign policy is not clear. But it is a fact that House returned to the matter in his diary in January 1918, here asserting that Wilson never took any steps in questions of foreign policy without first consulting him. And House continued: ". . . and since I am so much more interested in that than in domestic affairs, I have been willing to accept the situation as he has willed it"[7]). House had been shown his place.

All observers, and even Wilson himself, have agreed that the President had a "one-track mind." He could concentrate on only one set of problems at a time. It is also the general consensus of opinion that the problems of foreign policy were of very little interest to him in the beginning. He had been elected on the basis of a domestic reform programme, and that is what absorbed him.

House, on the other hand, had expressed great interest in foreign policy, even before the war. When war broke out and the U-boat problem threatened to overwhelm Wilson, he had his hands full enough with this and was, as we have seen, content to leave the question of peace policy to House. Far earlier than Wilson and even before the U-boat became a threat, House had seen the perspectives opened by American mediation, and the important role that he himself could come to play. Not until the U-boat policy had proved a failure did Wilson turn his full interest towards the policy of peace, and this resulted in a considerable reduction of House's role, for in the spheres to which Wilson at any given time gave priority, he took command himself.

Just such a sphere arose after American entry into the war. The war now came to the fore, and the mobilization of the American nation, both spiritually and physically, became his most vital interest. Wilson held weekly meetings with his newly established "War Cabinet" and almost daily meetings with George Creel, Chairman of the "Committee on Public Information". However, as we have seen, this side of the matter was practically closed to House. On the other hand, he was entrusted with a number of concrete assignments, all of which lay in direct continuation of his interests during the period of neutrality. He was requested to collect material on the domestic political conditions in the belligerent countries so that he could advise and assist in the framing of American ideological propaganda, and he was also the President's closest adviser in the preparation of the great speeches, in which Wilson formulated the principles for a future peace. In direct extension of this function, House was also entrusted with the organization of the American preparations for peace in the form of the establishment of "The Inquiry"[8]), and he further seems to have been the only person with whom Wilson was willing to discuss his very vague plans for the League of Nations. As mentioned earlier, House was at the same time in direct contact with the British Foreign Office, through Sir William Wiseman, and thus played an important part in all matters concerning the coordination of American and Allied policy. His two European missions, which were now official, had the same function. House's assignments were thus extremely comprehensive and important, but they did have certain drawbacks. It is characteristic that his tasks were connected more with the coming peace negotiations than with current policy, and that they lay more or less on the fringe of Wilson's immediate sphere of interest. However, there are signs that House, even in the fields in which he had the greatest influence, i. e. with regard to propaganda and peace policy, ran counter to Wilson's policy. As the war continued, House considered that Wilson showed a constantly increasing tendency to neglect the Liberal programme in favour an extreme, nationalistic–militaristic mobilization of the American people. And there is every reason to believe that House was extremely dissatisfied with this development. The first question to be clarified is therefore that of House's standing as a Liberal[9]).

The most penetrating analysis of this question is presumably Lasch's unfortunately somewhat impressionistic sketch: "Lincoln Colcord and Colonel House: Dreams of Terror and Utopia"[10]). Lasch, too, has come up against the facade of ambiguity and impenetrability that surrounds House's personality, but he has at least chosen to analyse the facade through the medium of a detailed study of House's novel of 1912: "Philip Dru: Administrator"[11]). Moreover, thanks to Lincoln Colcord's diary, he has also succeeded in getting a glimpse behind the facade. House's connection with Lincoln Colcord, William Bullitt, Walther Lippmann and other Left-Liberal forces is a very significant observation. It is obvious that House used these and other progressive young journalists to consolidate his own position, that he "convinced them by subtle inference that his own political ideas were more advanced than Wilson's, and that he himself, in fact, was the chief force impelling Wilson in a progressive direction"[12]). But was this purely a case of manipulation for the sake of prestige or were there realities behind it? Were there, in fact, more fundamental differences of political opinion between Wilson and House?

In the following brief entry in his diary, Ray Stannard Baker gave a penetrating analysis of House[13]):

"He is a liberal by instinct, though not at all a thinker. He is a conciliator, an arranger. He likes human beings—and so they like him. And he has a shrewdness, too!"

Baker has seen the dual nature of House, but has also clearly defined his political attitude: "He is a Liberal by instinct, though not at all a thinker." For this is presumably the real core of House's political affiliation: he had no hard and fast philosophical reference system, but his reactions to every situation were instinctively Liberal or, rather, Left-Liberal. However, his first, instinctive reaction was not necessarily his last, for other factors—tactical and psychological—influenced him: "He is a conciliator, and arranger. He likes human beings . . .". And precisely because he had no hard and fast philosophy, these other factors sometimes took him rather far off the Liberal standpoint that might have been expected of him. Indeed, it might even seem as though he had no standpoint at all. This explains how in February–March, he could enter deeply into negotiations with Georges Clemenceau and André Tardieu on a solution of the Rhine problem that lay considerably to the right of Wilson's standpoint, and at the same time send Bullitt to Russia with the task of concluding peace with the Bolsheviks, thereby providing a glimpse of an attitude that lay far to the left of that of the President[14]).

While the Peace Conference seems to provide the first example of House's enthusiasm for manipulation leading him to the right of Wilson, there are numerous examples from the war years of his taking a far more extremist Liberal view than the President, even though there are signs here too of the above-mentioned ambivalence. Whereas Wilson, after the American intervention, found it essential to make the continuation of the war to victory the crux of his policy, House, "even after the American declaration of war, continued to hope and strive for a peace of compromise"[15]). This standpoint can, of course, be attributed to House's declared ambition as a mediator[16]), but the fact remains that his persisting in Wilson's original programme lay quite in line with the Liberal forces whom Wilson had originally represented and on which the implementation of his peace programme would finally depend[17]). Thus, during the war, House stood clearly to the left of Wilson, regardless of motive.

The best example of just how difficult, if not impossible, it is to separate these motives is, perhaps, provided by House's reaction to the Pope's peace proposal[18]). This was a proposal for a status quo peace, and House, who was still hoping for a negotiated peace, advised Wilson to frame his reply in such a way as to leave the door open for further negotiations, while Lansing advised him to reject the Note. Wilson was at first determined not to reply at all, and House had to make do with giving vent to his feelings in his diary[19]):

"The President, I feel, has taken a wrong position and ... he will make a colossal blunder if he treats the note lightly and shuts the door abruptly. I wish I could be with him. I feel it is something of a tragedy to be heat bound at this moment."

He was, in fact, deeply hurt that Wilson would not follow his advice in the matter, because he considered his judgment to be better than that of both Wilson and Lansing[20]). However, he was soon reassured when Wilson decided to reply to the Pope's Note and sent him a draft of this, even though it was a rejection as proposed by Lansing[21]):

"The entire world has been on tip-toe concerning his answer, but he has taken no one into his confidence excepting me—his usual method in matters of grave moment."

House was thus now apparently satisfied with having been taken into the President's confidence at all, and when the press reaction to Wilson's reply proved to be favourable, he even went so far as to be ready to take the credit for it[22]):

"It is the culmination of an idea I have had for a long while. My diary will show the many times I have advised both the British and the French governments, as well as the President, to do what the President has now done."

Nevertheless, all this must not be allowed to conceal the fact that House actually took a different view than Wilson in the beginning—and for highly relevant political reasons[23]):

"It is important, I think, that Russia should weld herself into a virile republic than it is that Germany should be beaten to her knees. ... With Russia firmly established in democracy, German autocracy would be compelled to yield a representative government within a very few years."

Russia thus held a central position in House's deliberations, and its importance was certainly not diminished by the October Revolution. In general, the Bolshevik seizure of power put all Liberals in a serious dilemma[24]), and the Wilson Administration itself was split over the question[25]):

"... two broad approaches to the issues posed by war and revolution in Russia emerged within the Wilson Administration in the immediate aftermath of the Bolshevik Revolution. On the one side, Colonel House hoped to bring Russia back to liberal-nationalism through a policy of liberalizing Allied war aims. Presumably, in House's view, this change was to make possible the absorption of Bolshevism into a liberal war consensus. On the other, more conservative Administration elements surrounding Secretary of State Lansing were suspicious of the Allied Left and were also oriented more in the direction of an overtly anti-Bolshevik position in Russia. It was not long before the interaction of these two tendencies gave a somewhat erratic quality to Wilsonian efforts to contain Russian Bolshevik influence and power during 1917 and early 1918. By the time of the signing of the Brest-Litovsk Treaty, however, the balance had tipped in the direction of growing support in Washington for those anti-Bolshevik *and* anti-German Russian elements who wanted to bring Russia back into the war."

To the latent personal differences between House and Lansing, a clear political divergence was thus now added[26]). Lansing seems, moreover, to have had most of the State Department behind him[27]), while Newton D. Baker and the War Department appear to have had a leaning towards House's views[28]). However, what is even more important is the fact that Wilson himself seems to have vacillated between the two views. In the beginning, he appears to have leaned towards House's conception of Bolshevism as "an ephemeral expression of thoughtless radicalism soon to be reintegrated into a healthy democratic Russia committed to a crusade against German autocracy within the limits of the anti-imperialism of liberal order"[29]), and this seems to have been his stand during the framing of The Fourteen Points, but by the end of February 1918, Wilson seems finally to have accepted Lansing's anti-Bolshevik standpoint[30]).

It is admittedly correct that "House never intended his projected Wilson–Lenin fusion to be other than on Wilson's terms, whereby revolutionary-socialist passion would be moderated by the progressive controls of a pro-Allied version of anti-imperalism"[31]), but at the same time, House was indisputably to the left of Wilson on this question[32]):

"The point is that the President was only willing to adopt the House approach, of co-opting the Left by means of persuasion into the ordered pro-war framework of liberal anti-imperialism, up to a point. The heart of the matter was that Wilson was less prepared to compromise with the Left than either House or the *New Republic*-oriented liberals who went much further even than the Colonel in seeking to accommodate the American war effort to the values of radical anti-imperialism."

As will be seen from the above, the difference of opinion was not limited to Bolshevism, but applied in general to the relations between the Administration and the Left-wing forces—both in the United States and in Europe. The question is, however, to what degree House himself was aware of this difference.

In this connection, the relationship between House, Wilson and the *New Republic* people is very illuminating[33]). During the war, House acted as intermediary between this journal and the Administration[34]) and, as we have seen, he attached Lippmann to the Inquiry Directorate on the grounds, inter alia, that "the Administration had to cooperate with the extreme Liberals of the country"[35]). Even after Lippmann had left the Inquiry and gone to Europe as a captain in the Intelligence Service, House kept in touch with him, and it was he, together with Frank Cobb, who framed the interpretation of the Fourteen Points used by House during the pre-Armistice negotiations[36]). It is strange, however, that House should have given Lippmann this confidential task when he no longer enjoyed the full confidence of the President. That this was the case is shown by a letter from Wilson to House of 31 August, in which he wrote as follows on Lippmann[37]):

"I have found his judgment most unsound and therefore entirely unserviceable, in matters of that sort (propaganda) because he, in common with the men of The New Republic, has ideas about the war and its purposes which are highly unorthodox from my point of view."

Equally paradoxical is the fact that House, as we have seen, appears to have thought of giving Willard Straight a prominent position in the organization of the Peace Commission at a time when Straight himself seemed to have lost confidence in Wilson as the leader of Liberalism[38]). It was therefore perhaps not entirely fortuitous that "though Lippmann plunged into the work of the peace conference with great enthusiasm, he quickly found himself "shunted aside" by men closer to Wilson"[39]). Wilson quite obviously failed to share House's enthusiasm for the circle around the *New Republic*.

That House could be so far off target may perhaps have been due to the fact that Wilson, at least at times, seems to have given private expression to very extreme ideas that made House feel as though it were he that was the cautious one[40]):

"We discussed the trend of liberal opinion in the world and came to the conclusion that the wise thing to do was to lead the movement intelligently and sympathetically and not to allow the ignoble element to run away with the situation as they had done in Russia. He spoke of the necessity of forming a new political party in order to achieve these ends. ... Again let me say that the President has started so actively on the liberal road that I find myself, instead of leading as I always did at first, rather in the rear end holding him back. ...".

This, together with the fact that House was finding it increasingly difficult to differentiate between the President's private opinions and his official policies[41]), provides part, though by no means all, of the explanation.

Recent research[42]) has clearly placed the President as the man in the middle, the man who tried to present a Liberal alternative to both extreme Right-wing and extreme Left-wing forces. But it is also evident that he could only implement his political programme if he had the support of both the

Liberals and, more particularly, the European Socialist parties[43]). Vice versa, it is obvious that the Socialists had a real need for Wilson in their own domestic battle for political power, a battle whose aims were by no means identical to those of the President. Both parties thus needed each other, while neither of them intended, on the other hand, to be used solely in the service of the other's interests: "in spite of basic differences, Wilson and the Socialists sought each other out, all the time remaining on their guard"[44]). Of interest in this connection is not just the two parties' evaluation of each other, but also the fact that House and Wilson did not see completely eye to eye on the question of the European Socialists.

Arno Mayer has described the political situation as follows[45]):

"At first Wilson misjudged the European Socialists, exaggerating their strength, unity and radicalism. As a result, he was *extremely—excessively—cautious* in his approaches to and relations with the Socialists. He wanted to use them to cow the premiers into moderation without, however, furthering the Socialists' power, self-confidence and defiance. On the other hand, the Allied Socialists had no alternative but to remain loyal even to an overly cautious and compromising Wilson: Lenin was too far away, the Right and the incumbent governments were all powerful, the Socialist leaders were irresolute, and the immediate postwar crisis was considerably short of revolutionary in the victor nations."

The crux of the matter is that Wilson seems to have over-estimated the strength of Socialism and therefore to have hesitated to enter into more direct cooperation. However, there are excellent grounds for assuming that although House shared Wilson's incorrect assessment of the political influence of the Socialists, it made him extremely favourably disposed towards closer cooperation with them.

The misconception under which both Wilson and House were labouring as regards the strength of the Socialist movement was perhaps due to a great extent to the fact that their evaluation of the question was coloured by Ray Stannard Baker's excellent and well-informed, but at the same time biassed and over-optimistic reports on the European Socialist and Liberal movements[46]). Baker had been sent to Europe in the spring of 1918, at the initiative of House[47]), and he reported partly to Frank Polk at the State Department and partly directly to House. There is no doubt at all that Baker was not only extremely well qualified for this task, but that he was also strongly committed to the implementation of Wilson's political programme[48]):

"You may not fully realize it, that in sending me over here, but as a matter of fact, you've inaugurated something new! I have had a curious kind of delight in thinking that I was one of the diplomats of the New Order, . . .".

The theme that Baker played in one letter after another was then this[49]):

"Mr. Wilson can never hope for whole-hearted support upon the reconstructive side of his program from those at the moment in power either here (England) or in France, his true friends, the ones he must go to victory with, are the labour and liberal groups. I believe that we shall find that we shall have to be as *implacable* and *exacting* in securing *our* disinterested purposes—if we are to get anything at all out of our investment of blood and treasure—as these interests in seeking their purposes. The great source of Mr. Wilson's strength is that while each governing group over here can command a part of its own people, Mr. Wilson, in so far as his policy is disinterested and democratic, can command large and powerful groups in all the nations. They can never get real unity, because each has a separate policy, while he can. Therefore we must never let these democratic forces in England and France get away from us, . . .".

The problem was, however, how this influence of Wilson's on the Liberal and Socialist forces could be brought to bear as an active support for Wilson at the Peace Conference. Baker himself tried to answer this question in a letter he sent at the height of the pre-Armistice negotiations[50]):

Baker pounced on crucial points in Wilson's strategy: The President ought to come to Europe to establish direct, personal contact with the Liberal and Socialist leaders and "when the time comes he may have to make or thresten (!) to make an appeal direct to the people over the heads on (!) the obstructors." However, Baker realized that "(w)hile they (the Socialists) agree with us, generally, upon the Wilson program, they have a method of their own which they have by no means given over—to wit—an International Socialist Conference". Baker therefore also suggested that "(t)he President might throw his support in favor of some form of international conference of workers, not necessarily socialists, but all workers. . . . The President himself might address this assembly and bring them to the support of his method." In conclusion, Baker pointed out that "no one of the three countries (the Allies) is more fluid, or more open to our leadership, than Italy, or more willing to accept Mr. Wilson's program or to follow him to the end", and strongly recommended a visit to this particular country.

Baker here enumerated the political weapons Wilson could have used if he had been willing or able to take the full consequences of the ideological propaganda campaign of the war years, and he accentuated precisely the country that the President had apparently selected for a demonstration of what he could have done elsewhere if the political constellation had been the right one. Could the reason for this have been Baker's extremely favourable reports from Italy?[51]) In any event, Baker drew up here the main outlines of a policy that House seemed to think, at the beginning of the Conference, that the President should follow.

However, during the summer of 1918, House had already begun to conjecture on what might be the most favourable political constellation for the Peace Conference. He saw clearly that the best thing would be the establishment of "really liberal governments", not just in Germany, but also in Britain and France[52]), and he even went so far as to discuss the matter with the British Ambassador, Lord Reading[53]):

"He (Reading) thinks there will be a General Election in October and we worked out a plan which he is to propose to Lloyd George by which George will try to get Asquith Henderson and other liberals to work with him in order that George will not be dependent as now upon the reactionaries. Reading thought George would be willing to do this and that perhaps Henderson would be, but he doubted Asquith who thoroughly distrusts Lloyd George. *My purpose in this proposal was to wean George away from the conservatives and get a liberal government in England that would be more in harmony with our views at the Peace Conference."*

When, some months later, the Peace Conference and the British elections were imminent, House again took up the thread and drafted a new plan. This time he would try to influence Lloyd George by more indirect channels[54]):

"It has occurred to me that the General Election in England will afford us an opportunity to nail the British Government more securely to the President's program than we have already done here this week. I am arranging to have questions put to the Government during the campaign to which they will have to reply specifically, and come out squarely or repudiate what they have promised in the armistice to Germany. I am sending Frank Cobb over day after tomorrow to see the Liberal leaders and editors together with the Laborites, to tell them what is at issue."

Whatever one thinks of House's methods, his intentions are clear enough.

The direct contact with the "Liberal elements" in Europe was in general a task that deeply concerned House. When Ray Stannard Baker was sent to Italy in November "to keep in touch with Liberal elements there", House suggested to the President they should get Ida Tarbell to Paris in his stead, because she was "persona grata with the Liberal element here"[55]), and House himself had established contact with Briand through Elmer Roberts of Associated Press[56]). However, as pointed out by Baker, the decisive political manifestation had to be the direct, personal contact between the Liberal and Socialist leaders and Wilson. The French Socialists were well aware of the advantages of a publicly demonstrated alliance with the American President, and "the SFIO and CCT planned a huge public demonstration at Brest, a roaring welcome along the streets of Paris, a mammoth cortège in front of Wilson's residence in the capital, public rallies throughout France, and a special "Wilson" edition of 150,000 copies of *Humanité*"[57]). And when Cachin, Renaudel, Albert Thomas and others discussed the plan with House's secretary, they were told that "their demonstration would greatly hearten the President in his work"[58]). However, the President took quite another view when House informed him of the plans a few days later[59]): He did not wish to be identified "with any single element, and recalled the criticisms already made by those interested in opposing his principles with regard to the source of the popular support which he was receiving"[60]). Auchincloss now had to advise Renaudel, Laval, Longuet and Jouhaux that "we could not interfere in this matter at all"[61]). The official demonstration came to nothing[62]), but this was not House's fault. Still left, however, as also pointed out by Baker, was "The International". On this point too, Wilson shrank from a confrontation with the Allied Governments; he refused to use his prestige to effect the arrangement of an international Socialist conference in Paris at the same time as the Peace Conference[63]).

It is thus obvious that House, both during the war and in the period up to the Peace Conference, took a different political position than Wilson on a number of points. It is also clear that he found it increasingly difficult to hide his irritation and suppress his desire to act on his own initiative. This came to expression in September 1918 inter alia, when Wilson replied to the Austrian Note on "confidential, non-binding conversations over the fundamental principles of a peace treaty". The reply was a refusal, on the grounds that "the United States, having repeatedly stated its terms, could "entertain no proposal for a conference upon a matter concerning which it has made its position and purpose so plain". This "brusque" reply, Wiseman reported to Reading, was very popular with the American public, whose desire was "to march to Berlin and dictate terms". House, Wiseman said, considered that Wilson's answer, by alienating the "semi-pacifist, socialist and advanced labour group, constituted probably the biggest political mistake of the President's career"."[64]).

In other words, House was dissatisfied, both with his own position and with Wilson's policy. The question is, however, which was the more decisive, for although it is apparently incontrovertible that House stood clearly to the left of the President in most political disagreements prior to the Armistice, subsequent events were to show that when under pressure, he could—seemingly with just as little difficulty—place himself to the right of Wilson. On 5 October 1918, the German Government made a move that gave House the opportunity of once more acting on his own initiative—of giving a repeat performance of his role as American top negotiator and of demonstrating what he himself could do.

On 6 October, 1918, a Note arrived in Washington, in which the German Government requested the American President to institute peace negotiations on the basis of the Fourteen Points and later declarations, and to bring about an immediate cease-fire on all fronts[65]). The German Note placed Wilson in an extremely difficult position: Was the Note seriously meant and, if so, should the proposals be accepted or rejected? There was a considerable difference of opinion on these questions[66]), and Wilson himself was in a great quandary[67]). The reply was framed at meetings between Wilson, Lansing and House on 7 and 8 October, and it was, in Lansing's words, "Query not a reply"[68]). It is, of course, difficult to determine just how much influence House and Lansing[69]) had on the framing of the Note, but it is a fact that, as House reports[70]), Wilson actually tightened and accentuated the Note during the discussion. Wilson's papers include a draft, written on the President's own typewriter and with his own handwritten corrections[71]). The phrases used are here a shade more polite; the areas Wilson wished to see evacuated are expressly named (Alsace-Lorraine is not among them); and, most important of all, the last question of the Note, "whether the Imperial Chancellor is speaking merely for the constituted authorities of the Empire who have so far

conducted the war . . .", is omitted altogether, although this was a specifically
American requirement—a means of attempting to accommodate the "war mad-
ness" that was the dominant mood of the American people at this time[72]). And
it was this particular part of the Note on which the President concentrated
when he discussed it with the Cabinet[73]):

> "WW came into cabinet room whistling. In response to inquiry said he whistled because
> he thought he had done right in answering the German Note. Only one thing troubled
> him. How could we have correspondence with Germany under autocracy? Then we must
> go into G- and set up a government ourselves, something unthinkable. Unless some sort
> of gov. offers medium of communication, we might witness bolshevikism worse than
> in Russia. . . .".

The Note was despatched on 8 October[74]), and Wilson had thereby made
what was perhaps the most difficult decision of his entire period of office.

In its final form, the Note actually consisted only of three short and clearly
formulated questions: Was the German Note to be understood to mean that
the German Government accepted the Fourteen Points and later declarations
and only desired a discussion of their practical application? Was the Government willing immediately to initiate withdrawal from all occupied territory?
Was the German Government speaking only on behalf of the former rulers?

Wilson had framed and despatched the Note without at any time informing
or asking the advice of the Allies. These, for their part, had held a conference
in Paris from 5 to 9 October, at which they passed a number of resolutions
expressing their view of how the Armistice with Germany should be formulated[75]). In his first Note to Germany, the American President had limited
himself to demanding withdrawal from all occupied territory, and this was not
regarded by the Allies as providing a sufficient guarantee. In general, it was
considered best to leave the formulation of the terms for an Armistice to the
military authorities, and this view was made known to the American President
in a joint Note on 9 October[76]). General Tasker H. Bliss, the American
Delegate at the Supreme War Council in Versailles, refused to participate in
the Allied negotiations because he was well aware of their aim: To influence
the deliberations taking place at the same time in Washington[77]). Wilson himself was "much exercised" by the fact that the Allies had acted without prior
consultation with him, and he considered, moreover, that it was a mistake to
discuss details at this point. He feared that such a course would have a de-
moralizing effect on the peoples of the Allied countries and the United
States[78]). On their side, the Allies were, of course, equally offended by the
President's apparent autocracy[79]).

In the days following this, the Allied pressure continued. On 14 October,
Lansing received three telegrams from Balfour, which he immediately passed
on to the President[80]). These emphasized that the British Government doubted
whether Germany clearly understood that the Associated Powers would only
agree to the cessation of hostilities on such terms as would, in the opinion of

both the military and the naval experts, prevent the resumption of the fighting. "His Majesty's Government accordingly regard it as of the very greatest importance that an immediate and public notification should be given to the German Government as to how the matter really stands"[81]). The British Government further drew attention to the fact that the Fourteen Points had not been discussed between the Associated Powers, that the various Points were open to many interpretations, and that the British Government had to protest sharply against some of the Points; and further, that there were perhaps other conditions that Wilson had not mentioned, concerning, for example, the losses at sea, for which Britain must insist on full indemnity. It was the view of the British Government that it was important in the framing of the conditions for the Armistice not to limit the freedom of action of the Allies at the Peace Conference, and that immediate steps should be taken to negotiate the doubtful points so that agreement could be reached on these.

These telegrams were thus not just an effort to influence Wilson's negotiations with Germany, but also a clear accentuation of the special British views: British naval interest were not to be neglected in favour of French military interests. However, the telegram was also an obvious declaration of political programme and provided a foretaste of Lloyd George's final memorandum: there were certain points to which the British Government could not accede (i. e. freedom of the seas), and there were certain conditions that would have to be added (i. e. reparation for damage at sea).

In its response of 12 October, the German Government declared that it accepted Wilson's Fourteen Points and subsequent declarations, and that "its object in entering into discussions would be only to agree upon practical details of the application of these terms". The Government declared itself "ready to comply with the propositions of the President in regard to evacuation". It was further stressed that the present German Government had been formed in accordance with a majority of the German Parliament, and that the German Chancellor "speaks in the name of the German Government and of the German people"[82]). Wilson's first question had thus received an affirmative answer, but with this, the negotiations were, in fact, only just beginning.

The second American Note (14 October) represented a general tightening up[83]). Wilson now assumed the attitude desired by the Allies as regards a possible Armistice:

"It must be clearly understood that the process of evacuation and the conditions of an armistice are matters which must be left to the judgment and advice of the military advisers of the Government of the United States and the Allied Governments, and the President feels it his duty to say that no arrangement can be accepted by the Government of the United States which does not provide absolutely satisfactory safeguards and guarantees of the maintenance of the present military supremacy of the armies of the United States and of the Allies in the field. He feels confident that he can safely assume that this will also be the judgment and decision of the Allied Governments".

However, he at the same time pursued a goal that was quite his own[84]):

"It is necessary, also, in order that there may be no possibility of misunderstanding, that the President should very solemnly call the attention of the Government of Germany to the language and plain intent of one of the terms of peace which the German Government has now accepted. It is contained in the address of the President delivered at Mount Vernon at the Fourth of July last. It is as follows: "the destruction of every arbitrary power anywhere that can separately, secretly and of its single choice disturb the peace of the world; or, if it cannot be presently destroyed, at least its reduction to virtual impotency". The power which has hitherto controlled the German Nation is of the sort here described. It is within the choice of the German Nation to alter it. The President's words just quoted naturally constitute a condition precedent to peace, if peace is to come by the action of the German people themselves. The President feels bound to say that the whole process of peace will, in his judgment, depend on the definiteness and the satisfactory character of the guarantees which can be given in this fundamental matter. It is indispensable that the Governments associated against Germany should know beyond a peradventure with whom they are dealing".

Simultaneously, the Allies were advised "that the President has decided to send Mr. E. M. House to Europe as his special representative. Mr. House will start almost immediately"[85]).

While House started his journey and the Germans deliberated on the new American demands[86]), the Allies continued their efforts to press home their views; in a telegram dated 21 October[87]), the British Government pointed out that the German reply clearly had the aim of ensuring "a conditional armistice". As regards the military terms, Germany already seemed to assume that an unhindered retreat to its own borders was already accepted in principle and that all that remained was for agreement to be reached on a few supplementary details. "We are all well aware that this is not the President's view". The Experts were of the opinion that if this happened, it would give Germany the chance it most desired: time to reorganize a short front that could be defended. Peace negotiations under such conditions would never ensure fulfilment of the demands of the Associated Powers. It would mean a constant threat of a resumption of hostilities. Any Armistice therefore had to contain terms that would ensure against this "and probably against any violations of the final Treaty of Peace when that is concluded". According to the Experts, this could only be done if the Armistice included the following terms:

"A. That some enemy territory, including at least Alsace and Lorraine, be at once occupied by Allied troops, and
B. That adequate precaution be taken against the resumption of naval warfare".

It was greatly hoped that Wilson would not bind himself on these vital questions without prior consultation with the Allies. The British Government had thus now begun to follow the sharp military line: guarantees were demanded, not only against the resumption of hostilities, but also for the keeping of the Treaty of Peace, and so the demand for occupation now appeared.

Wilson again bowed to the Allied views: he finally passed his correspondence with Germany to the Allied Governments for detailed discussion and negotiation[88]), and, further, on 23 October, he advised the German Government "that the only armistice he would feel justified in submitting for consideration would be one which should leave the United States and the powers associated with her in a position to enforce any arrangements that may be entered into and to make a renewal of hostilities on the part of Germany impossible". But at the same time, he tightened the purely American demand as well: "the Kaiser must go"[89]):

"... Feeling that the whole peace of the world depends now on plain speaking and straightforward action, the President deems it his duty to say, without any attempt to soften what may seem harsh words, that the nations of the world do not and cannot trust the word of those who have hitherto been the masters of German policy, and to point out once more that in concluding peace and in attempting to undo the infinite injuries and injustices of this war the Government of the United States cannot deal with any but veritable representatives of the German people who have been assured of a genuine constitutional standing as the real rulers of Germany. If it must deal with the military masters and the monarchical autocrats of Germany now, or if it is likely to have to deal with them later in regard to the international obligations of the German Empire, it must demand, not peace negotiations, but surrender. Nothing can be gained by leaving this essential thing unsaid".

The Note was devised during a series of discussions between Wilson's political and military advisers[90]). Opinion was divided both as to the timeliness of now involving the Allies in the negotiations[91]) and as to the form of the reply. Tumulty—who always had a finger on the pulse of American opinion—stressed again and again that the popular demand was now for the resignation of the Kaiser[92]), and Lansing too recommended Wilson "to insist on political change as a guarantee of good faith and pointed out danger of submitting question of armistice on morale and public opinion ..."[93]). The President himself was aware that "(p)ublic opinion ... was as much a fact or a mountain and must be considered"[94]). All the participants in the discussion were incidentally in agreement that "(t)oday America can have more influence in peace meeting than in future. In July all Allies approved Wilson. If we continue to win the selfish aims will begin to be asserted"[95]).

By the time the third German Note arrived in the United States, House was on his way over the Atlantic. And as Admiral Benson advised against consultations by wireless, House was reduced to the role of spectator, and he was absolutely dissatisfied with the result. He had wanted Wilson just to send "a statement from the White House saying: "the President will immediately confer with the Allies concerning the German reply". The reason I would advise this is that it would keep down all intemperate discussion at home and would prevent another interchange of notes with Germany". What House now thought would follow were negotiations between the United States and the Allied military advisers "as to the military safeguards necessary before an armistice is granted"[96]). However, "(i)nstead of doing this he (Wilson) has gone into a long and effusive discussion which may have the effect of stiffening

German resistance and welding the people together back of their military leaders. If this should happen, the Labour and Socialist Parties in England, France and Italy would insist upon peace being made . . . He has taken, what seems to me, a reckless and unnecessary gamble. It might cost him the leadership in the Peace Negotiations, for it is conceivable that the Germans may approach some of the Entente Powers, believing that Wilson is more difficult to deal with . . ."[97]).

Nevertheless, it was Wilson, not House, who had taken the right view. The political developments in Germany could no longer be braked. An Armistice had now become vital to the country, and at the same time, the German–American negotiations had led a purely American policy to victory: Germany had accepted the principles embodied in Wilson's Fourteen Points and later declarations as the basis for the Peace, and shortly afterwards, the resignation of the Kaiser also became a fact. Indeed, the German–American exchange of Notes in October 1918 is generally regarded as a great personal diplomatic triumph for Wilson[98]).

Wilson sent the German–American correspondence to the Allied Governments *without any recommendations*. This point is very important: it was not the American President, but the Allied military experts (and politicians) who devised the Armistice[99]). The question is whether Wilson thereby jeopardized his victory.

In the deliberations concerning the framing of the American Notes, a number of different factors, relating to both domestic and foreign policy, had to be taken into account; but it must also be remembered that the situation itself changed during the negotiations. Whereas, at the beginning of October, Germany had still appeared as a formidable opponent, it was clear by the end of October which way things were going, and this could not fail to influence the balance of power between the United States and the Allies.

Wilson's decision to reply to the German Note at all was made practically in spite of public opinion in America, and the Republicans in particular continued with undiminished force throughout the negotiations, to call for unconditional surrender. However, there seems to be no doubt that during the exchange of Notes, the President won not only American but also Allied public opinion over to his policy[100]). Allied opinion in particular appears to have played a major part in the President's deliberations: He seems seriously to have feared the effect it would have on the morale of the Allies if he refused to negotiate with the Germans[101]). In addition, the fear that Bolshevism would spread to Eastern Europe, Germany and possibly to Western Europe was an additional factor in the considerations of Wilson and his closest advisers, although it is impossible to decide just how much weight was laid on this argument[102]). Finally, purely economic considerations, too, played a part: There was a limit to how long America could continue to finance not only its own war effort but also that of the Allies[103]).

The crucial development in the German–American negotiations took place with the despatch of the second American Note, since the President here bowed to the Allied wishes and stipulated that the framing of the Armistice should be carried out by the Allied and Associated military experts and that it would be framed in such a way as to ensure "the maintenance of the present military supremacy of the armies of the United States and of the Allies in the field"[104]).

This was a demand which, in the sharpened form it received in the third Note, would in actual fact put the victors in a position to dictate not only the terms of the Armistice but also those of the Treaty of Peace[105]). Seen from an American point of view, this development was not a completely unmixed blessing, but the question is whether the Americans were fully aware of this— and whether they could have prevented it while at the same time wanting to neutralize Germany.

In a confidential talk with William Wiseman on 16 October 1918[106]), Wilson said, inter alia:

"House and I have arrived at a formula which we think fairly sums up the positions: —'If the Germans are beaten, they will accept any terms; and if they are not beaten, we don't want them to accept any terms'. I think it should be possible to arrange an Armistice which would safeguard us against any possible treachery. It would be best for our Naval and Military experts to recommend terms for an Armistice. The heads of the Governments will probably have to modify the terms because the soldiers and sailors will make them too severe. We must not make them impossible, or even humiliating".

It must, of course, be remembered that this statement was made—however confidentially—to a spokesman for the Allies, so it is no good looking for a sign of Wilson's notorious distrust of his companions in arms. All the same, this and other statements[107]) bear witness to the fact that it was Germany that mainly occupied Wilson's thoughts at this time, although it is also clear from the final remarks that he was well aware that the *military* conditions would have *political* consequences.

During the negotiations on the framing of the third and last American Note, this problem was drawn up more clearly, and the mistrust expressed now seemed to be apportioned approximately equally between Germany and the Allies[108]).

"The President said that they (the Allies) needed to be coerced, that they were getting to a point where they were reaching out for more than they should have in justice. I (Secretary of State for the Interior Lane) pointed out the position in which the President would be if he proposed an Armistice which they (the Allies) would not grant. He said that this would be left to their military men, and they would practically decide the outcome of the war by the terms of the Armistice, which might include leaving all heavy guns behind, and putting Metz, Strasburg, etc., in the hands of the Allies, until peace was declared".

One week later, the development was an accomplished fact; on 28 October, Wilson telegraphed the following directions to House, who had now commenced the negotiations with the Allies in Paris[109]):

"My deliberate judgment is that our whole weight should be thrown for an armistice which will prevent the renewal of hostilities by Germany but which will be as moderate and reasonable as possible within those limits, because it is certain that too much success or security on the part of the Allies will make a genuine Peace Settlement exceedingly difficult, if not impossible. The position of Haig and Milner and Petain as reported by our Commander-in-Chief is therefore safer than Foch's . . .".

Wilson appears in general to have aimed towards a situation in which he could take the position of the exalted mediator at the Peace Conference: He had thus earlier most energetically discountenanced all attempts to involve the United States in the Allied plans on economic reprisals against Germany, also after the war, and steadfastly refused to discuss plans for the organization of the League of Nations with the Allies prior to the Peace Conference, since this would be "to construct a sort of Holy Alliance against Germany"[110]).

In his conversation with William Wiseman on 16 October, the President stated quite clearly that it was not his intention that House should discuss peace terms with the Allies. "He disliked the idea of settling peace terms without the enemy being present to state their case. It would give the impression of dividing the spoils amongst ourselves in advance"[111]).

The President was, in fact, busy arming himself for the Peace Conference—also against the Allies. They were not empty words he used when, at the War Council meeting on 17 October, during a discussion of Great Britain's "selfish policy", he said: "I want to go into the Peace Conference armed with as many weapons as my pockets will hold so as to compel justice"[112]). These weapons naturally included, first and foremost, America's mighty economic power in all its forms. This could be used both actively and passively, as food aid and/or loans, or as a threat (implemented or not) to withhold such assistance, and the threat was used in both ways[113]). It is from this angle that the heavy engagement of Wilson and House as regards the freedom of the seas should rightly be viewed. The freedom of the seas was only one aspect of Wilson's diplomatic armoury, and one that he was prepared to use in order to force Britain to accept his programme during the peace negotiations: the threat of building "a navy second to none". The fact that House, as we shall see, finally gave in and that Wilson accepted this[114]) was undoubtedly due to their realization that the Naval Act about to be laid before the Congress would be just as effective as a theoretical British acceptance of the freedom of the seas[115]).

It was thus now the Allies that took pride of place in the President's deliberations; it was *their* political ambitions he intended to check although *without* losing sight of the original aim—the weakening of Germany. It was this balancing act House was selected to perform, but if it were to succeed, there would have to be an exceptionally favourable political situation and a pre-eminent diplomatic effort, neither of which was at Wilson's disposal.

The German appeal came at the least convenient moment for Wilson; had it come eighteen months earlier, the United States would never have entered the war, and Wilson would automatically have taken the position as the neutral, unbiased mediator; had it come eighteen months or perhaps one year later, the Allies would have been so exhausted and impoverished that the United States would have been in a sovereign position to dictate terms to friend and foe alike. But as it was, the appeal came at a time when the whole of American Society was in highest war gear, while the Allies still retained their strength, and while Wilson's position at home was no longer as safe as it had been.

America was on the threshold of a mid-term Congressional Election, and the election campaign was already in progress. While such domestic problems as the Government's policy in favour of trade and its intervention in wheat prices but not in cotton prices, which favoured the South at the expense of the West ("the Sectional Issue") had hitherto taken first place in the debate, the problems of foreign policy now moved into the foreground[116]. The Democratic Party, which was once more facing a finally reunited Republican Party, found itself in serious danger of relapsing into its traditional minority role. Wilson and the leading tacticians of the party had already spent the summer considering various measures, and by the end of September the President seems to have decided to make a public appeal to the people to elect a Democratic Congress. However, the final decision was not taken until 10 October, when the Republicans made a sharp attack on the first Note to Germany, and, despite re-editing, the appeal was strongly coloured by the bitterness felt by the President[117]. The appeal was published on 14 October.

There is general agreement that the appeal was a tactical blunder[118], partly because it wounded many otherwise patriotic Republicans[119]—although these would hardly have been likely to vote Democratic anyway—and partly because the President stressed the fact that a Republican victory would be "interpreted on the other side of the water as a repudiation of my leadership". It is difficult to determine the actual effect of the appeal on the result of the election —which was a defeat for the Democrats[120], but most historians tend to take the view that it was local and regional questions, not national and international problems, that decided the election[121]. On the other hand, it can be said of the result that, appeal or not, a defeat would in any event have weakened the international standing of the President. However, as Thomas A. Bailey rightly remarks[122]:

"Foreign criticisms to the effect that Wilson was a repudiated leader were largely ill informed or for political effect, designed to humiliate or embarrass the President. Discerning Europeans knew perfectly well that Wilson was still a power to be reckoned with; they knew perfectly well that we did not have the parliamentary form of Government; they knew perfectly well that Wilson had not been legally repudiated".

The election took place on 5 November 1918, while the negotiations in Paris between House and the Allied Prime Ministers were being concluded, and the election campaign reached its climax just at the time of these critical negotiations[123]).

Edward House left the United States on 16 October, on a mission that marked the culmination of his remarkable career up to that time: as Special Envoy of the President, he was selected to head the American negotiations with the Allies on the conclusion of an Armistice with Germany[124]). The credentials he bore with him gave him, in fact, *carte blanche*[125]), and the President's farewell words were, as so often before, "I have not given you any instructions because I feel you will know what to do"[126]). Thus, while Wilson still seems to have retained the illusion of absolute community of thought, House himself was evidently more doubtful. Before his departure, he had a number of talks with the President, but his diary does not describe them in detail[127]). There are certain factors, however, that indicate that House was not entirely certain of Wilson's real intentions. It was thus House who had arranged the meeting mentioned earlier between Sir William Wiseman and the President[128]). The meeting took place on 16 October, after House himself had left Washington, and he later received both a written and a verbal account from Wiseman of the course of the talks. As for the reason for this strange arrangement, House himself said that he could in this way find out exactly how much Wilson wished the Allies to know of his plans. But he gave yet another reason: "he (Wilson) "thinks aloud" when with me and it is difficult to always catch what he has settled upon as a final conviction"[129]).

The German–American exchange of Notes had dealt with two matters, partly the assumptions for the conclusion of an Armistice, and partly the basis for a coming conclusion of Peace, Germany having accepted Wilson's Fourteen Points and later declarations as the basis for this Peace. However, the Allies had never officially bound themselves to this programme, and it was therefore House's task to reach agreement with them on both elements of this German–American correspondence—and this at a time when the mutual distrust between the parties was at its highest. Concurrent negotiations were held on the two components, but it was on acceptance of the Fourteen Points that House concentrated his main effort and it was here, in his own opinion, that he won his great diplomatic victory[130]). In the negotiations on the framing of the Armistice on the other hand, he seems to have remained far more passive and, indeed, almost to have regarded himself in the role of mediator[131]). He supported Foch's military terms, and the British terms as regards the German navy. However, this did not, as has been asserted, result in "a lessening of the severity of both the military and naval terms"[132]), but on the contrary, the most stringent requirements, at any rate as regards the military terms, which was clearly against the aim of the President, as expressed in the telegram to House of 28 October cited above[133]). Before the negotiations began, House had himself, in his diary, said that he shared Wilson's views[134]), so what was it that later made him change his mind?

As we have seen, Wilson's above-mentioned views were an expression of the realization that the Armistice terms would have not only a purely military but also a political content and that their framing would thus to a certain degree determine the course of the subsequent peace negotiations: it would to some extent be possible, by means of Armistice terms on occupation and internment, to discount in advance the final peace terms, and the bargaining positions at the Peace Conference itself would at the same time be fixed to the advantage of the Allies. And this is actually what happened. For France and Britain, the German Armistice represented the first step on the road to the realization of important war aims: the occupation of the Rhineland and the internment of the German fleet[135]). But it also meant a considerable weakening of the American negotiating position, as expressed sharply but appositely by K. D. Erdmann[136]):

"Mit seiner Zustimmung zur Entwaffnung und Rücknahme der deutschen Armee über den Rhein hatte sich Wilson der Möglichkeit beraubt, die Rolle des Friedensvermittlers zwischen den Gegnern spielen zu können, die ihm ursprünglich vorschwebte. Seine Hände waren gebunden".

Something similar happened in the case of the Austrian Armistice. The demarcation line that had been fixed between the Austro-Hungarian and the Allied armies, was identical to the boundary laid down in the Treaty of London, which the United States had refused to recognize[137]). At a meeting between the three Allied Prime Ministers and Edward House on the morning of 31 October, both Lloyd George and Clemenceau advocated the boundary of the Treaty of London as the demarcation line, although Lloyd George did not wish the Treaty itself mentioned, and Orlando signified his acceptance. House stressed the fact that America found it preferable for the necessary guarantees to be obtained without invoking the Treaty[138]); but he did not actually oppose the demarcation line itself. On the other hand, the Serbian representative, Vesnitch, who was present at the meeting held the same afternoon, most definitely did oppose it: he wanted Austria out of the whole of the Yugoslavian region. Clemenceau, however, stressed that the Armistice terms should not be mistaken for Peace terms, and House was not disposed to support Vesnitch either[139]). As we shall see later, it was on the basis of precisely the same assurances that House had the day before accepted the occupation of the Rhineland.

The military terms of the Armistice with Germany were mainly framed by Marshall Foch, working in close collaboration with Clemenceau[140]), and regardless of the differences that already seem to have been felt between the two men at this time[141]), it must be reasonable to regard these terms as an expression of official French policy. The main points had already been submitted to the Inter-Allied Conference in Paris on 9 October[142]). The three decisive terms were: "Germany was to evacuate the occupied zones, including Alsace-Lorraine." The Allies had to have a military vantage point against possible new attacks and therefore had to have three bridgeheads on the Right bank of the Rhine. And, as the third principal term: *"taken position of security for the reparations* to be exacted for the destruction perpetrated in Allied countries, the demand for which will be presented in the course of the negotiations of the Peace Treaty. For this the countries of the Left bank of the Rhine will be evacuated by enemy troops within a delay of thirty days; they will be occupied and administered by the Allied troops in concert with the local authorities up to the time of the signature of peace"[143]). With this formulation, the third point was thus clearly political, being aimed at ensuring guarantees for the terms the French wanted to have included in the Peace Treaty, and more disguised, at ensuring the boundary of the Rhine[144]). Of course, the purpose was not expressed as clearly as this in the official terms, nor in the draft House received from Clemenceau on 26 October[145]). Precisely on the question of the occupation of the Rhineland, Foch's proposal differed decisively from both the Resolution of the Allied Prime Ministers and the proposal submitted by the military advisers at the Inter-Allied Conference at the beginning of October[146]). Both these proposals demanded only evacuation of the occupied areas and withdrawal of the German army to their own side of the Rhine.

On 25 October, a conference was held in Senlis between Foch, Petain, Haig and Pershing, at which the three Commanders-in-Chief had the opportunity of presenting their views to the Marshall, while the latter does not seem to have expressed himself in any way. It was clear from the report on this conference that Haig opposed severe terms, while both Pershing and Petain went in for Allied bridgeheads east of the Rhine[147]). Foch then prepared his final proposal, which took no account of Haig's objections[148]). However, Haig's view did not express the official British standpoint, for the simple reason that there was as yet no such thing. On the contrary, opinion was very divided, both among politicians and generals[149]). Lloyd George himself does not seem to have finally fixed on a course of action, and it is at any rate a fact that he attempted in the subsequent negotiations to oppose the French occupation demands[150]). However, it is important to remember that in a memorandum to the Cabinet on 20 October, Balfour proposed "further points for the Armistice, such as the surrender of the German Navy, and the occupation of parts of Germany other than those it was proposed to detach—such as Alsace-Lorraine—with a view to holding them as pledges for payment of reparations and the settlement of the eastern frontier"[151]), and that Lord Curzon, in a memorandum of 15 October, had proposed "that the Armistice ought to contain in it a summary of the main items we should insist on in our peace terms . . .", and at that, not just the terms contained in the Fourteen Points[152]).

If Haig did not express the official British standpoint, then Pershing at any rate did not express the official American view, for Wilson questioned the necessity of occupying Alsace-Lorraine and also doubted the advisability of occupying the East bank of the Rhine "as this is practically an invasion of German soil under Armistice"[153]). Wilson was opposed to any form of occupation.

Both the French and the British thus now had a clear eye on the possibility of realizing parts of their political programmes through the Armistice, and in the American camp, Bliss at any rate was well aware of this possibility[154]). On the other hand, House and his colleagues were hampered by the short time available for judging the consequences of Foch's proposal. It is true that Bliss knew that Foch had presented his views at the Inter-Allied Conference at the beginning of October, but he was only partially orientated on the content[155]). In its entirety, this did not come to the knowledge of the Americans until 26 October[156]). And House's task was naturally not made any easier by the fact that Pershing took a different view.

On the other hand, House's negotiating position was by no means unfavourable: it was clear that he was not facing a united Allied bloc on the question of the Armistice. Indeed, House's diary bears witness to the fact that he spent most of the first two days after his arrival on winning supporters for the moderate Armistice that Wilson wanted[157]). After this, the diary is completely silent on this subject, and, as mentioned earlier, House took a rather passive role during the negotiations on the question. The explanation of this is that House's link with the British Government, Sir William Wiseman, arrived from England on 28 October and advised House that the British Cabinet "has been having some stormy sessions over the President's peace terms. They rebel against the "freedom of the seas" and they wish to include reparations for losses at sea"[158]). From this time on House concentrated all his efforts on getting the Allies to accept the Fourteen Points[159]):

"It seems to me of the utmost importance to have the Allies accept the Fourteen Points and subsequent terms of the President. If this is done the basis for a peace will already have been made. Germany began negotiations on the basis of these terms, and the Allies have already tentatively accepted them, but as Germany shows signs of defeat it is becoming every day more apparent that they desire to get from under the obligations these terms will impose upon them in the making of peace. If we do not use care we shall place ourselves in some such dishonorable position as Germany did when she violated her Treaty obligations as to Belgium".

However, while House was fighting this battle, he completely lost sight of the political aspects of the Armistice, and it was this that made possible the dualism that characterized the Armistice and pre-Armistice Agreement—the dualism that in fact weakened the American bargaining position even before the Peace Conference began. What Wilson had feared became a reality: "too much success or security on the part of the Allies will make a genuine peace settlement exceedingly difficult, if not impossible".

The question is then, whether the Americans had really not expected any opposition to the Fourteen Points? House's almost panic-stricken reaction indicates that he at any rate had not been prepared for it. He seems to have assumed that "The Allies have already tentatively accepted them". Another pointer in the same direction is the fact that it was not until this day, 28 October, that House requested Frank Cobb and Walter Lippmann to prepare an interpretation of the Fourteen Points[160]. This so-called Cobb-Lippmann memorandum was ready on 29 October[161], and House used it in his negotiations with the Allies on the same day. The German peace offer had admittedly come unexpectedly[162], and it is true that House had been forced to rush off to Europe, but it is still amazing that the definition of the very core of American policy had to be undertaken in greatest haste by two members of the American Delegation who may have been trusted colleagues but who were far from being au courant with Wilson's latest views[163].

It is also characteristic that it was not until after their arrival in Europe that the American Delegates realized that the Allies were now determined to take the initiative from Wilson[164]. And it must also be pointed out that House, at any rate during the preliminary stage of the German–American exchange of Notes, had completely misjudged the attitude of the Allies. He had believed that they would "want to throw the burden on you (Wilson)", and had therefore wanted to get to Europe as quickly as possible "to show them how unwise this would be"[165]. Finally, it must also be remembered that House had never shared the President's general distrust of the Allies but had, on the contrary, always advocated intimate collaboration, both in war and in peace[166].

Among Wilson's advisers it was House who had engaged himself most strongly in Wilson's ideological propaganda offensive in Europe[167], and both he himself and, to a certain extent also Lansing and Wilson, seem to have allowed themselves to be led astray by their own ideas, strongly supported by Ray Stannard Baker's reports and William C. Bullitt's interpretations[168]. Through his propaganda offensive, the President had intended not only to undermine the German Government, but also to fortify his own position as the leader of the Left-wing forces[169], in order to obtain sufficient strength to impose his own policy on the Peace Conference. Wilson's hold on the Left-wing forces was mainly ideological, and the Fourteen Points denote the climax of this alliance. The situation to which this programme was directed, a situation with strong and increasing unrest on the Left wing of the political spectrum, but with Bolshevism as the most serious challenge to Wilson's leadership[170], had, however, changed fundamentally. "Whereas in 1917–18, in the heat of the war, the Allied "parties of movement" (predominantly the Left) put their imprint on the diplomacy of the world crisis, in 1918–19, while peace was being made, "the parties of order" (predominantly the Right) reclaimed their primacy in the victor nations". It was a case of a "Right-wing resurgence[171]". The conditions under which Wilson's principles and aims came into being no longer applied[172]), and it was this new situation that now faced House and his colleagues[173]); House had to make a choice, and he apparently preferred to gather up the remnants of the old policy rather than attempt to formulate a new one.

The actual negotiations between House and the Allied Prime Ministers began on 29 October. They resulted in the framing of the Armistice terms to the Central Powers and in what is usually known in the American literature as the pre-Armistice Agreement, and in more neutral terms in the English literature, as the Lansing Note[174]). In this, the Allies declared themselves willing to conclude peace with Germany on the basis of the Fourteen Points, with two reservations: they reserved for themselves complete freedom at the Peace Conference in relation to the freedom of the seas, and they specified that the claim for reparations included "compensation ... for all damage done to the civilian population of the Allies and their property by the aggression of Germany by land, by sea and from the air". It was these reservations—and these only—that Britain had insisted on even before the Conference began.

The decisive negotiations on the Allies' approval of the Fourteen Points were held on 29 and 30 October. The meeting on 29 October is crucial to an understanding of the course of the rest of the negotiations because it was here that the procedure for the Conference was laid down[175]). The course of the meeting shows that the British had analysed the situation correctly even before negotiations started: the way in which the negotiations between the American President and the German Government had been conducted meant that two things were now required: 1. that the Allies make known their attitude to the Fourteen Points, and 2. that an Armistice be concluded with Germany[176]). Indeed, the meeting was dominated by Lloyd George; it was on his initiative that the actual procedure for the Armistice was fixed, viz. that Germany should get the Armistice terms direct from Foch and not through Wilson[177]). This meant that the subsequent negotiations were definitely in the hands of the Allies. It was also on his initiative that steps were taken right from the beginning of the negotiations to establish the Allied attitude to the Fourteen Points[178]). It was thus the British version of the procedure that decided the subsequent course of the negotiations.

Pichon and Clemenceau on the other hand, were only prepared to discuss the Armistice terms, and only interested in these[179]), and Clemenceau does not even seem to have realized that he had here an opportunity of evading Wilson[180]). He was primarily concerned with establishing that it was the Governments, not Foch, that should have the final word on the framing of the Armistice terms, since these would also contain political resolutions[181]). France was thus totally unprepared for having to take a stand on the question of the Fourteen Points, and this explains much of the events of the next day. On the question of procedure, House acted as a passive support for Lloyd George[182]), while Sonnino was apparently the only one interested in ensuring uniformity and simultaneity in the action taken as regards Germany and Austria–Hungary. However, his views were constantly swept aside by the others[183]).

The discussion of the Fourteen Points thus prompted by Lloyd George is equally interesting. Harold I. Nelson has asked whether Lloyd George here attempted to ensure "the postponement, if not rejection, of the Fourteen Points as the basis of peace negotiations and as the condition for an Armistice"[184]). If it is at all permissible to deduce the motives involved from the actual course of the negotiations, the answer has to be in the negative; at that time, Lloyd George already seems to have been prepared to support the Fourteen Points, with two reservations: freedom of the seas and reparations. Britain could not see her way clear to giving up her right to blockade and had, moreover, to insist on reparations both for the losses suffered by the occupied territories and for those suffered by the British merchant navy[185]). It was these that subsequently became the official British reservations, and they were already embodied next day in a memorandum prepared by Lloyd George.

That House understood the situation differently is quite another matter. The British attitude lay clearly in line with the views already expressed before House's arrival[186]). It was a policy that was intended to provide security as regards both the United States and Germany—as Balfour put it, it was feared that Germany would succeed in driving a wedge between the United States and the Allies[187]). In all events, Lloyd George had now provided the opportunity for a debate on Wilson's programme, and Clemenceau was not slow to pick up the thread: France had never been asked about its attitude to the Fourteen Points[188]). Pichon tried to get the question postponed until after the Armistice[189]), but was prevented from doing so by Balfour, and the Conference therefore passed to a point-by-point debate of the Fourteen Points[190]).

House's attitude during this entire discussion was comparatively reticent, but nonetheless crucial: he delivered a rather vague threat, which he interpreted, in reply to a direct question by Clemenceau, as a threat of the conclusion of a separate Peace between America and Germany if the Allies did not accept Wilson's programme[191]). The British report of the meeting shows that Lloyd George rejected this threat and that Clemenceau supported him. Lloyd George said: ". . . if the United States of America were to make a separate peace, we should deeply regret it, but, nevertheless, should be prepared to go on fighting. (M. Clemenceau here interjected 'Yes'.) . . ."[192]). The French version on the other hand, shows that Lloyd George perhaps failed to take this threat seriously: "Le Président Wilson agira selon sa conscience. Mais il ne crois pas que son départ—si l'on pouvait concevoir une chose pareille—nous empêcherait de poursuivre notre route et de continuer la guerre. . . ."[193]). However, Clemenceau touched upon the threat later in the talks, so it may anyway have made some impression on him[194]). House further made it clear that it was useless to discuss the Armistice terms before the situation as regards the Fourteen Points had been clarified[195]). Just as important is the fact that House seems to have suggested during the talks that the Fourteen Points were very vague and thus open to various interpretations[196]). It is clear, moreover, that this statement was not wasted on Lloyd George: "Je ferai observer que toutes les propositions du Président Wilson sont assez élastiques pour que sous puissions les accepter, sauf celle qui a rapport à la liberté des mers"[197]). On the other hand, care must be taken not to over-estimate the importance of House's statement, since the framing of the so-called Cobb-Lippmann memorandum can be regarded as an effort on House's part to give the points a definite interpretation. The debate ended with the Allies promising to have their reservations formulated in time for the next day.

Before the meeting broke up yet another couple of controversial subjects were touched upon. A statement by Clemenceau to the effect that he did not intend to participate in the near future in a League of Nations together with Germany produced an extremely sharp and cogent reply from House: 'Dans son discours du 27 septembre le Président a nettement indiqué son intention de stipuler l'établissement de sa Sté des Nations dans les clauses du traité de paix"[198]). The very crux of Wilson's programme now seemed to be in danger. Finally, the Armistice with Germany came up, and Balfour expressed fears that Germany would not accept such severe terms, whereas Clemenceau thought that it would do so, after some reflection. The naval terms were then read out[199]).

It is obvious that, after this meeting, House considered the situation to be extremely serious, and he apparently regarded Lloyd George's attitude as a stab in the back—a deliberate attempt to incite Clemenceau[200]). Before the actual meeting, House had had several talks with the British representatives on precisely those problems relating to the freedom of the seas[201]). He had himself, right from the start, taken a hard line and declared that the United States would not accept British naval dominance. If America were challenged, it would build a larger fleet than Britain, and it had the necessary resources to do this[202]). It was thus not just a question of international law. The controversy regarding the freedom of the seas was only a symbol of the deeper clash of interests that was now about to make itself manifest between the only two Great Powers left, one of them in a state of enterprise and progress, the other in a state of recession and stagnation. This is why the subsequent debate became so heated and why the problem arose again, although in another disguise, during the actual Peace Conference. All the same, House thought he had come close to a solution of the difficulties, on the basis of the Cobb-Lippmann interpretation, during a lunch-time meeting with Lloyd George, Balfour and Reading on 29 October[203]).

It is clear that House was being too optimistic, but this naturally only added to the shock he received during the subsequent discussion. House's report to Wilson was altogether dramatic, and he appears to have greatly over-estimated the effect of his threat of a separate Peace. "My statement had a very exciting effect upon those present". What House quite forgot to report was that, as shown by the concordant British and French texts, Lloyd George maintained his standpoint even after the threat[204]. House was further able to advise Wilson that neither the French nor the Italian Prime Minister sympathized with the idea of the League of Nations, and that the latter would possibly make many objections to the Fourteen Points. That House's report seems a trifle over-dramatized may be due to the fact that it was written not by himself but by Gordon Auchincloss[205]. This was unfortunate, because a more sober analysis might well have produced a less passionate reaction from Wilson than was actually the case[206].

House was thus in a very difficult position, being under pressure on two sides. Fear of precipitate action on the part of Wilson may well have contributed to the fact that House did not keep the President fully informed of the developments of the negotiations of the next few days, especially as regards the more difficult passages[207].

Meanwhile, House himself sent Wilson a direct telegram in their own private code; this was shorter and more realistic, and it shows far more clearly what House considered the real danger: not the British reservations, but the reaction these would produce in the other Allies[208]:

"The English I think will accept your Fourteen Points with some modification such as leaving open the question of reparation at sea and the making of the Freedom of the Seas conditional upon the formation of a League of Nations. The French are inclined not to accept your terms but to formulate their own . . .".

In the meantime, House sought new means of solving the critical situation. He must have realized that the threat of a separate Peace had not worked. At 3 o'clock in the morning he arrived at a new means of applying pressure: he would combine the threat of a separate Peace with a threat of publicity— if the Allies would not agree to Wilson's programme, the President would submit the Allied terms to Congress, which should then decide whether these were worth a continuance of the fighting[209]. House advised Wilson of his intention and at the same time proposed the following drastic measures: reduction of the troop transports, followed by a reduction of loans, food and raw materials. House was convinced that "we should play a strong hand", and, with Wilson's consent, he would do so in a "gentle and friendly" manner[210]. However, by the time House received Wilson's passionate agreement next day to the threat of publicity[211], the crisis had already been solved, and House noted in his diary: "the President's cable was intemperate and if I had read it to my colleagues it may have led to serious trouble"[212].

At a conference on the morning of 30 October, House presented his new plan to Frank Cobb and Admiral Benson, who both signified their agreement[213], and shortly afterwards, House had a meeting alone with Clemenceau and Lloyd George[214]. This was the most important meeting of the whole conference. What House had the day before interpreted as a British machination now actually proved to be an outstretched hand. Lloyd George spoke privately with House before the meeting and passed him a memorandum that was to all intents and purposes identical with the final pre-Armistice Agreement[215]). This memorandum contained the reservations mentioned earlier with regard to the freedom of the seas and reparations: Britain must reserve for herself complete freedom with regard to freedom of the seas at the Peace Conference and demanded compensation for all damage inflicted on the civilian populations of the Allies by the German aggression—on land, at sea and in the air.

House accepted this memorandum with a remark to the effect that he was afraid that Clemenceau would not agree to it as it was "in marked contrast to the position taken by George yesterday". This seems to indicate that House had completely misinterpreted the meeting of the day before, since the memorandum was in exact accordance with the arguments Lloyd George had presented there. At the same time, House aired his great concern: "I told George that I was afraid his attitude at yesterday's meeting had opened the flood gates; Clemenceau, Sonnino would have elaborate memoranda to submit containing their objections to the President's Fourteen Points, . . ."[216]). It also proved at once "that Clemenceau was having prepared an elaborate brief setting forth France's objections to the President's Fourteen Points". House therefore found it necessary to use his well-prepared threat. "As soon as I had said this George and Clemenceau looked at each other significantly". Clemenceau immediately gave up the idea of preparing a memorandum "and *apparently* accepted the proposed answer drafted by the British"[217]). If House's account is correct—and France did indeed accept the British memorandum—then the French policy seems to have been nipped in the bud by the joint Anglo-American onslaught. Was this due to House's threat, as already indicated at the meeting the day before, or had Clemenceau obtained promises in return?

As we have seen, the French Government concentrated on the Armistice terms; it was through these that the French intended to realize their political goals and they were therefore not prepared for a discussion of the Fourteen Points. General Mordacq asserts that House had a private meeting with Clemenceau before the meeting, and that Clemenceau here won House's support of the French Armistice terms[218]). House himself does not mention such a meeting, but it may well have taken place. House does not mention everything in his diary, and particularly as regards these negotiations, his entries are far from complete. It is at any rate a fact that when the conference passed to a discussion of the Armistice terms, House took a favourable stand on the question of the French wish for an occupation of the Rhineland territories: "I am inclined to sympathize with the position taken by Clemenceau". Lloyd George thought that such an occupation would be unwise, but Clemenceau asserted that he would be unable to maintain his position in the

Chamber of Deputies and as regards the army if the occupation did not take place[219]). When, on 1 November, Lloyd George again tried to prevent the occupation of the Rhineland, he received no support from House[220]). House took this standpoint: "Colonel House said that he was not disposed to take from Germany more than was absolutely necessary, but he was disposed to leave the matter in Marshall Foch's hands"[221]). Thus, as from 30 October, House seems finally to have given up his resistance to the Armistice terms proposed by Foch.

On the afternoon of 30 October, House again met the Allied representatives, and this time the Italians were also present. The events of the morning meeting repeated themselves, but now in the form of combined British–French–American pressure on Italy[222]). Sonnino had formulated a reservation to point IX, which he wished to have included in the memorandum that was to be sent to Wilson[223]). However, both Clemenceau and Lloyd George swept this aside with the argument that such a reservation did not belong in the Armistice with Germany, which was the question under discussion.

It is perhaps significant that while House elaborated at length on his negotiations with Clemenceau and Lloyd George in his reports to Wilson, he made no mention whatsoever of the extremely important Italian reservation. Only very indirectly did he suggest that he would, in the given situation, have preferred an evasion, not a solution, of this explosive question: "It was agreed that the terms of the military and naval Armistice to be offered Austria should be reviewed by the Allied generals and admirals, and when completed should be transmitted direct through General Diaz to the Austrian Commander-in-Chief. *This has the advantage of avoiding political discussion respecting Italian and other claims before capitulation of Austria (received)*"[224]). The next day he even went so far as to declare in a telegram: "it is my opinion that the submission of terms of Armistice to Austria in the circumstances and without any express qualifications, may be construed as an acceptance on the part of the Allies of the President's proposals"[225]). Not until 3 November did Wilson learn that the Italians had protested against point IX[226]).

After the meeting on 30 October, House held a conference with members of the American Delegation; with reference to this, Frank Cobb wrote: "House had won partial diplomatic victory at the conference of Prime Ministers who had accepted the President's Fourteen Points with two specific qualifications in respect to the meaning of Freedom of the Seas and reparation for property wantonly destroyed"[227]). If anyone is to be called a victor in this connection, it must surely be Lloyd George. It was his interpretation of procedure that decided the course of the negotiations and it was his reservations only that were included in the so-called pre-Armistice Agreement[228]).

However, all problems were far from having been solved at the meetings on 30 October. Twice more, on 1 and 3 November, the Italians tried in vain to win a hearing for their reservation[229]), and France was not yet altogether satisfied either. Clemenceau wanted the actual Armistice terms to include a section on the principle of the right of the Allies to reparations that went much further than the reservation proposed by Lloyd George in the pre-Armistice Agreement: "all future claims or demands of the Allies being reserved"[230]). Clemenceau advanced his wishes on both 1 and 2 November. On the first day, both Lloyd George and House opposed him, on the grounds that this was a Peace term and therefore had no place in the Armistice and further, that it had already been mentioned in the memorandum to Wilson[231]). However, the following day, Clemenceau got his own way[232]). Charles Seymour has commented as follows: ". . . upon this apparently innocent sentence was later based the French claim that, as regards reparations, they were not bound by the terms of the pre-Armistice Agreement, but were authorized to insert in the Conditions of Peace any terms that seemed to them justified by circumstances"[233]). Here, French policy thus stands out clearly: the French were seeking to get their demands realized via the Armistice terms and practically ignored the pre-Armistice Agreement. Whether House saw through this strategem is doubtful. Wilson was at any rate not advised of the French initiative. On the other hand, a French attempt to ensure, also through the Armistice terms, the establishment of a Poland with the 1772-boundary failed owing to British opposition[234]).

Nevertheless, the pre-Armistice Agreement had not solved all the problems in relation to Britain either. The American President was not satisfied with the reservation with regard to point II: "I am not clear that the reply of the Allies quoted in your 12 definitely accepts the principle of Freedom of the Seas and means to reserve only the free discussion of definitions and limitations. Please insist that that be made clear before I decide whether to accept the reply or go again to the Congress who confidentially will have no sympathy whatever with spending American lives for British naval control . . ."[235]). Incidentally, Wilson did recognize the special British position in this matter and realized the necessity for the freest possible exchange of views: he wanted a redefinition of the right to blockade, but he did not want it abolished. His attitude was thus by no means dogmatic, although he did demand a declaration of principle. However, he never actually got this, House only managing to force from Lloyd George the following modest promise: "we were quite willing to discuss the Freedom of the Sea in the light of the new conditions which have arisen in the course of the present war"[236]). And even this took quite a lot of getting.

The negotiations were conducted partly during the official meetings and partly outside, with Reading and Wiseman as intermediaries. A crisis already arose on 1 November; the afternoon meeting was held at Versailles, and here, the Belgian representatives were also present. The meeting began with Clemenceau reading out the memorandum to Wilson on which the other Allies had agreed on 30 October, and the Belgian representative immediately had a number of different objections to this[237]), particularly as regards points 3 and 5. Lloyd George joined in and asked House to elaborate on point 3. Orlando then drew attention to point 9, and the Fourteen Points thus came under debate once more. However, House refused to take a discussion on them at this time on the grounds that he did not have his notes with him—a deliberate diversion—[238]). The available minutes of the meeting thus seem to show that it was purely a question of a routine reopening of the discussion of the memorandum in order that the Belgians might have the opportunity of presenting their views. House, however, thought that it was Lloyd George who had brought the matter up again[239]). At all events, the discussion caught House completely unprepared. Wilson was not advised regarding this meeting[240]).

Immediately before the meeting, House had received the above-mentioned telegram from Wilson, demanding British acceptance in principle of the freedom of the seas, and immediately after the meeting, he took the matter up with Wiseman. The previous meeting had naturally not put House in a very sympathetic mood, and he at once took a hard line, simply informing Wiseman that unless Lloyd George "would make some reasonable concessions", "all hope of Anglo Saxon unity would be at an end". House even conjured up the war of 1812. The American Government and the American people would not tolerate that either the British or any other Government should dictate the terms on which American ships should sail the seas[241]). The ball was thus set rolling again, and the next day, Wiseman and Reading made great efforts to find a solution[242]). House reported as follows to Wilson: "I am insisting that they must recognize the principle that it is a subject for discussion at the Peace Conference or before, and I am having the greatest difficulty in getting them to admit even that much . . ."[243]). It is obvious here that House had already had to modify considerably Wilson's demand for recognition of the principle; House now only demanded that England should recognize that the matter was open to discussion at all.

Wilson again gave House the strongest support imaginable[244]):

"I suggest that you urge that if the British cannot, relying upon our friendship and good faith, accept the principle of Freedom of the Seas they can count upon the certainty of our using our present great equipment to build up the strongest navy our resources permit, as our public opinion has long desired".

Before this telegram arrived, however, a solution had been reached on the basis of the formula described above: "we were quite willing to discuss the Freedom of the Sea in the light of the new conditions which have arisen in the course of the present war". This occurred at a meeting on 3 November[245]). Here, House made one last attempt to get Lloyd George to accept the principle, and this produced exactly the same reaction in the British Prime Minister as that by which Clemenceau had, a few days earlier, justified the occupation of the Rhineland[246]):

"Mr. Lloyd George said he could not do this. If he did it would only mean that in a week's time a new Prime Minister would be here who would say that he could not accept the principle. The English people would not look at it. On this point the nation was absolutely solid. Consequently, it was no use for him to say that he could accept when he knew he was not speaking for the British nation".

Confronted with the vital interests of the European Great Powers, American policy had to give in unless it were to make use of drastic measures, and this House was not prepared to do[247]).

The British version took the form of a letter from Lloyd George to House, and no amendments were made to the formulation of the memorandum sent to Wilson and later to Germany. It was not found necessary either, to inform Germany of the amendment with regard to point III, which was agreed at the same meeting[248]). Next day, the Armistice terms were finally approved, and the negotiations were thus at an end.

It is obvious that House himself regarded the "battle" on the freedom of the seas as the most serious problem of the negotiations, and that he enjoyed Wilson's full support on this question. However, even bearing in mind that the dispute concerned more than merely a doctrine of international law, the heat with which the negotiations were conducted is still surprising, especially in view of the fact that the problem was not raised at all at the Peace Conference, or at any rate, not in that form. There are also signs that both the British and the Americans were themselves surprised by the violence of the discussion. Frank Cobb, who had participated in a number of the unofficial negotiations was, while these were being conducted, of the opinion that Lloyd George "(was) playing politics with issue", since the British elections were expected to take place in the period between the conclusion of the Armistice and the commencement of the Peace Conference. He further noted that the negotiations in Paris were accompanied by "(t)remendous propaganda ... in England against "Freedom of the Seas". Inspired of course". And Cobb was not prepared either, to exclude the possibility that Lloyd George was simply trying to delay matters until the result of the American election was known[249]).

Cobb was in all events interested in investigating the matter more closely, and when he went to London a little later, he thought he had found the answer. Talks with Lord Milner and with Government officials convinced him that the reason for the heavy British engagement was to be found in a speech made a little earlier by the Chairman of the American Shipping Board, Edward Hurley. In this he had said that "the United States intended to build *the greatest mercantile marine in the world*". Cobb therefore came to the conclusion that the British had intended to show America "that if we persist in building the greatest mercantile marine in the world, they intend to keep it at their mercy and dictate the conditions under which it shall sail the seas"[250]). He had another theory too, which Milner was not completely prepared to reject: "I told him I had found evidence of an organized attempt to drive a wedge (between) President and Lloyd George. He said it was undoubtedly true, but it could not succeed, unless they made it succeed"[251]). However that may have been, the fact remains that the climate of the negotiations had been influenced by public opinion on both sides of the Atlantic.

The British, on the other hand, seem to have been just as astonished by the strong American reaction. In a comment on the talks held by Wilson in London at the end of December, Lord Hankey wrote: "on the freedom of the seas, the President, *as we had expected,* 'was very vague'. There was *none of the missionary zeal that House had displayed* at the Armistice discussions . . ."[252]). This suggests that the British Government had other sources of information with regard to Wilson's interpretation of the Fourteen Points than the semi-official Cobb-Lippmann memorandum that House used in the negotiations. And this was indeed the case. Immediately before his departure from America, Sir Eric Geddes had had a talk with the American President, in which they had discussed precisely the question of the freedom of the seas. Geddes reported as follows to Lloyd George on 13 October[253]):

"In talking of his fourteen conditions conversation with me naturally turned on Freedom of the Seas upon which his views are obviously unformed but his intention appears to be to deal with that if possible in generalities and acceptance of principle that no one Power in League of Nations shall exercise its naval strength to crush a belligerent Power without consent of the League leaving until the occasion arises any decision as to nationality of Naval police force. I ventured to explain to him that of all belligerent Nations our views would naturally be strongest on this point on account of our geographical position and overwhelming Naval superiority".

However, of equal importance was a conversation between Wilson and Sir William Wiseman on 16 October, in which the President discussed his Fourteen Points in great detail. Wilson spoke here in favourable terms of the role the British navy had up to then played "as a sort of naval police for the world— in fact for civilization". He pointed out, however, the fear nourished by many countries in regard to this power, even though he himself did not share this. "I gathered that the President was searching for a remedy which he might suggest, but that he had found none; in his mind there is an idea that the great power of the British Navy might in some way be used in connection with the LEAGUE OF NATIONS and thereby cease to be a cause of jealousy and irritation". Wilson further considered that a conference on the maritime provisions of international law should be held soon after the conclusion of peace. In many ways, the submarine had made a great number of the old regulations obsolete, and the definition of blockade also required revision[254]).

John L. Snell has rightly asserted that Wilson's comments, particularly with regard to the freedom of the seas, were far more conciliatory than the Cobb-Lippmann memorandum. "This helps to explain how the British were brought to accept and support all the Points except that concerning Freedom of the Seas"[255]). However, on other points too, the President's statements were more moderate than the British might have feared; this applied first and foremost to the problem that was of such decisive importance to the Empire: the German Colonies. Regarding these, Wilson had namely said that it was clear that they should not be returned to Germany, and that he, for his part, would have nothing against their being administered by Great Britain, although he would like this to be done in trust for the League of Nations. Britain did not therefore raise the Colonial question officially during the negotiations, although Lloyd George discussed it in private with House at their very first meeting. The British Prime Minister here suggested that the United States should act as Trustees for the German East-African Colonies, while he held that South-West Africa and the Asiatic islands should go to the Federation of South Africa and Australia, respectively, as Britain would otherwise be confronted with a revolution in these Dominions. Furthermore, Britain would have to take over the Protectorate of Mesopotamia and possible also of Palestine. Arabia should become an autonomous State, while France might be given a sphere of influence in Syria. We do not know House's reaction to all this, but it can hardly have been completely negative[256]). In any event, the American views were not such as to deter Lloyd George from making common cause with House against the French and Italian Governments in the subsequent negotiations. It was in the British interests as well, to limit as much as possible the reservations to the Fourteen Points.

On 5 November, House sent a telegram to Wilson, in which he took stock of the negotiations to date[257]):

"I consider that we have won a great diplomatic victory in getting the Allies to accept the principles laid down in your January 8th speech and in your subsequent addresses. This has been done in the face of a hostile and influential junta in the United States and the thoroughly unsympathetic personnel constituting the Entente Governments.

I doubt whether any of the Heads of the Governments with whom we have been dealing quite realize how far they are now committed to the American Peace Programme. As far as the question of Freedom of the Seas is concerned, I think it fair to say that Balfour agreed with me and so in a lesser degree did Sir Eric Geddes. It is only the mischievous and reactionary blue water school that drove George to take his extraordinary attitude. Reading I think treated the matter from the lawyer's viewpoint and felt that George was his client. What he said did not impress me as being his own convictions. Both Clemenceau and George want to make the League of Nations an after consideration. Curiously enough, your speech of September 27th as published here was clearly open to this interpretation. I set them right about it, but did not press it further at the moment, for in accepting your terms they automatically accept this also.

If Germany accepts the conditions of our Armistice, the Peace Conference should be called for December 11th or thereabouts. It would be necessary for you to leave as soon as possible in order to hold some preliminary conferences here with Great Britain, France and Italy. This is essential. If Germany accepts by November 10th could you not sail on the 18th? I think Oxford may offer you the degree of D. C. L. This would give a reason for landing in England and also for making an address.

I am now bringing every force to bear to help win a people's victory, and your landing in England is an essential part of it. I send Cobb to London tonight. Wiseman has been splendidly helpful".

House, completely unawares, here discloses on just how slender a basis this so-called victory rested. The pre-Armistice Agreement was, in reality, one big diversionary manoeuvre, in which all parties had deliberately evaded actual confrontation; House, on the grounds that if he succeeded in binding the Allies formally, they would also be bound *de facto;* and the Allies, on the grounds that there was a difference between fact and form in any negotiating situation. The French tactics in this connection were especially characteristic. Clemenceau very quickly—indeed, astonishingly quickly—gave up all opposition to the Fourteen Points, and in the subsequent negotiations, he even supported House in his attempt to get Lloyd George to accept the freedom of the seas[258]). In return, he obtained very considerable, real concessions in the Armistice terms: recognition of the principle of reparations and the occupation of the Rhineland. There is no doubt that the American Delegation regarded the French demand for an occupation of the Left bank of the Rhine as a *sine qua non*[259]), but both Wilson and House, right from the commencement of the negotiations, had been fully aware of the political consequences if the Allies managed to get such demands through. They allowed themselves to be pushed by the situation[260]).

If the above account of the negotiations between the United States and the Allies on the conclusion of an Armistice with Germany is correct, it must have a bearing on any evaluation of House as a diplomat. It is clear that he was in a difficult situation and that any (verbal) instructions he may have received from the President before his departure completely failed to cover the situation with which he found himself confronted in Paris. It is also clear that Wilson's vehement reactions must have brought pressure to bear on him. Nevertheless, the President reacted in this way simply because House sent him over-dramatized versions of the meetings instead of sober evaluations of the situation. Both as regards feeling for a situation and tactical vision, House seems to have failed miserably, finding it difficult to comprehend the tangled and complicated state of affairs in Europe. Would it be too much to say that he lost his head? At any rate, he had shown obvious weaknesses of a nature that are not expected in an international top negotiator, weaknesses that did not augure well for the future.

*Chapter 2*

# Problems of Organization
# and Strategy

The so-called pre-Armistice negotiations had dealt with two questions: the framing of the Armistice and the basis for the coming peace. However, the preparations for a future peace conference had been going on for a long time. Woodrow Wilson had entrusted Colonel House with the organization of these preparations on 2 September 1917[1]). There seem to have been several moves in this direction, which ended in Wilson deliberately choosing House without prior consultation with the State Department[2]). There is no proof that House, right from the beginning, saw in "The Inquiry" the possibility of creating an instrument of personal power at the Peace Conference, but the "Executive Committee", which he himself appointed, does indicate something of this nature[3]). As director of the Inquiry, House chose his brother-in-law, Sidney E. Mezes, whose principal qualification apart from this was that of being President of New York City College, which presumably gave him a certain amount of administrative experience. Mezes was a religious philosopher by profession[4]). David Hunter Miller became the treasurer[5]). He was a law partner of House's son-in-law, Gordon Auchincloss, and was thus a personal acquaintance of House. Finally, House made Walter Lippmann secretary, for reasons that accorded perfectly with the policy on which House and Wilson had at that time based the American war and peace propaganda. House put it as follows in a conversation with Isaiah Bowman[6]):

"He said that the Administration had to cooperate with the extreme liberals of the country and that he could think of none who had so much influence and was at the same time so easy to get along with as Lippmann, and he had therefore selected him to represent the Liberals."

The obvious aim of this choice of men to lead the Inquiry was thus to ensure House's personal dominance and the implementation of his policies.

Beyond this, House did not interfere very much in the work of the Inquiry, and he did not participate in the appointment of the remaining members[7]). Both omissions were to have far-reaching consequences. In the course of the spring and summer of 1918, such serious, personal discord arose within the Inquiry that the organization was threatened with dissolution[8]). One result of this was presumably Walter Lippmann's transfer to Army Intelligence early in the summer of 1918[9]), but of greater import must have been the fact that the crisis was basically a crisis of confidence in Sidney Mezes[10]), whom House had personally appointed to lead the Inquiry and through whom he presumably wished to control the organization. The leader of the "revolt" seems to have been Dr. Isaiah Bowman, head of the American Geographical Society and an outstanding member of the Inquiry[11]), but he appears to have had the most prominent members of the organization behind him[12]), and, of greater importance in this context, he had the support of David Hunter Miller[13]). The triumvirate through which House had expected to control the organization was thus now totally split and partly dissolved, while, at the same time, a veritable battle was under way between Bowman and Mezes over the leadership of the Inquiry.

The situation facing House was fraught with danger; if he disavowed Mezes, he would lose his direct, personal control of the organization, but if he dismissed Bowman, he would run the risk of most of the other members of the Inquiry following him. As was his custom, he decided on a compromise—and a compromise of a somewhat ambiguous nature—. He seems to have given Bowman the *de facto* leadership of the organization, while Mezes retained the nominal leadership[14]). This happened at the beginning of August 1918. However, it soon became apparent that the compromise would not work, and a new crisis was about to culminate in the middle of October, when House had to leave the United States in great haste in order to act as America's representative at the pre-Armistice negotiations[15]). Thus, just as the battle of the Peace Commission was gathering force, House lost full control of the Inquiry, and as he himself had to leave the arena and hand over the subsequent negotiations to the already discredited Mezes, his chances were not very good. The whole affair could hardly have been more unfortunate.

The peace policy had been House's domain ever since 1914, and it was therefore no accident that Wilson had appointed him to lead the Inquiry. In House's diary we can read how his thoughts constantly circled around the Conference, which was to be the conclusion of the war. His views underwent a long period of development, starting with his early talks with Sir Edward Grey, while America was still neutral, but it is only the later phases of the development that are of interest to us.

During the autumn of 1917 and the spring and summer of 1918, House had a number of talks with both Wilson and Lansing on the organization and composition of the coming Peace Commission[16]). It is clear from House's talks with Wilson that the President himself wished to be a Delegate at the Conference[17]), and as early as January 1918, Wilson had already decided on the composition of the Delegation that he finally agreed with House in October 1918[18]). The Democratic members of the Delegation were to be Lansing, House, Newton, D. Baker and Wilson himself, while right up to the last minute, there was doubt regarding the choice of the Republican member. House was not in favour of Baker, on the grounds that one Cabinet representative was enough[19]), and moreover, he was not always certain that he would like to be an official Delegate if Wilson really attended too[20]). However, Wilson had his way, and before his departure, House was thus also able to advise Lansing and Baker of Wilson's choice[21]). Wilson, had at the same time, "tentatively assented" to Governor McCall of Massachussets as the Republican representative, as proposed by House[22]). The question of the top representation thus seemed to have been settled by the time House left.

However, this was far from being the case with respect to the remainder of the Peace Commission, the composition of which now had to be decided. From House's point of view, the decisive factors were how the Inquiry would be placed and who would be appointed to the key post of Secretary General of the Commission. House had delegated Sidney Mezes to look after his own and the Inquiry's interests in this matter. Immediately before his departure, House had a conference with Mezes, at which they agreed on a reorganization of the Inquiry with a view to the coming Peace Conference[23]). The result— and possibly also the aim—of this reorganization seems to have been to return to Mezes full control of the organization[24]). This took place at a time when the new crisis within the Inquiry was just coming to a head and when Mezes' position appeared to be definitively weakened[25]). It is not known how aware House was of this development[26]), but as he now seriously needed full control of the organization, he settled on the man he regarded as most loyal to him personally, regardless of suitability. Thus it was Mezes who came to lead the subsequent negotiations with the State Department on the composition of the Peace Commission.

Ever since its establishment, the Inquiry had cooperated with the State Department[27]), although relations could hardly be called particularly warm[28]). However, something similar was also characteristic of the relationship between House and Lansing. Wilson conducted a good deal of his foreign policy through House, without consulting the State Department, and this naturally placed the two men in a delicate situation that must, in the long run, become untenable. And indeed, House's diary is spattered with allusions to the Secretary of State, usually in a superior, parental tone, and with a carefully recorded list of his deficiencies. There is no reason for supposing that Lansing's feelings towards his rival were any warmer. And one thing is at any rate certain: the latent enmity between the two men now erupted.

In September, the Inquiry had prepared two memoranda on the organization of the Conference, and from these it appears that the representatives of the Inquiry expected to play a very prominent role[29]). House himself had discussed the matter with Lansing on 23 September and had here stressed the necessity of a large staff[30]). On 14 October, viz, immediately before his departure, House again discussed the Commission with Lansing and here estimated a strength of "over 100"[31]). Sparse though the details of these talks are in Lansing's diary, it must still be concluded that he had been informed of House's views before the latter left for Europe[32]).

On 24 October, Lansing and Mezes discussed the composition of the Commission in greater detail[33]). The content of their talks is mainly known only from the report Mezes sent to House[34]), but even though this is not complete, it does illuminate the plans of both House and Lansing at that time. Lansing now for the first time felt free to express his frank opinion of the Inquiry; in his view it was inexperienced, and the State Department had better people. What is more, Lansing considered that the Secretary General of the Commission should be a person of experience, and such a man was only to be found at the State Department. He had no objections to the Inquiry force being kept together but intended to take up the whole question of the composition of the Commission with the President. Mezes summed up the dangers as follows: "He *may* try to get more of his men and to influence the composition of the Secretariat."[35]) The two men apparently had a plan prepared by House as the basis for their discussions[36]). Mezes now had to modify this plan, after which he sent it to Lansing[37]). Lansing received the plan on 29 October[38]) and immediately took it to Wilson[39]).

It had evidently been Lansing's intention to subordinate the Inquiry to an organization dominated by the State Department, and he undoubtedly saw his chance of trumping this through in House's absence. House's plans were on a grandiose scale, although we only know them in the form of the modified plan, the core of which was quite naturally the Inquiry. House imagined the Delegation divided into three departments, all under the Commissioners. These departments were to be: Secretariat; Inquiry (Territorial and Trade Adjustments); and a group called Technical Advisers (economic questions, army, navy, international law, raw materials, etc.). The most interesting point about the plan is that House saw the Inquiry placed directly under his authority. And House had not wasted time either; on board the USS "Northern Pacific", he wrote to Wilson on 22 October[40]), enlarging upon his plans for the composition of the Commission. In this letter, he took the Inquiry for granted; what was troubling him was the above-mentioned group of "Technical Advisers", which he imagined should be composed of the chiefs of the various "War Boards", Baruch, McCormick, Hoover, Hurley, etc. However, the real reason for his letter seems to have been his wish to have Frank Cobb and not George Creel as Chief of the Press Bureau of the Commission. Yet another indication of House's plans is provided by the composition of the small group he himself took to Europe; besides Admiral Benson, Chief of Naval Operations, he was accompanied by Frank Cobb, Joseph Grew of the State Department, and his son-in-law, Gordon Auchincloss, who had been temporarily attached to the State Department during the war[41]). We have seen for which part Cobb was being considered and, as will be seen later, there is good reason for assuming that Auchincloss was intended for the post of Secretary General of the Commission—it is at any rate certain that House was *not* thinking of Grew for this—[42]), but it is obvious from Mezes' above remarks that House was concerned about this important appointment.

On 29 October, Lansing laid the entire question of the Commission before the President[43]), and this conversation redounded to the advantage of the Secretary of State. Like Lansing, Wilson found House's proposal "much too ambitious", and he seems in general at this time to have had very little conception of how the Peace Conference would work out:

"... it is so unlikely that anything but the main territorial, political and racial questions at issue will be settled at the peace conference and practically so certain that all detailed discussions of financial and commercial and other similar arrangements will be delegated by the conference to special conferences or commissions, ...".

Wilson therefore preferred a small force, and left it to the State Department to work out "the necessary minimum personnel and organization."[44])

In this letter Wilson thus gave Lansing the actual authority to prepare the organization of the Conference, and he did this without thinking to ask House's advice first. Whether he had received House's letter of 22 October at this time is not known, but he was conversant with—and rejected—House's plan. However we interpret Wilson's ambivalent attitude in this entire matter[45]), there is no doubt as to the result: Lansing now started planning the organization "from the Department's standpoint"[46]). At the same time, the following cable was received from Paris[47]):

"Colonel House wishes Mezes to be asked to send him a cable advising him of the progress and difficulties of "Inquiry" since his departure. He wishes further to be fully advised regarding this work by cable."

However, it was too late—House had lost the first round.

While House, in Paris, was reduced to following the situation through the State Department-censored telegrams from Mezes[48]), and letters[49]), which, although not censored, were a long time en route, Lansing got on with the organization of the Commission. On 4 November, his first draft was ready[50]), and in the next few days, the plan was worked out, apparently in close cooperation with Wilson[51]). After a long conference with the President on 12 November, Lansing noted in his diary that: "He approved my personnel plan"[52]). This plan must be identical with the undated "Memorandum by the Secretary of State", which gives the structure of the Commission, with the names of its most important members added in Lansing's handwriting. Wilson, too, made additions to the plan[53]). According to this plan, the Commission consisted of a Secretariat, with Joseph Grew as chief, assisted by Leland Harrison and Phillip Patchin; a group of "Specialists", which was identical with the part of the Inquiry that Lansing and Mezes had managed to agree to include[54]); and, finally, a group of "Technical Advisers", which did not, as House had proposed earlier, include any economic experts, but did include all of three specialists on international law.

Wilson was later to assert to House that he had never agreed to Harrison and Patchin as Assistent Secretaries and had not indeed even known that Grew had been appointed Secretary General, imagining, on the contrary, that House was constructing an organization in Paris "and that when they got here we could determine together who should officer it."[55]) There is, of course, the possibility that Wilson approved Lansing's organization plan before the names were included, but this does seem rather unlikely, especially when we compare it with the fact that shortly after his talk with Wilson, Lansing advised Patchin that he had been designated Assistant Secretary[56]). In this connection it may be worth mentioning another episode in which Wilson took a similarly ambivalent attitude; on 2 December, he signed a memorandum to Edwin F. Gay, leader of the Central Bureau of Statistics, in which he gave this organization the exclusive right to supply the Commission with economic data, expressly referring to an admission by the Inquiry members themselves that the organization's studies did not suffice[57]). Lawrence E. Gelfand has rightly characterized this as "a frontal attack on the Inquiry"[58]). However, this arrangement led to great confusion in the Commission and vociferous protests on the part of the Inquiry, and the matter ended in a compromise in favour of the Inquiry. Nonetheless, "Before a calm descended the President confessed to A. A. Young of the Inquiry that he had not "to his knowledge ever authorized the arrangement by which Dulles was to be the exclusive channel of statistical communication from Washington to the peace conference"."[59])

If Lansing was not in possession of Wilson's approval of the composition of the Secretariat, he at any rate managed to hide the fact effectively when he next day sent this telegram to Joseph Grew in Paris[60]):

"... After consultation with the President you are selected to act as Secretary of the United States Commission to the Peace Conference. Your assistant secretaries will be Harrison and Patchin ...".

Lansing's choice of Grew, quite apart from the man's qualifications, may well have been dictated by the fact that he was a candidate whom it might be presumed would be acceptable to House, who had himself taken him to Paris as one of his secretaries.

In Paris, the choice came as a shock. Grew had just been recommended by House as leader of "the entire political intelligence organization of the Peace Conference, with headquarters in Paris."[61]) A couple of days earlier, Willard Straight had been transferred from the army to House's staff[62]), and he and Auchincloss spent the next few days discussing various plans for the organization of the Conference[63]). It seems obvious that House had intended to place one of these two men in the post of Secretary, and at any rate Auchincloss reacted with bitter disappointment:

"This of course is the best selection. It would be immensely improper for me to do this work, and I do not want to do it anyway. I do not want to stay over here as long as the Peace Conference is going to last, and if it ever became known, as it would of course, that Colonel House was one of the Commission, that his son-in-law was the secretary of the Commission, and his brother-in-law was the chief man in the 'Inquiry', there would be an investigation and a bitter attack on the part of the Republican Members of the Congress that we would never get over. My job is going to be to act as private secretary to the Colonel and to help him look after the President when he comes. This is all I want to do, for a couple of months after the Peace Conference is called I am going back to the United States to resume the practice of law and make some money. We will help Grew all we possibly can to get the thing organized. Willard Straight 64) will be of immense assistance to him."65)

Despite many attempts at rationalization, Auchincloss did not completely succeed in hiding the fact that he had actually expected to get Grew's job. However, the reference is particularly interesting because it gives an idea of House's reaction. "My job is going to be to act as private secretary to the Colonel and to help him look after the President when he comes." This, namely, was House's answer to Lansing's conquest of the organization: to build up his own organization within the organization, in the hope that Wilson would use this and not the official one, and, in all events, to create out of this a personal instrument of power.

House himself waited another month before ventilating his grievances[66]):

"Some time ago I determined to let Lansing carry his own fortunes without help or hindrance from me. He has not been entirely considerate, after what I had done for him. On the other hand I always appreciate the fact that I have been what Gerard once termed "Super-Secretary of State", and Lansing has played a minor part and has done it without complaint."

Thus, the long-standing truce between the two men was finally broken even before the Conference started.

On 15 November, House sent the following telegram to Wilson[67]):

"... I have had in mind the fact that while you are in Europe you will wish to keep in close touch with governmental business in the United States and to receive and send cable messenges (!) from and to Washington respecting many matters. I am making arrangements to handle all this so that it will be unnecessary for you to bring a large staff ...".

Was this House's first countermove against Lansing? It was at any rate a clear expression of the policy House now began to follow: he would try to get Wilson to limit his own staff so that he would have to use that of House. This policy was crowned with success, at least during the preliminary phase of the Conference.

The composition of House's staff appears from an undated "Memorandum on the Personnel of the American Commission to Negotiate Peace"[68]), which appears from its contents to have been written at the beginning of February 1919[69]). This memorandum provides the following information:

"Commissioner House: Total personnel—32. Including eight civilians, two Army officers, three Naval officers, eighteen enlisted Navy, and one enlisted Marine. This office looks after the bulk of the Presidential correspondence, which is voluminous, and this accounts for the magnitude of the personnel."

For the purposes of comparison, the same memorandum gives Wilson's staff as 15, Lansing's as 13, White's as 12, and Bliss's as 14. Equally noteworthy, however, is the composition of the various staffs: while the other offices employed almost exclusively military personnel apart from a very few civilians, House alone included naval personnel in his staff. Or, in the words of the minutes of a meeting of the Personnel Commission: "General Bliss seemed to think that there were a great many Navy men in the offices of Colonel House."[70]) There can be no doubt that House had a definite reason for his preference for the Navy[71]) and it is not difficult to guess what it was: when House went to Europe, Secretary of War Baker had been appointed one of the American Commissioners, and it was therefore fairly evident that the Commission would get the stamp of the Army, especially as this was already in Europe. Therefore, if House wished to retain his independence, he would have to turn to the Navy, and that is precisely what he did.

When the American Delegation finally gathered in Paris in the middle of December, a struggle for power developed between the State Department on the one hand and the Military Intelligence Division, under the leadership of General Churchill, on the other[72]), i. e., a new battle between the State Department and a group of outside experts. It is significant that there seems to have been some degree of cooperation between the Inquiry and the M.I.D. in this matter[73]). The group of military experts had originally been organized by Baker at a time when he himself reckoned on participating in the Conference[74]), but although his expectations came to nought, he still kept loyally out of the conflict. Moreover, the whole Commission felt as though it were overrun by superfluous military personnel[75]). House, however, could view this development with the greatest equanimity—he was well on the way to having his own tight little organization ready, and with it, he soon achieved his aim: "This office looks after the bulk of the Presidential correspondence . . ."[76]), although, of course, he did not manage this without Wilson's consent.

On 14 December, Wilson made his brilliant entry into Paris, and on the same day, he had his first talk with House. During this he asserted, as mentioned above, that he had not authorized Lansing's organization of the Commission but had assumed that House was doing this. Indeed, according to House, the President even went so far as to say that House might dismiss anyone he wished in the organization. However, House refused to take advantage of this offer because he set great store by Grew[77]). We can, of course, only guess about what lay behind this complete volte-face on Wilson's part, but it may possibly have been due to Creel. Since the appointment of the Committee on Public Information, an exceedingly tense situation had existed between Lansing and Creel, because Lansing had refused to collaborate with Creel's committee and had instead built up his own organization within the State Department, under the leadership of Leland Harrison and Phillip Patchin[78]), precisely the two men that Wilson had told House he was particularly averse to. Of one thing we can at any rate be sure and that is that the conflict between Lansing and Creel broke out again immediately after Wilson's arrival, and from House's allusions to the battle, the cause appears to have been Lansing's organization in general, and Harrison and Patchin in particular[79]). In this situation, House seems to have supported Lansing[80]) and, considering the circumstances, had the satisfaction of a result that favoured himself most: Wilson requested Creel, Hugh Frazier and Auchincloss "to work ... as a sort of 'triple alliance' to handle his work."[81]) Auchincloss was to take care of "the economic end of it and the work of the departments in Washington."[82]) Thus, what began by looking like defeat at the hands of Lansing ended as a partial success for House, although there were signs that he would find it increasingly difficult to maintain his special position, and Wilson's attitude throughout the whole affair had been rather ambivalent. Nonetheless, House managed to fall out with yet another man before the Conference began, and this clash was to prove of some importance in the later course of events.

Frank Cobb had always been one of Wilson's warmest advocates, and 'The World' had supported his administration through thick and thin, so it was not at all surprising that House had decided on Cobb as head of the Press Department of the Commission[83]). However, when Wilson got to Europe, Cobb had just rushed home after a break with House. In 1937, Cobb's widow told the story to Ray Stannard Baker: Cobb had gone back convinced that "the "cards were being stacked" against the Americans, particularly by the French and Italians", and it had been his intention to warn Wilson personally regarding the situation and thus stop him from going to Europe. However, House had deliberately prevented Cobb from getting back in time. Cobb was, moreover, "convinced that Colonel House, for reasons unknown to him (Cobb), was withholding important information from the State Department and ... (was) holding the real key to the situation in his own hand." He was also certain that his own reports had never reached Wilson. According to Mrs. Cobb, Frank Cobb had asked House directly whether he was sure that Wilson was completely informed on the situation, and House had replied "Possibly not". It had also shocked Cobb to find that "in each US Embassy there was one member who was in direct contact with Colonel House and sent him a daily personal report which report did not go to the United States"[84]).

What Cobb had had the opportunity of observing at close range was, of course, the special "apparatus" through which House maintained his unique position. Although Cobb's account was probably somewhat exaggerated, it is correct that House had a comprehensive correspondence with the American Ambassadors[85]) and that he was also kept informed from London and Paris by William Buckler[86]) and Hugh Frazier[87]), and, further, that he had managed to place his son-in-law in a key position in the State Department[88]). The fact that the State Department was not being kept informed may have been news to Cobb, but it certainly was not to Lansing. House corresponded with Wilson in their own secret code, and the telegrams were usually deciphered by the President himself or Mrs. Wilson. None of this was new to those involved, but Cobb's observations show that the "apparatus" had now reached a stage of development at which it began to be dangerous to House: It had become visible.

The most serious of Cobb's accusations was though, that House had kept important information from Wilson—and had himself admitted this. Whether the latter assertion is correct is naturally open to dispute."Possibly not" is in the nature of an oracular reply, and House may have had his own reasons for not wishing to initiate others in his and Wilson's plans. However, that still leaves us with the former allegation. On 4 November, Cobb had given House a memorandum in which he practically pleaded that Wilson should stay in Washington and retain his exalted mediating position[89]) and he had repeated his views in a letter and a telegram[90]) sent ten days later. To this House had replied: "I am advising the President to land in France and to assess the situation here in respect to his movements after that"[91]). This was true enough and, in fact, the only thing House could have done in the circumstances. On 14 November, i. e. the same day as the telegram from Cobb, House telegraphed to Wilson[92]):

"Americans here, whose opinions are of value are practically unanimous in the belief that it would be unwise for you to sit in the Peace Conference. They fear that it would involve a loss of dignity and your commanding position".

In reply, House received one of the most impassioned telegrams Wilson ever sent[93]):

"Your 107 upsets every plan we have made. ... No point of dignity must prevent our obtaining the results we have set our hearts upon and must have. It is universally expected and generally desired here that I should attend the conference, but I believe that none would wish me to sit by and try to steer from the outside. ... The programme proposed for me by Clemenceau, George, Reading, and the rest seems to me a way of pocketing me. I hope you will be very shy of their advice and give me your own independent judgement upon reconsideration."

To this, of course, House could but reply: "... my judgment is that you should sail for France on December 3rd and determine upon your arrival what share it is wise for you to take in the proceedings."[94]) House later thought he saw in this, "the first flat and vital difference between Wilson and myself", the seeds of the subsequent break[95]).

However, Cobb's accusation went much further than this, in that he said House had been keeping valuable information from Wilson. The question is: who was to decide what was important, the Special Representative of the

United States or his subordinates, no matter how well qualified they were? And House and Cobb were miles apart in their evaluation of the entire diplomatic situation. While Cobb was not far from seeing an Allied plot against America, House's analysis, which he gave to the President on his arrival, was as follows[96]):

"I gave the President a brief summary of the situation, particularly the relations between France, England and ourselves, relations which seem to grow steadily better. Our relations with Italy have always been good."

This astonishing evaluation raises the question of whether House was right and thus whether he was really entitled to the confidence placed in him by the President. Cobb, at any rate, had no doubts on the matter and did not fail to say so when he returned to America. He could obviously not reach Wilson, since he had already left, but there were other influential men to whom he could report. Among these were Bernard Baruch and Henry Morgenthau, and Cobb's story made a deep impression on them both[97]). Baruch was thus already prejudiced against House when he arrived for the Conference in the middle of January, and Morgenthau did not stay silent during his visit to Paris for the last phase of the Conference[98]). Let us, however, see what was happening to House in the meantime.

The pre-Armistice negotiations were the culmination of House's previous careeer and, as we have seen, he valued his own contribution very highly[99]). However, the pre-Armistice negotiations were not the first occasion on which House had acted as official American representative in international negotiations. In the autumn of 1917 he had headed the so-called House Mission, which had the task of negotiating with the Allies on economic and military cooperation, and it is necessary to bring his experience from these two conferences into the picture if we are to understand House's activities at the Peace Conference.

At both these conferences, House won insight into how a big, international meeting was organized and manipulated: The really important decisions were made in narrow, intimate discussions between top negotiators, the so-called "steering committee". That is how it had been in 1917, and the system was perfected during the period of operation of the Supreme War Council, so that it functioned smoothly during the pre-Armistice negotiations. It was this procedure that was resurrected with the establishment of "The Big Four" at the end of March 1919[100]), and it was a form of negotiation that House found very attractive. He had always been an advocate of the "one man policy in diplomatic affairs"[101]),—he was the man of intimate, personal talks. Moreover, House had spent the whole of his career as the man in the background who pulls the strings. He was the grand manipulator. In his younger days he had "run" party conventions in Texas[102]) and now he saw his chance of trying his strength on a task of international dimensions. Thus, immediately after his return from Europe in 1917, he could advise Wilson that "the real work was done by the Prime Ministers of Great Britain, France, Italy and myself at private conferences. I thought I now understood how to handle the Peace Conference most effectively when it came . . ."[103]). It has earlier been described how House tried to control the organization of the American Commission, and we shall later see how, in January and February 1919, he went the whole length: It now became his ambition to be the man who manipulated the entire Peace Conference.

However, the House Mission in 1917 influenced House's later activities in yet another way. Here, for the first time, he participated in real negotiations with the top politicians of Europe, and thereby had the opportunity of getting a first-hand impression of their personalities. He had met Lloyd George previously, although not in his capacity of Prime Minister, and his opinion of him did not change with time[104]):

> "I cannot help dwelling upon the thought that my particular work might have been very much more effective if I had a different man to deal with other than Lloyd George. He makes an appealing speech, states his case well, has a charming personality, and there, as far as I can see, his usefulness ends. My experience leads me to believe that the world suffers from such men as Lloyd George."

House valued Balfour, whom he had met earlier, very highly and they worked smoothly together[105]). It therefore came as a great surprise to House that Wilson, after his negotiations in England at the end of December 1918, reached an entirely different view: "Strangely enough he (Wilson) said that if he could trust "the little man" he thought he could get along with him easier than he could with Balfour"[106]). However, by the end of March 1919, House was able to ascertain with satisfaction that Wilson was beginning to change his mind: "I think the President is beginning to realize how unreliable George is. George is so clever and has much charm, and is so quick and humorous that I do not wonder the President was deceived"[107]). In any case, House did not act as much as intermediary between Wilson and Lloyd George as he seemed predestined to do, because the antipathy was entirely mutual. Lloyd George preferred to negotiate direct with Wilson[108]).

However, the most decisive personal acquaintanceship was that between Clemenceau and House. House was literally taken by storm, he was overwhelmed: ". . . it seems to me now that Clemenceau is one of the ablest men I have met in Europe, not only on this trip, but on any of the others"[109]). It did not apparently detract from his pleasure that he was forced at the same time to recognize the fact that Clemenceau was "of the reactionary type". House therefore had high expectations as regards cooperation with Clemenceau during the negotiations on the Armistice and the conclusion of peace: ". . . if Clemenceau will cooperate with us as closely as he did last year at the Inter-Allied Conference, it will greatly shorten the life of the Congress. It merely needs a little organization and some understanding between the principals to have matters expedited in a way that it is quite unusual at such gatherings"[110]).

During the pre-Armistice negotiations, the friendship was sealed: as early as 26 October 1918, House was able to note in his diary that "He (Clemenceau) seems genuinely fond of me"[111]), and the culmination for the time being came on 9 November, when the two men had an exceptionally friendly talk[112]):

"This morning I had a conference with the President of the Conseil at the War Office. He was exceedingly cordial and said, "May I call you my dear friend, for I feel that you are. You have been so wise and so helpful that I beg you to believe that my friendship is sincere." He asked Pichon to be a witness, that he, Clemenceau, would not take up any matter at the Conference without having fully apprised me of it, and he intimated that if I objected, he would defer to my judgment."

Clemenceau took this opportunity of presenting the French plans for the annexation of the Saar to House, who "agreed to study it from a sympathetic viewpoint, but made no promise or comment". When House related the conversation to Wilson on the same day, he omitted all reference to the Saar[113]). House had entered upon a friendship that was, on his side, totally uncritical. This was in a later phase of the Conference to lead him to conduct that was, at the very least, on the borderline of disloyalty to the American President[114]).

House, meanwhile, in his two periods as American top negotiator, had acquired other experience that is far less easily weighed and measured. However, there is no doubt that House, who had all his life acted the part of the "Éminence grise", now acquired a taste for the limelight. He came to enjoy being the one to make the decisions, the man to exercise power. This comes to light in many ways in his diary, and can be seen most clearly in his reaction to Clemenceau's announcement that he no longer had any objections to Wilson participating in the Conference as American Delegate: "It was difficult for me to simulate a satisfaction I did not feel, but I did the best I could"[115]). All the same, he did not succeed in the long run.

We are finally left with the question of how House fulfilled his task as leader of a delegation and whether he managed to get everyone cooperating smoothly. As regards the House Mission in 1917, the answer is unreservedly in the affirmative. It is clear that he himself was well aware of the problem and that he did all he could to promote harmonious relations[116]). However, this was not the case in 1918. At a later phase of the Conference, when House's failings had become apparent to all, Vance McCormick put things as follows to Henry Morgenthau Sr.: "... he told me of House's inability to organize—and how they all worked together in 1917—in London ..."[117]). But General Bliss, too, who had been one of House's closest colleagues both during the pre-Armistice negotiations and later as American Peace Commissioner, was very critical of House's capabilities and methods as a leader. Bliss, who was otherwise a very careful man, finally aired his grievances in a letter to Secretary of War Baker, on 9 December[118]):

"Mr. House is by nature very secretive. . . . As a matter of fact he has not given me the slightest clue to the President's views on any matter whatever, even on those subjects which are to come before the Peace Conference. I doubt if any government in the world conducts business in regard to matters of vital interest to it in the careless way we do. . . .".

On the same day, Bliss wrote to General March, describing the organizational chaos by then reigning in the American Delegation, and he laid the blame for this at House's door[119]):

"There has been a great deal of confusion due to the fact that no one with any experience in such work has been placed in charge of the organization of the personnel for the American Mission. If anyone has the authority for this, it is Mr. House, but, as a matter of fact, the whole thing has been left to Mr. Grew. . . .".

Hard words indeed, and perhaps not entirely just, but Bliss could not have known that Wilson had disavowed House's organization plans and that House was presumably just as ignorant as he himself as to the President's intentions. However, the result was that House, even before the Conference began, had fallen out with two of his colleagues, first Lansing and now Bliss.

The period between the Armistice and Wilson's arrival was altogether a time of disappointment for House. It seems as though he lost contact with Wilson; time and again his initiatives were rejected in Washington until, at last, he was completely at sea as regards Wilson's actual plans.

The question that naturally arose first was when the Peace Conference should assemble. Right from the beginning, the Allies seem to have agreed that an inter-Allied conference should be held prior to the actual Peace Conference, with a view to concluding a preliminary Peace[120]). At first, however, this did not accord with the wishes of either House or Wilson. As early as 30 October, House informed Wilson of the Allied plans: Lloyd George thought the Allies should meet before the Peace Conference "and thresh out their differences". He himself thought that the conference would last a week, and the preliminary conference, 3–4 weeks. House's comment to this plan was: "I strongly advise against this procedure and for reasons which will be obvious to you"[121]). Wilson's view was just as clear[122]):

"Replying to your ten cannot agree to George's programme of a general settlement among ourselves before the general peace conference. I am entitled to take part in the real settlement and such preliminaries would make the final conference a mere form".

Thus, at the time, neither Wilson nor House was prepared for preliminary negotiations behind Germany's back, and it was, moreover, clear that Wilson was very much afraid of being left out. He was deeply suspicious of the Allies.

Nevertheless, House rapidly became convinced that the procedure proposed by the Allies was the right one, and on 5 November he telegraphed Wilson[123]):

"If Germany accepts the conditions of our Armistice, the Peace Conference should be called for December 11th or thereabouts. It would be necessary for you to leave as soon as possible in order to hold some conferences here with Great Britain, France and Italy. This is essential".

However, Wilson could not leave America before the yearly Message to Congress on 2 December and in any case, he considered it both wise and essential to postpone the Peace Conference until governments that could enter into binding agreements were formed in Austria-Hungary and Germany[124]). House then concentrated on at least getting the inter-Allied conference started on 16 December, immediately after Wilson's arrival[125]). He ensured British agreement, but the French Government hesitated over such an early date[126]).

F. S. Marston has rightly stressed the fact that "(t)he complete failure of American diplomacy to follow up its November success by securing the early embodiment and further elucidation of the Fourteen Points etc., in a treaty of Peace is one of the amazing features of this post-Armistice period"[127]). Admittedly, Lansing tried to force through the formulation of a plan in that he sent to Wilson on 18 November a number of questions on the principles for the framing of the Peace Treaty, but the President apparently failed to react to the very comprehensive and well thought out questionnaire[128]). We can see now that Wilson's reticence had its roots in the uncertainty engendered by his faltering political position both in the United States and in Europe. He simply needed a period of adjustment and orientation. However, House failed to understand the reason for Wilson's hesitance—and it was in any event much against his own wishes[129]). Despite this, he did not manage to alter the situation; the American initiative was at a standstill until the arrival of the President.

As we have seen, the French acceded astonishingly quickly and apparently without undue friction to the Fourteen Points. However, the offensive they now launched was aimed at repairing the damage or, in Binkley's words, "The French arrière pensée seems ... to have been the wish to shift the Peace Conference to principles which could be used to cover a strong Rhineland Policy"[130]). This became very apparent in the first of the so-called French November plans, Note sur le Congrès de la Paix, which House transmitted to Washington on 15 November. This said, inter alia[131]):

"Finally, this Congress, like all those which have preceded it, should adopt a basis of discussion. ... One single basis seems to exist at the present time: it is the solidary decision of the Allies upon their war aims, formulated January 10th 1917, in answer to the question of President Wilson, but it is rather a program than basis of negotiations. ... In a general way the questions to be discussed are segregated in two main series: First, settlement proper of the war, second, elaboration of the league of nations".

This comprised a frontal attack on the cardinal points of American policy; with the approval of the pre-Armistice agreement, the Fourteen Points had just been accepted by all parties as the "basis of discussion" for the Peace Conference, and it was Wilson's declared aim to make the League of Nations the cornerstone of peace[132]).

There was no official American reaction, either to this or to any of the subsequent French proposals, but a memorandum prepared by David Hunter Miller may possibly have been handed to the French Government[133]). This contained a sharp rejection of the French attempts to evade the Fourteen Points. In the following period, the French retreated, and a later revision of their proposal read[134]):

"Neither the four armistices ... nor the answer of January 10th, 1917, nor the President's fourteen propositions, can furnish a concrete basis for the labors of the Congress. That basis can only be a methodical statement of the questions to be taken up."

Other roads were open, however, and here, the so-called London Conference at the beginning of December 1918 played a central role.

On 15 November, House sent to Washington a copy of a telegram from Clemenceau to Lloyd George, which read, inter alia, as follows[135]):

"The coming of President Wilson naturally changes some of our plans in preparing for the Conference. ... I would suggest to you that we draw up some preparatory memoranda either in London or in Paris. ... If we should proceed thus, the President on arriving could make his observations without any delay and the task would find itself advanced. I expect to see Mr. Sonnino this afternoon. I do not doubt that he will assent."

Strangely enough, House did not comment on the telegram, but its meaning is clear enough—a French initiative for an inter-Allied Conference without the Americans. Did this constitute a French attempt to establish a joint front against Wilson?

If this was the aim of the French initiative, at any rate it failed in the first instance. On 25 November, House received an invitation from Lloyd George to come to London on 1 December, together with Clemenceau and Orlando[136]). Thus, it was evident that the British wanted American participation. However, House was supposedly ill and therefore had to send his regrets. The question is whether an indisposition was the real reason for his refusal; there are a good many problems attaching to House's attitude in this matter. On 18 November, House had a talk with the British Ambassador in Paris, Lord Derby, who advised that Clemenceau had invited Lloyd George to a conference but that the latter was too busy and had instead invited Clemenceau. "Derby expressed a willingness to go to London as often as necessary, which he thought would be better than for me to go. Personally, I have no thought of going"[137]). And in an earlier conversation with Derby, House had said that "if the President decides to come, his (House's) own hands would not be free in preliminary conversations and he (House) thinks they would not help matters"[138]). Thus, even before he fell ill, House seems to have decided not to participate in a possible conference. On 19 November House had another talk with Derby on the same topic: "Clemenceau, he (Derby) thought, was going to London to see Lloyd George, but just what they were to confer about, he did not know. If he could find out, he would let me know"[139]). After the telegram of 15 November and these talks, it must have been clear to House that it was a case of a French move.

In reply to the invitation on 25 November, House wrote that he was confined to bed with influenza, but that he hoped the doctor would allow him to travel[140]). And he wrote the same to Wilson: "I hope that my doctor will permit me to go to London on about December first for the conference in question. I am feeling better but am still weak, and I will not be able to tell before Thursday or Friday of this week whether I can make the journey"[141]). At this stage, House was thus still intending to go to London if he could, but two days later he changed his mind and now telegraphed Wilson[142]):

"As I have previously informed you George had asked Clemenceau, Orlando and myself to come to London on December first for a meeting of the Supreme War Council. I replied that while I hoped to be able to be present it would depend on my doctors decision. *I think it wise for reasons other than presented by my physical condition not to go to London for this conference.*"

Wilson had not replied to House's telegram of 25 November, and it may have been this that made him reconsider and remember that Wilson had already, on 31 October, expressly opposed any form of inter-Allied conference in which he did not personally participate. There was reason enough for House to be cautious, and in particular, the severe reprimand he had received from the President on 16 November after having advised Wilson against participating in the Conference must have provided him with plenty of food for thought. It is in any case remarkable that House received no directives whatsoever as to how he should react to the London Conference. Did the Americans simply not realize the danger inherent in the establishment of a joint Allied front against America? House was at any rate unaware of it, since on 16 November he analysed the situation as follows: "As far as I can see all the Powers are trying to work with us rather than with one another. Their disagreements are sharp and constant."[143]) And this view was identical with the one which, as mentioned earlier, he gave the President one month later, i. e. after the London Conference: ". . . the relations between France, England and ourselves . . . seem to grow steadily better. Our relations with Italy have always been good"[144]). The French move for an Allied conference without America should anyway have aroused House's suspicions, but it failed to do so; on the contrary, on 30 November, House "bought" Clemenceau's interpretation of the conference[145]):

"Clemenceau called on me this afternoon. He said that he had come to give me his solemn word of honor that he would discuss no question of any importance with George in London. He said that the meeting was of no importance whatever and that he thought George had asked him to come over simply for electioneering purposes. . . . He added that if Great Britain adopted during the Conference a grasping attitude, France would oppose it. France, he stated, would always be willing to submit her claims to the judgment of the conference. . . .".

On the same day, Lord Derby too—who should have known better—expressed the view to House that Lloyd George had called the conference "purely for election purposes"[146]). Was this a case of a common Allied attempt at pacification?

Thus, House did not believe that there was any possibility of the establishment of an Allied front against America, but there can be no doubt that as far as Clemenceau was concerned, this was the whole aim of the conference. On 26 November, the French Ambassador in London handed the British Government a number of proposals for a preliminary peace treaty with Germany[147]). Not until 7 December did these proposals by devious means reach the knowledge of the American Government[148]). One thing, however, was omitted from the copy received by the American Government—"the all-important preamble"[149]). Harold I. Nelson has managed to find the complete document and has thereby been able to prove that there was indeed a French move towards an Anglo-French agreement on the peace terms with Germany prior to Wilson's arrival. In other words, precisely the joint front. Moreover, when Clemenceau's talk with House on 30 November is brought into the picture, it will be seen that there was an attempt to play Wilson and Lloyd George against each other and in this way ensure greater freedom of movement for France[150]). The significant part of the preamble reads as follows[151]):

"When once the French Government have decided on the general principles which they themselves wish to assure, they will then come to an agreement upon them with his Majesty's Government.
The arrangement thus reached between the two countries will enable them both to appear with complete safety at the Conference which, immediately after the arrival of President Wilson, will be held at Versailles for the purpose of exchanging views and agreements among the greater allies".

It is, however, quite another question whether Clemenceau's policy succeeded.

In his memoires, Lloyd George has himself told how Foch, at a meeting with only the British representatives but not Clemenceau, presented his grandiose plans for an alliance between Britain, France, Belgium and the earlier German regions on the West bank of the Rhine as a permanent defence of the Rhine border[152]), and how the British rejected these proposals. Only German research has taken a sceptical view of the correctness of this rejection. Ferdinand Friedensburg took the whole problem up to discussion in an article in "Berliner Monatshefte" in 1938[153]). Here, he drew attention to a number of statements made by Tardieu, partly in the National Assembly in 1920 and partly in an article in "L'Illustration" the same year. In this article, Tardieu asserted that talks had taken place between Clemenceau and Lloyd George on the Sykes-Picot Agreement and that these had resulted in an amendment to the agreements whereby France now handed over to Britain the important oil-region of Mossul, which, according to the original agreement, lay within the French sphere of influence. The new agreement then read: "que la Grande

Bretagne soutienne sans restriction la France à la Conference sur la base inté-
grale de cet accord (moins Mossoul) et lui assure son plein appui dans le cas
d'objections américaines"[154]).

The article was published on 19 June 1920, and on 23 and 24 June, the
French policy in the Near-East was made the subject of a violent debate in
the Chamber of Deputies. During this, Tardieu made the following statement
(translated by Friedensburg)[155]):

"Es handelte sich vor allem anderen darum, sich mit England über gewiss wesentliche
Punkte zu verständigen. Es gilt von England das zu erhalten, was es um keinen Preis
geben will: Die Besetzung des linken Rheinufers. Es gilt die Saarkohle zu erhalten und
noch vieles andere. Sehen Sie, das sind die Umstände, unter denen Clemenceau nach
London gegangen ist!"

Friedensburg compared this statement with the conclusion of the article in
"L'Illustration": "Parce qu'il avait besoin, à la veille de la conférence, et
d'un accord général avec la Grande Bretagne et de son appui local en Syrie
. . . M. Clemenceau a jugé que ce compromis était sage"[156]). He then arrived
at the following conclusion: "Clemenceau hat sich damals mit seinen Nach-
geben die englische Zustimmung zu den französischen Forderungen an der
deutschen Westgrenze erkauft"[157]). And this was naturally precisely the conclusion that Tardieu hoped would be reached. He had made his statement in
a defensive position: Clemenceau had been attacked for appeasing Britain, but
Tardieu had said no more than could be read from the preamble cited above.
Through the talks in London, Clemenceau wanted to achieve prior agreement
with Britain. Tardieu advisedly refrained from all mention of the result, for
this was not nearly as positive as he hinted was the case.

However, Clemenceau himself also spoke of the negotiations with Lloyd
George. During a critical phase of the Peace Conference, he opened his heart
to House[158]):

"He (Clemenceau) was distressed at the turn matters were taking with the British. He
said Lloyd George did not keep his promises, that in England he had promised him
Syria just as the French now desired. He said he had broken his word as to the division
of the sum to be obtained from Germany, and again he had broken his word in declining to even discuss the Rhenish Republic and the proper protection of France".

Was this then the real content of the London talks: British promises to support
the French demands in Syria in return for having Mossul included in their own
sphere of influence? Agreement on the distribution between the Allies of the
German reparations, and a rather indefinable promise on the part of Britain
at least to be willing to discuss the French Rhine plans at the Conference? (It
must be remembered what a hard fight House had had to force the same
promise from Britain with regard to the freedom of the seas).

No Anglo-French bloc was created in London, but there was no reason
either, for taking the optimistic view of the situation that House took.

The meeting called by Lloyd George was not a real Supreme War Council meeting, but when General Bliss discovered that the Allied military representatives on the Supreme War Council were to attend the London meeting, he asked House for more information[159]):

"I then went to Mr. House and asked him if there was to be such a conference. He replied in the affirmative; he said that he had intended to go, but on account of his health he would probably send Mr. Miller to represent him. I asked him if he knew the subject-matters of the conference, in regard to which I could receive no definite information. I told Mr. House that the other governments were calling for their military representatives which indicated to me that some question would come up which would require their consideration and that if such should prove to be the case our government would have no military representation unless he designated someone. I then asked Mr. Miller if he knew what was going to be discussed in London and found that he, apparently, knew little about it. To cut the matter short, neither I nor any military representative went to London."

There is no doubt that Bliss felt he had been very badly treated, and it naturally did not improve matters when he later tried to discover what resolutions had been adopted at the London Conference and whether the United States was tied by these, that he could obtain no information on these points[160]).

House's attitude in this matter seems generally very strange. He did not himself wish to participate, either because he really was ill or because he thought his attendance would be contrary to Wilson's wishes. But what prevented him from giving Bliss a plain answer is a mystery, unless it was an attempt to hide his own uncertainty; simply a way of hiding the fact that he had no instructions from Wilson and therefore did not know how he should act.

America was not represented at the London Conference. House sent David Hunter Miller, but not apparently as an accredited observer. Miller's reports to House do not at any rate indicate that he was particularly well informed of what was going on at the official meetings of the conference[161]). However, House was advised of the course of the conference in another way. Balfour sent him details of the resolutions passed at the conference[162]), and when it was over he had talks with Clemenceau, Sonnino and Derby[163]). He then sent a detailed report to the President, in which he partly explained the various resolutions and partly recommended the steps that should be taken in this respect[164]). The consequence of the American absence from the conference was "that conclusions of conference should be regarded as provisional only and subject to the United States accepting those which require immediate action and do not concern the United States"[165]).

This applied to the following resolutions:

2 December, 11 am. 1st meeting:

A. Regret that illness had prevented House from attending.
B. Establishment of an inter-Allied commission with American participation, "to examine and report on amount enemy countries are able to pay for reparation and indemnity; form of payment also to be considered".

C. "... that Kaiser and principal accomplices should be brought to trial before international court."

D. Preliminary Peace Treaty should be signed at the Inter-Allied Conference at Versailles. Each of the Great Powers should have five delegates. The lesser Powers should only be present when questions of special interest to them were under discussion. New nations should be heard by this Conference.

2 December, 4 pm. 2nd meeting.

A. Foch authorized to renew armistice for one month on 10 December.

B. Measures regarding the German Baltic harbours.

C. Measures regarding interned German ships.

D. Establishment of an Inter-Allied Commission with American participation, consisting of four Admirals, "to inquire and report on existing situation and advise as to future activities to eliminate trouble in Adriatic territories occupied or to be occupied by Allied forces, ...".

3 December, 11,15 am. 3rd meeting.

A. Measures regarding the British occupation troops.

B. Measures regarding the costs involved in the occupation of Austria.

C. "British, French and Italian Governments agreed theoretically not to object to international labor or any other conference in relation to peace conference being held provided that until peace is signed it is held in a neutral country".

3 December, 4 pm. 4th meeting.

A. The question of food supplies (relief) to enemy, Allied and neutral countries referred to a special commission.

B. Measures regarding British troops in European Turkey.

C. Resolutions provisional until American approval.

House now advised Wilson (6 December) that, as regards the first meeting, he had informed the Allied Governments that the United States agreed to resolution B, with the exception of the word "indemnity", and that C. would be discussed on Wilson's arrival. With these exceptions, he recommended the President to agree to this meeting's resolutions. With regard to the second meeting, he had discussed the matter with Benson and Bliss and advised the Allies that the United States agreed. With reference to the third meeting, House proposed that Wilson should authorize him to agree. As regards the fourth meeting, House had suggested that resolution A. be amended in accordance with the procedure proposed in the American note on relief. With this exception, House recommended American agreement to these resolutions[166].

Thus, on such an important point as the future procedure for the Conference, House was willing to bind the American Government even before the arrival of the President. This was the more remarkable because, precisely with regard to the question of procedure, the London Conference signified a decisive turning point: "The London session had ... brought the idea of a preliminary Inter-Allied Conference officially to the fore, and there was now no possibility of the early and preliminary treaty that had been contemplated during November"[167]. This indicates just how far House had now let himself be influenced by the European ideas on procedure. However, Wilson was not yet prepared to take this step, appearing right to the end to have preferred a far more informal procedure than that now proposed and later approved[168]). He therefore asked House to postpone definitive acceptance of the resolutions from the first meeting until his arrival[169]). House replied: "I have not committed you to any of the resolutions"[170]).

The London Conference was far from the only instance in which Wilson disavowed House's decisions. It has been described earlier how, in the middle of November, the President rejected House's organization plans, and the consequences this had had. As soon as House came to Europe he began, at the request of Wilson to work for Switzerland as the venue of the Peace Conference, and House was well on the way to winning both the British and the French over when Wilson changed his mind and now went in for Versailles[171]). House saw only too clearly the dangers connected with holding the Conference in Paris and found, moreover, that Wilson's decision was "clearly against my judgment"[172]). However, even more disappointing to House was Wilson's choice of Peace Commissioners. As we have seen, House left for Europe with the conviction that the question had been settled: Wilson, Lansing, Baker, McCall and House himself. Nevertheless, Wilson was for several reasons unable to accept McCall as Republican Peace Commissioner[173]), and House then proposed instead to increase the number of Commissioners to seven so as to make room for another Republican besides McCall[174]). However, House was not consulted further in this matter; in fact, he was apparently not even advised beforehand of the final appointments[175]). Newton D. Baker abstained from becoming a Peace Commissioner on account of the retirement of McAdoo from the post of Secretary of the Treasury, and General Bliss was appointed in his stead[176]), and, after much deliberation, Wilson ended by appointing Henry White as the Republican representative on the Delegation[177]). Thus, the final Delegation differed considerably from that originally agreed between Wilson and House. House's diary entries on the matter are very bitter. On 1 December he wrote[178]):

"The papers of the last few days have been full of the President's appointments of the Peace Commissioners. Outside of himself and myself, there will be Lansing, Henry White and General Bliss. General Bliss is the best appointment, Lansing and White are weak and will be of little help. As a matter of fact, the President should have appointed a Republican of the standing of Root. He has made again one of his common mistakes".

House here disclosed an attitude that did not bode well for the future cooperation in the Delegation. Two days later he again commented on the appointments, in a manner that very clearly reflects his state of mind at the time[179]):

"I wish in my soul the President had appointed me as Chairman of the Peace Delegation with McAdoo and Hoover as my associates. I could have attended to the political end, McAdoo to the financial, and Hoover to the economic end. This distribution politically would have been perfect. Texas, New York and California with Hoover as the Republican member. If I could have had these two men as associates and only these, I would have been willing to guarantee results".

It is clear from these remarks that House's experience during the pre-Armistice negotiations had convinced him of his own capabilities as a political top negotiator and that he was fully aware of his own ambition: to become Chairman of the Delegation. This was why House, as we have seen, could assert that one of the seeds of the later break with the President was to be found in his telegram advising Wilson not to participate in the Conference. It was his own deep insight into the real character of the conflict and, most of all, into his own motives that House here revealed in a glimpse.

Now House was far from being the only one to criticize Wilson's choice of Peace Commissioners, and he was not alone in thinking that Wilson should not participate in the actual peace negotiations. On the contrary, this view was very widely held in America, especially among the President's friends[180]), and it was shared by many of the Allied representatives, primarily Clemenceau. It is remarkable, however, that House did not attempt to exploit his presumed influence with the French Prime Minister to get him to change his standpoint. On the contrary, from a conversation House had with Clemenceau on 5 December it appears very clearly that House was willing to try to persuade Wilson not to participate in the Conference itself but only to hold private negotiations with the Allied Prime Ministers[181]). And this was what House attempted to do after Wilson's arrival, and he himself believed that he had succeeded[182]). Just how far House was right in this assumption is doubtful, however, because at the first meeting between Wilson and Clemenceau on 15 December, the President made his attitude extremely clear[183]):

"Latter (Wilson) informed him (Clemenceau) that he was anxious to attend the Peace Conference. He added that if the Conference declared that they preferred that he should not attend, he would quite understand, but he nevertheless desired that his wishes in the matter should be known".

It is possible that Clemenceau here made Wilson's statements appear more ultimative than they actually were in order to cover up his own retreat, but it is at any rate a fact that Clemenceau changed his mind after this talk and accepted Wilson as official American Delegate[184]). The British Government then immediately agreed[185]). As we have seen, this was a source of deep disappointment to House: "It was difficult for me to simulate a satisfaction I did not feel, . . ."[186]).

However, apart from this, House had no reason for disappointment over Wilson's arrival. It is clear that he was looking forward to the moment with mixed feelings, for why should he otherwise have failed to meet the President in Brest or, if his health was not up to this, at any rate at the station in Paris[187])? If House harboured doubts as to whether his position with Wilson was the same as in the old days, these were immediately swept aside because, as described earlier, Wilson once more gave the whole of the organization into House's hands. The relief felt by House is clearly reflected in his diary[188]):

"I arranged with the President this afternoon to have his work done by Gordon (Auchincloss), Frazier, George Creel and the staff I have built up here. . . . He has never cabled me that he was relying upon me to look out for him while here, therefore, while I offered to do so in a cable, not having heard from him I presumed he was bringing some sort of organized help himself. In this he is like my brother T. W. who always expected me to know by intuition what he was thinking."

"(House) is in his best form and the PRESIDENT appears to be leaving everything in his hands. Whole situation is far more favourable than supposed"[189]), as Wiseman put it in a reassuring telegram to the Foreign Office.

After the President's arrival, two important problems had to be solved. The large and heterogeneous Commission had to be welded together to a smoothly cooperating unit, and the American programme had to be finally formulated. Neither problem was solved satisfactorily. As we have seen, all American initiative had been postponed until Wilson's arrival, and not even House had been initiated into the President's plans[190]). The first time Wilson lifted the veil was on board the 'George Washington', to the members of the American Inquiry[191])—and the result was disappointing. Most of the experts found Wilson's programme "too vague and inadequate"[192]). Wilson's conception seems to have centred on two points: if Europe was to be made safe against Bolshevism, a Peace must be concluded that was founded on the highest principles, since only in this way could the masses be won; and the League of Nations must be the core of this Peace. The President was "firm on broad, general principles, but flexible as to their precise application"[193]). Wilson does not seem to have been much more explicit in the account he gave House after his arrival in Europe. House's diary is silent on this point, and that we know the content of the talk at all is due only to the fact that House shortly afterwards gave a report of it to Wiseman, representing Wilson's plans as follows[194]):

"I do not think he has any specially cut-and-dried proposals to make regarding any of the important questions at issue, but will rather re-affirm his general principles and expect the Allies to make their definite proposals.

On the question of the LEAGUE OF NATIONS, he is, however, very strongly of the opinion that the formation of a League—at any rate definite agreement as to its form among the great Powers—should be the first work of the Peace Conference. He considers that almost all the difficult questions—Colonies, Freedom of the Seas, the Balkan difficulty, Russia and Reduction of Armaments—and, in fact, all the important problems that will arise, can only be satisfactorily settled on the basis of a LEAGUE OF NATIONS. . . . '.

The weakness of this strategy was formulated in almost classic manner by Henry White during the Conference itself[195]):

"The fact is . . . that the League of Nations, in which he has been more deeply interested than anything else from the beginning, believing it to be the best if not the only means of avoiding war in the future, has been played to the limit by France and Japan in extracting concessions from him; to a certain extent by the British too, and the Treaty as it stands is the result. The Italians overshot the mark . . .".

On the other hand, it is important to stress the fact that there really was a strategy and not, as might and, indeed, did seem to the Experts, just a lack of a programme: Wilson had deliberately chosen the defensive and elevated position of the arbitrator as a logical consequence of the policy he had maintained as an Associate—not an Ally—during the whole of the war, and as a logical consequence of his concept of America as the only disinterested nation at the Conference.

House seems to have understood and accepted this attitude of Wilson's, but if it was the intention of the President to impart a deeper understanding of his views to the other Peace Commissioners, he certainly failed. General Bliss's reaction is perhaps the clearest example of this; his reports to Washington during this period bear witness to his deep concern over the lack of an American programme[196]):

"Of course I should not feel worried if I knew the President's exact views on all questions that are to come up; but I do not know them. If there be any other member of the Commission who does know them he apparently does not feel at liberty to take them up *seriatim* and explain them . . .".

In this there lies a direct allusion to House, and a very serious, implicit criticism. The role House was predestined to play was precisely that of the mediator, not only outwardly, in respect of foreign politicians, but to the very highest degree also inwardly, as liaison officer between the President and the American Delegation. However, although he went in wholeheartedly for the former task, he neglected the latter altogether. Indeed, as we shall see later, one of the most serious complaints against House was precisely that he split the American Delegation.

It is from this angle that we should attempt to understand House's activities during the period from Wilson's arrival to the commencement of the Conference. Now that he was certain that his position with the President was well established, he concentrated all his energies on ensuring his own position of power within the organization of the Commission. McCormick saw this very clearly when he came to Paris at the beginning of January, and he also saw the dangers inherent in it[197]):

"Colonel active man of peace delegation, overlooking practically all political and economic work. Lansing legal. President real leader, however, and making tremendous impression. Fear trouble later over relationship of House and Lansing. . . .".

The plans for Wilson during the first weeks of his arrival included visits to both Britain and Italy. It must be assumed that great political importance was in advance attached to both visits, but House participated in neither of them. He stayed in Paris. Why? It is difficult to find any other explanation but that he was afraid of losing his grip on the Delegation if he left Paris. His refusal to go to England provides the clearest example of this.

House was the traditional link with the British statesmen, and nothing would have been more natural than that he should have introduced the President at the first, personal meetings, in the same way as he had done during the first talks between Clemenceau and Wilson[198]). And it was not for lack of invitations from either the President or the British[199]). However, House refused to go, and sent Auchincloss instead, who came to act as a kind of secretary to the President during Wilson's stay in England[200]). Whether this constituted a deliberate attempt on the part of House to manoeuvre Auchincloss into a position with Wilson is not known[201]), but if it actually was the aim, it at any rate failed, because Auchincloss managed to fall foul of both the President himself and his closest aides, especially the stenographer, Gilbert Close[202]). As soon as Auchincloss got to London and became oriented on the situation, he telegraphed House, entreating him to come to Britain with Wilson: "I am convinced that you will be making a grave mistake if you now announce that you have decided not to go to London." He put forward the following reasons, amongst others, for his advice[203]):

"2. Everyone here including George, Balfour and Cecil expects you and they are relying on you for assistance during the conferences.
3. It is more clear to me than ever that they plan to engage the President in important conferences and *if you lose touch now I believe it will make our work much more difficult . . .*".

Here, Auchincloss put his finger on the decisive issue: the danger that might lie in House losing contact with Wilson's innermost thoughts and aims, the danger that might lie in Wilson formulating his policies on premises unknown to House. But House had made his choice—he had found a task that was bigger than just being the President's counsellor—. With his refusal to accompany Wilson to England, House had finally taken the path that was to lead to the break.

It was obvious that these preliminary talks between Wilson and the British statesmen would be of extreme importance to the future of the negotiations, because here it would become clear whether there was any possibility of establishing an Anglo-American cooperation at the Peace Conference. House had already taken the first steps in this direction[204]); the plan was to establish close contact between House and Balfour, with Wiseman and Sir Eric Drummond as go-betweens. On the American side there was also a strong desire to see Lord Cecil as British representative at the negotiations on the League of Nations Covenant. Vice versa, the British seem to have been very interested in Anglo-American collaboration at the expert level[205]). However, the attitude of the two top statesmen, Wilson and Lloyd George, was naturally decisive. It is a well known fact that Wilson was far from being as pro-British as House during both the period of neutrality and the American participation in the war, but there is, on the other hand, no doubt that Wilson had now come to Europe with a really positive wish to realize cooperation with Britain. Newton D. Baker, who, both personally and by reason of his position, was very close to the President and must therefore, on this question, be presumed also to express Wilson's views, analysed the situation in a long letter to General Bliss. Baker said that the question occupying him most at present was the American relationship with Britain. He was convinced that the statesmen of both countries really desired to cooperate in the interests of peace. But Baker at the same time stressed the great difficulties relating to such cooperation: "For some strange reason, there is an underlying lack of real cordiality between the two peoples". The reasons for this were partly historical and partly very contemporary: the approaching economic and commercial rivalry between the two countries. However, Baker was convinced of the urgent necessity of reaching an understanding with Britain, despite the disparities. He had, moreover, found the same attitude in Lloyd George during his recent visit to Europe[206]). Thus, there was much at stake during Wilson's preliminary negotiations with the British.

The American sources do not provide much account of these talks, because the main source—House's diary—is, for good reasons, silent. On the other hand, such reports as there are concur in their evaluation of the result: Wilson was extremely satisfied with the talks, even though his old suspicion does not seem to have been completely overcome. Bliss described Wilson's reaction as follows[207]):

"He told us of the impressions which he had received at his various interviews with Mr. Lloyd George and Mr. Balfour. *In general he seemed very much pleased.* He was surprised at the mildness of the attitude of Mr. Lloyd George and his substantial agreement with him (the President) on various important points. He confessed that he could not feel quite sure as to the permanence of Mr. Lloyd George's views . . .".

Auchincloss summarized the situation as follows in a telegram to Frank Polk, Acting Secretary of State[208]):

"The President while he was in London had an opportunity to talk to practically all members of the present British Government. He was most favourably impressed with his conferences. You may rest assured that his relations with these gentlemen have been very much improved since his visit to England and that as a result close cooperation can be expected in the future . . .".

To House, too, Wilson expressed his great satisfaction with the results of the negotiations in England[209]), and in view of this it is strange to find House writing at the same time that he had some dificulty in convincing Wilson that "we would have to work with England rather than with France if we hoped to get the things for which we were striving through"[210]). The background for these statements by House was Clemenceau's famous "noble-candeur"-speech, which had shocked both House and Wilson[211]):

". . . we discussed Clemenceau's speech in the Chamber of Deputies. In my opinion it is the greatest diplomatic blunder that Clemenceau has made since the famous Sixtus letter. . . . After I read the speech I became convin(c)ed that the United States and England should get together closely and work to a common program in this Peace Conference rather than to depend on France."

From this we can deduce that House, possibly because of his friendship with Clemenceau, had tended to evaluate French policy far more favourably than warranted by the facts. Now he did an about-turn—although only for a short time—and argued in favour of a joint Anglo-American front. And it was this that Wilson apparently shrank from; his judgment of the situation was exactly the same as that of House, but his conception of his role as arbitrator prevented him from engaging himself as unilaterally as House here recommended. Nor was there really any definite political possibility for this.

On 30 December, Lloyd George submitted a report on the talks to the Imperial War Cabinet[212]). He started by emphasizing the fact that "there had been no attempt to arrive at anything in the nature of an agreement. There had simply been an informal interchange of views . . .". The question that had concerned Wilson most was the League of Nations; the British negotiators had got the impression "that that was the only thing that he really cared much about". But there was nothing in Wilson's views to impede Anglo-American agreement on this point. The crucial thing for the President was, moreover, that the League of Nations should be made the first item on the agenda for the Peace Conference, and both Lloyd George and Balfour were prepared to follow him in this, because it would facilitate treatment of a number of other questions. Wilson's views with regard to the freedom of the seas were "very vague", and he had not opposed postponement of this question until the League of Nations had been firmly established. It is thus worth noting that there seemed to be every possibility of Anglo-American agreement on these very vital points.

Furthermore, Lloyd George's report shows that the talks had covered almost all the questions that would be raised during the coming negotiations, and the difficulties that were later to occupy the Conference had already emerged clearly; the question that naturally enough interested the Imperial War Cabinet most was the German colonies. Wilson fully accepted the fact that they should not be returned to Germany, but there agreement ended. Lloyd George had argued that a differentiation should be made between "the German colonies conquered by the British Dominions and adjacent to them, and those in which the forces of the Empire as a whole had shared". Lloyd George was willing to entrust the latter category to the League of Nations, but considered that the former rightly belonged to the Dominions. Wilson seemed willing to accept this argument as regards German South-West Africa's relationship to the Union of South Africa, but not, on the other hand, as regards Australia's demands in the Pacific Islands, any more than he was prepared to approve the Japanese demands in these regions—demands which the Allies were under obligation of treaty to accept. In another connection, Lloyd George said of Wilson's attitude to Japan: "His whole attitude, in fact, was strongly anti-Japanese".

The same attitude had characterized the President's reaction to the Italian demands in the Adriatic:

"With regard to Italy, Mr. Lloyd George reported that he found President Wilson distinctly anti-Italian, as the consequence of the conversations he had had with Baron Sonnino. We had tried our best to state Baron Sonnino's case with regard to the strategical position of the Dalmatian Coast, but the President's only suggestion on that was that the Power to whom the Dalmatian Coast should be left should be forbidden to have a navy at all. ... Mr. Lloyd George said that in any case it was clear that the President would strongly support the Yugo-Slavs against Italy."

Wilson did not seem favourably disposed in regard to the French territorial claims either:

"With regard to FRANCE, he (Lloyd George) did not think the President was prepared to tolerate schem(e)s for the control of the West bank of the Rhine, though he might be prepared to accept the French annexation of the Saar Valley."

And the President took just as uncompromising an attitude in the case of war reparations:

"With regard to INDEMNITY, Mr. Lloyd George reported that he found the President, on the whole, stiffer than on any other question. The utmost concession he seemed inclined to make was that the claims for pure reparation should be tabled first, and that then other claims might possibly be considered afterwards."

Lloyd George had tried in vain to make Wilson understand that this would mean that the British Empire received nothing, while France and Belgium got the lot. "He had, however, failed to make any impression upon the President." This had also been the result of the discussions on the question of the German colonies:

"With regard to the Colonies, he (Lloyd George) had left the matter by telling the President that the question would have to be fought out at the Conference, where the Dominions would be able to present their own case."[213]

Thus, while there were no vital differences of opinion between America and Britain, there were, on the other hand, certain fundamental differences between the United States and the Empire as a whole, and it is in the light of this dualism that the Anglo-American relations at the Peace Conference must be viewed.

This dualism appeared very clearly during the opening phases of the Conference: on the one hand, intimate cooperation between Wilson and Cecil on the framing of the League of Nations Covenant, and on the other, serious clashes between Wilson and Lloyd George–Hughes over mandates and colonies. It is at the same time characteristic, however, that both sides showed a marked willingness to cooperate; the appointment of Robert Cecil as British representative on the League of Nations Commission must be regarded as a British gesture to America. Lloyd George's attitude towards the League of Nations was generally rather ambivalent, but he still chose Cecil, whose views lay very close to those of the Americans, whereby smooth Anglo-American cooperation was ensured. However, certain things indicate that Cecil was willing to, and perhaps even did, go further than the Prime Minister had actually intended[214]), although in the current situation, this was not decisive. In return, Wilson finally yielded on the Colonial question and accepted the compromise proposed by Smuts, even though this was far from according with the principles he himself had laid down[215]). We must not, however, anticipate events.

Besides his successful visit to England, Wilson also, as mentioned, paid an official visit to Italy. House did not accompany him on this occasion either, and Auchincloss's place was taken by Hugh Frazier[216]). By this time, the Adriatic question had already reached a critical phase. As we have seen, during the pre-Armistice negotiations, House had accepted the boundary laid down in the Treaty of London as the demarcation line, but he realized his mistake as early as 11 November[217]):

"... it would be well to assure the (Jugo-Slavs) in a very guarded way that the question of their territorial aspirations is a matter to be decided at the peace conference. This action is advised in order to reassure them in the face of the Italian occupation of the Dalmatian coast along the line of the convention of London, against which I protested and consented only upon the explicit promise that this territory should have the same status as the territory to be occupied under the terms of the German Armistice".

A series of episodes had already taken place between the Italians and the Yugoslavs in Dalmatia, and on the political plane, a tense situation had also arisen between France and Italy[218]). America here played a key role: foremost spokesman for the right of peoples to self-determination and *not* a signatory to the Treaty of London. Here, if anywhere, Wilson's principles were put to the test and—consciously or unconsciously—the President seems to have chosen exactly this question as the touchstone for his entire programme. In his Italian policy, Wilson acted as he would presumably have done in the case of the other Allied Great Powers if the political situation in Europe and America had been different.

Even on board the "George Washington", on his way to Europe, Wilson had been engrossed by the Adriatic problem[219]), and the very evening he arrived in Paris, David Hunter Miller was requested to provide him with a copy of the Treaty of London[220]), while House was given orders to have the Experts prepare proposals for a future borderline between Italy and Yugoslavia[221]). The first meeting between Wilson, Orlando and Sonnino took place on 20 December, with an exceedingly unfortunate outcome[222]), so unfortunate indeed that Wilson requested House to be present at a new meeting next day. Two days earlier the President had received his Experts' opinion[223]) and thus stood well armed from a technical point of view. The second meeting lasted two hours and, according to House's report[224]):

"The President talked well but he did not convince the Italians that they should lessen their hold on the Pact of London. On the contrary, Sonnino convinced the President that from a military point of view, Italy was pretty much at the mercy of the nations holding the Dalmatian coast.

The President afterwards said in talking with me that the next time they had a conversation he thought he would suggest some way by which their argument could be met. This might be done by insisting that the forts along the Dalmatian Coast should be demolished, and that the Jugo-Slavs should agree to have no navy and but a small standing army. I thought this would not meet the Italian objections, for the reason that they were not candid in their contention that it was for protection they desired this territory."

House here cut through to the heart of the matter, but Wilson was willing to accommodate the Italians in their demand for guarantees provided this—as he thought—could be done without violating the right of self-determination; he was prepared to wait and see if they meant what they said. It is possible, as Lloyd George maintained, that Wilson was already at this time "distinctly anti-Italian", but he was at any rate willing to seek a solution that could fulfil the rightful demands of all parties. It was this policy that he tried to implement in the time to come.

The supporters of Wilson's European policy were not the governments in power, but the forces that Arno J. Mayer has described as "the forces of movement"[225]), which means primarily the Liberal and Socialist parties. On 27 December, immediately prior to Wilson's arrival in Italy, the reform Socialist, Bissolati, resigned from the Italian Government[226]), and Bissolati was precisely one of the President's strongest supporters in Italy[227]). He resigned over the Adriatic question, since he thought that Italy should abandon the Treaty of London[228]). The aim of Bissolati's resignation seems to have been to provoke a "public debate over Sonnino's policy and to carry on his fight against it from the outside"[229]), but it may also have represented an attempt to draw Wilson's attention to the fact that the Italian situation offered other possibilities than cooperation with Orlando[230]). It was therefore natural that Bissolati wanted to meet Wilson when the President came to Rome[231]). What is strange, on the other hand, is the fact that Wilson accepted and, what is more, even took the initiative for a meeting himself[232]), thereby directly intervening in the domestic affairs of Italy. The meeting took place on 4 January[233]).

The talks took the form of a very free exchange of views[234]). Wilson asked Bissolati to explain "the heart of the Italian people towards the settlement of this war". Bissolati replied to this that: "The majority of the people have very little conception of geographical questions; but they felt that the Trentino, the Carso and Istria were justly Italy's heritage". To a direct question by Wilson regarding Fiume, Bissolati replied: "Fiume should be a free city, and a free port". Wilson then asked Bissolati to enlarge on his own views with regard to Istria, and Bissolati drew a rough sketch on a piece of paper. Wilson commented: "That is just about the line which was determined by our students". On the other hand, Bissolati made no claims on Dalmatia, and the following interesting views were exchanged:

"THE PRESIDENT: I have had a conference with Mr. Sonnino, who assured me that the Dalmatian coast and islands were a vital military necessity to Italy for defensive purposes. This I could not grasp, perhaps because of my somewhat old-fashioned ideas.

ON.BISSOLATI: Their military value is not so much for defensive as for offensive purposes. Dalmatia is really a bridgehead, from which an army could strike to the north or south, as occasion demanded.

THE PRESIDENT: I had thought, however, that the Islands might be held by them, if the following conditions were observed: First, that the Jugo-Slav nation should not possess any war fleet; secondly, that all the fortifications on the coast be dismantled; and thirdly, that the Italian and Slav inhabitants be assured equality of treatment. What is your opinion?

ON.BISSOLATI: I believe in the immediate abandonment of all Italian pretensions to Dalmatia. I insisted upon this in the Council of Ministers, and it was because of this stand that I took, that I was obliged to resign from the government. In September, Italy made a declaration of sympathy for the Jugo-Slav cause. In this declaration it was understood that the provisions of the Treaty of London would be used against Austria, but not against nations which might arise from the wreck of Austria.

THE PRESIDENT: (to the Ambassador) That is very interesting; I had not fully understood that.".

The conversation continued along the same lines and culminated with the following remark by Bissolati:

"We are waiting for the word from you, to solve these problems. This program, which I have indicated to you, with which Italy could be freed from all Imperialism, would render her a stronger ally of yours, Mr. President, in the struggle which you may have to maintain against the excessive pretensions of French and English nationalism, and therefore better able to aid you in your attempt to found the League of Nations".

Here we have, in fact, a direct offer to the President: Support me, support "the other Italy", and you will have ensured an important ally in the implementation of the American programme.

This conversation would have been remarkable under any circumstances, but it stands out particularly clearly when we remember that this was a talk between a foreign statesman and an opposition leader in a friendly country. Whether Wilson was already then contemplating direct intervention in Italian domestic policy must remain an open question. It is at any rate a fact that later on, when the crisis reached its climax, he seized upon precisely the means that Bissolati had recommended: "We are waiting for the word from you. . .", the appeal to the Italian people over the heads of the government in power. And it is highly probable that the talk with Bissolati had strengthened Wilson in the view that such an appeal would have the desired effect. However, in the immediate situation, the talk had no political consequences; two days later, on 6 January, the Conservative British "Morning Post" carried an interview with Bissolati in which he put forward the same views as in his talk with Wilson[235]). Bissolati himself asserted that the interview had been published against his wishes, but the possibility cannot be excluded that his talk with Wilson made him feel strong enough to attempt to take the initiative. However, if this was the case, he failed completely[236]):

"The fact that Bissolati's views appeared in a foreign newspaper, especially a Tory organ like the Morning Post, when his own resignation was due to his opposition to supposed imperialism in his own country, naturally created an unfavorable impression in Italy and reacted against him."

Bissolati's influence waned rapidly after this. Wilson was playing with fire.

Nonetheless, the significance of the Wilson–Bissolati contact did not pass unnoticed by the Italian Government; Page reported: "The fact of his (Bissolati's) visit to you has . . . made a deep impression here"[237]), and he continued:

"... I think that both Orlando and Sonnino appear somewhat anxious over the present political situation and I found Sonnino apparently readier to yield somewhat than he had been before. ... I do not know what he may claim when he comes to the final discussion, but I felt that he was ready last night to yield much more than I had ever believed he would yield before, and I thought this due to your suggestion about the guarantees against the fortification of the islands and the possession of a war fleet by Jugo-Slavia."

However, this compliant attitude was to prove to be of but a fleeting nature. As far as Wilson was concerned on the other hand, the talk with Bissolati had the effect of convincing him that Italy had no claim on either the boundary foreseen in the Treaty of London or Fiume. There were otherwise no important conferences between the Italian Government and Wilson during his stay in Italy, and Wilson found it impossible to have a private talk with Orlando; Sonnino was always present[238]).

However, Wilson was now ready to take the initiative: Immediately on his return to Paris he had a talk with Orlando, during which he handed him a memorandum setting out the American views[239]). The next day, he decided to go still further; he would explain the American views in a personal letter to Orlando. The letter should at the same time express the fact that Lloyd George and Clemenceau shared Wilson's views[240]). Wilson had originally imagined that House should lead the negotiations with the Allied Prime Ministers[241]), but he was ill at this time and instead, Wilson had a personal meeting with Lloyd George, Balfour and Bonar Law on 14 January. Lloyd George at once refused to commit himself[242]), and Wilson then seems to have given up his plan[243]). The letter is of interest, however, because it shows the Italian policy that Wilson had now formulated.

The President began by stressing the enormous advantages Italy had gained from the war: the recovery of terra irredenta, Trentino and Trieste, the destruction of the traditionally inimical Austria-Hungary. However, Wilson was willing to provide Italy with further guarantees; that is why he had proposed that Yugoslavia should refrain from having a fleet in the Adriatic, that the forts along the Adriatic coast and on the islands should be abolished, and Yugoslavia be under obligation not to rebuild them, that all new States should commit themselves to ensuring the equal status of minority groups with the other inhabitants of the countries, and, finally, that serious consideration should be given to making Fiume a free city and a free port. This was the offer; the warning was contained in the following:

"The "Pact of London", I respectfully submit, cannot wisely be regarded as applying to existing circumstances or carried out consistently with the agreements upon which the present peace conferences are based. The boundaries proposed in that agreement were laid down as a frontier against the Austro-Hungarian Empire; and that Empire no longer exists. It has been broken up into a number of states no one of which will be strong enough seriously to menace Italy. In order to hasten the break-up, Italy, along with the greater States associated with her in the war, encouraged the Jugo-Slavic peoples to break away from the Empire and assured them of her sympathy with their aspirations for independence and thus herself assisted in radically altering the circumstances which had justified the London agreement. As parts of the Austro-Hungarian Empire the Jugo-Slavic peoples of the Adriatic coast were Italy's enemies. They may now be made her friends, and the way of peace and permanent adjustment lies in arrangements of accommodation, not in military preparation. That, at least, the war has demonstrated."

It will be seen that this was precisely Bissolati's argument. Had Wilson played with the thought of publishing this letter? Whether he had or not, he still did not feel sufficiently strong or sufficiently committed to act without the backing of the other Great Powers. Instead, he began to seek other paths.

The foregoing may seem to be an unimportant digression in an account of House's activities at the Peace Conference, but it should not be so regarded; the two journeys made by Wilson after his arrival in Europe were of decisive importance to his subsequent policy, and the fact that House so often went counter to Wilson's aims during the Peace Conference was perhaps due to his failing to fully realize the extent of Wilson's commitment—because he had wasted the opportunity of being present when Wilson formulated his views.

While Wilson was measuring up the European leaders and the rest of the American Delegation were beginning to adapt themselves, the last members of the Delegation arrived. As early as 22 October, House had written to Wilson recommending that the leaders of the various "War Boards" be represented on the Delegation[244]), but Wilson had not reacted at that time. The question of ensuring America qualified economic representation was, however, a matter of concern to House, and in the following period Auchincloss tried to influence events through Polk[245]). In Washington, on the other hand, the problem does not appear to have been regarded as particularly urgent. Polk replied: "The President said he would telegraph for someone when he was needed. This seems to be the plan they are following"[246]). House then again tried to influence Wilson directly[247]), but still in vain. House finally took matters into his own hands, and Auchincloss reported to Polk[248]):

"With the approval of the Colonel I am informally trying to get the financial, shipping and general economic representatives of the United States in Europe prepared in some measure for the Interallied Conference and the Peace Conference. ... My personal opinion has always been (and this has been reenforced by information received since I have been here) that economic questions will be at the basis of almost every dispute which will arise at the conferences...".

The plan now being put into operation was the formation of "a small economic committee with Vance McCormick at the head of it to advise the delegates of the Peace Conference."[249]) At the same time, efforts were being made to get Norman H. Davis, who was already in Europe, attached to the delegation as representative of the Treasury Department[250]). As soon as Wilson arrived, Auchincloss submitted a memorandum to him proposing that word be sent forthwith to Vance McCormick, making him one of the economic advisers to the Delegation[251]). While House and Auchincloss had apparently only wanted McCormick, Auchincloss's talk with Wilson resulted in a telegram calling for both Vance McCormick and Bernard M. Baruch[252]). Baruch was thus Wilson's personal choice. He had already written to him on 7 December: "I am sure we shall need you within a very short time"[253]), and Baruch had long been ready to leave[254]). Auchincloss then prepared a new memorandum to the President, recommending Davis's attachment to the Delegation as representative of the Treasury Department[255]). Davis received his appointment on 31 December[256]). In addition, Thomas W. Lamont was attached to the Delegation, at the suggestion of Carter Glass, the new Secretary of the Treasury. Thomas W. Lamont was a partner in the firm of J. P. Morgan and owner of the New York Evening Post. He was a Republican. Glass gave the following interesting account of the reason for his choice[257]):

"Lamont's general standing as an international banker will ... tend to strengthen the confidence of our country in the ability of the Treasury Commission to meet the financial problems which are referred to it."

It was thus principally thanks to House that steps were taken to ensure that the American Delegation was provided with excellent economic advisers. From House's point of view, however, it was important that he himself should retain control of this part of the organization too. Auchincloss therefore submitted yet another memorandum, which Wilson approved on 3 January. The crucial passage in this reads as follows[258]):

"It is recommended that a council be set up, comprising Messrs. Hoover, Hurley, Baruch and McCormick and Davis with a Treasury Representative to be appointed by Mr. Glass, under your (Wilson's) chairmanship, to discuss and decide such joint policies as are necessary in both these phases and to coordinate it with the Peace Commission by inclusion of *Colonel House, General Bliss and Admiral Benson, Colonel House to act as chairman in your absence or inability to find time.*"

It is perhaps also important to note that Lansing was not made a member of this council.

With this group of economic advisers, a completely new element was added to the Delegation. The men were all prominent persons, who, either politically or administratively, had had quite a different degree of influence and position than the other "Experts" on the Commission. Their position can best be described as similar to the official position of the Peace Commissioners. And it is also obvious that the latter regarded the new arrivals with a certain degree of scepticism; on 31 December, they requested "a ruling as to the exact status in relation to the Commission of Mr. Hurley, Mr. Hoover, Mr. McCormick, Mr. Baruch and other similar advisers who have not been assigned as members of the Commission, but who will be in Paris during the Peace Conference in association with the American representatives"[259]). This group became officially designated "Technical Advisers", as opposed to the members of the Inquiry, who were called "Technical Experts"[260]).

The American Delegation thus comprised a number of different groups, whose only real link was the President, who had the final word. It may therefore be wise to give a brief account of these groups and of House's relationship to them:

1. Peace Commissioners Lansing, White and Bliss, who actually had no real influence. It was already clear from the beginning of the Conference that Wilson tended to neglect his Commission[261]). These three Commissioners met each day to discuss current problems, but House and Wilson seldom participated in their meetings[262]), and a close relationship developed between the three men in the course of the Conference[263]). House was well aware of the dangers inherent in the decisive difference between his position and that of his colleagues[264]). However, his situation was difficult because it was a combination of his own disinclination to accept a dominating influence and Wilson's tendency to neglect everyone but House[265]). At first, House did all he could "to keep them busy", but he apparently lost interest in the matter rather quickly and found the situation by no means unsatisfactory: "I have stopped trying to keep in touch with my fellow Commissioners on the American Commission. ... This Conference so far has been run by the President, Lloyd George, Clemenceau, Balfour, Tardieu and myself. Orlando has never been assertive ..."[266])

2. The Commission organization itself—staffed, as we have seen, by Lansing's people. This organization could have been an influential instrument in the hands of a strong man, but Lansing was not that man.

3. The Inquiry group, which was now, as mentioned, once more led by Mezes, House's man. The conflict between Mezes on the one hand, and Bowman and the other Experts on the other, was not at an end, however—quite the reverse[267]). Strife broke out at the beginning of April, when the Experts on the question of Fiume applied directly to the President over the heads of both Mezes and House[268]). This was the only time the Experts acted in concert, and it had a result, but apart from this, their influence varied from one question to another, depending on the personality and calibre of the individual Experts. However, it is still important to remember that House's influence over this group extended no further than that of Mezes.

4. The above-mentioned group of Economic Advisers, which, in this connection, means primarily Baruch, McCormick, Davis and Lamont—the four men

who led the extremely difficult and decisive negotiations on reparations. Their influence was very great and became even greater in the course of the Conference, even though Wilson could not always see his way, politically, to following their advice. We have seen that both Davis and McCormick, at any rate to a certain extent, owed their appointments to House, and we have seen how House, through the establishment of the Economic Council, tried to retain control of this group. It was, however, an attempt that was doomed to failure from the start. Baruch, Chairman of the War Industries Board, and McCormick, Chairman of the War Trade Board and a prominent Democrat, were both personal friends of the President. The relationship between House and McCormick was also exceedingly friendly at the beginning of the Conference, although it changed as House's weaknesses became more apparent[269]). On the other hand, relations between House and Baruch were rather cool, even before the Conference, although the two men kept up correct appearances. House had been one of those who advocated Baruch's appointment as Chief of the W.I.B., but his personal view was that "He (Baruch) is an able Jew but some people think he overrates his modesty"[270]), while Baruch regarded House as "a fellow who wants to be right, a kind of yes-man"[271]). House later came to look upon Baruch as one of the men behind his break with Wilson, perhaps because Baruch in many ways came to take House's place as Wilson's closest adviser. The foundations for a certain antagonism seem to have been laid as soon as Baruch arrived: "When I got to Paris, where Colonel House was the major-domo of the American Delegation, I was not one of his clique"[272]). Norman H. Davis was not personally known to Wilson before the Conference, but it is a measure of the confidence that developed between the two men that Davis, at the personal request of the President, followed Frank Polk as Under-Secretary of State in 1920[273]). Things went much the same way with Lamont, who, as Republican and financier, belonged to circles that were traditionally opposed to Wilson's policy; for him, the encounter with the President's ideas on foreign policy, primarily as regards the League of Nations, was of decisive importance. While he was in Paris he started, for his own account and at his own risk, through his partner in J. P. Morgan & Dwight Morrow, a propaganda campaign for the League of Nations in his paper, the New York Evening Post, and he similarly arranged for Morrow to send detailed analyses of the general feeling in the United States with regard to the League of Nations[274]). These analyses were passed to the President, and Lamont later threw himself into the fight for approval of the Covenant in America.

5. "The House Group"[275]), "the third floor front"[276]), "upstairs"[277]). Under such names was known the organization whose establishment we have followed in the foregoing and whose later fate is to be described in the following. This organization, not only in scope but also in size, was the largest

of the Delegation: "I have twice as many rooms as the other Commissioners put together", wrote House in his diary[278]). Thus, right from the beginning of the Conference, House had given up his anonymous, background position; his personal power was now clear to all, and dissatisfaction began to spread in the Delegation[279]). However, his position was safe as long as he continued to enjoy the confidence of the President.

*Chapter 3*

# Manipulating the Conference

The Inter-Allied Conference finally convened in the middle of January. It was organized so that all the Allied States were represented at the so-called Plenary Sessions, while the real power lay only in the hands of the Great Powers, whose representatives met each day in what was known as the "Council of Ten", which comprised the American President, the British, French and Italian Prime Ministers, the Foreign Ministers of these countries, and two Japanese delegates[1]). A procedure was then adopted whereby the Conference started with the minor Powers presenting their cases verbally to the Council of Ten, in this way the dissatisfaction felt by the countries in question over the organization of the Conference was subdued. At the same time, however, discussion of the big disputes between the Great Powers was postponed. At the end of January, the first commissions were appointed to deal with individual questions, but once again the problems between the Great Powers were evaded. Nevertheless, it was now that Wilson could mark up his first big victory: at the Plenary Session on 25 January, the Conference adopted a resolution in favour of the establishment of a League of Nations, which stated that this should be "an integral part of the general Treaty of Peace". At the same time, a commission was appointed to prepare a constitution for the League of Nations[2]). The American President became the chairman of this commission, and House was appointed the other American representative.

During the next few days, the President managed to consolidate his position still further by ensuring, through the adoption of the mandate system combined with the League of Nations, that the United States would be able to exercise influence on the settlement of territorial questions, even in areas in which America was not strictly involved from a legal point of view because she was not in a state of war with the countries concerned. This applied mainly to the Middle East[3]).

If House had hoped to play a decisive part in the organization of the Peace Conference, he was sadly disappointed; on 8 January he suffered an attack of gallstone and did not get up and about again until 21 January, "Just when the momentum was at its highest and the peace organization was being perfected, I fell ill . . ."[4]). By the time he was able to resume work, he found himself shunted onto a sideline. The decisive negotiations were held in the Council of Ten, on which Lansing, not House, had a seat. House gave vent to his frustration time and again in his diary in the time to follow[5]), but he also showed his feelings more publicly. McCormick relates[6]):

"Had an interesting talk in the afternoon with Gordon Auchincloss. Most amusing to note anxiety of Colonel's outfit over daily meetings of Council of five great powers at which Lansing sits with President. Colonel and Gordon both think things cannot possibly go right without the Colonel's presence and guiding hand. These little human weaknesses make interesting studies during these momentous days . . .".

House began to feel that his influence was being reduced because of his difficulty in maintaining daily contact with the President, who was busy with the negotiations in the Council of Ten[7]). As early as 23 January, House suggested to Wilson that they should change the system[8]):

"The Colonel has strongly advised the President to break up these conferences (Council of Ten). I (Auchincloss) have prepared a memorandum on the subject. The Colonel has suggested that two conferences of all delegates be held each week and that the time in between be utilized in private conferences. In this way it will be possible for a programme to be worked out and adherence to it secured in advance of each of the meetings. It is also suggested that particular subjects be delegated to committees of experts who should report back to the Prime Ministers after investigation. We hope that these suggestions will be adopted".

However, it would be a mistake to attribute House's impatience solely to jealousy and the thirst for power. The dissatisfaction expressed by House over the slowness and lack of organization of the Conference[9]) was shared by many others, including Lansing and Balfour[10]), who both had seats on the Council of Ten. From several sides now, the call came for the conclusion of a preliminary peace with Germany.

Even though House was thus prevented from participating in the official negotiations, he by no means lacked for something to do. As we have seen, he was, together with Wilson, elected to the League of Nations Commission. The first meeting of this commission was held on 3 February, but prior to this, a number of Anglo-American negotiations were held on a joint draft of the League of Nations Covenant. These negotiations were principally carried out between House and Cecil, the rest of the American Delegation being kept completely outside[11]). During and between the commission meetings, House acted as Wilson's right hand, and here he had the opportunity of exercising his organizational talents. There seems no reason to doubt that the two men enjoyed a perfect and harmonious cooperation, and House did a great and deserving job of work[12]).

In addition, House acted in his usual capacity of intermediary in the secret negotiations that accompanied the official meetings. We need only mention a single instance, which at the same time illuminates the secrecy and secretiveness that now reigned in the American Delegation. Ivo J. Lederer has demonstrated conclusively that the Yugoslavian request to Wilson at the beginning of February 1919 to mediate in the conflict between Yugoslavia and Italy was actually instigated by the President[13]). The contact with Yugoslavia was arranged partly through Hugh Frazier, who belonged to House's "organization", and partly through Wickham Steed, who was a personal friend of House. Steed reported as follows[14]):

"On February 2nd ... Major Bonsall, one of Colonel House's assistants, came to me with an important message ... Bonsall said also that the President wished to have the dispute between the Italians and Yugoslavia settled within a week. He urged me to extract from the Yugoslavs their final terms so that, if those terms were just, the President might insist upon Italian acceptance of them".

Apart from Wilson, House and Frazier, the only American to have been aware of the initiative seems to have been Douglas Johnson, one of the Inquiry's Experts on Italy. The other Peace Commissioners at any rate knew nothing about this, as is more than evident from the following letter from Joseph Grew to Gordon Auchincloss, dated 22 February, which is now in the National Archives:

"The American Charge d'Affaires at Belgrade telegraphs to the effect that the Yugo-Slav Government has received a confidential inquiry from the American Peace Commission as to whether it will consent to submit to the President of the United States for decision the questions between it and Italy. The Commissioners asked that the matter should be submitted to Colonel House, as Mr. Lansing desired to learn whether Colonel House has any knowledge that the President had given any such intimation. Will you please advise me on this point."

There are two pencil-written notes on the letter, both in Grew's handwriting: "Steed of London Times made the inquiry. Mr. Lansing informed Feb. 25"[15]). It is obvious that this sort of thing did not exactly promote concord in the American Delegation.

Wilson's mediation initiative is, of course, also crucial to an understanding of the development of his Italian policy. However, the point of principal interest in this context is that House was the only one to have been advised. He should thus have had every opportunity of knowing Wilson's views on the Italian question. It is important to bear this in mind when we later turn to House's various initiatives on the Adriatic question.

The draft of the League of Nations Covenant was adopted by the Plenary Session on 14 February, and that same evening, Wilson left Paris for a short visit to the United States. In the following month, House took the President's seat in the Council of Ten. Lloyd George and Orlando were also away from Paris during this period, and when Clemenceau was wounded by an assassin on 19 February, all the Heads of State were out of the picture for a while. This "interregnum" became a period of hectic activity, the remaining politicians doing their utmost to expedite solution of the big problems so that everything could be ready for a final decision when the Heads of State returned. The declared aim became now, the speediest possible conclusion of a preliminary peace with Germany.

The direct reason for the reappearance of the idea of a preliminary peace was the resumption of the negotiations on the Armistice[16]). At each new round, there had been a tendency, especially on the part of the French, to tighten the demands, while the Americans and, to a certain extent, the British were greatly opposed to such practice. On 12 February, the question was discussed in detail in the Council of Ten[17]). The naval and military Experts had expressed the wish for a decision on the *final* military and naval terms, and this was now advanced with great zeal by Balfour. Wilson was enthusiastic, finding "that Mr. Balfour's proposal for the first time seemed to suggest to him a satisfactory solution"[18]). Clemenceau, on the other hand, raised serious objections to the proposal: it was not possible to isolate the military from the political, economic and financial terms; the terms that would be considered in the military sphere depended to a great extent on those achieved in the other spheres. Nevertheless, the meeting ended with a resolution by Balfour in accordance with his proposal. The negotiations were resumed in the afternoon and Clemenceau, who now seemed more favourably disposed, expressed doubts as to whether the plan could be executed while Wilson was away. To this Wilson replied[19]):

". . . In technical matters most of the brains he used were borrowed . . . If his plan were agreed on in principle, he would be prepared to go away and leave it to his colleagues to decide whether the programme drafted by the technical advisers was the right one. He did not wish his absence to stop so important, essential and urgent work as the preparation of a preliminary peace. He hoped to return by the 13th or 15th March, allowing himself only a week in America. But he did not wish that, during his unavoidable absence, such questions as the territorial questions and questions of compensation should be held up. He had asked Colonel House to take his place while he was away".

Balfour's proposal was then adopted.

It is worth noting that Wilson touched on two points in his speech. The preliminary peace mentioned constituted the final military and naval terms, which were also denoted "these preliminaries of peace" in Balfour's resolution[20]), and it was in respect of these terms only that Wilson had given the go-ahead. On the other hand, however, he did not wish to prevent the negotiations from continuing on other points, and this was ensured by having House take his seat in the Council of Ten.

However, powerful forces were working for a speeding-up of the work of the Conference, so that an early peace could be brought about with Germany, and among the advocates of this course were, as we have seen, Lansing, House and Balfour. As early as 27 January, Lansing had discussed the possibility of a preliminary peace with House[21]), and on 9 February, he brought the matter up again[22]):

"... After dinner had a long conference with Col. House. I expressed much dissatisfaction at progress, said we ought to arrange a preliminary peace, told him my idea as to what it should contain, and asserted that delay in peace was causing Prest. to lose ground with people. House agreed with me, saying emphatically "You are right. You are perfectly right". I favor a resolution by the plenary conference as to contents of preliminary peace treaty ...".

The procedure indicated here by Lansing was that actually followed later, but just how much influence he had on the course of events is difficult to say; the combination, House, Balfour, Hankey, seems to have been dominant. However, it must still be remembered that House and Lansing were thus in agreement in their wish for a preliminary peace treaty.

On 5 February, House had had a talk with Bliss, who reported on the negotiations in the Armistice Commission and advised, to the great astonishment of House, that Foch was now in favour of "an immediate peace ... with Germany so that the wheels of industry should be started in motion throughout the world". House commented: "This has been my contention all the time"[23]). The next day he went further into the problem in a long entry in his diary, in which he explained his ideas on the terms for a preliminary peace treaty[24]). On 9 February, viz, the same day as the conference with Lansing, House had a long talk with Balfour, during which they both expressed their dissatisfaction over the slowness of the Conference[25]):

"Balfour and I determined that when the President, Lloyd George and Orlando left on their visits to their different capitals, we would try to get a program started which would include only articles necessary for a preliminary peace with Germany, and that we would work on these until they were finished".

Thus, on this day, the two initiatives formed a synthesis.

However, Wilson himself does not appear to have been advised of these plans until immediately before his departure, and his reaction was far from favourable. House laid his plan before Wilson: "I outlined my plan of procedure during his absence: we could button up everything during the next four weeks. He seemed startled and even alarmed at this statement. I therefore explained that the plan was not to actually bring these matters to a final conclusion but to have them ready for him to do so when he returned. This pleased him"[26]). Immediately after this talk, the President had a meeting with all the Peace Commissioners, and here Lansing asked him "if he had any instructions for the Commissioners during his absence concerning the settlements which should be included in the preliminary treaty of peace, as it was understood that the Council of Ten would continue its sessions for the consideration of the subjects requiring consideration and decision. The President replied that he had no instructions, that the decisions could wait until he returned, though the hearings could proceed and reports could be made during his absence"[27]). Nevertheless, Lansing definitely received the impression that Wilson was in favour of a preliminary peace treaty[28]).

Many misunderstandings might probably have been avoided if the two

Commissioners had only chosen a more convenient time than the day of Wilson's departure to present their views. As things stood, it is obvious that Wilson failed to appreciate the extent and scope of their plans, while, vice versa, neither House nor Lansing realized just how great the President's misgivings were with regard to the project.

In itself, the plan was both reasonable and obvious: the Conference had been assembled for a month, and the Armistice was three months old, yet none of the vital questions seemed to be anywhere near a solution—quite the contrary. And, at the same time, impatience was spreading all over Europe, and with it, the danger of revolution. What could be more natural than to seek a "speeding-up" of the whole procedure? Nothing more than that lay in the project, but the problem, seen from Wilson's point of view, was naturally that he might risk being faced with a kind of fait accompli on his return. And there was indeed a risk that this might be the case.

Immediately prior to Wilson's departure, relations with France had reached a crisis. The impression received by the American Delegation of French policy could be expressed in a single word: obstruction[29]. The French Government had an important weapon for its policy in the form of the press, and this had been used in the period up to Wilson's departure in a veritable campaign against the American President. Wilson had regarded the situation as so serious[30] that, with the approval of Lloyd George and Orlando, he had allowed rumours to seep out to the effect that if the campaign continued, a demand would be made for the removal of the Conference to another venue[31]. However, it was not only indignation over the French tactics that lay behind this threat, but also an evaluation of the aim of these tactics; both the British and the Americans were of the opinion that the French were deliberately delaying matters until Wilson had left, after which, with the help of a new press campaign, they would try to push the French demands through before the President returned[32]. It is therefore hardly surprising that Wilson reacted as he did to the plans submitted by House and Lansing, and it is perhaps also hardly fortuitous that Wilson had Admiral Grayson take care of the matter without advising House at all in advance[33]. Could it be that the President was already becoming aware of his adviser's failings?

Those left behind wasted no time, however; the day after Wilson's departure, Lansing started preparing "an outline for a preliminary peace treaty"[34], and similar deliberations were in progress in the circle around House[35]. At the same time, House entered into close cooperation with Balfour. On 16 February, the two men had a long conference to decide on the procedure best suited to promoting the rapid conclusion of a preliminary peace treaty. They also agreed that Balfour should discuss the matter with the Japanese, while House would take care of the Italians. "When this is done, I proposed that he and I should see Clemenceau and try and get him in line with us so that there might be no necessity to override him"[36]. The main obstacle to implementation of the plan was the French policy, and as we have seen, Clemenceau had great misgivings regarding a preliminary peace treaty comprising military and naval terms. However, during the following period, French policy seemed to change course.

One of House's first duties as American Delegate to the Council of Ten was to take a decision on the Russian question, which had again been raised on Churchill's unexpected arrival immediately prior to Wilson's departure[37]. This happened on 14 February[38]. What is interesting in this connection is not, however, Churchill's intentions, but Wilson's reaction; not only did he emphasize once more his opposition to continued intervention, but declared further that the purpose of the Prinkipo-proposal had not, for him, been *rapprochement,* but "fact-finding", and that this was still his view. "As far as he was concerned, he would be quite content that informal American representatives should meet representatives of the Bolsheviks". Nevertheless, no decisions were taken at this meeting, and Wilson left Paris the same evening.

Particular attention should be paid to these remarks of the President because they divulge something of great significance regarding his Russian policy and because an appreciation of this is essential to an evaluation of House's role in this matter. In recent years, Wilson's Russian policy has been subjected to renewed analysis[39], and several authors are agreed on the fact that Wilson was one of the few who really understood the dimensions of the Russian problem[40], even though, in the end, he did not act in accordance with this insight. Wilson's clearly defined standpoint, as expressed at the meeting of 14 February, was that neither his past nor his future policy towards Russia had included or would ever include *de facto* or *de jure* recognition of the Bolshevik regime[41]. His idea seems always to have been the re-establishment of the Liberal Government of the February Revolution[42], and his preferred means of achieving this aim was food[43]. "The real thing with which to stop Bolshevism is food"[44]. Behind this view lay the President's frequently admitted recognition of the fact that the Revolution could not be stopped by military force[45]. The power behind this economically oriented approach was, naturally enough, Herbert Hoover[46], but House fully shared the views of Wilson and Hoover:[47]

"... Bolshevism is steadily creeping westward. Intervention would only aggravate it. ... Not only would it aggravate it, but ... it would be impossible to realize even if it were advisable and just. There is not a western country that could safely send troops into Russia without creating labor troubles at home. It seems to me therefore that a barrier should be raised by helping the Central Powers to bring about stable, democratic governments of the right sort. To do this it is necessary to send food there and lift the blocade and other restrictions."

The question is, however, how deep this agreement went; did House also agree with Wilson on the fundamental question of non-recognition of the Bolshevik Government, or rather, did he realize at all that this was something fundamental and basic in Wilson's policy?

While the demand for intervention had its principal advocates in Conservative circles, with the French Government and Marshall Foch in the lead, and the policy of relief attracted a broad sector, both to the Right and to the Left of the Centre, the demand for recognition was an extreme Liberal and Socialist standpoint[48]). However, we have ascertained earlier that House placed himself clearly to the Left of Wilson on a large number of questions, including the problem of Russia[49]). This had also been the case in regard to the relations with the European Socialists, where Wilson had taken a far less accommodating attitude than House[50]). Nor had Wilson dared—or been prepared—to make full use of the International; he had not been prepared to force through the holding of an international Socialist conference in Paris at the same time as the Peace Conference[51]). "But while the Allied Governments meant to neutralize the International the U. S. Delegation sought to use this "safe" International to promote a Wilsonian peace settlement. This purpose was manifest in late January. It was then that the delegation made last-minute efforts to go to Berne and, having failed in these efforts, decided to send an unofficial observer to the Swiss capital"[52]). Consideration was apparently given to William H. Buckler[53]), but the final choice fell on William C. Bullitt[54]).

Bullitt must have seemed an obvious choice. During the war he had worked on the analysis of European Socialism and Bolshevism at the State Department, and in Paris it was his job, as head of the Current Intelligence Section of the Commission, to report personally to the four Commissioners[55]). However, it was not only his professional qualifications that were in order; politically too, he stood close to the Labour movement, whether one chooses to characterize him as "a frightened Radical"[56]) or, more suitably perhaps, as "the one representative of Left-Liberalism in the State Department"[57]). Nevertheless, what actually settled the matter was perhaps the memorandum on "The International Labour and Socialist Conference", which he submitted to House on 27 January 1919[58]). In a very penetrating analysis, Bullitt here wrote:

"The leaders of French and British Labor plan at Berne to draw up resolutions on three things: (a) League of Nations (b) Territorial settlements (c) International Labor legislation. They intend to follow definitely the lines the President has laid down. *It is possible, therefore, to steer the conference at Berne so that it will be an enormous support to the President in his work here.*"

Both Baker and Bullitt thus recommended the same course, but now as before, Wilson hesitated; he did not wish to lay direct pressure on Gompers, so the American Labour movement was not represented, and Bullitt was only present as an observer, but the green light was given for the American Socialists to participate[59]).

In December 1918 Wilson had rejected a proposed demonstration of welcome[60]) by the French Socialists, pointing out a number of political dangers involved in closer contact with the European Socialists, and the difficulties now came clearly to the fore: On 22 February, the four Peace Commissioners received a delegation of the American Federation of Labor, and Samuel Gompers took this opportunity of pointing out that "faddist parlor socialists were more agreeable to the Commission than the representatives of American labor", here referring to the "rumour that the Commission had supported the Berne Conference and sent representatives there". In reply to a direct question from Lansing, Gompers said that "he had heard that Mr. Bullard had gone to Berne to represent the Commission at the Conference. Mr. Lansing stated that this was absurd, that a Mr. Bullitt had gone to Berne as an observer to report the doings of the Conference to the Commission, and in no way as a representative to the Conference, that in the same way Mr. Bullitt was now going to Russia as an observer. Mr. Gompers stated that Mr. Bullitt was reported to be in sympathy with the Bolshevists. Mr. Lansing stated that he was not a sympathizer with the Bolshevists, nor was the Commission." This sharp exchange did not manage to deter Gompers, who referred instead to "other persons who were supposed to have great influence with the commission and to be of Bolshevist leanings—a Mr. Howe, and Captain Lippmann". Lansing again rejected this, and speaking of Lippmann, said that he only knew him "as editor of the "New Republic". Bliss now came to Lansing's aid, stating "that with the exception of Mr. Bullitt, the men whom Mr. Gompers had mentioned were not well known to the Commission". Gompers retaliated with an overall attack on the New Republic. The meeting was brought to an end by Mr. James Duncan, who "interrupted Mr. Gompers and gave a clear exposition of what the American labor delegation desired"[61]).

The most interesting point about this exchange of views is presumably House's total silence. For if the attacks were directed against anyone at all, they were against him. It was to House that Bullitt had addressed his memorandum and it was he who associated with the New Republic people. But he remained silent. Meanwhile, however, Gompers refused to give in. His first attack may have been founded on rumours and misunderstandings, but his next was both clear and concise[62]):

"Mr. Buckler stated that in a conversation which he had had with Mr. Gompers the day before, he had been alarmed to find that Mr. Gompers had a very definite charge to make against Mr. Bullitt. Mr. Gompers had first merely referred to Mr. Bullitt's general activities in Switzerland, but was finally pinned down to a statement of the exact information which he possessed against him. He produced a copy of a letter which he proposed sending to the Commissioners quoting a statement purposed to have been made by Mr. Bullitt to Mr. Frank Bohn in Switzerland. This statement was in substance that he, Mr. Bullitt, had been sent to Switzerland by the American Commission to Negotiate Peace in order to give his approval to the activities of the International Socialist Conference.

Mr. Lansing was of the opinion that there was nothing in this charge against Mr. Bullitt, but he felt that inasmuch as it was an extremely important matter, Mr. Gompers should be urged to put the thing in writing for presentation to the Commissioners, and that the charge should then be sifted. Mr. Buckler, agreed to inform Mr. Gompers that the Commissioners would like to have this whole question in writing."

As was most frequently the case[63]), House was not present at this meeting, but had he been there, he would have had every reason for concern, because, whether Bullitt had in fact said too much or not, the fact remains that he had really only put into words the thoughts entertained by the circle around House. And if he had indeed expressed himself as asserted, was he the right choice for so discreet and secret a mission to Russia as that on which he had recently been dispatched?

Recent research[64]) has clearly emphasized two points: The Conference regarded the solution of the Russian problem as absolutely vital to the establishment and preservation of peace, and, despite this insight, the Conference never had, and never arrived at, a real Russian policy. At best, it was never more than a series of partially self-contradictory attempts at one. This was due not only to the fundamental differences with respect to policy on Russia that existed between France and Italy on the one hand, and Britain and the United States on the other. It was also, to a high degree, due to the fact that even the most perspicacious of the Statesmen—Lloyd George and Wilson—were inhibited and unsure of themselves when it came to action. The result was an extremely variable course, depending on the changing initiatives of different persons.

The first attempt at a solution—the so-called Prinkipo-proposal, was the result of a British initiative[65]), with American support but energetic French opposition. Wilson was responsible for the final framing of the proposal, and it looked to the Liberals and Socialists as though the President had won the first round of the Conference[66]). Quite simply, the proposal was that representatives of all belligerent Russian parties should meet Allied negotiators on a small island in the Marmara Sea, although only on condition that all hostilities ceased beforehand. The convening of the meeting was approved by the Council of Ten on 22 January, and the meeting was arranged to take place on 15 February. However, the proposal came to nothing for many different reasons: the French opposed the idea more or less openly, and relying on this, the various "White" groups refused to be represented, while the Bolsheviks, on the other hand, agreed to attend, but worded their agreement so provocatively that both Wilson and Lloyd George regarded it as an insult. When Wilson left the Conference in the middle of February, it was obvious that this initiative had stranded.

The decision to convene the Prinkipo Conference had been reached at top level, and Wilson really does not seem to have had the rest of the American Delegation behind him[67]). It has been described earlier how the American Government was split over the question of its Russian policy, with Lansing and House on either side; but they both hesitated as regards the Prinkipo-proposal, although for vastly different reasons: "I hate the idea even of investigating those assassins. We know enough about them already. But what other course had we but to seek to bribe them to stop murdering by suggesting an investigation on condition that they stop fighting? . . .", wrote Lansing in a personal letter to Frank Polk[68]). House, on the other hand, feared the direct opposite: "The danger that we see in the communication issued with reference to Russia is that the Bolsheviks will simply ignore it or will say that they control Russia and that they don't need to submit to Allied Commission evidence of that fact"[69]). But for House, other factors also played a part[70]):

"Colonel House, who had been sick when the proposal was discussed and formulated, was annoyed that the conference had wasted so much time on it; his criticism obviously reflected a certain pique that the Prinkipo idea had been worked out without consulting him and without consideration of his own pet project for countering Bolshevism—food and economic relief".

He was, moreover, not particularly well disposed towards either of the American Delegates, William Allen White and—in particular—George D. Herron[71]).

To House, the Prinkipo-proposal was just one of many examples of how the organization of the Conference, with the Council of Ten as the determining organ, kept him away from the centre of action[72]). It was therefore hardly surprising that he took the first opportunity that presented itself not only to disclaim all responsibility for the project[73]), but also to take the initiative for an entirely new and, in his own view, far more promising attempt to get on speaking terms with the Bolsheviks[74]).

The Prinkipo-proposal was the result of a British initiative, and the British were naturally concerned over the possibility of it coming to nothing[75]). Lloyd George was therefore prepared to make an extra effort: ". . . I strongly urge that the delegates should insist on the Russian situation being cleared up before the President leaves on Saturday. If Prinkipo is to be abandoned then he ought to face the alternative and share the responsibility"[76]). Lloyd George was at this time in England, and the matter was taken up in the Cabinet[77]), where Churchill argued strongly in favour of "a definite decision to make war against the Bolsheviks", while "the principal arguments opposing Chruchill's came from Lloyd George". However, the Prime Minister was unable to find an alternative to Prinkipo, and wanted instead to leave the decision to the Peace Conference, which had to resolve the matter before Wilson left. Churchill was therefore sent to Paris: "one of Lloyd George's more serious tactical blunders at the Conference"[78]).

Churchill did not succeed in forcing a decision through before Wilson's departure, but he did get the President's "personal thoughts on the subject": the Allies and Associated Powers ought to withdraw their troops from all parts of Russia. On the question of Prinkipo, moreover, the President said, as described earlier, that the purpose of this should not be *rapprochement*, but "clear information", and that he was willing to have informal talks between the American and the Bolshevik representatives. Pressed to the extreme by Churchill, who "said that he would like to know whether the Council would approve of arming the Anti-Bolshevik forces in Russia should the Prinkipo Conference prove a failure", the President replied "that he hesitated to express any definite opinion on this question. He had explained to the Council how he would act if alone. He would, however, cast in his lot with the rest"[79]). From Wilson's earlier remarks, however, there was no reason for doubting his standpoint.

At the meeting of the Council of Ten next day, i. e. after Wilson's departure —Churchill submitted his own proposal, which was in two parts: "issuance of a ten-day ultimatum to the Bolsheviki to stop the fighting, with the understanding that if it was not accepted, the Supreme War Council would see what could be done about overturning the Soviet Government by force of arms"[80]). In other words, a last, although very limited, attempt to resuscitate Prinkipo, and, at the same time, joint planning of large-scale intervention. While Sonnino and Clemenceau took a favourable view of particularly the last part of the proposal, Lansing, House and Balfour demanded a postponement until Monday, 17[81]), and "(t)he weekend up to and through mid-day Monday saw feverish consultations between American and British officials, within the American and British delegations, and between Philip Kerr in Paris and Lloyd George in London"[82]). Wilson, on the other hand, was not brought into the deliberations, and indeed was hardly oriented on the situation[83]):

"The representatives of the five great powers met this afternoon at the Quai D'Orsay to continue the discussion of the two questions brought up by the British representatives at the meeting last evening.

. . .

The discussion of the Russian question will be continued on Monday afternoon."

"On Sunday, February 16, House discussed Russian policy with Lansing. He also met with Balfour to plan and coordinate the position Britain and America should take when discussion of Churchill's proposals was resumed the next day. Following these consultations, Auchincloss for the American side and Wiseman representing the British, together drafted an outline memorandum suggesting a modification of Churchill's first proposal".[84])

Next morning, this Auchincloss-Wiseman memorandum was laid before the other Commissioners by House, and was approved with a single amendment[85]). Lansing was then given the task of framing a telegram to the Bolsheviks on this basis, and Herter and Auchincloss were asked, to this end, to prepare "a statement of the principles constituting the policy of the United States"[86]). Both the Auchincloss-Wiseman memorandum and the Herter–Auchincloss declaration of principle were expressions of the same basic attitude: The Prinkipo policy should be given another chance, but if that failed, "the Associated Governments have firmly resolved to do all in their power to protect the newly constituted and friendly states bordering on Russia from the aggression of invading armies recruited from within Russia and to send to these states all assistance possible including food and other supplies"[87]).

There are two decisive points in this connection: from an American point of view, the alternative to Prinkipo was not increased intervention, but "containment"—and the Commission was unanimous on the policy—. The meeting of the Commission on the morning of 17 February is a clear example of this[88]); House, who was not otherwise in the habit of regular attendance at these meetings, was present on this day and opened the discussion by emphasizing that "in his opinion Winston Churchill was attempting by degrees to lead us into a position by which we would have to commit ourselves to enter war with Russia . . ."[89]). The Commission then agreed, as mentioned, to continue with the Prinkipo policy in accordance with the Auchincloss–Wiseman draft.

During this part of the discussion, House had taken the lead, but now it was General Bliss who took over the initiative, submitting "that we should be entirely prepared with an answer in case we were faced by the question of using armed force in Russia". He then read aloud a memorandum ("opinion") on the matter and asked for the views of the other Commissioners. Here, Bliss argued that "the Government and the people of the United States will be radically opposed to taking part in any hostile action in Russia so long as the present general conditions elsewhere continue to exist". "If we could make final and definitive peace *at once* . . . Then, and then only, the people of the United States might come to see that peace in Russia is the only thing necessary to secure universal peace; that her present condition is the only thing that menaces the peace of the world". Only then would America possibly participate in the pacification of Russia[90]).

Bliss thus disassociated himself from any plan for intervention, and in this he had the whole of the Commission behind him[91]):

"The Commissioners agreed heartily with General Bliss's statement of our policy, and decided that it should be read at this afternoon's meeting as a preliminary to suggesting that a statement should be made by all the Associated Governments in the sense of the outline which Colonel House had submitted at the beginning of the meeting".

While the American Delegation thus stood united in a rejection of Churchill's plans for intervention, the British Delegation was split. However, direct telegraphic intervention by Lloyd George enabled House and Balfour, at the meeting of the Council of Ten on 17 February, to act *en bloc* against Churchill and—more important—against Clemenceau[92]). At this meeting, House categorically rejected all plans for intervention and "faithfully reflected the view of President Wilson"[93]), but "(a)lthough House drew on the Bliss statement in his remarks before the Council that afternoon, neither he nor Lansing actually read it to the Council of Ten . . ."[94]), and he similarly "failed to submit a proposal along the lines of the Auchincloss–Wiseman memorandum, as recommended by the American Commissioners at their meeting that morning", perhaps because "he felt it would have no chance of adoption in the face of the interventionist bent of Churchill and the French"[95]).

Not until this meeting had been concluded did Wilson receive a more detailed report of the happenings of the last few days[96]). The President's reply[97]) clearly reflects his astonishment and anxiety over Churchill's unexpected move, but his standpoint was clear enough: "It would be fatal to be led further into the Russian chaos"[98]). However, the Commission could assure him that "Churchill's project is dead and there is little danger that it will be revived again by the Conference ..."[99]). Nonetheless, there were other projects brewing, and in one of these House was directly involved.

The Bullitt mission, ". . . this unfortunate mission"[100]), has in recent years been the subject of renewed, intensive analysis[101]), and a number of hitherto doubtful points have thereby been more or less clarified[102]). In the middle of January, the American and the British Delegations were already discussing the opportuneness of sending a "fact-finding body" to Russia. Wilson, House and Bliss were in favour, while Lansing did not like the idea very much[103]). However, these deliberations slipped into the background again in favour of the Prinkipo-project, and not until the chances of realizing this appeared slim, was the despatch of a mission taken up to renewed consideration. "It seems likely that Bullitt was largely responsible for renewed consideration of such a mission"[104]). It must further be regarded as highly probable, "although direct evidence is lacking", that House, immediately before Wilson's departure, "asked for, and received, discretionary authority to send a fact-finding mission to Russia, if and when such a course of action should seem desirable"[105]). However, and this is very important, ". . . it seems clear that in Paris only House of the American delegation and Kerr and Sir Maurice Hankey of the British delegation knew what terms Bullitt was planning to propose to the Soviet leaders. *President Wilson certainly did not;* in fact he was probably even unaware, until his return to Paris from Washington, that House had empowered Bullitt to *negotiate,* as well as to investigate"[106]).

What is important, however, is not only that House was agreeable to Bullitt negotiating with the Soviet leaders, but also that the knew—and accepted—the basis for negotiations that was to be used as the starting point. N. Gordon Levin, Jr.[107]) has proved that Bullitt left for Russia with a peace proposal that was to all intents and purposes identical with a Russian proposal made earlier[108]), and that had been finalized in talks between Bullitt and Phillip Kerr, and Bullitt and House. The Bolsheviks therefore had no difficulty in accepting the proposal since it was the one they themselves had previously submitted, and this was precisely the aim of the whole mission: the conclusion of peace with the Bolsheviks, viz, a *de facto* recognition[109]):

"The idea in the minds of the British and the American delegation was that if the Allies made another proposal it should be a proposal which we would know in advance would be accepted, so that there would be no chance of another Prinkipos proposal miscarrying."

However, there was no backing for this extreme Liberal standpoint in the rest

of the American Delegation; House had acted entirely on his own responsibility[110]). And what is more, not even Wilson was agreeable to such a policy
of recognition[111]).

The question that arises here is what motives House can have had for his
action in this matter. Firstly, it is obvious that the critical situation that arose
due to Churchill's initiative was the direct reason not only for the despatch of
the mission, but also for the decision to *negotiate*[112]). Although Lansing was
jointly responsible for the decision to send the Bullitt-mission[113]), he was not,
as we have seen, given any part in the detailed planning of the terms of
reference of the mission; this was done by Kerr, House and Bullitt alone,
and "(a)t this juncture House, Bullitt and Kerr, the three who planned and
organized the mission apparently considered it an alternative to the moribund
Prinkipo proposal; for on the following day, February 18, after arrangements
had been made for Lloyd George and House to attempt to renew the Prinkipo
proposal, the dispatching of Bullitt to Russia was delayed, although his orders
were prepared and signed. Only after the attempt to assassinate Clemenceau
and receipt of Lloyd George's message that the planned renewal of the Prinkipo
project would have to be postponed as a result, was it decided, on February 20,
to send Bullitt at once"[114]).

Churchill's initiative had indeed resulted in a close British–American contact
(Lloyd George–Kerr–House)[115]), which not only had the aim of a joint
manoeuvre to parry Churchill, but also led to a more fundamental exchange
of views between Kerr and House[116]). Following a talk with House on 17
February, Kerr gave the following report on House's views[117]):

"He (House) also asked me to say that the principal object of his policy was to prevent
the Germans and the Russians being driven together for that would inevitably mean a
great aggressive combination stretching from Yokohama to the Rhine. He thought the
French anti-Bolshevik policy would drive straight to this result and he could not imagine
what possessed them in advocating it. He was in favour of keeping in touch with the
Bolsheviks with the object of gradually bringing them to terms, restoring Allied influence in Russia and so composing the peace."

Next day, the talks were resumed at the initiative of House[118]). The two men
first discussed the successful averting of the intervention plans, after which
Kerr stated that Lloyd George was "anxious that if Prinkipo has to be dropped
some alternative policy should be put into its place". House then asked what
this policy was, but Kerr was unable to define it in detail beyond saying that
Lloyd George was against an attack on Soviet Russia but at the same time
felt "that we ought to stand by our friends until we could bring about some
reasonable settlement of the Russian problem". House then asked whether
Kerr had any suggestions, and Kerr replied that he personally "would be
willing to negotiate with the Bolsheviks provided that they signed an armistice
suspending hostilities on all fronts. I (Kerr) thought that we had the obligation
to defend our friends but that this did not include the obligation to refuse to

speak to the Bolsheviks, or to conquer Bolshevik Russia on their behalf. I thought that if we could negotiate a settlement which would secure to Koltchak, Denikin, the Archangel group and the small nations on the Western border of Soviet Russia the free control of their own affairs and at the same time allow Allied agents to penetrate European Russia with full guaranties for life and property, we should have amply fulfilled our obligations and at the same time have struck a deadly blow at the more violent and abominable forms of Bolshevism. If, on the other hand, the Bolsheviks refused to sign an armistice, or, having done so, refused to accept terms which the whole world would regard as reasonable, I thought that we then would have a clear case on which to ask Parliament to vote money and individuals to volunteer to help us to save non-Bolshevik Russia from Bolshevik aggression". House was in agreement with these views, "and would be prepared to support it in the Conference", and Kerr now asked Lloyd George his opinion, stressing at the same time the difficulties involved: ". . . it involves meeting the Bolsheviks which many people object to . . .". In his reply[119]), which was despatched after the attempted assassination of Clemenceau, Lloyd George did not take a direct stand on the question of negotiations[120]), but only on that of intervention: "Russia must save herself. Nothing else would be of the slightest use to her. If she is saved by outside intervention she is not really saved."

It is thus obvious that both Kerr and House were prepared to negotiate with the Bolsheviks and it is also probable, as mentioned, that they both looked upon the Bullitt mission as an alternative to the Prinkipo policy[121]). However, as we have seen, Wilson had not intended Prinkipo to be the preliminary to a *rapprochement* with the Bolsheviks[122]). Because of illness, House had, of course, been unable to participate in the framing of the Prinkipo policy, and it is therefore possible that he had simply misunderstood Wilson's intentions: ". . . it is highly probable that like the Soviets, but unlike the President, Bullitt and House had interpreted the first Prinkipo proposal as an indication of American readiness to recognize the Soviet regime"[123]). It is also possible that "the Colonel saw the projected mission in its various aspects but did not make clear his intentions, perhaps not even to himself"[124]).

On the other hand, it cannot be disputed that the policy of recognition of Soviet Russia was in keeping with the Left-wing line that House had, at any rate at times, made his own, and it is therefore extremely unlikely that he should have been ignorant of the fact that these views were far from being shared by all members of the Delegation[125]). In fact, the secrecy surrounding the actual aim of the mission and its despatch[126]) would seem rather to indicate that House deliberately took the opportunity of acting counter to all critics. On the other hand, his attitude after Bullitt's return does not indicate that he realized that, in advocating a policy of recognition, he had also acted against Wilson's intentions; the fact is that when Bullitt returned, House was the only one to receive his proposal favourably, and he only backed out of this policy when he realized that it was not only the members of the Commission, but also the President himself who opposed it[127]).

N. Gordon Levin, Jr. has given the following analysis of House's aims[128]):

"... House's approach to the Bullitt mission made clear that the Colonel hoped to extend *de facto* recognition to the Soviet regime in the context of an over-all effort to absorb the Soviets into an orderly Allied-dominated European settlement. House's rejection of another Prinkipo conference further suggests that his aim was to make peace in Russia, without consulting the anti-Bolshevik Russians, by means of a direct *rapprochement* with the Bolsheviks. In this regard, House's sophisticated diplomacy may be contrasted with the less realistic, but more ideologically principled, efforts of Wilson to create a Russian settlement at Prinkipo by bringing all the competing Russian political factions, including both the Bolsheviks and their opponents, together for rational truce discussions.
. . .
In retrospect, it is apparent that House was in favor of a policy which would have sought to contain Russian Bolshevism by extending *de facto* recognition to the authority of the Soviet regime over much of European Russia, in return for Bolshevik promises not to advance on Siberia, Poland and the Baltic States. In other words, House hoped to pacify Russia by a program of partition, a position he formulated as early as the fall of 1918:
"I am not in agreement with the President as to leaving Russia intact. She is too big and too homogeneous for the safety of the world, I would like to see Siberia a separate republic, and European Russia divided into three parts. The British Empire does not present the same menace to the world as would the Russian Empire under a monarchy"."

As we shall see, the Bullitt mission was only one of many instances in which House took initiatives during this period that resulted in policies directly opposed to the aims of the President. In some cases, House's actions were more than deliberate, while in others, they tended rather to express a lack of understanding and knowledge of Wilson's intentions.

We are faced with the problem of deciding what degree of responsibility should be attributed to the Bullitt mission, amongst all the other factors, for the much discussed break between the two men. And here it is worth remembering a few dates[129]): Bullitt left Paris on 22 February and arrived in Petrograd on 8 March. Next day he met Chicherin and Litvinov, and "(f)ollowing these conversations, Bullitt sent Pettit to Helsinki to dispatch a report to Lansing and House. Bullitt stated that the two Soviet leaders were "most favorably disposed toward the cessation of hostilities and a peace conference" ..."[130]), and he ended thus: "I am certain from conversations already held that the Soviet Government is disposed to be reasonable and that I shall have a communication of the utmost importance to transmit". This telegram was received in Paris on 12 March, 1919. Bullitt had already left for Moscow on 10 March to meet Lenin, among others. "The proposals agreed on were delivered to Bullitt on March 14, after five days of negotiating; they were approved by the Bolshevik Central Committee that same day. The proposals were in the form of an offer to be made by the Allies. The Soviet Government agreed to accept this offer provided it were made not later than April 10. The major provisions of the offer followed rather closely the outline terms given Bullitt by Kerr"[131]). The telegram containing these terms was despatched from Helsinki on 16 March and received in Paris at 10.50 p. m. on 17 March[132]). However, Wilson had arrived in Brest on 13 March, i. e. four days before the arrival of the telegram and at a time when it was impossible to know what would come out of the mission.

However, the despatch of the Bullitt mission was not the only initiative in the Russian policy that Churchill's 'offensive' gave rise to. The French, too, now began to make a move, no doubt encouraged by Wilson's absence.

It is particularly characteristic that the French initiative linked the German policy to the Russian[133]):

"If Germany could be compelled, in its current weakness, to accept crushing preliminary terms of peace, the Allies would then be free to support and supervise the creation of a coalition of East European forces to be directed against the Soviet regime; if necessary, the Allies might even enlist German assistance in this struggle. In this way the plague of Bolshevism would be eradicated at its source, and a ring of states under French domination would be securely established to surround and contain Germany in the East."

It is really hardly possible, at any rate as long as the French Archives are still inaccessible, to decide which of the two factors had top priority in the French policy. But there is in any case no doubt that the two motives were intimately linked when the French plans were first presented during this period, in a talk on 18 February (or 19 February?) between Foch and the British Chief of Staff[134]). The time chosen for this initiative was hardly fortuitous either: Wilson had left, the negotiations with the Germans at Trier seemed to show that "under existing conditions we can dictate terms of peace to Germany", and, finally, thanks to Churchill, the Russian problem had again become of immediate importance. It is worth noting that Foch's initiative coincided perfectly with Clemenceau's statement in the Council of Ten on 18 February[135]):

"M. Clemenceau proposed that there should be no meeting on the following day as he wished to devote the whole day to thought on the Russian question".

Next day, however, came the attempt on Clemenceau's life, and all official discussion of Russia came to a halt for the time being[136]). Nonetheless, on 15 February, Foch took the opportunity of an interview with the Council of Ten to present "a remarkable project which starting from the insignificant question of returning the Polish troops in France to Poland, unfolded with startling rapidity and seeming logic into a complete design both for the settlement of the German treaty and for the elimination of Bolshevism"[137]). The proposal submitted by Foch was actually identical with the thoughts he had expressed to the British Chief of Staff: rapid conclusion of peace with Germany, followed by a crusade to the east[138]). Thus the Marshall managed to add yet another dimension to the "speeding-up" efforts of the Conference[139]), and it was Balfour who assumed the task of replying to Foch[140]):

"He (Mr. Balfour) was most anxious to hasten the conclusion of the preliminary terms of peace. He had, himself, moved a proposition with that object in view. ... But when Marshall Foch asked the Conference to defer the sending of a Polish division to Poland until the preliminaries of peace had been concluded with Germany, he evidently underrated the difficulties of the latter task. A discussion with a view to bringing about a preliminary peace could hardly be brought to a satisfactory conclusion unless three or four such questions as the following were first settled, that is to say: financial questions, the question relating to the left bank of the Rhine, the question of Dantzig, etc., questions which could hardly be settled before President Wilson's return to Paris.

... (T)he Conference could not move a step until the reports of the Allied Commissions, which were now at work on these problems, had been received. Those reports could not, however, be expected before 8th March next. The Conference would then have a week to consider those reports before the return of President Wilson, and during that time no doubt some spade work could be done. It was evident, however, that, if the dates suggested by him were correct, it would be impossible to have the preliminary terms of peace ready ... It would be impossible to draft a peace ... at the earliest before the end of March, and even that would be a very sanguine estimate. He would, therefore, press for the acceptance of his original proposal ... As regards Marshall Foch's plan to mobilize the whole of Eastern Europe ... into a great anti-Bolshevik army to be hurled against Russia, he had no objections to offer, as he was not qualified to express an opinion. But the plan undoubtedly dealt with tremendous issues: it could not be regarded as part of the accepted policy of the five Great Powers, and the Conference could not be asked to settle that question before deciding to carry out the small and most desirable operation of sending General Haller's army to Poland. ...".

The French initiative was thereby halted, but the matter did not end there as far as the American Delegation was concerned.

Foch's plans for a crusade were the direct reason for the initiative now taken by General Bliss; it was on the afternoon of 25 February that Foch submitted his plans to the Council of Ten, but he had already tried a private campaign with General Bliss on the morning of that day[141]):

"On the morning of February 25th, after a meeting of the Committee in March (!) Foch's office, he detained me, after the others left, for a private conversation. He told me that he had now become convinced that it was absolutely necessary to make peace with Germany without a moment's delay. But I soon saw that his idea was not based on the same reason as mine (vis., that if we don't make peace with Germany very soon there will be no German Government with which to make peace), but that it was on account of his ulterior plans. He told me that he had formed a plan by which he would settle Bolshevism and the Bolsheviks as soon as peace was made with Germany. He was going to form an army of Greeks, Roumanians, Poles, Czecho-Slavs (!), etc., and he believed that this army together with the Russians that are already fighting the Bolsheviks would enable him to quickly occupy that entire country. It was also evident to me, as he talked, that he counted upon the assistance of the United States in order to carry out this plan".

The move on Foch's part gave Bliss occasion to indulge in a number of reflections on the proper course of American policy in this matter, on the basis of the idea "that if we are going to stand in with bankrupt Europe in order to finance future wars, our people ought to make up their minds to it right away; and if we are not going to do it, it would be part of wisdom to quietly but firmly let all people over here understand that fact"[142]). Bliss now prepared a memorandum in which he explained his views in detail[143]). The memorandum was then laid before the other Commissioners at their meeting on 28 February[144]).

In this memorandum, Bliss explained Marshall Foch's plans and asserted that "this plan would not have been formulated except in the hope that the necessary assistance would be given by the United States". The fact was that Europe itself was bankrupt and could do nothing without American aid. The time had therefore come "for a carefully guarded, but kindly and positive declaration of the purposes of the United States":

"... if, as is assumed by the Commission, it will not be the policy of the United States to participate in the settlement of these problems, the Commission believes that it would be wise for the government of the United States to enunciate that policy in such a manner that it will be clearly understood by every nation in Europe. The Commission suggests therefore that the government of the United States announce in a kindly but positive way that it will withdraw all of its military forces from Europe immediately after the conclusion of peace with Germany; that, from that time on, if it gives supplies of food or other supplies to any nation in Europe, it will be as a result of charitable contributions from the people of the United States; that, from that time on, appropriations of food and other supplies for government in Europe will be made only for cash or sound credit; and that loans to the government of Europe will be made only on the best of security".

It was primarily the French policy that was given as the reason for this isolationist doctrine:

"In its discussions with the French representatives on the question of the future military status of Germany, the Commission is constantly met by the statement that unless they can tie the United States to them by such a bond as will bring the latter to their assistance whenever they choose to have a war with Germany, they have no hope for the future; that they do not believe in the permanency of the present alliance. When the French are told that the League of Nations will afford them the protection of the world against wanton aggression from the Germans or anyone else, they intimate that the League of Nations is a dream while the friendship of the United States is a surety. If the French were told positively that after the signature of peace with Germany, the United States will with draw its forces from Europe and will not allow herself to be drawn into another war except as her own interests may dictate, the Commission believes that the French would become the most earnest and enthusiastic advocates of the League of Nations".

What Bliss wanted—and recommended—was thus a decisive confrontation between the French and the American standpoints. The Commissioners present at the meeting supported Bliss's views, and Henry White proposed that a telegram should be despatched to the President[145]). However, as usual, one of the Commissioners was absent from the meeting, and this decided the further course of events[146]):

"Mr. Lansing and Mr. White at once approved my suggestion, but for some time Mr. House "hung fire". Finally, he also approved it and the Commission asked me to draft it in the form of a telegram to the President, but I told them that it was then too late."

The purpose of the telegram had indeed been that the President should discuss the matter with all his political advisers and "the leading men of all parties" during his stay in Washington, so that agreement could be reached on "what will be the attitude of the United States in general, in both a financial and military way, towards the solution of these many after-the-war problems in Europe". But by the time Bliss finally received the go-ahead for sending the telegram, Wilson was about to leave Washington again, and would therefore not have time to discuss the matter with his advisers and might even be irritated "that such a subject should be unloaded on him when he would be unable to give it any attention"[147]).

It would be wise to pause a moment at this per se rather commonplace episode because it is one of the first, definite examples of the split in the Delegation that was to become so apparent during the last phase of the Conference: the division into advocates of and opponents of a compromise with the Allies. Paul Birdsall has made this question of a compromise the principal theme of his exposition, which makes House, in particular, the main scapegoat[148]), while N. Gordon Levin, Jr. has probed deeper, with his demonstration of how "reintegrationist" and "punitive" elements struggled for supremacy in Wilson's German policy[149]). Levin has also pointed out that the Delegation's most fanatical advocates of "the reintegrationist position towards Germany" were Lansing, Bliss and White, although he stresses their isolated position, which partly gave them grounds for dissatisfaction and partly gave them "general freedom from involvement in concrete situations demanding compromise"[150]). Most important of all is, however, the fact that "these three commissioners expressed their alienation at Paris in reintegrationist terms which fused opposition to Allied extremism with a pervasive concern lest Germany be overcome by Bolshevism"[151]). It might therefore be more apposite to classify Lansing, White and Bliss as the "Conservative" members of the Commission; the line they followed was an extension of the Landsdowne line during the war[152]). Nevertheless, as indicated above, we come closest to the truth if we term these three Commissioners as isolationists[153]).

It is impossible to ascertain now whether House's hesitance was a deliberate attempt to foil Bliss's initiative, but this seems highly probable, for the policy advocated by Bliss and the other Commissioners was diametrically opposed to that for which House was working. Where Bliss recommended isolation and confrontation, House went in for commitment and *rapprochement,* and this, as we shall see, primarily in relation to France.

On 17 February, Foch reported in the Council of Ten on the Armistice negotiations with Germany and at the same time advised Clemenceau that "in his opinion, the Germans were completely flattened out", and Clemenceau thought "it was a good time to press final peace terms." A meeting was therefore arranged between House, Clemenceau and Balfour for 19 February[154]). There thus seems to have been general agreement on the "speeding-up" process, whatever the motives behind the sudden French spirit of cooperation may have been. House thought the reason was "grave signs of unrest in the French army"[155]), but it is more likely that the French saw the chance of an initiative while Wilson was away and thought they now had the opportunity of evading the decision regarding a unilateral finalization of the military terms. It is at any rate certain that the French now started a heavy offensive to push through the French demands regarding the Rhineland.

The first indications appeared as early as 18 February. On this day, the British Chief of General Staff had a talk with Marshall Foch, who stated his conviction that Germany was now ready to accept any terms whatsoever. He therefore proposed that agreement be reached as quickly as possible on the three decisive terms: "1. The strength of her armed forces. 2. Her frontiers. 3. The indemnity she is to pay". "He is strongly in favour of saying to the Germans in this preliminary peace treaty that, whatever may be the fate of the Rhenish provinces and whatever form of government for these provinces the Allies may decide in favour of, under no circumstances will the German Empire extend beyond the Rhine. That in his opinion is essential for the security of France, and makes the settlement of the Western frontier a simple matter ..."[156]). House received this memorandum next day and immediately passed it on to Washington[157]), together with a comment in which he reported on the situation in general[158]). He advised that he and Balfour were to have had a talk with Clemenceau that day "to discuss plans for speeding up of conference". However, just before the appointed hour, an attempt had been made on Clemenceau's life, so the conference had had to be given up. He further advised that the "French have changed their position and now desire to hurry the signing of peace. ... I am doing everything possible to hasten work of Conference so that upon your return terms of preliminary peace will be ready for your consideration". This shows quite clearly that House believed himself to be in complete accordance with Wilson's views in working with Balfour for a speeding-up of the Conference. However, Wilson's reply should have given him cause to reconsider[159]):

"... Have just read the memorandum given you by the Chief of the British General Staff of an interview with Marshall Foch. It seems to me like an attempt on the part of the French to hurry us into an acquiescence in their plans with regard to the Western bank of the Rhine, a plan to which I could, as I now see the matter, in no case accede. I know that I can trust you and our colleagues to withstand such a program immovably, except that I am of course willing to have the strictly military and naval terms promptly decided and presented to the Germans. I am not willing to have anything beyond the military and naval terms decided and believe that the Conference of Ten would be going very much beyond its powers to attempt anything of the sort. The determination of the geographical boundaries of Germany involves the fortunes and interests of many other peoples and we should not think of being hurried into a solution arrived at solely from the French point of view. I beg that you will hold things steady with regard to everything but the strictly military and naval terms until I return".

This instruction could not possibly be misconstrued: Wilson wanted no further negotiations on any but the purely military questions, and he quite specifically warned against the French Rhineland plans.

Neither the attempted assassination on Clemenceau nor Wilson's words of warning, however, had any effect on the further course of events. With a view to the intended talk with Clemenceau on 19 February, Balfour had prepared a draft of a resolution that was, to all intents and purposes, identical with the one he later presented to the Council of Ten[160]). Because of the attack on Clemenceau, the talk came to nothing, but instead, House and Balfour reached agreement on the proposal, while Sonnino, as a condition of his participation, required that agreement should be reached on the question of the border between Italy and Yugoslavia[161]). In the meantime, Lansing continued work on his own draft, although he seems at the same time to have been kept informed by House[162]). A further result of the "speeding-up" efforts is also to be seen in a meeting held between the British and American Experts on Germany's boundaries, which was convened for 21 February[163]). House opened the meeting personally with a short address, in which he emphasized "that peace might have been made before Christmas"[164]). This meeting showed that there was a high degree of agreement between the two groups of Experts on a number of points. Thus, they agreed that France should have the full right of ownership and exploitation of the Saar coalmines, but that it would be necessary to ensure to the population "some special form of regime . . . with the object of avoiding the subjection of considerable German population to French institutions". It was, however, the task of France to present final proposals on this. Some form of local government under French sovereignty and in customs union with France was envisaged[165]). There also appears to have been agreement on Danzig's incorporation in Poland, although divergent opinions were heard[166]). However, the Experts arrived at no decision on the utterly crucial question of the Rhine provinces, but merely stated that if the Peace Treaty contained "a full guarantee to France that her frontier would be protected by the removal of all military establishments, fortifications and strategic railways from the left bank of the Rhine . . . it would not be necessary to secure to France a strategic frontier in advance of the former (1870) frontier of Alsace-Lorraine"[167]). This constituted a clear recognition of the fact that this question was a purely political decision. However, in general, the result of the meeting could only serve to support House's expectations regarding the possibility of concluding an early peace.

There were other spheres, however, where the situation appeared less promising. In the Reparations Commission, deep and fundamental differences had arisen between the American Delegation and the Allies on the question of the content of the concept of reparations. The American representatives maintained that the pre-Armistice Agreement was binding in this respect and that "war costs" could therefore not be included, while the Allies advanced the demand for "integral reparations". The reasoning varied, but the argument of the French representative is worth giving in detail. Klotz "contended that the real contract between the Allies and Germany was not contained in the terms of the Note of November 5th, 1918, but in the Armistice Convention of November 11"[168]). As will be remembered, this contained the clause whereby the Allies and Associates reserved their rights with regard to reparations. Here we thus catch a glimpse of the dualism of the supposed agreement. The American Delegates, Baruch, Davis, Lamont and McCormick, considered the question to be so important that they wanted to appeal directly to the President. They first talked to Lansing and then to House. McCormick, whose doubts as regards House seem to have been steadily increasing, reported as follows[169]):

"Talked to Colonel House about cable to President. He was not enthusiastic and I thought rather resented cable being shown first to Lansing, but approved".

The telegram was despatched[170]), and Wilson's reply was an unambiguous confirmation of the fundamental American standpoint[171]). If the American President intended to take the same firm stand on the other questions, there might anyway be reason for doubting the possibility of a rapid conclusion of a peace treaty.

Nevertheless, the efforts at hastening the work of the Conference proceeded unabated, and 22 February became a decisive date, in all senses of the word. On this day it was intended that Balfour's "speeding-up" resolution should be presented to the Council of Ten[172]), and shortly before the meeting, House received a message that Clemenceau wished to see him[173]). On the same morning, Clemenceau had also had a talk with Balfour[174]), and he seems to have given both House and Balfour the impression that he was willing to support the "speeding-up" resolution provided that "the entire terms should be given at once, and that the military terms should not be made now as at first planned"[175]), i. e. precisely what he had demanded in the discussion of 12 February. Both Balfour and House were prepared to accept this, although Balfour had his doubts about it[176]). At the meeting of the Council of Ten, Balfour submitted his resolution on speeding up the work on the conclusion of a preliminary peace with Germany, including "(a) The approximate frontiers of Germany: (b) the financial arrangements to be imposed on Germany: (c) Our economic relations with Germany after the war: (d) Responsibility for breaches of the Laws of War". In order to achieve this, all the committees should submit their reports latest 8 March[177]). The discussion extended over two meetings, because although there was agreement on the principle, there were some difficulties as regards the extent of the "speeding-up" process. Sonnino took the view that it should apply to all treaties. The result was therefore four separate resolutions, but as House pointed out to Tardieu and Balfour, "we would then sidetrack all these resolutions except with reference to Germany"[178]).

The "speeding-up"process was thus ensured, and it should be emphasized that it did not involve decisions, its sole purpose being to hasten the deliberations at Expert level so that everything could be ready by the time Wilson and the other leaders returned. House perhaps stretched his authority a long way but he did not exceed it. However, he now proceeded to do precisely this in private negotiations that he initiated in the following period.

If we wish to understand what was happening to House at this time, we can do no better than to cite his own words, from the entry in his diary for 26 February:

"I had a long meeting with Hankey. I decided instead of having a "steering committee" which we had thought should consist of Balfour, Tardieu and myself to have an entirely informal committee composed of myself alone. I am satisfied that I can do it better and with more harmony by consulting with first one and then the other".

And he added—by way of explanation—: "When I fell sick in January I lost the thread of affairs and I am not sure that I have ever gotten fully back"[179]). The development we have followed in the foregoing had thus reached its culmination. On this date, the break between Wilson and House actually took place. It was no longer the American policy that interested House, but his own role as leader and manipulator of the whole Conference.

On 25 February, Balfour analysed the political situation as it appeared at that time[180]). As the three vital problems he named: Italy's territorial ambitions, the West bank of the Rhine, and Poland's access to the sea, and he then pointed out that none of these problems could be solved before the American President returned to Paris. He went on to expound his views, particularly as regards French policy:

"This means that, however carefully the preliminary spade work may be carried out, the final discussions cannot take place until after the middle of March.

The French are as anxious as we are to arrange a preliminary peace with Germany. It is only Baron Sonnino who supports the impossible policy of deferring peace with one enemy country till peace with all enemy countries can be simultaneously accomplished. The French not only desire an early peace with Germany, but I suspect them, rightly or wrongly, of desiring to rush this peace in President Wilson's absence, and of using the present Military situation in Poland as one of the instruments for attaining this object.

On no other hypothesis can I explain the obvious reluctance of the French to allow the Polish troops in France to proceed to Poland . . .".

If Balfour's analysis of the situation was correct—and there is much to indicate that it was—House at any rate was not deterred from accepting the French tactics. As mentioned, House had had a talk with Clemenceau on 22 February. This had been one of the talks in which Clemenceau "spoke of me again as his "dear friend" and declared that he opened his heart to me"[181]). Clemenceau gave briefly, and to the point, a list of the French wishes, and House immediately referred this to Wilson; Clemenceau insisted on the establishment of a Republic of the Rhine that would include four million Germans. This Republic should be exempted from war reparations, it should have no army, and everything should be done "to make them prosperous and contented" so that the population would not wish to join the German Republic, and, if it did happen to nourish such aspirations, they would at any rate not be allowed to fulfil them. Clemenceau further considered that Danzig should be incorporated in Poland, and House added that this was also the view of the American and the British experts, but that the British Government was not in agreement on this point[182]). Finally, Clemenceau asserted his view that German-Austria would not seek assimilation in the German Republic if the Allies and Associated Powers opposed this[183]). What House thus sent to Wilson was a report, not an analysis, of the French policy, and not a statement of his own standpoint[184]). However, he can hardly have been prepared to agree to Clemenceau's very excessive Rhineland demands.

It is not possible to ascertain whether House had the opportunity of discussing the French Rhineland plans in greater detail with the President before he left Paris[185]), but it is certain that he had discussed the matter with Balfour before Wilson's departure. The initiative for the discussion seems to have come from the British Foreign Minister[186]). In this talk, House argued against the establishment of a Republic of the Rhine on the grounds that this would constitute a violation of the right of self-determination and would mean that Germany was treated in one way, and the rest of the world in another, with all the political dangers this might entail. Balfour shared House's opinion, "and yet we both have a profound sympathy for France and for the unhappy situation in which she finds herself". Nevertheless, House could see no other solution for France than to rely on the League of Nations[187]). His reaction to Clemenceau's proposal was therefore presumably the same.

The day after the conference with Clemenceau, however, House had a talk with Tardieu, who now presented an entirely new proposal. On this House reported as follows to the President[188]):

"Our territorial experts are in substantial agreement with the British and French respecting boundaries of Germany. Tardieu, who, since the attack on Clemenceau has become more prominent, said to me yesterday that France would be willing to have the Rhinish Republic set up only for a limited period of years, at the end of which the population would be permitted to decide for themselves what their future should be. He said that in this way a breathing space would be given us all and France would secure protection until she recovered from the present war. The principle of self-determination would be in this way safeguarded".

With Tardieu's new proposal, House's previous argument lost its force, but at the same time, a real possibility did seem to have been created for meeting the French wishes without compromising Wilson's principles. That is at any rate how it must have appeared to House, and he was not the only one to take this view.

House received no reply from Wilson to his two reports on the latest developments in French policy, his most recent line on the President's views being Wilson's above-mentioned vehement reaction to the talk between Foch and the British Chief of General Staff: ". . . a plan to which I could, as I now see the matter, in no case accede"[189]). House received this telegram on 24 February but as it related to the situation as it had been prior to Tardieu's new proposal, which House considered altered matters radically, he could not regard this standpoint as normative, except in as much as Wilson had, in the same telegram, warned him in general against entering into more detailed negotiations on the question of Germany's borders. But why did the President fail to react to House's reports? The fact is that he did reply, but in this manner[190]):

"Sorry to say new means of communication so far so unsatisfactory that I do not really clearly know anything you are trying to tell me. I am not in touch with your proceedings and unable to advise. The new code is extremely complicated, is imperfectly transmitted; and of such a character that when one word is lost it throws out all that follows".

Was the whole thing then, just one enormous misunderstanding?

This is a question that cannot be answered with any degree of certainty. It is quite clear, however, that there really were great communication difficulties owing to the fact that House and perhaps especially Auchincloss, in order to ensure the utmost secrecy in the correspondence between House and the President, had reverted to a plan for coding and communication that Auchincloss had earlier tried to put through, though without success. This plan covered the use of the naval coding system[191]), and the reason given for its use was that the codes used by the State Department were not safe from British decoding experts[192]). On the other hand, the plan in fact took control out of the hands of the State Department, and this was why the plan had stranded when Auchincloss first tried to get it adopted for all communications of the Delegation in November 1918[193]). However, the State Department was not involved in the internal communications between Wilson and House, and the difficulties that arose were entirely the fault of the instigators, as Auchincloss also admitted[194]):

"... as a result we had to recode all of the telegrams that had been sent to him (Wilson) under our new system which is green plus Navy cipher ... This is a perfect nuisance and we are partly responsible for the trouble ourselves. We should have sent back with the President to the United States one of our ensigns to do the coding for him."

What we can ascertain is that Wilson received the telegram on House's talk with Clemenceau (despatched 23 February) on 25 February[195]), and that the late reception was due to decoding difficulties, but that the message, once finally deciphered, was perfect as regards the part about the Rhine. On the same day the President also received the cable on the talk with Tardieu[196]), and here there were further decoding difficulties, also in the section on the Rhineland, although the meaning was clear enough. Nevertheless, a number of other points in both these and several other cables were very unclear or directly incomprehensible[197]). The first cables from House, including the report on the talk between the British Chief of Staff and Foch, to which the President had reacted so sharply[198]), was not coded according to the new system and therefore did not present the same difficulties as regards interpretation. It is therefore possible that Wilson did not see in the brief report of the talk with Tardieu any very great improvement—indeed, he may not even have realized that it concerned a new development since due to the decoding difficulties, he received this telegram simultaneously with the report on the earlier talk with Clemenceau[199]).

House maintained to the end that he did not understand what lay behind the break, and there is much that points to his being right, in the sense that he did not himself realize that he had exceeded his authority and acted disloyally to Wilson. He reflected on the break many times in his diary, and the closest he came to its real reason is presumably his account of a talk that he had in 1921 with Irving Hoover, former Chief Usher of the White House[200]):

"He said the President's change of feeling toward me began at Paris just after his return from the United States in March. Somewhat to my surprise and much to my regret Hoover laid it chiefly upon the President himself saying that those around him fanned the flame. Hoover recalled that the President had a jealous streak and he believes the feeling was primarily the cause of the slackening of his friendship for me. What he told agrees almost wholly with the conclusions I had already reached without having all the facts upon the subject, that is, there was no particular incident which caused the cooling of his friendship for me but that it began, as Grasty once told me, as my "pickening his vanity". From that time it was easy for others to increase this feeling".

In an interview with Charles Seymour in 1938, shortly before his death, he went one step further[201]):

"Upon his return to Paris in March I saw at once that there was a change. ... At the time I suspected with some reason that immediately upon his return the President had been told that I was disloyal ...".

A disloyalty, however, to which House never admitted.

House's reflexions on Wilson's character traits are unimportant in this context. What is decisive is the fact that he clearly dates the break to immediately after Wilson's return to France, and that he admits, indirectly, that he may have given the President grounds for jealousy by his behaviour. However, this behaviour was, as we have seen, apparent to all in the Delegation, even *before* the President left in February—apparent to all, that is, except Wilson himself. Other and harsher means were needed to open the President's eyes; House had to overstep his powers in a really big way, to show definite disloyalty. And the reasons for his managing to do this—so to speak with his eyes closed —are to be sought in his psychological situation at this time, as demonstrated in the foregoing.

The blame for what followed was, however, not only House's, but also, to a great degree, the President's. To leave the Delegation without directives, in blind trust to absolute communion of minds with his closest adviser, was irresponsible, to say the very least.

On 25 February, the French made a new move, with Tardieu's "Mémoire du gouvernement français sur la fixation au Rhin de la frontière occidentale de l'Allemagne et l'occupation interalliée des ponts du fleuve"[202]). This was in many ways a remarkable document. The French "case" was here presented more convincingly than ever: in Tardieu's memorandum, the argument took up 20 pages—the concrete proposals, on the other hand, only three lines:

"1. La frontière occidentale de l'Allemagne doît être fixée au Rhin. 2. Les ponts du Rhin doivent être occupés par une force interalliée. 3. Les mesures ci-dessus ne doivent entraîner au profit d'aucune puissance aucune annexion de territoire."

This was thus an introduction to negotiations that appeared to leave several possibilities open, and it was perhaps not entirely fortuitous that the English translation among House's papers has been given the following wording by means of a handwritten addition[203]):

"c) The above measures ought not to carry with them any territorial annexation *(against the will of the peoples)* to the benefit of any power".

That is, a direct reference to Tardieu's new proposal.

The French views were amplified in two addenda, in which the French plans for an independent Republic of the Rhine were explained, together with the economic aspects of such a solution. However, this proposal did not contain the clause on the right of self-determination included in Tardieu's earlier proposal[204]), and this was not an accidental omission. Tardieu seems to have submitted his own modified proposal quite on his own responsibility and at his own risk—and without having made it clear to House and Balfour that it did not represent Clemenceau's views[205]). If he intended in this way to create a more fertile soil for reception of the mémoire, he certainly enjoyed some degree of success. Balfour's reaction was astonishingly favourable[206]):

"Since our conversations with Clemenceau and Tardieu, I have had two long talks with the latter, and have received from him a written argument upon the subject. This is an able paper and not very long, I strongly recommend its perusal.

My general conclusion from all these sources of information is that while the French are still profoundly impressed by the dangers they and Belgium will run if the Rhine is not made the Military frontier of Germany, they are ready to modify their schemes for neutralizing the left bank of the river so as to make them more tolerable to British and American opinion. To this end they would be ready, I think, to abandon any plans for the permanent dismemberment of Germany. The administrative separation of the German provinces on the West from those on the East, and the occupation by Allied Forces of the Rhine bridges, would be regarded as a temporary measure, justified by Military necessity, which would only last so long as Germany remained suspect among the peoples of the world, and was not permitted to enter the League of Nations. If, when this probationary period came to an end, the German-speaking population of the left bank of the Rhine desired that their separation from the rest of Germany should be permanent, that would be another matter to be decided when the time came. For the moment the Associated Powers would only be concerned with securing from German aggression France, Belgium and the Channel Ports until the League of Nations had consolidated the civilized world into a peaceful organization of States".

House restricted himself for the time being to advising Wilson that he had received a memorandum from Tardieu and would cable details when he had

had an opportunity of studying it[207]). In the meantime, he discussed the matter in great detail with Balfour on 27 February[208]):

"I brought up the question of a Rhenish Republic, and we practically came to an agreement as to what the United States and Great Britian would do as to that question".

On the basis of the two passages cited here, Paul Birdsall has concluded that[209]):

"While there is no evidence of any formal commitment to the French program, Tardieu had led both men pretty far in the direction of approving French projects "in principle" and as a temporary expedient, and, at least in the case of House, in the face of explicit warning against precisely that course from his chief".

However, neither of the arguments in Birdsall's conclusion can be said to be valid. For the first thing, it is not possible on the basis of House's not particularly adequate and, as usual, very optimistic diary entry, to conclude that Balfour really had been prepared to accept Tardieu's proposal; the most that can be ascertained is that he was favourably disposed towards it—more favourably indeed than most of his Delegation[210]), and, of greatest importance, more favourably disposed than Lloyd George. Secondly, it is not right to say that House acted "in the face of explicit warning against precisely that course from his chief", for as demonstrated above, House had no instructions regarding the new situation that had arisen with the arrival of the modified French proposal. Finally, it is only partially correct that "there is no evidence of any formal commitment to the French program".

On 2 March, House had a talk with Tardieu, on which he reported with his usual brevity in his diary[211]):

"I had a long talk with Tardieu, and we got nearer together on the question of the Rhenish Republic and Luxembour(g) . . .".

However, McCormick was himself present at this meeting, and his diary provides a far fuller account[212]):

"At 5.00 Colonel House and Tardieu came for tea, also Aubert with Tardieu. They agreed on plan for Rhenish Republic and discussed method for getting Lloyd George's approval, also on Saar Coal Basin. Agreed Poland should have Danzig and Belgium Luxembourg, all of these, of course, with proper reservations. Agreed to push to conclusion work of committees so that reports would be ready for President upon his arrival the (1)4th, and Tardieu said Foch very anxious to get the Germans at conference, Versailles, 26th. Colonel agreed and they both hope it can be wound up May 1. This program is an ambitious one but I believe it can be done and should be, although I still see rocks ahead, particularly on questions of priority as to reparation payments."

During this meeting, House thus gave his consent to the whole of the French programme—to the Saar, to Danzig and to the Rhenish Republic—in accordance with Tardieu's modified proposal. Although not "a formal commitment", this was at least a "commitment" with very far-reaching consequences. If it was Tardieu's intention, by means of the modified proposal, to establish a joint Franco-American front against Lloyd George, he must be said to have enjoyed the greatest success. However, both negotiators had calculated without their hosts: Clemenceau was not supporting Tardieu's proposal, and Wilson was definitely not backing House's acceptance, and, finally, it was no easy matter to make a fool of Lloyd George.

When McCormick sent a copy of his diary to Ray Stannard Baker in 1928, he himself drew attention to this remarkable meeting in his accompanying letter, commenting as follows[213]):

"I think he (House) had two purposes in arranging this interview in my office; one was to avoid the newspapermen and any publicity and the other was possibly to be a bit flattering to me. You will note that at this conference "They agreed on plan for Rhenish Republic and discussed method for getting Lloyd George's approval". As I had not been sitting in with the political groups and had never discussed these questions with President Wilson I did not know at the time of the strong position he had taken, which I subsequently learned, against the Rhenish Republic or I would certainly have paid closer attention to the discussion in my room. But the facts remain, however, that at that time, in my rooms, House had agreed with Tardieu on going along in the creation of a Rhenish Republic which I understood later was absolutely contrary to the President's policy and, of course, I think we all agree now would have been fatal.

I mention this because it appears to me to be one of the instances in which House overstepped his authority in agreeing to something which was not approved by the President. This may mean nothing but it seems to me it was quite a significant occurrence and I thought you would be interested in knowing about it.

If I had known on that particular day what I have since learned my diary entry would probably have been considerably amplified."

It is worthwhile analysing McCormick's comments.

McCormick seems here indirectly to imply that House may have had reasons for wishing to make a favourable impression on him, and it would probably not be unrealistic to see in this an indication that House was aware of the scepticism with which McCormick regarded him in this period. However, it must be considered as exceedingly unlikely that House should have tried to regain McCormick's confidence by attempting to make him privy to a deliberate ultra vires act—such a course of action would indeed only have served to undermine House's position. The conclusion must therefore once more be that House was not aware of just how far he was exeeding his authority at this time, for there can be no shadow of doubt that he did exceed it. Of course, his action did not constitute such a signal breach of faith as thought by McCormick—it is quite clear that he remembered nothing more of the episode than related in the diary, i. e. he did not quite perceive that what House was agreeing to was Tardieu's modified plan, and thus *not* the Clemenceau version of the Rhenish Republic in its original intention that Wilson had so definitely opposed. All the same, it is quite clear that House here acted if not against the letter then against the spirit of Wilson's instructions. This was not just a case of hastening the process at expert level—even though House, both as regards Danzig and the Saar, did indeed follow exactly the recommendations of the American Experts, but a case of exceedingly detailed negotiations that might well result in decisions that would, in fact, present Wilson with a *fait accompli* on his return. House may possibly have had a feeling about this deep down; he at any rate took care not to report on this conference to Wilson.

Quite apart from this, the diary entry and comment are interesting from another angle, since they witness to the horrifying degree of ignorance that reigned in wide circles of the American Delegation as to Wilson's actual programme. Not even House, who must have been closest to it, could thus be sure. That the Delegation could be so ignorant in this respect was, of course, due amongst other things, to the fact, that Wilson had never attempted to explain his standpoint to the rest of the Delegation, so matters developed as General Bliss had much earlier forecast: "I think that our present course is dangerous, dangerous to the point of threatening the success of the commission"[214]). However, this was not the only reason. If there had been the slightest degree of unanimity in the American Delegation, or in the American public, as to what interests America was supposed to be looking after in the solution of the European question, the conditions mentioned would have been unthinkable. That such "common agreement" did not exist was, however, not only the fault of the President—the cause of it must also be sought in the historical situation itself: America was now finally confronted with the alternatives, commitment or isolationism, and strong forces pulled in both directions. This became more than apparent in the debate to which Wilson's presentation of the draft of the League of Nations Covenant gave rise in the United States.

Wilson's neutrality and war policy has often been criticized on the grounds that he gave it far too moralistic-legalistic and idealistic-utopian a line instead of stating clearly the considerations of *Realpolitik* that lay behind it, and that he thereby failed to "educate" the American people towards a deeper understanding of both the balance of power and the concept of collective security, and the United States' interest in a stable Europe and a strong League of Nations[215]). This is, however, a criticism that to a certain extent defeats itself, since the self-same critics have to admit that there was simply no basis in the American public in the given situation for the "realistic" arguments they so desired. Quite simply, Wilson showed the line of reasoning that seemed to provide the only possibility of ensuring a strong national line[216]). At the same time, this idealistic appeal also became a valuable weapon in the ideological propaganda that became so important an accompaniment to the actual military operations during the last year of the war[217]).

However, the war released other forces in American Society than the crusading spirit and idealism: a strong isolationist trend began to make itself felt. This was supported in many circles and was, of course, linked to the most honourable of all American political traditions.

In his penetrating analysis of the phenomenon of modern American isolationism, Selig Adler has tried to sum up its various sources as follows: The declaration of war was, per se, the first step towards the foundation of a new isolationism, because a not inconsiderable minority of the American people never accepted the necessity for this decision. To this could be added the possibilities for reaction inherent in the far too inflamed feeling that was the background for the crusading spirit. However, the war also rekindled American nationalism, which came to expression in many quarters as pure chauvinism, a "red, white and blue Americanism", which considered its most vital task to be to back up the Monroe Doctrine. Regional, geographical and economic factors also played their part: "The First World War crystallized the phenomenon called midwestern isolationism", which nevertheless also had national roots, since a considerable part of the population was of German or Scandinavian descent. Most important of all, however, was the fact that politics entered the matter. The Presidential elections were on the horizon, and after two terms with a Democratic President, it was the duty of every Republican to back any alternative to Wilson's programme. However, no attack on Wilson's policies could succeed in the long run as long as the Liberals supported the President, and this they were still doing, even though there were increasing signs of dissatisfaction[218]).

Wilson, of course, was well aware that his programme would meet heavy Republican opposition purely for political motives, and his entire strategy, right or wrong, was calculated with the aim of presenting the Senate with a *fait accompli:* If the League of Nations Covenant were an integral part of the whole Treaty with Germany, and the majority of the American people supported the concept of collective security, then the idea of rejection would be unthinkable. And indeed, there is every indication that "in March 1919, the American people were on the whole strongly if not overwhelmingly favourable to the League"[219]). Nonetheless, there was not the slightest indication that this had any effect at all on Wilson's political opponents—quite the contrary[220]):

"At two minutes after midnight on the morning of March 4th, Senator Lodge presented to the Senate an extraordinary document that has come to be known as the Round Robin. This was a pronunciamento, drawn up by the Republican leaders at the instance of Senator Brandegee, which announced to the world that the signatories did not find the Covenant of the League acceptable "in the form now proposed". The Round Robin further urged that the Conference address itself to the urgent task of making peace with Germany, while deferring such proposals as the League for later "careful consideration". The document was signed, or soon signed, by thirty-nine Republican Senators or Senators elect. Only thirty-three votes were needed to defeat a treaty".

This remarkable step has rightly been termed an ultimatum[221]), but there was more to it than that—it was a direct appeal to the Peace Conference over the head of the President, an open attempt to make common cause with the European opposition to Wilson's programme. It was a warning to the European Statesmen that America—regardless of what its President might claim—was not behind his policies, and that they would do well to draw the relevant conclusions from this[222]).

Wilson replied to the threat with a promise that "When that treaty comes back gentlemen on this side will find the Covenant not only in it, but so many threads of the treaty tied to the Covenant that you cannot dissect the covenant from the treaty without destroying the whole vital structure . . ."[223]). However, the opposition to the League of Nations had had its effect, and when the President again landed at Brest, it was clear that "practically the entire press of the United States had concluded that some amendments would be necessary out of deference to the critics of the Covenant and to lessen the doubts which had naturally been aroused in many people by their campaign"[224]). The question was, however, whether Wilson would agree to this demand.

No-one in Paris knew the answer to this question, but speculation was rife, and the American Delegation followed the developments in the United States with steadily increasing concern. It is clear that House had had the Senate's reaction on his mind even before Wilson left; it was at his suggestion that Wilson decided at the last minute to arrange a dinner for the Foreign Relations Committee of the Senate[225]), and even while the President was still at sea, the first of a number of telegrams from House arrived, with advice on the debate with the Senate and the other opponents of the League of Nations[226]). Wilson, on the other hand, did not discuss the situation in his correspondence with House[227]), and the Delegation was thus forced to seek information by other means.

A decisive difficulty here was the distance, which made it impossible to gain a first-hand impression of the press reaction in the United States. The daily summary received by the members of the Delegation was typical of this. Such summaries were prepared for Germany, France, Britain and the United States, but the last-mentioned simply did not compare with the others, possibly because the American summary was prepared on the basis of press cables. No attempt was made at interpretation, the summary being just a selection from various newspapers. The weekly summaries were better, although they showed clearly that the author, NJB, was an optimist—in the rare event of there being an interpretation at all, it was always favourable[228]). The first attempt at a coherent survey of the American reaction was available on 16 February[229]). The first impression was "general approval", although there were signs of the growth of criticism against the omission of the Monroe Doctrine. On the other hand, the author had to admit "that editorial opinion frequently makes one ask himself if the people of the United States actually desire to form a real league". However, he saw no danger to ratification, public opinion being too strong, although he at the same time admitted that the reports from Washington showed "that an organized Republican effort to block ratification could easily provide the necessary one-third vote".

The same views appeared in the survey for the following week[230]): "the pendulum of American popular opinion has swung over decisively to approval of the League of Nations", although at the same time, it was "only fair to assume that the man in the street has not delved deeply into the problem". And the opponents did their utmost to stress the fact "that American sovereignty is in danger of impairment". "With all these powerful forces appealing to the American's patriotism to block the League, it might be felt that a revulsion of feeling on the idea might take place ... but still it may be predicted that, in the long run, the honest desire of the American people to see a peace-enforcing League established will triumph ...". But this was surely a case of wishful thinking when, in the same breath, the author had to admit that the New York World, Wilson's strongest and most optimistic supporter, had carried out an investigation that resulted in the conclusion that ratification in the Senate would be rejected by at least 15 votes. One conclusion was, however, unavoidable, and that was that "American public opinion will bear heavily on the President to modify the Covenant in several phases". The most serious objection was in respect of the Monroe Doctrine, which seemed to be annulled through the League of Nations Covenant. And even the optimism of the author could not hide his anxiety:

"To sum up, America now is in favor of the League. There is strong opposition that is increasing and will increase to the point that ratification of the treaty will be obtained only after a real struggle. The President's battle at the peace conference is a skirmish compared to the drive he must make for the support of his own people".

This dualism continued in the subsequent surveys, and its cause was obvious enough. The opposition that was rearing its head in America was of such unexpected dimensions that the only solution seemed to be faith in Wilson's personal power, his ability to carry the people with him in any situation—even the most difficult one. In the survey of 2 March, it was precisely this tune that was played: The American people stood behind the League of Nations Covenant, but not so strongly that victory would be easy. "But, the President is bringing every ounce of his strength, which has proved powerful in every international crisis, slowly but surely to bear on the feelings of the American people. And, the American people are responding favourably, if the daily press is to be taken as a criterion"[231]). Optimism was on the wane.

After Wilson's departure, however, a certain clarification seemed to take place, and on 7 March, according to the daily survey:

"A sudden flood of newspaper dispatches from Washington, hinting of the President's willingness to consider American claims for revisions of the present draft, bear out earlier intimations of a compromise. The sudden appearance of stories of this kind lends color to the belief that they probably are inspired by some authoritative person. This conjecture is strengthened by the announcement that Hitchcock, presumably the administration representative, conferred with Knox, the whip of the Senate opposition, on the question of changes in the League covenant ...".

It thus looked as though Wilson was finally ready to give in, but it also appeared that he had waited until the very last moment, for the same survey could now report that the conflict concerning the League of Nations had developed into the bitterest fight for generations[232]):

"Although it is asserted emphatically that there is good reason for the President's declaration that he has American popular support on the League question, it cannot be overlooked that, although the American people are firmly resolved to have a League, they object strenuously to the non-inclusion in the present covenant of provisions safeguarding the more important of America's sovereign prerogatives".

The optimism had thus turned to a clear recognition of the fact that the opposition had had sufficient strength to force Wilson to accept amendments. The next question was whether these amendments would be sufficient to ensure ratification.

The author attempted to answer this question in his weekly summary of 9 March[233]). He came to the conclusion that the "hysterical opposition" to the League of Nations had culminated with the Lodge Resolution (Round Robin). However, this resolution should not be interpreted as meaning that all signatories had bound themselves to vote against the League of Nations Covenant in any form—on the contrary, "The slightest alterations in the League draft will permit of a speedy disintegration of the now formidable opposition". For the signatories included both those who were against the League of Nations under all circumstances and those who were prepared to accept it with certain modifications. "Over and over again, it is claimed by editors in every part of the country, that the President's appeals to the people at large will bring such pressure to bear on the Senate obstructionists that their front will crumble". And the survey ended with the following optimistic evaluation:

"All the American wrangling about the covenant may serve a useful purpose abroad, inasmuch as foreign delegates who are greatly desirous of the formation of the League, but who have amendments to offer, may refrain for fear of giving more fuel to the opposition in America—thus increasing the possibilities of America coming in".

The British newspaper, "The Daily Telegraph", wrote with far greater realism in its analysis of the consequences of events in the United States[234]):

"Wilson is now en route for Europe leaving behind *a situation very different from that existing in December.* The difference is perhaps not overwhelming as is assumed in some quarters, but it is serious enough and it is undeniable that the League of Nations is surrounded with difficulties and dangers which apparently were never anticipated by many of his friends in Europe. ... the President is meeting the situation in a bold and some think rashly defiant manner. The essence of his attitude is his reliance on the determination of the American people to see a League created. Whether he is entirely upon safe ground it is not for us to say, but *it is evident that his "mandate" from his countrymen for this and other matters will no longer be put in the definite form which was given it by some enthusiasts here and his position at the Conference will be correspondingly affected ...".*

This hit the nail right on the head: When Wilson once more landed at Brest, an entirely new diplomatic situation had arisen, and in this new situation, his political influence was decisively weakened.

The British press was generally less optimistic in its evaluation of the situation in the United States and—naturally enough—more critical of the President's tactics. On 7 March, "The Times" published a penetrating analysis of the situation, written by its Washington correspondent[235]). The correspondent established the fact that the President "has not succeeded in the chief object of his visit to Washington" and that "in its present form the Covenant is doomed as far as American participation in it is concerned". However, he pointed out at the same time that if Wilson decided to agree to alterations, there was a chance of turning the tide. Three days later came a new analysis by the same correspondent; his conclusion was again that "there is but little doubt not only senatorial but public opinion is against the acceptance of the Covenant in its present form, and for Paris to ignore this fact, may result in America's declination to join the League". He had carried out an opinion poll on the basis of 50 newspapers distributed over the entire country with the exception of the Pacific coast and had found "a formidable majority proclaiming belief in the League, but counselling alterations in the Covenant"[236]).

On 12 March, several British newspapers carried the news "that a wireless from the George Washington (the boat taking Wilson to Europe) says that the President is not averse to certain unspecified changes in the Covenant", and it was at the same time advised that The New York World "devotes its first leading article to proving by excerpts from the utterances of the President and his colleagues at Paris that the Covenant was never regarded as anything but a draft"[237]). Next day, The Times' Washington correspondent informed his readers that a telegram had been received from Paris requesting either Lodge or Knox to advise the amendments they wished to have incorporated in the League of Nations Covenant, but that neither seemed prepared to comply with the request[238]). The criticism thus seems to have had its effect on both the President and the Delegation in Paris.

The French press too, was inclined to take a pessimistic view of the situation in the United States, and there was a clear tendency, even in the Right-wing section of the press, to see the dangers inherent in the situation: ". . . if Mr. Wilson himself be not supported strongly, the United States might drop away from European society altogether and leave it to settle its quarrels alone", for which reason the press there supported the President[239]). However, the general view was that the opposition would not be able to stand up to public opinion, although, on the other hand, alterations were necessary[240]). And the French correspondents too, cited rumours to the effect that "Mr. Hitchcock is drawing up a series of amendments for the League of Nations project, which indicates that Mr. Wilson in preparing to make important concessions"[241]).

Of course, the press was not the Delegation's only source of information; it had, inter alia, the chance of receiving private advice. To give an impression of this, we can take a look at Thomas W. Lamont's correspondence with his partners, Dwight Morrow and J. P. Morgan, and the correspondence of Robert Lansing and Gordon Auchincloss with Frank Polk. Both these sources were favourably disposed towards the League of Nations project and both were in positions that can best be described as extremely well informed. Otherwise, they differed considerably; Morgan and Morrow were Republicans and belonged to the world of high finance, while Frank Polk was a Democrat and an official of the State Department. Nevertheless, their conclusions were practically identical.

As behoves a Government official, Polk was rather reticent, but his pessimism still shines through clearly: "General opinion is that the public are misinformed in regard to how the League will (function?)." It was regrettable that the President did not hold more speeches out in the country in order to explain his standpoint. "Question becoming rather political"[242]). The Republicans were raising objections in all spheres, and the Democrats were split[243]). Polk was convinced that the only thing that could change the picture was an energetic, personal campaign on the part of the President to explain his views to the people, because they were only prepared to listen to a man who had himself participated in the negotiations, "and until he can unlimber and get into action himself, it is not going to be very hopeful"[244]). " ... I am afraid that unless something is done to meet the objections, that those opposed to it (the League) are going to be able to hold public sentiment against the President"[245]).

Both Morgan and Morrow were far more explicit in their evaluations. Morgan judged the situation as follows: "Politics in most awful mess I have ever known them ... President ... has on the whole, done badly since his return, because he has not been intelligent in his answers to criticisms on League of Nations plan, and has not put it forward in anything like as favorable light as it deserves ..."[246]); and Morrow took the same line: " ... The situation here has been most confused during the last two weeks. Opposition to proposed Covenant much more bitter, on the part of many Republican and some Democratic Senators, than any of us had expected ... One of the primary troubles is that there is a complete misunderstanding of what the plan means ... The main difficulty is, in my mind, that no one has authoritatively explained for the Peace Commission what the plan really means ... I assumed there will be some amendments to the Covenant. When those are made it ought to be possible to prove to some of the Senators already committed against the plan, that the document does not mean what they say it does". Morrow further proposed that Elihu Root should be attached to the American Delegation in one capacity or another[247]).

Optimists or pessimists, they all agreed in their evaluation of the situation: opposition to the League of Nations Covenant had assumed far greater dimensions than anyone had expected—so great indeed was the opposition that it would take an extremely energetic effort on the part of the President to change the atmosphere, and concessions were unavoidable. For the Delegation in Paris there was only one conclusion, viz, that the Senate had now become an active partner in the negotiations and was a factor that would have to be taken into account.

On 14 February, Wilson had submitted the draft of the League of Nations Covenant to the Plenary Session of the Conference. Clemenceau concluded this meeting by declaring "that the Report presented and commented on by the President of the United States had been deposited with the Bureau of the Conference for examination and discussion by the interested Powers. The date on which the discussion could take place would depend on the completion of the preliminary examination of the scheme . . ."[248]). The Covenant was thus not approved, but only presented to the Conference for careful consideration and it was therefore removed from the agenda for the time being. However, the fact that it was laid on one side did not mean that it had been forgotten.

During the next few days, House negotiated with Lord Cecil on the appointment of a committee to discuss the Covenant with representatives of the neutral countries[249]) and, at the same time, he initiated negotiations with the Swiss representatives regarding the housing of the League of Nations either at Lausanne or at Geneva[250]). In the "speeding-up" resolutions proposed by Balfour on 22 February, the League of Nations was not mentioned, these providing only that the Preliminary Peace Treaty should include not only military and naval terms, but also boundaries, financial and economic factors, and war crimes[251]). At the suggestion of Lansing, however, an "inter alia" was inserted in the resolution[252]), and House advised in his diary that Lansing had submitted this proposal at his, House's, instigation[253]):

"My thought was that we would want to include in the treaty with Germany the Covenant for the League of Nations. I did not want to bring this up at the time, and I explained to Lansing, that if we did, it would cause an interminable discussion with the French, and that we had better merely leave room for that and any other subjects without mentioning them by name."

As usual, House had chosen to postpone the difficulties until a later date, with all the possibilities for misunderstandings inherent in such a postponement.

Soon, the heavy opposition to the League of Nations in the United States began to make itself felt on the other side of the Atlantic. This apparently made House decide that something should be done, and he therefore suggested[254]) bringing the League of Nations into function with immediate effect. To David Hunter Miller, he expressly stated that his reason for this step was that "he would like to see how any Republican could object to the League of Nations after it ever got started in advance"[255]). On 27 February he discussed the matter with both Cecil and Balfour. Balfour "was sympathetic but did not understand the subject well", while Cecil and House "found ourselves in entire agreement"[256]). At the same time, David Hunter Miller was given orders to investigate the juridical problems involved in the plan, and he was further asked to look into the different proposals for amendments to the League of Nations Covenant, which Frank Hitchcock, who was in Paris at the time, had brought up[257]). Finally, House sent a very detailed account of his plan to the President[258]). The plan was as follows:

"Let the members of the Committee which formed the Covenant act as the provisional executive council proposed in the Covenant. Have the Council of ten (!) which sits at the Quai d'Orsay or the Plenary conference refer certain matters to the League. Have the League report back to the Council of ten or the Plenary conference as the case may be with recommendation. In the meantime, it is our purpose to call in the neutrals and explain the Covenant to them and say that an invitation is soon to be extended to them to become members. We will not call the committee together unless the French, Japanese and others agree not to offer amendments to the Covenant until you return. I anticipate no difficulty in this . . .".

House further advised that the British had expressed the wish to have Hankey as Secretary General of the League of Nations, and House recommended this, inter alia on the grounds that it would increase Lloyd George's enthusiasm for the League of Nations. House had, in fact, offered Hankey the post that very day[259]).

Next day, Miller delivered a draft of a protocol for the provisional League of Nations[260]). This stated, among other things, that[261]):

"The Powers Signatory hereto, represented at the Conference at Paris, have agreed that in order *to facilitate the ending of the existing state of war there shall be forthwith constituted temporarily, and until the Preliminaries of Peace shall take effect, a Provisional League of Nations* composed of the aforesaid Powers".

It is clear from this that it was at least Miller's view at this time that the League of Nations in its final form should constitute part of the Preliminary Peace Treaty.

However, the optimism expressed by House on the first day soon cooled. At a meeting between Wiseman, House and Miller on 28 February, at which Miller's draft protocol was discussed, Wiseman raised a number of objections to the project. The nature of these objections is not known, but they may well have been political, for Miller advised that Wiseman "did not think it would be adopted but he thought it ought to be submitted to Cecil to see what he thought of it"[262]). And Auchincloss noted in his diary: "This is not going to be as easy as it first seemed"[263]). House himself now admitted that there were difficulties, but he hoped it would be possible to overcome these[264]). Perhaps, after all, he had over-estimated the favourable attitude of the British politicians the day before?

After this, the project seems to have been abandoned, and this was probably all to the good because, on 4 March, House received a telegram from the President expressing deep misgivings about the whole idea. He feared "that some advantage would be given to the critics on this side of the water if they thought we were trying in that way to forestall action by the Senate and commit the country in some practical way from which it will be impossible to withdraw".

Precisely, in fact, what lay behind House's idea. Then, for the first and only time before his return, Wilson gave *his* evaluation of the situation in the United States[265]):

"The people of the United States are undoubtedly in favor of the League of Nations by an overwhelming majority. I can say this with perfect confidence, but there are many forces, particularly those prejudiced against Great Britain, which are exercising a considerable influence against it, and you ought to have that constantly in mind in everything you do."

Depressing words indeed, providing plenty of food for thought, and House replied immediately that the plan had been shelved and that nothing would be done before Wilson returned to Paris[266]).

This exchange of cables coincided approximately with a critical phase in House's entire view of the peace negotiations. It is not possible to establish a direct, external cause, but is is nevertheless a fact that on 3 March, he "confided" to his diary one of the most pessimistic analyses of the situation that he was ever to give: "It is now evident that the peace will not be such a peace as I had hoped, or one which this terrible upheaval should have brought about". The reasons for this were manifold—some were purely personal: none of the leading politicians except the President appear to have been of the necessary calibre to solve the great tasks facing them, and even Wilson had his faults. However, there were other, equally important difficulties: "The American delegation is not in a position to act freely". Whereas the British elections and the vote of confidence of the Chamber of Deputies had given Lloyd George and Clemenceau a strong position, the November election had weakened the American position decisively. It was true that Wilson could use his influence in Liberal and working-class circles, and he could possibly in this way overthrow the Governments of the Allied countries, but he would still have his own people to reckon with, and there was, moreover, the possibility of such a step bringing chaos in its wake. This was a responsibility none could take. "I dislike to sit and have forced upon us such a peace as we are facing". Even the League of Nations was, in House's view, "an imperfect instrument". "All our Commissioners, Experts and Economists tell of the same impasse and come to me almost hourly for consultation and advice. No one can ever know how hard pressed I have been during the last months . . .". However, House would not complain if only the negotiations were characterized by a more unselfish spirit[267]).

There was, of course, a goodly portion of sentimentality and self-absorption in this analysis, but there was something else as well. There was deep anxiety, and a feeling that events had run away from American policy, together with a clear understanding of the fact that the forces which could be mustered behind Wilson's programme were anyway too dangerous to be used because this would open the door to Bolshevism. And at the same time, there was a clear recognition of the fact that the opposition in the United States had weakened the President's position decisively. In this connection it is worth remembering that House had, the day before, actually given his consent to the entire French programme, and if he did this in the same frame of mind as characterizes this analysis, it must have been because he had drawn the conclusion that it was no use fighting any longer. But could he be sure that Wilson would reach the same conclusion in his evaluation of the situation?

We must at any rate assume that it was in this pessimistic frame of mind that House received the message regarding the Lodge resolution of 4 March, and this apparently made a deep impression on him. Lansing's laconic comment really states the case: "very ugly situation"[268]), but House's reaction bears the print of desperation, and he even discussed with Auchincloss "the question of having the Covenant in a separate treaty so as to concede something to the Senate"[269]). Miller was consulted, and he expressed "an opinion very unfavorable to this"[270]) and prepared a memorandum on the matter[271]). Miller had been very heavily involved in the framing of the draft of the League of Nations Covenant and was presumably the American Delegate who was best acquainted with Wilson's thoughts on the subject, so it is worthwhile analysing the views he expressed in this memorandum.

He began by establishing that "We are agreed that the Covenant of the League of Nations is an integral part of the Treaty of Peace in reality, whatever it may be in form, and that the Peace itself is one whole agreement including the Covenant of the League of Nations". If the two parts were now separated, the Senate would, at least theoretically, have the possibility of rejecting the League of Nations and accepting the Treaty. But the fact of the matter was that the Treaty under preparation had been created on the express assumption that the League of Nations was a reality. "If it were not for that creation (League of Nations) they (the Allies) would insist, and would rightly insist, on a very different peace":

"To permit the possibility of the acceptance of those portions of the Peace to which the Allies have agreed only because of the Covenant and at the same time the rejection of the Covenant which is their consideration for the rest of the agreement, would in my opinion be a reproach to the honor of the United States".

If, on the other hand, the peace were an integrated whole, then it was true that the Senate would be able to reject it, but in that case the state of war would, formally, still exist and it would be possible to conclude a Peace Treaty "satisfactory to the European Powers on whose side we have fought, based upon the essential condition of a policy of isolation of the United States":

"But to make a peace which had been agreed to upon the belief that our policy of isolation was ended but which came into effect with the knowledge that our policy of isolation was not ended, would be so unjust as to be difficult of characterization".

After this powerful contribution, Miller heard no more of the plan[272]).

The problems dealt with here by Miller were certainly crucial, but his reasoning was, in a way, already outdated. It had fitted the situation before Wilson's departure, but it did not suit the new situation, which had been given concrete expression in the Lodge resolution, for after this declaration, the Allies had absolutely no guarantee that American isolationism would be given up, and their only hope was to ensure that the Treaty contained sufficient gurantees for the purpose of their security requirements, regardless of whether American policy returned at a later date to isolationism. And the question was whether Wilson would, in the long run, have the political power to resist these demands.

In the foregoing we have seen how House conducted a very hesitant policy with regard to the fate of the League of Nations Covenant. Firstly, he failed to specify that the Covenant should form part not only of the final Peace Treaty but also of the Preliminary Peace Treaty that was now under preparation. And his choice of words seems to indicate that he was fully aware that at any rate the French did not share this view[273]. Indeed, David Hunter Miller has clearly admitted that "(u)ndoubtedly, while Wilson was away from Paris (February 14–March14), the idea of separating the Covenant from the Treaty revived, despite the resolution of the Peace Conference of January 25. . . ."[274], although he also disassociates himself sharply from R. S. Baker's assertions of a more or less regular and well defined "plot", a plot in which both House and Balfour were involved and in which the "speeding-up" resolution played a central role[275]:

"Mr. Baker's thesis is that the moment the President left Paris, the anti-Wilson forces mobilized; the resolutions presented by Mr. Balfour on February 22, calling for speeding-up of work on economic and territorial problems connected with the German Treaty, he regards as an attempt to frustrate the proposal for an immediate military treaty, which the council and Mr. Wilson in particular had approved. He accuses Mr. Balfour of presenting the resolutions under instructions from Lloyd George, "who began to think he had gone too far with this League business". Colonel House, he avers, yielded to Mr. Balfour's suggestions because he did not wish to enter into a quarrel with the Allies and because "there was nothing hard, clear, sure, definite in his intellectual processes". Mr. Balfour's suggestion of hastening decisions on points other than the military terms, Mr. Baker insists, "would wreck the entire American scheme for the peace. . . . Thus, while it is too much to say that there was a direct plot, while Wilson was away, to kill the League or even cut it out of the Treaty, one can affirm with certainty that there was an intrigue against his plan of a preliminary military and naval peace—which would have indirectly produced the same result" ".

However, the sharpest refutation of Baker's views is to be found in the fourth volume of Charles Seymour's Intimate Papers, in which he published, inter alia, an exchange of letters between House and Balfour in 1922. The fact is that House felt himself forced by Baker's accusations to place the question before Balfour: "If my memory serves me rightly", wrote House, "you and I were moved solely by a desire to accelerate the Treaty . . .". And Balfour took the accusations so seriously that he asked Hankey to investigate the matter and reject Baker's allegations. By studying the minutes of the meetings of the

Council of Ten, Hankey reached the conclusion that "(t)he suggestion that there was anything savouring even remotely of a plot against the League of Nations in President Wilson's absence is supported by no evidence whatsoever. "The League was scarcely mentioned in the conferences until just before the President returned", complains Mr. Baker. Why? Because the text of the Covenant had been formally laid before the Peace Conference in Plenary Session by President Wilson, as Chairman of the appropriate Commission of the Conference, on February 14th, the day before he sailed for America. To tamper with it in the absence of the President, one of its principal authors, was unnecessary and undesirable. Its further consideration and final acceptance was reserved until after Mr. Wilson's return".

However, as we have seen, this conclusion was both right and wrong. House simply left the question open at the official level. His actual action in the matter had the form of either private negotiations with the British representatives or internal American discussions, and none of these initiatives apparently got beyond the verbal stage. Moreover, both initiatives were based on an erroneous interpretation of Wilson's reaction to the American situation, i. e. on the view that the President, under the impression of the violent American opposition, would be prepared to make concessions of one type or another.

It was House's personal view that concessions were unavoidable, and he had even told the President so before the latter left for America[276]):

"I asked him to bear in mind while he was gone that it was sometimes necessary to compromise in order to get things through; not a compromise of principle but a compromise of detail; he had made many since he had been here. I did not wish him to leave expecting the impossible in all things".

Wilson had apparently not reacted at the time, and his later reaction to House's negotiation bulletins, both as regards the Rhineland and the League of Nations was, as mentioned, either silence or direct rejection. There are therefore several possible explanations of why House still, as we shall see, continued his policy of compromise in his negotiations with the Allies in the time to come.

House may have trusted the veracity of the many reports from the United States at the time of the President's departure regarding his apparently newly adopted favourable attitude to negotiations on amendments to the League of Nations Covenant with both the Senate and the Allies[277]). However, these reports in no way corresponded with the instructions House had already received and later—much later—received[278]), but he may, in theory, have believed himself to be acting in accordance with a presumed changed attitude in the President, and the temptation to believe this was very great since such an attitude must have appeared to House to be the only logical one.

Nevertheless, the interpretation proposed in the foregoing and following pages of this exposition is a different one, viz, that in February-March, House came to the end of a personal development that had been in process for quite a long time—a development that, in this period, freed him from consideration to the President and American policy in general, and instead led him onward to the position—in his own imagination—of manipulator and director of the entire Conference[279]).

However, these two interpretations are compatible, although on another level, namely, that of self-delusion. For as we have seen earlier[280]), House never at any time admitted that he had acted disloyally to the President. He may thus have disguised the extent of his actions to himself as well by deluding himself that he was acting in accordance with Wilson's intentions[281]).

As House's attitude to the League of Nations is described in the foregoing, it must be characterized as unsure and irresolute, but one thing is certain and that is that he deliberately neglected to insist on a detailed definition of the relationship between the Preliminary Peace Treaty and the League of Nations Covenant, although his diary gives no other reason for this than that he wished to avoid "an interminable discussion with the French"[282]). The question is now, whether it is possible to produce other sources to illustrate House's attitude than those already reported. The answer to this must depend on whether we can be persuaded to accept the fact that, besides Seymour's account in "The Intimate Papers of Colonel House", there is another presentation of House's view, which may not bear the stamp of official approval, but which is, on the other hand, not hampered by the considerations to discretion that characterize Seymour's work. This "other" version is Wickham Steed's memoirs from 1924[283]).

In the next chapter we shall see how House and, to an even greater extent, Auchincloss stood in very close contact with Wickham Steed for most of the Conference, culminating with the crisis in April, and how at any rate Auchincloss tried to engage directly in politics through Steed, whose editorials in the Paris edition of the "Daily Mail" were frequently directly inspired by talks with Auchincloss[284]). The "Continental Daily Mail" was "the chief newspaper written in English available there (in Paris) every morning", and its influence was great[285]):

"It was normally read over breakfast by most of the British and American delegations: more important, it was regularly read by the head of each. Neither Steed nor Northcliffe was slow to realize the importance of such an opportunity; and Steed was regularly employed in the congenial task of writing the leading article of the *Continental Dail Mail*. *These articles represented the weightiest contribution by the Press of any nation to the shaping of the Treaty of Versailles.* By comparison *The Times*'s influence on the process of peace-making was slight. The chief reason was technical: copies of the paper could not arrive in Paris until late on the day of publication; sometimes they could not be made available until late in the afternoon of the following day. . . .".

During this period Steed was in almost daily contact with Auchincloss and had frequent talks with House[286]). Steed's presentation bears the heavy imprint of this intimate contact, and, in its penetrating polemic against R. S. Baker's theses, assumes practically the character of a defence of House[287]).

When the "New York World" printed an attack on House in December 1919, "The Times" immediately ran an editorial in which Steed defended him, and, at the same time, Wiseman wrote from London[288]):

"Of course people here blame the President for his handling of the situation (the failure to bring about the conclusion of the Treaty) and many of our friends have fallen by the way. Most of them, however, still stick up for you. Among the latter is Wickham Steed, who is contemplating the publishing of his own account of the Peace Conference, in which he will describe how the whole thing would have been satisfactorily finished in March if they had adopted your programme; I should think this little book of reminiscences might create quite a stir . . .".

House wrote to Steed and thanked him for the editorial, and Steed replied[289]):

"I am glad to know that the few lines we published upon the World's diatribe were not displeasing to you. I should have wished to say much more, but thought it best so to write that your adversaries could not find in our words any handle against you.

I think I understand, and I certainly sympathize very deeply with your feelings; but having put our teeth into this business, we must keep them there and hold on. It's a long lane that has no turning. You, at any rate, can have no personal cause for feeling humiliated. If ever a man did his duty and more than his duty, you did it. I hope it may be possible one day to put things in their true light. I do not feel at all sure whether, at the right moment, you ought not to speak out. Posterity is all very well, but there is sometimes a duty to contemporaries and to one's own self. In any case, you may be quite sure that Lord Northcliffe and I will cherish among our happiest memories that of the weeks and months during which you allowed us in some measure to collaborate with you."

Finally, after completing his memoirs, Steed wrote a letter to House in 1924—a letter bearing the stamp of having been written "for the record" and "for posterity", but nevertheless, seen in connection with the other data, disclosing more than it hides[290]):

"From time to time rumours have reached me that, in some way or other, the friendly and confidential relations which, thanks to your kindness, have existed between us since the closing years of the war, were responsible for the later attitude of President Wilson towards you and for the astounding ingratitude with which he treated you. He, or those about him, seem to have imagined that you were responsible, directly or indirectly, for the views which, in my journalistic capacity, I expressed in *The Times* and in the Paris *Daily Mail* during the Peace Conference.

I have dealt with this matter in my book, "Through Thirty Years", and it will be published by Doubleday Page in the autumn. I have made it clear that at no time did you ever attempt to circumscribe the independence of my judgment or to influence the expression of my individual views. I have also explained in my book that, by a singular coincidence for which neither of us was responsible, I got you into trouble once or twice during the Paris Peace Conference; but that was because, on some questions if not on all, our thoughts were running in the same direction and that we happened to express them simultaneously but quite independently of each other in different places. It has now been represented to me that a despatch which I wrote from Paris to *The Times* of April 7, 1919, was brought to the notice of President Wilson and wounded so deeply his susceptibilities that his estrangement from you began at that date. He, or those about him, seem to have suspected you of have (!) inspired me to extol your work as a Peace delegate and to disparage that of the President. I do not know what mean-souled wights can have attributed to you so monstrous a proceeding. All I know is that never, at any time, by implication or otherwise, did you criticise to me, much less disparage, the work or the ideas of President Wilson.

Nor did you at any time suggest, directly or indirectly, that I should write one about you. What I wrote was written on my own responsibility and based on my own observations —and, truth to tell, I did not much care whether what I wrote pleased you or anybody else as long as I was convinced that it was the truth.

If I am in any way responsible for the (!) President Wilson's treatment of you and for an estrangement which I have always regarded as one of the misfortunes of the Peace Conference, I regret it for the sake of the good of which that estrangement prevented the achievement; but no journalist who writes sincerely at moments of stress and crisis can subordinate the discharge of his public duty to the possible misinterpretation of his work by petty or jealous folk."

Everything thus points to the fact that Steed actually gives House's version of events, just as Baker gave Wilson's. It should therefore be possible, through Steed, to penetrate deeper into House's thoughts on the League of Nations at this time. Steed's version is particularly interesting because it hints that behind the apparently close cooperation between House and Wilson on the framing of the League of Nations Covenant, there lay—here too, one is tempted to add—conflicting views, which House admittedly tried to conceal while Wilson was still in Paris[291]). Steed explains the divergence as follows[292]):

"The full story of Colonel House's efforts to serve the President, the United States and the interests of peace, amid difficulties almost insuperable, could be told by himself alone, and he is probably too modest ever to tell it. He may not have had the President's hard grasp upon the principles of the kind of peace Wilson desired, but he was no less devoted than he to the League of Nations as the only international safeguard against a recurrence of war. Like Wilson, too, he wished the League to be inseparable from the Peace though he did not think it essential that every "i" should be dotted and every "t" crossed in a complete Covenant before the League were allowed to work. He seems to have conceived the framework of the League as something more closely akin to the British Constitution than to the Constitution of the United States, something that could grow from small beginnings into a large beneficence and gain authority and experience from work actually done. In a word, he was a practical as distinguished from a philosophical idealist; and President Wilson never did a worse day's work for himself, or for the cause he wished to serve, than when he overrode House's views on March 13, 1919."

Whereas Wilson "wished to plant a full-grown oak, to make a complete league of nations with a rigid constitution fixed in advance", House went in for the "acorn method"[293]):

"Having secured a decision on January 25th that the League of Nations should be an integral part of the Peace Treaty, President Wilson was anxious to subordinate the making even of a preliminary peace to the elaboration of a complete League of Nations Covenant. Colonel House, on the other hand, with much stronger practical sense than Wilson possessed, wished to conclude the main points of a general peace as quickly as possible, to set up a working league of nations in some form and to let it cooperate in making the final peace."[294])
"But when he met the President (on March 13th), he met also a bitter disappointment. He found him determined to put the whole Covenant into the text of the Treaty before any Peace were concluded, and to secure the adoption of all amendments to the Covenant before other and more pressing matters were settled."[295])

And this was the result[296]):

"Many efforts had been made before to drive a wedge between Wilson and House. Some American financial interests had done their worst without success. Mr. Lloyd George had repeatedly sought to eliminate the influence of Colonel House so that he might deal the more easily with the President. But until the President was induced to suspect that, in his eagerness to conclude a satisfactory preliminary peace and to set the League of Nations to work at once, House was departing from "Wilsonian principles", these efforts were of little avail. Thereafter, Wilson gradually gave ear to other counsellors, until the final breach was affected by the influence of those who were jealous of House's eminence, and by gossip mongers, who alleged that Colonel House's son-in-law, Gordon Auchincloss, who worked with him at the Hotel Crillon, had committed the unpardonable sin of speaking disrespectfully of the President. The idea of lèse-majesté might have been overthrown in Europe by the war, but it certainly survived in the immediate neighbourhood of President Wilson during the Peace Conference. One of its effects was to cause Colonel House to be condemned unheard. . . .".

The important thing in this context is that Steed clearly admits that House agreed, in Wilson's absence, that the Preliminary Peace Treaty should not include the League of Nations Covenant[297]), and that this was the reason for the break between the two men. It is further clear that this break can be dated to 13 March, immediately upon the arrival of the President and the first talk between the two men, i. e. the date that House himself has indicated on several occasions[298]) and that R. S. Baker has argued for with such strength[299]).

It remains to investigate how the Allies evaluated the significance of developments in America. While it is impossible to say anything definite about the French reaction, the British reaction can, at any rate, be intimated. Shortly before Wilson's departure, Lord Reading had also left the Peace Conference to resume his post as British Ambassador to Washington. On 7 March, he sent Wiseman a very penetrating analysis of the American situation[300]), and it is highly probable, not to say certain, that this is identical with the analysis that Reading sent to Lloyd George two days later[301]). Reading commenced by stating that Wilson's speech on his arrival (at Boston) had had a great effect, but that his speech on departure (from New York) had not had the same effect, "as something more precise was desired". He further emphasized the fact that the President's dinner for members of the Foreign Relations Committee had apparently had no effect on the Republican Senators: "They have been playing politics violently." With regard to the Lodge resolution, he asserted that there were probably 52 Senators in all who would oppose the treaty "if the League were made part of the treaty without fundamental change". On the other hand, he took the view that "(t)he present attitude of the Senate should not be regarded as necessarily final. ... Moreover, the Lodge resolution is said to be meant primarily as a warning to the Peace Conference that they must not disregard the view of the United States Senate". And he further advised that "(o)pposition to the League has to some extent taken an anti-British aspect". He then listed the leading opponents and analysed their positions.

As regards the general sentiment in the population, however, he was forced to agree with Wilson:

"The President states confidently that he has the country behind him, and there is reason to think that he may be right, and that he would win if the League were put to a popular vote."

He based this opinion on, inter alia, the fact that the "New York Sun" (an energetic opponent of Wilson) had sent an enquiry to all 48 Governors regarding local feeling, and although 26 of them were Republicans, "the result was so greatly in favour of the League that the "Sun", which is strongly opposed to it, was forced to forego printing what it hoped to be a sign of failure". Reading continued that the fears expressed in Europe that America might leave it in the lurch had had a favourable effect. Finally, he said that the general consensus now seemed to be that Wilson "will return with a new draft embodying some of the points suggested to him by opponents, and that he will thus counter their opposition". However, standpoints were generally still fluid and much would depend on the developments of the next few weeks.

This generally rather favourable evaluation of the situation produced a very vehement counter-plea. The memorandum is not signed, but it was written by a man with a very extensive knowledge of American politics, and the author advised that he had left the United States on 18 February[302]). It was already clear at this early hour "that the project in that form was still-born; that is to say, it would not have the remotest chance in the United States", because it involved "the impairment of the Congress's absolute right to declare war". The author found the analysis of Wilson's speeches and the significance of the dinner for the Senators correct, but he found it necessary to stress the fact that Wilson's New York speech and his attack on the Senators had played a not inconsiderable part in the mobilization of the opposition. "The thing to bear in mind throughout this matter is that the standpoint of the Republicans is correct in the view of this matter. What is at stake now in this whole discussion is the President's desire for a third term". The Republicans considered that Wilson had been campaigning ever since he went to Paris, and "to accuse them of "playing politics" in the situation is not quite impartial".

Regarding the Lodge resolution, the author concluded that "It is a veto by the power of veto on that project so far as the United States is concerned". However, he had to agree with Reading that the attitude of the Senate was not final except on a single point: "that the present project is condemned. That is final":

"If the Allies do not look out they are running the following risk: that by carrying out the President's New York speech policy of having the Peace Treaty and the League project so completely interwoven that they cannot be dealt with apart, they will run the practically certain chance of having no action on either".

This was, in fact, the warning that the author read in the Lodge resolution, but the same resolution also opened the opportunity of execution of the following plan, which would ensure "prompt and favourable" action on the part of the Senate:

"Draw up the Peace Treaty, at the foot thereof add measures adopted by the co-belligerents to enforce the terms of the Peace Treaty (not of a new order of things in the World). These military measures taken between co-belligerents need not to be deifned (!) as either alliance or anything else. ... These measures should specify that they will continue until replaced by such arrangements as may be made as part of the League of Nations. Then, as a distinct matter, adopt a League of Nations plan ... if the project is separate and distinct, and if the Treaty has added there to measures which maintain the military cooperation of the United States with the Allies, the situation is safe. The Senate will proceed to ratify the Peace Treaty with these measures. It will then adopt the League of Nations project, and whatever may be its fate the actual condition of force will be such that the military cooperation of the U. S. with the Allies for an indefinite time will have been provided for ...".

In other words, the author recommended the policy of separating the League of Nations and the Treaty, while at the same time maintaining America's commitment in Europe through the military guarantees of the Treaty, and he stressed that this was a policy to which the Republican Senators would be able to agree. He added: "Undoubtedly the Lodge resolution is a warning to the Peace Conference that they must not (dis)regard the views of the U. S. Senate. It would be suicidal to do it."

The author admitted that the opposition in the United States had, to a certain extent, assumed an anti-British aspect, but said that it was therefore in the interests of Great Britain to make it clear that it was France, not Britain, that would be receiving the greatest benefit from the League of Nations: "This should be done by the French, and as they are themselves thoroughly convinced that it is true there is no doubt that they will be quite convincing in the discussion!" The author seems to reveal here that he has a greater knowledge of American than of European politics.

Turning to Reading's report, the author further stated that the President may have been right when he asserted that he had the American people behind him, but that "there is nothing more difficult to determine than that." The only thing that could be established was that Wilson had asked for a blank cheque in November, but that it was the Republican party that had got it, and as there was every indication that Wilson's entire handling of the situation "is nothing but a disguised campaign for his re-nomination", it was not surprising that all Republicans were turning against his policies.

"Therefore, for the Allies to continue to appear to accept the dictation of the President would involve the risk of discontenting those who wield real power in the U. S. for all the purposes of the Peace Conference, save only negotiations."

The best thing would therefore be for a "Senatorial sub-committee" to come to Paris "solely for the purpose of gathering and transmitting to the Senate accurate and timely information enabling that body to discharge its constitutional duty in such a way as will not involve dangerous delays." And the author concluded with the following urgent appeal:

"The Sun and everybody else would veer round if the Allies would make up their own programme, taking into account the considerations pointed out above, and then invite the President to present it as his own, with the plain alternative that if he did not they would. ... This is the Allies' opportunity."

This is a very strange document, at one and the same time an extremely penetrating and an extremely biased analysis of the American situation, and the author also spoke very authoritatively on the Republican standpoint. This, combined with his wish to get a Senate committee to Paris, makes it more than probable that the author was an American! This view is further strengthened by a talk which David Hunter Miller had with Wiseman on 11 March[303]):

"Wiseman spoke about the Americans who had recently come to Paris and were saying that the Republican Party was the real friend of Europe and that the British and the French ought to get together with their leaders and compel the President to do what the British and French wanted."

In other words, the same argument as presented in the above-mentioned memorandum, and it is, of course, possible that it was precisely to this document that Wiseman was referring—it is at any rate found among his papers. The matter would, perhaps, not have been of much importance had not the title of the memorandum been "Comment on Despatch of March 10th". This means, in fact, that the telegram on which the memorandum commented was not Reading's report to Wiseman of 7 March, but his apparently identical report to Lloyd George of 9 March, which must be assumed to have been received in Paris on 10 March. (Lloyd George returned on 6 March). In view of the above, the author of the document must have had connections right up to the closest circles around the Prime Minister, and his views must have come into the possession of at least some of Lloyd George's closest attendants. Just how great an influence the Republican argument had is naturally an open question, but it is a fact that, immediately before and after Wilson's arrival, the British and French were busy trying to push through at least one of the proposals contained in the document—the division of the Treaty and the League of Nations Covenant[304]), although, of course, this policy need not have been prompted by the Republican proposal, but by a general evaluation of the situation. However, it is worth establishing that the Allied Governments had well-informed Republican sources of information at their disposal and that the Senate was now in more ways than one an active participant in Paris.

At the same time, internal discussions were in progress in the British Delegation as to the tactics to be followed as regards possible amendments to the League of Nations Covenant. On 7 March, Lord Eustace Percy made an analysis of the American situation, which concluded that Lord Cecil ought to issue a declaration on the alterations that should be made to the Covenant. It was, moreover, Percy's view that the Republicans controlled the vote in the United States[305]). On 11 March, Wiseman submitted a memorandum to Cecil, with objections to his proposal[306]). He began by agreeing that Wilson had indeed challenged the Republican leaders, but did not find that this necessarily meant that the League of Nations had been compromised. Nor did Wiseman think that "it will be necessary for us to tell the President when he arrives that we will not sign the draft as it stands. He will probably tell us that himself. Certainly we had better hear his views before suggesting amendments; and surely it would be difficult for us to say we have been influenced by criticism in the United States."

Further, Wiseman did not share the view apparently expressed by Percy that the American Delegation was not representative—it was in any event with the President that negotiations should be carried out, and it could be left to him to manage American public opinion. Wiseman expected Wilson to continue to take a sharp stand against the Republican views in public, but thought that he would anyway seek to get amendments through in order to comply with the criticism. These alterations would primarily concern the Monroe Doctrine, the question of immigration and "the question of voting power or unanimity". In addition, Wiseman found it unlikely that the Senate would refuse its approval of ratification of the Treaty, and he advised Cecil in any event to await the President's arrival before making any public statement.

The views of Percy and Wiseman are interesting because they show that the British Delegation was divided in its evaluation of the American situation and the conclusions that should be drawn from this. In the present situation it was Wiseman's views that won: Cecil remained silent. However, the final decision on the British policy lay with neither Cecil nor Wiseman, but with Lloyd George.

On 6 March, Lloyd George returned to Paris, and by this time Clemenceau had recovered sufficiently to participate in the meetings again. The negotiations then entered a new phase.

For each of the three Great Powers, the Peace was a unity. We have seen how Wilson did everything in his power to make the League of Nations Covenant an integral part of the Treaty. By incorporating the principle of collective security in the conclusion of peace itself, it should be possible to avoid the territorial guarantees required in earlier times. If the League of Nations could be given the role of the 'Great Mediator', the Peace would assume a completely new character. Neither part could be separated from the other without both assuming a different form. And we have seen how Clemenceau too, regarded the Treaty as a single entity, although from quite another angle: The military terms could not be separated from the territorial terms. The guarantees that France had to demand for her security were an integral whole. What the French were prepared to accept on the one point would depend on what they could achieve on the other, although for them, as for the British, the Peace settlement had to be an overall solution—in the case of Britain, of course, from other standpoints than those of the French and the Americans

—. She had vital interests to protect elsewhere than Europe, interests that, for the Empire as a whole, appeared to the British to be just as decisive as, for example, the question of the boundary between France and Germany. Thus, in a report to Lord Reading dated 2 March, Wiseman wrote[307]):

". . . Tardieu has written very able paper presenting French case regarding the Rhine. It made a considerable impression with House and Balfour but although moderately stated does not present very practical solution. . . . We cannot however make final settlement with French until Syrian and Moroccan claims are settled, and these cannot be settled by arbitration (? until we) know whether America will accept mandate in Turkey".

Furthermore, there was at least one point in the Treaty with Germany in which Britain and the entire Empire had a vital interest, and that was the question of reparations. What is more, this was a question on which British and French policy could meet; and finally, it was a question of such enormous domestic importance to the two countries that the political fate of their Governments hung on it.

This rough outline shows clearly that when the Treaty with Germany was to be framed, each of the three Great Powers would be bound by considerations on which it would come into conflict with at least one of the other Powers, and it also shows that the threads were so tangled that there was no possibility of any two of the Powers establishing a joint front on *all* questions; for each separate point, new constellations would have to be formed.

When Lloyd George returned to Paris, he too seems to have taken the view that the time had come for the real negotiations that had been postponed for so long. Not only did he immediately throw himself into very energetic negotiations in the Council of Ten, with a view to pushing through amendments to the military terms that had been resubmitted just before his return[308]), but he also entered into a number of secret, top level negotiations with House and Clemenceau.

House seems to have had certain misgivings with regard to Lloyd George's return; at any rate, he tried to put off his arrival as long as possible because he thought the British Prime Minister "would only hinder us in our work because he would be certain to waste time and introduce a lot of extra subjects for discussion"[309])—a fear that proved to be not entirely unfounded.

The last preparations before Lloyd George's arrival were agreed on at a meeting between Clemenceau, Balfour and House on 4 March. There were several questions on the agenda: The situation in Germany, particularly Bavaria, had developed in a dangerous direction, and House at any rate was pessimistic about the situation: "We have deliberately run the risk of having them turn to Bolshevism"[310]). It now appeared to be a matter of immediate urgency to open the way for the supply of food to Germany in order in this way to seek to contain the revolutionary forces. France had hitherto been the stumbling-block in the way of implementation of this policy, but at the conference on 4 March, House finally thought he could see a gleam of hope:

"I believe I have Clemenceau thoroughly frightened. He agreed as to Germany"[311]). However, Clemenceau had not yet given his final consent, asking once more for a postponement in order "to bring the French public to a realization of the importance of sending food into Germany", but he promised "earnest cooperation with us in that direction"[312]).

The main item of the negotiations was, however, the continued "speeding-up"process. House reported to Wilson that "Everything has been speeded up and I feel confident that by the time of your arrival all questions will be ready for your approval"[313]). At the conference, both Clemenceau and Balfour promised "to drive ahead at full speed so that everything might be ready by the 14th", while House for his part "undertook to get decisions from the President upon every subject relating to a Preliminary Peace with Germany by the 20th[314]). House did not inform Wilson of this last promise, but that he gave it at all is presumably due to his belief that he had the President behind him in the "speeding-up" efforts. The atmosphere at this meeting seems generally to have been very optimistic: the date of the Germans' arrival at Versailles was also discussed, and House proposed that this should be just after 20 March, to which Balfour and Clemenceau appear to have agreed[315]). Seen against the developments of the subsequent period, House's optimism is a complete mystery. Did he really imagine that the long list of complicated problems that had hardly as yet even been thoroughly discussed at expert level, and not at all at top level, could be solved in the course of two short weeks?

Immediately after his arrival, Lloyd George had a conference with House in the form of a "working lunch". There is no doubt that House was here exposed to a veritable "charm offensive" by Lloyd George, and that he himself was well aware of this fact[316]). House was, as usual, optimistic in his evaluation of the situation: "We had a fairly complete understanding regarding matters of interest between our two governments". "He wishes to work with us, and I am more than willing . . ."[317]). The question in which Lloyd George was particularly interested was that of reparations[318]):

"He was especially interested in the question of reparations and said that if I would help him out in this direction, he would be extremely grateful. By helping him out, he meant to give a plausible reason to his people for having fooled them about the question of war costs, reparations and what not. He admitted that he knew Germany could not pay anything like the indemnity which the British and French demanded. He said that my ideas and his were not different as to the actual sum she should pay, but he wanted the amount named to be large, even if Germany could never pay it, or even if it had to be reduced later. He said it was a political matter in which the English were greatly interested and he did not want to let the Conservatives "throw him" on a question of such popular concern".

Here, with astonishing frankness, Lloyd George went to the crux of the matter. We have no means of knowing what House replied to this, but from the context, it may be presumed that he did not refuse to consider the matter.

The question of reparations was the only problem of controversy between the Great Powers that had been referred to an expert Commission, and the reason for this was presumably that the questions were so involved that expert aid was absolutely essential, and that several of the minor Powers also had interests to look after in this respect. As mentioned, the preliminary discussions in the Commission immediately revealed a clear, fundamental difference between the American and the Anglo-French viewpoints: were the Allies and the Associates bound by the pre-Armistice Agreement or had they the right to demand "integral reparations" ("war costs")? It will be remembered that Wilson had backed his experts up unreservedly, but when it proved impossible to reach agreement, the Commission had referred the question to the Council of Ten. The case came up on 1 March, and here it was easy for House to get it postponed until Wilson's return on the grounds that the question would anyway not be touched upon in the Preliminary Peace Treaty[319]). House seems to have calculated that if the question could be postponed until after the drawing-up of the Treaty, it would "die a natural death"[320]). And in this he was correct[321]).

However, the matter was reincarnated in a new form, i. e. as a question on the amount of the compensation that should be demanded of Germany. This problem was treated in the 2nd Sub-Commission of the Reparations Commission, where Lamont was the American representative. It was the task of this Commission to determine Germany's capacity to pay, but it rapidly proved impossible to reach agreement on this on the basis of purely economic considerations, because the entire question was politically loaded. The negotiations then entered into the phase termed by P. M. Burnett "direct bargaining for a figure", i. e. direct negotiations to arrive at a sum that would be politically acceptable all round. Here, the differences between the proposals seemed practically insuperable. Lord Cunliffe, the British representative, demanded an amount of 480,000 mill. Mark, and in this he was backed up by Louis Loucheur, the French representative. The American calculations resulted in a figure of 60–100,000 mill. Mark, but during the negotiations, Lamont allowed himself to be pressed to increasing this to 120,000 mill. Mark. The negotiations then continued outside the Commission, between the three representatives of the Great Powers, and here Loucheur proved willing to agree to a figure of 160,000 mill. Mark, although he made it clear that, with a view to public opinion, he could not recommend a lower sum than that demanded by Britain, so everything depended on Cunliffe. For a while, he appeared willing to agree to 190,000 mill. Mark, but he retreated again and refused to compromise[322]).

This was the situation when Lloyd George had his conference with House, at which he flatly stated that the political life of his Government depended on this question, although he admitted that the British demands were really unreasonable. In other words, he could not give in. After this it was clear that the question was fraught with the danger of conflict between the United States and Great Britain[323]).

At the meeting on 6 March, House and Lloyd George further agreed to meet with Clemenceau next morning in order to discuss the military terms, and specifically, conscription[324]). The naval terms were also touched upon, and here House delivered the threat that if Britain did not agree to the sinking of the German fleet, it would lead to an extensive shipbuilding programme in the United States[325]). It was finally agreed to call Orlando to Paris as quickly as possible, and that "he (Lloyd George), Clemenceau, Orlando and I should thresh out everything before the President came *and arrive at decisions. The President could agree or point out wherein his views were not as ours.* In this way I thought matters might be greatly expedited"[326]). With this, House had shown his readiness definitively to exceed his instructions. He was now ready for *decisions,* which, although they could not be binding on the President, were still of a nature to ruin his bargaining position in the event of his taking a different standpoint—and House thus appears to have reckoned with this possibility. From the above passage it also seems clear that the initiative for this step came from House, and there is no reason to doubt this because, of course, it was just the logical consequence of the "speeding-up" process of which he had been so enthusiastic an advocate. With this, the wheel had turned full circle.

Next day, Clemenceau, Lloyd George and House had a conference, with which House was exceedingly satisfied[327]):

"We did our work rapidly and both George and Clemenceau felt encouraged that so much could be done so quickly. It was agreed that we should meet again in a day or two to decide matters before going to the Quay d'Orsay. We also decided to send for Orlando, George remarking that "We four Prime Ministers can quickly finish up the business that is before us."

When the President is away *I never hesitate to act and to take as much responsibility as either of the others.*"

The "steering committee" that had been in function during the pre-Armistice negotiations was thus re-established, and House was once more engaged in the private top-level negotiations that he preferred and in the efficiency of which he had such faith[328]). At the same time, however, he was getting deeper than ever into an over-interpretation of his own powers.

House sent Wilson a very detailed report on the meeting, from which it appears that a number of the points of controversy between the Great Powers were discussed, together with a number of questions requiring early decisions[329]). Lloyd George returned to the sum to be paid by Germany in reparations, this time from the point of view of distribution, and he proposed a distribution schedule, which House was prepared to approve, while Clemenceau wished to give the matter further consideration[330]). Besides the question of reparations, there were—at this stage of the negotiations—two other problems of vital importance to the mutual relations of the Great Powers: the question of the establishment of a Rhenish Republic and the question of the fate of Syria.

It has been described earlier how House to all intents and purposes agreed to Tardieu's modified Rhineland scheme at the conference of 2 March and promised to aid him in persuading Lloyd George. Meanwhile, with Clemenceau's return, the situation entered a new phase[331]):

"The left bank of the Rhine was discussed, but no tentative agreement was reached because of Clemenceau's very unreasonable attitude. He wants the Rheinish Republics to be perpetually restrained from joining the German Federation. Tardieu tells me he will urge him to modify this view."

Thus, if Clemenceau had proposed Tardieu's modified plan again, House would have been willing to accept it on behalf of America as one of the decisions to be taken by Wilson on his return. However, it was only one aspect of the problem that he had mentioned in the telegram to Wilson. Just as vital was Britain's attitude in this matter. Auchincloss gave a far more lucid evaluation of the diplomatic situation[332]):

"The French are very insistent upon the creation of a Rhenish Republic, the size of this republic and its length of life as a buffer state have not as yet been decided upon. ... *The British are trying to whittle down the size of this Rhenish Republic and of course we are supporting them.* Clemenceau wants the republic to have perpetual existence. Tardieu is willing to have its existence limited by period of years at the end of which a plebiscite would be held to determine the wishes of the population."

The initiative in the negotiations had now passed to Lloyd George.

As we have seen, the British were apparently prepared to "bargain" on the Rhineland problem for a solution of the Syrian question and, as pointed out earlier, such a correlation was perhaps the result of the London Conference in December 1918. In any event, it was clear that Anglo-French relations were at this time approaching a critical phase as regards Syria. France demanded the mandate over Syria and thought that they had received a British promise in this respect in December, when the Sykes-Picot settlement had been amended as regards Mosul"[333]). The matter was further complicated by the fact that Britain not only had obligations to France, but also to King Hussein, whose troops had played a prominent part in the battles with the Turks[334]. By the Anglo-French declaration of November 1918, the two Allies had promised "The complete and definite emancipation of the peoples so long oppressed by the Turks and the establishment of national governments and administrations deriving their authority from the initiative and free choice of the indigenous populations"[335]), and the Arabs did not want a French mandate. Here was, therefore, an obvious possibility of a conflict between the right of self-determination and a "secret treaty", and in this situation America might, in more ways than one, come to play a key role.

In Dr. Howard S. Bliss, the American President of the Syrian Protestant College in Beirut, the Arabs had a spokesman whose views got straight to President Wilson. Bliss was of the opinion that the people, given the opportunity of deciding for themselves, would choose either the United States or

Great Britain, but not France, as mandate Power. He proposed that an Inter-Allied or Neutral Commission should be sent to Syria to investigate conditions on the spot before a decision was taken[336]). On 13 February, Bliss had the opportunity of presenting these views to the Council of Ten[337]). However, no decision was reached before Wilson's departure for America, and in the meantime, unrest increased i Syria.

When Lloyd George returned to Paris on 6 March, he seems to have taken the attitude that some kind of compromise now had to be found[338]), and at the meeting on 7 March he told Clemenceau that "if France insisted upon going in without having an understanding with the Prince of Hedjas(!), ... there would be a long and bloody war ...", while Clemenceau, for his part, wanted to send for General Allenby[339]). The confrontation had finally taken place.

Whereas the problems relating to the three principal questions, reparations, the Rhineland and Syria, were thus as yet only outlined, agreement on certain of the current problems was reached at the meeting. Clemenceau still refused to consent to supplying Germany with food, but on the other hand, he and Lloyd George reached agreement on the abolition of conscription in the military terms. With regard to the German fleet too, a settlement seemed at hand, Lloyd George agreeing to sink the ships in British possession provided the United States and Japan did the same, and a meeting was arranged between Admirals Wemyss and Benson. France, on the other hand, refused to participate in these measures[340]).

Nonetheless, if everything was to be ready for Wilson's arrival, it was essential that the views on the two vital points in the Treaty, reparations and the Rhineland, should be brought considerably more in line with each other than had hitherto been the case. The first step to this end was taken the same day, a luncheon meeting being arranged between Lloyd George, Lamont and Davis, at which the problem of reparations should be discussed[341]).

For the next few days, the initiative continued to lie with Lloyd George, and on 9 March he advised House that he wanted to have a new meeting with him and Clemenceau. This took place next morning, and proved to be of decisive importance to the subsequent course of the Conference[342]):

"At Colonel House's suggestion it was agreed that after the President's arrival the three Prime Ministers and the President would meet morning and afternoon until the various peace terms with Germany have been agreed upon and that the meetings at the Quay d'Orsay should be discontinued."[343])

and, in House's own version:

"I earnestly urged that after the President's return, the Quay d'Orsay meetings should be, if not discontinued, held only at intervals, and that the three Prime Ministers and the President should continue the meetings we have held in the President's absence. Both Clemenceau and Lloyd George expressed the hope that I would attend these meetings whenever I thought necessary. However, I shall probably not do so."[344])

This was the origin of the Council of Four.

F. S. Marston has pointed out the continuity as regards procedure between the Council of Four and the "steering committee" that had developed during the meetings of the Supreme War Council during the war and the pre-Armistice negotiations, and emphasized the fact that it was particularly the British who pressed to get the organization of the Conference altered[345]), while Hankey has directly indicated Lloyd George (and himself) as "the prime mover in this development"[346]). However, Hankey's account of the origin of the Council of Four relates solely to the period following Wilson's return[347]), and there is really no reason for denying to House a considerable portion of the initiative in this matter, even though it is admittedly correct that his inspiration came from his experience from the earlier Inter-Allied conferences. As we have seen, House had already proposed to the President in January that the Council of Ten should be dissolved and private conferences held instead[348]), and there was nothing that happened later that could have made him change his mind; quite the reverse: when the President returned, House would have to relinquish his seat in the Council of Ten and would again find himself in the vacuum that had so frustrated him during the first four weeks of the Conference. There is no doubt either, that he intended to utilize this change in the organization to retain his grip on things. Thus, House managed to arrange for the first meeting between Wilson, Lloyd George and Clemenceau after the President's return to be held at his own rooms at Hotel Crillon[349]):

"The reason I wanted them to meet in my rooms was to keep my hands on the situation. If they go to the Quai d'Orsay or the Ministry of War or to the President's house, matters get out of hand."

However, as it happened, House was unable to prevent matters from getting out of hand.

In the meantime, on the political plane too, a number of important decisions were reached at this meeting. The critical questions were still the Rhineland, reparations and Syria, and although the discussions on the last of these seemed to have reached an impasse, energetic efforts were at any rate made to solve the first two through direct negotiations at the expert level.

"The Syrian question was discussed but no agreement arrived at because Clemenceau asked for more time. The French insist on getting all of Syria. Lloyd George said he would consent to give France Lebanon but that there should be a break in the line north of Lebanon so as to allow the English and the Arabs an outlet to the sea. George does not want the French to occupy any of the railroads running north and which Foch demands. Clemenceau asked for more time to consider this."[350])

Lloyd George's proposal for a compromise was not accepted.

On the other hand, the participants agreed to appoint two commissions, both of which should be secret and both of which should submit their findings on 13 March, i. e. the day before Wilson returned to Europe. One of these commissions, consisting of Montagu for England, Loucheur for France and Davis for the United States, was to discuss the question of reparations:

"Both Clemenceau and George said they hoped a large sum of money would be agreed upon because of the political situations in England and France. ... Lloyd George declared that he had not purposely misled the English people, but somehow, during the recent elections, there was a perfect ground-swell for the Germans to pay for the cost of the war, and while he knew it was an impossibility to realize such expectations, he followed and was one of the most vociferous of the lot in demanding that the cost of the war should be paid by Germany."[351]

"They were perfectly willing to have the sum called reparation."[352]

The Allies thus now aimed at a compromise that would ostensibly keep within the framework of the pre-Armistice Agreement, but which would, in fact, constitute the fulfilment of their most extreme demands.

That the commission on reparations should be secret was due first and foremost to the fact that Lloyd George had chosen Montagu instead of Cunliffe or Sumner, who would have been a more natural selection. It was partly due to House that Montagu was appointed: he recommended him because he knew he did not belong to the extremists on this point[353].

The second commission "should *definitely* formulate the boundary lines of Germany"[354]. It comprised Tardieu for France, Philip Kerr for England and Sidney Mezes for America. The reasons for keeping this committee secret were to all intents and purposes the same as in the first case[355]:

"George stated he did not put Balfour on the limitation of boundary Committee because if he put Balfour on Clemenceau would have to put Pichon on."[356]

And, we could add, "House would have to put Lansing on."

In a sense, Mezes was a natural choice as he was, after all, the nominal head of the Experts and enjoyed House's trust, but he was weak as a negotiator and did not come to play any part at all in the work of the committee. This developed into a duel between Kerr and Tardieu. It is, of course, quite another question whether House had any authority whatsoever, without at least consulting his three colleagues on the Commission, to agree to the appointment of these committees or indeed to participate at all in private top negotiations with the two Prime Ministers. Here, the answer must be in the negative. House was not, in this situation—as in so many before—, the authorized representative of the President; he was not the President's deputy, but Commissioner Plenipotentiary, in line with Lansing, White and Bliss, and it was as Peace Commissioner that he had his seat in the Council of Ten in this period, just as, for instance, Milner and others had deputized for Lloyd George and White had sometimes taken the place of House or Lansing. Whatever he did beyond this had to be for his own account and at his own risk, and if he gave his actions the appearance of being other than private, non-binding talks, then he was exceeding his authority. We can only ascertain that something of this sort is what actually happened.

At the meeting, the Italian-Yugoslavian boundary was also discussed, and neither Clemenceau nor Lloyd George seemed prepared to grant to Italy the boundary line foreseen in the Treaty of London. On the contrary, they expressed their satisfaction with the boundary proposed by the American Experts. The two Allies were not willing either, to give Fiume to Italy, although they were prepared, if necessary, to agree to internationalize the city[357]). It thus seemed that Wilson could depend on Anglo-French support for his Italian policy. But now Lloyd George introduced an entirely new element in the already tangled negotiations[358]):

"George spoke of the sinking of the ships and the necessity for an agreement between England and America not to rival each other in naval building."

This was the answer to the American threats.

That same afternoon, the military terms were discussed in the Council of Ten, and here it was finally decided to relinquish the principle of conscription for the quid pro quo of a reduction of the Germany army to 100,000 men. The military terms contained two further provisions of direct relevance to the Rhineland problem. Chapter 2, article 8, required Germany to destroy all fortifications west of a line drawn 50 km east of the Rhine, while article 9 called for the "demilitarization of all territory on the left bank of the Rhine which may remain as part of Germany." This meant that the inhabitants of the region could not receive any form of military training or be incorporated in any military organization, either compulsorily or voluntarily, and further, that this region was not to contribute either financially or in other ways to Germany's army[359]).

In this way, France would at least be ensured a "buffer zone" in the area in question[360]). At the suggestion of Clemenceau, however, it was agreed to omit the last article because the fate of the region had not yet been decided and it would therefore "be of no use to ask the Germans to agree to any terms regarding it before its final allotment."[361]) Thus the French did not wish to prejudice the work of the committee just appointed.

At the same meeting, the following agenda was agreed for the next meetings[362]):

"It was decided that the Military and Naval Convention should be discussed on Wednesday (12.3), and that the eastern and northern frontiers of Germany should be discussed on Thursday (13.3.). ... It was further decided that Germany's western frontier should be discussed on Friday (14.3)."

If this agenda were followed, it had therefore to be assumed that all questions relating to the territorial terms in the Preliminary Peace Treaty with Germany would have been discussed and perhaps also provisionally agreed before the American President returned, for he could hardly have been expected to be present on the date of his arrival. The question is, however, what real possibility there was for realizing this programme or, in other words, how the "speeding up" process was getting on.

The question has both an organizational and a political aspect. F. S. Marston has pronounced harsh judgment on the development from an organizational point of view: "By the end of February it was probably too late to change the whole direction of the Conference and to adapt its machinery for the purpose; the resolutions of the 24th were certainly not sufficient to bring about such a change." The only organizational innovations were the appointment of a committee to examine the question of the boundary between Poland and Germany on 26 February and the appointment of the Central Territorial Committee on 27 February, while other vital questions, such as the Saar and the Rhineland, were not subjected to committee treatment. The "speeding-up" resolution had no effect either, on the committees already in existence, for "having passed the resolutions ... the Council of Ten appears to have taken no effective steps to ensure that they should have definite results", and the effect seems in general to have been "very slight". "The only commission which responded, though rather tardily, to the new policy of the Council of Ten and changed its whole direction was ... that dealing with Ports, Waterways and Railways"! The whole thing was purely fictitious[363]).

However, it must in this connection be mentioned that whereas the aim of the Balfour resolution was primarily organizational, the development after Lloyd George's arrival entered a new phase in which, as we have seen, an attempt to accelerate the process on the political plane as well can be observed. An effort was now made to reach decisions, partly through top level negotiations and partly through the appointment of ad hoc committees intended to produce their findings with a minimum of delay. In this way, it should have been possible, at any rate in theory, to balance the organizational weaknesses mentioned. Whether it was possible in practice too was entirely a political question, the decision on which did not, however, lie solely with Paris. On 11 March, House received the following telegram from Wilson[364]):

"10 March 5 p. m. Your cable of March 8th. 11 p. m. (report on meeting of 7.3.) just deciphered. Am made a little uneasy by what you say of the left bank of the Rhine. I hope you will not even provisionally consent to the separation of the Rhenish Provinces from Germany under any arrangement but will reserve the whole matter until my arrival."

House must have realized, when he received this, that he had gone too far.

Meanwhile, the two secret committees had convened. The economic committee discussed both the question of the distribution and the magnitude of the sum to be paid by Germany, and on both points it proved possible to reach a compromise. The distribution was: 55 per cent to France and 25 per cent to Great Britain, but "Nothing definite came out of this because of another change of procedure."[365]). With regard to the actual amount, agreement was finally reached on the American proposal of 120.000 mill. Mark[366]). However, the committee did not submit its report as planned on 13 March, first after Wilsons's return, possibly because no report was requested since no new "summit meeting" took place on that date.

The other committee did not submit a report to the two Prime Ministers and House either. The meetings took place on 11 and 12 March[367]), and both the German-Polish boundary and the French demands regarding the Rhineland were discussed. The treatment of the Polish question did not take very long, the committee seeming to agree to recommend the report of the Polish Commission, which, inter alia, gave Danzig to the Poles[368]). However, it was the Rhineland that took the committee's time. As a basis for the negotiations there was a proposal by Tardieu[369]), which contained the "familiar general considerations"[370]): Germany's boundary should be fixed at the Rhine and Germany should relinquish all rights of sovereignty and customs union west of the Rhine. The Rhine-line should be occupied by an Inter-Allied force under a mandate from the League of Nations, while the conditions for the continued occupation of the Bridgeheads on the East bank should be laid down in the Peace Treaty, and further, Germany was not to be permitted to maintain fortifications in a zone 50 km east of the western frontier of Germany. The left bank of the Rhine should constitute one or more independent States under the protection of the League of Nations. The former top German and Prussian officials in this region should be evacuated, and detailed provisions should be framed, under the guarantee of the League of Nations, for the German economic interests in the region. Finally, Germany should be responsible for supplying coal to the region, and this would be credited to Germany's reparations account.

"M. Mezes parle peu, Ces huit heures de discussion son un dialogue entre M. Kerr et moi", writes Tardieu[371])

and this is also how it appears from the reports of the meetings. The situation after the talks of the first day did not look too bad[372]):

"Of the four main points in Tardieu's project Kerr had given unqualified support to none, but the gulf can be exaggerated. They agreed on the Rhine as the military frontier and on German disarmament. As for an occupation, Kerr had only said that British support for a permanent occupation could not be expected. He told Tardieu near the end of the meeting: "So far as I could see the difference between our views centered upon the question of the occupation of the Rhenish provinces". In other words, they were not necessarily divided over the question of the separation of the Rhenish provinces . . .".

Something similar could be concluded from Mezes' remarks[373]):

"Mezes assured Tardieu of American concern for French security. The American government could more easily meet the French point of view if Allied troops were not maintained on German soil proper and if the proposed Allied occupation was only temporary."

Equally important was perhaps the fact that during the talk, Kerr indicated for the first time the possibility of a French-British-American Alliance as the best means of guaranteeing the security of France[374]).

The first meeting may have given grounds for a certain optimism, but this was definitely not confirmed next day, because Kerr then declared that the British Government could not agree to the separation of the Rhineland any more than it could agree to Inter-Allied occupation[375]). "Kerr failed to see why the French Government could not accept the alternative proposal for security: German disarmament, the demilitarization of the Left bank, and confidence in joint action by Great Britain, the United States and France"[376]), but Tardieu maintained the French viewpoint. Mezes summed up the situation as follows[377]):

> "Tardieu, after seeing the Premier, yielded the bridge-heads proposal, accepting, as a substitute, rigid military inspection in Germany.
>   Kerr was holding out *against* political independence and interallied occupation of the Rhine Provinces if intended as any more than a very shortlived measure winding up the war.
>   Tardieu holding out for *both,* mentioning first a 15 to 20-year term, later a ten-year term, and at the end alluding to, but not accepting (*he* would), a five-year term."

Strangely enough, Mezes made no mention of the British alternative proposal, and his reaction to this is not known, but we do know that he requested during the meeting that all decisions on the fate of the Rhineland should be deferred until after Wilson's arrival[378]). The President's cable had had its effect.

Mezes' role in this exchange had been that of a passive onlooker, and it could hardly have been otherwise in the circumstances, for what took place, so to speak before his very eyes, was a serious aggravation of the latent Anglo-French crisis, which was completely independent of American policy. This appears clearly from talks that House had on this day, 12 March. In the middle of the meeting of the Council of Ten, Lloyd George asked House to join him outside, and here he initiated him in his difficulties: "He said he was seriously troubled concerning the French." He could not agree to the French plans for a Rhenish Republic, but was willing to provide them with protection in other ways. "He would also be willing to say that in the event of an invasion, the British would come at once to the rescue ..."[379]). Here the idea of an Alliance came up again, but—if House's report is correct—Lloyd George's statements made no mention of America; the British Prime Minister was reserving this proposal for Wilson himself[380]). There was also disagreement in the economic sphere, over the question of distribution, on which Lloyd George found the French attitude unfair[381]). And finally, there was the question of Syria, which was perhaps the decisive element in the crisis[382]).

On the same afternoon House also had a visit from Clemenceau[383]):

> "He was distressed at the turn matters were taking with the British. He said Lloyd George did not keep his promises, that in England he had promised him Syria just as the French now desired. He said he had broken his word as to the division of the sum to be obtained from Germany, and again he had broken his word in declining to even discuss the Rhenish Republic and the proper protection of France.

... I soothed the old man by telling him that we would straighten it out in some way and not to worry."

Broken promises and unacceptable demands: the crisis was a reality, and at last even House had to look the facts in the face: "Now that everything is closing and the different questions which have been discussed have to be settled, I can see trouble."[384]). However, in this critical situation, House—and America—were placed in a key position. As things stood on 12 March, it looked as though Wilson would walk straight into the role of disinterested mediator on his return—the position of "arbiter mundi", which, as we have seen, seems to have been an important part of his original strategy. The question was, however, whether he would be allowed to play this role—and whether he *could*. Did the President really regard America as being so disinterested that the mediatory position was a realistic possibility?

The answer is to be found in a cable that Tumulty sent to Wilson from Washington on 13 March, which Wilson must thus have received immediately before or after his arrival in France[385]):

"Country greatly disturbed over stories appearing in Paris and elsewhere under Associated Press head that League of Nations is not to be included in Peace Treaty."

Three days later, the situation was reported to be as follows[386]):

"Much excitement has been caused by statements in the press here (USA) that it had been decided to conclude the preliminary treaty of peace without incorporating the League of Nations. A definite statement ot this effect has appeared here in all newspapers from Tardieu, followed in the next edition by a telegram from the President to Tumulty to the exact opposite and with the intimation that the plenary council had already so decided, obviously referring to the January meeting."

When Wilson again set foot on French soil, he was not only greeted by an acute Anglo-French crisis, but also ran straight into an Anglo-French offensive, aimed at his weakest point.

The "speeding-up" process which House and Balfour had started and which Lloyd George, with his hectic activity, had accelerated so violently, had brought all the latent political differences to a climax just in time for the arrival of the President, and this whole complex of problems now included, thanks to the opposition in America and to House's sins of omission, an entirely new element: the threat of a separation of the Peace Treaty and the League of Nations Covenant. This was a political weapon that the Allied politicians neither could nor would leave unused, especially as it became apparent to all that the President would, on his arrival, be forced to seek serious—and perhaps unacceptable—amendments to the League of Nations Covenant.

Thus, when Wilson landed at Brest, he found himself in the middle of an entirely new diplomatic situation, and in this situation, his position was seriously weakened because his political position at home had been catastrophically shaken. The role of "arbiter mundi" was no longer politically possible.

*Chapter 4*

# The Break and the Crisis

When, in 1923, Ray Stannard Baker published his treatise on Wilson's policy at the Peace Conference: Woodrow Wilson and World Settlement[1]), he presented an interpretation of the break between House and Wilson[2]) that is worthy of detailed analysis. Baker claimed that "while it is too much to say that there was a direct plot, while Wilson was away, to kill the League or even cut it out of the Treaty, one can affirm with certainty that there was an intrigue against his plan of a preliminary military and naval peace—which would have indirectly produced the same result"[3]), and went on to write that "Colonel House met the President when he arrived at Brest and rode up to Paris with him. From this time onward there began to grow up a coldness between the two men to which I shall refer again, for it had an important and unfortunate bearing upon the Peace Conference"[4]). At the same time, he emphasized that this coldness could not be attributed to "trivial personal causes" or "little, mean jealousies", but "was based upon far deeper failures in understanding and action":

"So long as Colonel House was what Clemenceau called "an ear, but not a mouth", silent, listening, reporting veraciously and voluminously to the President, everything went well. His help was great and valuable . . .
. . .
But when Colonel House was placed in a great position where action based upon utterly clear thinking and sharp and definite decisions were required, he began to suffer from the defects of his own qualities. Instinctively and emotionally he was as truly liberal as the President and he was a loyal supporter of the League of Nations: but he had never thought through. He never knew quite where he was, but he was always optimistic. There was nothing hard, clear, sure, definite, in his intellectual processes . . .
. . .
He never intended for a moment to be disloyal to the President; thought he was serving the cause of a speedy peace; sent the President long cablegrams as to what was going on at Paris. But the real effect of his action here, as later in the Conference, was to confuse everything, and in action in this case at least to serve exactly the contrary purpose from the one the President had in view. This judgment is based not alone upon the writer's own conclusions growing out of personal contact at Paris with both men, but upon careful survey of the entire record of the Peace Conference".[5])

Baker further stressed the fact that it was "the dispatches from Colonel House that gave the President the first inkling of the course of affairs at

Paris—and no doubt sharpened the challenge in his great speech of March 4, at the Metropolitan Opera House in New York, just before sailing again for France, in which he asserted that the Covenant must be knit into the Treaty"[6]). Then, after describing in more general terms how "the course of the Council (of Ten) during that crucial month was more stupid than designing", Baker continued "(t)he foes of the League were doubtless too quick to jump to the conclusion they desired—that the League was done for, cut out of the Treaty, and left to perish of inanition. But there was a real kernel of truth in their predictions. These were repeated eagerly, reached the United States, and inspired Tumulty to cable in alarm (March 14) warning the President on his return to Paris of what was being cooked up against him"[7]). As a purely personal recollection, Baker further advised that "(a)lmost the first well-informed man the writer talked with after landing again on French soil said, with a smile: "Well, your league is dead":

"And that was, indeed, the conviction of the French Press. At least the League was sidetracked—put off until the real settlements could be made. So Pichon was quite frankly saying; so even Lord Robert Cecil, a true friend of the League, was admitting; so the London Times was assuming, arguing that the peace as now planned was in reality only a kind of enlarged armistice".[8])

Baker's thesis regarding a more or less clearly defined "February plot" and a more or less pronounced attempt to "sidetrack the League" has often been both discussed and rejected, most recently by Alexander L. George and Juliette L. George[9]). Nevertheless, there may still be good grounds for a re-analysis, for although it is true that Baker accompanied Wilson to America and was thus out of the picture for a while, he was, as we shall see, very directly involved in the events immediately following the President's return, and had, moreover, the opportunity of discussing the problem not only with the two men directly concerned, but also with the other members of the Commission.

The interesting thing about Baker's treatise is not just that it is the work of a man who was very close to the events about which he writes, but also—and particularly—that it can be regarded as the "official" account. For Baker was not only given access to Wilson's papers during the preparation of the book; he also lived with the Wilson family, partly at the White House and partly at S Street, while he studied the material, and "(a)lthough Wilson insisted that the Peace Conference book be entirely Baker's, the President granted him frequent interviews to clear up difficult points"[10]). It must therefore be assumed that Baker's treatise is at least in approximate accordance with the version of the story that Wilson's immediate circle wished to have disseminated.

It is true, as Robert C. Binkley has pointed out[11]), that Baker had already formulated his thesis in 1919, when he published his booklet "What Wilson did at Paris"[12]), viz, before Wilson's papers had been made available to him.

However, it is possible to reverse this argument: As this version was left un-
altered in the new, greatly extended and revised edition, it must have had the
approval of the President[13]). And in this connection, it is perhaps worth
noting that George Creel's version of the events tallies with Baker's[14]):

"A full report of this action (Lodge-resolution 4. 3. 1919) was cabled to Europe, as a
matter of course, and when the President arrived in Paris on March 14th, ten days
later, he was quick to learn of the disastrous consequences. The Allies, eagerly accepting
the orders of the Republican majority, had lost no time in repudiating the President and
the solemn agreements that they had entered into with him. The League of Nations was
now discarded and the plan adopted for a preliminary peace with Germany was based
upon a frank division of the spoils, the reduction of Germany to a slave state, and
the formation of a military alliance by the Allies for the purpose of guaranteeing the
gains. . . .".

When Seymour's edition of House's papers was published in 1926, Baker
wrote to Creel, commenting as follows on, inter alia, the first volume: "I
regret that he did not go on through to the end, for I know mighty well what
happened at the Peace Conference"[15]). Creel, who was at this time working
on a psychological study of House, immediately took the opportunity of posing
the following question[16]):

"It was also my conviction, although I always forgot to ask the President about it, that
the Colonel went still further in the matter of the League; that while the President was
on the water, returning to Paris in March, 1919, that the Colonel gave assent to the attempted repudiation of the League as an integral part of the Peace Treaty. Was this
true? . . .".

However, Baker did not really wish to come clean; he replied by drawing
attention to his presentation of the matter in "Woodrow Wilson and World
Settlement". He referred partly to the version cited above of the events during
Wilson's absence: "the period in which Colonel House utterly failed him."
And he stressed his description of House's attitude during the Italian crisis and
the critical phase of the negotiations on reparations[17]). Nevertheless, on
22. 12. 1926, he finally got around to speaking his mind[18]):

". . . I feel certain of my position—the more so because I know that Mr. Wilson himself
thought that Colonel House had surrendered while he was absent in America. I know
that Mr. Wilson found out the true situation on the train up from Brest. I was on that
train. And the first he did upon reaching Paris was to knock over what had been done.
I myself wrote the statement by which he did this, talked it over with him, and gave it
publicity. There is not the shadow of a doubt in my mind that this was the beginning
of the break with Colonel House".

As will be seen below, the "statement" mentioned is the declaration on the
League of Nations. It is thus once more the problems relating to the incorporating of the League of Nations in the Treaty that are given priority in the
explanation of the causes of the break. The question is whether it is possible
to verify Baker's account of the points that are of importance and whether we
can possibly amplify his views.

As described in the previous chapter, not only did Wilson land right in the middle of an inter-Allied crisis, he also ran straight into a situation that very quickly developed into an Anglo-French offensive aimed at his weakest point: the tie-up between the League of Nations Covenant and the Peace Treaty. That this was his most vulnerable point was however also due to his having made it the very core of his political strategy at home: Wilson wanted to exploit his foreign policy as a weapon in his domestic fight for power[19]). As described earlier, Wilson had left the United States just at the climax of a crisis over precisely this relationship between League and Treaty. And when, as we have seen, either immediately before or just after his arrival, he received the following telegram from Tumulty[20]): "Country greatly disturbed over stories appearing in Paris and elsewhere under Associated Press head that League of Nations is not to be included in Peace Treaty", he must have realized that his opponents on both sides of the Atlantic were well on the way to uniting. This was the common front that Senator Lodge had much earlier tried, without avail, to establish[21]), a front that the anonymous Republican author of the memorandum mentioned in the last chapter had warmly recommended, and a front that the bulletins from America now seemed to indicate was becoming a reality[22]). This was a terribly dangerous situation for the President; what was a stake was not just an idealistic vision but—as he himself had structured the situation—the very foundation of his political existence, both in Europe and in America. His reaction was therefore a foregone conclusion, and he could not help but feel that House had totally failed him—regardless of whether House had been involved at all in the events in question or had in general had any chance whatsoever of influencing them— and the more so as House was apparently never given the opportunity of explaining himself, either on this point or on his other actions during the President's absence.

The accounts of the first meeting between House and Wilson are rather inadequate, but a number of them do display common features that seem to permit a new interpretation. The most dramatic account is that of Mrs. Wilson[23]), but it was written a number of years after the event and is partly incorrect on a number of peripheral details[24]), that have been checked in other ways, and partly self-contradictory in its presentation of the content of the talk. This has brought George and George to the conclusion "that Mrs. Wilson correctly reports the gist of her husband's irritation with House sometime *after* his return to Paris"[25]). What Wilson said, according to Mrs. Wilson, was, inter alia: "House has given away everything I had won before we left Paris. He has compromised on every side, and so I have to start all over again and this time it will be harder, as he has given the impression that my delegates are not in sympathy with me"[26]).

However, we also have three contemporary reports, by House, Lansing and Auchincloss. On 14. 3. 19. House wrote in his diary:

"I went up on Wednesday evening, after our dinner and reception, on the President's special train to meet him at Brest. ... I arranged that none of the people who went to meet the President before should go this time, with the exception of the French Ambassador and Mme. Jusserand, whom I could not prevent going if I would. I desired to have the President alone so as to place him *au courant* with the situation here during his absence. I did not go out to the George Washington to meet the President and Mrs. Wilson but met them at the landing stage. I had but little talk with them that night because Jusserand thought it necessary to entertain the President.

However, I had ample opportunity this morning to go over the entire situation with him and to get from him his story of his visit to the United States. He said, 'Your dinner to the Senate Foreign Relations Committee was a failure as far as getting together was concerned'. He spoke with considerable bitterness of the manner in which he was treated by some of the Senators. Knox and Lodge remained perfectly silent, refusing to ask any questions or to act in the spirit in which the dinner was given. However, I told[27]) the President that the dinner was a success from my viewpoint, which was that it checked criticism as to his supposed dictatorship and refusal to consult the Senate about Foreign affairs. He admitted this. I told[27]) him that it also had a good effect upon the people, even if it had failed to mollify the Senators themselves.

The president comes back very militant and determined to put the League of Nations into the Peace Treaty".

On 19. 3. 19, Auchincloss sent a cable to Frank Polk[28]), saying, inter alia:

"On trip from Brest to Paris the President had only about half an hour's conversation with the Colonel who was able to inform him only respecting the high points dealt with by the conference during his absence".

And as early as 15. 3. 19., Lansing had himself written to Polk[29]):

"Jusserand went to Brest also, and sat and talked with the President until 11.30 p. m. much to the Colonel's disgust. The latter went to Brest so he could explain the present situation to the President, and he never got a chance. He seemed decidedly peeved".

It is clear that all three acounts are from the same source, viz, House himself, although his own diary version deviates on one important point from the other two: House and Lansing agreed that Jusserand had that evening prevented House from having the talk with the President that had been the whole purpose of the trip. And Lansing and Auchincloss further agreed that House never had an opportunity of a detailed discussion of the situation with Wilson: "He never got a chance", "only about a half an hour's conversation", "able to inform him only respecting the high points". House, on the other hand, asserts that even though he did not manage to talk to the President during the evening, he had "ample time this morning to go over the entire situation with him."[30]) The question is, which account is most probable? Or rather: Can House have had any reason for deceiving not only the Secretary of State but also his own son-in-law? And, if everything had gone according to plan, why did he "look decidedly peeved"?

The answer seems obvious: the talk had been extremely unsatisfactory for both House and Wilson. The only thing they managed to discuss in detail was the situation relating to the League of Nations, and the President was not satisfied with this. Of his other political manoeuvres, House only had the opportunity of giving a brief account, which was by no means complete and certainly did not reassure Wilson. House never had the chance of going into detail on the situation. The President was to be informed of this and of House's part in it through other channels.

There is, however one more factor that should be taken into account: the last chapter described how House—partly, although by no means solely, because of the poor communication between Washington and Paris—embarked upon detailed negotiations on the French Rhineland programme. It also described how the last hectic days before Wilson's arrival were taken up with, inter alia, discussions on just this programme between Mezes, Tardieu and Kerr. These discussions had not produced any results, partly because of Kerr's opposition and partly because Mezes had finally requested a postponement of all decisions on the fate of the Rhineland until after Wilson's arrival[31]): House had apparently got cold feet on receiving Wilson's cable of 10. 3. 19., in which the President said "I hope you will not even provisionally consent to the separation of the Rhenish Provinces from Germany under any arrangement but will reserve the whole matter until my arrival"[32]).

The Kerr–Mezes–Tardieu negotiations gave no result, but we now know that House took with him to Brest Tardieu's proposal of 12. 3. 19[33]), which he had promised to pass to the President at the first opportunity[34]). It is therefore reasonable to assume that House must, in connection with this, have had the opportunity of accounting in brief to Wilson for his rather compromising negotiations with, inter alios, Tardieu[35]). Even if this account were incomplete, the President would still have had plenty of opportunity to supplement his information the same day, for immediately after his arrival in Paris, he had two important meetings, first with Lloyd George alone and then with Lloyd George and Clemenceau[36]). It was at the first meeting that Lloyd George presented to Wilson his plan for an Anglo-American guarantee to France to make up for the French Rhineland plans, and it was at the following meeting that Lloyd George and Wilson presented the plan to Clemenceau[37]). It has always seemed strange that Wilson should so quickly have consented to such a radical deviation from the traditional American foreign policy of non-committance[38]), but viewed against the background of his prior talk with House, the President's reaction may become more understandable: He felt the foundation of his previous policy shaking and simply grabbed at the first thing to hand. However, here we have not only to a certain extent anticipated events, but have also entered on conjecture. All the same, it would not be out of place to conclude by citing the words of Admiral Grayson written in 1926[39]):

"It was upon Mr. Wilson's return to France that he found to his amazement that Colonel House had consented to a plan for the separation of the Peace Treaty from the Covenant of the League of Nations. He had assented to Premier Clemenceau's wishes and suggestions about this matter. He had also agreed to the establishment of a Rhenish republic that would act as a buffer state between Germany and France, the creation of which would have been in absolute contradiction to President Wilson's Fourteen Points.

So President Wilson had no sooner arrived in France than he found it necessary to repudiate practically everything that had been done during his absence. On March 15, 1919, he gave out a strong newspaper statement to the effect that he would never assent to splitting the League from the Peace Treaty.

From that time on, the relationship between the President and the Colonel ceased to be close and confidential".

If this interpretation is correct, then it was the situation concerning the League of Nations, in connection with House's compliance with the French Rhineland plans, that first instilled doubts in Wilson's mind as to House's capabilities. What he learned during the next few days regarding his adviser's other transactions, simply increased this mistrust—and increased it to such an extent that House was never given the opportunity of defending himself[40]). It is thus to the brief talk in the train that we must assign the "break". After this discussion, the personal trust between the two men was broken and the friendship damaged beyond repair. Nevertheless, House was still a Peace Commissioner and, on a number of points, he was still the only qualified negotiator.

Seen from Paris, the whole affair was not nearly as dramatic as Wilson's sharp and immediate reaction made it appear. On 14 March, to mark Wilson's return, The Times printed a statement of affairs, written by the paper's political correspondent in Paris[41]). After describing the progress made regarding the framing of the preliminary Peace Treaty, the correspondent wrote: "The situation with regard to the League of Nations is not, so far as the immediate work of the Peace Conference is concerned, a pressing matter now". There would undoubtedly be discussions and amendments, but "The main thing for the present is to make the preliminary treaty with Germany. When once that has been done, work on the League of Nations and consideration of all outstanding questions of expediency rather than of policy, can be quietly and properly taken in hand".

To Wilson, however, things looked quite different. He had never envisaged so comprehensive a preliminary Peace Treaty—and this he had also written to House—but only a speedy decision on the military terms[42]); and in particular, he had never imagined any form of Peace Treaty that did not include the whole of the League of Nations Covenant. That is why he reacted so promptly. The President arrived in Paris at lunch-time on 14 March[43]), and met Clemenceau and Lloyd George the same afternoon to discuss the major controversial questions of policy that now finally had to be solved. "They discussed the question of the left bank of the Rhine but came to no conclusion. They also discussed the question of reparation but came to no conclusion", reported Auchincloss, and he continued "David Miller came over to discuss with Sir Maurice Hankey a clause by which the League of Nations would be brought into the Peace Treaty and made a part thereof"[44]).

However, Wilson did not leave the matter at this internal discussion—he also brought it into public—yet another indication that it was primarily the situation in America that he had in mind. On 15 March, he issued a press bulletin establishing the fact that the decision of the Plenary Session of 25 January 1919 "to the effect that the establishment of a League of Nations should be made an integral part of the Treaty of Peace, is of final force and that there is no basis whatever for the reports that a change in this decision was contemplated"[45]). Ray Stannard Baker, who was himself actively involved in the framing of this bulletin[46]), has reported as follows on the motives and considerations on which it was based[47]):

"... The President called me on the telephone about 11 o'clock and asked me to deny the report, now being circulated, that there would be a separate preliminary treaty with Germany excluding the League of Nations. *Partly this report represents a genuine belief in some circles that such a preliminary peace would be valuable in helping solve immediate difficulties, but it is also being used by enemies of the League here and in America to delay and obstruct the whole League of Nations plan.* I drew up a statement in accordance with the President's ideas and submitted it to him after the noon conference. He approved it and we put it out ...".

Wilson may have had a dual purpose in issuing this declaration—the situation both in the United States and in Paris—but if so, it had, to a certain extent, the opposite effect of that intended: it made no very great impact on the League of Nations controversy in America[48]), whereas in Paris, it raised a veritable political storm—"... (T)he President's statement fell like a bomb ..."[49])—a storm that had a most unfortunate effect on the whole negotiating position of the President. Whereas Wilson had earlier been given a very favourable reception by the French press[50]), apparently in anticipation of great decisions, the President's proclamation on the League of Nations led to a virulent press campaign against him in the French Right-wing press[51]), the official inspiration for which was revealed when Pichon too, in a press interview, threw down the gauntlet on the question of the incorporation of the League of Nations in the Peace Treaty[52]). This resulted in all the blame for the crisis in the negotiations that had developed during the first week after Wilson's return being laid at the President's door for insisting on having the League of Nations included in the Peace Treaty. The truth of the matter was probably that "the real questions which are holding up the peace are (1) the left bank of the Rhine, (2) economic questions involved in reparation, (3) military terms, (4) entirely extraneous matters such as Syria and Morocco which have been injected into the discussion not by us (USA) but principally by the French and in part by the British"[53]). This development aggravated the President's situation because he was already on the defensive in another way: the American situation had made it vitally important to amend the League of Nations Covenant, and it soon became clear that the Allies were not going to agree to this without a suitable quid pro quo. Moreover, there were at the same time signs that Wilson's colleagues on the American Commission did not share his view of the prior importance of the League of Nations[54]).

Despite this, Wilson did not limit himself to a public proclamation of the incorporation of the League of Nations Covenant in the Peace Treaty—he also upset all the plans for a preliminary Peace Treaty, with or without the League of Nations[55]). And the way he did this shows how uncertain he was of the whole situation on his arrival[56]). It had been planned that the first meeting of "The Council of Ten" after Wilson's return should deal with and, if possible, finally agree on the military, naval and air terms. Shortly before the meeting was to be held (15 March), however, the President advised that he was unable to attend. His decision seems to have been taken in haste, and House had to deputize at very short notice and without having been included in the prior deliberations[57]). Not until 17 March did the planned meeting take place in "The Council of Ten", and here a question of procedure was now raised, which meant that not only the military, naval and air terms, but also the question of a preliminary Peace Treaty, were postponed indefinitely at the request of Wilson: M. Fromageot of the Drafting Committee here requested "a ruling as to the character of the document that the Conference wished to present to the Germans." Were the present terms to be regarded "merely as a set of military clauses for immediate execution by the Germans" or "were (they) to be considered as final Peace Conditions?". If the latter were the case, "it would be necessary for them to be ratified by the legislators of the various countries, parties to the agreement". Herewith, in other words, the Senate was brought into the picture, and Wilson reacted at once[58]):

"PRESIDENT WILSON ... said that the paragraph as it now read indicated that these terms would be part of the Armistice. But if they were to constitute the Preliminary Treaty of Peace, the wording was not correct. In this matter he found himself in considerable difficulty, and he would be compelled to seek legal advice. He had assumed that this preliminary Convention would only be temporary until the complete Treaty was prepared, and that it would have the character of a sort of exalted armistice, the terms being re-included in the formal Treaty. If this Preliminary Convention would have to be submitted to the Senate for a general discussion there, he knew from the usual slow processes of legislatures that it would be several months before it could be ratified.
...
PRESIDENT WILSON said he did not feel quite sure of his ground, and he proposed that the question be postponed until he could consult with the Constitutional lawyers, in whose opinion he had more confidence than in his own.
..."

Wilson then consulted Lansing, who in turn brought in Scott and Miller, the Commission's Experts on international law. The nature of the President's deliberations becomes apparent from Lansing's report[59]):

"SWC met ... Prest. astounded me by practically saying that he had not thought that preliminaries of peace ought to go to Senate. I told him it was a treaty of peace and he could not avoid it ... 10 pm Miller and Scott on necessity of submitting treaty of peace, whatever it is called, to Senate. They agreed. Asked them to give me memo. Gregory[60]) (10,50–11,30) on ditto. He agrees and promised to see Prest."

Gregory later told Miller that "it was true that the President had had an idea that he could make a treaty with Germany and put through the League of Nations, military terms etc., without having it ratified by the Senate, but he said that he had no such idea any longer"[61]). It is thus clear that the ideas of both Wilson and other top politicians regarding the legal and procedural consequences of a preliminary Peace were rather vague to say the least[62]), but it is also clear that the Senate had played a decisive role in Wilson's deliberations, no matter how his statements to Lansing and Gregory are to be interpreted. At the same time, however, Wilson was undoubtedly taking purely tactical steps: he wanted to prevent all discussion of the preliminary Peace Treaty until the question of the incorporation of the League of Nations in this had been solved. And finally: House was not consulted at all on this question, despite the fact that it was in reality his achievements that were here negated[63]).

House was altogether a worried man. It is true that he now backed up the President's League of Nations policy to the full, but he too was extremely anxious over the critical negotiating situation, and even more anxious over his own total isolation: "White said to Bliss and me (Lansing) that House told him that he (House) had not had talk alone with Prest. for over a week and that he was becoming greatly disturbed at the way things were drifting . . ."[64]). A study of House's diary for the days following Wilson's return shows that his above statement to White was not just empty words. Apart from the negotiations between Wilson, Cecil and House on amendments to the League of Nations Covenant, House was not involved in the top level negotiations now in progress between Wilson, Clemenceau and Lloyd George, and for the initiation of which he himself had been largely responsible[65]). And it is extremely characteristic of the whole situation that when Wilson attempted, with some success, to counteract Pichon's negation of the relationship between the League of Nations and the Peace Treaty, it was Cecil—not House—who was asked to take action[66]). House himself tried to intervene, but the attempt was not particularly successful and indeed, was hardly even taken seriously. On 20 March, he gave an interview to the Paris Daily Mail, "guilded with optimism." He declared that the whole Treaty would be ready by 29 March and that he would be disappointed if the Germans did not come to Versailles within three weeks. Furthermore, in the significant part of the interview, he held that "The League of Nations Covenant has not held up the work of framing the Peace Treaty in any way . . . It has never taken up time needed by other Commissions. We sat at night, or when the Council of Ten was not meeting.". However, the interview had no particular effect: "Very little editorial comment was spared it. A few organs of the conservative-nationalist press took occasion to characterize it appropriately . . . The Figaro (March 22) put it somewhat more baldly: "The entire peace within three weeks? What a beautiful dream!" "[67])

All that was left to House now was to make a direct approach to Wilson, and this he did on 24 March, in an obvious effort to regain the President's confidence[68]):

"I saw the President for nearly an hour at his residence and pointed out the necessity of forcing the Conference out of the rut into which it had fallen. He asked what I had to suggest. I said it was necessary to tell George, Clemenceau and Orlando that immediate peace was not only imperative, but if we did not make it in a reasonable time we would find ourselves with a peace treaty and no one excepting ourselves to sign it. Hungary went over to Bolshevism yesterday, and other states are tottering while we sit here trying to satisfy the greed and fears of certain of our Allies. I urged him to settle once and for all the question as to whether the League of Nations was to go into the Peace Treaty. He, Cecil and I wanted it in and I thought it would go in. George and Clemencau do not want it in and have intimated that it would not be in. I advised a showdown.

In making the argument, I suggested that he tell them that the Covenant for the League of Nations would either be written into the Treaty of Peace or we would have none of it; that the only excuse we could give for meddling in European or world affairs was a League of Nations through which we hope to prevent wars. If that was not to be, then we would not care to mix again in their difficulties.

The other three questions I thought should be put to the Prime Ministers were:
1. The amount of reparation;
2. What was necessary to satisfy France and safeguard her future;
3. What should be the boundary lines between the old Austria-Hungary and Italy.

I advised doing away with the Quai d'Orsay meetings and for him to meet with the Prime Ministers in continuous session until these three essentials to peace har been determined. He said he would do it, and he did do it after a fashion; not as thoroughly as it should be, but still the Quai d'Orsay meetings are at an end for the present, and the Prime Ministers and himself meet tomorrow at eleven to get at grips with the questions I have outlined".

On the face of it, House's proposal may appear to have been superfluous: after all, he was saying no more than Wilson had fought for ever since his return. However, it was of course clear that the talk had the primary purpose of showing the President that House—regardless of what he had previously said and done—now went in for the hard line. "I advised a showdown." House's proposal was not without effect: on the same day, the Council of Four was formally established, although, as House himself has indicated[69]), this presumably had no direct relation to the talk. Nonetheless, it is noteworthy that Wilson opened the first official meeting of the Council of Four with what was practically a repetition of House's arguments[70]):

"C'est en ce moment une véritable course entre la paix et l'anarchie et le public commence à manifester son impatience . . .

Je serais d'avis que nous prenions en main les questions les plus difficiles et les plus urgentes, telles que la question des réparations, celle de la protection de la France contre l'aggression, celle de la frontière italienne du côté de l'Adriatique, afin de les discuter entre nous quatre. Les questions les plus importantes et les plus difficiles une fois réglées, la route sera délayée et le reste ira vite".

Further, at the meeting next day, Wilson ensured the consent of the three Prime Ministers to the incorporation of the League of Nations Covenant in the Peace Treaty[71]). House himself felt that "I have the thing moving in the right direction and I hope there will be no further delay." The question is whether he had any reason for this optimism.

Wilson's vehement reaction to the question of the incorporation of the

League of Nations Covenant in the Peace Treaty clearly bears the stamp of the passion with which the battle was now being fought in the United States, a passion of a depth that had apparently not previously been appreciated on the other side of the Atlantic. That House, as we shall see, failed to understand a number of the vital points of the policy followed by the President after his return is not only due to the fact that he was ignorant of the factors behind its formulation. The reason is more fundamental than that: House quite simply failed to appreciate the depth of Wilson's commitment to his battle with the Senate; he had not realised that consideration of the political situation at home was now a decisive element of Wilson's policy. House had always been "much more European than American in his diplomatic thinking"[72]), and his stay in Europe since the Armistice had accentuated this tendency. Since November, he and Wilson had gone separate ways, and now the breaking point was reached.

It is at any rate a fact that from this time on, Wilson reacted with extreme sensitivity to the mood in the United States[73]); of this, the correspondence with Joe Tumulty provides, perhaps, the best example because, through his cables, Tumulty acted as a kind of barometer of public opinion[74]). An analysis of the correspondence between Tumulty and Wilson from the time of the President's return to Paris in the middle of March until the crisis abated at the end of April[75]) shows that, in a number of critical situations, Wilson acted, except in a single instance, in accordance with Tumulty's directions—i. e. with Tumulty's interpretation of American public opinion—.

In the foregoing we have seen Wilson's energetic and resolute reaction to a crisis that seemed to threaten his position both at home and abroad. The relationship with the American situation—as interpreted by Tumulty—is clear: from his cable of 13 March concerning the unrest awakened by press reports of a separation of the Treaty and the League of Nations Covenant[76]) and from Wilson's prompt reaction in Paris, as described above, and his equally prompt reply to Washington[77]):

"The Plenary Council has positively decided that the League of Nations is to be part of the Peace Treaty. There is absolutely no truth in report to the contrary".

On 16 March there was a new cable from Tumulty, in which he emphasized just how critical the situation was in the United States: "Opposition to League growing more intense from day to day" and added: "Know you will not be drawn away from announced program to incorporate League Covenant in Treaty. You can afford to go any length in insisting upon this"[78]). To this Wilson again replied in the affirmative[79]).

The same quick reaction came again a few days later, when Tumulty sent a further warning: "I can see signs that our enemies here and abroad would try to make it appear that you are responsible for delay in peace settlement ...", and Tumulty now wanted Wilson to place the blame for the delay[80]).

Wilson reacted promptly once more: Two days later, 27 March, he issued a public declaration to the effect that it was not the League of Nations that had delayed the negotiations[81]). And Tumulty could immediately assure the President that "Your statement of March twenty-seventh has had a fine effect here."[82]) As we shall see later[83]), it is possible to trace a similar connection between Tumulty's messages and Wilson's decision to summon the "GEORGE WASHINGTON" and perhaps also his later hesitation after all to take the consequences of this action. It can further be proved that Wilson at least asked Tumulty's advice before he issued his Italian proclamation[84]), while on the other hand, both the President himself and Cary Grayson[85]) did their utmost to explain to Tumulty—and thus also to American public opinion— why Wilson was forced to run counter to practically his entire Delegation on the Shantung-question[86]).

It is thus clear that Wilson's thoughts and actions were directed towards the American scene, and the anonymous Republican author of the memorandum cited earlier was not far wrong when he pointed out that Wilson's attitude was "nothing but a disguised campaign for his renomination."[87]) The consensus of the reports from America stressed the importance of party politics to standpoints and the personal bitterness that characterized the situation in the United States. The Presidential campaign for the 1920-election had started and, what is more, Wilson's third term was at stake. It was not only the Republicans who realized this; House himself had been well aware of the situation for a long time. As early as 16 August 1918, after a talk with the President, he had concluded that Wilson would stand for yet another term[88]), and in the period that followed he discussed the matter with both Grayson and McAdoo[89]). House was at that time favourably disposed towards the idea, but does not, apart from this, appear to have spent much time on the matter. However, he had been "warned", so he knew what was at stake for the President—or, at least, he *had* known it[90]).

The speculation regarding a possible third term had already started in January 1918, and the result of the November election 1918 had given the Democrats new food for thought. To many, Wilson's renomination appeared to be the only possibility for victory in the Presidential election, and "(i)n February 1919, the White House denied that he (Wilson) had renounced another race."[91]) The question of the League of Nations played a crucial part in these deliberations. Homer Cummings, the future chairman of the Democratic National Committee, predicted that if the League of Nations were rejected, "the pressure brought to bear on the President to run again would be very great."[92])

"It was thus in an atmosphere surcharged with presidential politics that the Senate decision on the Treaty of Versailles was made. If Wilson's league were ratified unchanged, his prestige might become unbeatable at the polls. Furthermore, a belief that he would be needed to inaugurate league participation might prompt a "draft" for a third term. To prevent the league from becoming the vehicle of Democratic victory, Republicans, per-force, had either to so amend it as to give it a bipartisan character or defeat it".

However, by March 1919, the League of Nations question was already so interwoven with the American inter-party conflict that it was clear that not only the political future of the President himself but also that of the whole Democratic party, depended on the policy he chose to follow in this matter. And just at the time of Wilson's return to Paris, he himself seems to have been in doubt as to the right course to choose. At the time of the President's departure from America, the American press had published rumours to the effect that he was now prepared to seek revisions to the League of Nations Treaty, and that it was advised that Senator Hitchcock had had negotiations with Senator Knox[93]). Indeed, Wilson did take with him to Paris a letter from Hitchcock dated 4 March, in which the latter listed a number of amendments to the League of Nations Covenant that would, in his opinion, make it accept-able to some of the Republican senators who had signed the Lodge Resolu-tion[94]).

The American Delegation had apparently also reckoned on finding the President willing to compromise. On 7 March, White wrote to Lodge and asked for proposals for amendments, and two days later, he even telegraphed the Senator, but Lodge's reaction appears to have been negative[95]) and Thomas Lamont tried to get Elihu Root's views through his partners, Morgan and Morrow[96]). However, when Wilson arrived, he was not prepared to make any sort of change in the League of Nations Covenant: "The President, with his stubbornness in such matters, desires to leave it as it is, saying that any change will be hailed in the United States as yielding to the Senate, and he believes that it will lessen rather than increase the chances of ratification. Of course, I totally disagreed with him, and so did Lord Robert, but rather more diplomatically than I"[97]), wrote House of the first meeting between Wilson, Cecil and House. Nevertheless—two days later—these same three men dis-cussed proposals for amendments on the basis of Hitchcock's letter, inter alia[98]).

However, this was not the only matter on which the President vacillated. In fact, it was the rule rather than the exception. Might this have been partly due to the fact that House was no longer being consulted?

If the above description of the circumstances of the "break" between Wilson and House is correct, there is every reason for taking a second look at House's statements in his last interview with Charles Seymour in 1938[99]):

"Upon his return to Paris in March I saw at once that there was a change. ... At the time I suspected with some reason that immediately upon his return the President had been told that I was disloyal ..."

The fact of the matter is that the above interpretation is based on the assump-tion that House was never given the opportunity of explaining and defending his actions, the President being informed of these through other channels. The question is then whether there is any possibility of identifying the person or persons who influenced Wilson?

In later years, House tended more and more to the view that it was Wilson's immediate circle—Mrs. Wilson, Admiral Grayson and Bernard Baruch—that was chiefly responsible for the break[100]). It is, of course, a fact that relations between Mrs. Wilson and House were strained by both jealousy and antipathy[101]), that Grayson was already talking quite openly of House's "fall" during the last phase of the Conference[102]), and that Baruch—despite his great discretion—could not contrive to hide his true opinion of House in the years following the Peace Conference[103]); indeed, he may already have expressed himself to Frank Polk immediately upon his return from the Conference[104]). Nevertheless, it must at the same time be remembered that both Mrs. Wilson and Cary Grayson were away from Paris during the critical February-March period, only Baruch staying behind. However, there was at least one other person in Paris, who was just as close to the Wilson's as Grayson and Baruch, and whose constantly increasing irritation with House we have earlier had the opportunity of observing[105]).

As we have seen, as soon as Vance McCormick arrived in January, he took note of the fact that House had built up his own organization within the Commission[106]), and realized that House's son-in-law, Gordon Auchincloss, was an important prime mover in this undertaking[107]). His indignation over the situation seems, however, to have been considerably greater than suggested by the entries in his diary. There was one incident, in particular, which he not only passed on, at any rate to Cary Grayson[108]), but which he also remembered—and still considered important—nine years later[109]):

"McCormick thinks that a marked change came over House after he reached Paris and became a member of the Peace Commission. His near friends flattered him. McCormick said that when he reached Paris, at the beginning of the Peace Conference, and went up to call on House, Auchincloss met him and said to him: "Vance, the Colonel is the greatest man here. Everybody comes to him and nobody goes to Lansing".
McCormick said that he thinks House was changed by the flattery and adulation which he received".

This incident, or rather, perhaps, McCormick's anger, also made such a deep impression on Grayson that he too remembered it several years later[110]):

"There can be no question that his son-in-law, Gordon Auchincloss, had an evil influence upon the Colonel. Auchincloss never showed any loyalty toward the President, but made it his business to exalt Colonel House . . .
Auchincloss said that "Kings, and Prime Ministers, and Plenipotentiaries come to the Colonel to get the dope and then we have to tell Woody what to say to them". He came near getting into serious trouble on one occasion by this kind of talk when stalwart Vance McCormick threatened to punch him in the face if he spoke in that disrespectful manner of the President of the United States".

It is impossible now to establish whether McCormick took advantage of, for example, his private visit to the Wilson's on 16 March[111]) to expand on the subject of House. On the other hand, it is a well-known fact that House was at this time trying to get rid of McCormick by sending him to Syria as a member of a commission[112]). In this connection, McCormick contacted Lansing to ask his advice, and the two men got together in their indignation over House's behaviour:

"Took ride in auto in Bois after church with Secretary Lansing. He is a bit disturbed at the way things are going with Colonel House, who is trying to "hog" it. Worried at the slow progress being made, and talked of resigning."[113])
"We talked over present situation and he (McCormick) agrees fully as to unwisdom of present course and as to secrecy of the House Group and the President. He blames Auchincloss for it. Asked my opinion as to his going to Syria on Inter-Allied Commission. I advised against it because of his work here. He felt the same way about it".[114])

The various groups in the Delegation were thus beginning to make common cause against House, and House himself was well on the way to being made scapegoat for all delays and all mystery-mongering, precisely at the time when he actually no longer had any influence at all on the course of events. In this way, the foundation was laid for the most persistant of all the House-myths: that he was responsible for all Wilson's compromises during the final phase of the Conference.

However, if it is true that the "break" between the two men occurred immediately after Wilson's return to France, it must also be possible to prove that House was not, in fact, in the confidence of the President in the following period and no longer participated in the decisive political deliberations. We must therefore seek to ascertain House's role in the critical negotiations immediately following Wilson's return. Due principally to Lloyd George's offer of guarantees, the problem of the Rhineland became one of the major issues of the first few days' negotiations. There has hitherto been a tendency to attribute a key position to House in the preliminary stages of the framing of the Treaty of Guarantee[115]), although his strangely ambivalent attitude has also been emphasized: when he was together with the other Commissioners, he appeared to share their scepticism, but when he was with Wilson, he took another view[116]). The most recent contribution is that of Harold I. Nelson, who has advanced a new interpretation that seems entirely to support the theory of a "break" immediately after Wilson's return[117]):

"On the American side between March 14 and April 2, Colonel House's efforts to arrange a compromise dominated the Rhineland negotiations. As he defined his purpose, 'My main drive now is for peace with Germany at the earliest possible moment'. Initially, the Colonel suggested on March 17 a temporary Rhineland buffer state. Events, however, had outrun this idea. After Clemenceau sent House a copy of the French note of March 17, the Colonel bent his efforts towards seeking a solution along the general lines drawn by Tardieu. *Although absolute proof is lacking, apparently House did not know until March 27 that Woodrow Wilson had committed himself to a special guarantee of American aid for France.* This was the first major breach in the intimate relationship between the two men".

However, if we also consult Auchincloss's diary, which Nelson has not done, we can give the picture greater depth and shading, although it is still impossible to arrive at a completely unambiguous interpretation of House's rather bewildered and bewildering behaviour in this matter.

At the meeting between Clemenceau, Lloyd George and Wilson on 14 March, the British and American negotiators had offered the French Prime Minister "à la place de l'occupation inter-alliée d'une Rhenanie indépendante. l'engagement de la Grande-Bretagne et des États-Unis de venir immédiatement apporter leur aide à La France, si celle-ci était l'object, de la part de l'Allemagne, d'une agression non provoquée"[118]). It is impossible to ascertain whether House knew more about the summit meetings on this date than that the problems of the Rhineland and reparations had been discussed without agreement having being reached[119]. On the other hand, it is certain that on 17 March he received from Clemenceau a copy of the French reply to the offer of a guarantee that was sent that day to Wilson and Lloyd George[120]). After reading this Note, House cannot have been in doubt that France had received an offer of a guarantee that "la Grande-Bretagne et les États-Unis s'engageraient, dans le cas d'une agression de l'Allemagne, à apporter sans délai à la France le concours de leurs forces militaires . . ."[121]), although, of course, in the light of his talk with Lloyd George on 12. 3.[122]), he may have believed that this was a purely British proposal.

On the same day, 17. 3., House drafted "a plan for the settlement of the left bank of the Rhine question which I thought might meet the President's, Lloyd George's and Clemenceau's views. This suggestion was that a buffer state should be created for a period of five years and then the League of Nations should decide whether the buffer state should exercise self determination or should continue for another five year period"[123]). If this proposal was submitted before he received the French Note, then it shows that House had not been advised of the offer of a guarantee before receipt of the Note, and if it was submitted after this, it shows that he must have completely misunderstood not only the Note but also the entire situation. However, regardless of which of these interpretations is correct, the very nature of the proposal still indicates that House was not only poorly informed but was also losing the last remnants of his once so well-developed powers of assessment.

On 18 March, House and Robert Cecil attended a dinner[124]) given by the President as the overture to a discussion on amendments to the League of Nations Covenant. When coffee was served after dinner, Wilson sat beside Cecil and spoke of his great irritation over the French. He said that nothing would make him agree to a division of the country on the West bank of the Rhine, "but he was prepared to agree to something in the nature of an alliance between America and France to protect her against sudden aggression, in addition to the protection which she would already have by the League of Nations. But he appears to have rather spoiled the effect of this conversation by pointing out to Clemenceau that it really amounted to very little more than Article 10 of the Covenant"[125]). We cannot know whether House heard this conversation, but even if he did, or was advised of its contents by Cecil, it is very unlikely that it helped to clarify Wilson's intentions. Even Cecil seems to have been in doubt as to the extent of Wilson's offer. On the other hand, we can establish the fact that Wilson was here ready to discuss matters with Cecil that he did not wish to discuss with House[126]). Thus the situation on the evening of 18 March was still that House was not officially informed of the American policy and was apparently very uncertain of the situation in general.

On 19 March, House finally became personally involved in the negotiations, although in a somewhat different manner than might have been imagined: At 10 a. m. he was called to Clemenceau's office. "Clemenceau told him of the troubles he was having with Lloyd George, particularly with reference to the left bank of the Rhine, and asked for his assistance. This the Colonel promised to give him"[127]). House had thus once more implicated himself in the French efforts to establish a joint French-American front against Britain, i. e. to break the collaboration between Wilson and Lloyd George that had hitherto characterized the Rhineland negotiations.

Compared with the situation during Wilson's absence, however, there was a decisive difference in House's behaviour now, which shows how isolated and insecure he had actually become. He immediately laid the matter before the other members of the American Delegation[128]), although he does not seem to have been entirely open in his statements, giving his colleagues the impression that Clemenceau wanted a guarantee undertaking *within* the framework of the League of Nations Covenant: "The French were apparently not satisfied with the League of Nations as it stood and desired a more explicit guarantee that both England and the United States would come to the assistance of France in case of her invasion at any time in the future. M. Clemenceau had practically threatened that in case such a clause were not added to the League of Nations, the French Government would assume a waiting role and do nothing to further the signing of peace". House therefore asked his colleagues "to consider the matter very earnestly and endeavor to draft, if possible, some modification to the Covenant of the League of Nations which might satisfy the French views"[129]).

House's own activities show clearly, however, that what Clemenceau wanted, and what House was working for, was really an *independent* treaty: the very next day, House submitted the first draft of such a treaty to Clemenceau, who "read it with keen delight . . .". House himself had his doubts as to "the Senate accepting such a treaty but that is to be seen. Meanwhile, it satisfies Clemenceau and we can get on with the real business of the conference. It is practically promising only what we promise to do in the League of Nations, but since Clemenceau does not believe in the League of Nations, it may be necessary to give him *a treaty on the outside*. When he read it he said "A monument ought to be erected to you"[130]). House was thus willing to become Clemenceau's tool—in the service of French policy[131]), but he again sought backing in the American Delegation: he showed the draft treaty to Henry White, who submitted it at the daily meeting of the Commissioners on 20 March. House's colleagues carried out a number of amendments to the draft, but also expressed their view that "the subject matter thereof was most prejudicial to the whole structure of the League of Nations, and to the ideal for which the United States entered the war, and that they therefore would desire further time to consider it"[132]). House's far too tardy attempt to establish cooperation with his colleagues had not met with success, and his isolation was now complete.

The French reaction to the Anglo-American offer of a guarantee was a conditional acceptance: in a Note of 17. 3.[133]), the French accepted the political guarantee, but demanded that this should be supplemented by a number of physical guarantees. In other words, the French relinquished the demand for an independent Rhenish Republic, but demanded instead, inter-Allied occupation of the West bank of the Rhine and bridgeheads on the East bank for 30 years; demilitarization of the West bank of Rhine and a 50 km wide zone on the Eastside; permanent inspection commission in this zone; the right of reoccupation if Germany did not fulfil its obligations; and finally, for the first time, an official demand for the 1814-border, with occupation of the part of the Saar-region not included in this border. This was the proposed compromise on which the negotiators now concentrated. The most difficult and also the most decisive negotiations concerned the latest component of the compromise: the Saar. However, at this early stage of developments, it was the relationship between the demilitarization terms and the offered guarantee on which the negotiations concentrated[134]):

"The real purpose of an agreement with the French is to create a strip of territory which will extend from fifty kilometers east of the Rhine to the western German frontier, in which military operations shall be prohibited, and into which an entry of German military forces would be regarded as an invasion of France in the sense that it should call forth the same responsibilities of Great Britain and the United States as would be called forth by an actual invasion of French territory".

On 21 March, House received from Tardieu a summary of the French demands, and he then asked Wiseman, Miller and Auchincloss to prepare a memorandum on this basis[135]). Both Miller and Auchincloss sympathized with the French demands for physical guarantees, but they were doubtful as to the possibility of fulfilling these effectively. This is clearly stated in the very fine analysis of the situation, which David Hunter Miller gave in a letter to Thomas Lamont on 19 March[136]):

"The question discussed is not only one of the highest political importance but of immediate importance. France does not think that our interest in a future attack of Germany

on France is secondary but primary, and feels that that possibility should be the first concern of the world in general and of America in particular, while admitting that no such
attack for the next few years is possible. Whether this feeling on the part of France
is right or wrong is not the question, for it exists in a degree which it is almost impossible
to overstate, and any attempt to limit our responsibility in the matter would defeat the
whole Covenant, for France would prefer then to make a different kind of peace with
Germany and not have a League. Certainly without the League we could hardly refuse
her the right to make a peace with Germany which would let her feel secure, but such
a peace would then be made as would be contrary to everything we have stood for.
The position of France is that our guarantees must be strengthened and however desirable
it might be it seems impossible in a League of Nations to devise a formula which would
recognize the wishes of France and not give, at least technically, the same sort of guarantees to Poland or Greece.
    It would be possible, of course, to make an alliance with France to that effect but any
such idea is the opposite of the League of Nations".

Despite this, it rapidly appeared that Miller and Auchincloss differed fundamentally as to the procedure to be followed[137]):

"My (Auchincloss's) idea would be to set up fully and frankly the situation in the
treaty of peace itself and not to refer to the League of Nations any more than is absolutely
necessary. David's idea was to have the executive council of the League of Nations pass
a resolution recommending that in the event of aggression by Germany against France
a military force on the part of England and the United States would be deemed the proper
method of meeting this aggression . . .".

Thus whereas Miller's memorandum expressly tied the guarantee to the
League of Nations[138]), Auchincloss—as emphasized by Nelson—wanted to
omit the specific offer of guarantee altogether and simply term violation of
the demilitarization conditions "as an hostile act directed against the signatories of the present Treaty and such act shall be regarded as calculated to
disturb the peace of the world". Otherwise, both authors did their best to fulfil
the French demands, apart from that concerning inspection[139]).
    House preferred Auchincloss's proposal[140]), and he apparently submitted
it to his three colleagues, who "accepted it without reserve, excepting Bliss
who made a tentative reservation."[141]) In the meantime, however, Auchincloss
was becoming very nervous over his father-in-law's transactions:

"Tardieu came in to see the Colonel this afternoon. He and Clemenceau are very much
excited about the settlement of the left bank of the Rhine question. *I am afraid that the
Colonel got them a little too much worked up by holding out to them the hope that
they might get something like this from the United States and England:*
    "Because of the havoc which Germany has brought upon the world by her attack
upon France and Belgium in 1914, and in order to prevent as far as possible such another
disaster to humanity, we hereby solemnly pledge to one another our immediate military,
financial, economic and moral support of and to one another in the event Germany should
at any time make a like unprovoked and unwarranted invasion of the territories of either
one or more of the subscribing powers". *The Colonel has not really discussed this matter
with the President yet and so he cannot tell what the attitude of the United States
will be*".[142])

Here we are thus presented with definite proof that House carried out this
whole series of very far-reaching negotiations without direct contact with Wil-

son. Did House act in desperation? It is at any rate quite clear that the connection between the President and himself was broken at this time and that House was aware of this; he was impatient of the way in which the negotiations between "The Big Three" were dragging on, and he thought he knew the reason for this—that he himself was no longer involved: ". . . I am discouraged at the outlook. We are not moving as rapidly now that the President and Lloyd George are back as we did before. I have no authority to decide questions on my own initiative as I did while the President was away. . . ."[143]). Now something had to happen.

As we have seen, on 24 March, House finally had a talk with the President, and on this occasion he handed to him "a draft which Gordon drew as a solution of the French desires,"[144]) but we are not informed of Wilson's reaction to this plan[145]). As regards the guarantee project itself, however, House was still in two minds, presumably due mostly to the reaction of both colleagues and advisers. In a talk with Orlando on 26 March, for instance, House said that he—like Orlando—felt that a guarantee "would be in contradiction with the League of Nations."[146]) However, that very same evening he found out that the President did not share this view: "He surprised me by saying that he was willing to guarantee with Great Britain that we should come to France's rescue in event of an attack by Germany. I had not shown him the memorandum on this subject which I had drafted, and which Lloyd George, Balfour and Clemenceau had accepted. . . ."[147]).

It is true that when Wilson finally submitted a written proposal to the French Government on 28 March, he followed Auchincloss's suggestion that "(v)iolations of these conditions (governing demilitarization) to be regarded as hostile acts against the signatories to bhe (!) treaty and as calculated to disturb the peace of the world". But despite this, the formulation of the offer of guarantee was entirely his own and did not in the least resemble the various drafts on which House had negotiated with the Allies[148]). On the same day, however, Wilson and Clemenceau clashed in the Council of Four on the question of the Saar, and with this, the negotiations entered a new phase.

The following passage is indicative of the entire situation[149]):

"I spoke to the President about seeing our Commissioners. I have the greatest difficulty in making them feel that I am as much in the dark as to his movements and intentions as they are. They are becoming sensitive and it will be necessary for the President to see them. He promised to do so tomorrow".

This, then, characterized House's activities in the period following Wilson's return: his contact with the President was broken, and he found it impossible to establish contact with the rest of the Delegation; all that now remained to him was the role of independent political adviser to any buyer, as now, for example, Clemenceau[150]), or entirely on his own initiative. House really seems to have taken his decision as early as 14 March, i. e. after his first talk with the President[151]):

"My main drive now is for peace with Germany at the earliest possible moment, and I am determined that it shall come soon if it is within my power to force action. I have the Northcliffe Press at my disposal in this effort, and every day editorials and articles appear which have a tendency to frighten, persuade and coerce".

House had realized that his former position was lost, but he was willing to pursue his own policies, simply for the sake of feeling in on things, or, as he wrote during a phase of the Adriatic crisis: "I am delighted to have the matter coming back into my hands"[152]). All this is, in general, most clearly reflected in the Italian crisis, but it characterizes all his undertakings: the combination of isolation, uncertainty and independence. In this respect, his Russian policy, around which his activities now centred for a while, provides an excellent example.

William C. Bullitt arrived back in Paris on 25 March, and reported that same evening to House, filling him with enthusiasm. He finally thought he could see a solution to the Russian problems and got down at once to the framing of a plan[153]). This he presented next day to Orlando, "and it succeeded admirably." House argued that "Russia had become orderly and wanted to resume relations with the outside world. If we met her in a reasonable way she would agree to leave the boundary lines as they stand today; to stop all fighting on all fronts, and to agree not to use any propaganda in any of the Allies countries, provided propaganda was not used by them in Russia". "It seemed to me footless to say we preferred some other plan. As far as I could see there was no other". It was necessary either to accept the *de facto* government or to remain at war. But everyone agreed that it was not possible to intervene because the troops would not go and fight in Russia. "I suggested that we proceed to draw up a treaty with Russia practically upon our own terms, provided they were just, and send this treaty to Moscow for their signatures, promising to sign it ourselves in the event it was agreed upon here"[154]).

What House was proposing here was, quite simply, *de facto* recognition of the Bolshevik Government[155]). But in this, House was quite on his own; neither his colleagues[156]), nor his closest personal advisers[157]), any more than Wilson himself, shared this view, and next day, House himself abandoned his plan, for "no one wanted to deal with such as Lenine and Trotsky."[158]) House had wanted to take the matter up with the President on 26 March, but he found in a telephone conversation that "his (Wilson's) "one-track" mind is against taking up this question at present,"[159]) and when House finally succeeded in talking to Wilson on 27 March, the Russian policy took an entirely new direction: Wilson asked House to contact Hoover and "see whether we could get ships and food to Russia in the event we wished to do so,"[160]) and House immediately did as requested. The Hoover-Nansen plan[161]) had replaced the House-Bullitt plan.

The fact that Wilson did not wish to discuss the Russian question with

House and Bullitt on 26 March was due neither to his "one-track" mind preventing him from thinking of anything else nor to his having had a headache[162]), but to the fact that he had been won over, presumably that day, to the policy of relief long advocated by Vance McCormick[163]). John M. Thompson has substantiated the fact that this plan, thanks to a report from the State Department (11 March), had once more become a topic of immediacy at this very time; the question had been discussed at a Commission meeting on 20 March, and at meetings between Lansing and McCormick on 24 and 25 March, and Hoover had also been implicated. On 26 March, McCormick had then asked the President for "an appointment to take up important matters in connection with a message he has received from the Secretary of State with regard to Russia".[164]) However, Thompson has not succeeded in providing indisputable proof that McCormick did actually talk to the President on 26 March, but only managed to present "one telling bit of circumstantial evidence:"[165])

"... on March 27 ... when House discussed with Wilson the proposals brought back by Bullitt in the context of the general problem of policy toward Russia, the President suggested that House consult Hoover concerning the possibility of getting food to Russia, a suggestion which led directly to the formulation of the Hoover-Nansen plan. Since there is no indication that Wilson himself was thinking about relief to Russia at this time, it seems not unreasonable to assume that sometime on March 26 or early on March 27 McCormick planted the idea with the President, perhaps not even at a formal appointment, but in a brief conversation held in the corridors, or in Wilson's quarters. The President in turn passed the idea on to House who promptly took it up with Hoover. Although from this time on the proposal for relief to Russia was taken over by Hoover and House, and McCormick faded into the background, it is clear that McCormick, not Hoover, was the inspirer of the plan for feeding Russia subsequently adopted by the peace conference...".

Thompson's evidence of probability can, however, be further supplemented by an observation made by Mayer: "On March 26—the same day that House thought that Wilson was otherwise preoccupied—the President asked Hoover for "a memorandum on (his) information and opinion on the Soviet problem"[166]). And Wilson's request resulted in Hoover's extremely comprehensive memorandum of 28 March[167]). It thus seems clear that, on 26 March, Wilson deliberately made a decision without consulting House, and even though, for a while, House was apparently ready to go his own way on this question as well—"I have telephoned the President, but as usual find that his "one track mind" is against taking up this question at present (Bullitt's report). I would have preferred to have taken it up first with the President, but since he is not in a frame of mind to do so I shall take it up with Lloyd George and see whether I cannot commit him as I have Orlando"[168])—he immediately fell in line[169]) and allowed himself next day to be enrolled in loyal cooperation with Hoover. House was no longer a politically determining factor, but had to content himself with being a mere tool.

All the same, there were certain negotiations from which House, because of his expertise, was not completely excluded. This naturally applied first and foremost to the question of the League of Nations, but he was also still in constant touch with the negotiations on reparations, although only at the Expert level[170]). During the conversation on 24 March, the President also directly requested House "to keep in touch with our financial experts and not let them agree to the absurd figures which some of the French and British financiers still have in mind. ...", and the very same day we hear that House "advised Davis and Lamont and Strauss not to go beyond thirty-five billions, and to agree to such an amount only in the event that a large part of it could be paid in depreciated marks, and a commission appointed with authority to make reductions in the event it was later considered necessary."[171]) Nevertheless, House's increased involvement was still only at the Expert level, and it is typical that he was not engaged at all in the negotiations that led to the inclusion of pensions and separation allowances[172]), the first decisive step on the road of compromise[173]).

At this time, the negotiations had long been in a critical phase[174]): Both Clemenceau and Lloyd George were bound by domestic policy to maintain their astronomical demands[175]), while the American position was primarily based on the pre-Armistice Agreement. However, the American attitude was to prove more flexible than that of the Allies for several reasons: seen from an American viewpoint, the question of reparations was entirely a European affair[176]), and, apart from the purely economic criteria[177]), the standpoint of the American Experts was based mainly on considerations of justice and reasonableness: What could Germany actually pay? "We should give the German people an opportunity to work, but must make them pay to the fullest extent possible for the terrific damage done to the devastated countries"[178]).

America's interests were, therefore, not directly at stake in this question and there was no pressure from domestic politics—on the contrary, America felt considerable sympathy for the Allies—. Everything thus indicated that Wilson's choice would be based on considerations of policy, not principles. His decision to include pensions[179]), despite the attitude of his Experts, which was based on the pre-Armistice Agreement, points clearly in this direction, and a number of his statements during this period seem to show that he was open to a compromise on the entire question[180]); McCormick wrote as follows on 31 March:

"Met with Lamont and Davis on Reparations before going to President's house. Found the President, Lloyd George, Clemenceau, and Orlando closeted. President came out for a few minutes and gave us an opportunity to explain to him that under Lloyd George's plan we would still have to face the question of principle. We showed him the difficulties to be encountered. *He told us to try to overcome them that we should try to meet Lloyd George's and Clemenceau's suggestions as otherwise, he was told by them, their ministries might fall and we would have no government to make peace with for some time to come.* Their plan is to postpone the fixing of the amount Germany is to pay and leaving determination of claims to commission to report upon later ...".

It is worth bearing this in mind as we now attempt to evaluate House's role in the reparations negotiations during the critical phase of the Conference at the beginning of April.

On the evening of 3rd April, Wilson fell ill and had to go to bed, and House was now given the task of deputizing for him during the negotiations in the Council of Four[181]). "Some historians, notably Charles Seymour, interpret Wilson's reliance on House during his illness as a sign of his continued regard for the Colonel. Another explanation suggests itself when one scrutinizes the facts in terms of just what task it was that the President wished his substitute to accomplish for him. Wilson felt he must capitulate to Clemenceau in order to obtain French approval of the Monroe Doctrine amendment. Since this was personally distasteful, Wilson seems to have turned to House to make the necessary concessions", according to Alexander and Juliette L. George; Wilson needed a scapegoat[182]).

It is, however, possible to put a different and possibly equally reasonable complexion on the matter: firstly, it must be realized that if the President needed a deputy, he could only choose House because he was, quite simply, the only American Commissioner with the least idea of what was really going on[183]). Secondly, Wilson actually approached House even *before* his illness, i. e. on the evening of 2 April[184]). This is precisely the date that R. S. Baker also stressed as the critical date, and besides the grounds mentioned above, there is particular reason to concentrate attention on Baker's words because he had had daily talks with the President in this period and was, in general, perhaps the member of the Delegation who best understood Wilson's ideas at this time[185]). Baker wrote[186]):

*"On April 2 the President was at the end of the tether.*
I find in my notes for that day:
"He (the President) said that it could not go on many days longer; that if some decision could not be reached by the middle of next week, he might have to make a positive break. . . .
I spoke of the feeling of unrest in the world, the new revolts in Germany and in Hungary, and of the blame of delay that was everywhere being charged, unjustly, against him.
"I know that", he said, "I know that". He paused. "But we've got to make peace on the principles laid down and accepted, or not make it at all"."

Even more typical, perhaps, of Wilson's state of mind is this entry, which Baker omitted[187]):

"I found the President to-night again much discouraged. . . . He looks tired. He said that it began to seem to him that the French were intentionally delaying the proceedings by endless talk: for what purpose he could not see. . . .
I suggested that the time might come soon when he would have to speak out. The other day when I made a similar proposal he said: "That would break up the Peace Conference. Must do everything I can to keep things together." But tonight it was plain that he had been thinking of the possible necessity of making such a move. "If I speak out", he said, "I should have to tell the truth and place the blame exactly where it belongs—upon the French"."

Wilson had thus now begun seriously to contemplate breaking off the negotiations, but was at the same time prepared to try one last expedient, viz, indirect negotiations through House. House himself regarded it as a turning point[188]):

"Frazier, Gordon, Wiseman and practically all of my entourage have been worried for the last day or two because they did not think I was pushing the President as hard as I ought, and that I was letting matters drift. I have done this deliberately. I saw that things were coming to an impasse and the more I let them alone, the quicker this impasse would come. Frazier was urging me yesterday to see the President. I replied that when the President really needed me he would not hesitate to call. This call came about eight o'clock tonight and we talked for three quarters of an hour over the telephone.

We went over the situation from start to finish. The Sarre Basin, The Rhenish Republic, the protection of France, Dantzig, Fiume, Reparations and whatnot. He declared that the old man was stubborn and that he could not get him to come to a decision. What he really means is that he cannot get Clemenceau to come to his way of thinking.

He asked if I would see Tardieu and find what could be done in that direction. I have asked for Tardieu to be here at ten in the morning. The President asked if I thought Lloyd George was sincere with him. I had my doubts. The general impression is that George is playing him for a rupture with the French. I told the President I could see trouble ahead with George. When one talks of the sea, shipping etc. an Englishman becomes as crazy as a Frenchman when a German is mentioned. He asked to what I referred. I replied "the merchant fleet and the navy building program". He talked as if he would stand firm on both propositions. If he does he will find that the row he is having with Clemenceau is a frolic compared to that which he will have with Lloyd George.

He wishes me to outline to Orlando the boundary and other terms for Italy. I do not relish the job but I promised to do it. I shall see Orlando on Friday and tell him just where we wish the northern and eastern boundaries of Italy to be.

The President tried to get me to admit that the solution which our Experts have proposed and which Clemenceau might be willing to take as to the Sarre Valley, was inconsistent with the Fourteen Points. I replied that there were many who thought otherwise.

I told the President that I intended to tell Tardieu that unless a conclusion was reached within the next ten days that he, the President, would probably go back to America and that we would all go with him. I suggested that I would use the necessity of calling in Special Session Congress and passing appropriation bills as the reason why it would be necessary for his early return. I asked him if he had anyone at the Council of Four meetings who was taking notes. Professor Mantoux is there to do the interpreting for Signor Orlando. The President admitted that he thought Mantoux did not like him. He said, "indeed, I am not sure that anybody does". Mantoux is a Frenchman having a chair at the London University. I consider the President imprudent and reckless to go into these acrimonious meetings with no member of his own staff there to actually report what goes on".

An attempt has been made in the foregoing to demonstrate that in the period following Wilson's return, House found himself in an isolated position, out of contact with the decision-making; that he tried to re-establish this contact through his talk with Wilson on 24 March; but that it was not really established until 2 April, and then on Wilson's initiative. Before we analyse this rapprochement in detail, we must spend a little while considering the contact that had actually taken place before this date. On 25 March, i. e. the day after the assumed "thaw talk", House noted: "I have been in close touch with the President over the telephone", and his diary entries show that he was well informed on the meeting of the Council of Four on this date[189]). However, over the next few days, House's contact with the President became more and more sporadic: 26–27 March: rejection of House's Russian initiative[190]), and short talk with Wilson on 26 March in connection with the meeting in the League of Nations Committee on the Monroe Doctrine and the Guarantee Treaty, respectively[191]). 27 March: formulation of League of Nations Declaration together with Wilson and R. S. Baker[192]). 28 March: talk with Wilson on the Saar. This talk came about on House's initiative and at the request of Lloyd George under the impression of the morning's clash between Clemenceau and Wilson[193]). However, for the next three days—during which the crisis steadily worsened—House had no contact at all with Wilson on the political plane[194]), although he could, as a sort of consolation prize, note in his diary on 1 April[195]):

"The President and I confer quite frequently over our private telephone. This morning I arranged with him to send Colonel Sherman Miles to Monte Negro in response to Mr. Balfour's letter of last night . . .".

However, the President now finally seemed prepared once more to confide in House.

Wilson's talk with House on the evening of 2 April apparently had a dual purpose. The President wanted a general discussion of the entire situation, and at the same time, he entrusted House with two concrete tasks: to negotiate with Tardieu and Orlando, i. e. he wanted to see whether House's speciality, the unofficial, personal negotiations, could save the now almost hopelessly critical situation. He was thus once more prepared to rely on the loyalty of his adviser in this, his moment of extreme need. House was given one more chance. However, if Wilson had been aware of House's comments to the talk, he would probably have been a little more sparing with his trust. The fact of the matter is that House was now not only critical of the President's views but actually took an almost diametrically opposite attitude on points of importance. This applied primarily—now as earlier—to relations with France: House wanted a Franco-American rapprochement and did not consider Lloyd George to be a stable partner, while Wilson had hitherto acted on the basis of the opposite premises.

The principal components of the crisis that was now rapidly approaching its culmination were listed as follows by House: "The Sarre Basin, the Rhenish Republic, the protection of France, Dantzig, Fiume, Reparations . . .", but the question is whether this covered all the controversial points and how the Great Powers stood in relation to each other on these. As we have seen in the foregoing, the League of Nations[196]) formed the crux of Wilson's conception, for reasons of both domestic and foreign policy. To the above list it is therefore necessary to add yet another component: the inclusion of the Monroe Doctrine in the League of Nations Covenant[197]):

"Three of the four amendments which the President sponsored were quickly conceded by his fellow negotiators at the Peace Conference. At the same time, however, they made it clear that they would withhold their approval of the most important amendment of all, that acknowledging the validity of the Monroe Doctrine. Now, there was nothing in the Monroe Doctrine amendment significantly at variance with the interests of either Britain or France. But the perceptive Allied leaders correctly concluded that their power to obstruct Wilson's amendments and, indeed, to withhold support of the League as it was finally constituted, was the most effective bargaining weapon at their disposal. Faced with the formidable task of getting Wilson to agree to their various demands, Clemenceau and Lloyd George let it be known that their approval of the Monroe Doctrine amendment would be contingent upon Wilson's making concessions on the matters uppermost in their minds".

There was, however, no question of a joint Allied front against the United States, or—which might also have been a possibility—of an Anglo-American alliance: The threads were far more tangled than that.

The question of reparations was presumably the field in which a joint Allied front came closest to being formed: "The negotiations over reparations took the form of a series of contests between the United States on the one side and Great Britain and the continental Allies on the other, with the latter usually successful". It is true that the British policy was not very clearly defined, and that there were conflicting views in the Delegation, but "when decisions had to be made, the pressures of British public and parliamentary Opinion drove the Prime Minister to take his position for large or undefined sums". "On no issue at the Peace Conference did British and American policies conflict more directly and more fundamentally than on the question of reparations"[198]). The problems of the French security demands—The Rhenish Republic and the Treaty of Guarantee—were, on the other hand, the questions on which the British and the Americans cooperated best[199]). The problem of Fiume was characterized by a more or less favourable Anglo-French attitude to Wilson's uncompromising standpoint; but it proved difficult —due to the Treaty of London, to translate the goodwill evinced into concrete political terms[200]).

The vital issue was now how these conflicting demands could be combined with the basic elements of the American policy, viz, the League of Nations and the Fourteen Points. In this context, two questions became of particular interest: the Anglo-American naval negotiations and the conflict relating to the French demands on the Saar. However, whereas Lloyd George simply made an Anglo-American naval settlement a condition of signing the League of Nations Covenant[201]), the Saar-conflict was principally Wilson's own choice —a fact that historians have tended to overlook—[202]). Wilson chose the Saar as a symbol of the Fourteen Points and as a proof of their observation, and he also saw his chance of using the Saar as a quid pro quo for French consent to the incorporation of the Monroe Doctrine in the League of Nations Covenant.

The President's approach to House came at a time when the latter was rapidly losing patience[203]), and he immediately grabbed the chance he had been given: on 3 April he had long talks with Tardieu and Orlando, as agreed with Wilson[204]). That very evening, the President fell ill[205]):

"Mrs Wilson telephoned tonight that the President was sick with a cold and had gone to bed. She wished to know whether I thought he had better remain in bed or try to have a meeting of the Council of Four tomorrow. I advised remaining in bed since as far as I can see, it would be just as effective as any meeting they might have".

Was House perhaps relieved and did he begin to see a chance of once more having a final say in matters? In any event, he behaved so strangely that evening that he inspired Ray Stannard Baker to make the following, almost clairvoyant entry in his diary[206]):

"I had a long talk this evening with Colonel House who was sitting in his long lounge with a figured blanket on his chilly legs—quite serenely dictating his diary to Miss Denton. More and more he impresses me as the dilettante—the lover of the game—the eager secretary. Without profound responsibility—he stands in the middle of great events, to lose nothing. He gains experiences to put in his diary, makes great aquaintances, plays at getting important men together for the sheer joy of making them agree. He is a matchless conciliator but with the faults of his virtue for he conciliates over the border of minor disagreements into the solid flesh of principle. I found him tonight quite cheerful: quite optimistic. Told me that if he had it to do he could make peace in an hour! Were the Italians going home: well and good, let them go! Was Lloyd George going to issue a defense (as I intimated to him) which might compromise the President—all right let him issue it! I told him of the President's illness (of which I had just been talking with Grayson) and said that Grayson told me that the President had probably contracted his cold from contact with Clemenceau who coughs fearfully. "I hope", said the Colonel genially, "that Clemenceau will pass on the germ to Lloyd George". The Colonel had conferences today with Tardieu and Orlando and told them (as he assured me) just what the American position was—Thus, a bright kindly little man, optimistic in the presence of tragic events! . . .".

Next morning House received orders from the President "to take his place in the Council of Four which was to meet at his residence."[207]) Here was his chance! Auchincloss wrote[208]):

"The Colonel also told me that the President was sick in bed with some fever and a bad cold and that it was necessary for him to go to the Big Four meetings in the President's place. *The President's illness may help break the impasse now existing*".

It is, at any rate, a fact that House approached his new assignment not only fully determined that something should happen now, but also fully determined that it should happen in close collaboration with Clemenceau. The events of the very first day (4 April) provide ample proof of this:

The morning meeting of the Council of Four was devoted to the Belgian King's presentation of Belgian views. And House was frustrated: "I can easily see how the time has been wasted in the Council of Four. . . . It was all talk and a promise to look into matters later"[209]). House himself insisted that he "tried to get Lloyd George down to the matter of priority[210]) but it was impossible. That was too near accomplishment"[211]). However, Mantoux's minutes of the meeting do not indicate special activity on the part of House in this matter[212]). Nevertheless, the Belgian King's speech of presentation also led to a discussion of the Rhineland problem, and here House got the opportunity of showing that he would be willing to take a far more favourable attitude to the French demands than President Wilson: Clemenceau now raised once more the question of surveillance against possible German rearmament, saying, inter alia[213]),

" Le Président Wilson n'aime pas l'idée de commissions permanentes surveillant l'état militaire de l'Allemagne. Je ne tiens pas à des commissions permanentes, mais il nous faut un moyen d'enquête immédiate en cas de besoin".

House willingly replied[214]):

" Je dois dire que je ne partage pas le sentiment du Président Wilson sur les commissions. A mon avis, si une puissance ne fait que ce qu'elle a le droit de faire, elle n'a aucune raison de s'offenser d'une inspection quelconque ".

Lloyd George, on the other hand, was unsympathetic[215]), and no decision was reached.

After the meeting House reported to Mrs. Wilson, but declined an invitation to lunch: He had a prior arrangement with one of his colleagues[216]). At the afternoon meeting, it had been agreed that the future borders of Czechoslovakia should be discussed, and now the House–Clemenceau contact had already been systematized[217]):

". . . Our Experts had drawn a line which ran in and out of the old territory, (the Bohemian border—the Sudetenland) throwing some of the old Austria into Germany and placing many Germans in Austria. The French and English agreed upon the entire line.

I reached the Ministry of War five or six minutes in advance of George and Orlando and by the time they arrived, Clemenceau and I had agreed to adopt the old historic boundary line and not attempt the new one. It was so much simpler and less full of possibilities for trouble. We had but little difficulty in persuading both George and Orlando to accept our conclusions, George seeming to know but little about it . . .".

Thus, on this question too, House made common cause with Clemenceau, even going against the advice of his own Experts.

In this instance Lloyd George had given his consent, but he was fully aware that a continuation of the newly established Franco-American collaboration would have unpleasant consequences for British policies. House described the situation as follows to his son-in-law[218]):

". . . It is very clear that George is not satisfied with the turn affairs are taking. The Colonel admitted what I (Auchincloss) have always contended that George was trying to undermine the Colonel's influence and was fighting him just as hard as he could. George took the position that a number of these things had better be deferred because he wanted to have the President decide them. He is going to try to take the position that the Colonel is not competent to decide these questions and that he wishes the President to be present at the conferences before taking them up. George sees that the Colonel and Clemenceau can play together and that they can put the steam roller over him, while with the President George has a much better chance of getting away with his side of the argument. It is an exceedingly interesting game that is being played here now. Tomorrow the Colonel is going to try to force through a decision on the reparation question. George will not want to sign it but the Colonel is going to insist upon it".

House was now determined to get the negotiations moving, and he did not try to hide the fact that he was aiming at a solution of the reparations question: "Le Colonel HOUSE estime que le moment est venu de prendre une résolution et qu'il est possible de la faire à bref délai"[219]). At the same time, however, the next meeting was planned to take place at Wilson's house "pour que le Colonel House puisse prendre immédiatement l'avis du Président Wilson,"[220]) and the same evening, House explained his view to the American economic Experts[221]). The stage was therefore set for the big break-through in the negotiations next day.

However, even before he had managed to benefit from his regained influence, the situation began to disintegrate, and on 4 April, everything apparently collapsed, House himself wrote[222]):

"I was glad to hear, in talking with Mrs. Wilson over the telephone that the President was better. I explained what I had done at the two meetings. After she had told the President, he was evidently alarmed at the rapidity of the decisions and had her telephone me back that he hoped I would not commit myself in the question of the Sarre Valler (!) and the left bank of the Rhine. I replied that these question(s) had been up with Tardieu only and I was not committed any further than that Tardieu knew my views and knowing them, had prepared the memorandum".

And R. S. Baker exploded[223]):

"The Colonel would make peace quickly by giving the greedy ones all they want!"

From other quarters too, dissatisfaction with House—and Auchincloss—began to make itself felt. McCormick wrote[224]):

"Baruch and McFadden came in before bed. Baruch very sore at our Allies on account of unfair tactics at Economic meeting, also sore at Colonel's crowd, which he thought too free in criticising President to outsiders.
    These are strange days and everyone tired and irritable and we will have to keep our heads and keep cool for we are just passing over the peak and still have some rough going before we land".

At the same time, Auchincloss, writing in his diary, lifted a corner of the veil concealing his various transactions[225]):

"After the meeting of the Big Four (morning 4.4) I had a short talk with the Colonel and Lloyd George. George referred to Steeds attacks and said that Steed had been using matter that we (looking at me) had no doubt given him in confidence and that he, George, thought that was the worst thing a newspapersman could do. I did not comment but just stared George back. He is playing a slick game and is getting nervous on account of the attacks in the Daily Mail and London Times. I happen to know that he sees Steed almost raily. *Of course, I realize that I am playing with fire also but I may be able to escape getting burned*".

Soon the air was thick with rumours. On 7 April, Josephus Daniels, the American Secretary of the Navy, who was staying in Paris at the time, reported after a talk with McCormick that "He and Baruch are doing very important work and will compromise anything except principle and justice. Others here have compromised and shifted so long think frank statement sensational"[226]). And two days later, Lord Reading advised Wiseman from Washington that "(e)xtraordinary statements are appearing in press from noted correspondents in Paris for example Frank Simonds and Frederick Moore that Wilson and Lloyd George are at loggerheads, that Wilson has thrown over House, that Lloyd George is aligning himself with France against United States. The main points are said to be (a) Reparation (b) Saar Valley (c) recognition of Russia . . ."[227]).

Two months later, the rumours had taken more concrete form. Thus, Henry Morgenthau wrote after a talk with William H. Buckler, that "House's stock (has) been going down . . . partly due to fact that through Steed he had arranged adjustment. Wilson refused to conform as it was contrary to his basic principles—it made H(ouse) mad and he said he can't comprehend Wilson's actions all the time . . ."[228]) while Buckler himself wrote to his wife[229]):

"I rode yesterday morning with Rear Admiral Grayson, (The President's A. D. C. and constant companion), who confirms my impressions as to the waining of the 'Colonel's' (i. e. House) influence. *This is partly due to his own mistakes, but more to the indiscretion and boastfullness of his son-in-law*".

What was it then, that happened not so much within as outside the Council of Four during the days of Wilson's indisposition?

In the latest accounts of "the break" between Wilson and House, and particularly in George and George's very penetrating analysis of the friendship between the two men, the view is taken that there was actually a gradual development caused by a complicated set of factors[230]):

"It was an unfortunate combination of circumstances—Wilson's increased sensitivity to House as a possible competitor and House's overpowering desire to "come into his own" —that contributed heavily to *the gradual waning* of the President's enthusiasm for his closest collaborator. *No one incident marks the end of the friendship between Wilson and House*. The relationship was never terminated in a clearcut fashion. Rather, Wilson gradually withdrew his affection and gradually ceased to consult House".

For Paul Birdsall, on the other hand, it was the events during the Italian–American negotiations on Fiume in the middle of April that were crucial[231]). He did, however, also stress the decisive difference between the views of the two men on the strategy and tactics of negotiations, and he became one of the severest critics of House's enthusiasm for compromise: House was willing to agree to everything in order to get the League of Nations through[232]). However, Birdsall's argument is considerably weakened by the fact that he has to admit that Wilson suffered from the same fundamental weakness[233]):

"Henry White suggests that Colonel House was responsible personally for fatal concessions to nationalist greed in order to purchase support for the League, but he said more generally of Wilson: "The fact is that the League of Nations in which he has been more deeply interested than anything else from the beginning . . . has been played to the limit by the French and Japanese in extracting concessions from him; to a certain extent by the British too, and the Treaty as it stands is the result. The Italians overshot the mark" ".

196

It is perhaps also typical that the compromise that awakened the greatest indignation of all, i. e. the Shantung decision—was reached after House had lost every scrap of influence over the President[234]).

Nevertheless, the problems of compromise did undoubtedly play a serious part both during the Conference and in the entire subsequent debate: the obvious discrepancy between the Fourteen Points and the pre-Armistice Agreement on the one hand, and the final form of the Treaty[235]) on the other, was important in this respect, but of equal importance, as far as American criticism was concerned, was the notion that Wilson could have dictated peace terms on *his own conditions*. Research in recent years has, however, resulted in a rather different perspective: The Fourteen Points were not eternal principles to Wilson, but weapons for use in his political propaganda[236]); and the President's views on Germany were not just "that a settlement of moderation which did not seek the destruction of Germany as a World Power would best serve the interest of all,"[237]) but a far more composite synthesis of "reintegrationist" and "punitive" tendencies[238])—in reality, a self-contradictory policy based on a subtle balance between Allied and German extremism[239]), and a policy whose inner tensions could only be released through the successful implementation of the League of Nations[240]):

"Since he (Wilson) was unwilling to risk either the control of Germany or world liberal order by openly moving toward solidarity with the non-Bolshevik Left in opposition to German and/or Allied imperialism at Paris, Wilson was forced to devise another policy for the defense of his international goals. . . . Somehow a program would have to be devised which, while permitting Germany to be punished and controlled, would nonetheless retain enough reintegrationist features to assure the gradual reabsorption of Germany into a viable non-Bolshevik world of liberal order. Moreover, such a program would also have to be able to legitimize ideologically the co-opting of American power into the maintenance of a basically anti-German peace settlement, by providing a liberal vision going beyond mere punitive righteousness. .. Ultimately such a program was available to Wilsonians in the form of the League of Nations. . . . (F)or the President, the League seemed to resolve all the contradictions latent in his policies at the Paris Peace Conference".

Seen in this perspective, the difference between the aims of Wilson and those of House were, perhaps, not so very great.

However, it is essential for the present analysis to decide whether Wilson felt that House had failed him, whether he had reasons for thinking so, and, in the affirmative, when he was given these reasons. In the foregoing, it has been argued that the "contemporary" accounts, principally those of Baker and Steed, which date the "break" to immediately after Wilson's return to Paris, come closest the truth, i. e. that both the theory of a "gradual development" and the theory of the decisive importance of the Italian question must be rejected, because it has been possible to demonstrate that House actually had no influence at all on vital decisions after Wilson's return and that Wilson only used him in top negotiations again in a moment of desperation. As we shall now see, there is every indication that this new period of trust was of extremely short duration. It began on the evening of 2 April and ended on 4 or 5 April. And the reason for the abrupt end is to be sought in the combination of factors indicated by the passages quoted above.

In his memoirs, Wickham Steed stresses how impossible it is to reproduce the atmosphere in Paris during the Peace negotiations, "and without knowledge of the atmosphere, many of the words and deeds of the leading actors in that historic tragi-comedy must ever be incomprehensible"[241]. And it was Wickham Steed, more than any other man, who came to influence the atmosphere during the most critical phase of the Conference, because just at that time, Lord Northcliffe[242] began his frontal attack on Lloyd George, and his most important weapons for this purpose included Steed's editorials in the (Paris) Daily Mail and The Times[243]. What began as an attack on Lloyd George for his presumed policy of recognition in respect of the Bolsheviks and his "taking a "soft" line on Germany and ... not extracting the largest possible reparations from the defeated enemy"[244], soon developed into an attack on the American President as well: Wilson was accused of supporting Germany and failing France, and Lloyd George was attacked for preferring a pro-American line rather than supporting France[245]. R. S. Baker regarded the attack as a deliberate effort to split Lloyd George and Wilson and drive Lloyd George straight into the arms of Clemenceau[246].

"High policies are being played a desperate effort is being made to separate Wilson and Lloyd George. Northcliffe and his press are attacking George bitterly for his "kindness" to the Germans and his effort to work with the Russians. ... It is a struggle between Northcliffe and Wilson for the soul of Lloyd George—who has no soul".

In this dangerous game, Auchincloss was very directly implicated, even though, as we have seen, at an earlier stage House had also played with the idea of exercising influence over the Conference through the Northcliffe-Press[247].

It was Auchincloss who provided Steed with a considerable part of the ammunition with which he thwarted all attempts by Lloyd George to support Bullitt's peace plan[248], and he went even further than that. In talks with Northcliffe and Steed, he encouraged them to bring pressure to bear not only on Lloyd George but also on Wilson[249]. However, in this extremely illoyal behaviour, Auchincloss appears to have been acting entirely on his own initiative and House was apparently not involved. All the same, as we have seen, this conduct did not escape the notice of either Lloyd George[250] or Wilson's closest advisers[251]. Both Lloyd George and Bernard Baruch reacted on 4 April, and there is really no reason for thinking that Wilson was kept ignorant of matters much longer than this. Even though House can hardly have been personally involved, it is obvious that the responsibility for his son-in-law's irresponsible actions must, in the end, rebound on him, especially as the policy recommended in Steed's articles: an approach to Clemenceau and implementation of the French demands, was precisely the same as that advocated by House. And it is the recognition of this that R. S. Baker expresses so vehemently on 4 April: "The Colonel would make peace quickly by giving the greedy ones all they want!"[252]) and that he repeated some days later in more considered terms[253]):

"I had a long talk with Colonel House. He is *still* working with Clemenceau and North-cliffe and opposes Lloyd George, while the President works with Lloyd George—and finds Clemenceau his hardest opponent".

By 28 March, Franco-American relations had finally reached a critical phase. It was on this date that the big clash took place between Wilson and Clemenceau on the question of the French demands on the Saar:[254]) "It seems that they were near an open rupture." On that date, Tardieu submitted the French demands in the Council of Four: "His minimum demand was the 1814 frontier; the maximum, the entire Saar Basin."[255]) The French demands were based on both economic and historical arguments, the first of which made the deepest impression: "Comme réparation spéciale de la destruction de ses mines aussi bien que comme élément necessaire de la réparation total, la France est fondée à revendiquer le bassin de la Sarre"[256]). Both Wilson and Lloyd George recognized the fact[257]) that France was entitled to compensation for the devastation wrought by the Germans, but there agreement ended. While Lloyd George drafted the idea of the Saar as an autonomous state, with its coalmines the property of the French, Wilson began a discussion of principles. He made it clear that his views were dictated by the principles involved in the pre-Armistice Agreement and the right of self-determination[258]), while Clemenceau met this with a demand for "une justice non mathématique, mais qui tienne compte du sentiment."[259]) The lines were thus sharply drawn up, and the American President had now placed himself in a position of isolation, not only as regards Clemenceau, but also as regards Lloyd George and his own Experts. Indeed, more than that, his uncompromising attitude represented a change in his own standpoint as well. The question is: Why?

Both Lloyd George and Wilson emphasized on 28 March that they had heard nothing about the French Saar-demands until after the Armistice[260]), so these were not covered by either mutual agreements or promises to Germany. However, right back in November, Clemenceau had discussed the problem with House, who had promised to give the matter sympathetic attention, but had failed to advise Wilson of what had passed[261]). Nonetheless, the American Experts had given their views on the problem on several occasions— and these views had always been favourable to the French demands[262]), while House had apparently given the go-ahead for the French plans in his talk with Tardieu on 2 March[263]). Indeed, the President himself, in his talks with Lloyd George in December, had apparently expressed approval although not in final terms: ". . . he might be prepared to accept the French annexation of the Saar Valley."[264])

However, on 28 March, the whole thing took on quite another complexion. The day before, the Council of Four had discussed the question of the Rhineland, and the negotiations had revealed that the distance between the parties was still great: ". . . Clemenceau faced an almost solid Lloyd George–Wilson front."[265]) In fact, however, Anglo-American agreement at this time was not all that it appeared, the meetings in the League of Nations Committee having been discontinued for the time being, primarily because Lloyd George had decided to exploit Wilson's desire for incorporation of the Monroe Doctrine in the League of Nations Covenant as a quid pro quo for an Anglo-American naval settlement[266]). Wilson's unfavourable negotiating position was now generally apparent. The political situation in the United States was forcing him to push through a number of amendments to the League of Nations Covenant, and both the British and the French[267]) were determined to use these amendments—first and foremost, the Monroe Doctrine—as bargaining counters. It is then, from this angle that the Saar-negotiations should rightly be considered[268]).

The demands relating to the Saar were thus presented at a time when both Clemenceau and Wilson needed an opening, and whatever the motives behind the French "timing", it is obvious that Wilson here saw a chance of forcing the French Government to accept the addition of the Monroe Doctrine and of once more bringing his fundamental principles into the limelight. The American President needed, quite simply, to reassert his position as the leader of Liberalism, a position that was becoming seriously endangered[269]). There was certainly no lack of exhortations that he should make a public stand[270]). However, the President was fully cognizant of the dangers of such a course— it might well entail the collapse of the Conference and the dissolution of the Alliance, and these were risks that he was unwilling to take—at any rate, in the first instance[271]). What he could do, however, was to make an example. The Saar provided a suitable object as far as the French were concerned, and Fiume, as far as the Italians were concerned[272]). But House apparently failed to realize this.

House learned of the clash between Clemenceau and Wilson during a lunch with Lloyd George on the same day (28 March), and at the request of the Prime Minister, he then sought out the President and urged him "to bring the British into harmony with his position on the French boundary proposals." House considered that it would be a tactical error for the Americans to take a special standpoint and "advised yielding a little in order to secure harmony so that the accusation could not be made that we were unreasonable". According to House, Wilson promised this[273]). House thus here appears to have misunderstood Wilson's attitude completely, due partly to lack of information; what looked to House like a simple tactical question was in fact, a point of principle to Wilson. It is further important to note that House does not seem to have received any invitation from the President to participate in the negotiations at any level at all. Yet House was already in conference with the American Experts next day "(to) see what could be done to straighten out the situation between the President and Clemenceau." However, this fresh initiative on the part of House was made not at the request of Wilson, but of Tardieu and Clemenceau[274]). Therefore, in order to understand House's attitude in the days to come, it is essential to remember that his information on the matter came from Haskins, the American Expert, and from Tardieu—and Haskins' views lay very close to those of the French[275]):

"I sent for Haskins and Mezes. Haskins believes the President too severe and that the economic reasons for letting France have the Sarre Valley are fairly reasonable. I saw Haskins several times during the day and also Mezes and Bowman. They had conferences with Tardieu, with the British and with the President, and each time reported back to me for information and instructions. Haskins and Tardieu have tentatively thought that if France could get a ten or fifteen year total occupation of the Sarre Valley and then have a plebicite (!) held, it would perhaps be the best solution. I am inclined to think so myself. I do not like the latest proposals to let France have the ownership of the mines and work them while the territory remains in German hands. It would certainly lead to trouble".

On 31 March, Wilson gave his consent to "French ownership of the coalmines and a special economic regime to facilitate French exploitation of their resources. ... (T)he major problem (now) became the issue of sovereignty"[276]). This became the cardinal point for Wilson—here, the principle of the right of self-determination of the people was involved and here, an example had to be made[277]). The plan House now instigated in collaboration with Steed was therefore most unfortunate. It came from the desire of the two men to establish a rapprochement between Clemenceau and Wilson, and was born during a talk on 31 March[278]): ". . . If I (Steed) could persuade Clemenceau to come closer to the President, he House, would do his utmost to get the President closer to Clemenceau so that contact between the two men might be reestablished. "At present", concluded House, "your little Welshman has manoeuvered the President so skilfully against Clemenceau that the two are not on speaking terms"."

Steed approved of the plan, and visited Clemenceau next day (1 April)[279]). Both before and afterwards, he had long talks with Auchincloss[280]). Steed's talk with the French Prime Minister showed clearly the distance between Clemenceau and Wilson at this time, but Clemenceau was still willing to make one more effort if Steed could ensure Wilson's acceptance of the proposal that Steed, by agreement with House, had taken with him[281]). House was enthusiastic about the result: "I have rarely seen the Colonel more pleased,"[282]) and Steed got to work straight away on the written formulation of the proposal, which was then sent to Wilson with House's handwritten recommendation[283]). Steed's proposal comprised two sections: One of these dealt with the Saar, and the other with the question of the Rhineland, and it was characteristic of both proposals that they lay far closer to the French viewpoints than to Wilson's. The Saar proposal had been arrived at after discussions not only with House, but also with Haskins[284]), and it was practically identical with a letter sent by the American Expert to Wilson as the result of his discussions with the British and French Experts[285]). The Rhineland proposal distinguished itself by adopting the right of occupation, precisely one of the decisive points separating France and United States-Britain at this stage of the negotiations[286]). Steed's letter was passed to Wilson by Hugh Frazier, who reported to Steed next day (2 April) on Wilson's reaction[287]):

" "He turned me out", said Frazier.
  "Who?" I (Steed) asked.
  "The President", he answered. "I took your letter and formulas up to him last night. He had hardly glanced through them when he flew into a terrible rage. He threw them on to the table and shouted, 'I will not have it. I will not have it. Unless my principles are accepted integrally I will order the "George Washington" at once and go home. What do you mean by bringing me things which are in flagrant contradiction with my principles?'—and, literally he turned me out of his room".
  "Then Clemenceau is quite right", I replied. "Your President is an utterly impossible fellow. How do my formulas violate his principles?"
  "I cannot guess, and he did not say", answered Frazier.
  "He explained nothing, but just bundled me out" ".

Even though Steed's version must naturally be taken for what it is—in particular, the mention of the "George Washington" smacks more than a little of rationalization after the event—it can hardly be doubted that it does cover the core of Wilson's reaction: blank rejection on grounds of principle, a reaction that fits in well with the entire attitude of the President at this time, as described in the foregoing, and that seems to confirm the passages cited earlier: "House's stock (has) been going down ... *partly due to the fact that through Steed he had arranged adjustment. Wilson refused to conform as it was contrary to his basic principles*—it made H(ouse) mad and he said he can't comprehend Wilson's actions all the time ..."[288]). Nevertheless, Wilson's rage can hardly have been entirely objective in view of the fact that he received an almost identical proposal from Haskins on the same day without finding due reason therein for casting him off as Expert[289]). The only explanation seems to be that Wilson's agitation was due only in part to the actual content of the proposal; what particularly infuriated him was its author: Steed— the man behind the press campaign that was still going on[290]). At the same time, however, Wilson did not yet seem to realize just how deeply House was involved, since on 2 April he once more took House into his confidence[291]). It was not until he became aware, a few days later, of the full extent of House's complicity that the last link in the chain of evidence was forged.

Steed reacted to Wilson's rejection with an editorial in "The Daily Mail" on 4 April[292]), which revealed a thorough knowledge of the negotiations in the Council of Four and contained a very direct and pronounced attack on President Wilson. As we have seen, both Lloyd George and Bernard Baruch reacted sharply to this attack, which they apparently connected with Auchincloss[293]), and Wilson's reaction can hardly have been less vehement. At the same time, it became clear to the President that House's negotiations with

Tardieu had not given the result desired by Wilson but had, on the contrary, been continued on the same lines as those proposed by Steed, i. e. with the aim of achieving a French-oriented compromise[294]) or, as Baker wrote, "The Colonel would make peace quickly by giving the greedy ones all they want!"[295]) The wheel had now turned full circle.

On 5 April came the decisive breakthrough in the negotiations on reparations, just as House had promised at the meeting the day before[296]). The demand for a time limit for German reparations was now finally abandoned, just as the idea of a definite sum for the reparations had been abandoned earlier. Here, House acted counter to the advice of the American Experts, but —and this is the significant point that even his strongest critics have stressed— Wilson gave his consent to this[297]). As described above, House's policy of concessions on the question of reparations was completely in line with that already begun by Wilson himself: the Alliance must not be jeopardized on that account[298]).

Although there is thus no reason for thinking that it was this question that proved to be the last straw for the President, there is every reason to point out that it was at any rate the last important decision in which House was allowed to participate. It is true that he was entrusted with the task of negotiating with Lord Cecil on a naval settlement with England in return for British acceptance of the incorporation of the Monroe Doctrine in the League of Nations Covenant, but this was at the initiative of Lloyd George[299]), and House was not even informed of the most important step Wilson took in this entire period: the summoning of the USS "George Washington", viz, the threat to leave the negotiating table[300]).

While House himself apparently regarded the solution of the question of reparations as the big breakthrough in the negotiating crisis[301]), the President and the other Commissioners obviously took another view. The 6 April was a Sunday, there were no meetings in the Council of Four, and Wilson was still confined to bed. Nevertheless, in the afternoon he summoned *all* the Commissioners to a meeting at his home. This was in itself a serious sign of crisis: it had been a long time since the President had last felt himself prompted to inform his colleagues on the Commission of his policy, let alone ask for their advice[302]). It is also significant that House was astonished to find the other Commissioners participating, and it is characteristic of the situation in which he once more found himself that he had not been advised in advance of either the meeting or its purpose[303]).

It was at this meeting that House got the consent of the President to the reparations compromise[304]), but it is clear from all contemporary reports that this was only a collateral circumstance, which he may even have brought up himself; the real purpose of the meeting was something quite different: Wilson wanted to sound out the feeling of the Commission as regards a possible discontinuation or threat of discontinuation of the negotiations with the Allies[305]).

The President seems to have operated with the alternatives of either convening the Plenary Session of the Conference, i. e. full publicity in the negotiations, or of threatening to go home. There had been no lack recently of encouragement to initiate one of these measures under some form or other, but Wilson had time and again refused to go so far. However, by the evening of 2 April, i. e. the evening on which he again restored House to favour for a short while, he appears to have changed his mind. At any rate, R. S. Baker reports as follows on a talk he had with the President[306]):

"I found the President tonight again much discouraged ... He looks tired. He said that it began to seem to him that the French were intentionally delaying the proceedings by endless talk: for what purpose he could not see ... I suggested that the time might come soon when he would have to speak out. The other day when I made a similar proposal he said: "That would break up the Peace Conference. Must do everything I can to keep things together". But tonight it was plain that he had been thinking of the possible necessity of making such a move. "If I speak out", he said, "I should have to tell the truth and place the blame exactly where it belongs—upon the French".

"The downfall of a government in France", I said, "is not as serious a matter as it would be in England".

He said that it could not go on many days longer: that if some decision could not be reached by the middle of next week, he might have to make some positive break.

...

I spoke of the feeling of most of the world: and of the blame that was everywhere being charged against him. "I know that", he said, "I know that". He paused. "But we've got to make peace on the principles laid down and accepted or not make it all". ....".

i. e. once again the alternatives, public statement or return home, with an open break as at least a likely result.

The predominant opinion in the American Delegation was as follows[307]):

"We are all hoping that the President will announce to his colleagues that if they do not promptly come to an agreement he will go home and let Congress decide for itself what it will do. If anything will bring them to time, such an announcement will do it."

From America too, an opinion was signified, when Tumulty telegraphed on 5 April[308]):

"In my opinion the President must in some dramatic way clear the air of doubts and misunderstandings and despair which now pervade the whole world situation. He must take hold of the situation with both hands and shake it out of its present indecision, or political sabotage and scheming will triumph. Only a bold stroke by the President will save Europe and perhaps the world. That stroke must be made regardless of the cries and admonitions of his friendly advisers. He has tried to settle the issue in secret, only publicity of a dramatic kind can now save the situation. This occasion calls for that audacity which has helped him win in every fight".

But Tumulty's appeal was not explicit: was it a public statement or a break, or threat of a break, that he recommended?

When Wilson finally made his choice, it was a compromise: he sent for the USS "George Washington", the ship that had been taking him back and forth over the Atlantic, but he took care that the press notice covering this was worded in quite neutral terms[309]). Nevertheless, the message was understood for what it really was, viz, a threat[310]). The question is now whether it is possible to elucidate the background for Wilson's choice of time and form of threat, and the priority given to the individual elements of his policy[311]). Ray Stannard Baker has, rightly, I think, stressed the direct connection between Wilson's decision and Tumulty's telegram[312]), i. e. the very great importance Wilson laid on American opinion. However, the step the President took was not the public appeal to which Tumulty seemed inclined, but a step that left the door ajar for further negotiation—although negotiation under pressure[313]), i. e. he was willing to give the Alliance one more chance, but it would have to be on *his* terms.

We have innumerable witnesses to the fact that it was primarily the French obstruction that weighed on the President[314]). It was the French demands in respect of the Rhineland, including the Saar, that were mainly responsible for blocking the negotiations, and it was House's conciliation on precisely these questions that had made Wilson react so strongly on 4 April[315]). It is also clear that the French "got the message": On the morning of 8 April "there even appeared one of those extraordinary little items in *Le Temps* which everyone recognized at once as inspired. It was headed "France's Claims", and ran as follows:

"Contrary to the assertations spread by the German press and taken up by other foreign newspapers, we believe that the French Government has no annexationist pretensions, openly or under cover, in regard to any territory inhabited by a German population. This remark applies particularly to the regions comprised between the frontier of 1871 and the frontier of 1814."

This latter region was of course the Saar Valley, and this statement, although upon close examination, somewhat ambiguous, symbolized a turning point in the Conference"[316]). The question is whether the threat had had the desired effect—whether Wilson had anyway managed to force an opening in the negotiations.

On 31 March, the Council of Four had appointed a commission comprising Tardieu, Headlam-Morley and Haskins, with the following terms of reference[317]):

"1. That full ownership of the coal-mines of the Saar Basin should pass to France to be credited on her claims against Germany for reparation.
 2. That for the exploitation of these mines the fullest economic facilities shall be accorded to France, including particularly:
    (a) Exemption from taxation on the part of Germany, including import and export dues.
    (b) Full mobility of labour, foreign and native.
    (c) Freedom for the development of adequate means of communication by rail and water.
 3. That the political and administrative arrangements necessary to secure the foregoing results be enquired into".

On 6 April, this commission presented "an elaborate draft embodying the principle of French ownership of the Saar mines. The proposals were based upon Tardieu's initiative. Headlam-Morley and Haskins signed them"[318]). In an accompanying note it was stated, inter alia, "If these articles, the substance of which appears economically and socially necessary, were to be applied without the establishment of some special political and administrative regime, serious friction and conflict would inevitably arise"[319]). However, at the meeting of the Council of Four on the morning of 8 April, the committee's report was rejected by Lloyd George. "The combination of French ownership of the mines and German sovereignty would only produce disputes. Instead, he favoured an independent state under the League of Nations but joined to the French customs union. ... House, representing the ailing Wilson, seemed to react favourably. Clemenceau was non-committal, merely observing Wilson had granted that the political and administrative implications of a special economic regime required study"[320]). Lloyd George's new proposal placed him in a position in which "his views ran counter to both Clemenceau's and Wilson's current opinions. The former wanted the Saar within France; the latter saw the establishment of a separate Saar state or special political regime as a violation of the right of selfdetermination"[321]).

While this was going on, Wilson was busy finalizing his own plan for the Saar. The details of this had been left to David Hunter Miller, and what Wilson considered crucial is clear from Miller's covering letter[322]): "I am of the opinion that such provisions regarding the Saar Basin as are indicated in the papers submitted are in accordance with the principles of the President and in particular in accordance with those stated in the fourteen points and that these provisions would be so generally regarded". Miller's plan included ". . . the principle of German sovereignty over the Saar and the maintenance of the political and civil rights of German subjects in the area. To settle conflicts arising out of the special economic regime, Miller advised a Permanent Commission of Arbitration. His proposal also provided for a plebiscite at the end of fifteen years to determine the issue of sovereignty"[323]).

As a basis for his deliberations, Miller had not only the committee's draft with Wilson's comments and a memorandum from Haskins on the extent to which the Saar should be annexed to France, but also a memorandum from Bernard Baruch, commenting as follows on the report of the Saar-committee: "that this seems to him unfair to Germany from the facts that he has. He would like to get first of all the reasons why the coal mines of the Saar Valley should be given to France and then if the reasons are sound we should consider the method of their transfer"[324]). In other words, Wilson wanted a proposal in which all views had been taken into consideration and which was, above all, unassailable on grounds of principle.

The afternoon meeting of the Council of Four—the first attended by Wilson after his indisposition, began most auspiciously: agreement was practically reached on the question of responsibility for the war and, in particular, on the possibility of bringing the German Kaiser to trial. This was a question on which the American representatives, especially Robert Lansing, had taken an entirely unresponsive attitude. However, it appeared in the course of the discussion that Wilson was now prepared to compromise[325]). This raises the question of whether Wilson's threat had been pure bluff. The answer must be that this is not necessarily the case. It was common knowledge that Lansing's uncompromising attitude was not shared by the President, and Lloyd George, the driving force in this matter, had made sure that the question would not be brought up in the Council of Four while Wilson was still ill, thereby excluding any possibility of his letting Lansing deputize for him[326]). In other words, this was not one of the President's pet projects, and this was known to his negotiating partners in advance.

However, Wilson then took up the question of the Saar by presenting his new plan[327]). If he had expected an opening in the negotiations as hinted in the morning's press[328]), he was due for a disappointment. Clemenceau seemed more intransigent than ever[329]):

"M. Clemenceau.—La grande chose est de rendre l'exploitation possible. Je ne crois pas que ce système nous donnerais la sécurité nécessaire.
. . .
M. Clemenceau.—Nous examinerons cela; mais je crains qu'un tel système ne puisse conduire qu' à des disputes sans fin.
Le President Wilson.—Je vous demande instamment de ne pas suspendre la paix du monde à cette question de la Sarre.
M. Clemenceau.—Non, mais la paix du monde exige que nous établissions d'abord la justice entre nous".

That same evening, Clemenceau, Loucheur and Tardieu met at the Ministry of War. Tardieu reports[330]):

"Nous pesons la gravité d'une décision négative. Nous décidons pourtant de ne pas céder. Une note, que je rédige dans la nuit, expose les raisons de notre résistance. Cette note, distribuée le lendemain dès l'aube aux chefs de gouvernements, affirme, en même temps que notre esprit de conciliation, l'impossibilité ou nous sommes d'aller plus loin".

It thus appeared that 9 April would prove decisive. One of the parties had to give way or Wilson would have to carry out his threat, break off negotiations and go home. The situation was now[331]) that the French delegation had accepted a plebiscite under the League of Nations to determine the final fate of the Saar, but had at the same time maintained their demand for permanent ownership of the mines. The French hoped that by accepting the British alternative, they would win British support for an attempt to get Wilson to agree to a special administrative and political regime for the Saar. Wilson was isolated on this question and his position, therefore, was a difficult one. He had opposed a semi-independent Saar state, and was not prepared either, to accept the idea of a French political mandate. On the other hand, he had agreed to both the French right to use the mines and the establishment of a special economic regime. "Both logic and the combined pressure of

Lloyd George, Clemenceau, and of men like Haskins within his circle of advisers were pushing him towards accepting special political–administrative arrangements".

The decisive meeting took place at 3.30 in the afternoon, and it became clear from Wilson's introductory remarks that he had made his decision[332]): ". . . comme je l'ai déjà dit très franchement, j'ai peur d'une solution de ce genre pour des raisons de principe. Je ne veux cependant pas m'attacher avec raideur à la lettre du principe, si l'on peut arriver à une solution raisonable . . .". The President then submitted his proposal for the settlement, that formed the basis for the compromise achieved during the next few days[333]). The conflict over the question of sovereignty ended with an evasion of the problem: "The Four agreed to avoid specifically posing the issue of sovereignty. The word would be dropped, and 'administration' changed to 'government' "[334]). On the other hand, the French accepted "the American delegation's position on the transfer of the mines from French to German ownership in any areas remaining to Germany after the plebiscite"[335]). On the evening of 10 April, the League of Nations Committee met for the first time for a fortnight, and at this and the meetings of the following evenings, the Covenant, including the section of the Monroe Doctrine, was finally approved[336]).

The inevitable conclusion is therefore, that it was Wilson who took the decisive step on the path of compromise[337]), that he did this on the afternoon of 9 April, and that the final decision was made on the morning of 10 April. The question is then whether the summoning of the USS "George Washington" had anyway been a piece of bluff, and this is something that we have no means of knowing with certainty.

As early as the evening of 8 April, Wilson, in a talk with R. S. Baker, put a favourable construction on the events in question[338]):

"I saw Wilson this evening. He is much more hopeful. His gesture in ordering the G. W. was effective. He is driving toward a settlement: but he will say nothing!"

This, however, was self-deception, as Baker himself was the first to realize[339]), even though, in his account of the Peace Conference, he was later to play his part in the adoption of the favourable interpretation that Admiral Grayson, Wilson's mouthpiece, was already doing his best to make the official one[340]). The fact is, however, that the man who had given in at the meeting that day was Wilson, not Lloyd George or Clemenceau[341]), and now the President had even also abandoned any idea of a public appeal—the alternative to leaving the Conference. It is not possible to demonstrate any change in the political situation between 6 and 8–9 April, the conflict was the same on both occasions: Without a satisfactory solution of the Saar conflict, there was no prospect of the French accepting the incorporation of the Monroe Doctrine in the League of Nations Covenant, but this was vital to acceptance of the Treaty in the United States. Conversely, conciliation on the question of the Saar—which

Wilson had already made into a pet project—would mean that he not only definitely compromised with his principles, but also with his earlier position as the leader of Liberalism[342]). And he can hardly have been aware, before sometime on 9 April[343]), of the American reaction, which definitely prevented him from making use of his threat if he wanted to retain his position at home. It is therefore tempting to conclude that the summoning of the "George Washington" served primarily as a means of overcoming a psychological crisis in Wilson himself. It created an imaginary cover for him in the same way as the purely formalistic compromises on the questions of the Saar and the responsibility for the war. As regards the latter, Fritz Dickmann has hit the nail right on the head[344]):

"Das war ein typisch Wilsonscher Kompromiss: Der Sache nach war den Alliierten eigentlich alles zugestanden, was sie wünschten, der amerikanische Rechtsstandpunkt faktisch aufgegeben und dafür eine bedeutungslose Formel eingeflickt, die den Präsidenten erlauben sollte, das Gesicht zu wahren und sein Gewissen zu beruhigen".

But what was House's position during this, the most serious crisis of the Conference? He was in fact totally on the outside: he was not advised in advance of the critical meeting between Wilson and the Commissioners[345]), he had no prior knowledge of the summoning of the "George Washington"[346]) and, what is more, when he found out what had happened, he did his utmost to lessen the effects by means of soothing press bulletins[347]). Indeed, he even tried to influence the judgment of posterity by carefully omitting all mention of the episode from his diary. Incidentally, this omission later caused Charles Seymour to conclude that the episode had therefore been of no significance![348]). House was kept out of the Saar negotiations too, his role being solely that of messenger boy[349]).

However, the matter did not end there. On 7 April, "The Times" carried an article on "Colonel House's Services", which contained the whole of the myth also found in House's own diary[350]): if any progress at all had been made at the Conference, it was thanks to Colonel House, who, owing to Wilson's illness, had now once more placed his "savoir faire" and "conciliatory temperament" at the disposition of the peace-makers. House was one of the few Delegates who had made good at the Conference, and it was possible that peace would have been concluded long ago if he had not unfortunately fallen ill right at the beginning of the Conference. By the time he recovered, the Council of Four had already got into bad habits and had begun to waste time on elementary courses in ethnography and geography. It had been impossible to change this state of affairs before Lloyd George went to England and Wilson to the United States. "During their absence Colonel House, who has never found a difficulty in working with his colleagues (implication: contrary to Wilson), because he is a selfless man with no axe to grind, brought matters rapidly forward. The delay that has occurred since the return of President Wilson and Mr. Lloyd George has been due chiefly to the upsetting of the good work done during their absence . . .". If there now once more seemed to be a chance of bringing the Conference back to relatively safe ground, "it is mainly due to the efforts of Colonel House and to the salutary effect of the feeling that the Allied peoples are becoming seriously alarmed at the secret manipulations of their chief representatives".

Historians have later wished to attribute decisive importance to this article for the break[351]), and this may indeed be the case as regards Mrs. Wilson, but not as regards the President. Even though Steed—the author of the article —was an erratic person[352]), neither he, nor Auchincloss, or House, were so naive as to believe that anything of this sort would pass unchallenged[353]). The article was an epitaph on something recognized by all parties as being passé, but it was at the same time House's own contribution to yet another myth, which within just a few weeks was given the following form[354]):

"The President, unfortunately, has not dealt with the Commissioners or taken them into his confidence, but has done everything in private with Colonel House, and Colonel House is what somebody called Cicero, "a great trimmer". In each case under discussion he has compromised, in order that he might get through the thing he was interested in, and I cannot see that he was really interested in anything except the League of Nations".

While the Conference seemed about to be disrupted by the critical Franco-American relations, a series of delicate Anglo-American negotiations were in progress on an informal naval settlement. And Lloyd George saw no reason whatsoever for hiding the fact that as far as he was concerned, British consent to the incorporation of the Monroe Doctrine in the League of Nations Covenant was conditional upon a solution satisfactory to Britain being reached on the Anglo-American naval race that was now beginning[355]). We saw what an important role the naval problems played even during the pre-Armistice negotiations, and we saw too, that the Americans were also prepared to use this potential weapon in the negotiations with Britain[356]). House himself had not refrained from using the threat[357]), and as early as 10 March, Lloyd George had declared at a meeting with House and Clemenceau that "an agreement between Great Britain and the United States must be reached not to rival one another on naval building"[358]). The negotiations between Admiral Wemyss and Benson only led to further complications, and when Daniels, the Secretary of the Navy, arrived in Paris at the end of March 1919, he found it necessary to intervene in order "to restore the urbanities between the quarreling Admirals[359]).

At the express wish of Lloyd George, Daniels then initiated negotiations with the British First Lord of the Admiralty, Walter Long[360]), and in these talks, the positions became sharply drawn up[361]):

"I (Daniels) explained that so far as programme already authorized, could do nothing but build those ships. The larger programme (for 3 years) that passed House was dependent upon League of Nations and would not be necessary if League was firmly established and all nations agreed to reduction of armament. He (Long) said L(loyd) G(eorge) could not support League of Nations if US accompanied it by big building programme, for GB could not consent to any other nation having the supremacy of the sea. I pointed out that GB would still have more ships than America. . . .".

At the request of Wilson, Daniels then took the matter up directly with the British Prime Minister[362]). This meeting took place on 1 April, and it clearly showed that Daniels could not be used as a tool for any sort of private agreement or informal understanding: "I (Daniels) told him (Lloyd George) I could not make such agreement or understanding, for anything done must be public and printed in all papers"[363]). If the two statesmen wanted such an agreement, they would have to seek other means of achieving it.

After the meetings, Daniels went to Rome in accordance with an earlier agreement, and did not return to Paris until 7 April[364]). Here, he discovered that the British were very eager to resume negotiations, but Daniels first wished to have a talk with the President, and Wilson, who had that same morning sent the previously mentioned orders to the "George Washington" took an uncompromising attitude[365]):

"He (Wilson) said: Please say you (Daniels) have seen the President and have found him deeply concerned about the whole method with which the whole peace programme is being handled and that you have been instructed by the President to say that he cannot make any sort of agreement until he sees what the outcome is going to be".

The subsequent talks between Daniels and Long were therefore doomed to failure, and it was agreed that Wilson and Lloyd George should now take the matter up again[366]).

The initiative for this came from Lloyd George, perhaps as an indication of a result of Wilson's "George Washington"-threat. At all events, on 8 April, Lloyd George had a meeting with Philip Kerr and Robert Cecil. Cecil, the British top negotiator on the League of Nations Commission, had been very indignant over Lloyd George's pressure methods in this matter[367]), but the situation had now developed in such a way that Lloyd George needed his help[368]):

"Unfortunately the matter has now got into a mess. The P. M. has entrusted Walter Long with the negotiation, and he has got across the US naval authorities, with the result that neither can retreat without a certain amount of loss of face. At breakfast the P. M. showed some conciousness that he was in a mess, and *suggested that I should take the matter up with House, which I agreed to do*".

House was thus once more directly involved in important top level negotiations, *but this happened at the initiative of Lloyd George, not of Wilson.*

After a talk with Wiseman, Cecil now framed a letter to House, explaining the British standpoint[369]). The actual crux of this was:

"Would it be possible, for instance, for you to say that when the Treaty of Peace containing the League of Nations has been signed you would abandon or modify you(r) new naval programme? I am sure that the British Government would be only too ready to give corresponding assurances. That would be what the French call a 'beau geste' with which to inaugurate the League; and if you could also intimate, however informally, that the two governments would consult together from year to year as to their naval programmes, and that the British sentiment on the matter would not be disregarded I feel confident that the present very genuine anxieties on the point could be completely removed".

In his reply, House tried carefully to define the exact scope of the American promise[370]):

". . . I am sure you will find the United States ready to 'abandon or modify our new naval programme', by which I understand you to mean our programme not yet provided for by law, as our naval bill for the next fiscal year has not yet passed. I am also certain that you will find us ready and willing to consult with the British Government from year to year regarding the naval programmes of the two Governments".

However, Lloyd George was not satisfied: "(He) objected to my letter and wanted it to include ships still not under construction but provided for by law"[371]). Cecil therefore called on House, and their meeting resulted in a memorandum, the crucial passages of which are as follows[372]):

"I (Cecil) asked him (House) whether it would not be possible for the President to postpone the commencement of those ships which had not been actually begun until after the Treaty of Peace had been signed so that we might have time to discuss and consider the matter together. He said he thought that might be possible, and would see what could be done in that direction. At the same time he repeated more than once that there was no idea in the mind of the President of building a fleet in competition with that of Great Britain. That was entirely foreign to his purpose. . . .
. . . He then urged that it really would be much better to leave the thing as it was left by his letter to me: that we might fully rely on the intention of the President not to build in competition with us; and that he thought that some arrangements as to the relative strengths of the fleets ought to be arrived at; and that conversations with that object might well be begun as soon as the Treaty of Peace was signed. But he added that he was very much afraid that if the matter were stirred in public at all now, national spirit on both sides would be aroused and no accommodation would be possible".

Wilson gave his consent to the memorandum the same evening[373]), and the Monroe-Doctrine was also approved (10 April). Two days later, House gave the American Secretary of the Navy a verbal report on these negotiations[374]). The most recent research on the matter has judged the agreement as an American diplomatic victory: Lloyd George was given no promise on a reduction of the 1916-programme, but only in respect of the 1918-programme—towards which the American Congress was anyway not particularly favourable —together with certain vague promises that he would probably have achieved in any case. On the other hand, "the Americans . . . got something tangible," viz, the Monroe Doctrine[375]).—Which they might have achieved anyway? In any event, engagement in this entire matter seems to have been heaviest at the Expert level, and here, heaviest on the American side, with Admiral Benson as the driving force[376]).

While House still had an independent position in these negotiations, although he was only seriously brought into matters on British initiative, his role in the subsequent Rhine negotiations was further reduced. With the solution of the Saar problem and the passing of the League of Nations Covenant, such a favourable climate had apparently been created for the negotiations, that sufficient courage was found to take the decision to call the German Delegation to Paris. Therefore, although decisive questions still stood open, there was no longer any doubt as to the continuance of the Alliance[377]. On 12 April, the very day on which Lloyd George, speaking in the Council of Four, proposed summoning the German Delegation for 25 April, and the day following the final completion of the League of Nations Covenant in committee, Wilson made a move on the question of the Rhineland.

While the crisis in the Conference had been at its height, the Saar negotiations had held the centre of the stage, and the Rhineland question had apparently slipped into the background for a while[378]. Up to then, the Rhineland negotiations had been characterized by a joint Anglo-American front, first against the French wish for an independent Rhineland, and then against the French demand for inter-Allied occupation of the West bank of the Rhine and bridgeheads on its East bank for 30 years, and the right to continued occupation or reoccupation beyond this period in the event of Germany not fulfilling the terms of the Treaty[379]. However, Wilson now took the matter up again, apparently on his own initiative and without prior negotiations with Lloyd George.

We know that the American Delegation was at this time very dissatisfied over the way in which Lloyd George had behaved during Wilson's illness. It was felt that, partly by means of his statements to the press, he had attempted to join forces with Clemenceau behind Wilson's back[380]. Similarly, his attitude on the Saar question had been more than ambiguous and he had only swung over to the American standpoint at the last minute[381]—and the naval negotiations had naturally not exactly promoted constructive Anglo-American cooperation. These factors may perhaps explain why Wilson, in the time to follow, carried out his negotiations on a Rhineland compromise with the French on his own—or perhaps the explanation is simply that everyone knew that if the United States and France could agree, then Britain would have to follow suit. In any event, it is one of the ironies of fate that just at the time when House had finally lost all influence on Wilson's decisions, the President entered upon the policy that his adviser had recommended in vain for so long[382].

On 8 April, i. e. the day on which the President seems to have decided to compromise in the Saar negotiations[383], he also took up the problem of the Rhineland for renewed consideration[384]. This he did in the form of a memorandum on the French note of 2 April[385]. Wilson maintained his earlier standpoints[386], and further stressed:

"I beg very respectfully to urge upon the French Government this reflection: The proposals that I made jointly with Mr. Lloyd George with regard to assuring the safety of France on her eastern frontier (offer of guarantee) were made after mature reflection, after full consideration of all other plans suggested, and necessarily represent the maximum of what I myself deem necessary or possible on the part of the United States".

In other words, if Wilson were to give in with regard to the Saar and with regard to a Treaty of Guarantee, he would at any rate stand firm on the question of the Rhineland itself.

This still seems to have been his attitude on 12 April, for on that day, he sent his memorandum to House with the following comment[387]):

"My dear House.
Since I received at your hand from Mr. Tardieu the memorandum which is herewith returned, I am going to ask if you will not hand this reply to Mr. Tardieu with the very solemn warning that it is necessary for him to induce his chief to accept these terms as drawn, pointing out to him that this is an extraordinary step for the United States to take, and that there will be no possible hope of my obtaining the proposed treaty, if the additions he suggested were made. It would be well for him to understand that this is the only obtainable solution of the problem of the protection for France of her eastern frontier.

Affectionately yours,
Woodrow Wilson."

There are several points of interest in this connection: House was apparently never brought into the deliberations forming the basis of Wilson's memorandum. Indeed, he was so far outside the negotiations that Wilson even found it necessary to explain why he was now being brought in again. From the text of the American Note, Wilson seems to have maintained the ultimative attitude he had already taken in this question on 8 April, but we must ask ourselves whether his reason for involving House in the negotiations was not that he actually desired that a compromise should now be reached, and from the further development of the negotiations, we must conclude that this was indeed the case. Clemenceau at any rate wasted no time in taking advantage of this new opportunity, and House functioned gladly as messenger between the two statesmen.

On 14 April, Clemenceau sought out House: ". . . it was . . . in the nature of a love-feast[388]):

"He said he would agree to the President's terms for the protection of France and the west bank of the Rhine. It was not what he wanted but with the guarantee of the United States he thought it sufficient. He would have to fight Foch and his other Marshals but he was willing to make the fight provided the President would agree to let the French occupy three stratas of German territory. The first strata for five years, the second for ten years, and the third for fifteen years. The first strata to include Coblentz, the second Maintz and the third would come closer to the French frontier. He said in the Treaty of '71 Germany insisted upon occupying France for five years or until indemnity was paid. The indemnity was paid sooner, therefore the troops were withdrawn sooner, nevertheless, it set a precedent for his demand.
If the President would consent to it he, Clemenceau, could beat his Marshals in the Chamber of Deputies and the Senate, and he would also take occasion to state the generous action of the President toward France in the Peace Conference".

Here, finally, was a constructive move on the part of the French, and Wilson gave his consent to their proposal the very next day[389]). House was permitted to take the news to Clemenceau and receive the usual embrace[390]).

Nevertheless at no time had he had any influence on the content and framing of the compromise itself[391]). And House himself was well aware of this. When he claimed praise after the talk with Clemenceau, it was not for having brought about a compromise, but for having stopped the French press campaign against the President[392]).

The critical phase of the Conference was now over, and with it, a decisive period of House's life. Nevertheless, with restless energy he was already seeking new spheres of action, while at the same time, attempting to influence the negotiations of the Conference, principally in the crisis that was now blowing up over the question of the Adriatic.

*Chapter 5*

# Myths

During the last phase of the Conference it gradually became apparent to all that Wilson and House were no longer on the same intimate terms as earlier, and there was ample opportunity for the more peripheral participants to advance hypotheses. Amongst others, House's three colleagues on the Peace Commission availed themselves of this and thereby came to give a very influential version of what can be termed the House-Myth. They saw, knew and sensed a certain amount, but it all related to the period after the actual break. However, their position gave their testimony greater weight than was justified by their actual influence and level of information. Henry White's statements were of particular importance because they became, through Allan Nevins' account, one of the cornerstones of Paul Birdsall's interpretation, which in turn, influenced the picture presented by Alexander and Juliette George[1]). It is therefore necessary to take a closer look at this version of the events.

As early as 1 May, Lansing wrote as follows to Frank Polk at the State Department in Washington[2]):

"White, Bliss and I, who confer together every morning (The Colonel never joins us), heartily approve the decision in regard to Fiume and as strongly disapprove submitting to Japan's demands. The President knew our views in both cases. The first was courageous and right; the latter was quite the contrary. Kirk brought in the decision in regard to Japanese claims last night and told me that the President had authorized Ray Stannard Baker to say to the Chinese that he was sorry that he could not do more for them but he had to compromise with the Japanese in order "to save the League of Nations". He meant by that that the Japanese had threatened not to sign the Covenant if they did not get what they wanted. The "compromise" was conceding all Japan claimed. I may be wrong but I anticipate a storm of protests from the United States when it is known that we have abandoned China and given in to Japan.

The League of Nations has become a veritable millstone about our necks. First France threatened to defeat it unless she got all she wanted. So a "compromise" was effected by giving her everything. Then Italy obtained nearly everything she asked by the same tactics, but being a little too greedy got into difficulties. Now comes Japan with the same threats and puts through her unconscionable demands, though I can assure you that we did all we could to prevent this grave injustice to poor helpless China.

I don't know how the Colonel feels about all this, because he remains isolated from his colleagues unless they go to see him, and they don't seem disposed to do it these days because they rather resent his aloofness.

Having already written you my views as to the folly of secret diplomacy I am not going to repeat them, but Cellere ... (the Italian Ambassador in Washington) was intensely bitter saying that secret interviews and lack of frankness were to blame for the Fiume affair. I am really distressed about the reputation for intrigue, the President has made over here. It is being openly discussed by everyone, and (most confidentially) House is considered the high priest of the mysteries and is being blamed in no small measure for the position in which the President has been placed.

The feeling is that the principles, which the President laid down in the "Fourteen Points", and in his speeches, have been destroyed by compromises and concessions, that a victor's peace rather than a just peace is being sought, and that cupidity backed by threats of refusal to sign the Covenant controls the situation. . . .".

And a few weeks later, Tasker H. Bliss, in a conversation with William C. Bullitt, said[3]):

". . . I (Bliss) personally have had no influence whatever on the treaty. Since December 13th, I have actually seen the President for less than twenty minutes in all, except at a dinner party, where I was seated at the opposite side of the table. The President, unfortunately, has not dealt through the Commissioners or taken them into his confidence but has done everything in private with Colonel House, and Colonel House is what somebody called Cicero, "a great trimmer". In each case under discussion he has compromised, in order that he might get through the thing that he was interested in, and I cannot see that he was really interested in anything except The League of Nations".

The myth was then given its final version in a letter that Henry White wrote to Robert Lansing on 8 November 1919. White was still in Paris as American Delegate, while Lansing was in Washington. However, as the letter deals mainly with subjects with which, as will be seen from the passages quoted above, the other Commissioners were not unfamiliar, there may perhaps be grounds for regarding White's letter as addressed to posterity rather than to Lansing[4]):

"I have been thinking of writing you for some time past about one or two situations which seem to me important with reference to the immediate or near future . . .

I was not aware until recently of the extent to which intrigue went on "upstairs" during the earlier months of the Conference, with a view to preventing any of the views of our experts, which happened to be contrary to those held there, from reaching the President. Still less had I any idea of the attempts made to get some of the experts to change their views and adopt those advocated in the small upper chamber previously mentioned.

Since your departure I have realized more and more how grievously misled the Italians and others were by the tendency to compromise and by the assurances of friendship and sympathy, of a general nature at least if not actually with their particular views, expressed during their interviews upstairs; and there is no doubt in my mind that the Fiume and other questions would have been settled while the President was still here, if they had been left in your hands, or kept in the President's, and had not been hampered by a feeling upstairs that no decision should be attempted, much less reached, which would in any way be likely to cause jeopardy to the adoption of the Covenant of the League of Nations.

I am afraid the Shantung decision which, as you, the General (Bliss), and I felt, would arouse such serious opposition to the Treaty at home besides being wrong in itself, was another case in point.

Under these circumstances, and in view of the undue influence which I cannot but think our British friends exercise over our late colleague, I cannot help feeling anxious —and to a certain extent sharing the anxiety evidently felt in the Senate—about our participation in the League of Nations if we are to be represented there by a man (and a series of feeble advisers) given to compromise and not strong enough and willing to make a fight on every question in which our interests (which besides being commercial are those of world peace as against special national interests such as the land-grab-bing and sphere-of-influence capturing now rife in Europe) are likely to be overridden unless carefully guarded and defended. And of course during the next few years such questions will constantly be arising in respect to commercial and financial matters in which our interests will be in jeopardy, and attempts will be made to make use of our influence at the League Council for the furtherance of European intrigue.

It seems to be generally assumed that Colonel House will be our first representative on the League of Nations Council, and if such be the President's decision of course there is, I suppose, nothing to be said. But I see no reason why it should follow that he have the selection of all American members of the staff, and I do not think . . . and . . ., to whom he has promised places on the mandates section, are suitable men for the purpose . . .".

The three Commissioners thus seemed to have been agreed on condemning the many compromises of the Conference and on giving House a large part of the blame for these, attributing his eagerness to compromise to the fact that he was only interested in the League of Nations. The two territorial questions stressed particularly are the problems of Fiume and Shantung. If, however, we subject House's position on these questions to a detailed analysis, we will see that the Commissioners not only overshot the mark with their accusations but actually also gave a lopsided picture of the situation, especially as regards Shantung, because they assigned to House responsibility for a policy on which he no longer had any influence at all. However, that House deliberately let himself be used as a scapegoat was due not only to his wish to keep up appear-ances at all costs, but also to the fact that the actually sympathized with Wilson's intentions. Baker, with his usual vision, seized on the ambiguity of the whole affair when he wrote, at the culmination of the Shantung crisis[5]):

"(The League of Nations is a matter of *faith:* and the President is first of all *a man of faith.* He believes in the League of Nations as an organization that will save the world. On the commission House is the only one who supports this view and House only feels it, when the President *sees it,* grasps it, feels it with the mighty tenacity of a great faith. He is willing to compromise even desperately for it—he is the only Man here)". . . .
. . .
"House is with the President, he favors all compromises, while the President knows when to compromise and when not to. . . .".

With the solution of the questions between "the big Three", all problems were far from solved. The two lesser Great Powers, Japan and Italy, had long been waiting impatiently for their turn. And although only the Japanese claims had a direct relationship with the Treaty with Germany, it was no longer possible to postpone consideration of Italy's problems. In both cases, the secret, wartime treaties formed part of the pattern for the negotiations, i. e. both France and England had their hands tied beforehand, and the way was clear for an almost exclusively American–Italian and American–Japanese conflict. However, right from the beginning, other factors than the secret treaties played a part in both problems.

It has earlier been suggested that Wilson, in his Italian policy, played through the entire register that would, in a more favourable political situation also have been at his disposal in the case of America's other Allies. It seems as though he had, right from the beginning picked this particular country as an object for demonstration. This may have been because R. S. Baker's reports[6]) on his overwhelming popularity in Italy had given him an exaggerated idea of his possibility of gaining support among the population, but he was certainly also encouraged by the fact that a severe attitude towards Italy would be safe from a domestic point of view and might indeed even be popular in the United States. The conflict was, however, fundamentally one of principle: "Nowhere else did the new theories of international policy championed by President Wilson come so definitely to an issue with the elements of pre-war and war-time diplomacy"[7]).

However, the distinctive feature of American policy in this matter is not just that Wilson here played through the entire register at the disposal of the "New Diplomacy", but that he was also backed up by an energetic lobby of Experts, who literally bombarded the Commission with memoranda[8]). Had House understood the extent of Wilson's commitment and that of the Experts, he would perhaps have kept himself in the background—or would he?

On 21st January 1919, the so-called "Black Book", viz. the recommendations of the American territorial experts with regard to the solution of the territorial questions[9]), became available. These recommendations included the proposal for the frontier between Italy and Yugoslavia that became Wilson's guide in all the subsequent negotiations[10]). The author was Douglas Johnson, Chief of the Division of Boundary Geography, and he seems all the way through to have been the driving force behind the uncompromising attitude of the Experts in this matter. René Albrecht-Carrié has described the American proposal as "a sane and fair-minded analysis of local situations" and has further emphasized the fact that "(t)he American Report took into account first ethnographical, then economic and strategic considerations, and struck a moderate compromise between them"[11]). Only on one point did Wilson prove willing to go beyond the Experts' proposals, in that he was prepared to make Fiume an independent port[12]).

The Italian Delegation, for its part, adopted a strangely ambiguous policy, demanding not only the frontier laid down in the Treaty of London, but *also* the port of Fiume, which the Treaty expressly assigned to Croatia[13]). With this attitude, the Italians weakened their own bargaining position not only from a legal point of view but also because Britain and France were by no means willing to support the Italian claims beyond the provisions of the Treaty of London, and, at the same time, laid the scene for a head-on collision with Wilson on the question of the right of self-determination[14]). Fiume became a symbol for both parties. Wilson himself explained his position as follows[15]):

"First: There can be no profit in our covering again the field of discussion which we went over so often with Signor Orlando and Baron Sonnino. Our position has remained exactly the same throughout all the discussions, because, though we have the most cordial good will towards Italy and the most sincere desire to meet her wishes in every possible way, we do not feel at liberty to depart, in respect of the territory, from the principles which have been followed throughout all the other settlements in which we have taken part. Second: There is no longer any use in insisting upon the Treaty of London, because the United States is now an essential guarantor of all the settlements made, and no action of Great Britain or France could be effective without her. There is no means except that of the general settlement by which *any* territories could be handed over to Italy.

Third: Fiume can in no circumstances go to Italy, it must serve the uses and necessities of the several states behind it to the North and East, and can do so in our judgment only as a free state. . . .".

We have seen how the American President flirted quite openly with the Opposition[16]), during his stay in Italy and how he afterwards did not restrain himself from seeking direct collaboration with the Yugoslavs on a solution[17]). However, neither of these moves had any result, and when Wilson left Paris in the middle of February, the situation was already becoming critical, due partly to the fact that Italy constantly laid obstacles in the way of the relief aid to South-East Europe via Trieste. By 12th February, the leader of the relief work, Herbert Hoover, had finally lost his patience, and he now placed the matter before Wilson[18]), suggesting, with Norman Davis' backing[19]), that economic sanctions be applied. At exactly this time the Italians were negotiating a big American loan to cover purchases in neutral countries and, above all, to maintain the exchange rate of the lire[20]). The possibility of effective economic pressure was therefore present, but on this occasion, Wilson chose to support the granting of the loan[21]); the question was, however, whether he would maintain this attitude in a more acute crisis.

The Italian Prime Minister, Orlando, took the opportunity provided by Wilson's absence to go to Rome himself, and no decisive new political moves could therefore be expected in this period. On 10th March, House had a meeting with Clemenceau and Lloyd George and found that both preferred the American proposal for the Dalmatian frontier to that foreseen in the Treaty of London and that they did not find an Italian annexation of Fiume desirable although they were prepared, as a compromise, to accept internationalization[22]). Two days later, House had a private talk with Orlando, during which he was extremely cautious in his statements on the Adriatic question[23]). However, towards the end of the conversation, House invited Orlando "to appeal to him whenever he needed help,"—an invitation for which Orlando was exceedingly grateful since he thought that his life would be in danger if he went home without Dalmatia! "Colonel House said that he hoped that his (Orlando's) life could be preserved." House had in other words signified his good will towards Orlando—neither more nor less—but there is much to suggest that this attitude was to a high degree dictated by ignorance of the extent of Wilson's commitment in this matter[24]).

The situation on Wilson's return was now "that the Italians had just submitted to the Council a new Memorandum in which they extended their claim in Dalmatia to cover Spalato. Another Italian Memorandum drew a dire and rather exaggerated picture of the situation of inferiority which confronted Italy in the Adriatic", while the American Delegation was divided on the question of the Italian demands[25]. On the one side stood the group of Territorial Experts within whose sphere the Italian question belonged: Charles Seymour, Chief of the Austro-Hungarian Division; Clive Day, Chief of the Balkan Division; W. E. Lunt, Chief of the Italian Division; and Douglas W. Johnson, Chief of the Division of Boundary-Geography; and backing them up were A. A. Young, Chief of the Division of Economics, and Isaiah Bowman, Chief Territorial Specialist. They all recommended an uncompromising attitude towards Italy, as described in the foregoing. On the other side stood a more heterogeneous group, composed of Sidney Mezes, the nominal leader of the Inquiry and American representative on the Central Committee on Territorial Questions; David Hunter Miller, the "legal adviser" to the Commission and a prominent member of the original staff of the Inquiry; Gordon Auchinloss, House's son-in-law and secretary; George Louis Beer, expert on colonial questions; and, for a short period, James Shotwell, librarian of the Inquiry. While the first group acted en bloc, the other group tended to act in a series of more or less independent moves. However, common to all these was the wish to reach a compromise that would be satisfactory to Italy, based on the view that it was Italy that was the Great Power, both politically and culturally. When the crisis culminated in the middle of April, the schism went all the way up, the Commissioners being divided as well, with Lansing, White and Bliss on the side of the first group, and House on the other side[26].

Both Paul Birdsall and Lawrence E. Gelfand have emphasized the fundamental, or rather, ideological, nature of the split as a conflict between two groups of Experts, one academic and idealistic, the other "realistic"[27]. Birdsall's sympathies lie with the first group and, thanks partly to a number of interviews with representatives of this group, he sees the conflict through their eyes and thus quite naturally tends to overestimate its importance[28]. And this in turn colours his evaluation and timing of the House–Wilson break. Gelfand, on the other hand, tends to take a far more critical view of the academic Experts, who, in his opinion, "clung tenaciously and inflexibly to Wilsonian principles in the face of the new power structure rising out of the war"[29].

It is obvious, however, that purely personal motives also played a part. On 27th February, the Conference had established a Central Committee on Territorial Questions, and House, who was at that time in charge of the American Delegation, had placed Sidney Mezes as the American member of this co-ordinating organ. This, however reignited the old Inquiry-conflict, Mezes again coming into conflict with Dr. Bowman, the actual leader of Inquiry: "this issue was one of principle as well as personality, for, while Dr. Mezes was eager to coordinate Dr. Bowman held that the specialists of the various separate committees were more competent to decide concerning contentious issues than the non-specialists of the coordinating body"[30]).

It is further obvious that the Italians consciously set out to find sympathizers among the American Delegation[31]), and men like Miller and Beer felt sufficiently independent to participate in negotiations on solutions running counter to those proposed by the official Experts[32]), while the Experts on their side formed a remarkably coherent and militant group, who did not shrink from appealing directly to the President when they felt their views threatened[33]). The whole affair is first and foremost characteristic of the unrest and dissatisfaction that now dominated the entire Conference, but it is important to our discussion because it was here that House for the first time committed himself openly against Wilson, thereby publicizing, so to speak, the rupture that was already a hard fact.

It was Sidney Mezes who brought up the internal Inquiry-conflict, when on 16th March, he sent House a memorandum in which he advocated a solution of the Adriatic question that was completely contrary to the views previously advanced by the American Experts[34]). And two days later these retaliated with a memorandum to all Commissioners in which they made their position amply clear: "... (e)very memorandum hitherto submitted to the Commissioners, about which any of the heads of the above-named divisions have been consulted, recommends that Fiume and all of Dalmatia should go to the Jugoslavs. We are still unanimously of that opinion for the reasons here set forth"[35]). However, the crisis did not become acute until the beginning of April.

The Italians had tried throughout to assert the principle that peace should be concluded simultaneously with all the Central Powers, but in reality, the other Allies were still postponing treatment of the Italian demands, and this continued even after Wilson's return. As the questions regarding the Treaty with Germany gradually approached a settlement, it became impossible any longer to ignore the Italian demands, and on 1 April, Lloyd George promised in "The Council of Four" that the question would be dealt with the following week, but already on 3 April, he created a state of almost panic in "The Council of Four" by bringing up the Adriatic question, thereby giving occasion to a rather sharp confrontation between the Italian and the American viewpoints. The debate turned primarily on Fiume. Orlando demanded Italian annexation, while Wilson argued in favour of the free city solution[36]). On the same afternoon, the Yugoslavs had the opportunity of presenting their views, while Orlando preferred to stay away[37]). However, before things went that far, a number of more or less informal contacts had been arranged, in which House too was involved. As early as 15 March, Orlando had had two conversations with Wilson, on which R. S. Baker reported as follows[38]):

"The Italian situation is now acute and full of dynamite. Orlando had 2 interviews with the President today. Orlando and his associate Sonnino are not on speaking terms. Something has got to break soon."

House had himself talked to Orlando on both 19 and 26 March. We know practically nothing about the first conversation[39]), but it appears clearly from the report of the second that House continued the sympathetic but non-comittal line followed in the period before Wilson's return[40]). It is obvious, on the other hand, that the Italians, especially through their Washington ambassador, di Cellere, worked hard on two men close to House, Sidney Mezes and David Hunter Miller, and that these both proved to be exceptionally sympathetic[41]). However, House himself does not appear to have gone too far at any time.

The situation soon came to a head. Not only was the matter now finally raised in "The Council of Four", but on 1 April, Wilson had yet another conversation with Orlando, which did not seem to go well either[42]). As will be remembered[43]), it was the day after this conversation that Wilson, after a long period of silence, once more contacted House and instructed him, among other things, "to outline to Orlando the boundary and other terms for Italy. I (House) do not relish the job but I promised to do it. I shall see Orlando on Friday and tell him just where we wish the northern and eastern boundaries of Italy to be"[44]). Incidentally, on the same day, Orlando expressed the wish to see House[45]).

On 2 April, Sidney Mezes also had a talk with the President. Mezes was working with the English Expert, Headlam-Morley, on the preparation of proposals for the solution of the Danzig question, and just that day, Lloyd George and Wilson had agreed "that a free, autonomous city of Danzig should be established with a High Commissioner appointed by the League of Nations"[46]). Mezes now learned the details of this solution and was at the same time informed by the President that he desired a solution of the Fiume-question along the same lines[47]). House was, therefore, acquainted with Wilson's latest views when he met Orlando on the afternoon of 3 April, and the—admittedly onesided—material available on the course of the conversation affords no grounds for doubting that House tried loyally to present the President's views[48]). The meeting ended, incidentally, without any result.

The literature on the Italian question mentions two direct appeals by the territorial Experts to the President, one dated 4 April, 1919, and the other, 17 April. According to Albrecht-Carrié[49]):

"Mezes' proposed scheme of settlement ... caused not a little indignation among the American territorial experts ... they now addressed themselves to Wilson ... In a memorandum dated April 4, they repeated once more the usual arguments. The most interesting part of this memorandum is the last, which gave a list of conditions necessary to safeguard Yugoslav interests if Fiume was to be, for other reasons made a free city. It contained the germ of the idea which was to become the basis of a later negotiation and indicated the extent to which Wilson would eventually be willing to compromise. ...".

Birdsall, on the other hand, writes[50]):

"The real conflict originally lay between the experts and Mezes, their titular chief. ... to make perfectly certain that Mezes' views should not be regarded as their own, the four chiefs of division (and the economist Allyn A. Young) addressed themselves directly to Wilson on April 4, at the very height of the controversy over French claims. Wilson accepted the views of the experts and his firm stand upon them in his interview with Orlando on April 14 ... lead to complete deadlock with the Italians".

And in Lederer, we read[51]):

"Meanwhile, the American experts added a new dimension to the problem. Appealing directly to Wilson on April 4, they proposed for the first time the idea of an "independent" city or state for Fiume, an idea that was to play a central role in the critical days that followed".

On this basis, we cannot avoid getting the impression that it was the conflict with Mezes which lay behind the appeal to the President, that the appeal was made on 4 April, and that it was the Experts who put the idea of a free city solution in Wilson's head, and that it was on their initiative that Wilson adhered to this idea. Nevertheless, this interpretation does not hold good on a number of important points, and as the entire question surrounding the two appeals to the President are important to the present thesis on the events connected with the House–Wilson break, we must analyse the problem in greater detail.

First, there is a decisive difference between the two appeals. Whereas the second appeal, of 17 April, was formulated as a real letter, addressed personally to Wilson: "Dear Mr. President"[52]), the former was only written as a standard memorandum: From–To-Subject. The memorandum concerned Fiume, but it is not correct that the idea of a free city was here presented for the first time—because Wilson had, in fact, advocated this solution on 2 April. On the contrary, the memorandum argued in favour of giving Fiume to Yugoslavia: "1) That Fiume should be given to the Jugo-Slav State without restriction. ... 2) That the interests of the Italian minority of greater Fiume should be assured by the establishment of adequate guarantees of protection. ... 3) That it is unwise to make of Fiume a free city. ... 4) That if for reasons not connected with the best interests of the city and its hinterland it is deemed necessary that Fiume be made a free city, its right of local self-government should be accompanied by the following safeguards of the interests of the Jugo-Slav State. ..."[53]). It was, therefore, above all, the President's own view that the memorandum argued against.

Very little is known of the background for the memorandum. However, rumours were flying at the time that the Italian Delegation would leave the Conference if Italy did not get Fiume, and it is possible that the memorandum must be seen as a reply to this[54]). One thing is certain and that is that Wilson cannot have received it before 6 April; this is indicated by the fact that the memorandum was accompanied by a letter from David Hunter Miller to Major Johnson, fulfilling the latter's request for Miller's arguments against making Fiume an "independent territory"; this letter was written on 5–6 April[55]), and dated 6 April 1919[56]), and as reference is made to it in the memorandum, the letter can hardly have been given its final form before 6 April, even though the original date was retained. In Wilson's papers, the two documents are now separate, each being placed under its respective date but in R. S. Baker's collection of documents, they are printed together, in the way he must have found them among the President's papers[57]), and they were also filed together in the archives of the Peace Commission[58]). We can thus exclude the possibility of the memorandum in question having had any influence whatsoever on the "explosion" around House on 4 April described in the previous chapter.

On the other hand, there can be no question that House, in the following period, engaged actively in the innumerable attempts to establish a compromise on the Adriatic question that would be acceptable to all parties, and that he now acted in such an obviously independent manner and along lines contrary to those of the President that R. S. Baker could already write on 19 April[59]):

"The rift between the President and Colonel House seems to be widening. The Colonel compromises everything away—He has gone so far with the Italians that they are now heralding him as the great man of the conference and comparing him unfavorably with the President. It makes it difficult now for the President. The Colonel is still declaring that if he had the peace to make it could all be done in a day or so—and it could—by giving away everything we came to fight for".

Baker states here, clearly and concisely, that the rupture which for other reasons was already a fact was now, thanks to House's attitude in the Italian question, fast becoming a public secret. The period 17 to 19 April was decisive in this connection[60]).

On 7 April, Orlando had submitted a new proposal for a compromise to House, which included the establishment of "a free city to the west of Fiume and give the Jugo-Slavs a chance to develop a flat and sandy beach as a port". House found the plan "a perfectly foolish suggestion", but anyway promised to submit it to the President, who "turned (it) down as quickly as I did myself"[61]). Two days later, Orlando requested another meeting with House, but the latter delayed: "It is a mere waste of time since I cannot come to his way of thinking. The whole interest centers around Fiume. It seems quite clear that they do not care for Fiume itself or for its Italian population, but the purpose is to strangle it in order to make a greater Trieste. . . ."[62]).

The next few days saw a number of attempts at confidential negotiations between the Yugoslavs and the Italians, with the Americans as arbitrators, in which House too was engaged[63]). For the time being, nothing came of these attempts, and instead, Wilson and Orlando had two personal meetings on 14 April, in one of which Andrea Ossoinack, the former Delegate for

Fiume in the Hungarian Parliament, participated[64]). The stenographic report of the conversation between Wilson and Ossoinack shows the President in sharply polemic form. He often interrupted Ossoinack and brought out all the arguments we know so well from Johnson's memoranda, arguments that were mainly of an economic nature—consideration to the hinterland—and that showed that it was not Fiume itself that was crucial, but the question as a whole, reflecting at the same time a deep distrust of Italian motives[65]).

On the same day, Wilson handed Orlando a memorandum in which he argued on the basis of more fundamental principles[66]). He stated here that he "felt bound to square every conclusion that I should reach as accurately as possible with the fourteen principles of peace", the principles that "were formally adopted, with only a single reservation, by the powers associated against Germany and will constitute the basis of peace with Germany. I do not feel at liberty to suggest one basis for peace with Germany and another for peace with Austria". In other words, he declared himself to be personally bound by the Fourteen Points, but said nothing on Italy's position in this matter. On the contrary, he declared a few days later that "(h)e fully realised that Italy was not bound by the Fourteen Points, but his position was that he could not make peace with Germany on one set and with Austria on another set of principles"[67]).

In his memorandum Wilson further expressed the fact that he was "quite willing that Italy should be accorded along the whole length of her Northern frontier and whereever she comes into contact with Austrian territory all that was accorded her in the socalled Pact of London, but I am of the clear opinion that the Pact of London can no longer apply to the settlement of Eastern boundaries". Here, an entirely new situation had arisen due to the Austro-Hungarian collapse. And with special reference to Fiume, the President declared: "Just because it is an international port and cannot with justice be subordinated to any one sovereignty, it is my clear judgment that it should enjoy a very considerable degree of genuine autonomy and that, while it should be included no doubt within the customs system of the new Jugo-Slavic state, it should nevertheless be left free in its own interest and in the interest of the states lying about it to devote itself to the service of the commerce which naturally and inevitably seeks an outlet or inlet at its port". Wilson's viewpoint was in fact just as split between fundamental and politico-economic considerations as that of Orlando, and if he had had the will to compromise, an acceptable solution could undoubtedly have been found. But Wilson did not have the will, and it was this that House failed to understand, or perhaps refused to understand. He simply could not refrain from taking a hand.

When Orlando visited House again the day after the abortive meetings with Wilson, he therefore enjoyed his usual favourable reception. House reminded him of how great the problems had been with regard to France, and pointed out that these had finally been solved to general satisfaction and that the same could be the case with the Italian question "provided there was a disposition to yield a little by all parties . . .". And on the same day he recommended Wilson to negotiate a solution "that was not permanent but which would tide over the present and give passion time to cool".

Later that day, he also asked Clemenceau to inform Orlando that the only solution Wilson could see "was for the League of Nations to take over the disputed territory for a given time"[68]).

However, House did not leave matters there. Next day, 16 April, David Hunter Miller was set to work on a proposal for a compromise for the solution of the Fiume-problem[69]). His starting point was as follows[70]):

"1. To Italian Sovereignty.
2. Commission to rule Fiume district, etc. under League.
   One Jugo-Slav, one Italian, one American.
3. Provision for free port, etc.
4. No taxes to Italy.
5. No military service".

The first line alone shows that this proposal was bound to be completely unacceptable to Wilson. House's diary is silent in regard to this initiative, so we know nothing of his reasons for it, but a remark by Auchincloss gives the impression that House somehow imagined that he would thereby be able to achieve the postponement that he had recommended the day before to both Wilson and Clemenceau[71]). However, it is at the same time clear that he had no authorization from the President for his initiative, and it is reasonable to ask why, if House was at this time in the confidence of the President, he did not go directly to him with his proposal instead of attempting by various roundabout means to give the impression that it had the backing of both Commissioners and Experts.

It was, in fact, a singularly clumsy method that House used. Paul Birdsall has described in detail how Douglas Johnson, much against his will, became involved in the deliberations, how Auchincloss tried to present Mezes and Miller to Lansing as "Experts" in the Italian question, and how the real "Experts" reacted by sending the direct appeal of 17 April to the President. The letter was sent "at exactly one minute past midnight (18 April), together with a copy addressed to Mezes. By 10 a. m. of that same day, April 18, Wilson's reply was on Bowman's desk, offering complete support to his experts' view"[72]). The Experts were evidently afraid that Wilson might, in order to ensure Italian support for the carrying into effect of the League of Nations, enter into a compromise that would not only jeopardize his prestige with the English and French Liberals, but also disillusion the American Delegation. They felt that "the President never had such an opportunity in his career

for striking a death blow to the discredited methods of Old World Diplomacy"[73]). And even after receiving Wilson's extremely friendly reply, they were
still in doubt as to his attitude. On the other hand, they were convinced that
Lansing, White and Bliss shared their view, while they apparently had more
difficulty in judging House's position[74]).

"House claims that he agrees with us in principle, but that his hands are tied. Actually I think that he is behind the President in making any sacrifice in order to get full
support from Italy for the League.
So you have Wilson and House deciding everything, the six of us territorial specialists
and the three Commissioners being bitterly opposed to yielding".

It was not only the Experts who felt the need to make their positions
clear; the Commissioners too, opposed all forms of manipulation. The situation actually had considerable points of similarity with the events surrounding the Guarantee Treaty: here too, House went to his Commission colleagues
with his proposal instead of to Wilson, and here too, he changed his mind
when he noticed the mood of the other members of the Delegation. I took
it then as an expression of the fact that the relationship of trust between him
and the President was broken, and can see no reason taking a different
view now[75]).

On 17 April, House sent his proposal for a compromise to the Commissioners,
who disassociated themselves altogether from the views set forth, replying
"(1) that it was entirely inconsistent to say that the sovereignty of Fiume
should revert to Italy, whereas its administration was to be international
and many concessions in the city itself were to be granted to the Jugo-Slavs,
and (2) that the whole question involved was one of principle and that it
was impossible to compromise with a principle. In this question, either the
city should be granted to the Italians and the Jugo-Slavs kept out, or else
it should be granted entirely to the Jugo-Slavs and the Italians kept out. The
latter solution was the one favored by the Commissioners"[76]).

At the Commission meeting on 18 April, at which Lansing, White and Bliss
were present, Christian Herter, Secretary to the Commissioners, advised that
he had conveyed this answer to Gordon Auchincloss, who "took exception
to the views of the Commissioners as stated by Mr. Herter, on the grounds
that it was perfectly practicable to place the sovereignty of the city in the
hands of the Italians while making the administration international, since such
a procedure was recognized in law with regard to many questions of property
or estates. He likewise felt that in this matter, and in view of the fact that
the American experts on this question differed as to its rights and wrongs,
a compromise was the only possible solution. When asked what American
experts believed that Italy had any valid claim to the city of Fiume, Mr. Auchincloss asserted that both Dr. Mezes and Mr. Miller were of this opinion,
but that it was also undoubtedly true that some of our other experts were
not"[77]).

General Bliss then advised "that on the previous night Dr. Bowman had shown to him a letter to the President signed by the Chiefs of six Sections of the Bureau of Inquiry, in which those experts expressed to the President their absolute conviction that the Italian claims to the city of Fiume were absolutely unjustified. General Bliss felt that possibly this letter had been instigated because of the feeling among those experts that some compromise was being contemplated"[78]). House then joined the meeting.

He explained to his colleagues that "the memorandum which he had sent down on the previous day had merely been a suggestion, and that it had not been shown even to the President (Mr. Auchincloss had told Mr. Herter on the previous afternoon that the substance of this suggested compromise had been informally brought to the attention of the Jugo-Slav representatives in Paris and that the indications were that it would be satisfactory to them). Colonel House added that he personally felt that there could be no such solution as a compromise, that the time had gone by when any further compromise could be made"[79]). In other words, House did a volte-face when he became aware of the feeling among the Commissioners. His tactics had failed, and he did not even give himself the time for an orderly retreat.

However, Bliss was not satisfied with this assurance, but "wished to go on record as being absolutely opposed to any settlement such as that suggested in Colonel House's memorandum, that in his opinion such a settlement would bring upon Europe in a very short time a war the proportions and length of which could not be foreseen but which would undoubtedly be most extensive and most disatrous"[80]). And this perhaps provides the reason why the otherwise short and insignificant minutes of the meeting on this date have been provided with a supplement in the form of an extremely detailed memorandum, from which the above passages are taken[81]).

The meeting ended with House asking "if the other Commissioners were definitely agreed that Fiume should remain in the hands of the Jugo-Slavs, to which Mr. Lansing, General Bliss and Mr. White affirmed most categorically that it was. Colonel House then added that he was of the same opinion as the other Commissioners, and that it would be best to have the matter out with the Italians as soon as possible, preferably on the next day"[82]). House's second attempt at making common cause with his colleagues on the Commission had also failed.

House did not mention this meeting either, in his diary. However, on the same day, he had the opportunity of discussing various problems including Fiume with the President: ". . . I urged him to settle it one way or the other. I have about come to the conclusion that since we cannot please the Italians by compromise, we might as well do what seems best in the judgment of our experts, and that is to give it directly to the Jugo-Slavs, safeguarding the rights of all those contributory to the port. This solution appealed to the President. . . ."[83]). It was naturally not surprising that Wilson felt attracted to this solution, since it was what he himself had recommended all the time! The whole entry in the diary has indeed the stamp of having been written "for the record", as a cover and a compensation for the events at the day's meeting of the Commission and the Experts' appeal to Wilson. What House actually said to the President, we have no means of knowing[84]). Wilson himself was at this time expecting a break with Italy[85]).

In the afternoon of 19 April, Wilson held a conference with all the Commissioners, during which he advised that the Italians were threatening to leave Paris if they did not get Fiume, but that he would never give his consent to this[86]). Before the President left the meeting, he requested the Commissioners to send "any suggestions which might occur to us (Commissioners) as a possible way of assisting the Italian Government in tiding over its apprehended political difficulties"[87]). And this they did in a memorandum of the same date, in which they submitted proposals for a temporary postponement of the decision for a period of one year, during which the areas in dispute should be governed by an international Commission[88]). House asserted that it was he who stood behind the proposal, while Lansing's diary entry does not state who took the initiative. However, House wished to make quite sure that Wilson should know that it was at his initiative, and he therefore sent a letter himself to the President, setting out the same proposal. He concluded with the words[89]):

"I proposed this to the other Commissioners after you left and they all agreed. At White's suggestion, it was decided to draw this up in the form of a letter for us all to sign. I asked Lansing to prepare it, but since I cannot lay hands on him for the moment, I am sending this in advance".

Was this just a clumsy attempt to regain Wilson's favour, or was it posterity he had in mind? In any event, all efforts at solidarity were laid aside, and House really appears to have been very angry with both Commissioners and Experts[90]).

In his diary, House gives the following reason for his attitude, and it is a reason he must often have repeated, for precisely the attitude it expresses became one of the most important grounds for recrimination against both Wilson and House by both the Commissioners and the Experts[91]):

"The only reason I suggest such a compromise, if indeed it may be called one, for it merely postpones the action which we have decided upon now, is because if Italy refused to sign the Treaty with Germany and if Japan also refused, and there is some danger of this too, then conditions would be serious. . . .".

However, House had for the second time misjudged Wilson's attitude in a fundamental matter: he had believed that the President was willing to arrive at a compromise in the Saar-question, and he believed it in this case too, but in fact Wilson took the opportunity of finally making an example. Since his return in the middle of March, he had received innumerable exhortations to make a public statement, but he had restrained himself as long as the matter concerned France. In the case of Italy, however, which was not really a Great Power, he was willing to take the risk of a break[92]).

At a meeting on 21 April with the other four American Commissioners, he read aloud a declaration that he intended to publish in the event of a break with Italy, and this was "cordially approved by everyone"[93]). On 23 April he published it, four days after taking another step from which he had shrunk in the case of France: direct economic sanctions. On 19 April, he wrote to Norman Davis[94]):

"We have come to a rather difficult issue with the Italians, and I am going to beg therefore, that you will cooperate with me in delaying our reply to the Treasury about the fifty million dollar advance to the Italian Government for a few days until the air clears—if it does".

While Wilson prepared himself for the decisive break, House continued his confidential negotiations with the Italians to the bitter end[95]), possibly because he, like Auchincloss and Wiseman, was of the opinion that the Italians were really bluffing[96]). R. S. Baker was at any rate already of the opinion that House's "compromising spirit and his assurances to Orlando, communicated to Italy, has served to fan the flame of Italian nationalism and make it harder for Wilson, now that the real issue is joined"[97]), and with Baker's close relationship with Wilson during this period, the possibility cannot be excluded that his remark actually reflected the view of the President. As mentioned earlier, it was also one of the recriminations later made against House by Henry White and Paul Birdsall[98]).

As long as a detailed analysis of the Italian material is lacking, it is scarcely possible either to verify or refute this assertion. It is obvious that the Italians did everything to flatter House and strived to make him "their man", and it is also clear that House completely misjudged the resolution of both the Italians and Wilson, and at the same time, manipulated quite irresponsibly with the various Expert groups in the Delegation. On the other hand, however, the Italians were undoubtedly at this moment playing such a complicated diplomatic game that most observers felt repelled by it. Nevertheless, it is not until later that we have direct proof of the fact that House deliberately played on his supposed position with Wilson in his negotiations with the Italians[99]). But by that time the situation had changed again. House had in advance ensured the President's (very unwilling) consent to his new plan, and his motive appears to have been a very personal one. He wanted to rehabilitate himself: "... It would be a great triumph if I could bring about a settlement of this difficult, delicate and dangerous problem"[100]). However, after Wilson's Italian manifesto and the subsequent withdrawal of the Italians from the Conference, new proposals for a compromise fell on stony ground, and the negotiations came to nothing.

The President's public declaration on the Italian question has been described as "a capital error in judgement"[101]), and this was undoubtedly the case as far as concerned its effect in Italy. If Wilson imagined that his declaration of principles would arouse public feeling that would either engender the fall of the Orlando Government or improve its will to negotiate, he was vastly mistaken. The reaction outside Italy, on the other hand, was far more favourable, and in particular the American reaction was extremely favourable. The President could not, of course, hope by a single blow to regain his enormously successful position as the leader of Liberalism that he had held at the beginning of the Conference, but he could make a last, wholehearted attempt to rally the scattered forces.

The reaction of the French press was, as usual, extremely polarized, but still surprisingly favourable: "while the reactionary Press denounces with bitterness the attitude Mr. Wilson has taken in the Italian claims, moderate opinion indulges in hopes that the situation may yet be smoothed over, and the Left wing Press in general rings with approval of Mr. Wilson's message"[102]). The reports from England were even more favourable. "The most influential editorial opinion in England supports Wilson in the present crisis", according to the daily press report[103]) and "British liberal opinion was enthusiastic"[104]). "In both Britain and France the political as well as the trade union arms of the labor movement formally and publicly endorsed the President's appeal, calling on their premiers to return to the straight and lofty path of the Fourteen Points"[105]).

Most noteworthy of all, however, was the American reaction. After R. S. Baker, Tumulty had been one of those who had tried hardest to get the President to break the silence he had kept too long[106]), and it is also characteristic that Tumulty should be one of the first to be asked his opinion when the decision was finally taken[107]). It was, of course, still on the other side of the Atlantic that the decisive battle had to be won. And Wilson could hardly have wished for a better reception of his declaration[108]):

"The President's stand on Fiume has the support of practically every shade of unbiased American opinion.

For the first time in months, Mr. Wilson finds himself backed without reservation by the great body of the press. And, there is every indication that closer unaninimity of approval is given by the people at large. Congress is overwhelmingly sympathetic, even the familiar dissenters to any Administration program being found among the endorsers of the President's position. The latest to approve are Senators Johnson, Smoot and Cummins".

Tumulty reacted enthusiastically: "This is your supreme hour and I have never been so proud of you"[109]), and encouraging telegrams flooded in from the United States[110]). It looked as though Wilson had, at any rate for a time, closed the mouth of the American Opposition[111]).

The day after publishing this Italian manifesto, Wilson received the following telegram from Tumulty[112]):

"As we see it from this distance, the selfish designs of Japan are as indefensible as are those of Italy. The two situations appear to parallel each other in their bearing upon the fate of weak and helpless nations. Would it not be an opportune time to cast another die, this one in the direction of Japan that the whole world may know once and for all where America stands upon this greatest issue of the peace we are trying to make! Now is the time to use your heavy artillery and emphasize danger of secret treaties and selfish designs of certain big nations".

And it is clear that Wilson shared this view completely[113]). Nevertheless, on 30 April, he entered into a compromise agreement with Japan that seemed quite contrary to the principles he had so clearly formulated hardly one week earlier.

In 1914, Japan had conquered the German possessions, Kiaochow and the Shantung railroad in China. On 18 January 1915 Japan had presented her "21 demands" to China, "which required Chinese consent in advance to any ultimate arrangement between Japan and Germany regarding the German rights in Shantung and which contained other provisions for the recognition of pre-eminent Japanese interests in Manchuria and northern China". The United States protested, but on 25 May of the same year China consented. In February 1917, "formal agreements were concluded between Japan and Britian, France and Russia which bound the European Allies to support at the Peace Conference Japanese claims to the German rights in Shantung and to the German islands of the North Pacific". In the Lansing-Ishii settlement of 2 November 1917, the United States recognized that Japan had "special interests" in China on account of its territorial proximity, and both Powers disclaimed any intention of violating the independence and territorial integrity of China, and promised to maintain "the open-door policy". However, on 24 September, 1918, "secret notes were exchanged between China and Japan conceding various Japanese privileges in Shantung, including police functions, joint Sino-Japanese management of the Kiaochow-Tainan railroad, and concessions for railroads to be built by Japan in Manchuria and Mongolia as well as in Shantung. Japan thus came to the Peace Conference fortified in her demands by valid international legal engagements as well as by her position as the dominant military power of the Far East. Moreover, Japan was in possession of Shantung"[114]).

China had the sympathy of the United States, not only on moral grounds, but also for important economic and political reasons. The free and unimpeded access to the enormous Chinese market had long been a declared American policy, and if we have to point to a vital, long-term, American interest at the Peace Conference, it must have been the maintenance of the balance of power in the Pacific. American opinion was undoubtedly against the Japanese demands[115]). That Wilson gave in was due to the fact that he gave the League of Nations priority over everything else and considered it important to have Japan as a member. When the organization had been established it would provide the instrument for the correction of all injustice. And the President took at face value the Japanese threat of refusing to sign the Covenant if an acceptable Compromise were not reached.

Later research has shown that his evaluation of Japanese policy was correct[116]). In the Treaty, Japan demanded—and was given—all Germany's concessions in the Shantung Province. In return, the Japanese representatives declared, partly in the "Council of Four" on 30 April and partly in a press announcement on 5 May, that it was Japan's intention only to retain the economic privileges, but to assign to China full sovereignty over the leased area of the Bay of Kiaochow. China refused to sign the Treaty on this basis[117]). Balfour played an important part in the implementation of the compromise[118]).

Wilson himself, the Experts Hornbeck and Williams, Commissioners Lansing, White and Bliss, and R. S. Baker—all, in fact, except House—sympathized with China[119]). This became quite clear at the meeting Wilson held with his Commissioners on 26 April, at which only House seems to have been in favour of a compromise with Japan, on the grounds that "it would be a mistake to take such action against Japan as might lead to her withdrawal from the Conference"[120]). This was the argument that, in the end, proved decisive for Wilson's acceptance of the Japanese demands. But was this due to House's influence? There is nothing, in fact, to indicate that House had any influence at all on Wilson's decision in this matter. His standpoint should rather be taken as support for the view that House was, in spite of everything, the only adviser whose aims harmonized well with the fundamental principles behind Wilson's policy.

After the meeting, however, it was not House, but Lansing who was ordered to contact the Japanese Delegates[121]). Typically enough, House's only involvement in the matter occurred on British initiative[122]). Wilson reached the final decision during the morning meeting of the "Council of Four" on 28 April[123]). At the afternoon meeting, the Covenant of the League of Nations was placed before the Plenary Session of the Conference, and the Japanese Delegate, who had already been advised of Wilson's change of attitude, "confined himself to an academic speech on Japan's racial clause (which had been rejected) and did not refer to the Shantung subject"[124]). Lansing had the opportunity of talking to Wilson and got the impression that "a bargain had been struck by which the Japanese agreed to sign the Covenant in exchange for admission of their claims. If so, it is an iniquitous agreement . . . I believe House is at the bottom of it. I said to him today that to give Kiau Chau to Japan was to barter away a great principle. He replied, "we have had to do it before". . . ."[125]). To Bliss too, House had expressed the opinion during the meeting "that it would be a satisfactory "compromise" "[126]).

After the Plenary Session, Bliss took the initiative to call a meeting with White and Lansing. They were all opposed to the contemplated compromise, and they had the impression that Wilson was under House's influence in the matter: "he is influenced solely by Mr. House who is a trimmer". Bliss therefore decided to send a personal letter to the President before he reached his final decision, and the others supported Bliss in this line of action[127]). In reality, however, House was just as ignorant of Wilson's intentions as his colleagues. He too, composed a letter to the President, although at the instigation of Lloyd George and Balfour, and with quite a different content than Bliss's letter[128]). His choice of words is clearly characterized by the devil-may-care attitude that now seemed to have taken hold of him:

"My feeling is that while it is all bad, it is no worse than the things we are doing in many of the settlements in which the Western Powers are interested. I feel too that we had best clean up a lot of old rubbish with the least friction, and let the League of Nations and the new era do the rest".

House was not advised when the final decision was taken[129]), and it is doubtful whether his letter had any effect whatsoever, since the President had, as we have seen, reached this decision by 28 April. Nevertheless it was against him rather than the President that everyone directed their anger: "House is with the President, he favours all compromises, while the President knows when to compromise and when not to"[130]).

The rest is really just an epilogue. Apart from one last, hectic, but extremely brief and fruitless engagement in the Italian negotiations in the middle of May[131]), House did not participate in any of the decisive political negotiations during the last phase of the Conference, and on 30 May, he himself admitted as much in his diary: "I seldom or never have a chance to talk with him (Wilson) and, for the moment, he is practically out from under my influence"[132]). And the next day, he disclosed the fact that while Hankey's reports of the meetings in the "Council of Four" had been distributed among the British and French Delegations, Wilson did not wish his American colleagues to see them. "I have never seen a copy of it. Hankey proposed sending it down to me, but the President vetoed it by saying he was afraid to let it come to the Crillon because there were so many newspapermen around"[133]).

However, House continued to allow himself to be used by Clemenceau, for instance, at the beginning of June, when Lloyd George demanded considerable changes in the Treaty on account of German protest[134]). House sympathized to a certain extent with a number of the alterations proposed by Lloyd George, but "I (House) wanted to fight it out when the Treaty was being made and not now after it had been unanimously agreed upon"[135]). The same attitude, incidentally, as that of Wilson himself[136]). House was thoroughly depressed during the last phase of the Conference: "he was so sick of the Paris game before he left that it almost hurt"[137]). He was isolated in the Delegation and the gossip regarding his person thrived unhindered, with Admiral Grayson himself joining in[138]). Even the post he had prepared for himself to fall back on seemed to be slipping out of his hands:

As the President's right-hand man in the League of Nations Commission, it was natural that it should also be House who became the representative of the United States on the "Committee on the Site of the League of Nations"[139]). And House soon began to lay plans for the location and architecture of the buildings[140]):

"I have followed the fortunes of the League too long to wish to leave it until it is a safely going concern. I have in mind the kind of home it should have on the banks of Lake Geneva; the style of architecture it should have, and I would like one of the best architects in the world to draw the plans. I do not want anything official looking; it should be like a private residence of the nobler kind, something of the kind we find so often here in France and even in Paris. I have in mind, too, to use this home merely for committee rooms and meetings, and to have drawn for erection residences throughout the park to house the different nations, very much as embassies or legations. These to be drawn some on a modest scale and some more pretentious so that the great nations may have homes suitable to their rank, and the smaller nations may have something artistic and in keeping with the general style of the park".

Indeed, he had even got as far as considering the design of the flag, deciding that it should be "similar to the flag of my native State, Texas"[141]).

However, what was just as important was the fact that House tried to achieve the dominating influence on the organization of the League of Nations. Not only was he the United States representative on the "Organization Committee of the League of Nations"; he also tried, through the framing of the draft resolution, to get "the direction of the organization, the preparation of the agenda for the first meeting of the league, and the place of the meeting largely in my hands"[142]). It was originally House's wish that the first meeting of the League of Nations should be held on 1 October in Washington, under the Chairmanship of President Wilson[143]). On 28 April, the Plenary Session passed the resolution on the organization, and House now thought that his influence was ensured[144]). In the following period House was therefore heavily engaged in meetings in connection with the organization[145]). Behind this comprehensive activity lay the apparent expectation of becoming the first representative of the United States on the League of Nations Council.

We do not know when, or even whether, the President ever gave such a promise, but we do know that House at one time asked D. H. Miller whether he could become the United States representative on the Council "without confirmation by the Senate"[146]), and that he hinted to Bullitt that he would be the American representative, and that the rest of the Delegation considered it a matter of common knowledge that House should be the American top Delegate[147]). However, we also know that Admiral Grayson said at the end of June that he was not certain whether the President "would permit House to take position of US on League of Nations ..."[148]), and that Lansing refused to make a grant from the Emergency Fund for a London office for House until the Senate had consented to the Covenant of the League of Nations[149]). Thus, personal and political factors combined to interfere with House's plans, and later that summer, he complained bitterly that the situation regarding the Senate approval was uncertain, for otherwise, "the entire organization of the League of Nations . . . would have been in our hands, may I say, in my hands"[150]).

There was really nothing but disappointment left for House in his official, international career. Immediately after the signing of the Treaty with Germany, Wilson left Europe, while Lansing took over the leadership of the Delegation until, later that summer, he was succeeded in this capacity by Frank Polk. When Wilson left, House went to London, where he was to participate, in inter alia the meetings of the Mandate Commission[151]). However there is much to indicate that Wilson had not intended that House should leave Paris so quickly. At any rate, House felt obliged a little later to send the President a detailed explanation of his action. It was a very personal and a very humble letter, and was the closest House ever came to admitting his faults. It constituted an outstretched hand, but the President failed to take it[152]):

"I hope you will not think that I shirked the work in Paris by leaving when you did. I thought the thing out carefully and came to the conclusion that it would be nearly impossible to continue there after you had gone and keep cordial relations with the other Commissioners. You may or may not know that there was considerable resentment that you did not consult them sufficiently and I cann (!) in for my share of this feeling. With you away and Lansing in charge, and with Lansing gone and White in charge, my position would have been untenable. It seemed therefore on the whole, better to leave them to work things out alone. The members of the other delegations would almost surely have brought their difficulties to me and I would have been under the necessity of having to decline to take them up or to have created friction with my colleagues. I suppose you understood that it was really this that brought me over here" (to England).

Thus House admitted here that his position in Paris had become untenable, but he asserted in his diary that ". . . I would have been entirely willing to have remained with the Conference provided I had been left in absolute charge which, in the circumstances, was hardly possible"[153]). When his work in London came to an end, House therefore wanted to go home, but he was instead ordered back to Paris[154]). At the same time, press rumours regarding a break between Wilson and House were again circulating. House telegraphed Wilson concerning an official denial, but Wilson just sent the noncommittal answer: "the best way to treat it is with silent contempt"[155]). At the beginning of October, House left Europe anyway, without the consent of the President[156]). Clemenceau went to the railway station to say goodbye, but none of House's colleagues from the Commission was present[157]). House's official career was finally at an end.

The Peace Conference saw the conclusion of an epoch in House's life. However, there is no mystery in the fact that things went the way they did. The break was the logical culmination of a course of events for which House himself was, to a great degree, responsible. There is no need to seek scandal and intrigue—though they were doubtless to be found: House acted with his eyes wide open—he knew what he was doing.

It is obvious that he felt himself provoked, forced out by Mrs. Wilson and by developments in general. This was his last chance and he grabbed it with both hands. However, that does not constitute an excuse. The Peace Conference was a deadly serious matter, not an exciting past-time; House forgot this. His situation was by no means easy—quite the reverse—but it was a situation and a position that he himself had brought about.

House dug his own grave.

# Conclusion

In the foregoing I have tried to draw a portrait of Colonel House during the time he spent in Paris up to and during the Peace Conference. At the same time I have aimed at presenting as diversified a picture as possible of the political events in which House took part, not only because I believe that this is something that previous research on House has neglected[1]), but also because I share the view that diversity is vital to the historical presentation[2]). Nonetheless, the book has still acquired the character of a thesis, which although presenting me with a constant challenge, I have frequently felt as an unnecessary restraint. It is therefore with the greatest hesitation that I shall now attempt the very converse of diversity: to give a conclusion.

Alexander and Juliette George's dissection of House's diary has shown that a consistent analysis of the diary is a necessary but insufficient condition for an understanding of House's conduct at the Peace Conference. What is also needed is a concurrent and partially independent assessment of the political situation and the political environment in which House acted. Such an analysis of House's activities at the Conference seems to point to the fact that his conduct was of such a character that, regardless of possible psychological motives, on Wilson's part too, a break with the President was practically unavoidable, i. e. the scapegoat theory is superfluous. On the other hand, R. S. Baker's thesis on the causes and "timing" of the break appears increasingly plausible.

It is clear from the diary that, both personally and politically, House was already in opposition to Wilson at the time of his departure for Europe in October 1918. He was frustrated because his real influence on the President appeared to be waning (partly because of Mrs. Wilson's position), and he at the same time felt himself to stand considerably more to the Left of the political spectrum than Wilson. Furthermore, before commencement of the Conference he had had a number of experiences that were to have a decisive influence on his conduct during the Conference itself. Both in the so-called House Mission in the autumn of 1917 and during the pre-Armistice negotiations in 1918, House had been the chief negotiator on the American side, with very wide powers invested in him. At these two conferences, though perhaps principally the former, House had obtained insight into how a big inter-Allied meeting was organized and manipulated, and he had acquired a taste for being the man to make the decisions.

Another important factor relating to these two conferences was that House here came into contact with Clemenceau for the first time, and was undoubtedly highly influenced by this strong personality. This in turn had the effect of leading him to favour the French views on a number of points, whereby he came to take steps that neither his position as an American nor his standing as a Liberal could ever warrant. He became disloyal to Wilson and to American policy, partly through his own personal attraction to Clemenceau, partly through the feeling of superiority engendered in him by his earlier conference experience, and partly through the frustration born of his increasingly precarious personal relations with the President. On the other hand, the original difference in political interests between Wilson and himself does not appear to have played a significant part in the course of events. On the contrary, in the situations in which House acted in a definitely illoyal manner, he stood clearly to the Right, not to the Left, of the President.

The pre-Armistice negotiations provided the last opportunity for House to act completely independently, and they reveal quite clearly his obvious weaknesses as a negotiator. He seems totally to have underestimated the political consequences of the negotiations and to have accepted formal rather than real concessions. On the other hand, it is clear that he was acting under double pressure, partly from the Allies in Paris and partly from the President in Washington, and there is no doubt that both during the negotiations themselves and in the subsequent period, House was very uncertain as to the President's intentions. He simply did not know what Wilson wanted.

However, it was not only the President's policy of which House was uncertain in this period, but also his own position. He would obviously be given a formally prominent place in the American Delegation, but the question was how much real influence he would have. Even before the end of the war an internal struggle for power had been played out between House and Lansing on the dominant role in the coming American Peace Delegation. In the period up to Wilson's arrival in Paris at the beginning of December 1918, the second phase of this struggle took place, ending, after a first serious setback, in the most favourable result for House. He apparently re-established his position with the President and at the same time ensured himself a solid position of personal power by building up his own organization within the Delegation. However, this was also the beginning of the end. He became so absorbed in consolidating his own key position not only in the American Delegation, but also in respect of the Conference as a whole, that he failed to keep himself au courant with Wilson's policy. He never succeeded in regaining the awareness of the President's innermost thoughts that he had apparently lost during the pre-Armistice negotiations. In addition, he fell ill during the decisive political manoeuvres before the Peace Conference opened, and he thereby lost the influence that he had hoped to exercise.

When Wilson left the Conference in the middle of February 1919 for a short visit to the United States, House threw himself into restless action to regain lost ground, but he seems to a certain extent to have lost touch with the realities of the situation. He saw himself in the role of grand manipulator of the Conference and forgot that his primary task was to act as mouthpiece for American policy. There can be no doubt at all that during this period, House acted in clear contradiction of Wilson's intentions, both as regards the League of Nations and as regards the French demands in respect of the Rhineland; he failed to counter the efforts that were once more being made to separate the League of Nations Covenant from the Peace Treaty, and he allowed himself to become very heavily involved in negotiations on a compromise on the French demands.

The consequence of House's attitude here was a prior weakening of Wilson's bargaining position, a weakening that was further accentuated by the domestic developments in the United States, where Wilson was encountering heavy opposition to his League of Nations policy. Indeed, all indications point to the fact that the close personal relationship between House and Wilson came to an abrupt and definite end as soon as the President returned to France, the "break" evidently taking place during the very first talk between the two men. Wilson here apparently learned enough about the events of the previous month to feel that House had failed him, while House, for his part, would have liked an opportunity to explain matters in detail. This opportunity was never granted to him; from now on, as clearly shown by a detailed analysis of American policy in the subsequent period, he was left out in the cold. After the return of the President in mid-March 1919 House was without any real influence upon American policy-making. He was, in fact, as much in the dark regarding Wilson's thoughts and intentions as his three fellow-Commissioners; although, thanks to his connections in the French and British Delegations and his contacts with the American Experts, he was better informed of the work of the Conference as a whole than were Lansing, White and Bliss.

There is no reason to attribute the break itself to exterior intrigues, although there is no doubt that even before Wilson left Paris in February, House was in a rather isolated position in the Delegation. His energetic efforts to gather all power in his own hands seem to have had a marked effect on the working climate in The American Commission to Negotiate Peace, and House's fellow-Commissioners, in particular, felt both frustrated and bitter. The most influential group in the Delegation, apart from House, appears to have been the economic Experts, several of whom (Bernard Baruch, Vance McCormick) were already personal friends of the President. However, it is not possible to prove that any intrigues on their part or on that of others contributed to the break itself. As long as House enjoyed Wilson's trust he was unassailable. On the other hand, it is naturally possible that after his talk with House in March, Wilson became more heedful of information that may have helped to deepen the cleft. All the same, this is pure hypothesis.

However, it can be ascertained that for a short time during the height of the crisis of the Conference at the beginning of April, House was once more taken into favour. Again he failed; it was not his policy of concessions in the negotiations on reparations during Wilson's illness that proved decisive —here he was only continuing a policy already initiated by the President—but once more his pro-French policy, this time on the question of the Saar. In this serious crisis Wilson deliberately chose to stand firm on this question, he wanted—at least for a time—to demonstrate the strength of his principles, and this, House did not understand. A not insignificant part in the course of these events was also played by Gordon Auchincloss, House's son-in-law, and Wickham Steed of "The Times". The explosion took place on 4 April.

After this, House's role was, in fact, played out. It is true that he was later involved in the negotiations on a compromise with Italy, but this was apparently mostly on his own initiative. House's conduct during the Italian negotiations finally exposed his total isolation in the Delegation, but it did not appear to affect his personal relationship with the President; that, as House was only too aware, had already been broken. On the other hand, several members of the American Delegation, especially House's fellow-Commissioners Lansing, White and Bliss, were still under the illusion that House was a person of influence. They, therefore, made him responsible for the solution of the Shantung-question although it was actually Wilson himself who had decided on this against the wishes of nearly all other members of the American Delegation. House was almost the only one who understood—and approved—the decision, but his advice was not sought by the President. Incidentally, during the last phase of the Conference House seems to have devoted himself increasingly to building up the League of Nations. Besides having a truly idealistic interest in the concept of the League, he saw, in the possibility of a prominent post within this organization, a consolation for the position he had lost with the President. But here too, he was disappointed.

It is evident, in the wider perspective, that any interpretation of Colonel House's influence at the Peace Conference is also an evaluation and interpretation of the policies of Woodrow Wilson. I hope that the foregoing pages may have thrown some new light on this aspect—and, particularly, on the President's stand on the Italian question and his thoughts and actions in the period from mid-March to mid-April 1919. On the whole, this rough sketch of House's activities in Paris reflects only one side of my aim in the present thesis. The more I tried to penetrate into the problems of the Peace Conference, the more fascinated I became by this fantastic play, in which people and ideas were cast hither and thither in a complicated diplomatic game, and I became obsessed with the necessity of untangling the threads down to the minutest details. The most enthralling aspect of it all is perhaps the ideological dilemma in which Wilson found himself. The hard-pressed centre position of Liberalism was a vital element of both his Russian and his Italian policy, and the whole fundamental principle of Wilsonianism was at stake durring the decisive crisis in April. All this House appreciated far better than any of Wilson's other advisers, yet every time it really mattered, he gave in:[3])

"He is a liberal by instinct, though not at all a thinker. He is a conciliator, an arranger. He likes human beings—and so they like him. And he has a shrewdness, too!"

# Dansk resumé

Hovedpersonen i nærværende afhandling er Oberst Edward M. House, der gennem en længere årrække var Woodrow Wilsons nærmeste ven og rådgiver. Det venskabelige forhold mellem de to mænd fik en brat ende under fredskonferencen i 1919, og om dette celebre »brud«, dets årsager og betydning har der siden stået en heftig debat. Den her foreliggende bog er at betragte som endnu et indlæg i denne strid.

Når spørgsmålet har været så hidsigt diskuteret, skyldes det ikke alene den psykologiske tiltrækning en sådan gåde altid udøver på forskeren, men også at i det større perspektiv har den fortolkning man giver af såvel årsagerne til »bruddet«, som tidspunktet for dets ikrafttræden, betydning for den samlede vurdering af Woodrow Wilson og den politik han førte på fredskonferencen i 1919.

Mange fortolkninger er da også blevet fremsat i årenes løb, skylden er skiftevis blevet tillagt House og Wilson, og nogle har søgt årsagerne på det principielle og politiske plan, andre på det personlige og psykologiske, eller eventuelt en kombination af begge dele. Også om dateringen af selve »bruddet« har meningerne været delte: Fandt det sted umiddelbart efter Wilsons tilbagekomst til Paris (efter et kort ophold i USA) i marts 1919, eller var der tale om en gradvis udvikling – og hvornår begynder og afsluttes da denne udvikling? Hvilket atter vil sige: Havde House overhovedet nogen indflydelse på den politik Wilson førte under konferencens kritiske fase? Hvem var ansvarlig for den serie kompromis'er præsidenten i den sidste ende måtte indgå for at få gennemført hvad han selv regnede for kernepunktet i sit program: Folkeforbundets indlemmelse i traktaten.

Når jeg har ment det rimeligt endnu engang at tage hele problemet op til en nærmere undersøgelse skyldes det ikke blot, at gåden stadig har uløste aspekter og at alt relevant kildemateriale nu på det nærmeste er tilgængeligt, men også at forskningen i de seneste år er bragt ind på et helt nyt spor af Alexander og Juliette L. George. De to forfattere (henholdsvis en political scientist og en psykolog) har i bogen Woodrow Wilson and Colonel House. A personality Study, analyseret House's dagbog i dens fulde kronologiske omfang og derigennem klart demonstreret, at House's venskab for Wilson var noget i høj grad villet, noget yderst bevidst. House havde erkendt præsidentens psykologiske behov for sikkerhed, opmuntring og smiger og var villig til at opfylde dem, fordi han derigennem kunne opnå en indflydelse og magt, han ikke på anden vis ville kunne få del i.

Der kan ikke herske tvivl om, at venskabet i begyndelsen (november 1911) var baseret på virkelig gensidig sympati og tillid, men George og George's analyse af House's dagbogsnotater viser, at der i disse så tidligt som i 1913 kan iagttages en vis irritation hos House overfor Wilson, en irritation, der som tiden går tiltager i styrke og akcentueres efter Wilson's bryllup i december 1915, i takt med den voksende spænding mellem House og den nye Mrs. Wilson. Denne irritation hos House giver sig udslag i en række kritiske kommentarer i dagbogen, både om Wilson selv og om hans politik, ledsaget af udredninger af, hvad House *selv* ville have gjort i præsidentens sted.

Spørgsmålet er nu om House's voksende distancering fra Wilson alene er psykologisk betinget eller om den også afspejler reelle politiske modsætninger, eventuelt af mere principiel karakter? Dette spørgsmål har de to forfattere ikke besvaret eentydigt, men har nøjedes med fra gang til gang at anføre, at uoverensstemmelser var tilstede, uden nærmere at analysere, af hvilken karakter de var. Jeg mener imidlertid at kunne godtgøre, at der i krigens løb udvikledes principielle politiske modsætninger mellem de to mænd, men at det på den anden side ikke var disse spørgsmål, der havde betydning for »bruddet«.

Svagheden ved George og George's analyse set fra en historikers synspunkt er den, at de med hensyn til deres vurdering af House's politiske virksomhed udelukkende har baseret sig på den tidligere forsknings (ikke mindst Charles Seymour's) resultater. En forskning, de imidlertid selv takket være deres dagbogsstudier, har gjort forældet. M. a. o. hvis man vil præstere en virkelig tilbundsgående fremstilling og diskussion af House's virksomhed på fredskonferencen i 1919 kræves der ikke blot en konsekvent analyse af dagbogen, men også en sideløbende og delvis uafhængig analyse af den politiske situation og det politiske miljø, House agerede i. Det er en sådan dobbelt undersøgelse der er forsøgt i nærværende afhandling, og den har efter min mening vist, at House's optræden på fredskonferencen var af en sådan karakter, at et brud med præsidenten var på det nærmeste uundgåeligt, uanset eventuelle psykologiske motiver også fra Wilsons side. Den teori at House blev »syndebuk«, d. v. s. at han blev ofret a. h. t. de kompromis'er, præsidenten måtte gå ind på, er altså overflødig. Til gengæld forekommer Ray Stannard Bakers allerede 1923 fremsatte these om »bruddets« årsager og »timing« mere og mere plausibel: Det fandt sted umiddelbart efter Wilsons tilbagekomst til Paris i midten af marts 1919, og den direkte anledning var den politik House under Wilsons fravær havde ført m. h. t. Folkeforbundet og m. h. t. de franske Rhinkrav.

Spørgsmålet er da: hvorfor og hvordan?

Den tyske regering anmodede i begyndelsen af oktober 1918 den amerikanske præsident om at foranledige fredsforhandlinger på grundlag af De fjorten Punkter, og medens Wilson gik ind i en noteudveksling med Tyskland mødtes de allierede premier- og udenrigsministre i Paris med en udsending for den amerikanske præsident for at komme overens om en fælles politik m. h. t. den kommende våbenstilstand. Den amerikanske repræsentant i disse såkaldte pre-Armistice forhandlinger var Edward House.

Det fremgår af dagbogen klart, at House allerede inden sin afrejse til Europa i midten af oktober 1918 både personligt og politisk var i opposition til Wilson. Han følte sig frustreret fordi hans rent faktiske indflydelse på præsidenten syntes at blive stadig mindre (bl. a. på grund af Mrs. Wilsons position) og han følte sig samtidig placeret betydelig mere til venstre på den politiske arena end Wilson. Inden selve fredskonferencens begyndelse fik House lejlighed til at gøre en række erfaringer, der skulle få afgørende indflydelse på hans senere optræden. Både på den såkaldte House Mission i efteråret 1917 og under pre-Armisticeforhandlingerne i 1918 havde House været den ledende forhandler på amerikansk side med meget vidtgående beføjelser. På disse to konferencer og måske især på den første, fik House et indblik i, hvordan et stort interallieret møde organiseres og manipuleres, og han fik smag for at være den, der træffer beslutningerne.

De to konferencer fik også betydning på den vis, at House her for første gang kom i direkte kontakt med Clemenceau, og ganske givet i høj grad blev påvirket af denne stærke personlighed. Dette betød igen, at han på en række punkter blev særdeles franskorienteret, og at han derfor under fredskonferencen kom til at tage skridt, som hverken hans position som amerikaner eller som liberal kunne bære. Han blev illoyal overfor Wilson og overfor den amerikanske politik, dels p. g. a. den personlige tiltrækning mod Clemenceau, dels p. g. a. den følelse af overlegenhed hans tidligere konferenceerfaringer havde indgydt ham, og dels p. g. a. den frustration hans stadig mere usikre personlige position hos præsidenten affødte. Derimod synes det oprindelige politiske modsætningsforhold mellem ham og Wilson ikke at have spillet nogen rolle, tværtimod. I de situationer hvor House på afgørende vis optrådte illoyalt, stod han klart til højre, ikke til venstre for præsidenten.

Pre-Armistice forhandlingerne var sidste gang House optrådte helt på egen boldgade, og de afslører klart hans åbenbare svagheder som forhandler. Han synes ganske at have undervurderet forhandlingernes politiske konsekvenser og have affundet sig med formelle snarere end reelle indrømmelser. På den anden side er det givet, at han var under dobbelt pres, dels fra de allierede i Paris, dels fra præsidenten i Washington, og det er tydeligt, at House såvel under selve forhandlingerne som i perioden derefter har stået meget usikker overfor præsidentens intentioner. Han vidste ganske enkelt ikke, hvad Wilson ville.

Det var imidlertid ikke alene præsidentens politik House i denne periode stod usikker overfor, det var også sin egen position. Det var klart at han formelt ville få en fremskudt placering i den amerikanske delegation, men hvilken indflydelse ville reelt blive ham til del? Allerede inden krigens afslutning var første fase af en intern magtkamp blevet udspillet mellem House og udenrigsminister Lansing om den dominerende rolle i en kommende amerikansk fredsdelegation. I perioden indtil Wilsons ankomst til Paris i begyndelse af december 1918 udspilledes nu anden fase, der efter et alvorligt tilbageslag i starten, fik den for House gunstigt tænkelige afslutning. House genvandt tilsyneladende helt sin position hos præsidenten og sikrede sig samtidig, gennem opbygningen af sin egen organisation indenfor delegationen, en solid personlig magtposition. Dette blev imidlertid også begyndelsen til enden. Han blev nu så optaget af at konsolidere sin egen nøgleposition, ikke alene i den amerikanske delegation, men på hele konferencen som sådan, at han forsømte at holde sig au courant med Wilsons politik. Den kontakt med Wilsons inderste tanker han tilsyneladende havde mistet under pre-Armistice forhandlingerne lykkedes det ham aldrig at etablere igen. Samtidig blev han imidlertid syg under de afgørende politiske manøvrer inden fredskonferencens åbning, således at han heller ikke her fik den indflydelse, han havde håbet på.

Da Wilson så forlod konferencen i midten af februar 1919 for at tage til USA for en kortere periode, kastede House sig ud i rastløs aktivitet for at genvinde det tabte terræn, men samtidig synes han i nogen grad at have mistet kontakten med realiteternes verden. Han så sig selv i rollen som konferencens store manipulator, og glemte at hans opgave primært var at være talerør for den amerikanske politik. Der kan da heller ikke herske tvivl om, at House i denne periode både m. h. t. Folkeforbundet og m. h. t. de franske Rhinkrav førte en politik, der var i modstrid med Wilsons intentioner: Han undlod en klar imødegåelse af de bestræbelser, der under præsidentens fravær atter var i gang for at skille Folkeforbundspagt og Fredstraktat, og han indlod sig endog meget dybt i kompromisforhandlinger om de franske krav.

Konsekvensen af denne holdning hos House var en forhåndssvækkelse af Wilsons forhandlingsposition. En svækkelse der yderligere akcentueredes af den politiske udvikling i USA, hvor Wilson netop i sin Folkeforbundspolitik mødte heftig opposition. Alle indicier peger da også på, at det nære personlige forhold har fået en brat og definitiv afslutning straks ved Wilsons tilbagekomst. Åbenbart er »bruddet« indtruffet under den allerførste samtale mellem de to mænd. Wilson erfarede tilsyneladende her tilstrækkeligt om den foregående måneds begivenheder til at føle sig svigtet af House, medens denne på sin side kunne have ønsket sig en mulighed for at forklare sig nærmere. Denne mulighed fik han imidlertid aldrig. Fra nu af var han udenfor. Dette fremgår klart af en nærmere analyse af den amerikanske politik i den følgende periode.

Efter Wilsons tilbagekomst til Paris i marts 1919 var House uden reel indflydelse; ja, han var i virkeligheden lige så uvidende om Wilsons tanker og handlinger som de øvrige kommissærer, selv om han fortsat, takket være sine forbindelser i de engelske og franske delegationer, og sine kontakter »nedad« med eksperterne i den amerikanske delegation var mere velorienteret end Lansing, White og Bliss om hvad der overhovedet foregik på konferencen.

Der synes ikke at være nogen grund til at tilskrive selve »bruddet« intriger udefra, selv om der på den anden side heller ikke kan herske tvivl om, at House allerede inden Wilson i februar forlod Paris stod temmelig isoleret i delegationen. Hans energiske forsøg på at samle al magt i egne hænder synes i høj grad at have sat sit præg på arbejdsklimaet i The American Commission to Negotiate Peace, og ikke mindst House's kommissær-kolleger var frustrerede og forbitrede. Den mest indflydelsesrige gruppe i delegationen ud over House, synes at have været de økonomiske eksperter, hvoraf flere (Bernard Baruch og Vance McCormick) i forvejen var præsidentens personlige venner. Det er imidlertid ikke muligt at påvise, at intriger fra deres eller andres side skulle have været medvirkende ved selve bruddet. Sålænge House havde Wilsons tillid var han urørlig, uanset om hans svagheder var åbenbare for alle andre. Derimod er det naturligvis ikke udelukket, at Wilson efter marts-samtalen har været mere lydhør overfor informationer, der kan have bidraget til at gøre kløften dybere. Dette er dog kun gisninger.

Hvad der står fast er derimod, at House en kort stund under selve konferencekrisens højdepunkt i begyndelsen af april 1919 atter blev taget til nåde. Men igen svigtede han. Det var ikke hans eftergivenhed i krigsskadeserstatningsforhandlingerne under Wilsons sygdom, der var udslaggivende – her videreførte han blot en politik Wilson allerede var slået ind på, men derimod atter engang House's fransk-venlige politik, denne gang i Saar-spørgsmålet. I denne, den yderste krise, valgte Wilson at stå fast just i dette spørgsmål, her ville han – i hvert fald for en stund – demonstrere sine princippers bærekraft. Og dette forstod House ikke. En ikke uvæsentlig rolle i begivenhedsforløbet spillede også Gordon Auchincloss, House's svigersøn og Wickham Steed fra The Times. Eksplosionen indtraf den 4. april.

Derefter var Houses rolle faktisk udspillet. Ganske vist var han siden involveret i de italienske kompromisforhandlinger, men det var tilsyneladende mest på eget initiativ. House's optræden under de italienske forhandlinger blotlagde definitivt hans totale isolation i delegationen, men på det personlige forhold til præsidenten havde den ingen indflydelse. Forbindelsen var afbrudt inden, og det var House også ganske på det rene med. Derimod lå en del af de øvrige delegationsmedlemmer, fremfor alt House's kommissær-kolleger Lansing, White og Bliss, fortsat under for den illusion, at House stadig havde noget at sige. Derfor tillagde de ham også ansvaret for det Shantung-kompromis, som Wilson gennemførte på trods af på det nærmeste hele den amerikanske delegation. House var ganske vist een af de få, der forstod – og billigede – Wilsons handlemåde, men han var ikke på noget tidspunkt blevet spurgt til råds. House synes iøvrigt under den sidste del af konferencen mere og mere at have helliget sig opbygningen af Folkeforbundet, idet han bl. a. – udover en virkelig idealistisk interesse for sagen – i en fremtrædende position indenfor denne organisation så en erstatning for sin tabte stilling hos præsidenten. Men også her blev han skuffet.

Det er tidligere nævnt, at i det videre perspektiv har den fortolkning man giver af House's indflydelse på fredskonferencen også betydning for den samlede vurdering af Wilson og den politik han førte. Det er da også mit håb, at nærværende afhandling har kastet nyt lys over sider af præsidentens politik, ikke mindst hans holdning i det italienske spørgsmål og hans optræden under konferencens mest kritiske fase i perioden fra midten af marts til midten af april 1919. I det hele taget afspejler denne yderst råt tilskårne sammenfatning af House's virke i Paris kun den ene side af det jeg har villet med nærværende afhandling. Jo mere jeg søgte at trænge ind i fredskonferencens problemer, jo mere fascineret blev jeg af dette fantastiske skuespil, hvor mennesker og ideer slynges hid og did i et indviklet diplomatisk spil, hvis tråde det i visse afgørende situationer blev mig magtpåliggende at rede ud i de mindste detailler. Måske det mest fascinerende af alt, var det ideologiske dilemma, hvori Wilson så sig placeret. Liberalismens betrængte centrumsposition var et væsentligt element i såvel hans russiske som hans italienske politik, og hele wilsonismens principielle indhold var på kant under den afgørende krise i april. Alt det forstod House måske bedre end nogen anden af Wilsons rådgivere, og alligevel – hver gang det for alvor gjaldt, bøjede han af.

# Appendices

*Appendix I*

In order to simplify the text I have taken the liberty of referring to Appendix I a number of problems relating to Wilson's foreign policy touched upon earlier. This appendix is identical to part of my outline in Historisk Tidsskrift, 12. rk. bd. IV, pp. 107–138: Nyere Synspunkter paa Woodrow Wilson's Udenrigspolitik, which follows in English translation:

American policy during the war and at the Peace Conference has been made the subject of more thorough study in recent years, and it is in many ways within this field that the most "exciting" development in the research has taken place. A number of authors have shown a tendency to approach the problems from untraditional angles—angles that are not entirely unrelated to the current political situation. These authors have been particularly fascinated by the ideological aspects of Wilsonian foreign policy, and one of the foremost results is a deeper appreciation of the importance of this element.

However, this recognition of ideology as an independent and vital factor in the formulation of American policy is closely related to another shift in the formulation of the problems; whereas research in the years between the wars and the first few post-war years naturally concentrated primarily on relations with Germany, a new generation of historians has felt itself drawn by a totally different and, for it, more pressing problem: the reaction to the challenge presented by Bolshevism. However, Bolshevism was not just an ideological challenge—Bolshevik Russia was itself a problem of the first order —and Russia has thus moved to the centre of research[58]). It must be remembered, however, that the Russia of 1917 was revolutionary Russia, and the ideological message that Bolshevism brought to Europe was the call to revolution, once more a theme of the greatest relevance to our own times. That the research side of this development has proved so fruitful is due primarily to the fact that this inclusion of new themes has taken place parri passu with a methodological new-orientation: foreign policy is no longer regarded as an isolated phenomenon but as a function of domestic policy.

Of course, the new tendencies are far from being equally represented by all authors; in fact, we find them all in only one case, but nevertheless, there are important common characteristics. The ideological dimension of Wilsonian policy is the main theme of two such different books as *Lawrence W. Martin: Peace without Victory. Woodrow Wilson and the British Liberals*[59]), and *Victor S. Mamatey: The United States and East Central Europe: A Study in Wilsonian Diplomacy and Propaganda*[60]). As indicated by the title of this book, Martin has analysed the ideological correlation between Wilson's public proclamations on the aim of the war and the formulation of the Peace Treaty and the thoughts expressed by the British "Radical" circle rallying round the Union of Democratic Control. He has further investigated the purely factual contact between the two parties, a contact that was arranged partly by Edward House. With this, Martin has also made a decisive contribution to the revaluation of the ideological content of Wilsonian policy: after this, it is no longer possible to regard Wilson's proclamations as an expression of a special American "moralistic-legalistic"[61]) tradition and thought. On the contrary, the ideas expressed by Wilson were the common chattels of American-European Liberals and, as shown by, for instance, Mamatey's study, these ideas had a very high degree of political force.

Mamatey's analysis of the propaganda-political effect of Wilson's ideology, partly as regards the "new" national states being born in South-Eastern Europe, constitutes an extension and a refinement of the views already propounded by Charles Seymour in 1934[62]) regarding the effect of the American propaganda on the domestic situation in Germany. Mamatey puts it as follows: "Unlike his (Wilson's) attitude towards Russia, the President's policy towards the Central Powers was unwavering. His well-known formula for breaking down Germany's will to fight, "Peace to the German people, war to the end on the German Government" has already been mentioned. Less well known is his propaganda addressed to Germany's Allies. Yet the two formed a logical and coherent whole. The formula was really "Peace to the German people *and the German Allies,* war to the end on the German Government". For about a year, until the spring of 1918, Wilson hammered on this theme with great consistency and eloquence. Its objective was clear: to isolate the German Government from its people and its allies and constrain it to peace"[63]). In other words, a highly differentiated policy.

One of the most pressing problems of our time: the confrontation between the Liberal and the Marxistic philosophies, has become the principal theme of a number of the most recent and important contributions to the research on Wilson. In his book, *The American Liberals and the Russian Revolution*[64]), *Christopher Lasch* has analysed the first confrontation, and this approach to the problem has also been made the supporting pillar of the basic works of *Arno J. Mayer* and *N. Gordon Levin.*

With his book, *Political Origins of the New Diplomacy, 1917–1918*[65]), the then 33-year old Arno Mayer managed with a single stroke to bring Wilsonian research onto an entirely new course. "The principal" of the book is not actually Wilson, but the domestic political situation in Europe[66]) against which Wilson's ideological drive was directed and in which it partly had its fount. While Martin has demonstrated the ideological communion between Wilson and the British "Radicals", Mayer has now developed the picture to include not only the European Liberals, but also the European Socialists: as regards the ideals of foreign policy, there was also a close fellowship of thought between the latter and Wilson, but it did not extend to the aims of domestic policy. The Russian revolution therefore placed Wilson in a serious dilemma, because Lenin herewith stepped forward as a dangerous rival for the loyalty of the Socialists; he could offer communion of thought not only in the field of foreign policy but also in that of domestic policy, and Wilson's problem was that he needed the support of both Liberals and Socialists if he was to have any hope at all, at the coming conclusion of peace, of forcing his programme of foreign policy through against the Conservative and Imperialistic Governments of Europe. It would therefore be taking too narrow a view to consider Wilson's ideological appeals as solely directed at the Central Powers —they were also—indeed mostly—aimed at Russia and, perhaps more important, they were directed at the Liberal and Socialist forces in the Allied countries, the forces whose support was essential for the implementation of Wilson's peace policies.

With this approach, Wilson's "idealism" is put in an entirely new perspective; not only has Mayer been able to demonstrate that Wilson's proclamations were dictated by "objective conditions"[67]) in the European political situation; he has also established the fact that this propaganda was an extremely "realistic" political instrument in the internal battle for power with the coalition parties on the formulation of the Peace Treaty. In later books, Mayer has further emphasized yet another dimension of Wilson's policy: a victory for the Liberal programme at the Peace Conference would put the President in a position to crush the Conservative opposition in the United States and to resume the Liberal reform programme halted by the war. Foreign policy and domestic policy thus seem in this connection to be two sides of the same coin[68]).

Mayer's reinterpretation of Wilson's policy is most clearly expressed in his analysis of the most celebrated proclamation of the war: the Fourteen Points[69]). This manifesto, which has since fallen into such disrepute, cannot be properly understood if it is torn from the context in which it originated. The Fourteen Points (8 January 1918) were composed in a specific political situation, viz, the Russian crisis (Brest-Litovsk negotiations), and their content was to a great degree directed at precisely this siuation; in other words, they were a time-related phenomenon. Their vague wording, in the nature of slogans, was precisely a function of this; they were propaganda, and propaganda aimed in several directions. They were aimed at the domestic political situation of the Central Powers: an attempt to support the forces opposing the militarism of Ludendorff; and they were aimed at Russia: "Wilson . . . hoped that a war aims offensive could forestall a separate peace in the East"[70]). Finally, they were also aimed at the Allied domestic political situation: Wilson had to recover the initiative that Trotsky's fiery peace appeals threatened to wrest from him, and at the same time, he attempted to force the Allied Governments to liberalize their war aims. "Thus Wilson's Fourteen Points had an eminently realistic diplomatic origin"[71]).

In the paperback edition of his book, Mayer has changed the title from *Political Origins of the New Diplomacy* to *Wilson vs. Lenin,* on the grounds that this title "reveals the content and nature of the book more accurately than the original title"[72]), thus anticipating to a certain extent the accentuation of the approach to the problem that can be observed in his latest book, *Politics and Diplomacy of Peacemaking. Containment and Counter-Revolution at Versailles, 1918–1919*[73]). The book is in many ways a direct continuation of the former. The method is precisely the same—comparative and with heavy emphasis on the interaction between domestic and foreign policy, and the sphere of interest is the same—not the daily negotiations but "the political and diplomatic context and climate"[74]), i. e. not so much the negotiations in Paris as the European situation constituting their subject. The keywords in Mayer's exposition are "Containment and Counter-revolution".

Whereas, in the period 1917–1918, it was the Left-wing forces that had a decisive influence on the political and diplomatic developments[75]), the period following the Armistice was characterized by a strong move to the Right, a development that also contributed to a further radicalization of the Left wing. Political life polarized at the expense of the Centre, and the Centre was represented by Wilson. When the President went to Paris, his position was undermined, not only at home, but also in Europe: the forces supporting him were on the retreat; the conditions under which his aims and principles had been formulated no longer existed. But even so, the Fourteen Points were not entirely dismissed: ". . . until May 1919 the Allied governments could not afford to disavow Woodrow Wilson publicly . . . Without the still potent spell of Wilsonianism the swing towards Leninism within the Left might well have assumed considerable proportions"[76])—Wilson was a kind of hostage!

The adherents of the American President were on the defensive on both sides of the Atlantic, and his hesitation about going over the heads of the coalition partners may well have been due to his narrow political basis. "The issue is hardly whether or not Wilson was sincere about his principles and aims; nor is the issue one of the quality of his strategic and tactical skills as diplomatist and politician. Even assuming Wilson scored exceptionally high on all these counts, a prior question must be considered: how pertinent and consequential was Wilson's reformist project in the crisis setting of 1918–

1919. Unlike Clemenceau, the President strained to understand this crisis in its world historical context. . . . Wilson's concern was less with the importance of the Revolution for Russia than for Europe and the world"[77]). This passage expresses the central theme of Mayer's conception of Wilson and the principal thesis of the book. He therefore goes the whole way when he emphasizes the fact that it was precisely because Wilson saw the wider perspectives of the threat of revolution that he "spearheaded various Allied efforts to tame the Russian Revolution. In fact, these efforts came to be central to Wilson's overall peacemaking strategy"[78]).

Mayer's aim has been to present not just a new interpretation of Wilson's policy in Paris, but a new interpretation of the entire Peace Conference: "The constellation of political forces in the Allied and Associated nations was more decisive for the course and outcome of the Paris Peace Conference than the personalities, negotiating skills, and historical culture of the members of the major delegations. Similarly, the near-anomie throughout Central and Eastern Europe rather than deficiencies or mistakes in the planning, organization, and running of the conference shaped the erratic peace and agenda of the negotiations"[79]). "Hence, even though the Conference was convened to settle the fate of the defeated powers, the German question was not the first substantive issue on the agenda of the Peace Conference: instead "it was mutually agreed that the strongest most pressing question and the one to be considered first by the representatives of the Five Great Powers was the Russian situation, with particular reference to the Bolsheviki question" "[80]). The crucial problem in 1919 was not Germany, but Russia; the dreaded enemy was not the German army, but the spread of the Revolution.

Of course, this perception is not new: "Thorstein Veblen was the first to note that the compact to reduce Soviet Russia and contain Bolshevism "was not written into the Text of the Treaty (but) may rather be said to have been the parchment upon which that text was written" "[81]), but it was a realization that rapidly slipped into the background to make way for the disillusioned Liberal interpretation represented by such names as John Maynard Keynes[82]) and Harold Nicolson[83]), and it was, moreover, superseded by the actual political developments in the interwar years, when Germany's adjustment quickly became the problem that overshadowed all others. However, it is important to note that it was a perception that was shared by contemporary observers; Ray Stannard Baker perhaps, provides the clearest example of this.

Baker, Wilson's later biographer[84]), was present in Paris as Press Secretary to the American Delegation. At that time, he was one of America's most prominent Liberal journalists, and he had, moreover, spent the last couple of years of the war in Europe as a Special Envoy of the State Department on a mission to collect material on the European Left-wing forces[85]). Baker thus had every opportunity of observing and understanding the forces that were beginning to make themselves felt in Europe, and this, combined with his extreme sensitivity and brilliant style, make his diary[86]) from the Peace Conference one of the most fascinating documents of this period. The impression gained from a study of Baker's diary can best be described in his own words: "The effect of the Russian problem on the Paris Conference ... was profound: Paris cannot be understood without Moscow. Without ever being represented at Paris at all, the Bolsheviki and Bolshevism were powerful elements at every turn. Russia played a more vital part at Paris than Prussia! ..."[87]). This is the view that Mayer has now made his own[88]), and there can be no doubt that Mayer stands in debt to Baker[89]), not only as regards his main thesis, but on a number of other points as well.

Mayer has undoubtedly touched upon a crucial point in his analysis of the political climate of the Peace Conference. The question is, however, whether he has also managed to provide a new interpretation of the diplomatic conflict as promised by the title, "Politics and Diplomacy". In his interpretation, Mayer draws a decisive line at the Hungarian Revolution, which he links with the March-April crisis at the Conference under the very appropriate title, "The Peace Conference Shaken"[90]). However, Mayer's thesis is compromised by the fact that the March-April crisis actually arose before the Hungarian Revolution[91]), as he himself admits.

In the chapter, "Storm Signals"[92]), which directly precedes the description of the effect of the Hungarian Revolution, Mayer analyses the political climate at the Conference and lays heavy stress on the fear of revolution: "In retrospect the chances of a collapse of order and authority may appear to have been quite small; at the time, however, the specter of revolution was ever-present"[93]), and he directs special attention to the conditions in Germany, where he emphasizes the fact that the increasing unrest here at the end of February and beginning of March had a decisive effect on the decision to ease the blockade[94]). At the same time, however, he admits that "No doubt elements other than this crescendo of alarm went into the decision to loosen the blockade in mid-March"[95]). He further stresses the fact that the situation in Eastern Europe was still undecided, and the whole situation still in suspense: "These apprehensions also rose to the surface in official circles"[96]), and as an example of the increasing feeling of "a race between peace and anarchy", Mayer then quotes heavily from Baker's diary: "Starting around March 18 the Press Secretary of the American Delegation registered a decided change in mood and outlook"[97]). However, what Mayer completely overlooks, or at any rate fails to mention, is that this reversal, not only in Baker but in everyone else as well, was related to both the European situation and, perhaps even more closely, to the simple fact that Wilson's return on 13 March did not bring with it the long awaited progress in the negotiations but, on the contrary, "deadlock"[98]). Indeed, the fact that Mayer does not mention Wilson's return at all must be viewed as an effort to strain the evidence in order to fit it to the thesis.

Exactly the same views apply to Mayer's presentation of the formulation of the Fontainebleau Memorandum: the offer of guarantees and the unacceptable counter-demands made by France meant the initiation of a new round of talks, and the result was the Fontainebleau Memorandum. "What cannot be overlooked is that this review, which culminated in the remarkable Fontainebleau Memorandum of March 25, got under way *before* Paris was shaken by Bela Kun's takeover in Budapest. Henry Wilson initiated it on March 18 by engaging Phillip Kerr  and Maurice Hankey in wide-ranging discussions"[99]). But that is just the point: it happened *before* the spectre of revolution again reared its ugly head, and it might therefore seem reasonable to attribute it to other causes. However, as Mayer does not do this, his emphasis of *"before"* is incomprehensible. And Mayer further stresses that the circle behind the formulation of the Memorandum (with the exception of Henry Wilson) "now reflected the growing opinion which, intimidated by the specter of Bolshevism, tended "toward a fairly moderate treatment of Germany, in order not to crush her morally, the idea (being) that a reasonably strong German state was a healthy thing for Europe" "[100]). But is this not also stretching the argument a little too far? Had not this view always been fundamental to British policy?

If there is reason to doubt the universal nature of Mayer's thesis, then the same applies to its specific application to the interpretation of Wilsonian policy. In this connection, the interpretation of Wilson's negotiations at the height of the March-April crisis must be critical, i. e. the significance we are to attribute to the summoning (on 7 April) of the SS. "George Washington", with the implicit threat of leaving the Conference and thereby breaking up the Peace negotiations. As we know, Wilson never fulfilled this threat, and Mayer explains why: "This thinly disguised pressure instantly moved Clemenceau—but not Orlando—to a more conciliatory position. Between April 8 and 13, the Franco-American stalemate over the Saar, the Rhine frontier and reparations was broken and the press campaign against Wilson began to subside"[101]). It is Baker's interpretation that Mayer has "bought"[102]) and it is at the same time the interpretation naturally desired by the circle around Wilson[103]). Nevertheless, it is definitely not an interpretation that is allowed to stand undisputed: "According to Ray Stannard Baker, this "bold gesture" intimidated both Clemenceau and Lloyd George, who now became more conciliatory. However, as Seymour has pointed out, it was Wilson, not Clemenceau nor Lloyd George, who conceded most in the negotiations of the following week"[104]). And indeed, in previous research, the hectic week in the middle of April has been regarded as the period in which Wilson entered into a series of compromises with the Allies, which resulted partly in the Treaty of Versailles and partly in the final acceptance by the Allies of the League of Nations. That Mayer anyway accepts Baker's assessment without reservation can only be because he agrees with Baker's conclusion that "When it came to the crisis, then, the need to hold the world steady, keep order, and fight both extremes—militarism on the one hand and Bolshevism on the other—the responsibility of breaking up the Conference became too great"[105]), since to Mayer, the main element of Wilsonian policy was, as we have seen, precisely the "containment" of Bolshevism[106]).

The question is, however, which problem had top priority in Wilson's policy at this critical point: Europe or America. As mentioned earlier, Mayer himself has stressed very heavily the domestic aspects of Wilson's foreign policy: "Fatally weakened by the outcome of the congressional elections, the President looked for political support to Europe, where the non-revolutionary Left was eager to follow his leadership. . . . A partial but nevertheless distinct diplomatic victory in Europe might give Wilson the strength and momentum to initiate a revival of the New Freedom in Washington"[107]). But just as it would seem most relevant to marshall this argument, Mayer is silent. In two chapters sharing the title, "Intrusion of Politics"[108]), he discusses in detail the influence of the British and the French domestic developments, but he leaves the American situation untouched, despite the ample evidence that Wilson was primarily, indeed perhaps exclusively, concerned with this situation after his return in the middle of March[109]).

Wilson's "barometer" with regard to the mood in the United States was Joseph Tumulty, his secretary for many years, and a detailed analysis of the telegraphic correspondence between the two men illustrates the close interaction between Tumulty's interpretation of the mood in America and a number of Wilson's actions[110]). And Tumulty's interpretation of the American reaction to the "George Washington" episode was clear and unambiguous: "The ordering of the GEORGE WASHINGTON to return to France looked upon here as an act of impatience and petulance on the President's part and not accepted here in good grace either by friends or foes. It is considered as evidence that the President intends to leave the conference if his views are not accepted. I think this method of withdrawal most unwise and fraught with the most dangerous possibilities here and abroad, because it puts on the President the responsibility of withdrawing when the President should by his own act place the responsibility for a break of the Conference where it rightly belongs. . . . A withdrawal at this time would be a desertion"[111]). This very sharp attitude must have hit Wilson hard. It showed beyond a shadow of a doubt that the door to withdrawal was finally closed because such withdrawal would not be understood in America. If he took this course, he would finally have destroyed his position at home[112]).

Now Mayer's main interest does not lie in the motives of the individuals but in the forces and structures conditioning the actions of the actors, and with this mode of regarding matters, this environmental approach, he has achieved a great deal. In the foregoing it is suggested, however, that the unification of the two "layers" of his interpretation is not altogether convincing in the last book, although it is in the first. And this is, to a certain degree, due to the method adopted by Mayer.

Mayer adheres to the "analytical" rather than the "narrative" school of historical writing[113]), which is surprising inasmuch as the form of his presentation is not analytical, but descriptive. He makes use of an almost "impressionistic" method: representative passages rather than real analysis. However, the danger of this method is that the entire interpretation tends to become somewhat unprecise, not only in that the nuances disappear, but also in the fact that important problems become dislocated or contracted. These weaknesses were of no significance in the first book because there, analysis and description were two sides of the same coin: the description of the European political developments permitted a simultaneous analysis of significant features of Wilson's policy; and at the same time, the problem dealt with was clearly defined. The same is not true of Mayer's last book; the problem here is so complicated and the subject so enormous that greater analytical precision would have been appropriate. The example that particularly comes to mind in this context is the total lack of analysis of Wilson's political conception—the more so as the author has actually intended to provide a new interpretation of the President's policy. This lack is most obvious in the presentation of Wilson's policy in respect of the Bolshevik Government: Mayer's evaluation here becomes incomplete because of the insufficiency of his analytical apparatus. However, this is best illustrated in connection with a detailed discussion of the latest and perhaps the most significant contribution to the literature on President Wilson.

With his book, *Woodrow Wilson and World Politics. America's Response to War and Revolution*[114]), *N. Gordon Levin Jr.,* has provided the analysis of the Wilsonian conception of foreign policy called for above: "... an integrated analysis of the theory and practice of Wilsonian foreign policy in the 1917–1919 period"[115]) As in the case of Mayer and Lasch, Levin finds his motivation in the parallel he discerns between Wilson's situation and our own, and he concludes that Wilson's political aims laid the foundation for "a modern American foreign policy[116]). "This ultimate Wilsonian goal may be defined as the attainment of a peaceful liberal capitalist world order under international law, safe both from traditional imperialism and revolutionary socialism, within whose stable liberal confines a missionary America could find moral and economic pre-eminence. In our own time this basic Wilsonian vision, at once progressive and conservative, continues to motivate America's foreign policy decision-makers"[117]).

Wilson's policy was aimed at the establishment of a stable world order, based on Liberal-Capitalistic internationalism. He thus offered a middle-of-the-road solution between imperialism on the Right and revolution on the Left. And precisely because such a solution would at the same time ensure optimum

conditions for American economic development, Wilson perceived no divergence, but on the contrary, concordance, between the national interest of
the United States and the internationalism whose spokesman he was. "The
heart of the matter is that Wilson's conception of America's exceptional mission made it possible for him to reconcile the rapid growth of the economic
and military power of the United States with what he conceived to be America's unselfish service to humanity"[118]—Levin's analysis thus represents a
development and refinement of Mayer's views[119], although it must be borne
in mind that Levin reached his result independently of Mayer's second book.

Unlike Mayer, Levin has not proposed an order of priority for the various
elements of Wilsonian policy, but has analysed the policy in relation to Germany, to the League of Nations and to Russia, as equal components of the
total conception[120]. This approach, combined with Levin's extremely penetrating analysis of the interplay of "reintegrationist" and "punitive" tendencies
in Wilson's German policy has resulted in an exceedingly original contribution
to our understanding of the President's policy at the Peace Conference[121].
Thus, unlike Mayer, Levin has not made anti-Bolshevism the crucial element
of Wilsonian policy[122], and on other points too, his conception of this policy
in relation to Russia deviates from that of Mayer—primarily on the fundamental question of whether Wilson was at any time prepared to recognize the
Bolshevik Government[123]. In this respect, the interpretation of the so-called
Bullitt-mission becomes decisive: was it sent with Wilson's knowledge and
was he in agreement with its aim?

Mayer's attitude on these questions is not clear[124]. At one stage of his
interpretation he seems to think both that Wilson agreed to the Bullitt-mission
and that he really wanted an approach to the Bolsheviks if this were politically feasible[125]. A little while later, however, Mayer changes his mind, now
seeming to attribute the initiative for the mission to House and Lansing[126],
although he does maintain that the aim of mission – to arrive at a modus
vivendi with Lenin – was "compatible with the key tenets of the Wilsonian
formula"[127]. And finally, he explains the abandonment of the plan as follows: "Paradoxically the March-April crisis strengthened rather than weakened
the opponents of an accommodation with Lenin. For the first time since the
German elections the specter of Bolshevism was once again haunting Central
and East Central Europe.... Caught between a strong and established Right
and an impatient but fledgling Left, and themselves baffled and frightened by
events, Wilson and Lloyd George lost their nerve... they abandoned the
Kerr-Bullitt plan in favor of the Nansen plan"[128]. Mayer must thus believe
that Wilson was really prepared for a *de facto* recognition of the Bolshevik
Government, but that this was made impossible due to the March-April crisis,
whereby he has at the same time provided himself with further confirmation
of one of his principal theses.

Against this we have Levin's completely new interpretation of the Bullitt-mission: it is Levin's clearly substantiated view that Wilson was at no time prepared for a *de facto* recognition of the Bolshevik Government[129]), and that he was therefore not at any time favourably disposed to the proposal Bullitt brought home from Moscow[130]). Bullitt went to Russia with a peace proposal that was in principle identical with a Russian proposal made earlier[131]) which had been given its final form in talks between Bullitt, Phillip Kerr and Edward House. The Russians therefore had no difficulty in accepting once more a proposal that they themselves had previously presented, and that, of course, was precisely the whole idea of the mission—the conclusion of peace with the Bolsheviks. However, there was no backing at all for this extreme, Liberal standpoint in the rest of the American Delegation: House had acted entirely on his own responsibility[132]). There was, therefore, no question of a change of course on Wilson's part when he adopted the Nansen plan; he had simply never accepted the premises of the Bullitt-mission[133]).

Although it is thus possible, on a crucial point, to play the two authors against each other, it is still more important to stress the high degree of agreement in their evaluation of Wilson. It is certainly no accident that Levin expressly mentions Arno Mayer, Louis Hartz and William Appleman Williams[134]) as his sources of inspiration. As we have seen, his debt to Mayer is evident, although no more decisive than the influence exerted by the publisher of Studies on the Left seems to have been[135]).

*William A. William*'s book, *The Tragedy of American Diplomacy*[136]) is a further contribution to the continuing discussion of American foreign policy. His interpretation of Wilsonian foreign policy has a rather one-sided economic orientation, but precisely this bent enables him to provide an account that totally lacks the traditional "idealistic" views. To Williams, Wilson's foreign policy was a consistent continuation of the views on which John Hay's formulation of the open-door policy was based: the insurance of unrestricted American economic expansion. And in a way, the League of Nations was the culmination of this policy: "Wilson aimed to use American power, inside and outside the League of Nations, merely to order the world so that such classical competition could proceed in peace. If this could be done, he was confident that American economic power could take care of the United States—and of the world"[137]).

As regards the interpretation of Wilson's policy at the Peace Conference too, Williams can also be said to anticipate to a high degree certain facets of the analyses of both Mayer and Levin, in that Williams also regards the threat of revolution as a decisive challenge to Wilson's policy: "The crisis completely disrupted Wilson's original peace program, making it necessary to delay the work of reforming the world under American leadership as part of sustaining America's own democracy and prosperity. First priority had to be given, at least temporarily, to the problem of checking the revolution"[138]). "Though it sometimes appeared vague, even irresolute and contradictory,

Wilson did develop a general program to cope with the complex crisis. His objective was to structure the peace settlement so that America could provide the intellectual, moral, economic, and military power and leadership to reinvigorate and sustain the liberal way of life throughout the world. So strengthened, liberalism would effectively undercut, and ultimately defeat, its revolutionary and radical antagonists"[139]).

Thus, Wilson's position as defender of economic and political Liberalism against attacks from both the Right and the Left is given a central place in the analyses of Mayer, Williams and Levin. "Wilson's personal dilemma symbolized the broader difficulties faced by classical liberalism"[140]), and it is therefore hardly surprising that Levin names as his third source of inspiration, *Louis Hartz,* whose book, *The Liberal Tradition in America*[141]) is, in fact, one long discussion of the basic constituents of the special American form of Liberalism and the society built upon this basis. Hartz finds it of decisive importance that the American society, unlike its European counterpart, has not arisen on the basis of a feudal structure of society: as Tocqueville put it, America has never had to undergo a democratic revolution[142]), the Americans have never been faced with the task of building a new society on the ruins of the old. "We are reminded again of Tocqueville's statement: The Americans are "born equal" "[143]).

The consequences of this quite special form of development are manifold, but one of the most important of these, in this context, is the inability of Socialism to find a foothold in the United States[144]). If Socialism and Progressivism are as far apart as Hartz asserts[145]), there must be good reasons for asking whether this in fact was not the real cause of Wilson's fiasco. Was he, for ideological reasons, pre-doomed to failure? Was there no possibility of bridging the gap between American Liberalism and European Socialism?[146])

It is, therefore, possible to conclude that the debate on Wilsonian foreign policy is equally relevant today, not only because we too are faced with the very same problems as Wilson, but to an even greater extent because he himself and all he stood for were the very incarnation of American Liberalism.

*Appendix II*

The Republicans and the Allies.

The Resolution of the Senate of 4 March 1919 and the anonymous memorandum from the same period (cf. above pp. 147–149) were both attempts on the part of the Republicans to influence the Allies. This was not, however, the first time they had tried such tactics. Right back on 1 November 1918, i. e. even before the American election had taken place, Ambassador Sharp reported from Paris that "(f)or some-time past there have appeared in some of the Paris French Papers as well as in both the Herald and the Daily Mail despatches emanating from American (!) purporting to quote men in high official positions which have had a tendency in my judgement to mislead the French public as to the position of the American Government on questions affecting the war and particularly the granting of an Armistice. In nearly every instance these expression(s) of opinions have come from prominent Republicans and the whole effort would seem to point out the conclusion that such news were sent over with a definite design. The various agencies transmitting it, judging from its uniform and sinister character, seem to be under the direction of parties not in sympathy with the administration. I believe the tendency of such despatches has been at least to create doubt as to the real policy of the administration if not indeed to misrepresent it. Senator Poindexter's recent radical utterances widely quoted over here furnished an illustration. Senator Lodge's criticisms are also given much prominence . . ." (763.72119/2449: Sharp to Secr. of State 1.11.18, received 2.11. 5660. midnight. urgent.) (Microscopy No. 367, roll 386, National Archives).

At the end of November 1918, Henry Cabot Lodge tried out a direct approach, partly through the British and French Washington Embassies and partly by means of a personal letter to Balfour. Here he emphasized that the Wilson-Government had suffered a defeat in the elections, and that the Republicans had demanded the unconditional surrender of Germany, that the party desired physical guarantees against future German agression, and that the proposed League of Nations seemed to him to be "hopelessly impracticable in many respects". A League of Nations, "if such a thing can be made", that sought to exercise control of the immigration laws, customs, laws, the Monroe Doctrine, or the army and the navy, would meet "great and probably effective opposition". It would therefore be unfortunate if agreement were reached on linking the League of Nations with the Peace Treaty, "for it might lead to great and most undesirable delays and probably amendments to the treaty of peace, which would be greatly to be deplored." In his letter to the British Embassy, Lodge further emphasized that the election victory meant that the Republican party would have "a good deal to say as regards the reconstruction policy after the peace", and this could naturally be read as a threat of possible economic reprisals. Other prominent Republicans too, including Theodore Roosevelt, attempted to make their influence felt with the Allied Statesmen, but apparently without success. (Fowler, pp. 228–235 with references, passages pp. 229–230, cf. also Garraty, pp. 343 and 348–349).

At the same time, Lodge tried to make Henry White, the American Peace Commissioner, his contact man with the Allies. White, however, who was a personal friend of Lodge's, refused to collaborate. Although the attempt thus came to nothing, there may be good reason to study more closely the memorandum sent by Lodge to White on 2 December 1918, because this shows clearly his political standpoint with regard to the Peace Treaty with Germany—a standpoint that very closely approximated that of the French. Lodge suggested that White should show the memorandum to Balfour, Clemenceau and Nitti, all of whom were personally known to the Senator, asserting that they would in this way become acquainted with "the real feeling of the people of the United States, and certainly the Senate of the United States. This knowledge may in certain contingencies be very important to them in strengthening their position". The constant theme of the memorandum was that "it was necessary in every way to cripple Germany in order to prevent future war." Furthermore, Lodge advocated the view that the United States should act as "a part guarantor of many elements of the European settlement." "(I)ndemnities, . . . he wished to be very large", and he also considered that the German Reich should be split up into its various components. Regarding the League of Nations, he repeated that this should under no circumstances be a part of the Treaty, not only because this would mean an unnecessary postponement, but also because it would make ratification by the American Senate doubtful. (Nevins, pp. 252–253, cf. Alan Nevins to R. S. Baker, 12.9.1937, R. S. Baker papers, Ser. I).

When it became clear that the repeated Republican feelers were not having any result and that, on the contrary, Wilson would succeed in forcing his policy through with regard to the correlation between the Peace Treaty and the League of Nations Covenant, the Republican party began to speak with another voice: a pronounced anti-British attitude now made itself felt. By the end of April 1919, such a situation had been reached that Lord Reading, the British Ambassador in Washington, felt that he had occasion to talk to Frank Polk, Acting Secretary of State. On this meeting we have Polk's report: "He has discovered that the Republicans are very resentful of the fact that Lloyd George has been getting on pleasantly with the President, and they are disposed in their desire to embarrass the President to make it disagreeable for Great Britain as long as Great Britain's representatives stand with the President".

"In strict confidence, he told me the name of the man who called on him and told him this in so many words, and intimated it would be necessary for the Republicans to tie up with the extreme Irish, and even with the Germans, in order to embarrass the President in his relations with Great Britain. The organization that is back of this movement, although probably the heads of it are not aware of the exact line that they are taking, is the organization of which old Henry Watterson is President and George Wharton Pepper Vice President. I do not know whether Beck is a member or not, but Henry Wise Wood and others of that kind are active. You undoubtedly can judge the situation from the fact that Lodge was driven to come out for Italy's claim in regard to Fiume because the President had apparently taken the other end of the argument."

"I understand that there is a split among the Republicans as to how far they should go. Root and some of those men don't want the League of Nations to be made a political issue. They tell me that Will Hayes also feels the same way. Lodge is uncompromising in his opposition. I think he is going so far that if they would let him alone he would hang himself." (Polk to Auchincloss 5.5.19, Polk papers 74/8; see also Polk diary 26.4.19 and Polk to Lansing 7.5.19, Polk Papers 78/11).

*Appendix III*

In chapters 1 and 3 of this book, I have attempted to show that House stood to the left of Wilson politically, and here, as elsewhere, I have made frequent use of the concept "Liberal" without providing a detailed definition of the term. This has been deliberate, for the simple reason that I find myself unable to give a clear and unambiguous definition, and—probably just as important in this connection—I have been unable to find a satisfactory solution to the problem elsewhere.

The fact of the matter is that just at this time, Liberalism was in the melting-pot both in Europe and in America. "At the cost of considerable semantic confusion, the old nineteenth-century liberalism of individual rights and laissez faire (was) gradually (giving) way to a different pattern of thought that also claims the name of liberalism. ... The earlier emphasis on individualism (was being) replaced by a concern for individuality, a desire to resist the conformity exacted by an ever more integrated technological society. Equality (was being) expanded to mean not merely formal equality before the law but also social, religious and racial equality insured by considerable legal coercion. Liberty (was being) redefined through a total social view that comprehends how much one man's liberty may be another's bondage. The new liberalism, in sum, has turned away from a dream of automatic progress by the free-wheeling exercise of individual rights to a conviction that only the conscious, co-operative use of governmental power can bring reform" (Forcey, p. xiii–xiv).

The problem is further complicated by the fact that "Liberalism" is not, and never has been, one and the same thing on both sides of the Atlantic. Louis Hartz is presumably the writer who has best analysed this question, in his book on The Liberal Tradition in America (cf. also Appendix I), while Charles Forcey, in his book, The Crossroads of Liberalism, in which he analyses the journal, "The New Republic", and the men behind it, is the writer who has most clearly described what was happening to American Liberalism in this period. Both these books are "intellectual history", whereas there are really only two comparative political studies, Arno Mayer's Wilson vs. Lenin (cf. Appendix I) and Hans F. Pettersson's Power and International Order. However, in both books, the comparative analysis is limited to the European material, and neither author provides us with the concise and, therefore, valid definition we are seeking.

Nevertheless, if we cannot give a definition, at least we can attempt to isolate the concept, and that is precisely what Christopher Lasch has succeeded in doing in the preface to his book, The American Liberals and the Russian Revolution: "The term "liberal" is surely one of the most baffling in political discourse. It can mean almost anything, from a belief in rugged individualism to a belief in the welfare state. ... All Americans are liberals, by virtue of the fact that they have no feudal past against which to rebel; but Americans at the same time are conservative in their liberalism, as Europeans keep reminding us, and as we ourselves have now begun to realize. One finally despairs of investing the term with any meaning at all. But efforts to find a substitute are equally unavailing. . . . Liberalism, then as now, was less a set of attitudes toward specific issues than a set of assumptions about human affairs. The liberal of 1900–1920 was an optimist; he believed that human reason could ultimately order the world so as to eliminate poverty, disease, discomfort and war. He did not think men had to be coerced into sociable behavior; that is why he was for self-determination, the removal of external restraints, in every area of human activity. . . . He believed, in short, that it would be possible in the not too distant future to substitute the rule of reason for the rule of force in the relations among men, in international as well as in domestic affairs."

The war—the victory of force over reason—had, however, to lead to a demand for self-reflection. It not only made its mark among Conservatives and Liberals, but "also brought to light a cleavage within liberalism itself." "It drove a wedge between those who, while critical of their own country in peacetime, eagerly closed ranks in time of war, and those who continued to doubt, throughout the war, that any nation or group of nations could be regarded as the repository of all political virtue." Wilson could also contain this group as long as he was able to convince it that "the war should not be used to further the interests of British and French imperialism, as embodied in the secret treaties." It was for this reason that the whole question of the war aims became of such vital importance (cf. Appendix I).

The schism created by the war was deepened further by the Russian Revolution. The men who were already opponents of the war were also those who "from the beginning insisted that the revolution would prove a blessing to the world". Vice versa, the Liberals who supported the war joined the Conservatives in deploring "the revolution as a menace to civilization—that is to the successful prosecution of the war against Germany." "So deep, indeed, did the division within liberalism itself become that the division between liberals and conservatives seems at times, to the student of these events, to become insignificant. But whatever their differences, liberals were trying to work out a solution to the problems raised by the revolution within the context of certain assumptions which conservatives did not share. All of them looked with horror on the suggestion that Bolshevism be crushed by force . . . All of them could find a common denominator of agreement in the eighth of Wilson's Fourteen Points, with its promise of forbearance, if not of sympathy, for the revolution." (Lasch, pp. vi–xvi).

*Appendix IV*

The following list of the Saar-negotiations is contained in the National Archives, RG 256, Doc. No. 185.113/34. The document bears the handwritten designation, "Docket". The author, who appears to have been extremely well informed, is possibly Haskins, cf. also chapter 4, note 315.

"March 29, 1919. Messrs. Bowman, Johnson and Haskins were called into conference at 11.00 A. M. by the President on the question of the claims of France in the region of the Saar. Thereafter Messrs. Johnson and Haskins drafted with Mr. Headlam-Morley of the British Delegation a statement of points which was sent to the President at 1.00 P. M. and by him subsequently transmitted to Clemenceau. (Annex A).

April 2. The Council of Four appointed a special committee on the Saar, consisting of Messrs. Tardieu, Headlam-Morley and Haskins. A first meeting was held that afternoon, and meetings continued until April 30.

April 6. A draft of the economic articles was sent to President Wilson (Annex B).

April 7. This draft with certain notes of the President, was referred through Colonel House to Mr. D. H. Miller, who proposed the addition of articles establishing a Commission of Arbitration and arranging for a final plebiscite. (Annex C).

April 8. These additional articles were sent by the President to M. Clemenceau, and drew forth in reply Annex D, drafted by M. Tardieu.

April 9. M. Tardieu's observations were sent to Mr. Miller by the President, who instructed Messrs. Miller and Haskins to prepare articles providing for a Commission of Administration and a plebiscite at the end of fifteen years.

The matter was discussed throughout the afternoon and until after midnight with the co-operation, after 5.30, of Messrs. Tardieu and Headlam-Morley. The discussion resulting in a draft (Annex E).

April 10. This draft was sent to the President early in the morning. From 11.00 to 12.30 the Committee sat with the Council of Four, and the articles were with certain amendments (Annex E1), approved, save for the reservation by M. Clemenceau of the question of selling out the mines after fifteen years. It was understood that the Committee would modify of Annex I to conform to the regime established by Annex II.

April 11. The Council of Four instructed the Committee to report:

1. A plan for a plebiscite with a third alternative, that of continuing under the Commission;
2. An article to be agreed between Messrs. Baruch and Loucheur respecting the supply of coal to France after the plebiscite;
3. The boundaries of the Territory of the Saar Basin, fixed upon the basis of the map (No. 1) which had formed the basis of the Council's earlier discussion.

April 13. Committee's report on these three points accepted by Council of Four (Annex F and Map 2). . . .". (Omission: mine).

# Notes

*Introduction*

1. Doubleday, Page and Co., New York. See also the discussion in chapter 4.—In a review in Historisk Tidsskrift, 12. rk., bd. IV, p. 107–138, I have discussed the post-World War II debate of Woodrow Wilson's foreign policy. The relevant parts of this article are given below as Appendix I.
2. Through Thirty Years II, London, William Heinemann, 1924. For further information, see below chapter 3.
3. I–IV. Ernest Benn, London, 1926–1928. For further information on Seymour's views, see below chapter 4.
4. Int. Pap., p. 392–393.—Italics are Seymour's.
5. Seymour's thesis was well received by Robert C. Binkley (Ten Years of Peace Conference History, The Journal of Modern History I, 1929, pp. 607–629): "Baker's theory is that House weakened Wilson unnecessarily; Seymour's theory is that Wilson ruined the peace with fruitless intransigence. This is an issue clearly joined, and well worthy of further study. It can be tested by examining the proceedings of commissions and the records of the political currents of the time. It is to be hoped that the attention of historians will follow such an issue as this, and not pursue further the fate of the melodramatic "February Plot". Ten years later, Paul Birdsall gave his answer (The Second Decade of Peace Conference History. The Journal of Modern History XI, 1939, pp. 362–378): "But the conflict of principle and personality will not down. Indeed it becomes clearer and clearer that such conflicts were not only entirely real, but were a fundamental factor in shaping the treaties. . . . (E)verything that has appeared in the category of memoirs and letters, as well as much purely historical writing, has tended to increase the stature of Wilson while substantiating more and more the early charges made by Ray Stannard Baker that Colonel House created serious difficulties for the President by his disposition to compromise on essential principles".
6. New York, Reynal and Hitchcock, 1941. For further information on Birdsall's views, see below chapters 4 and 5. Birdsall did not quite overlook the possibility that the break had started earlier. See especially pp. 329–330.
7. Thomas A. Bailey: Woodrow Wilson and the Lost Peace, New York, MacMillan Co., 1944, pp. 361–362.—Seymour indeed put forward the thesis of the gradual cooling of the friendship, but at the same time, he tried hard to minimize the problem. He accepted, "that the relations of Wilson and House had undergone a certain change during the course of the Peace Conference", but at the same time, he not only refuted Baker's "February plot", but also stressed the fact that Wilson continued to use House during the last part of the Conference and sought his advice on several occasions, and during the summer he signed all letters to House "affectionately yours". It was only after he fell ill—and after a long period of silence—that this affectionate greeting was exchanged for more cool expressions (in no more than three letters in all): "Thus the friendship lapsed. It was not broken" (IP IV, pp. 526–533).
8. See Alexander L. George and Juliette L. George: Woodrow Wilson and Colonel House. A Personality Study, John Day Company, New York, 1956, pp. 242 and 246.
9. See, for instance, the article written by Cary Grayson in 1926, which was published

posthumously: The Colonel's Folly and the President's Distress, American Heritage XV, Oct. 1964, pp. 4–7 and pp. 94–101; George Creel to R. S. Baker 27.3.1926, R. S. Baker papers, Series I, Library of Congress; Memorandum of Interviews with Dr. Cary T. Grayson on February 18, 19, 1926 at Washington, ibid.; Memorandum of a Conversation with Vance C. McCormick 15.7.1928, ibid.

10. Pocket edition 1964 in Dover Publications, New York, see above note 8.—In 1967, just before he died, William C. Bullitt published a book written by himself and Sigmund Freud: Thomas Woodrow Wilson. Twentyeigth President of the United States. A Psychological Study, Houghton Mifflin Company, Boston. If the book had been published before the scholarly analysis by George and George it probably would have been both a sensation and a catastrophe; now it was only a catastrophe. Freud and Bullitt met each other in 1930 and for several reasons they started co-operating on a study of Woodrow Wilson. At this time Freud was 74 and Bullitt 39. Bullitt writes of the procedure (p. vii): "From these private documents and conversations I compiled notes which ran to more that fifteen hundred typewritten pages. When I returned to Vienna, Freud read the notes and we discussed thoroughly the facts they contained. We then began to write. Freud wrote the first draft of portions of the manuscript and I wrote the first draft of other portions. Each then criticized, amended or rewrote the other's draft until the whole became an amalgam for which we were both responsible". In 1932, when the book was ready for publishing, Freud, wished certain changes to be made, to which Bullitt would not agree. Not until 1939, just before he died, did Freud give his assent to publication. This was further postponed until the death of Mrs. Wilson, and even after that Freud's relatives tried to stop publication, inter alia because they found the manuscript "perplexingly unlike any other that Freud had written. ... That is, Freud's psychoanalytic guidelines had been badly formulated and misapplied". This view was also put forward by the reviewer in the New York Times Book Review: "From general interpretations supplied by Freud, Bullitt seems to have managed a distorted weapon of revenge". (Robert Sussman Stewart: Posthumous Analysis, The New York Times Book Review, 21.1.1967, pp. 3 and 42–44. From this review I have also taken the information about Freud's relatives).

11. Alexander L. George is a political scientist and a "senior staff member of The Rand Corporation", and Juliette L. George, his wife, is a sociologist with war-time experience in analyzing foreign propaganda and editing political affairs reports (George and George p. 362). With reference to further discussion of the book, it is probably important to emphasize that neither is either a historian or a psychiatrist, the two sciences which they try to combine.—In Danish, on the other hand, the historian Povl Bagge has made the following experiment: He wrote a political biography of Johan Nicolai Madvig (Copenhagen, Ejnar Munksgaard, 1955) and showed the chapters in which he described Madvig's personality to a psychiatrist, Ib Ostenfeld. Ostenfeld then made his evaluation on the basis of this material, and this was published as an appendix to the biography.

12. The dedication is taken from Seymour's American Diplomacy During the World War, Baltimore, Johns Hopkins University Press 1934.

13. See, for instance Bernard Baruch to Carter Glass 17.3.1926, Baruch to Glass 22.9. 1926, Glass to Baruch 16.10.1926. Baruch Papers, Princeton University Library.

14. Peace Moves and U-boat Warfare, Stockholm Studies in History II, Stockholm 1958, pp. 223–225 and pp. 365–366.

15. A. O. Sarkissian ed., Studies in History and Historiography, p. 90.

16. Edward H. Buehrig ed., Wilson's Foreign Policy in Perspective, Indiana University Press, Bloomington, 1957, pp. 11–33.

17. ibid. pp. 15–16.

18. ibid. p. 33.

19. ibid. p. 26.

20. Harold Nicolson; Peacemaking 1919, Constable and Co., London 1943 (33); University Paperback, Methuen, London 1964, p. 15.

21. Wilson: Confusions and Crises. 1915–1916, Princeton, Princeton University Press,

1964, pp. 101–141, for further information, see Appendix I.—The so-called House-Grey memorandum was a memorandum prepared on February 17, 1916 by Sir Edward Grey after a conversation with Edward House. During this conversation, House told Grey "that President Wilson was ready, on hearing from France and England that the moment was opportune, to propose that a Conference should be summoned to put an end to the war. Should the Allies accept this proposal, and should Germany refuse it, the United States would probably enter the War against Germany". It was further stated that the possible peace terms would be "not unfavorable to the Allies". When House returned to the United States, President Wilson confirmed the memorandum. While the American revisionist writers during the 'thirties in this found ample proof of Wilson's and House's willingness to lead America into war on the side of the Allies, post-World War II historians have viewed the British motives with scepticism, and wondered how it was possible for House to take these negotiations seriously at all.

22. ibid. p. 141.—It has been of great importance to Link's evaluation that he was allowed to use "an important French diplomatic archive" (presumably Ambassador Jusserand's). In this way he got a chance to see the French memoranda of the important conversations between House and Jules Cambon, former French Ambassador to Germany, February 2, 1916, and between House and the French Prime Minister, Aristide Briand and Jules Cambon February 7, 1916. He was thus able to make an evalutation of House independent of his diary and telegrams to Wilson. Ernest R. May has tried a similar comparison in another connection: The World War and American Isolation 1914–1917, Harvard University Press, Cambridge, Mass., 1959, pp. 79–80. In January 1915, just before leaving on his first peace mission to Europe, House had a conversation with the Allied Ambassadors in Washington. May compared the report of the Russian Ambassador (Mezhdunarodnye Otnosheniya v Epokhu Imperializma. Series III, VII, no. 8, Moschou 1930) to House's diary entry (Int. Pap. I, p. 352) and concluded: "The difference between these two documents does not suggest that House's diary is an inaccurate record, but it does indicate *that the Colonel is not always to be trusted as an interpreter of others' moods and thoughts.* In any case, the Colonel had made his effort and thought he had succeeded". (Italics mine). However being "an interpreter of others' moods and thoughts" was exactly the task House was supposed to fulfil.

23. Link, Wilson: Confusions . . ., pp. 89–93.—House also gripped the political situation in England at once, even though he did not take the consequences: Grey's position was now seriously shaken, Lloyd George was the strong man. (Int. Pap. II, p. 133 and p. 141).

24. Link, Wilson: Confusions . . ., p. 93.

25. But none of these writers knew the French material to which Link had access (see note 22).

26. Bloomington, Indiana University Press, 1955, chap. 6 and 7.

27. ibid. pp. 186–187.

28. Chapter XVL, see also note 22.

29. ibid. p. 352.

30. Princeton, Princeton University Press, 1957, pp. 81–85 and passim. For Mamatey's discussion of the diary, see below p. 00.

31. This characterization is very similar to that given by Ray Stannard Baker, see below pp. 28, 164 and 192.

32. Op. cit., pp. 84–85.

33. Int. Pap., pp. 3–4. Italics mine.

34. ibid. p. 4.

35. Mamatey, op. cit. p. 82. Mamatey does not give any references, but many examples can be found: see note 36. Cf. also Burton F. Beers, Vain Endeavor. Robert Lansing's Attempts to End the American-Japanese Rivalry. Duke University Press, Durham, N. C., 1962, pp. 187–188: "All materials, especially the Diary, must be used with caution. House seems to have had the historian constantly in mind as he produced his record".

36. House diary 28.6.1918; 24.9.1918; 12.11.1918; 20.12.1918; 2.4.1919. Seymour tells us that the diary was begun on September 9, 1912, at a time, thus, when House was beginning to be seriously involved in important political events (IP, I, p. 75).
37. Cf. note 10.
38. In the following, I have purposely refrained from any evaluation of this aspect of the book, not being a psychologist myself. To a historian, at any rate, the analysis seems rather heavy-handed.
39. George and George, p. 340, Cf. p. 323.
40. Ibid., chapter 5.—The authors base their description of House's pre-Wilson period rather uncritically on his two autobiographical essays. House always preferred a "behind the scenes" function, and the authors ascribed this to his notoriously bad health. But was he not also afraid of the burdens of responsibility?—A very positive evaluation of House's Texas years and indeed of House in general is given by Rupert Norval Richardson: Colonel Edward M. House. The Texas Years, 1858–1912, Hardin Simmons University, Abilene, Texas, 1964.
41. Ibid. chapter 6.
42. See especially chapter 7.
43. This analysis is found ibid. chapter 10.
44. Wilson's first wife, Ellen Axson Wilson, had accepted her husband's special relationship with House with great understanding. She died in August 1914, and left Wilson in a state of deep depression. "In his grief, Wilson needed his friends more than ever. His emotional dependence upon House, to judge from House's diary and the letters which the President wrote him, seems to have reached its peak in the period between the death of Ellen Axson Wilson and Wilson's marriage to Edith Bolling Galt in December 1915" (George and George, p. 155). The new Mrs. Wilson did not show the same tolerance, she thought House a "yes, yes man", and in the long run she did not keep her antipathy to herself "She seems however, not to have comprehended that House's "yes, yes" characteristics were implicitly demanded by Wilson as the price of maintaining his status as presidential adviser". (Ibid. p. 187).—See also George Sylvester Viereck: The Strangest Friendship in History. Woodrow Wilson and Colonel House, New York, Liveright, 1932. Viereck's book is a curious combination of insight and hearsay.
45. ibid. p. 187.—Seymour analyzed the Wilson-House correspondance and found that the way Wilson titulates House and the formulas for greetings he used indicate a considerable change following the reelection. Seymour therefore concluded that the personal relationship between the two men was most intimate before 1917, while on the other hand, the American participation in war brought a vast increase in House's responsibilities (IP I–IV, passim).
46. Cf. below chapters 3 and 4.
47. "House confided to his diary..." (George and George, p. 127); "... the privacy of his diary..." (p. 128); "... House confided to his diary ..." (p. 183); "... the safety of his diary..." (p. 185); "... the intimacy os his diary..." (p. 190). Italics mine.
48. ibid. especially chapter 9, but also chapter 13.
49. ibid. p. 158.—For further discussion of this element, see my review in Historisk Tidsskrift (cf. note 1.).
50. Robert E. Osgood: Ideals and Self-Interest in America's Foreign Relations, Chicago, 1953. On Buehrig see note 26.
51. George and George, p. 163.
52. ibid. p. 336.
53. ibid. pp. 160–161.
54. Harper and Row, New York, 1954.
55. George and George, p. 336, Link op. cit. p. 203.
56. George and George, p. 168. For Link's views, see above pp. 15–16.
57. George and George pp. 168–170.
58. Cf. George and George, p. 337, note 23.
59. ibid. pp. 191–192.

60. ibid. chapter 13.
61. ibid. pp. 192–193.
62. ibid. p. 242.
63. ibid. p. 246.

## Chapter 1

1. For this aspect of Wilson's wartime diplomacy see especially David F. Trask: The United States in the Supreme War Council. American War Aims and Inter-Allied Strategy, 1917–1918, Wesleyan University Press, Middletown, Conn., 1961; Daniel M. Smith: The Great Departure. The United States and World War I. 1914–1920, John Wiley and Sons, New York, 1965; W. B. Fowler: British-American Relations, 1917–1918. The Role of Sir William Wiseman, Princeton University Press, Princeton, New Jersey, 1969. Quotation Fowler, p. 5.—For further literature on Wilson's foreign policy see my survey in Historisk Tidsskrift, 12. rk., bd. IV, pp. 107–138. 21.7.17. Wilson wrote to House (House Collection, Yale University Library): "England and France have not the same views with regard to peace that we have by any means. When the war is over we can force them to our way of thinking because by that time they will, among other things, be financially in our hands: but we cannot force them now, and any attempt to speak for them or to our common mind would bring on disagreements which would inevitably come to the surface in public and rob the whole thing of its effect.
Our real peace terms,—those upon which we shall undoubtedly insist, are not now acceptable to either France or Italy (leaving Great Britain for the moment out of consideration)". Italics in the original, the letter is quoted from Trask, pp. 7–8.
2. Cf. the introduction p. 15.
3. For the neutrality period see especially the ealier cited works by Buehrig, Link and May and volume 5 in Link's Wilson-biography: Campaigns for Progressivism and Peace, 1916–1917, Princeton University Press, Princeton, New Jersey, 1965.
4. House must share the honours with A. J. Balfour, the British Foreign Secretary and with Sir William Wiseman who acted as a kind of liason-officer between the British Government, and House and Wilson. See Seymour's and Fowler's above cited works and also Arthur Willert: The Road to Safety; A Study in Anglo-American Relations, London, 1952; and Arthur Murray: At Close Quarters, A Sidelight on Anglo-American Diplomatic Relations, London 1946. Fowler is much more critical in his evaluation of Wiseman and House, than either Seymour or Willert.
5. Originally, the Americans had counted on being asked only to give economic help (Fowler, pp. 127 ff), but by the end of the war, there were about 2 mill. American soldiers in Europe.
6. See especially Arno J. Mayer: Political Origins of the New Diplomacy, 1917–1918, Yale University Press, New Haven, 1959; and Lawrence W. Martin: Peace without Victory. Woodrow Wilson and the British Liberals, New Haven, Yale University Press, 1958; Victor S. Mamatey's above quoted work and Christopher Lasch: The American Liberals and the Russian Revolution, Columbia University Press, New York and London, 1962. For a further discussion of these problems see Appendix I and below pp. 31–35.
7. George and George, p. 189.
8. See Lawrence E. Gelfand: The Inquiry. American Preparations for Peace, 1917–1919, Yale University Press, New Haven and London, 1963; and cf. also below chapter 2. pp. 61–62.
9. For a further discussion of the term "liberal" see Appendix III.
10. Christopher Lasch: The New Radicalism in America. 1889–1963. The Intellectual as a Social Type. Vintage Books, New York, 1967 (1965), pp. 225–250.
11. A Story of Tomorrow, 1920–1935. New York, B. V. Huebsch, 1912.
12. Lasch, The New Radicalism, p. 234.

13. 23.6.19. Baker notebook XXV, R. S. Baker papers, Ser. II. Library of Congress. For Baker's very changing view of House see also Robert C. Bannister, Jr.: Ray Stannard Baker. The Mind and Thought of a Progressive. Yale Publications in American Studies, 10, New Haven and London, Yale University Press, 1966, p. 211 and cf. below chapter 4.
14. cf. below.
15. Mamatey, op. cit. pp. 81–85.
16. ibid. and see also the discussion of George and George in the introduction.
17. About these problems see Martin, Peace without Victory, passim; Lasch, The American Liberals, passim; and Mayer's two books, passim.
18. The following discussion is based principally upon Mamatey, op. cit. pp. 143–147, but see also Lasch, The American Liberals, pp. 46–54 and Mayer, Wilson vs. Lenin, pp. 229–236. Lasch and Mayer especially stresses the influence of the Russian question upon House's stand.—The Pope's proposal was put forward in August 1917.
19. House diary 18.8.17, cited in Mamatey, op. sit., p. 145. House stayed at Magnolia, his summer-home.
20. Cf. the diary entry 15.8.1917. Mamatey, op. cit. p. 145.
21. House diary 24.8.17. Mamatey, op. cit., p. 146.—Incidentally, Mamatey also shows that Wilson actually had asked Lansing's advice.
22. House diary 29.8.17. Mamatey, op. cit., p. 146.
23. House to Wilson 15.8.17, cited in Lasch, The American Liberals, pp. 46–47. Lasch, furthermore, gives the following quotation from Lincoln Colcord's diary 30.7.1917: "What I (House) am afraid of is that if we don't make a peace, and if the Russian situation gets worse and worse, there will be a world-wide reaction from democracy. I (House) think that on this count alone, peace must be made this fall if possible" (Lasch, p. 229). Cf. also chapter 3 below.
24. About these problems see especially the works of Lasch, Levin and Mayer.
25. The following discussion is based on Levin's very penetrating analysis, Levin, op. cit., pp. 50–73. The quotation pp. 50–51.
26. About the relations between House and Lansing see chapter 2, and also Mamatey, op. cit., p. 83 and 146, and Arthur S. Link, Wilson, Confusions and Crises. 1915–1916, Princeton, N. J., Princeton University Press, 1964, p. 174.
27. For an analysis of the attitude of the State Department toward Bolshevism see: Williams, American-Russian Relations, chapters 5 and 6, passim. Especially Basil Miles seems to have played an important role. William C. Bullitt was an exception, he was "the one representative of Left-Liberalism in the State Department" (Levin, op. cit., p. 90).
28. Levin, op. cit. p. 63; George F. Kennan, The Decision to Intervene, Soviet-American Relations, 1917–1920, II, New York, Atheneum, 1967 (1958), p. 381.
29. Levin, op. cit. p. 58.
30. ibid. p. 62 and pp. 70–71. The cause was probably the dissolution of the Constituent Assembly by the Bolsheviks, this made a deep impression.
31. ibid. p. 64.
32. ibid. p. 66.
33. About the New Republic's relations with the Administration during and after the war, see Charles Forcey: The Crossroads of Liberalism. Croly, Weyl, Lippmann, and the Progressive Era, 1900–1925, New York, Oxford University Press, 1961, chapters 7 and 8, and Lasch, The New Radicalism, chapter 6.
34. Forcey, op. cit. pp. 265–266, and Lasch, The New Radicalism, pp. 220–221.
35. Cf. chapter 2, p. 61.
36. For the war-time career of Walter Lippmann, see Forcey, op. cit. p. 278; about the Cobb-Lipmann memorandum see p. 48.
37. Cited in Lasch, The New Radicalism, p. 221. – But see also Wilson to Lansing 5.9.18. Wilson papers, Series II: "... I have a high opinion of Lippmann, but I am very jealous in the matter of propaganda ... I want to keep the matter of publicity entirely in my own hands ...".
38. For House's plans regarding Straight, see pp. 66–67 and about Straight's opinion

of Wilson see Forcey, op. cit., pp. 284–285: "By the end of the war Willard Straight was more convinced than ever that Wilson was, "not a leader". "He's no more ready for peace than he was for war", wrote Straight. "We stand in fair way of having fought the war, lost thousands of lives and millions of dollars, upsetting everything, and of not getting the peace we started for" ".

39. Forcey, op. cit. pp. 288–289.—Cf. Lansing diary 26.11.18: "Patchin on *not* employing Lippmann". Lippmann left Paris in February 1919.

40. House diary 24.2.18. Cf. chapter 2, p. 61. For another radical Wilson-statement see Forcey, op. cit., pp. 286–287.

41. Cf. House's reasons for arranging an interview between Wiseman and Wilson in the middle of October, cited below p. 44 (House diary 22.10.18).

42. See Appendix I.

43. For the following see especially Mayer, Politics . . ., pp. 167–177.

44. ibid. p. 169.

45. ibid. p. 170, italics mine. Also Levin discusses Wilson and Socialism, Levin, op. cit., pp. 161–168.

46. Baker's letters from Europe to Frank Polk in the State Department and to House is found in R. S. Baker papers, Library of Congress and/or in Polk papers and House papers, respectively, both at Yale University Library. For Baker's reports see also Mayer, Politics . . ., pp. 33–40; about his overestimation of the strength of the Socialists, see especially pp. 37 and 40. About Baker, see also Appendix I.—Also William C. Bullitt seems in his analysis of the European political situation to have overrated the Socialistic strength, Mayer, Politics . . ., p. 386.

47. See Norman Hapgood to R. S. Baker 7.2.18: "This is extremely confidential. Our sources of information about popular feeling abroad are not what they ought to be. Our government wants the right man to go to England on that mission. Will you permit Colonel House to suggest your name to the State Department?" (R. S. Baker papers, Library of Congress). See also House diary 2.2.18 on a conversation with Frank Polk.

48. Handwritten draft of letter no. 21 (Baker to Polk 12.9.18) dated 3.9.18. R. S. Baker papers.

49. Baker to Polk 10.8.18, no. 16. R. S. Baker papers, italics Baker's.

50. Baker to House 1.11.18, no. 18. R. S. Baker papers.

51. See especially his "Memorandum for the President", 18.12.18. Baker papers.

52. House diary 28.6.18.

53. ibid. 28.7.18. Italics mine.

54. ibid. 4.11.18.

55. House to Wilson no. 119, in Auchincloss diary 18.11.18.

56. House diary 16.11.18.

57. Mayer, Politics . . ., p. 172.

58. Auchincloss diary 4.12.18.

59. House to Wilson, no. 19, 9.12.18. PC I, pp. 148–149.

60. ibid. pp. 146–147.

61. Auchincloss diary 10.12.18.

62. Cf. Mayer, Politics . . ., pp. 174–177.

63. ibid. p. 379.—For the Berne Conference se also ibid. pp. 373–409.

64. Fowler, p. 221 with references. Lord Reading, the British Ambassador in Washington, was at this time in London.

65. FR18SI, 1, 338—About the German policy see for example Gerhard Ritter: Staatskunst und Kriegshandwerk, IV, R. Oldenbourg Verlag, München, 1968; and Rudin and Renouvin mentioned below. See now also the important work by Klaus Schwabe: Deutsche Revolution und Wilson Frieden. Die amerikanische und deutsche Friedensstrategie zwischen Ideologie und Machtpolitik 1918/19, Droste Verlag, Düsseldorf, 1971, which, unfortunately, arrived after I had finished my manuscript.

66. Tumulty for example recommended a refusal (Tumulty to Wilson 8.10.18, Wilson papers, Ser. 2), while House recommended a more sophisticated method: ". . . An armistice such as the Germans and Austrians ask for seems to me impossible, and

yet a refusal should be couched in such terms as to leave the advantage with you. ... Our position I think should be one of delay without seeming so" (House to Wilson 6.10.18, Wilson papers, Ser. 2.).

67. Lansing desk book 7.10.18: "Conference 9–12,15 (pm) with Prest. and Colonel House on reply to peace proposals. Difficulties multiplied with discussion". House diary 9.10.18 (about the same meeting 7,10 pm): ". . . The President had prepared his reply to the German Chancellor, Prince Maximilian of Baden, and read it to us (House and Lansing). He seemed much disturbed when I expressed a decided disapproval of it. I told him I had thought of something quite different; that I did not approve of what he had written. After arguing the matter some half an hour or more, he said that I might be able to write something and embody what I had in mind, but he had to confess his inability to do so. He suggested that I have a try at it. ... We then began to amend his draft and before we finished with it the next day, there was no much left of the original". The next morning (8.10) House and Wilson met again: "We read what the papers had to say: I called attention to what the French socialists convention said upon the subject in Paris, and the comments of the Manchester Guardian and London Daily News. He, on his part, read the debate which took place in the Senate Monday. I found the President's viewpoint had changed during the night and he had come around to mine. He did not seem to realize before, the nearly unanimous sentiment in this country against anything but unconditional surrender. He did not realize how war mad our people had become.... The President thought if such an offer had been made by a reputable government, it would be impossible to decline it...." (ibid.). "The President was not happy at this effort of ours, and neither was I, and yet it is the best, that our combined judgment could produce. That it has taken with the public as well as it has makes me content..." (ibid.).

68. Lansing desk book 8.10.18.

69. House sought to eliminate the role of Lansing: "Lansing took little or no part in our discussions" (House diary 9.10.18 about the evening meeting 7.10).

70. Cf. note 67.

71. Wilson papers, Ser.2. Actually, there are two versions, a draft and a fair copy with minor (insignificant) deviations. The note as sent: FRI8SI, I, p. 343.

72. Both Lansing and Tumulty recommended this step: Pierre Renouvin: L'Armistice de Rethondes. 11. Novembre 1918, Gallimard, Paris, 1968, p. 121. For the American public opinion see ibid. pp. 115–116. The Allied governments, on the other hand, were very sceptical towards this intervention in German internal political conditions (ibid. p. xx). Also House wrote, as noted above, that Wilson in the beginning did seem to have realized "the nearly unanimous sentiment in this country against anything but unconditional surrender".

73. Josephus Daniels diary 8.10.18, Library of Congress; E. David Cronon (ed): The Cabinet Diaries of Josephus Daniels 1913–1921. University of Nebraska Press, Lincoln, 1963, p. 339.—There was no real discussion of the note in the Cabinet, see The Letters of Franklin K. Lane. Personal and Political, edited by Anne Wintermute Lane and Louise Herrick Wall, Boston and New York, Houghton Mifflin Company, 1922, p. 293.

74. FR18SI, 1, p. 343.

75. Guy Pedroncini: Les Négociations secretes pendant la Grande Guerre, Flammarion, Paris, 1969, pp. 93–105; War Memoirs of David Lloyd George, Ivor Nicholson and Watson, London, 1936, VI, p. 3263, pp. 3274–3278 and 3280–3283; Harry R. Rudin: Armistice 1918, New Haven, Yale University Press, 1944, pp. 89–109.—The meeting was originally called for other reasons.

76. See the "joint note" which Frazier forwarded to the State Department 9.10.18 (received 10.10.). Wilson papers, Ser. 2, FR18SI, 1, p. 353. See also Frazier to Lansing 8.10.18 (received 8.10), ibid. pp. 344–345, Frazier to Lansing 8.10.18, ibid. pp. 345–346, Frazier to Lansing 8.10.18 (received 9.10) ibid. p. 346, Frazier to Lansing 9.10.18 (received 10.10) ibid. pp. 351–352 and Frazier to Lansing 9.10.18 (received 10.10.) ibid. p. 352.

77. Bliss to Newton D. Baker 9.10.18, no. 28, Wilson papers, Ser. 2, and Bliss to War Department, telegram no. 244, 8.10.18, ibid.

78. House diary 13.10.18, see also Lansing desk book 9.10.18: "General March (the American Chief of Staff) on astounding proceeding of Lloyd George, Clemenceau and Orlando at Paris in formulating terms of an armistice with Germany". And ibid.: "Conferred at House with French and Italian Amb.'s on extraordinary proceeding of premiers at Paris. Asked them to find out what it means"....."Barclay on armistice terms. He telegraphs his Govt.".".

79. See for example Frazier to Lansing 7.10.18 (received 8.10.), FR18SI, 1, pp. 344–345, and Frazier to Lansing 8.10.18 (received 9.10.), FR18SI, 1, p. 346, and Renouvin, Armistice, pp. 122–127. On October 11 Wilson had a conversation with the French Ambassador Jusserand, during which he "affirme qu'a ses yeux; comme à ceux des gouvernements alliés, l'évacuation des territoires envahis n'est pas une conditions suffisante, et il reconnait que les chefs militaires sont "seuls compétents" pour étudier les modalités de cette évacuation". Renouvin concludes: "Voila donc un résultat acquis" (ibid. p. 126). See also Balfour to Barclay 14.10.18, no. 2, presented to Lansing 14.10., and forwarded by him to Wilson the same day (Wilson papers, Ser. 2). The conversation is explicitly referred to, and it is taken as evidence of "that he (Wilson) never contemplated the grant of an armistice merely on the promise of Germany that she would withdraw her troops from the accepted territories. . . .".—Hankey's diary shows very clearly the irritation of the Allies. Stephen Roskill: Hankey, Man of Secrets, I, 1877–1918. Collins, London, 1970, pp. 608–611 (diary, 5., 6. and 9.10.18).

80. Lansing to Wilson 14.10.18. Wilson papers, Ser. 2, cf. note 10.

81. The paragraph quoted here is thrown into relief in the copy in the Wilson papers by a pencil-line, and in his covering letter Lansing wrote: "I would particularly call your attention to the last paragraph of the second telegram, which has sufficient merit to warrant careful consideration".

82. FR18SI, 1, pp. 357–358.

83. FR18SI, 1, pp. 358–359.—The American note was drawn up in conferences between Wilson, Baker, Daniels, House and Lansing, and Wilson, House, Polk, Tumulty and Lansing. See House diary 15.10.18, partly in IP IV, pp. 82–83, and Lansing desk book 14.10.18. In Wilson papers, Ser. 2 is a draft, written on his own typewriter and with his own handwritten corrections. This draft is almost identical with the note as sent. ibid. is also an outline written on Wilson's own typewriter. A copy of the note, written on Wilson's own typewriter is also found in the National Archives: 763.72119/2313. The note also required the termination of the U-boat war.

84. It is possible that Wilson in this accentuating of the way he presented the problems compared with the first note, was influenced by an analysis of American public opinion which David Lawrence sent him on October 13 (Wilson papers, Ser. 2). Lawrence argued that, "America has been fed war-hate or rather hatred of the Kaiser and the Hohenzollerns ... To a surprising extent the Kaiser has become the single issue". "The man on the street today doesn't believe Germany "has been licked enough" ". By this he (the man in the street) primarily meant that the present German rulers had to be removed. "It has the appearance of a personal issue but it is a fundamental principle". Lawrence therefore recommended—and this is underlined in the original in Wilson papers: "Judging by what I have seen and heard, I set it down most solemnly as my humble judgment that anything short of a positive definition of the issue as between the "constituted authorities who have thus far conducted the war" and the elimination of those authorities before condition one and two of your inquiry can be further considered, would be disastrous not merely to the prestige of the man whom the world acclaims as its leader but disastrous to the further application of moral force itself. No, Mr. President, rightly or wrongly, our people have been fed intolerance and personalities for eighteen months. British and French propaganda has intensified that feeling and today you have behind you a nation ready to follow you to the finish for the extermination of the men

responsible for the things the people have read about. ... You have described so splendidly the origin of this war in secret counsels and selfish groups. You have argued so effectively that such groups must never be permitted to disturb the peace of the world. You have said we cannot come to terms with the present German Government and you are privileged to call the attention of the German people to that section of your speech of September 30th in New York in which you so described the attitude of the American people. If they accept the principles laid down in your speech of January 8th and "subsequent addresses" would it not be in order to make your answer to the German note of last night a single question, asking, in effect, if the German people read and if their answer means they have agreed to that portion of your speech of September 30th referring to the present Government of Germany....". Wilson chose instead an example from his July 4 speech, but at least he used the idea.—The Allies on the other hand were not quite convinced of the appropriateness of mingling in German Internal affairs. Cf. Renouvin, Armistice, pp. 134–135.

85. FR18SI, 1, p. 361. At the meeting of the War Cabinet on 23.10. Wilson said that he had used a memorandum by Newton D. Baker, the Secretary of War, in preparing the note, "but the last part he wrote himself". Josephus Daniels diary 23.10.18; Library of Congress; Cronon, p. 344.

86. For further information see Renouvin, Armistice, pp. 138–163. The German answer (FR18SI, 1, pp. 379–381) was known in Washington 21.10. (Cf. Daniels diary 21.10.18; Cronon, p. 342, and Lansing desk book 21.10.18).

87. Balfour to Barclay 21.10.18, presented to Lansing 22.10. and forwarded by him to Wilson (Wilson papers, Ser. 2). The French Government, too, now decided to put pressure on Wilson. See about this Renouvin, op. cit., p. 133.

88. FR18SI, 1, p. 383. In the National Archives 763.72119/2368 1/2 is found Wilson's draft of the note to the Allies, written on his own typewriter and the different amendments proposed by Lansing. Wilson wrote in his covering letter to Lansing (23.10): "Here is my idea of the form in which we should submit our correspondence with Germany to the governments with which we are associated as belligerents. What do you think of it? I dare say we should send the correspondence to each of them as promptly as possible". See also Lansing desk book 23.10.18: "At 10 (pm) received proposed communication to Allies from Prest. Worked it over into different form ...".

89. FR18SI, 1, pp. 381–383. In National Archives 763.72119/2368 1/2 is found Wilson's draft of the note, written on his own typewriter. Except for certain changes of editing, the draft is identical with the note as sent ibid. 763.72119/2371 1/2 (21.10.18) and 2372 1/2 (22.10.18) is found several drafts by Lansing, inter alios the following penetrating analysis (dated Oct. 21): "The President laid down three conditions to the negotiation of a peace which were cumulative in effect.

*First.* There must be an actual evacuation of all invaded territory. (This means on every front.) Until that is done the President will not consider submitting the question of an armistice to the military advisers of the associated governments.

*Second.* The submission of the question of an armistice, even after evacuation, is entirely discretionary. If it is submitted and an agreement reached by the military authorities, then the question of peace terms may be considered.

*Third.* All discussion of peace depends, however, on the entire acceptance of the principles laid down by the President in his address of January 8, 1918, and subsequent addresses, and also on the imperial autocracy of Germany has been completely supplanted by a democratic government which unquestionably represents the popular will.

The cessation of devastation of occupied territory during evacuation and of submarine warfare are only evidences of good faith which is essential to any consideration of the German proposals and immediately affect the question of considering an armistice".

Lansing's different drafts, except the above quoted handwritten analysis, are also found in the Wilson papers, Ser. 2. ibid. is also located several drafts written in Wilson's handwriting or on his own typewriter. These drafts are basically in agreement with the note as sent.

90. For the meetings about the drafting of the note see Lansing desk book 21., 22. and 23.10.18, and Daniels diary 21., 22. and 23.10.18, and Renouvin, pp. 133–134.

91. Daniels wrote about the Conference 21.10.18 (Cronon, p. 342–343): "German note came by radio.
Long conference at White House. WW, Lansing, Baker, JD, March. WW read it over and commented on it. General opinion that Germany had accepted WW's demands. Was she in good faith. Lansing first thought should put it up the military men as to armistice. Baker thought G.had accepted. Why not ask Allies for their views? March thought WW ought to act without conference with Allies. WW felt it well to sleep over it. House on way to France. Benson with him. Wish they were there now so as to get view of Prime Ministers there. But the sentiment here wants blood or to put Kaiser on St. Helena. This was regarded as "ridiculous" said WW".

92. See Lansing desk book 22.10. and 23.10.18. The viewpoint is also found in several letters to Wilson, see for example Anita McCormick Blaine to Wilson 22.10.18, Homer S. Cummings to Wilson 22.10.18, John Sharp Williams to Wilson 22.10.18, and Key Pittmann to Wilson 23.10.18, all in Wilson papers, Ser. 2.

93. Lansing desk book 23.10.18.

94. Daniels diary 23.10.18, Cronon, p. 344. The discussion at this meeting (it was a War Cabinet meeting) turned, inter alios, on the probable influence of the note on the approaching election.

95. Daniels diary 22.10.18; Cronon, p. 343.

96. House diary 22.10.18.

97. ibid. 24.10.18.

98. FR18SI, 1, p. 381.—This is the opinion of so different authors as Renouvin, L'Armistice .... pp. 136–137; Richard W. Leopold: The Growth of American Foreign Policy. A History, New York, Alfred A. Knopf, 1962, p. 357; and Daniel M. Smith, The great Departure, p. 103.

99. Thomas A. Bailey, Woodrow Wilson and the Lost Peace, MacMillan, New York, 1944, p. 42. The parenthetical addition mine.

100. Renouvin gives a very penetrating discussion of public opinion in the United States, as well as in the Allied countries, (pp. 113–137). See also Bailey, pp. 40–41 and Mayer, Arno J.: Politics and Diplomacy of Peacemaking. Containment and Counter-revolution at Versailles, 1918–1919, Weidenfeld and Nicolson, London, 1968, pp. 53–89.

101. Lansing gives the following interesting account of the motives behind the first note in a letter to Edward N. Smith, 12.10.18 (Lansing papers, Library of Congress, vol. 39):
"I was sorry that I had to rush away from the Grand Central Station on yesterday morning in order to catch the first train for Washington, as I should have liked to breakfast with you and talk over the international situation. *It presents some problems which are most perplexing and which acquire adroit handling. These do not appear so much on the surface but arise largely from secret information* which I could talk about but cannot write about except in a general way. I have read this morning the editorial in the Standard of Wednesday last on the Note of Inquiry and I congratulate you on the grasp of the situation and the reason for the note. I assume that you wrote or that it emanated from you. You struck the nail squarely on the head. Much better than many of our Solons in Congress who can see only red and would have us do exactly what the German Government wants us to do. *A flat rejection would have united all parties in Germany and would have cost great dissatisfaction among considerable elements in Great Britain, France and Italy.* The people of those countries are weary, almost beyond endurance, after four years of war. They long for peace at the earliest possible moment, and would go far in stopping bloodshed at once. They are full of rejoicing at the desire of the Central

Empires for peace, and see no good reason for continuing the war. *Confidentially*. When the German note was published many of the principal cities of Italy had peace demonstrations and in Milan a holiday was declared and all labor ceased while parades and music evidenced the popular desire an the resentment which would have followed had there been a flat refusal to the overture. In Paris the German note and military successes were received with quiet elation, but as our informant says, "not so much because of ultimate victory as of the near approach of peace". In England also a large group of labor are influenced by the same spirit.

The foregoing, which I must ask you to keep confidential, shows what we are up against. *Today our people as a whole are the most bellicose and most sternly opposed to giving any consideration to the future of Germany.* They wish Germany crushed and peace made in Berlin. *It is hard to deal with this intense feeling, which approaches fanaticism, because the situation in the Allied countries cannot be publicly explained. Furthermore in Eastern Germany Bolshevism is raising its abominable head, and a Germany crushed might become a prey to that hideous movement. If it did, Europe might become a seething mass of anarchy. Who can tell?* We must take no changes on this war culminating in such a frightful catastrophe, beside which "the Terror" of 1792 would be a happy epoch. *The horrors of Bolshevik Russia must not be repeated in other Lands. The doctrine is spreading as it is.* It is in all the nations of Europe and is (I say it with regret) gaining a foothold in this country. It must not be allowed to master the people of Central Europe, where it would become a greater menace to the world than Prussianism.

What I have written you I know you will treat as secret, but I wished you to understand the many conditions and influences which have to be considered in dealing with the international situation, and with what caution we have to travel. The vast majority of Americans think that an appeal for peace requires only a "yes" or "no". Even some of our distinguished Senators seem to have no greater comprehension of the difficulties. I wished you to understand all this not only on your own account but because you would be in a position to explain the truth to my friends at home for I especially want them to be satisfied with my work."

Lansing to Edward N. Smith 12.10.18, Lansing papers, vol. 39. Library of Congress. (The italics, except *"Confidentially"* are mine). Smith belonged to a circle of friends in Watertown, New York, where Lansing spent his childhood and youth. During his later years, Lansing remained on intimate terms with these friends. (For further information see Burton F. Beers: Vain Endeavor. Robert Lansing's attempts to end the American-Japanese rivalry. Duke University Press, Durham, N. C., 1962, pp. 9–15). Lansing expressed the same views to other of the friends: "You are quite right in saying that this is a very critical time in our international affairs. It is in certain ways far more critical than the public can know. I could explain this to you if I saw you, but I do not wish to write upon the subject. *Many thought that we should have answered the first note of Germany with a peremptory refusal, but we had to consider the political situation in various European countries, and took the course which seemed to us wise in view of that situation.* This may sound a little blind, but I really cannot explain more fully. In this as in other cases the people must take something on faith and believe that we are not fools and that our hearts are in the right place" (Lansing to Gary M. Jones, Watertown, New York, 17.10.18, Lansing papers, vol. 39—italics mine). "The international pot is boiling these days, and no one can tell from one day to another what will happen. While we are having great successes on the western front, *I believe that the political possibilities for Germany's cracking are greater than they are in a military way.* The German army is still a powerful and well organized machine, and the German retreat is being conducted in a very orderly manner. *Naturally we watch the internal affairs of Germany with the greatest interest, as it seems that that is the place where the break will come*". (Lansing to W. C. Stebbins, Watertown, New York, 18.10.18—italics mine). See also Mayer, Politics and Diplomacy . . ., pp. 53–89.

102. Cf. note 101, and see for example Daniels diary 8.10.18 (Cronon, p. 339); Daniels

diary 17.10.18 (ibid. p. 342). Daniels was the American Secretary of the Navy and he took part in the discussions both in the ordinary Cabinet, in the War Cabinet, and in the inner circle discussions Wilson had with his most intimate advisers. No minutes were taken of the Cabinet meetings. the notes taken by Daniels, as well as by Lane, the Secretary of the Interior, therefore, are of a special interest. Lane wrote among other things of these problems in his account of the Cabinet meeting 22.10.18: "I said that we were in a confidential relation to France and England, (and) that they were in danger of troubles at home, possible revolution . . .". "He (Wilson) said he was afraid of Bolshevism in Europe . . .". (The Letters of Franklin K. Lane, p. 295); see also William Wiseman's "Notes of an Interview with the President at the White House, Wednesday, October 16th, 1918. Very Secret", printed in John L. Snell: Wilson on Germany and the Fourteen Points. Journal of Modern History, 26, (Chicago 1954), pp. 364–469 and Fowler, pp. 283–285. For a further discussion of Arno Mayer's thesis about Bolshevism and the Peace Conference see chapter 3 below, and especially Appendix I.

103. See Secretary of the Treasury, McAdoo's remarks, Lane, p. 295; Daniels diary 15.10. (Cronon, p. 341) and Daniels diary 22.10.18 (Cronon, p. 343). McAdoo did not think that the Treasury would be able to finance the war for two more years.

104. Cf. above pp. 37–38.

105. Cf. above pp. 38–39.

106. Cf. above note 102.

107. It seems to have been especially this aspect Wilson discussed in his conversations with House regarding the drafting of the first two notes. House diary 9.10.18; 13.10.18; 15.10.18; 22.10.18 and 24.10.18. House refers to the "formula" in this way: (15. 10.18, partly in IP IV, p. 83): "We fell back time and again on the theory which I offered when the last note was written, that if Germany was beaten, she would accept any terms. If she was not beaten, we did not wish to make terms with her".

108. Lane's notes of the Cabinet meeting 22.10.18. (dated 23.10.), Lane, p. 295; see also Daniels's notes, above p. xx, note 95.

109. Baker, Ray Stannard: Woodrow Wilson: Life and Letters, VIII, New York, Double-day, Doran, 1939, p. 523. House seems to have received this telegram in a somewhat garbled version, cf. W. Stull Holt: What Wilson sent and what House received . . ., American Historical Review, 65, 1960, pp. 569–571. Wilson gave as his reasons to Pershing that too severe conditions would strengthen the military party in Germany. Newton D. Baker to Pershing 27.10.18, Baker VIII, p. 521.

110. Fowler, pp. 209–216, quotation p. 215. It is the period August-September 1918.

111. Snell, pp. 364–369; Fowler, pp. 283–285. For Wilson's original dissociation from negotiations with the Allied before the Peace Conference see below chapter 2, p. xx.

112. Daniels diary 17.10.18; Cronon, p. 342. The remark covered British economic policy and the quotation continues: "England has agreed to trade conditions as I proposed. We must pool raw material and not permit it to be used for speculative purpose". November 6 Daniels also wrote about a War Council: "Baruch said France wanted much steel, England wanted many things. "I (Wilson) wish no ships and nothing done till peace. I intend to carry as many weapons to the peace table as I can conceal on my person". I will be cold and firm. GB selfish. He looked for League of Nations to settle freedom of the seas" (Daniels diary 6.11.18; Cronon, p. 347).

113. For a further analysis and account of this aspect of American policy see Mayer: Politics and Diplomacy . . ., pp. 260–283, and Levin: Woodrow Wilson and World Politics, pp. 139–150. Mayer stresses inter alios that "US foreign aid was multipur-pose: it helped stem the Bolshevik tide in Central and Eastern Europe; it placated and served interests at home; and it facilitated the reconversion of the American economy to peace conditions. But there was a fourth function of equally great magnitude. As America's military and naval power began to count for less with the Allies, her economic and financial resources counted for correspondingly more. Allied as well as American leaders expected these resources to assume considerable political weight in the impending peace negotiations. Whereas the Allies thought

to curtail the thrust of this untried instrument of power, the Americans prepared to harness it for their own national purposes" (p. 273). See also Carl P. Parrini, Heir to Empire. United States Economic Diplomacy, 1916–23, Pittsburgh, 1969.

114. Daniels wrote of Wilson's acceptance: "Decided to accept inasmuch as GB agreed to all other 13 points and did not actually dissent from that in order to have unity. But he is resolved in later conference to win over the other countries to our point of view and secure it from League of Nations . . .". (Daniels diary 4.11.18).

115. The bill came before Congress in December 1918. For at further analysis of the American Naval policy, with a heavy stress upon the foreign policy motives behind it—"The Administration's purpose, as intimated in Secretary Daniels's statements before the House Naval Committee, was primarily to fashion a club to hold over the European Allies in general, and over Great Britain in particular, pending their adherence to President Wilson's comprehensive plans for reduction of armaments and creation of a new world order"—see Harold and Margaret Sprout, Toward a New Order of Sea Power. American Press, Princeton, N.J., 2. ed. 1943 (1940), pp. 36–103 (quotation p. 59). Other motives for the Administration were the wish to give the League of Nations a strong—and politically and nationally balanced—naval force; and also the wish to create an effective support behind the growing American mercantile marine. See also George T. Davis, A Navy Second to None. The Development of Modern American Naval Policy. New York, Harcourt, Brace and Company, 1940, pp. 204–260. See further below about the Anglo-American naval negotiations during the critical phase of the Peace Conference at the beginning of April 1919, chapter 4, pp. 209–211.

116. Seward W. Livermore: Politics is adjourned. Woodrow Wilson and the War Congress, 1916–1918, Wesleyan University Press, Middletown, Conn., 1966, pp. 206–247, and Mayer: Politics . . ., pp. 119–139. Livermore's book is a refutation of the myth that politics was ever adjourned during the war. Also Bailey stresses this (Woodrow Wilson and the Lost Peace, p. 60).

117. Livermore, pp. 206–223; see also Mayer: Politics . . ., pp. 119–125.

118. Bailey, p. 57; Livermore, pp. 209 and 220–222; Smith: The Great Departure, p. 111. —House called the appeal "a political error" and thought that Wilson, "has taken a great gamble" (House diary 25.10.18), but originally (July 1918) he had been receptive to a like proposal, and when he was told about the actual plans (in September 1918), he had only showed his disagreement by remaining silent. Later on he admitted—and regretted—this (Livermore, p. 208; 217–218, and Mayer: Politics . . ., p. 124).

119. On this Edward N. Smith to Lansing 28.10.18 is a splendid example. Lansing papers, vol. 39.

120. Before the election the Democrats had a majority of three in the House of Representatives and of ten in the Senate. After the election the House of Representatives consisted of 237 Republicans, 193 Democrates and 5 representatives of smaller parties. In the Senate the Republicans had a majority of 2 (two). If the Democrats had won but one more State they would, thanks to the decisive vote of the Vice-President, have been able to occupy all chairmanships of the important committees.

121. Bailey, pp. 62–70; Livermore, pp. 224–247; Smith. pp. 111–112.

122. Bailey, pp. 69–70.

123. It is an open question whether the election campaign in itself had any decisive influence upon Wilson's stand in the negotiations with Germany as well as with the Allies. House, for example, wrote, that Lansing during the discussions regarding the drafting of the second note "started the discussion by saying that we had to keep in mind the coming elections", but was rebuffed (House diary 15.10.18.) While on the other hand Tardieu, in a report from the United States recommended the French leaders to take a positive stand to the Fourteen Points before November 5. Tardieu thought it to be in France's interests that the Democrats succeeded, and he added that Wiseman had been asked to present the same view to the British Government (Tardieu to Clemenceau and Pichon 1.11.18. kindly shown me by Karl Christian Lammers).

124. On October 9, the Allies asked if an "American representative possessing the full confidence of the United States Government could be sent to Europe to confer . . .". House was the only possible choice (Frazier to Secretary of State, 9.10.18. FR18SI, 1, pp. 353–354). In a conversation with Frazier on October 7, Lloyd George said that he "earnestly hoped that the President would send Colonel House over at the earliest possible moment". (FR18SI, 1, p. 344). Cf. also above p. xx and note 139.

125. House's credentials is printed IP IV, pp. 87–88. On carte blanche see Joseph Grew, Turbulent Era, I, Boston, Houghton Mifflin Co., 1952, p. 332. House's own estimation was the following: "The President certainly gives me the broadest powers. It virtually puts me in his place in Europe". House diary 15.10.18.

126. IP IV, p. 88.

127. House diary 9.10.18; 13.10.18; 15.10.18.

128. House diary 22.10.18. Wiseman's report of the meeting is printed in Snell, pp. 366–369, and Fowler, pp. 283–290.

129. House diary 22.10.18.

130. FR18SI, 1, p. 381.—About the distrust generally see Trask and Fowler passim. William Wiseman to Lord Reading 3.9.18, (House Coll.) gives a good insight into the situation just before the opening of the negotiations. Lloyd George's irritation at this time is well known, see for example Murray to Wiseman 23.10.18, Wiseman papers; Henry Wilson diary 21.10.18, C. E. Callwell, ed.: Field-Marshal Sir Henry Wilson: His Life and Diaries, London, Cassell, 1927, II, p. 139.—About the "diplomatic victory" see House to Wilson 5.11.18, House Coll.; Wilson papers, Ser. 2; partly in IP IV, p. 188 ("great" is here left out in "a great diplomatic victory"). Henry Wilson had this bitter comment to the course of the negotiations: "We are intercepting all cabelgrams from House to Pr. Wilson and Lansing and vice versa and they are most amazing reading. I believe Wilson to be an unscrupulous knave and a hater of England and House to be a poor miserable fool. Luckily I don't believe Wilson has any real ability". (Henry Wilson diary 9.11.18, transcript from the original, lent to me by Jørgen Sevaldsen).

131. Trask, p. 162. House wrote in his diary 4.11.18: "I frankly told him (Sir Eric Geddes) . . . that I would have followed England in the naval terms as I had followed Marechal Foch in the Military terms". House actually went so far that he volunteered to leave the negotiations while the Allies drafted the armistice conditions: "Colonel House asked why the terms of an armistice should not be drawn up now? All the Allies were agreed on the principle. The President was prepared to leave it with Marshal Foch and with Generals Pershing, Petain, and Field-Marshal Haig to prepare a draft. He asked if he should withdraw from the conference during the forthcomming discussions?
M. Clemenceau said certainly not. . . .".
"Notes of a conversation in M. Pichon's room at the Quai d'Orsay, Paris, on Tuesday, October 29, 1918, at 3 p. m. IC 83 (about the sources see further below note 175).

132. Trask, p. 164.

133. Cf. above pp. 41–42.

134. House diary 26.10.18 and 27.10.18 27.10. he wrote after a conversation with Admiral Benson: "He agreed with Haig, Bliss and that school of thought which, indeed, is my viewpoint and that of the President."

135. W. Deist, Die Militärischen Bestimmungen der Pariser Vorortsverträge, Helmuth Rössler (ed.), Ideologie und Machtpolitik, Musterschmidt Verlag, Göttingen, 1966, pp. 190–191.

136. Adenauer in der Rheinlandpolitik nach dem Ersten Weltkrieg, Ernst Klett Verlag, Stuttgart, 1966, p. 16. As would seem reasonable, these aspects of the Armistice has been stressed primarily in the German literature, see also Ernst Keit: Der Waffenstilstand und die Rheinfrage 1918/19, Ludwig Röhrschied Verlag, Bonn, 1939, passim, and Deist, p. 191.

137. Victor S. Mamatey: The United States and East Central Europe 1914–1918, Princeton Un. Press, Princeton, 1957, p. 362.

138. Jacques de Launay: Secrets Diplomatiques 1914–1918, Brepols, Bruxelles et Paris, 1963, p. 105.
139. ibid. p. 110. Gabriel Terrail (Mermeix): Les Negociations secrètes et les quatre armistices, aved pieces justificatives, Fragments D'Histoire 1914–19, V, Ollendorff, Paris, 1921, pp. 209–210.
140. The French preparations is described in Général H. Mordacq: L'Armistice du 11 Novembre 1918, Paris, Librairie Plon, 1937, pp. 150–172.
141. 27.10.18. Haig wrote in his diary: "It seems that Clemenceau and Foch are not on good terms. Foch is suffering from a swollen head, and thinks himself another Napoleon! So C(lemenceau) has great difficulties with him now". (Robert Blake ed., The Private papers of Douglas Haig 1914–1919, London, Eyre and Spottiswoode, 1952, p. 237). Mordacq says that Foch on October 19 demanded to be currently informed about the negotiations with the Allies, and that Clemenceau rejected this. This should be the cause of the disagreement (Armistice, p. 153). At the first meeting between House and the Allied Prime Ministers Clemenceau declared that the governments, not Foch, were to have the decisive influence upon the drafting of the armistice terms (Launay, p. 85). He wished, in other words, to keep Foch away from the political considerations. House thought that Clemenceau himself was moderate, "but is influenced by Foch, who believes Germany is absolutely beaten" (House to Wilson 27.10.18, Baker VIII, pp. 519–520). If so, House did not try to play upon these supposed differences. About the relations between Foch and Clemenceau see also Frederick J. Cox: The French Peace Plans, 1918–1919: The Germ of the Conflict between Ferdinand Foch and Georges Clemenceau, p. 83.
142. Mordacq: Armistice, p. 152; Lloyd George: War Memoirs VI, pp. 3276–3278. Lloyd George gives the date 8.10., but Mordacq says this is the date of the drafting of the document, the meeting itself was held 9.10.
143. Lloyd George, ibid. italics Lloyd George's. Lloyd George says, that both he and Sonnino thought that Foch desired too much, and, besides, the conference thought it too early to take a definite stand in this matter. (ibid. 3278). Mordacq says that even if Lloyd George had objections, he "n'insista pas d'une façon particulière" regarding the demand of occupation which was heavily stressed by Clemenceau Armistice, p. 152).
144. Pétain expressed himself very clearly to Haig 25.10.18 in Senlis: "Petain spoke of taking a huge indemnity from Germany, so large that she will never be able to pay it. Meantime, French troops will hold the left bank of the Rhine as a pledge". Blake, p. 336.
145. House forwarded the terms to Wilson 27.10.18. (House Coll., Wilson papers, Ser. II), see also the diary 26.10.18.
146. Lloyd George prints the proposal of the Prime Ministers in War Memoirs VI, pp. 3275–3276. The proposal of the military experts is found in Rudin, pp. 95–96.
147. Pershing gives a concise survey of the different views in Pershing to Adjutant General (War Department) 25.10.18. Wilson papers, Ser. 2. Pershing was no advocate of "leniency" towards Germany.
148. The proposal is printed in IP IV, pp. 145–148.
149. The British policy is discussed in Harold I. Nelson: Land and Power, London, Routledge and Keagan Paul, 1963, pp. 53–87.
150. Before the negotiations began House thought Lloyd George belonged to the irreconcilable wing: "Haig and Milner are exceedingly reasonable. George, I understand, is not". House to Wilson 27.10.18. Baker VIII, pp. 519–520.
151. Loyd George: War Memoirs, p. 3305. The British communication to Wilson 21.10.18 contained a like demand: "That some enemy territory including at least Alsace and Lorraine, be at once occupied by Allied troops . . . .. Balfour to Barclay 21.10.18. Wilson papers Ser. 2.
152. War Memoirs VI, p. 3291.
153. Newton D. Baker to Pershing 27.10.18. Wilson papers, Ser. 2. The letter was an answer to Pershing's report of the Senlis meeting. Wilson does not mention the occupation of the left bank of the Rhine, because this was not mentioned in Persh-

ing's telegram. But the whole tone of Bakers telegram seems to indicate that Wilson was against any form of occupation.

154. See Bliss to Newton D. Baker 23.10.18. Wilson papers, Ser. 2.
155. Bliss to Newton D. Baker 23.10.18, Wilson papers, Ser. 2. Bliss knew that Foch desired four Allied bridge-heads east of the Rhine.
156. Cf. note 81.
157. House diary 26.10.18 and 27.10.18.
158. House diary 28.10.18. IP IV, pp. 164–165. Wiseman was well advised: These were exactly the objections Lloyd George raised during the negotiations, and it was these objections which became part of the official Allied memorandum to the President.
159. House diary 28.10.18. IP IV, p. 155.
160. Auchincloss diary 28.10.18.
161. House to Lansing for Wilson 29.10.18. FR18SI, 1, pp. 405–413. Wilson accepted the interpretation as "satisfactory", but besides, he only wanted it to be considered illustrative; the definitive decision in his opinion belonged to the Peace Conference. Wilson to House 30.10.18. FR18SI, 1, p. 421.
162. Already on September 9, 1918, House had urged Wilson to try to pledge the Allies to his program: House to Wilson 3.9.18. House Coll.
163. About this see Snell, p. 365.—Actually, Wilson seems to have felt himself bound by the memorandum, at least in the case of the Brenner-frontier, see René Albrecht-Carrié: Italy at the Paris Peace Conference, Columbia University Press, New York, 1938, pp. 63–65.
164. Journal of Frank J. Cobb, Library of Congress, 26.10.18; 28.10.18; Auchincloss diary 28.10.18; House to Lansing for Wilson 29.10.18, FR 18SI, 1, p. 413.
165. House to Wilson (telegram) 6.10.18, IP IV, pp. 75–76.
166. Cf. above p. 25.
167. See above pp. 25–35 and Appendix I.
168. See further pp. 25–35, 106–108, Appendix I and Mayer: Politics . . ., passim.
169. See the references in note 168.
170. Cf. Appendix I.
171. Mayer: Politics . . ., p. vii.
172. ibid. pp. 15–16.
173. See for example the following diary entries by Frank Cobb: "Lunched with Col. House and discussed situation with him. It is plain that while the British and French have no programme of their own, there is a certainty that the chauvinistic elements will try to wreck the President's programme" (26.10.18). "Will see William Wiseman at Col. House's. He feared the President's programme was in danger of shipwreck as events had moved too rapidly for the White House. We shall see what we shall see, but it is certainly time the British laid their cards on the table" (28.10.18).
174. For the text see Lansing's note to the German Government 5.11.18, FR18SI, 1, pp. 468–469. Cf. also IP IV, p. 152 ff, Rudin, p. 318 f., and F. S. Marston: The Peace Conference of 1919, London, Oxford University Press, 1944, pp. 13–27.
175. Launay, pp. 85–93.—The negotiations took place in connection with a session of the Supreme War Council, and they were held in Paris as well as in Versailles. Several of the meetings had the character of more informal conversations, in a so-called "steering committee" composed of House, and the Italian, French and British Prime Ministers (IP IV, p. 99). About the sources: There are two seemingly independent sets of minutes. An English version made by Sir Maurice Hankey and his staff: IC 83–95, House Coll. The Hankey-minutes have been used by Charles Seymour (IP IV) and by Lloyd George (The Truth about the Peace Treaties, I, London, Victor Gollancz, 1938), and both authors give extensive quotations. The Hankey-version is the official one. The other is a French version made by Paul Mantoux, the interpreter. His original notes are not konwn, but a transcript was found among the papers of Louis Loucheur, the French Minister of War Industries, and this transcript was published by Jacques de Launay in 1963 (cf. note 138). Launay wrote (p. 83) that "ce dernier (Loucheur) en a recopié laborieusement à la main les données essentielles". The French minutes are held in direct speech contrary to the English.

In addition to these two more or less complete sets of minutes is found, in the House Collection, a set of minutes in English and in direct speech comprising three meetings 29.10; 30.10. and 3.11. These minutes seem to be independent of the two other versions and are probably made by either Gordon Auchincloss or Arthur Hugh Frazier who both were present at the meetings as secretaries to Colonel House. These minutes have been used by Charles Seymour. On the other hand, the minutes published by Mermeix (Les Négociations Secrètes, cf. note 139), are no independent source, but the official French version of the Hankey-minutes. The sources, thus, present a reasonable chance to follow the negotiations as a whole. The different sets of minutes show a high degree of accordance, although, at several points they are differing regarding the length of text given (see further below). The course of the negotiations is also known from the reports made by Colonel House to President Wilson (Wilson papers, Ser. 2 and House Coll.; FR18SI, 1 and Baker VIII). These are important because they show how House evaluated the situation, or at least how he wanted the President to see it; and also because among the reports we have the most important source of the morning meeting of October 30, at which only Lloyd George, Clemenceau and House himself were present. The negotiations have also been discussed in several works, of which some have been mentioned above or will be mentioned below.

176. Lloyd George in Launay, p. 89; IC 83 and the American minutes 29.10.18.
177. Lloyd George's remarks in Launay, p. 85–87. IC 83 and the American minutes 29.10.
178. Lloyd George in Launay, p. 89, IC 83 and the American minutes 29.10. Both Lloyd George (Truth I, pp. 75–80) and Seymour (IP IV, pp. 166–172) gives excerpts from the British minutes for the 29.10.
179. Pichon in Launay, p. 89, and Clemenceau ibid. p. 85; IC 83 and the American minutes 29.10.18.
180. Clemenceau, Launay, p. 86; IC 83 and the American minutes 29.10.18.
181. Clemenceau, Launay, p. 85; IC 83 and the American minutes 29.10.18. Cf. note 141.
182. House, Launay, p. 86; IC 83 and the American minutes 29.10.
183. Sonnino, Launay, pp. 85–93 passim; IC 83 and the American minutes 29.10.
184. Nelson, p. 78 n.
185. Lloyd George in Launay, p. 91; IC 83 and the American minutes 29.10. Was the British memorandum already set up at this time?—My colleague, Jørgen Sevaldsen, who is working on a book about the British policy during the Peace Conference, has told me, that in his opinion Lloyd George at this time viewed an Allied acceptance as unavoidable, but that he was ready to take a firm stand behind the British reservations.
186. Cf. above pp. 36–37.—Already on October 9, during the Inter-Allied conference at Paris, Lloyd George had pointed to the necessity of getting a discussion of the Fourteen Points with the American Administration. In his opinion the points were vague, and especially regarding the freedom of the seas he wanted further explanation. If the Allies neglected to make their stand quite clear, it could be construed as acceptance, and they would be bound by those terms. Clemenceau did not seem to have the same kind of hesitations, his interest seems to have been concentrated about the Armistice itself (Pedroncini, pp. 93–105 and Lloyd George, War Memoirs VI, pp. 3280–3282), which both quote from the minutes of the conference.). The discussion is interesting, because it shows exactly the same pattern as in the pre-Armistice negotiations.
187. Balfour in Launay, p. 92; IC 83 and the American minutes 29.10.
188. IC 83 (Truth I, p. 76; IP IV, p. 167); the American minutes 29.10.18. Launay does not have this remark.
189. Pichon in Launay, p. 89; IC 83 and the American minutes 29.10.18.
190. Launay, p. 90; IC 83 and the American minutes 29.10.18.
191. Launay, p. 91; IC 83 (Truth I, p. 78 and IP IV, p. 170) and the American minutes 29.10.
192. IC 83 (Truth I, p. 78). The version Seymour prints in this case (IP IV, p. 171), has

no verbal correspondance with the IC version, but on the other hand, it is much nearer the IC version than the American minutes of 29.10.18, which, as is also the case with the French version, do not mention the interjection by Clemenceau. Seymour's version is probably a rewriting of the IC 83 version. The American minutes give Balfour, not Lloyd George as the originator of the remark, the text is: "... If the US made a separate peace, we would be sorry but we could not give up the blockade ... as far as the British public is concerned, we will fight on even if everyone else gives up the war ...". Hankey gives this version in his diary (29. 10.18): "... House looked very sick. There were many criticisms of the 14 pts. At last Col. House declared that it amounted to this, that the President in his next communication to Germany and Austria would have practically to clean the slate. In this case America would have to consider whether (they) would take up these matters with the German and Austrian Govts. only. Clemenceau—"Do you mean that you will make a separate peace?" House—"It might amount to that—it depends on how far your criticisms go". Ll. G.—"We shall be very sorry if you won't—but we shall fight on". Sensation! After that, Ll. G. having made it clear we were not to be bullied, things went better, and eventually we agreed to put up a draft....". (Roskill, Hankey, p. 623).

193. Launay, p. 91. The French minutes does not mention the interjection by Clemenceau.
194. Launay, p. 93. Clemenceau's remark is found only in the French version, and here it has apparently been abridged.
195. Launay, p. 91; IC 83 and the American minutes 29.10.18.
196. This observation was first made by Nelson (p. 79), who refers to Lloyd George, Truth, I, p. 80. Lloyd George here quotes the English minutes, which at this point are much more comprehensive than the French, which only have the first part of House's argumentation: "Les termes employés par le Président sont très larges ..." (Launay, p. 92). The English version reads: Colonel House said that the President's conditions were couched in very broad terms ... He (Wilson) had insisted on Germany's accepting all his speeches, and from these you could establish almost any point that anyone wished, against Germany" (IC 83). Lloyd George, himself, also stresses the remark as "a significant reply, which has a much wider application" (Truth, I, p. 79). Seymour does not mention this phase of the negotiations at all. The American minutes say: "The President's terms are broad ... every word he has used in his speeches since the war began is an indictment of Germany....".
197. Launay, p. 93. The English version (IC 83) reads: "Mr. Lloyd George said that apart from Clause II, the others of the fourteen points appeared to him sufficiently elastic to enable us to put our own interpretations upon them ..."; and the American minutes 29.10.: "I think the other points are sufficiently elastic to enable us to reconcile all our points of view".
198. Launay, p. 92; IC 83.
199. Launay, p. 93 (IP IV, p. 120); see also IC 83 and the American minutes 29.10.
200. House to Lansing for Wilson 30.10.18, no. 8 FR18SI, 1, pp. 421–423.
201. Meeting with Reading and Wiseman 28.10 (House diary 28.10.18). Meeting alone with Lloyd George in the morning 29.10. (Auchincloss diary 29.10.18 and House to Lansing for Wilson 30.10.18, no. 10, FR18SI, 1, p. 424), and lunch with Lloyd George, Balfour and Reading the same day (Auchincloss diary 29.10.18 and House to Lansing for Wilson 29.10.18, no. 8, FR18SI, 1, pp. 421–423). On the meeting between House and Lloyd George alone, the main topic seems to have been colonial problems.
202. House diary 28.10.18.
203. House to Lansing for Wilson 30.10.18, no. 8. FR18SI, 1, pp. 421–423. The Cobb-Lippmann memorandum had foreseen a solution in connection with the League of Nations.
204. ibid. IC 83, Lloyd George, Truth, I, p. 78 and Launay, p. 91.—It is worth noting that the House diary does not mention this critical meeting at all. The meeting that is mentioned under the date of 29.10. is very definitely the meeting held the following morning with Clemenceau and Lloyd George. Internal evidence shows

that the entry must have been dictated immediately after this meeting, and through an oversight, the date has not been changed.

205. Auchincloss diary 29.10.18.
206. Baker VIII, p. 529. The original in the Wilson papers is undated, but the date proposed is: "c. Oct. 29, 1918?", the correct date however, must be 30.10., as it must be an answer to House no. 8.
207. At the afternoon meeting of November 1, Lloyd George again took up the question of the acceptance of the Fourteen Points, a question, which House thought had found a solution on 30.10. Auchincloss wrote in his diary: "We did not send a report of the meeting this afternoon. inasmuch as nothing was definitely decided and any report we would send would be sure to mislead and confuse the President ...". For further examples see below. House's fear is very evident in his answer to Wilson's excited telegram: "It is exceedingly important that nothing be said or done at this time which may in any way halt the armistice ...". IP IV, p. 174, Baker VIII, p. 534.
208. House to Wilson no. 4, 30.10.18, House Coll. In Wilson papers is an attempt, in Mrs. Wilson's handwriting, at the deciphering of the code. This bears the date of 29.10.
209. House diary 30.10.18. IP, p. 169.
210. House to Lansing for Wilson 30.10.18. no. 9. FR18SI, I, pp. 423–424.
211. Wilson to House 30.10.18. FR18SI, 1, p. 423. Wilson authorized House to state that he could not give his consent to any peace which did not contain the freedom of the seas and the League of Nations, and he threatened to publish this.
212. House diary 31.10.18.
213. Journal of Frank Cobb 30.10.18. Library of Congress.
214. This conversation is known only through House's report to Wilson 30.10., no. 12, FR18SI, 1, pp. 425–427, IP IV, pp. 170–172. There is almost verbal correspondance between the telegram and the diary entry of 29.10. Internal evidence shows that the entry has been dictated immediately after the morning meeting of October 30, and the date given, therefore, wrong. The meeting of 29.10. is only indirectly referred to. It is evident from the diary, however, that House has been working behind the scenes: "The memorandum was so different, both in temper and substance, from his and Clemenceau's talk yesterday that what I said at (!) to the President's probable action, and what Gordon (Auchincloss), Wiseman and others did on the outside by working through Eric Geddes, Balfour etc., has had its effect ...". (ibid.).
215. For the text of the memorandum see IP IV, pp. 170–171 and FR18SI, 1, p. 425.
216. FR18SI, 1, p. 425.
217. ibid. pp. 425–426. Italics mine. See also House diary 29.10. (30.10.)18.
218. Général Mordacq: Le Ministère Clemenceau, II, Paris, Librairie Plon, 1930, p. 297–298, and Mordacq: Armistice, pp. 166–167. In the last account, Mordacq is not as categorical as in the first, he does not say directly that House had been convinced before the meeting.
219. FR18SI, 1, p. 426; House diary 29.10.18 (30.10). In his report to Wilson House wrote that the discussion had turned about the *right* bank of the Rhine, while in his diary he wrote the *left* bank. Mordacq asserts, moreover, that House during the negotiations supported Clemenceau against Lloyd George. (cf. note 164).
220. IC 87 (IP IV, pp. 121–127). See further Nelson's penetrating discussion of the British standpoint (Nelson, pp. 80–82). The meeting was held in the morning and is not reported in Launay.
221. IC 87 (IP IV, p. 123).
222. IP IV, pp. 172–174; Launay, pp. 94–95, see also Albrecht-Carrié, pp. 60–62.
223. This reservation is printed in IP IV, p. 173. In the French minutes it is mentioned, but not quoted. (Launay, p. 95).
224. FR18SI, 1, p. 427. House of Lansing for Wilson 30.10.18, no. 13. Italics mine.
225. IP IV, p. 178. Seymour prints the original version from the House Coll. While the telegram received by the State Department has a misleading "not". (FR18SI, 1, p. 431).

226. House to Lansing for Wilson 3.11.18. no. 38. FR18SI, 1, p. 448.
227. Journal of Frank Cobb 30.10.18.
228. See in this connection also Nelson, p. 85. Nelson has reached the same conclusion upon another basis: "... Lloyd George and Balfour secured at Paris a substantial victory".
229. Albrecht-Carrié, p. 62.
230. IC 91. Cf. IP IV, p. 128. Seymour's version, which is given in quotation marks, has no verbal correspondance with the IC version, although the meaning is the same.
231. Launay, pp. 119–120.
232. According to the English version (IC 91) House followed the wishes of Clemenceau, because he had the support of the Belgian, Serbian and Italian representatives: "Mr. House proposed that as the matter appeared important for all, the amendment should be accepted". While House, according to the French version, did not take part in the discussion at all (Launay, p. 129).—Seymour does not mention House's remark, although he prints the discussion which directly precedes it (IP IV, p. 128).
233. IP IV, p. 128.
234. Nelson, p. 83. House here supported Balfour. See also IC 91 (Mermeix, p. 246–248) and Launay, pp. 132–133.
235. Wilson to House 31.10.18, no. 6, private series. Wilson papers, Ser. 2. An incomplete version (the paragraph from "Please insist ..." has been left out) is printed in FR18SI, 1, pp. 427–428. Baker, on the other hand, prints the whole telegram (Baker, VIII, pp. 537–538). The original, written on Wilson's own typewriter, shows that the President had originally written: "British naval supremacy".
236. House to Lansing for Wilson 3.11.18, no. 41, FR18SI, 1, pp. 455–457.
237. Launay, pp. 116–117 and IC 88 (Mermeix, pp. 226–228).
238. House diary 1.11.18.
239. House diary 1.11.18. See also Auchincloss diary 1.11.18.
240. Cf. note 207.
241. House diary 1.11.18. IP IV, p. 185.—Frank Cobb and Sir William Wiseman had a discussion which lasted for two hours with Colonel House. Thereafter, they wrote the memorandum, which was rejected by Lloyd George. Cobb was convinced that Lloyd George was "playing politics with issue" (Cobb diary 1.11.18).
242. House diary 2.11.18; Auchincloss diary 2.11.18. House was wery irritated over the part played by Reading in these negotiations.
243. IP IV, p. 181. A slightly different version is found in FR18SI, 1, p. 448, House to Lansing for Wilson 3.11.18, no. 38. The difference undoubtedly stems from the decoding. This was the first telegram which gave Wilson any knowledge of the Belgian and Italian protests.
244. Wilson to House 3.11.18, no. 8, private series. Wilson papers, Ser. 2.
245. IC 92 and the American minutes 3.11.18. The meeting is not found in Launay. Seymour also prints a detailed minute of the meeting (IP IV, pp. 187–190), but it has no verbal correspondance with any of the other versions. For House's report see House to Lansing for Wilson 3.11.18, no. 41, FR18SI, 1, pp. 455–457; and the commentary in his diary 3.11.18, in which he seems to project his own excitement on Lloyd George.—Hankey also mentions the meeting and the negotiations in his diary (3.11.18 Roskill, Hankey, p. 627).
246. IC 92. Seymour's rendering of this quotation (IP IV, p. 189) is a combination of IC 92 and the American minutes 3.11.18.
247. During the negotiations House made use of a paraphrase of Wilson's telegram no. 6, 31.10.18 (cf. p. 55 and note 235). The decisive paragraph, in which Wilson threatened to go before Congress, "who confidentially will have no sympathy whatever with spending American lives for British naval control", was left out (IP IV, p. 188). But Wilson's use of "confidentially" in this connection undoubtedly shows that he himself did not want the threat used directly.—Wilson to House 29. 10.18, Wilson papers, Ser. 2. House's strong engagement in this matter is also clear from the diary entry of 3.11.18: "This has been a red letter day. I brought Lloyd George to terms concerning the "freedom of the seas" ... When the P. M.'s met

at my headquarters this morning we at once went into the President's Fourteen Points. When Lloyd George and I began discussing Article Two relating to the freedom of the seas, he showed visible signs of excitement and nervousness. I have never seen him exhibit quite as much agitation before. Our debate was not heated and not unpleasant, but both he and I have been keyed up to a high pitch ever since this subject has been under discussion. We were at it all day, in one way and another, and when we sat at the table, I think we both felt that a crisis had come. I feel I have won a distinct victory. . . .". It seems very likely that it was his own feelings he was in this way projecting into the situation.—Nelson's evaluation of the result is this: "House suffered a severe defeat in this phase of the negotiations" (p. 84n).

248. "They (the Allies) wish it to be understood that the words ("so far as possible") qualify the entire point. This they suggest could be accomplished by transposing them to the beginning of the point, so that point 3 would read: "So far as possible the removal, etc. etc.". I assented to this suggestion and stated that I thought it would probably be unnecessary for the President to point out this change to Germany . . ." (FR18 SI, 1, p. 456). Wilson, naturally, was informed of both changes.

249. Cobb diary 1. and 2.11.18.

250. Cobb to House 9.11.18, House Coll. Italics Cobb's. In a conversation with Cobb Lord Milner admitted that Hurley's speach was an essential cause (Cobb to House 11.11.18, House Coll.).

251. Cobb to House 11.11.18, House Coll. The reference here is probably to the activities of the Republicans. For further information about this see below chapter 3, pp. 146–149 and Appendix II.

252. Lord Hankey, The Supreme Control at the Paris Peace Conference 1919, London, George Allen and Unwin, 1963, p. 16. Italics mine. See also Lloyd George, Truth I, p. 186.

253. Geddes to Prime Minister 13.10.18, Wiseman papers. Lloyd George in his War Memoirs (VI, pp. 3290–3291) wrote: "In talking of his Fourteen Points, the President's views on the Freedom of the Seas appeared to be unformed". See also House diary 13.10.18 about the difficulties House had in getting Wilson to see Geddes. See also Haig diary 26.10.18: "I asked how the President interpreted "Freedom of the Seas". He (House) replied by saying that the President took him aside and told him what Geddes had said to him on the subject, and similarly Geddes told him what the President had said to him. And it all amounted to nothing!" (Blake, p. 337).—Geddes was First Lord of the Admiralty.

254. Snell, pp. 366–369; Fowler pp. 283–290. Wiseman has confirmed that Lloyd George saw this memorandum, before the negotiations with House in Paris (Snell, p. 366 n). Immediately after the conversation Wiseman sent a shorter report to Lord Reading and Sir Eric Drummond (Wiseman papers), cf. above p. 44 and note 128).

255. Snell, p. 365.

256. House to Lansing for Wilson 30.10.18, no. 10, FR18SI, 1, p. 424. House's only commentary to Wilson was that Lloyd George put forward the proposal regarding East Africa, because, "the British would like us to accept something so they might more freely take what they desire".

257. House to Wilson 5.11.18, no. 6, private series, House Coll.; Wilson papers, Ser. 2. The copy in Wilson papers, written on the President's own typewriter, shows that the decoding had been difficult. There are several omissions, but none that disturbs the meaning.

258. At the meeting 3.11.18 (IP IV, p. 189). Clemenceau also supported House in his manoeuvre of escape during the discussion of the Fourteen Points 1.11. (Launay, p. 117 and Mermeix, p. 228).

259. Bliss to Newton D. Baker 10.11.18, no. 33, Bliss papers. Library of Congress.

260. On the other hand it is true, as Thomas A. Bailey has stressed that "(n)o matter how many or how powerful the clubs (the Americans might have used), the mental reservations (on behalf of the Allies) still remained; and they were bound to come out around the peace table" (Bailey, p. 47–48).

*Chapter 2*

1. Wilson to House 2.9.17. R. S. Baker: Woodrow Wilson, Life and Letters, Garden City 1927–1939, VII, p. 254.
2. For a discussion of this see Lawrence E. Gelfand: The Inquiry, American Preparation for Peace, 1917–1919, New Haven and London, Yale University Press, 1963, chapter 1.
3. That the "Executive Committee" was in the beginning made up of only Mezes, Lippmann and Miller is evident from the "Notes on the Inquiry, November 30, 1918", presumably written by Isaiah Bowman, and given as appendix VI in Gelfand, pp. 350–353. From Lippmann to Division Chiefs of the Inquiry 11.12.17 (PC I, p. 26), it is further evident, that the "Executive Committee" was now made up of Mezes, Miller, Lippmann and James T. Shotwell (as head of "research"). It is thus certain that Bowman became a member only later on.
4. Gelfand, p. 38.
5. ibid. p. 51.
6. This quotation is taken from the above-mentioned "Notes on the Inquiry", and I see no reason to doubt its valitidy. For a further discussion of the relationship between Wilson, House and the Liberals see Laurence W. Martin: Peace without Victory, Woodrow Wilson and the British Liberals, New Haven, Yale University Press, 1958; Christopher Lasch: The American Liberals and the Russian Revolution, New York and London, Columbia University Press, 1962; and Arno J. Mayer: Political Origins of the New Diplomacy, 1917–1918, New Haven, Yale University Press, 1959, and for example, the following diary entry by House after a conversation with Wilson: "We discussed the trend of liberal opinion in the world and came to the conclusion that the wise thing to do was to lead the movement intelligently and sympathetically and not to allow the ignoble element to run away with the situation as they had done in Russia. He spoke of the necessity of forming a new political party in order to achieve these ends ... Again let me say that the President has started so actively on the liberal road that I find myself, instead of leading as I always did at first, rather in the rear and holding him back ...". House diary 24.2.18, Yale University Library.—See also above pp. 28–35, and below pp. 106–108 and appendix I.
7. Gelfand, p. 98.
8. For a discussion of this crisis, see Gelfand, chapter 3. For Bowman's version see his "Notes on the Inquiry. November 30, 1918" and "Statement made by Dr. Isaiah Bowman concerning the reorganization of the Inquiry, notes taken March, 14, 1932", given by Gelfand as appendix VI and VII.
9. Gelfand, p. 96.
10. ibid. p. 96.
11. ibid. p. 94.
12. ibid. p. 96.
13. See Bowman's above-mentioned memoranda. It was also Miller who brought the matter to House.
14. The main sources are the above-mentioned Bowman-memoranda, but these ar not only biassed, on this matter they also differ from each other. For a discussion of this, see Gelfand, pp. 94–95. The new organization is evident from the "Memorandum on the Organization of the Inquiry (PC I, p. 104). The memorandum is undated but it seems reasonable to date it ca. 3.8.18 (cf. ibid. p. 103–104), where the composition of the "Research Committee" is given). The new organization is as follows: "Chief" was Colonel House. Under him was an "Executive Committee" made up of Mezes (Director), Miller (Treasurer) and Bowman (Executive Officer). The work of the organization was delegated to several committees: an "International Law Committee" under Miller; "Problem Areas" under Bowman; "International Economics" under A. A. Young; an "Editorial Committee" under Shotwell, and a "Research Committee" with C. H. Haskins as Chairman and Young, Shotwell and Bowman as the other members. Besides being "Executive

Officer" Bowman thus had several key-positions in the organization, while Mezes seems to have been merely a figure-head.

15. On this new crisis see below.
16. House's diary 13.10.17, 18.12.17, 12.1.18, 27.1.18, 28.1.18, 15.8.18, 24.9.18, 6.10.18, 13.10.18, 15.10.18, 16.10.18.
17. ibid. 13.10.17, 27.1.18, 13.10.18,
18. ibid. 27.1.18, 13.10.18
19. ibid. 5.8.18.
20. ibid. 15.8.18.
21. ibid. 15.10.18.
22. ibid. 13.10.18.
23. Mezes to Haskins 19.10.18, PC I, pp. 109–110. The Committees, including the "Research Committee", were now cancelled.
24. This at least was the way Bowman saw it (cf. the above-mentioned memoranda). —Bowman's assertion, that it was only after leaving America that House telegraphed the order about the reorganization must be a misunderstanding. See Mezes to Haskins 19.10.18 (ibid. p. 108). In both places Mezes mentions a conference with House on the reorganization of the Inquiry.
25. See the two Bowman-memoranda. Gelfand, appendix VI og VII.
26. House diary 1.10.18. "I went to the Inquiry rooms ... I am giving this work much closer attention now that the war seems in its last phase and because of the differences which have arisen in its circles". House had talks on the Inquiry with Miller 15.9.18, with Miller and Mezes 29.9.18, with Mezes alone 13.9.18, with Bowman and Mezes 1.10.18, with Bowman alone 28.8.18 and 18.9.18, he also had a conversation with Wilson on the same matter on 17.8.18—see diary entries on the above-mentioned dates.
27. House diary 13.10.17, 12.1.18 and 20.1.18, see also Gelfand, p. 100.—At least at times House seems to have been positive.
28. Gelfand, p. 106: "Ordinarily, Inquiry members received from the State Department information they requested, it was not furnished voluntarily".
29. Gelfand, pp. 156–158.
30. Lansing desk book 23.9.18. Library of Congress.
31. ibid. 14.10.18.
32. House and Mezes actually thought there was a positive agreement: "I am not sure that I mentioned yesterday Colonel House's statement to me that he thought that some seventy-five or eighty individuals should compose the force of the Inquiry, an estimate he said he had reached after discussing the matter with you". Mezes to Lansing 25.10.18. PC I, p. 111.
33. Lansing desk book, 24.10.18.
34. Mezes to House 26.10.18. The letter is paraphrased and partly cited in Gelfand, p. 161.
35. ibid. Mezes's italics.
36. Mezes to Lansing 25.10.18. PC I, p. 111: "I am sending you a copy of the chart prepared by Colonel House and submitted to you yesterday, with the modifications discussed at our conference".
37. ibid. The modified plan is given p. 112.
38. The receipt stamp on Mezes to Lansing 25.10.18 shows this date. National Archives, Record Group 256, 184/11.
39. Lansing desk book 29.10.18, Lansing to Mezes 31.10.18. PC I, p. 115.
40. House to Wilson 22.10.18. Wilson papers, Ser. 2. Library of Congress. The letter, but without the crucial paragraph on Cobb vs. Creel, is in PC I, pp. 155–156, from a copy in House's papers.
41. Joseph Grew, Turbulent Era I, pp. 326 and 335. Auchincloss diary 18.10.18. Yale University Library. House's diary 22.10.18.
42. House had already appointed Grew chief of a newly established intelligence organization for Central Europe. when the news arrived from Lansing that he had been appointed Secretary-General of the Commission. Grew I, p. 355–356.

43. Wilson to Lansing 29.10.18. PC I, p. 113. Lansing to Mezes 31.10.18. PC I, p. 115. Lansing desk book 29.10.18.
44. Wilson to Lansing 29.10.18. PC I, p. 113.
45. Gelfand does not think there was any "departure of policy", Wilson delegated the organization of the Commission to the State Department: There was simply no other government organ that could manage the job. (p. 162).
46. Lansing to Mezes 31.10.18. PC I, p. 115.
47. House to Lansing 30.10.18, received 31.10. PC I, p. 115.
48. See Mezes to House 2.11.18. PC I, pp. 115–116: A telegram in which absolutely nothing is said about the difficulties between Mezes and Lansing, although the theme of the telegram is exactly these negotiations.
49. See Mezes to House 15.11.18 (House Coll.) and Mezes to House 1.11.18 (ibid.), a hand-written letter, in which Mezes writes inter alios: "L(ansing) is having frequent conferences these days and will plan the organization personal in large measure. Of course I cant say such things in cables".
50. Lansing desk book 4.11.18: "Preparing outline of personnel to go to Peace Conference".
51. Lansing desk book 5.11.18 and 7.11.18.
52. ibid. 12.11.18.
53. PC I, pp. 113–115, cf. note p. 113.
54. The negotiations between Mezes and Lansing on the place of the Inquiry in the Commission are discussed by Gelfand, pp. 163–168. Mezes seems to have tried to exclude Bowman from those going to Paris, but he failed.—However, this was not the policy of Colonel House himself, but must be related to purely personal reasons: In his letter to Wilson 22.10.18 (Wilson papers, Ser. 2) House mentioned Bowman as well as Mezes and Miller among those he wished to take to Paris.
55. House diary 14.12.18.
56. Lansing desk book 12.11.18.
57. Gelfand, p. 167.
58. ibid. pp. 167–168.
59. ibid. pp. 177–178.
60. Auchincloss diary 14.11.18. See Grew I, pp. 355–356.
61. Grew I, pp. 355–356. The above-mentioned Central European post had been cancelled in the meantime (ibid).
62. Auchincloss diary 11.11.18.
63. Auchincloss diary 11.11.18: "Willard Straight was assigned to us to-day and he is going to work with me on the problems connected with securing accommodations, etc for the American representatives coming from the United States for the Peace Conference".—This, among other things, was the job of the Secretary-General of the Commission.
    Auchincloss diary 12.11.18: "During dinner Straight and I talked over a whole lot of plans for the organization of the American representation at the Peace Conference".
64. Willard Straight died from the flu on 1.12.18 (Auchincloss diary 1.12.18).
65. Auchincloss diary 14.11.18.—In this connexion see the quotation below, note 201.
66. House diary 14.12.18.—This entry follows a description of a conversation with Wilson on organization-problems.
67. Auchincloss diary 15.11.18.—As early as 16.10.18 House had written Wilson: "I want to let you know that there will be ample trustworthy people to do the coding, stenographic and other special work which you may need to have done at the Peace Conference without your having to trouble with it". (Wilson papers, Ser. 2).
68. National Archives. Record Group 256.
69. The memorandum mentions two commissions on personnel: "The Commissioners' Committee on Personnel" held its first meeting on 3.2.19. (See minutes in Henry White papers, Box 64, Library of Congress). The Committee on Personnel was established on 1.2.19 and made up of Bliss, White, Patchin and McNair. (White to Bliss 1.2.19, Bliss papers, Library of Congress.—See also Lansing desk book 1.2.19.).

70. Minutes of the initial daily meeting of the Commissioners' Committee on personnel. 3.2.19, Henry White papers, Box 64. Bliss' quotation is given only in the draft of the minutes (ibid.).

71. Auchincloss to Commander A. F. Carter 6.12.18: "It is the Colonel's purpose to depend entirely on Navy Personnel to constitute his office during his work as one of the peace plenipotentiaries". (Auchincloss diary 6.12.18). This was in line with House's personnel policy during the pre-Armistice negotiations: See A. F. Carter to Auchincloss 6.12.18, (ibid.) and Auchincloss to Polk 5.11.18 (Auchincloss diary 5.11.18).

72. A very penetrating description of this is given in the letters of Ralph Hayes to Newton D. Baker: 18.12.18, 18. (?) 12.18., 22.12.18, 26.12.18, 28.12.18, 31.12.18, 4.1.19. Newton D. Baker papers, Library of Congress.

73. Hayes to Baker 18.12.18, ibid.

74. Baker to Hayes 7.1.19, ibid.

75. See for instance Hayes to Baker 18.12.18, 22.12.18 and Baker to Hayes 7.1.19, ibid. —This was the problem which brought about the establishment of the above-mentioned Committee on Personnel.

76. Cf. note 69.

77. House diary 14.12.18.

78. See unpublished chapter of Lansing's War Memoirs: "Publicity and Secrecy Lansing papers, Box 1, Princeton University Library, cf. also War Memoirs of Robert Lansing, 1935, pp. 322–324 and George Creel: Rebel at Large, New York, G. P. Putnam's Sons, 1947, pp. 158–160.

79. House diary 16.12.18: "I told him (Woodrow Wilson) that a "head-on collision" was about to occur with Creel on the one side and with Lansing and the State Department on the other. I advised him to see Lansing and not allow the thing to get into an impossible condition. He said he would do so. I told him that Lansing's dislike for Creel was only equalled by Creel's dislike for Lansing. I urged him not to disrupt the organization which Lansing had suggested to Grew because while Harrison and Patchin were perhaps not the best selections, yet their removal at this time would be unfortunate".

80. See note 79.

81. Auchincloss diary 15.12.18, see also House diary 14.12.18.—Auchincloss thought that Creel was disappointed over not being appointed secretary to Wilson. In his memoirs Creel wrote: "While I was deep in the liquidation of CPI, President Wilson was kind enough to ask me to go with him to the conference in a personal capacity". (Rebel at Large, p. 205). Was he offered the post as private secretary to the President? However that may be, everything was blurred when Postmaster General Burleson shortly thereafter took the cables, and public criticism was focused on Creel. His role as intimate adviser to the President was thereafter impossible, but Wilson sent him on a face-saving trip to Europe (ibid. p. 205). Creel accompanied Wilson to Rome (ibid. p. 207), and was thereafter sent to Czechoslovakia, Poland and Hungary (ibid. p. 207), and later on to Ireland (ibid. p. 214). Creel left Paris around March 1 (ibid. p. 222). Creel's story is probably not the whole truth, but however that may be, he was a controversial person, and it was symptomatic that House backed Lansing in the conflict between the two, as he had earlier tried to get Cobb, not Creel as the press-secretary of the Commission. (see above note 40).

82. Auchincloss diary 15.12.18.

83. Cf. note 40.

84. Memorandum made by Mrs. Frank I. Cobb, November 9, 1937, giving her recollection of what her husband, Frank I. Cobb, told her on his return from Paris, December, 1918. Frank I. Cobb papers, 1915–1923, Wilson papers, accession 6161, Library of Congress. For the right date of this memorandum see Mrs. Copp to R. S. Baker 9.11.1937 (R. S. Baker papers, Series I, 26, Library of Congress): "I am enclosing a memorandum which is a copy of one I wrote out at the time of President Wilson's death".—Even though this memorandum is written some years after the events took place and at a time, when Cobb himself was dead, I see no reason to doubt that Mrs. Cobb put down the situation, as Cobb saw it, correctly.

85. See, for instance, his rather voluminious correspondance with Thomas Nelson Page (House papers) and cf. the following diary entry: "I censured Willard (the American ambassador to Spain) for his lack of cooperation and failure to keep in touch with me by letter . . . He promised to do better in the future". (House diary 24.11.17).

86. Regarding Buckler see Martin, pp. 115–123, 137–139, 145, 158, 166 and 179.

87. Mrs. Cobb's memorandum, regarding Frazier see also Trask, pp. 65, 185 and 186.

88. See, for instance House diary 23.7.18: "William Phillips (Ass. Secr. of State) came in the afternoon and we had a long conference about existing conditions in the State Department. Phillips thinks that Frank Polk (Councellor of the State Department) and Gordon (Auchincloss, House's son-in-law) are building up too much of an organization within the Department, about which the other officials are not informed. I rather believe this is true".

89. Confidential Memorandum from Mr. Cobb for Colonel House, dated Paris, November 4, 1918. IP IV, pp. 219–221.

90. Cobb to House 14.11.18. Handwritten letter and telegram, House Coll.

91. Auchincloss diary 15.11.18.—In Cobb papers (House to Cobb 16.11.18) the vital sentence is corrupted: ". . . and to compromise the situation . . .".

92. House to Lansing 14.11.18. PC I, p. 130.

93. Wilson to House 16.11.18. ibid. pp. 134–35.

94. House to Wilson 16.11.18. ibid. p. 135.

95. Charles Seymour, End of a Friendship (memorandum about a talk with House 5.1.38), American Heritage XIV, Aug. 1963, pp. 8–9.

96. House diary 14.12.18.

97. Bernard M. Baruch: The Public Years, New York, Holt, Rinehart and Winston, 1960, p. 142. Henry Morgenthau diary 18.12.18, 25.3.19, 6.5.19. Library of Congress.

98. See especially his noteworthy conversation with Vance McCormick 6.5.19. (Morgenthau diary 6.5.19 and Vance McCormick diary 6.5.19, Yale University Library). Morgenthau came to Paris 24.3.19.

99. 18.12. he wrote Thomas W. Gregory: ". the thing I did that was of value to the President, to the United States, and I dare hope, the world, was the incorporating in the armistice the American war aims" House Coll. 9/4. See also the diary 9.12.18 and cf. chapter 1, pp. 59–60.

100. See Lord Hankey: Diplomacy by Conference, London 1946, pp. 11–39. F. S. Marston: The Peace Conference of 1919, London, New York, Toronto, Oxford University Press, 1944, pp. 1–12, 13–27, 151–64; and David F. Trask: The United States in the Supreme War Council, Middletown, Conn., Wesleyan Un. Press, 1961, pp. 20–53.

101. House's remark to Henry Morgenthau 24.5.19. Henry Morgenthau diary 24.5.19. Library of Congress.

102. "House again described how he used to run Conventions in Texas". Wiseman diary 22.1.19. Yale.

103. House diary 18.12.17.

104. House diary 11.12.17. See also House diary 11.12.18, where House, in a conversation with Lord Derby, explained that Lloyd George was "the stumbling block" in Anglo-American relations.

105. For House's estimation of Balfour, see for instance House diary 8.11.17, 4.12.17, 31.12.18.

106. House diary 31.12.18.

107. ibid. 27.3.19.

108. Lloyd George: Truth I, p. 244.

109. House diary 29.11.17. See also the entry 6.12.17.

110. House to Wilson 22.10.18. Wilson papers, Ser. II.

111. See also the entries 29.10.18 and 31.10.18.

112. House diary 9.11.18.

113. PC I, p. 344, cf. Nelson, p. 134.

114. Seymour gave a very understanding description of the friendship in IP IV, p. 196–198; but Lloyd George possibly came nearer the truth when he wrote: "Clemenceau's use of House" (Truth I, p. 244).

115. House diary 21.12.18.
116. "There has not been a discordant note struck, either in public or private. This is the one thing I have been insistent upon and anxious about". House diary 18.11.17.
117. Henry Morgenthau diary 6.5.19.
118. Bliss to N. D. Baker 9.12.18. Bliss papers. Baker answered inter alia (23.12): "I realize that Colonel House is secretive and I have several times found myself embarrassed just as you found yourself in this instance, by reason of not having been told things I ought to have known to make my own course clear and consistent . . .". Bliss papers.
119. Bliss to March 9.12.18. Bliss papers.
120. The evolution of the procedural question in this period is traced in Robert C. Binkley, New Light on the Paris Peace Conference I, Political Science Quarterly, XLVI, 1931, pp. 335–361, and Marston pp. 28–53.
121. House to Lansing for Wilson 30.10.18, no. 10. FR18SI, 1, p. 424. Baker VIII, p. 528.
122. Wilson to House 31.10.18, no. 6. private series. Wilson papers, Ser. 2.
123. House to Wilson 5.11.18, no. 6. private series, House papers. Wilson papers, Ser. 2.
124. Wilson to House 10.11.18. no. 12 private series. P. C. I., p. 128.
125. Derby to Balfour 18.1118 House Coll 6/26. Derby refers to conversation with House.
126. Polk to Lansing from House 5.12.18. nr. 2. PC I, p. 126.
127. Marston, p. 31.
128. "Plans for the Peace Conference", 16.11.18; sent to Wilson 18.11.18. Wilson papers, Ser. 5 A. (to be found among the documents Wilson took with him to Paris).
129. IP IV, p. 211.
130. Binkley, p. 343. An analysis of the French policy in this period is given in Binkleys above-mentioned article, and also in an article by Frederick J. Cox, The French Peace Plans, 1918–1919: The Germ of the Conflict between Ferdinand Foch and George Clemenceau.
131. House to Lansing 15.11.18. no. 109. PC I, p. 344–352. The quotation is taken from p. 350.
132. In this matter France had the backing of the British Government: see Harding to Balfour 10.10.18: ". . . it seems desirable to separate at the Congress, so far as possible, matters which neutrals are entitled to discuss from those which only concern the belligerents, and, above all, to stipulate categorically that, until the questions directly arising out of the war have been settled, no attempt shall be made to handle so difficult a question as that of the machinery for maintaining peace afterwards . . .", i. e. a direct allusion to the League of Nations (House Coll. 21/9).
133. Binkley, p. 346. Binkley wrote (p. 343), that House in his telegram of 15.11. to the State Department left out this vital French attack, but this seems to be a misunderstanding on the part of Binkley.
134. ibid. p. 347.
135. PC I, pp. 131–132. House to Lansing for Wilson 15.11.18, no. 108.
136. House to Lansing for Wilson 25.11.18, no. 173. PC I, p. 333. IP IV, p. 250.
137. House diary 18.11.18.
138. Derby to House 12.11.18. House Collection 6/26.
139. House diary 19.11.18.
140. House to Lloyd George 25.11.18. House Coll. 12/32.
141. House to Lansing for Wilson 25.11.18. no. 173. PC I, p. 333.
142. House to Lansing 27.11.18. no. 188. PC II, p. 637.
143. House to Wilson 16.11.18. no. 15. PC I, p. 135.
144. House diary 14.12.18.
145. House to Lansing for Wilson 30.11.18. no. 203. PC I, pp. 333–334. At the same time Clemenceau delivered a memorandum on the French demands in the Saar region. But this time also House did not tell Wilson. House diary 30.11.18, Cf. Nelson, p. 134.
146. House diary 30.11.18.
147. Nelson, p. 130.

148. PC I, pp. 371–378.
149. Nelson, p. 136 n.
150. Nelson pp. 135–136.
151. Nelson, p. 135. Nelson gives the whole preamble.
152. Lloyd George: Truth I, pp. 132–136.
153. Die geheimen Abmachungen zwischen Clemenceau und Lloyd George vom Dezember 1918 und ihre Bedeutung für das Zustandekommen des Versailler Vertrages. Berliner Monatshefte, 1938, pp. 702–715.
154. ibid. p. 710.
155. ibid. p. 710.
156. ibid. pp. 710–711.
157. ibid. p. 709.
158. House diary 12.3.19. See also Auchincloss diary 12.1.19: "Wiseman told me that Clemenceau had made a definite proposition when he was last in England that an alliance be formed between France, England, Italy, Spain and Portugal against Germany and without paying any attention to the United States, and that Clemenceau was very much upset when his proposals were turned down", and Miller diary I, 11.3.19, pp. 162–163: "Wiseman told me in confidence that right after the Armistice the French had asked the British to virtually support each other in their demands about the peace, which the British had declined". During the secret negotiations in the middle of March between Kerr, Tardieu and Mezes about the French demands on the Rhine, Tardieu expressed his disappointment over the British resistance against Allied occupation and the separation of the Rhineland, and he alluded to the fact that this was a departure from an understanding between Lloyd George and Clemenceau (Nelson, p. 217). Zeine N. Zeine has treated the Syrian question at the London Conference from a different angle (The Struggle for Arab Independence, Beirut, Khayat's, 1960, pp. 55–58). He concludes: "Actually, because of the rising tension between the two governments concerning the situation in Syria, what Clemenceau was most anxious to obtain from Lloyd George was a *confirmation* of the French rights in Syria and Cilicia as already laid down in the Sykes-Picot Agreement. This confirmation was obtained at a price: Mosul and Palestine". (ibid. p. 58, italics Zeine's).—On the Mosul compromise at the London Conference, see also Jukka Nevakivi: Britain, France and the Arab Middle East 1914–1920, University of London, The Athlone Press, 1969, pp. 89–93.
159. Bliss to Newton D. Baker 11.1.19. Bliss papers. See also Bliss to N. D. Baker 9.12.18. ibid.
160. Bliss to N. D. Baker 11.1.19. Bliss papers.
161. PC I, p. 334–340.
162. Balfour to Grahame 2.12.18, 3.12.18. Balfour to House 4.12.18, Balfour to Grahame (?) 4.12.18. Balfour to Derby 4.12.18. House Coll. 2/23. Derby to House 5.12.18. ibid. 6/26.
163. House diary 4.12.18 and 5.12.18.
164. PC I, pp. 340–342, sent 6.12.18.
165. ibid. p. 342.
166. ibid. p. 342.
167. Marston, p. 46.
168. Marston, p. 48.
169. PC I, p. 343, sent 8.12.18. See also Lansing to Polk for House 7.12.18: "President suggests that arrangements for meeting of Inter-Allied Conference be postponed until preliminary informal discussions have shown just what would be best in all the circumstances". PC I, p. 127.
170. PC I, p. 343, sent 8.12.18. House had already advised Lord Derby on 6.12. that the American Government was favourably disposed towards the Reparations Commission and the Adriatic Commission, but he had not given any binding assurances. (House to Derby 6.12.18. House Coll. 6/26).
171. PC I, pp. 119–121. FR18SI, 1. p. 426. IP IV, pp. 226–228.
172. House diary 8.11.18.

173. McCall was sharply criticised by his fellow-Republicans because of his backing of Wilson during the election campaign. PC I, p. 157 and IP IV, p. 234.
174. House to Wilson 10.11.18, no. 10. PC I, p. 158.
175. Cf. Bliss to March 30.11.18, Bliss papers: "To my amazement he (House) told me that I had been selected as one the Peace Commissioners. He said that an Associated Press dispatch had been received to that effect and also that the French Ambassador in Washington had telegraphed it to his Government".
176. Lansing desk book 26.11.18.
177. Lansing desk book 26.11.18, 19.11.18 and 20.11.18 shows, how fortuitous it all was.
178. House diary 1.12.18.
179. House diary 3.12.18.
180. A good review of the arguments for and against is given in Key Pittman to Wilson 15.11.18 (PC I, pp. 132–134). Polk and McAdoo, for instance, were against (House diary 13.10.18), and so was Lansing.
181. "(Clemenceau) wondered again whether the President would sit with the other delegates. That, I told him, was a matter the President would determine after he reached France; the President was a man of sense and could be relied upon to do the sensible thing. Clemenceau said he would be willing to go to the President's house in the mornings; ... and then have more formal meetings of the delegates at the Quay d'Orsay to endorse what was done in the morning meetings. I thought the President might be willing to accept this compromise". House diary 5.12.18.
182. "I had previously told Clemenceau that I had talked the President out of sitting in. I did this in less than ten minutes. It is a question now whether the President will want to sit in since I so thoroughly convinced him it was not the right thing to do. However, after the three of us (House, Clemenceau and Wilson) had finished talking it was decided to leave the matter for final decision later". House diary 15.12.18. See also Wiseman to Drummond 16.12.18, Wiseman papers: "The President is not anxious to sit at the Peace Conference. On the contrary, he thinks it would not be wise". Wiseman's source of information is doubtless House. See also memorandum on conversation with House (Wiseman) 15.12.18 in Wiseman papers: "The President came over with the intention of sitting at the Peace Conference as Chief American delegate, but House has persuaded him to abandon this idea, and he will remain in Paris in close touch with his own representatives and the Allies for informal conferences. The President does not want to stay much more than a month".
183. Derby to Balfour 16.12.18. PC I, pp. 149–150. Derby is forwarding Clemenceau's memorandum of the conversation with Wilson.
184. ibid.: "He (Clemenceau) feels sure that if it became known that the President had expressed a wish to be present and had been refused the effect would be very bad, at any rate in France".
185. Drummond to W(iseman) 17.12.18. House Coll. 6/26, and Derby to House 18.12.18. ibid.
186. House diary 21.12.18.
187. House diary 13.12.18 and 14.12.18.
188. House diary 14.12.18. See also memorandum on conversation with House 15.12.18 (Wiseman?), Wiseman papers: "I had a long interview today with Colonel House. He it quite recovered from the influenza, and very satisfied with the result of his talks with the President. As soon as he arrived the President seems to have turned to House for advice, and asked him to arrange his Secretariat and map out his program of work".
189. W(iseman) to Drummond 15.12.18, Wiseman papers. Se also Auchincloss diary 14.12.18: "The Colonel had a talk with the President and a much longer one with him this afternoon and so far as I could see everything is satisfactorily fixed up".
190. See in this connection also Auchincloss diary 13.12.18: "I tried to get from him (Cary Grayson, Wilsons medical doctor and confidential) an indication as to what the President's plans were, but he said that he did not know anything about them and that no one else did".

191. Several participants of the meeting took notes: Bowman's are given in IP IV, pp. 280–283. Gelfand used among others (pp. 171–174) Bullitt's and George Louis Beer's versions. Seymour's own notes are now available in: Charles Seymour: Letters from the Paris Peace Conference, Yale University Press, New Haven and London, 1965, pp. 22–26. And Klaus Schwabe has used Charles Swem's stenographic notes (pp. 312–324).

192. Gelfand, p. 175. Only Seymour seems to have been more optimistic: Letters, p. 23.

193. George Louis Beer's evaluation. Gelfand, p. 174.

194. Memorandum, 15.12.18. Wiseman papers.

195. Henry White to William Phillips 8.5.19. Allan Nevins, Henry White. Thirty Years of American Diplomacy, Harper and Brothers, New York and London, 1930, p. 446.

196. Bliss to N. D. Baker 11.1.19. Bliss papers. See also Bliss to Lansing 26.12.18. PC I, pp. 297–298, Bliss to Lansing 15.12.18, Bliss papers, Bliss to Mrs. Bliss 18.12.18, ibid, and Bliss to N. D. Baker 18.12.18, ibid., and Robert Lansing, The Peace Negotiations, Constable and Company, London 1921, pp. 169–189.

197. McCormick diary 13.1.19, Yale. House was not blind to this either: "I told Gordon (Auchincloss) not to allow the papers to announce that Pichon, Foch, Clemenceau, the President and Lord Robert Cecil had been my visitors during the day. I am afraid to hurt sensibilities". House diary 7.1.19.

198. House diary 15.12.18. It was very important to House that the first meeting should be a success, and he had worked on the two main actors beforehand.

199. House diary 19.12.18, 24.12.18 and 25.12.18.

200. Auchincloss diary 22.12–28.12.18.

201. House wrote in his diary 27.12.18: "It is a great opportunity for him and if I had gone to London, he would have missed most of it". Several years later Lansing had a conversation with Stephen Bonsal (one of House's aides in Paris who worked for the State Department during the War): "I (Lansing) asked him (Bonsal) if he had ever heard of an intrigue among some of the President's intimates to get rid of House and to break his influence. He said that he had heard the story and was convinced that it was so, but that he doubted very much if it would have succeeded except for the foolish conduct of Auchincloss.
I said that I had understood that the plan had been to make Auchincloss the President's confidential secretary during the Peace Conference, but that the President would have none of it as he took a personal dislike to House's son-in-law. Bonsal said that my understanding was correct and that it came about through Auchincloss' officiousness when he accompanied the President to London. He said that, as he understood it, the young man called up Mr. Wilson one night about 11 : 30 to tell him something of a social nature which he should do and that the President was furiously angry about it and would have nothing to do with him after that. Bonsal went on to say that Colonel House now felt that he had made a great mistake in taking Auchincloss and Mezes to Europe as the President resented it and thought that House was endeavoring to control everything by surrounding the President with members of his family. I replied that I was entirely in agreement with the Colonel's opinion as it had been the subject of much talk and adverse criticism. That everybody knew, I said, that Mezes was a mere figurehead and that Bowman was the real head of the experts. I added, "You ought to include Auchincloss' law partner, David Hunter Miller, in this family group. Everybody else does". Bonsal assented saying his name was also mentioned.
There can be little doubt, I think that Colonel House did attempt to get control of the negotiations and to keep President Wilson isolated so that everything had to go through him or his group. Possibly he did this with the best of motives; possibly because of personal reasons. I do not pretend to say what was the real course which he adopted". (Lansing Confidential Memorandum, 14.10.1921: The Break between House and President Wilson. Lansing Papers).

202. Auchincloss diary 26.12.18, 28.12.18 and 1.1.19.

203. Auchincloss diary 24.12.18, italics mine.

204. See House to Balfour 16.12.18. House Coll. 2/23, cf. Auchincloss diary 16.12.18.

205. See D. H. Miller to House 4.12.18 on conversation with Sir William Tyrrell. P. C. I, p. 338–339.
206. N. D. Baker to Bliss 23.12.18. Bliss papers.
207. Bliss to N. D. Baker 4.1.19. Bliss papers. Italics mine.
208. Auchincloss diary 2.1.19.
209. "He is rather full of his trip to England and seems to have had a thoroughly satisfactory time". House diary, 1.1.19.
210. House diary 31.12.18.
211. House diary 1.1.19.
212. "Imperial War Cabinet 47. Draft minutes of a meeting held at 10 Downing Street, S. W., on Monday, December 30, 1918, at 3–30 p. m.". Wiseman papers.
213. The question is, however, whether Lloyd George really presented the matter to Wilson in such clear-cut terms: "George advanced a rather indefinite program under which Australia would be permitted to take over the control of certain of the German Colonies. The President was most opposed to this and the matter was not vigorously pressed on the part of the British". Auchincloss to Polk, Auchincloss diary 2.1.19.
214. See Wiseman diary 31.1.19, 5.2.19 and 7.2.19.
215. See Paul Birdsall, Versailles Twenty Years After, Archon Books, Hamden, Conn. 1962 (1941), pp. 58–77 and George Curry, Woodrow Wilson, Jan Smuts and the Versailles Settlement, The American Historical Review, 66, 1961, pp. 968–986.
216. Auchincloss diary 1.1.19.
217. House to Lansing for Wilson 11.11.18, no. 89, PC II, p. 287.
218. Victor S. Mamatey: The United States and East Central Europe 1914–18, Princeton Un. Press, Princeton, 1957, pp. 359–375, and Ivo J. Lederer: Yugoslavia at the Paris Peace Conference, Yale Un. Press, New Haven and London 1963, pp. 54–78.
219. Seymour, Letters, p. 20. W. E. Lunt to Professor Young (both Inquiry Experts on board the George Washington) 12.12.18: Lunt forwarded a memorandum on three possible frontiers between Italy and Austria: The Treaty of London-frontier and now the demarcation line of the Armistice: Brenner, was strategically best, but not justifiable on grounds of history or language. (Wilson papers, Ser. 5 A).
220. Albrecht-Carrié, p. 79.
221. House diary 15.12.18: "The President cheerfully unloads matters upon me. I am having worked out the boundary lines between the Jugoslavs and the Italians...".
222. House diary 20.12.18, see also Auchincloss diary 20.12.18.
223. Auchincloss diary 18.12.18. This must be identical with a memorandum on "Suggested boundary between the Italians and the Jugoslavs", which in Wilson papers, Ser. 5 A is put together with the letter mentioned in note 219 from Lunt to Young. The conclusion of the memorandum was as follows: "The line granted to Italy by the Pact of London, 1915, and coinciding with the line limiting the occupation of Austria according to Armistice, includes much territory almost purely Jugo-Slav in character and which is not essential to the interests of Italy either on strategic or commercial grounds. A boundary further to the west, lying between the Pact of London line and the linguistic frontier, is suggested".
224. House diary 21.12.18, see also Auchincloss diary 21.12.18.
225. Political Origins of the New Diplomacy, Yale Un. Press, New Haven 1959.
226. Albrecht-Carrié, p. 71.
227. Albrecht-Carrié characterizes Bissolati's views as follows: "... favoring a peace of compromise with the Slavs, a sincere devotee of the Wilsonean ideal, and one who placed high hopes in the future League of Nations", p. 70.
228. Albrecht-Carrié, pp. 71–72 and Lederer, p. 65.
229. Lederer, p. 65.
230. Bissolati's secretary told Gino Speranza, that "The last straw for Bissolati was the discovery that Orlando had told Wilson that the entire Cabinet shared his—Orlando's—views on the Adriatic question". See Speranzas diary 29.12.18. Albrecht-Carrié, p. 82; and The Diary of Gino Speranza, Italy, 1915–1919, edited by Florence Colgate Speranza, II, New York, Columbia University Press, 1941, pp. 232–233.

231. "Bissolati wants to talk to Wilson, and there is no reason why he shouldn't". ibid.
232. "I did what I could to make sure that Wilson would see Bissolati in Rome ... Bissolati had asked me, if he had an interview with the President to interpret for him. After his resignation, he let me know that, since he was no longer a member of the Cabinet, he could not make any move to see the President. He could not go unless he were invited. Late on the second day of the President's stay in Rome, Bissolati was summoned ...". Speranza diary 17.1.19. Albrecht-Carrié, p. 83. Speranza, pp. 237–239.
233. On January 7, Ambassador Page forwarded to Wilson "the only copy I have of minute made by Lieutenant Lawrence G. White of the conversation between Bisolatti and yourself". Page had asked White to show the minute to Bissolati, which he had done. "It, therefore, expresses Bisolatti's mature presentation of his views as expressed on the occasion of the interview". Bissolati had asked that it must be "kept entirely confidential". Wilson papers, Ser. 5 A.
234. "Digest of the President's conference with On. Bissolati", in Page to Wilson 7.1.19. Wilson papers, Ser. 5 A.
235. Albrecht-Carrié, pp. 71–72.
236. Ibid., p. 71 n.
237. Page to Wilson 7.1.19, cf. note 233.
238. Auchincloss to Polk, Auchincloss diary 9.1.19. It seems reasonable to think, that Auchincloss related what Wilson told House (House's own diary is, as so often before, silent). It is possible, however, that it actually was during his stay in Italy that the President gave his assent to the Brenner frontier: Cf. Albrecht-Carrié, p. 85 n.
239. See Wilson to Orlando 10.1.19 (not sent): "Supplementing the memorandum which I gave your Excellency yesterday ...". Wilson papers, Ser. 5 A.
240. The letter is found in three versions in Wilson papers, Ser. 5 A: the first one, dated 10.1., is very short (cf. note 140), while the other two (dated 13.1 and 15.1.) are longer and identical except in the conclusions. 13.1. the version was: "I am glad to be able to assure you that the statesmen who represent France and Great Britain unite with the representatives of the United States in entertaining the earnest hope that Italy will accept this just settlement as her contribution to the longed for peace of the world".
   In the letter of 15.1. this was exchanged for less positive assurances because, as we shall see, Wilson failed to get the co-operation of the Allied Prime Ministers. The 15.1.-version is the original with the President's original signature, and it therefore seems reasonable to assume that neither of the letters were sent.
241. Auchincloss diary 12.1.19.
242. Auchincloss diary 14.1.19.
243. Cf. note 141.
244. House to Wilson 22.10.18. Wilson papers, Ser. 2, partly in PC I, p. xx, cf. above p. xx.
245. Auchincloss to Polk 16.11.18, Auchincloss diary 16.11.18; Auchincloss to Polk 18.11.18. Auchincloss diary 18.11.18.
246. Polk to Auchincloss, Auchincloss diary 22.11.18.
247. House to Wilson, Auchincloss diary 23.11.18.
248. Auchincloss to Polk, Auchincloss diary 30.11.18.
249. Auchincloss diary 2.12.18, and Polk to Auchincloss, Auchincloss diary 17.12.18.
250. Auchincloss diary 28.11.18, 5.12.18 and 6.12.18.
251. Auchincloss to Irving Hoover 17.12.18. Wilson papers, Ser. 5 A. See also Auchincloss diary 18.12.18.
252. Auchincloss diary 18.12.18, 19.12.18 and 20.12.18.
253. Wilson to Baruch 7.12.18. Baruch papers, Princeton University Library.
254. Polk to Auchincloss, Auchincloss diary 17.12.18: "Baruch is planning to go over with a large staff. His departure indefinite apparently he is awaiting for some word from the President".

255. Auchincloss diary 20.12.18 and memorandum (no author) 21.12.18 Wilson papers, Ser. 5 A, and House to Glass, Auchincloss diary 26.12.18.
256. Carter Glass to Norman Davis 31.12.18, received 2.1.19. Norman H. Davis papers, Library of Congress and Auchincloss diary 31.12.18.
257. Glass to House 9.1.19, received 10.1.19. Davis papers, see also Glass to Wilson 6.1.19, received 8.1.19. Wilson papers, Ser. 5 A, and Wilson to Glass, Auchincloss diary 12.1.19.
258. Auchincloss diary 3.1.19, italics mine. This memorandum is also found in an undated version in Davis papers. See also Lansing to Polk 7.1.19, Wilson papers, Ser. 5 A.
259. Commissioners to Wilson 31.12.18. Wilson papers, Ser. 5 A.
260. See "List of Technical Advisers to the American Commission to Negotiate Peace", 2.4.19, 184/97 National Arvhives and "List of Technical Experts of the American Commission to Negotiate Peace", 2.5.19. 184/97 National Archives.
261. See, for instance, Lansing desk book 20.1.19: "Had a few moments with Bliss and White who are becoming dissatisfied at the President's secretiveness about the League of Nations . . .". See also House diary 3.1.19, 8.1.19, 24.3.19.
262. "Minutes of Meetings of the American Commissioners Plenipotentiary and of the Commissioners and Technical Advisers of the American Delegation". PC XI, pp. 1–479.
263. See Lansing to Polk 26.7.19. Polk papers, Yale.
264. House diary 3.1.19, 8.1.19, 28.1.19, 14.2.19, 19.2.19, 28.3.19 and 23.6.19.
265. On Wilson see, for instance, House diary 14.2.19 and 24.3.19 On Bliss's frustration over not being "used" see Frederick Palmer: Bliss, Peacemaker. The Life and Letters of General Tasker Howard Bliss, New York, Dodd, Mead and Company, 1934, pp. 363–379.
266. House diary 5.4.19.
267. See, for instance, Memorandum: To Captain Newton re Dr. Bowman, from Stephen Philbin, 3.2.19. National Archives 184/93: Dr. Bowman wants himself to appear as head of a separate department apart from Dr. Mezes".
268. Birdsall, pp. 264–288. For further information see chapter 5.
269. See, for instance, Henry Morgenthau diary 6.5.19: Got impression that V(ance McCormick) does not admire House as much as formerly—and resents A(uchincloss) and H(ouse) not being quite loyal to W(oodrow) W(ilson)". A good review of Mc Cormick's personality, career and friendship with Mr. and Mrs. Wilson is found in Ray Stannard Baker's "Memorandum of a conversation with Vance C. McCormick", 15.7.1928, R. S. Baker papers, Ser. I, Library of Congress. The friendship with Wilson dates back to the election campaign in 1916, which McCormick headed for the Democratic Party.
270. House diary 18.2.19. In Baruch's papers (Princeton Un. Library) there are copies and photo-copies of all the entries in the House diary in which Baruch is mentioned, which makes it easy to follow the relationship through the years as seen with House's eyes. In the beginning House had nothing to criticize, but after Baruch got his first official assignment in the last part of 1916, his entries became more and more critical.
271. Baruch to Ray Stannard Baker 19.10.1928. Baruch papers.
272. Baruch: The Public Years, Holt, Rinehart and Winston, New York, 1960, p. 142. See also Auchincloss diary 23.1.19: "At the present time Baruch's job is not exactly defined and there is a very small amount of friction which needs to be straightened out".
273. See Wilson to Bainbridge Colby 2.4.1920 and 12.4.1920 with the very appraising words about Davis.
274. The correspondence between Lamont and Morrow is in Polk papers, Yale, see also Lamont to Wilson 19.3.19, 5.6.19, 10.6.19, 11.6.19, 13.6.19, 21.6.19 and 23.6.19 and Wilson to Lamont 24.3.19, 7.6.19, 16.6.19, 17.6.19 and 23.6.19. Wilson papers, Ser. 5 A.—On Lamont, see also his autobiography: Across World Frontiers, New York, Harcourt, Brace and Co., 1951.

275. Lansing desk book 23.3.19. Lansing papers.
276. Henry Morgenthau diary 11.6.19. House's offices were situated on the third floor of Hotel Crillon. The whole of the Hotel was taken over by the American Delegation during the Conference.
277. White to Lansing 8.11.19. Nevins, p. 475. The offices of the other Commissioners were situated on lower floors than those of House.
278. House diary 24.3.19.
279. See Lansing desk book 5.1.19.—Lansing has given a very penetrating description of House's organisation in a letter to Frank Polk on 26.7.19 (Polk papers, Yale, copy in Lansing papers, Princeton). He wrote about the intrigues and the secrecy that had damaged the whole Conference. He also pointed out that the efficiency of the Commission had been very much impaired because of the personal organisation that House had built up. An organisation that acted independent of, and sometimes against the official Commission, with the result that intrigues and jealousies split the American Delegation. He also mentioned that House's organisation had the character of a family-firm, including, as it did, both Mezes and the other Experts (for further information on this see below). Lansing also pointed to the unlucky role played by Auchincloss and his propaganda for House, which made co-operation even more difficult.—Lansing was certainly no neutral observer, but it seems clear to me that what he wrote was not far off the mark.


*Chapter 3*

1. About the organization and procedure of the Conference, see Marston, pp. 69–83.
2. PPC III, p. 201.
3. I am here following Lawrence Evans: United States Policy and the Partition of Turkey, 1914–1924, Baltimore, The Johns Hopkins Press, 1965, pp. 105–107 and 132–141. In the immediate situation, it was naturally the British Dominions who gained most from the compromise. For further information see Evans, pp. 89–107, and Seth P. Tillman: Anglo-American Relations at the Paris Peace Conference of 1919, Princeton, Princeton University Press, 1961, pp. 85–100.
4. House diary 21.3.19.
5. House diary 21.1.19., 22.1.19, 23.1.19, 26.1.19, 28.1.19, 30.1.19 and 6.2.19
6. McCormick diary 29.1.19.
7. Auchincloss diary 29.1.19:
   "The fact that the President is continuing to hold meetings twice a day with the Allied Prime Ministers makes it impossible for anyone else to see him and for him to get advice from the various members of the Commission (read House). This is becoming very embarassing and is working against the President. He is in a position of carrying on the whole alone because Lansing gives him no help whatever and he has no intercourse with the rest of his advisers".
8. Auchincloss diary 23.1.19, see also Wiseman diary 22.1.19.
9. Cf. note 4.
10. Lansing desk book 16.1.19, 17.1.19, 27.1.19, 6.2.19, (on Balfour's views), 9.2.19. See also Lansing, The Peace Negotiations, London, Constable and Company, 1921.
11. See for example Lansing desk book 20.1.19: "Had a few moments with Bliss and White who are becoming dissatisfied at the President's secretiveness about the League of Nations ...".
12. House's role in the making of the Covenant of the League of Nations is described in IP IV, pp. 1–54, and pp. 290–331, and in David Hunter Miller, The Drafting of the Covenant I, New York—London, G. P. Putnam's Sons, 1928. Vol. II gives the texts of the several drafts of the Covenant, and also minutes of the meetings of the Commission. Miller, the legal adviser of the American Commission to Negotiate Peace, also played an important role in the framing of the Covenant.—See also House diary, passim.

13. Lederer, pp. 146–155.
14. Through Thirty Years II, London, William Heinemann, 1924, p. 278.—See also Auchincloss Diary 10.2.19, about a conversation with Steed.
15. Nat. Archives 186.3411/212. See also Minutes of the Daily Meetings of the Commissioners Plenipotentiary, Thursday, February 20th, 1919, PC XI, p. 62. The minutes have almost the same wording as the above cited letter, but it is furthermore related, that "Mr. Lansing stated that he had no knowledge that any such inquiry had been made by the American Commission".
16. Marston pp. 123–136.
17. PC III, pp. 970–1012, cf. furthermore Marston.
18. PC III, p. 972.
19. PC III, pp. 1003–1004.
20. PC III, p. 1005.
21. Lansing desk book 27.1.19.
22. Lansing desk book 9.2.19. About the content of the treaty Lansing had thought of see Lansing, The Peace Negotiations, pp. 185–186. See also Lansing to Polk 11.2.19. Polk papers, Yale.
23. House diary 5.2.19. IP IV, p. 336.
24. House diary 6.2.19.
25. House diary 9.2.19, cf. also Auchincloss diary 9.2.19.
26. House diary 14.2.19, partly in IP IV, p. 340. Stephen Bonsal has a strange diary entry which is worth mentioning in this connection. It is dated 13.2.19. (Unfinished Business, London, Michael Joseph, 1944, pp. 49–50). Bonsal writes, that the President in the presence of Bonsal, gave House "very definite instructions for his guidance while he was away". Wilson said: "During my unavoidable absence I do not wish the questions of territorial adjustments or those of reparations to be held up". This is almost verbatim the same wording as is rendered in the minutes of the meeting of the Council of Ten the day before. One possible interpretation is therefore that the President regarded his statement in the Council of Ten as his official authority, and simply quoted it in front of House. Bonsal further relates that he afterwards discussed the matter with House. Bonsal interpreted the President's words as meaning, "that the President left House in control", but House did not agree with this interpretation. He said: "The President does not mean that I am authorized to definitely settle anything, but he does hope that I will get the problems, one and all, in such a shape that on his return they can be submitted to him for final judgment. I am glad for these limitations of my powers ...". The interpretation House gives here, corresponds closely to the one he renders in the diary, but, in reality, it tells us nothing about Wilson's intentions, only *what House was thinking* the President had in mind. During the conversation Bonsal also said that in his opinion House was taking "quite a risk in accepting merely verbal instructions from his chief", and House answered that he, too, would have preferred written instructions, but that the President never gave them. In an entry dated February 15 (ibid., p. 63) Bonsal further relates, that in House's opinion it would be very difficult for him, House, to propose to the President that he should extend "the period of his (House's) authority and greater responsibility". House did not want any repetition of the episode of 14 October (November?), when he had clearly expressed the opinion that the President should stay away.
27. Lansing, The Peace Negotiations, p. 181. See also Lansing, Appendix to Diary 14.2.18. Lansing papers: He (Wilson) said before he left that he was in favor of a preliminary peace treaty provided it contained the covenant complete. To do that means to delay drafting the Treaty until the President returns from the US, ... I asked the President if he had any instructions for the Commission while he was away. He said that he had not only that I should continue as the head of the Commission and that House might sit with one in the Council of Ten. I asked him if he had no instructions as the contents of the preliminary treaty. He said, no, that that could wait till he returned ...". Lansing is the only source: The minutes of the meeting of Friday, February 14th, 1919, are missing from the Department's

files". (PPC XI, p. 38). House mentions the meeting, but says nothing about what happened. (House diary, 14.2.19).

28. Lansing writes about the meeting in his diary: "President plans to leave tonight. Spoke of preliminary peace which he favors". (Lansing desk book 14.2.19). Cf. also Lansing's memorandum of 30.3.19, printed Peace Negotiations, p. 185.

29. See for example Lansing desk book 27.1.19, 31.1.19, 10.2.19 and McCormick diary 10.2.19.

30. For Wilson's evaluation of the situation see for example Wilson to Swope 1.2.19. Wilson papers Ser. 5 A, Wilson to Hoover 3.2.19, ibid. Wilson to Swope 7.2.19, ibid. Wilson to Melville A. Stone 11.2.19, ibid. and McCormick diary 10.2.19.

31. See Polk to Auchincloss 12.2.19. Auchincloss diary 13.2.19, and Auchincloss's report to Polk 13.2.19. Auchincloss diary 13.2.19. Cf. further Cambrun's report from Washington 12.–14.2.19, House Coll. 5/4.

32. Kerr to Lloyd George 11.2.19. Kindly made available to me by Jørgen Sevaldsen.

33. Auchincloss to Polk 13.2.19. Auchincloss diary 13.2.19, and Kerr to Lloyd George 12.2.19, op.cit.—House actually succeded in stopping the publication in France (ibid).

34. Lansing desk book 15.2.19.

35. See anonymous memorandum "Confidential for E. M. H." 15.2.19. (Is also found both in Wiseman papers and in Wiseman's correspondence with House, House Coll 20/48, so possibly the author is Wiseman.

36. House diary 16.2.19, partly in IP IV, p. 341. See also Auchincloss diary 16.2.19. Already 31 January Balfour had circulated a memorandum in the British Delegation, in which he argued in favour of the establishment of a more fixed procedure, for example by beginning with the territorial questions. At a meeting of the British Empire Delegation on February 20 Balfour's "speeding up" resolution was discussed and it was agreed that the demand for a rapid decision of the military conditions should be maintained, and the efforts regarding the economic and territorial conditions confined to "pressing on as quickly as possible". Balfour doubted, inter alios, that the economic and territorial conditions could be worked out quickly and stressed that if a preliminary peace should "cover the whole ground", it could first be ready for signature "some time after Wilson's return". Balfour also sent his draft-resolution to Lloyd George, who telephoned his consent 21. February 9.35 am. (Hankey to Lloyd George 20.2.19, LGP F 3/4/13. On Lloyd George's consent see also Hankey to Lloyd George 23.2.19, LGP f 23/4/22).—Jørgen Sevaldsen has kindly made the above discussed material available to me.

37. The following discussion of House's role in relation to the Russian policy of the Conference is based primarily on the following of the latest expositions of the Russian problem during the Peace Conference: Beatrice Farnsworth: William C. Bullitt and the Soviet Union, Bloomington and London, Indiana University Press, 1967; George F. Kennan: Russia and the West under Lenin and Stalin, New York and Toronto, Mentor Books, 1960; Christopher Lasch: The American Liberals and the Russian Revolution, New York and London, Columbia University Press, 1962; N. Gordon Levin, Jr.: Woodrow Wilson and World Politics, America's Response to War and Revolution, New York, Oxford University Press, 1968; Arno J. Mayer: Politics and Diplomacy of Peacemaking. Containment and Counterrevolution at Versailles, 1918–1919, London, Weidenfeld and Nicholson, 1968; John M. Thompson: Russia, Bolshevism and the Versailles Peace, Princeton, N. J., Princeton University Press, 1966; Richard H. Ullman: Anglo-Soviet Relations, 1917–1921. Britain and the Russian Civil War. November 1918—February 1920, Princeton, N. J., Princeton University Press, 1968; William Appleman Williams: American Russian Relations. 1781–1947, New York and Toronto, Rinehart and Co., 1952.—For a discussion of the background for Churchill's initiative see Thompson, p. 131–135 and Ullman, p. 117–120. Churchill travelled with the consent of Lloyd George (Ullman, p. 120).

38. PPC III, p. 1041–1043 and FR, Russia 1919, pp. 56–59.

39. Cf. note 37 above and see further Appendix I on Mayer and Levin.

40. See for instance Williams, op. cit., p. 162, Mayer, Politics . . ., pp. 20–21, Levin, op. cit. p. 190 and Kennan, Russia and the West, pp. 118–119.

41. See about this Levin's very comprehensive and convincing discussion: op. cit. 197–220, see also Williams op. cit., pp. 157–175 and Lasch, The American Liberals ..., p. 172.—Incidentally, Arno Mayer does not at all face this problem clearly, cf. Appendix I.

42. See for example Mayer, Politics ..., p. 329 and Levin, op. cit. pp. 197–210.

43. See about this Mayer's very comprehensive discussion of this element in American policy: Politics ..., pp. 17, 24–27, 261–281, and the references in connection with the Bullitt mission. See also Levin, op. cit., pp. 184–197. Levin goes as far as talking about a "proto-Marshall Plan tendency" in Wilson's policy (ibid. p. 191). See also Williams, op. cit., p. 159.

44. Wilson to Lansing 10.1.19. Wilson papers, Ser. 5 A.

45. See for example his remarks at the meeting of the Council of Ten 16.1.19. (PPC III, pp. 581–584 and 589–593) and 21.1.19. (ibid. p. 647–653 and 663–668).

46. Cf. note 5 and see below in connection with the Bullitt mission.—Also McCormick was a driving force. See McCormick diary, passim.

47. House to Norman Hapgood 6.1.19, cited in Thompson, op. cit. p. 97, omissions Thompson's. For a very early example of House's recommendation of this policy see House to Wilson 21.6.1918, Baker VIII, p. 225.

48. About the American liberals see Lasch, The American Liberals pp. 127–157, pp. 173–174 and 191–192, and Levin, op. cit. pp. 211–212. About the European Socialists see Mayer's two books, passim.

49. Cf. chapter 1, pp. 28–35.

50. ibid. pp. 28–35.

51. ibid. p. 34, see further Mayer, Politics ..., p. 379—About the Berne Conference ibid. pp. 373–409.

52. ibid. p. 384.

53. ibid. p. 384.

54. ibid. p. 387.

55. See Farnsworth, op. cit. pp. 3–31 and Mayer, Politics ..., passim, and cf. below in connection with the Bullitt mission.

56. Mayer, Politics ..., p. 387.

57. Levin, op. cit. p. 90.

58. Printed in Mayer, Politics ..., pp. 385–386 (Bullitt's italics). Bullitt was ordered to Berne on 29 January (ibid. p. 387).—It cannot be determined for sure that Wilson has seen the memorandum, but House certainly has.

59. Cf. above Chapter 1, p. 34.

60. Cf. above chapter 1, p. 34.

61. PPC XI, pp. 70–71.

62. ibid. pp. 115–116: Minutes of the Daily Meetings of the Commissioners Plenipotentiary, Thursday, March 13th, 1919.

63. He had only contempt for these meetings: "I spent much of the morning with the Commissioners ... It is the kind of work I dislike and I only do it in order to placate the other Commissioners". (House diary 28.1.19).

64. Cf. note 37.

65. About the Prinkipo-proposal see for example Kennan, Russia and the West, pp. 122–125; Ullman, op. cit. p. 99–135; Thompson, op. cit. pp. 82–130; Mayer, Politics ..., pp. 410–449; Levin, op. cit. pp. 206–218.

66. Mayer, Politics ..., p. 440, Thompson, op. cit. p. 111.

67. Thompson, op. cit. p. 111.

68. Lansing to Polk 11.2.19. Polk papers, Yale University Library, cf. Thompson p. 112.

69. Auchincloss to Polk 23.1.19. Auchincloss diary 23.1.19. Also in Polk papers, here it ends: "... evident from that fact".

70. Thompson, op. cit. pp. 111–112, with references.

71. House seems to have been rather jealous of Herron, for his views on Herron see House diary 27.1.19 and 12.5.19. About Herron see also Mitchell Pirie Briggs, George D. Herron and the European Settlement.—Neither Herron nor White was

Russian policy House initiated during Wilson's absence: see House
.3.19.

.g of the Council of Ten after Wilson's departure, at which Chur-
his proposal (15.2.19), House said, "that he had never been in
kipo proposal . . .". (PPC IV, p. 18 and FR, Russia, 1919, p. 65).
Balfour and Sonnino disclaimed any responsibility.
mission see below.
1 George 11.2.19 and Lloyd George to Kerr 12.2.19. (Jørgen Sevald-
ent me his transcripts of both letters). Kerr said about the American attitude that "I understand that House and Lansing are . . . not very keen on
it (Prinkipo proposal) I am also told that the President is now lukewarm, though
prepared to stand by his guns".

76. Lloyd George to Kerr 12.2.19 (Cf. note 75).
77. For the following see Ullman, op. cit. pp. 118–120.
78. ibid. p. 120.
79. PPC III, pp. 1041–1043 and FR, Russia, 1919, p. 56–59.
80. Kennan, Russia and the West, p. 125; cf. PPC IV, pp. 13–21 and FR, Russia, 1919, pp. 59–67.
81. PPC IV, pp. 13–21 and FR, Russia, 1919, p. 59–67.
82. Mayer, Politics . . ., p. 454.
83. Lansing to Wilson 15.2.19. Wilson papers, Ser. 5 A. The passage left out treats a telegram to Holland. House does not seem to have sent any telegram.
84. Thompson, op. cit. p. 140, with references. The memorandum reads (Auchincloss diary 16.2.19, also printed in Mayer, Politics . . ., pp. 454–455):
   "1. Don't say negotiations are broken off.
   2. Issue statement saying B's have not complied with conditions for meeting and have misinterpreted the Allies' Note.
   3. Allies will now make another statement to clear the issues.
      *What we will do if they come.*
   a. Don't want to interfere in Russia.
   b. Foreign loans, concessions, etc. are *not* our only interests in Russia.
   c. In favor of peasants having land.
   d. Want to be of service to Russia.
      *What we will do if they don't come.*
   (a) Conclude Russia does not want to join in world peace.
   (b) Will protect neighboring states from their *terrorist* armies.
      1. By sending forces to these states;
      2. Drawing an economic cordon around Russia.
   BUT
   We will at any time be ready to meet Russian Delegates when they inform us they are prepared to join with us in seeking peace and the free development of peoples under democratic principles".
85. Thompson, op. cit., p. 140. The amendment was a proposal from House "to send food and other supplies to Russia on condition that the Russian factions attend the proposed conference" (ibid.).
86. Auchincloss diary 17.2.19.
87. ibid.: quotation from the Herter-Auchincloss memorandum.
88. PPC XI, pp. 42–45.
89. National Archives, RG 256, Doc. no. 184.00101/14. This part of the minutes is left out in PPC XI, p. 43.
90. PPC XI, p. 44. See also "Memorandum for Mr. House", 17.2.19, Bliss papers.
   —It is interesting to note that Bliss here links up the with for an early peace with Germany, with the possibility of fighting Bolshevism. It is exactly the same argumentation we find by Foch.
91. ibid. p. 44–45.
92. About Lloyd George's intervention see Ullman, op. cit. pp. 124–127; Thompson, op. cit. pp. 141–143; and Mayer, Politics . . ., pp. 455–458. The discussion during

the meeting of 17.2. was so "acrimonious" that it was left out of the minutes, but see the several reconstructions: Thompson, op. cit. pp. 143–145; Mayer, Politics . . ., pp. 458–459 and Ullman, op. cit. pp. 127–128.

93. Ullman, op. cit. p. 127.
94. Thompson, op. cit. p. 141.
95. ibid. p. 144.
96. House to Wilson 17.2.19, no. 14, House Coll. 49/12. Also in Auchincloss diary 18.2.19 and Wilson papers, Ser. 5 A, here provisionally dated 19.2.19 probably because it was received at this date. Note also that the telegram was drawn up by Auchincloss: "Prepared by G. A. Approved by G. A."; and Lansing to Wilson 17.2.19 (received 18.2.19), FR, Russia, 1919, pp. 68–69, also in Wilson papers, Ser. 5 A.
97. Wilson to Ammission 19.2.19, FR, Russia, 1919, pp. 71–72, also in Wilson papers, Ser. 5 A., and with minor changes caused by the decoding in House Coll. 49/20 and Auchincloss diary 19.2.19.
98. ibid. See also Wilson to House 21.2.19. Wilson papers, Ser. 5 A. The date in the Wilson papers is provisionally given as 20.2., but the right one must be 21.2., because on this date the President received the memorandum about the conversation with Foch, which is mentioned later on in the telegram. (The telegram is found—with minor changes caused by the decoding—in House Coll. 49/20 and Auchincloss diary 24.2.19): "Hope you will be very plain and decided to the effect that we are not at war with Russia and will in no circumstances that we can now foresee take part in military operations there against the Russians. I do not at all understand why Churchill was allowed to come to Paris on such an errand after what Lloyd George had said with regard to the British sending troops to Russia. . . ." (quoted after Wilson papers).
99. Ammission to Wilson 23.2.19, FR, Russia, 1919, p. 73; also Wilson papers, Ser. 5 a.
100. National Archives, RG 256. Doc. no. 184.022/25: To: The President. Subject: Statement concerning the Bullitt-mission". 16.4.19. "Unfortunate" is again deleted from the text. Author unknown.
101. Cf. note 37, and see Appendix I for a further discussion of the views of Mayer and Levin.
102. The following is mainly based on Thompson's very detailed and well documented account (Thompson, op. cit., pp. 131–162).
103. Thompson, op. cit. p. 150.
104. ibid. p. 151.
105. ibid. p. 151.
106. ibid. p. 155.—Italics mine. The mission itself, on the contrary, "for information purposes solely" seems to have been decided by Lansing and House together on 16.2. But House apparently did not tell Lansing that Bullitt was intended to discuss peace terms with the Bolsheviks, cf. ibid. pp. 151–152 and 156.
107. For the following see Levin's discussion of the Bullitt-mission, Levin, op. cit. p. 213–220 and cf. Appendix I.
108. The result of the so-called Buckler-Litvinov conversations in January 1919. It is by comparing the proposal Bullitt brought back, with the result of the Buckler-Litvinov conversations, that Levin has reached his new interpretation. (Beatrice Farnsworth, op. cit. p. 192, n. 15, has made the same observation, but not drawn as far-reaching conclusions).
109. The Bullitt Mission to Russia. Testimony before the Committee on Foreign Relations United States Senate of William C. Bullitt, New York, B. W. Huebsch, 1919, p. 38.
110. "Taken all in all, the evidence suggests, that House and Bullitt were probably alone among the American Peace Commissioners in seeking to co-operate with the British in finding a *rapprochement* with the Soviets during February-March, 1919, on the basis of a *de facto* recognition of Lenin's regime in European Russia" (Levin, p. 215).—Mayer puts far less stress upon House's role in connection with the Bullitt-mission, he only talks about the Kerr-Bullitt proposal. (Mayer, Politics . . ., pp. 478–479).
111. Cf. note 41.

112. Thompson, op. cit. pp. 151–152.
113. The decision was made during a conversation between Lansing and House the 16.2., and House asked Bullitt 17.2. (ibid. pp. 151–152).
114. ibid. p. 152.
115. See especially Ullman, op. cit. pp. 124–128 and Lloyd George, The Truth about the Peace Treaties, I, pp. 370–77.
116. See especially Kerr's memorandum to Lloyd George 17.2.19 (The Truth, I, pp. 372–374) inter alios about a conversation with House; and Kerr to Lloyd George 18.2. 19 (Jørgen Sevaldsen has kindly lent me his transcript of this from the Lloyd George papers) about conversation with House; and further Kerr to House 21.2.19 (House Coll. 12/41) in which Kerr transmits the views of Lloyd George regarding Russia, and House's answer of 22.2. (House Coll. 11/55); see further House to Wilson 23.2. (House Coll. 49/12, handwritten attempt at transcription in Wilson papers, Ser. 5 A) which gives quotations from Kerr's letter; and Lloyd George to Kerr, 19.2.19 (The Truth, I, pp. 375–377).
117. The Truth, I, pp. 373–374, cf. note 116.—It is worth remembering that as Kerr himself was also interested in negotiations with the Bolsheviks, there is the possibility that his rendering of House's views were coloured by this fact.
118. The following is based on Kerr's report to Lloyd George the same day (18.2.) mentioned note 117.
119. Lloyd George to Kerr 19.2.19 (The Truth, I, pp. 375–377), quoted in Kerr to House 21.2.19 (House Coll. 12/41).
120. But he had probably got the answer by telephone already. (Cf. Kerr to Lloyd George 18.2.19). mentioned note 116): "Perhaps you (Lloyd George) would tell J. T. to telephone me (Kerr) on the subject".
121. Cf. note 114, see also Lasch, The American Liberals, pp. 187–188.
122. See also Levin, op. cit. pp. 212 and 214.
123. Levin, op. cit. p. 214, cf. ibid. p. 218: "In short, the Bullitt mission was probably doomed to failure from its inception, because both Bullitt and House had structured the mission around the mistaken assumption that Wilson's intention was to use a Prinkipo conference as a way to recognize a moderate Bolshevik regime in European Russia".
124. Farnsworth, op. cit. p. 37 with references. Se also Thompson, op. cit. p. 158: "Actually, it is doubtful if anyone, from Wilson and House down, ever considered the mission as anything more than an exploratory effort, with the possible exception of Bullitt himself . . .".
125. Cf. also note 111 and Levin, op. cit. p. 215.
126. As we have seen, not even Lansing was informed about the negotiation-aspect of the mission. Inter alia, when the designated Prinkipo-delegates George D. Herron and William Allen White went to see House on 1.3., he refused to discuss Russia with them (Lasch, The American Liberals, p. 187).
127. See more about this below pp. 185–187 and cf. especially Levin, op. cit. p. 215–218.
128. Levin, op. cit. p. 216–219, the diary quotation: House diary 19.9.18.
129. For the following see Thompson, op. cit. pp. 162–177.
130. ibid. p. 163, cf. "Bull. 4. For Secretary Lansing and Colonel House only". Dated "Petrograd, March 10th", sent Helsingfors 11.3. and received Paris 12.3. from which also the following has been taken. (FR, Russia, 1919, pp. 76–77).
131. Thompson, op. cit. pp. 167–169.
132. The telegram is "Bull. 5. For the President, Secretary Lansing and Colonel House only". Sent Helsingfors 16.3. 5 pm and received in Paris 17.3. 10.50 pm. FR, Russia, 1919, pp. 77–80.—Judging by the numbers: "Bull. 4", "Bull. 5", Bullitt did not send any other reports between 11 and 16 March.
133. Thompson, op. cit. p. 178.
134. House to Wilson 19.2.19, House Coll. 49/12 (also Wilson papers, Ser. 5 A). House transmits memorandum by the British Chief of Staff about conversation with Foch.
135. PPC IV, p. 56.

136. Cf. Thompson, op. cit. pp. 147–148.

137. ibid. p. 183, cf. PPC IV, pp. 121–125.

138. "Marshal Foch replied that what he had meant had been that the Preliminaries of Peace must be signed, and that could be done with Germany alone in a fortnight's time: and the same thing could be done as soon as possible with the other enemy countries. In other words, his plan would be to settle all the important outstanding questions on the Western side in order to enable the Allies to use the resources thus made available for the solution of the Eastern questions" (PPC IV, p. 122).

139. See further below.

140. PPC IV, pp. 123–124.

141. Bliss to Newton D. Baker 4.3.19. Bliss papers. See also Bliss to Newton D. Baker 3.4.19. Bliss papers.

142. ibid.

143. Bliss diary 26.2.19. Bliss papers, and, in a slightly different version, addressed to the American Peace Commission and dated February 26, as appendix to Bliss to Newton D. Baker 3.4.19, Bliss papers. This version is summarized in PPC XI, pp. 83–84.—The version in the diary has the form of a recommendation from the whole Commission, and it seems reasonable to assume that this is Bliss's draft of the telegram to the President (cf. further below).

144. PPC XI, pp. 83–84.

145. ibid. p. 83.

146. Bliss to Newton D. Baker 3.4.19. Bliss papers, cf. also Bliss diary 26.2.19, Bliss papers: "The foregoing memorandum was approved by Mr. Lansing and Mr. White but action by Mr. House was delayed so long that it (!) was unable to get the memorandum in the form of a telegram to the President before he sailed from the United States on March 5th on his return to France. The following draft of a telegram was therefore not sent".

147. Bliss to Newton D. Baker 3.4.19. Bliss papers. See also Bliss to Lansing 2.3.19. Bliss papers, where Bliss withdraws the telegram.

148. Paul Birdsall, Versailles Twenty Years After, passim. Cf. the discussion in the introduction and see below chapters 4 and 5.

149. Levin, op. cit. pp. 123–182.—It must not be overlooked, however, that the majority of examples on Wilson's "reintegrationist" approach is found during the first phase of the Conference, while the "punitive" aspects becomes more dominating during the last phase of the Conference.

150. Levin, op. cit. p. 136.

151. ibid.

152. Another possible parallel is the appeasement-policy: ". . . the problem of Germany's borders at the Paris Peace Conference contained in embryonic form many of the issues that would evolve into the full-grown appeasement debates of the 1930's, in which fear of Communism and fear of Germany would be dialectically intertwined" (Levin, p. 152).

153. Cf. also Levin, op. cit. p. 174: "In part, then, Lansing, Hoover, and Bliss became somewhat "isolationist" in their reactions to events at Paris, in that they sought to keep America free from entangling economic and political ties to the Allies".

154. House diary 17.2.19.

155. House diary 19.2.19. See also House to Wilson 19.2.19, no. 20. PC XI, p. 511.

156. Memorandum dated 18.2.19, in House's correspondance with Hankey. House Coll. 9/33.

157. House to Wilson 19.2.19, House Coll. 42/12, and Wilson papers, Ser. 5 A, 21.2.19.

158. House to Wilson 19.2.19, PC XI, p. 511.

159. Wilson to House, date uncertain, but possibly 21.2.19 (cf. note 158), Wilson papers, Ser. 5 A. The version in the House Collection (49/20) has a slightly different wording in a few points, probably because of the coding, but it in no way changes the meaning.

160. Hankey to House 19.2.19, House Coll. 9/33. It contains both the draft-resolution and a memorandum for Balfour with a view to the conversation with Clemenceau.

The documents are also found in House's correspondance with Balfour, House Coll. 2/24, cf. PC IV, p. 85.

161. House diary 19.2.19. Se also Auchincloss diary 19.2.19.

162. Lansing desk book 20.2.19 and 21.2.19.

163. See House diary 21.2.19: "This committee is a part of the plan to speed up things". Cf. also Auchincloss diary 21.2.19. Minutes of the meeting of the Committee is found in House Coll. 30/165.

164. House diary 21.2.19.

165. The minutes cited above, note 163.

166. ibid. Nelson has made a penetrating analysis of the different opinions in the two delegations regarding this question (Land and Power, p. 151).

167. The minutes cited above, note 163.

168. James Mason Burnett, Reparation at the Paris Conference, New York, Colombia Un. Press, 1940. p. 24. For a discussion of the problem of "War costs", see ibid. pp. 17–30.

169. McCormick diary 19.2.19.

170. Lansing, House, Baruch, Davis, McCormick to Wilson. Wilson papers, Ser. 5 A. The date is uncertain, in Wilson papers the date 15.2.19 is proposed but McCormick's diary shows, that it is rather the 19. or 20.2.19.

171. Wilson to Lansing 23.2.19. Burnett, pp. 613–614.

172. In the Council of Ten on 21.2. Balfour stated that he would circulate a resolution the same evening on, "the general conduct of business". PC IV, p. 67.

173. Auchincloss diary 22.2.19 and House diary 22.2.19.

174. Balfour referred to this on the meeting in the Council of Ten 22.2.19, PC IV, p. 86.

175. House to Wilson 23.2.19, no 3. PC XI, pp. 512–513, cf. also the discussion in the Ten 22.2.19, PC IV, pp. 85–97.

176. See the discussion PC IV, pp. 85–97.

177. PC IV, p. 85. For the following see partly the minutes of the Council of Ten 22. and 24.2.19. PC IV, pp. 85–97 and 101–107, partly the very penetrating analysis in Marston, pp. 137–150, cf. also House diary 22.2.19.

178. Auchincloss diary 22.2.19.

179. House diary 26.2.19.

180. "Brief Notes on the Present Conference Situation. By Mr. Balfour. February 25th, 1919". Transmitted to House 26.2.19. House papers.

181. House diary 22.2.19.

182. For an analysis of the British view see Nelson, p. 151.

183. House to Wilson 23.2.19, no. 3, PC XI, pp. 512–513, (received 25.2.19, Wilson papers, Ser. 5 A).

184 The diary gives no hint of House's reaction: I shall embody in a cable to the President our conversation, therefore, I will not repeat it here". House diary 22.2.19.

185. Bonsal writes, however, that House in a conversation with Bonsal 13.2.19 said: "The President has been so absorbed in his struggle for the Covenant that he does not fully appreciate the obstacles that still beset his path. Let me give you but one illustration. The President is unalterably opposed to the creation of the Rhenish Republic, and justly so, because if we acquiesced it would torpedo our doctrine of self-determination upon which the future of our better world depends. And yet if we close an eye but for a moment there it is—rearing its ugly head". (Unfinished Business, p. 53).

186. Wiseman writes about this: "Lunched with Mr. Balfour . . . Afterwards I stayed behind with Mr. Balfour, and he explained to me Clemenceau's view about an independent Republic on the Left bank of the Rhine. I am going to discuss this with House". Wiseman diary 7.2.19.

187. House diary 9.2.19.

188. House to Wilson 24.2.19. no. 4. PC XI, pp. 513–514, (received 25.2.19, Wilson papers, Ser. 5 A). In his diary House further elaborated the conversation: "This, of course, relieves that question of one of its most objectionable features since

otherwise it would be quite contrary to the policy of self-determination". House diary 23.2.19. IP IV, p. 357.

189. Cf. note 160. Auchincloss diary 24.2.19 shows that House received the telegram on this date.

190. Wilson to House 27.2.19, Wilson papers, Ser. 5 A. Auchincloss diary 28.2.19.

191. Mission 300, Benson to Opnav 20.2.19; Mission 304, Benson to Opnav 23.2.; Mission 306, Benson to Opnav 24.2.19; and House to Wilson no. 1, 23.2., received 25.2. All in Wilson papers, Ser. 5 A.

192. Auchincloss diary 5.11.18. Auchincloss was right in this, cf. Henry Wilson diary 9.11.18, quoted above in chapter 1, note 130.

193. Auchincloss diary 28.10.18; 29.10.18; 3.11.18; 4.11.18; 5.11.18; 8.11.18; 9.11.18; 12.11.18; 13.11.18; 30.11.18 and Polk to Auchincloss 3.12.18, Leland Harrison papers, Library of Congress, AC 9619, box 115.

194. Auchincloss diary 28.2.19, cf. Wharton to Close (Wilson's stenographer) 25.2.19. (Wilson papers, Ser. 5 A): "Rush very urgent. For Close. 25. February, 1919. Reference your service my one, two, three and four sent in special naval cipher. Naval Officer from Op. Nav. Should report to White House for duty as per arrangements. Suggest you telephone. Op. Nav. and reserve officer to report immediately. Wharton. EDWARD HOUSE". And Close's commentary: "The messages have been sent to Commander Ingersoll, Naval Communications, who is trying to decipher tham. G. F. C.".

195. Cf. above p. 124 and note 183.

196. Cf. above p. 124 and note 188. The section about the Rhine reads: "(2) Our territorial experts are in substantial agreement with the British and the French respecting the boundaries of Germany. Tardieu who since attack on Clemenceau has become more or less (omit) said to me yesterday that France would be willing to have the Rhenish republic set up only for a limited period of years, at the end of which the population would be permitted to decide for themselves what the future should be. He said that in this way (a breathing) space would be given us all (and France) would secure protection (until she) had recovered from the present war. The principle of self-determination would be in this way safeguarded". (Brackets in the original, showing doubtful passages in the transcription).

197. The House-Wilson correspondence, Wilson papers, Ser. 5 A, with several attempts of decoding.

198. Cf. above p. 120 and note 159.

199. In his article on "Woodrow Wilson's plans to enter the League of Nations through an executive agreement" (cf. chapter 4, note 63) Kurt Wimer also discusses this telegram (p. 804), in connection with his treatment of the negotiations regarding a preliminary peace treaty. He quotes Wilson to House 20.2.19: "I am not willing to have anything beyond the military and naval terms settled ... we should not risk being hurried", and House to Wilson 22.2.19 writing that "the entire terms should be given at once, and that the military terms should not be made now as at first planned", and then he (Wimer) writes: "Two days later a resolution was passed in the Council of Ten which went on record to include additional issues such as frontiers and economic and financial conditions in the preliminary treaty without mentioning the League of Nations by name. Wilson, obviously at a loss for an adequate explanation of these procedures, refrained from giving House further advice on this point, explaining to him that he was out of touch with his proceedings. It appears that the President counted on taking personal charge upon his return to Paris". Obviously, this is a possible interpretation, and it goes along fine with Ray Stannard Baker's stressing that it was "the dispatches from Colonel House that gave the President the first inkling of the course of affairs at Paris" (cf. chapter 4, pp. 164–165); on the other hand it is a fact, that there were *also* very real difficulties of decoding behind the President's reaction.

200. House diary 14.10.21.

201. Charles Seymour, End of a Friendship, American Heritage XIV, Aug. 1963, p. 9.

202. Tardieu, pp. 165–184. A translation is found in House Coll. 25/13.

203. Italics mine.
204. Tardieu discusses these pp. 184–188, but does not print them verbatim. They are not found in the translation in the House Collection.
205. After a conversation with Lloyd George and Clemenceau 7.3.19 House cabled Wilson: "The left bank of the Rhine was discussed, but no tentative agreement was reached because of Clemenceau's very unreasonable attitude. He wants the Reeinish Republics to be perpetually restrained from joining the German Federation. Tardieu tells me he will urge him to modify this view". (House Coll. 49/12, also Wilson papers, Ser. 5 A., 8.3.19) cf. also Nelson, p. 204: "Tardieu consistently pursued a more moderate line than did his chief".
206. "Brief Notes on the Present Conference Situation". 25.2.19., cf. note 181.
207. House to Wilson 26.2.19, PC XL, pp. 516–517. House does not seem to have made any comments.
208. House diary 27.2.19.
209. Birdsall, p. 203. Birdsall's last sentence alludes to Wilson's telegram 21.2.19.
210. Cf. Nelson, p. 209.
211. House diary 2.3.19. Auchincloss writes: "Returning to the Ritz at five-thirty I stopped at McCormicks room where the Colonel was having a conference with Tardieu and Aubert. They talked of the problem of the left bank of the Rhine and of Luxembourg. The Colonel urged that Luxembourg should be given to the Belgians". Auchincloss diary 2.3.19.
212. McCormick diary 2.3.19. Italics mine.
213. McCormick to R. S. Baker 16.7.28. R. S. Baker papers, Ser. I. Library of Congress.
214. Bliss to Lansing 26.12.18. PC I, pp. 297–298.
215. George F. Kennan, American Diplomacy 1900–1950, Chicago, Chicago Un. Press, 1951; Hans J. Morgenthau, In Defence of the National Interest, New York, 1951; Robert E. Osgood, Ideals and Self-Interest in America's Foreign Relations, Chicago, Chicago Un. Press, 1953; See further Appendix I.
216. Kennan, pp. 72–73 and Osgood pp.
217. See Mamatey, passim and especially Mayer, passim, and Appendix I.
218. Selig Adler, The Isolationist Impulse. Its Twentieth Century Reaction, London and New York, Abelard-Schuman, 1957, pp. 32–53.
219. Thomas F. Bailey, Wilson and the Peacemakers, Woodrow Wilson and the lost Peace, pp. 203–205. New York, The MacMillan Company, 1947.
220. ibid. p. 206, cf. further D. F. Flemings very penetrating analysis: "The United States and the League of Nations, New York and London, G. P. Putnam's Sons, 1932, pp. 153–171.
221. Fleming, p. 153.
222. This came out very clearly in Washington Post, 5.3.19, quoted in Fleming, p. 158. See also the following quotation from the resolution itself: "Resolved further, that it is the sense of the Senate that the negotiations on the part of the United States should immediately be directed to the utmost expedition of the urgent business of negotiating peace terms with Germany satisfactory to the United States and the nations with whom the United States is associated in the war against the German Government, and that the proposal for a League of Nations to insure the permanent peace of the world should be then taken up for careful and serious consideration". George Creel sees a direct connection between the Lodge-resolution and the development in Paris:
"A full report of this action (Lodge-resolution) was cabled to Europe, as a matter of course, and when the President arrived in Paris on March 14th, ten days later, he was quick to learn of the disastrous consequences. The Allies, eagerly accepting the orders of the Republican majority, had lost no time in repudiating the President and the solemn agreement that they had entered into with him. The League of Nations was now discarded and the plan adopted for a preliminary peace with Germany was based upon a frank division of the spoils, the reduction of Germany to a slave state, and the formation of a military alliance by the Allies for the purpose of guaranteeing the gains...". (George Creel: The War, The World

and Wilson, Harper and Brothers, New York and London, 1920, p. 205)—More about this later. See also Appendix II.

223. Quoted from Bailey, pp. 207–208.
224. Fleming p. 173.
225. House diary 14.2.19, IP IV, p. 326. See also Wilson to Tumulty 14.2.19, Wilson papers, Ser. 5 A.
226. House to Wilson 18.2.19, PC XL, p. 509. 25.2.19, House Coll. 49/12. Wilson papers, Ser. 5 A, 27.2.19, ibid. 27.2.19 House Coll. 49/12. 2.3.19, House Coll. 49/12, Wilson papers, Ser. 5 A, 4.3.19, PC XI, p. 521.
227. Except for one instance, which is discussed further below.
228. Copies of these daily reviews are found in the Bullitt papers, Yale. The author of the reviews of the French press was George Bernard Noble, who later wrote: Policies and Opinions at Paris, 1919. New York, The MacMillan Company, 1935.
229. Current Intelligence Division, American Section, Weekly Review, 16.2.19. Bullitt papers.
230. ibid. 23.2.19.
231. ibid. 2.3.19.
232. ibid. 7.3.19.
233. ibid. 9.3.19.
234. Great Britain, Daily Summary, 6.3.19. Bullitt papers. Italics mine.
235. ibid. 7.3.19.
236. ibid. 10.3.19.
237. ibid. 12.3.19.
238. ibid. 13.3.19.
239. Current Intelligence Summary—France. Weekly Review, 3.3.19, see also Noble, pp. 124–125.
240. ibid. 7.3.19.
241. ibid. 8.3.19.
242. Polk to Auchincloss 27.2.19 (telegram), Auchincloss diary 27.2.19.
243. Polk to Auchincloss 1.3.19 (telegram), Auchincloss diary 1.3.19.
244. Polk to Auchincloss 3.3.19 (letter) Polk papers. See also Polk to Lansing 3.3.19 (letter) ibid.
245. Polk to Lansing 18.3.19 (letter) Polk papers. See also Polk to Auchincloss 18.3.19 (telegram) ibid.
246. Morgan to Lamont 4.3.19 (telegram) Polk papers.
247. Morrow to Lamont 7.3.19 (telegram) Polk papers.
248. PC III, p. 230.
249. House diary 18.2.19. Cecil to House 25.2.19, House Coll. 4/38.
250. House diary 21.2.19 and 12.3.19.
251. PC IV, p. 85.
252. ibid. p. 96.
253. House diary 22.2.19.—Lansing did not vizualize the League of Nations Covenant included in the Preliminary Peace Treaty, see Lansing to Edward N. Smith 19.2.19, Lansing papers, Princeton University Library.
254. House calls the initiative "my idea" (House diary 27.2.19), and as no one else claims the copyright, it is possibly true.
255. Miller Diary I, 28.2.19, pp. 141–142.
256. House diary 27.2.19.
257. Auchincloss diary 27.2.19, Miller Diary I, 28.2.19, pp. 141–142.
258. House to Wilson 27.2.19, House Coll. 49/12, also Wilson papers, Ser. 5 A, received 28.2.19.
259. Auchincloss diary 27.2.19.
260. Miller Diary I, 28.2.19, p. 143. "Protocol of Agreement of Powers represented at the Conference at Paris. March 1919". Wiseman papers.
261. Italics mine.
262. Miller Diary I, 28.2.19, p. 143.

263. Auchincloss diary 28.2.19.
264. House diary 28.2.19.
265. Wilson to House 3.3.19, Wilson papers, Ser. 5 A, House Coll. 49/20. Auchincloss diary 4.3.19 shows, that the cable was received at this date.
266. House to Wilson 4.3.19, PC XI, p. 521.
267. House diary 3.3.19.—Both Mayer and Schwabe states, that at this time—the beginning of March—the Conference was shaken by signs of a coming "second revolution", i. e. a Bolshevik revolution in Germany, and they both relates House's pessimism to this situation (Mayer, Politics . . ., p. 501 and Schwabe, p. 344).
268. Lansing desk book 5.3.19.
269. Miller Diary I, 6.3.19, p. 154.
270. ibid.
271. "Memorandum for Mr. Auchincloss", 6.3.19, House Coll. 14/16. Miller, Drafting the Covenant I, p. 100.
272. The Drafting of the Covenant, I, p. 100: "I never heard anything more on the subject . . .".
273. Cf. above, p. 137.
274. Miller, The Drafting of the Covenant, I, pp. 92–93.
275. ibid. p. 98. The following quotation, which relates Baker's thesis is from IP IV, pp. 373–374. The discussion of Seymour's views is based on IP IV, pp. 373–391. In Seymour's reproduction of the correspondance between House and Balfour, Hankey's name is left out, but it is found in the original in House papers (Balfour to House 17.7.22, House Coll. 2/23). For Baker see the discussion in the following chapter.
276. House diary 14.2.19, IP IV, p. 341.
277. Cf. above, pp. 133 and 135.
278. Cf. below, p. 160.
279. See especially above p. 123.
280. Cf. above, p. 126.
281. Wickham Steed thus states, that House in a conversation on 6.3.19 inter alios said, that "(h)e was full of hope that, when he should meet the President at Brest, on March 13th, the work which had been done would receive full approval, and that matters would then go forward rapidly to a successful conclusion". Steed, Through Thirty Years, London, William Heinemann, Ltd., II, p. 291.
282. Cf. above note 273.
283. Steed, II, pp. 259–338.—It was during this period that Steed followed Dawson as Editor of the Times. Up till then he had been foreign Editor of the paper. Cf. The History of the Times, 1912–1920, I, London, The Office of the Times, 1952, pp. 361–393.
284. Cf. Auchincloss diary 29.3.19: "In reading over this diary it occurs to me that it would be very illuminating to have handy a file of the Daily Mail since January first. The editorials so often are part and parcel of my discussions with Steed that they would help one very much in understanding the sequence of events".—Se also IP III, p. 384.
285. History of the Times, I, p. 324. italics mine.
286. Auchincloss diary, passim. House diary, passim.—Characteristic for House's relation to Steed is thus the following diary entry: "My main drive now is for peace with Germany at the earliest possible moment, and I am determined that it shall come soon if it is within my power to force action. I have the Northcliffe Press at my disposal in this effort, and every day editorials and articles appear which have a tendancy (!) to frighten, persuade or coerce" (House diary 14.3.19). Two days later he relates, how Steed as usual came to him to get inspiration for his editorials in the Northcliffe papers. "I told him of our attitude on the League of Nations and assured him that there would be no delay because of it and that it was intended to make it a component part of the permanent peace. I also told him of Lloyd George's intended departure Thursday and asked him to do what he could to stop it. His editorials which will come out tomorrow will deal with this subject and I will attach them" (ibid. 16.3.19).

287. The first chapter of Steed's account of the Peace Conference (Through Thirty Years, II, pp. 259–294) is thus built up around House. He is seen as the predominant figure of the Conference, and he is constantly thrown into relief at the expense of Wilson: The problem of the organization of the Conference: If House had not fallen ill, he would have seen to it that the Conference had been organized much more effectively (pp. 264–266). (This was House's own interpretation, too). Wilson did not know—as House did—the European statesmen and their methods (p. 267).—If House had not been ill when the Prinkipo-decision was made, Wilson would probably not have made this (in Steed's opinion) mistake (p. 271). House was worried about Wilson's declining influence among the lesser powers—imply: because of the wrong tactics used by the President (pp. 273–274). Wilson did not treat the Republican Senators the way House had advocated (p. 284). House was "the ablest peacemaker at the Peace Conference" (p. 285). House's speeding-up attempt is seen as the only right thing to do in the situation (pp. 288–291). The controversy between Wilson and House after the President's return is seen as the second catastrophe of the Conference, the first being House's illness at the beginning of the negotiations (p. 292). It would have been better if Wilson had stayed in Washington and let House direct the American Delegation in Paris. (p. 292).—For Baker's account see the discussion in the following chapter.

288. Wiseman to House 12.12.19, House Coll. 20/48. The editorial was composed by Steed and Wiseman together (ibid.).

289. House to Steed 13.12.19, House Coll. 17/57, printed in History of the Times I, p. 415. Steed to House 5.1.20, House Coll. 17/57.

290. Steed to House 31.7.24, House Coll. 17/57. About the article in The Times on 7. April 1919 see further below in the following chapter.—Observ, too, how Steed very carefully avoids any mentioning of Auchincloss, who actually functioned as the link between House's thoughts and Steed's articles.

291. See especially Steed II, p. 284 about the episode just before Wilson's departure.

292. ibid. p. 293.

293. ibid. p. 284.

294. ibid. p. 289.

295. ibid. p. 291.

296. ibid. pp. 293–294.

297. It is naturally possible to argue, that Steed's demonstration of the two men's fundamentally contradictory conceptions is an after-rationalization, but this does not change the fact that Steed actually admits that during Wilson's absence, House was willing to separate the Covenant from the Treaty.

298. Cf. above p. 126.—In the following chapter we shall see that also Steed's other information: The role of Auchincloss and the fact that House was "condemned unheard", can be verified from other sources.

299. See further the discussion in the following chapter.

300. Reading (Nathan) to Wiseman 7.3.19, Wiseman papers.

301. Reading to Wiseman 10.3.19.: "I sent a report to the Prime Minister on the 9th explaining my views on the situation here". Wiseman papers. The references and quotations in the 'Comment on Despatch of March 10th" mentioned below corresponds very closely with Reading's telegram of 7.3.19, which, thus, must be identical with the telegram to Lloyd George, sent two days later. ("March 10th", because a telegram sent 9.3. would first be received 10.3.).

302. "Comment on Despatch of March 10th", Wiseman papers.

303. Miller Diary I, 11.3.19, pp. 162–163.—Of the Republican activities see further Appendix II.

304. More about this later.—Also the treaty of guarantee is in a way anticipated in the argumentation of the anonymous author.

305. Percy's memorandum is mentioned in Miller Diary I, 11.3.19, pp. 162–163 and in (Wiseman) to Cecil 11.3.19. Wiseman papers.

306. (Wiseman) to Cecil 11.3.19, Wiseman papers. Wiseman had discussed the matter with Miller beforehand. Miller Diary I, 11.3.19, pp. 162–163.

307. Wiseman to Reading 2.3.19. Wiseman papers.

308. These negotiations are often described, see for example Tillman, pp. 161–166. The question was, if Germany was to have a standing army of professional soldiers, or an army of conscripts. Lloyd George wanted the first thing, and won. Foch preferred the latter alternative. See also Jere Clemens King: Foch versus Clemenceau. France and German dismemberment, 1918–1919, Harvard University Press, Cambridge, Mass., 1960.

309. Conversation with Hankey, House diary 27.2.19.

310. House diary 3.3.19.

311. House diary 4.3.19.

312. House to Wilson 4.3.19, PC XI, p. 521.

313. ibid.

314. House diary 4.3.19.

315. House diary 4.3.19, IP IV, pp. 366–367.

316. "It always amuses me to have Lloyd George say in his *naive* way that he has done this or that or the other for political effect, but that he really knew better. He does not seem to have any ingrown sense of right or wrong, but only looks at things from the standpoint of expediency. He wishes to work with us and I am more than willing, for with all his faults, he is by birth, instinct and upbringing, a liberal". House diary 6.3.19.—italics House's.

317. ibid.

318. ibid.

319. PC IV, pp. 178–179.

320. "I was delighted at being able to postpone again the question of reparation, damage, cost of the war, or whatever term is to be applied to that question ... The matter is now postponed until after the President arrives and I think there will be no difficulty in postponing it until after the peace terms have been offered Germany, and then it will die a natural death. If this question had not been finessed out of being it might have cast serious differences in our councils". House diary 1.3.19. —Here we have, thus, another example of House's tendency to postpone controversial subjects.

321. Burnett I, p. 28: "By the end of the first week of March, 1919, it seems likely that pressure from the Allied delegations to include war costs claims in the Treaty no longer existed".

322. This section is based on Burnett I, pp. 47–50. For the situation in the first subcommission which treated the question of evaluation of damages, see Burnett I, pp. 31–36. Neither in this case was it possible to reach agreement. In this subcommission it was the French delegate Lebrun who proved to be the stumbling block, while the British representative, Lord Sumner, backed McCormick.

323. Tillman remarks rightly of the reparations negotiations: "On no issue at the Peace Conference did British and American policies conflict more directly and more fundamentally that on the question of reparations". (Tillman, p. 229–230).

324. House diary 6.3.19.

325. ibid. partly in IP IV, p. 367. See further about this in chapter 4, pp. 209–211.

326. ibid. partly in IP IV, p. 367. italics mine.

327. House diary 7.3.19, italics mine. Cf. also Auchincloss diary 7.3.19: "Apparently everything had been discussed and agreed upon".

328. Cf. Auchincloss to Polk 12.3.19 (letter) Polk papers: "The Colonel has, as usual, been holdning a lot of small conferences at which the real work has been done. If we were permitted to continue this method of procedure we would clean up this work in a very short time".

329. House to Wilson 7.3.19, House Coll. 49/12 and Wilson papers, Ser. 5 A.

330. "George said he could not sustain himself with his people if on question of priority all of this sum should go to France and Belgium for reparation. He suggested that it be apportioned as follows: three parts for reparation and two parts for costs of war. France, Belgium and all countries at war with Germany should participate in these two parts as well as Great Britain. I thought this proposal of George fair but there must be no demand on Germany inconsistent with our terms of armistice

with Germany and the fourteen points. Clemenceau seemed to think the proposal just, but reserved final judgment until he could consult his financial experts". ibid.

331. ibid.
332. Auchincloss to Polk 11.3.19 (telegram), Auchincloss diary 11.3.19, italics mine.
333. See also the section about the London Conference, chapter 2, pp. 76–82.
334. For the following see Zeine N. Zeine, The Struggle for Arab Independence, Beirut, Khayat's, 1960, pp. 45–83.
335. ibid. p. 47.
336. Memorandum 8.2.19, Wilson papers, Ser. 5 A. Wilson to Bliss 11.2.19, ibid. Bliss to Wilson 11.2.19, ibid., see also Zeine, pp. 69–70.
337. PC III, pp. 1015–1021, Zeine, pp. 69–71.
338. See Milner to Lloyd George 8.3.19. "You asked me last night what kind of compromise I thought possible . . .", Truth II, p. 1047.
339. House diary 7.3.19.—House did not mention this in the telegram to Wilson.
340. House to Wilson 7.3.19, House Coll. 49/12, Wilson papers, Ser. 5 A. About the naval negotiations see also Auchincloss diary 7.3.19, and Hankey to Auchincloss 7.3.19 with Hankey to Admiral Wemyss 7.3.19, House Coll. 9/33 and House diary 8.3.19.
341. Auchincloss diary 7.3.19.
342. Two accounts of the meeting are known, but they both have House as a source: His diary entry for 10.3.19; and the account Auchincloss set up immediately after the meeting on the basis of House's (verbal?) report. Auchincloss diary 10.3.19. Miller prints Auchincloss's account, Miller Diary VI, Doc. 489, pp. 316–317.
343. Auchincloss op. cit., Miller op. cit.
344. House diary op. cit.
345. Marston pp. 161–162. Marston, oddly enough, does not make any thorough analysis of the meeting of 10.3. (p. 161).
346. Hankey, p. 107.
347. ibid. pp. 97–106.
348. Cf. p. 100 above.
349. House diary 14.3.19. See also House diary 12.3.19: "I made an appointment for the President, Clemenceau and Lloyd George to meet here in my rooms at three on Friday, and to cut out the Quai d'Orsay meeting, which he (Clemenceau) readily promised to do. I have a regular program in mind which I outlined to Clemenceau and which he said was satisfactory to him. I thought it was best not to have Orlando at all the meetings but to let him come in only when the interest of the Italians wer(e) involved".
350. Miller op. cit., Auchincloss op. cit. House writes (diary 10.3.19): "We discussed the Syrian question at considerable length, but no agreement was arrived at. Clemenceau asked for more time. The French want all of Syria. George produced a map which Milner had prepared. This gave Lebanon to France, allowing Great Britain and the Arabs an outlet to the Mediterranean. Clemenceau did not like this, neither did he like the fact that the Milner line did not give the French the railroad running north (!) and south. He declared that Foch said this was necessary for strategic reasons. George replied that it was no more necessary for France than it was for the others. Clemenceau asked for time to consider it further".—For the further development of the Syrian question on the Peace Conference, see Nevakivi, pp. 126–171, and Evans, pp. 132–189. Evans, furthermore, puts forward this for the present thesis very interesting interpretation of House's attitude to the Syrian question during Wilson's absence (p. 134): "Throughout these discussions House had remained on the sidelines, letting the British and French leaders fight it out between themselves and intervening only to soothe ruffled feelings. He did not press the American point of view, that the settlement of the Syrian problem should be under the mandate system. He felt, in fact, that the injection of the League of Nations into the dispute would serve only to complicate and extend the problem. Wilson had succeeded in drawing the highly controversial subject of the disposal of conquered territory under the aegis of the League and thus within the reach of the United States. But

House had so conducted himself in the Conference that territorial disputes were being openly discussed in terms of the secret treaties, and Clemenceau was appealing to House to help him with the British in Syria because they were not keeping the promises they had made in the Sykes-Picot agreement. When Wilson returned to Paris on March 14th, "very militant", he was faced with the problem of re-establishing American Control over territorial questions. Syrian problems were shelved for a week as matters concerning the German settlement, which House had also dealt with after his own policy, were considered by the chief delegates, but on March 20, at the first regularly constituted Council of Four meeting, the Syrian question was the chief topic".

351. House diary 10.3.19.
352. Auchincloss, op. cit.; Miller, op. cit.
353. House diary 10.3.19.
354. Auchincloss, op. cit., Miller, op. cit. italics mine.
355. House diary 10.3.19.
356. Auchincloss, op. cit.; Miller, op. cit.
357. Auchincloss op. cit.; Miller op. cit., see also House diary 10.3.19, and IP IV, p. 370.
358. Auchincloss op. cit.; Miller op. cit., see also House diary 10.3.19.—Of this more below.
359. PC IV, pp. 295–311. Cf. Nelson pp. 210–211.
360. "A buffer zone, but not a buffer state, would exist". Nelson, p. 211.
361. PC IV, p. 300.
362. ibid., p. 304.
363. Marston, pp. 145–150.
364. Wilson to House 10.3.19., House Coll. 49/20, also Wilson papers, Ser. 5 A. From Auchincloss diary 11.3.19 is evident, that the telegram was received on this date.
365. Norman H. Davis, Peace Conference Notes, 5.7.19. Norman H. Davis papers, Library of Congress.
366. ibid. and Burnett I, pp. 54–55. Burnett's account is based on personal conversations with Norman Davis.
367. There are three sources to the meetings of this committee, which took place 11. and 12.3.19: Tardieu's rather retorical and antithetical account in La Paix, pp. 190–195; Mezes's very short and summarized memorandum on Kerr's and Tardieu's (but not his own) views, House Coll. 30/166 (In Wilson papers, Ser. 5 A this memorandum is wrongly placed under the date of 26.2.19—the date of Tardieu's memoire); and finally Kerr's very comprehensive account: "Notes of Discussion between Mr. P. H. Kerr, M. Tardieu and Dr. Mezes", Papers respecting Negotiations for an Anglo-French Pact. Cmd. 2169, London 1924, pp. 59–68.—For the following see also Nelson's discussion: Land and Power, pp. 212–218.
368. Only Papers respecting Negotiations for an Anglo-French Pact mentions this discussion (Nelson, pp. 165–166). The Polish report was presented on 19.3., but the content was known beforehand. About the negotiations in the Polish Committee see Nelson, pp. 145–175. Cf. furthermore Auchincloss to Polk 11.3.19 (telegram) in Auchincloss diary 11.3.19: "It is virtually agreed that Danzig shall go to Poland".
369. Tardieu, pp. 194–195. Tardieu states that he delivered these demands verbally and first presented his written proposal at the breakdown of the negotiations 12.3.19 (p. 193), while Kerr says that the document was on the table already 11.3. (Papers, p. 59 and Nelson, p. 212). Tardieu dates the document 12.3. But whether it was presented verbally or written at the beginning of the negotiations, it was the French proposal, which formed the basis of the discussion.
370. Mezes, op. cit.
371. Tardieu, p. 191.
372. Nelson, p. 214.
373. ibid. p. 213.
374. ibid.
375. Tardieu, p. 193. Nelson, p. 214.
376. Nelson, p. 215.

377. Mezes op. cit., Mezes's italics.
378. Nelson p. 218.
379. "In the first place he would not agree with them upon the question of the boundary of the Rhine and the creation of a Rhenish republic upon the terms they had in mind. He was willing to give them protection in other directions. For instance England would build a tunnel which would put English troops in France within forty-eight hours without having the vicissitudes of the sea to contend with. He would also be willing to say that in the event of an invasion, the British would come at once to the rescue, but he was not willing to maintain an army indefinitely at the Bridgeheads of the Rhine and to do the other things the French desired which we both agree will eventually lead to another war". House diary 12.3.19, partly in IP IV, p. 371.
380. During the conversation Lloyd George arranged to see Wilson the 14th at noon, i. e. immediately upon the President's arrival in Paris. House diary 12.3.19.
381. "He said the financial question was another difficulty. He thought the French were unfair. However, according to Davis, George is not living up to his promises to Clemenceau, that is, making the division three to two, with the French also participating in the two". House diary 12.3.19, partly IP IV, p. 371.
382. "Another difficulty is Syria. George declares the French are making troubles for themselves and war is sure to come if they insist upon their present plans". House diary 12.3.19, partly IP IV, p. 371.
383. House diary 12.3.19.—See further the discussion of this quotation in the section relating to the London Conference, chapter 2, p. xx.
384. House diary 12.3.19.
385. Tumulty to Wilson 13.3.19, Wilson papers, Ser. 5 A.
386. Reading to Wiseman 16.3.19. Wiseman papers.


*Chapter 4*

1. I–III, New York, Doubleday, Page and Co.
2. Chapter XVII, While Wilson Was Away, I, pp. 295–313.
3. ibid. p. 296.
4. ibid. p. 307.
5. ibid. pp. 306–307.
6. ibid. p. 307.
7. ibid. p. 308.—For further information on Tumulty's telegram see chapter 3 and note 385.
8. ibid. pp. 308–309.
9. Woodrow Wilson and Colonel House. A Personality Study, New York, Dover Publications, 1964 (1956), pp. 241–242, with references to the debate. The two authors have given the latest lengthy discussion of the "break" (Chapter XIII, the "Break"), and they are, after all, heavily influenced by Seymour.—Kurt Wimer has very rightly written that "(w)hile the dramatic presentation given by Ray Stannard Baker is primarily responsible for the belief in a "sidetrack" plot, a careful reading of Baker's articles reveal that too much has been read into his words". Baker actually wrote: "It is too much to say that there was a direct plot, ...". On Wimer's thesis with relation to an eventual preliminary peace treaty, see below note 63.
10. Robert C. Bannister, Jr., Ray Stannard Baker. The Mind and Thought of a Progressive, New Haven and London, Yale University Press, 1966, p. 201.—See also ibid. pp. 200–230 for Bannisters interesting description of how the book was written.
11. Ten Years of Peace Conference History. The Journal of Modern History I (1929), pp. 607–629.
12. Garden City, New York, Doubleday, Page and Company. Chapter V: What happened at Paris during the month that President Wilson was away.

13. It is not clear how closely Baker co-operated with Wilson and the people around him during the writing of the first book: Bannister tells us that Baker wrote to Wilson on 20.11.20 to get his permission "to look at all the records of the Peace Conference which Wilson possessed, *only some of which* he had used in preparing What Wilson Did at Paris" (p. 200, italics mine).
14. The War, The World and Wilson, New York and London, Harper and Brothers, 1920, p. 205.
15. R. S. Baker to George Creel 23.3.26, R. S. Baker papers, Ser. I, Library of Congress.
16. George Creel to R. S. Baker, 27.3.1926, ibid.
17. R. S. Baker to George Creel 29.3.1926, ibid. See also Baker to Creel 23.11.16, ibid. Here Baker, in connexion with a letter from Charles Seymour, repeats these references as representative of his own interpretation of the problem.
18. R. S. Baker to George Creel 22.12.26, ibid.
19. For a further analysis of this, especially with relation to Mayer's views, see appendix I.
20. Cf. chapter 3. p. 163, and see also Baker's description cited above.
21. For further information see appendix II.
22. Cf. chapter 3, pp. 148 and 163, on inter alia Tardieu's interviews to American newspapers.
23. Memoirs of Mrs. Woodrow Wilson, London, Putnam, 1939, pp. 293–294.
24. Especially in relation to place and timing. Internal contradictions particularly in relation to the League of Nations.
25. George and George, op. cit. p. 241 (italics G. and G.'s). The foregoing discussion of Mrs. Wilson's description is based on G. and G.'s analysis pp. 241–243 and pp. 344–345.
26. Mrs. Wilson, op. cit. p. 293.
27. In Seymour's version this was in both places given as the more polite "I said": IP IV, p. 401.
28. Auchincloss diary 19.3.19.—Auchincloss was in Brest together with House.
29. Lansing to Polk 14.3.19, this part of the letter was written 15.3.19. Polk papers, copy in Lansing papers, Princeton.—Lansing himself met Wilson at the station in Paris.
30. The fact that House writes nothing about what he himself told Wilson is not indicate of anything; he seldom did that.
31. Cf. chapter 3, pp. 161–162.
32. Cf. chapter 3, p. 160.
33. Cf. chapter 3, p. 161.
34. Frazier to Tardieu 13.3.19, House Coll. 18/34: "On the point of leaving for Brest, Colonel House directed me to acknowledge *receipt of your communication of Wednesday,* and to say that the enclosed letter would be handed to the President at the earliest opportunity. He also begged me to say that he too found the note of General Fayolle in regard to the left bank of the Rhine very interesting".—Italics mine. 12.3. was Wednesday.
35. Cf. chapter 3, pp. 126–130.
36. Auchincloss diary 14.3.19.
37. Lloyd George, Truth, I, p. 403.—Cf. Birdsall, op. cit. p. 207; Nelson, op. cit., p. 221; Yates, Louis A. R.: United States and French Security, 1917–1921, Twayne Publichers, New York, 1957, pp. 49–50.
38. House related it to "a moment of enthusiasm", House diary 27.3.19.
39. When Intimate Papers were published in 1926, Cary Grayson, Wilson's physician and a close friend of the family, wrote down his version of the House-Wilson relationship and the underlying causes of the break. This article was published posthumously in 1964 by Grayson's 3 sons as an answer to Charles Seymour's publication of a memorandum from 1938 of his last conversation with Colonel House (American Heritage XIV, August 1963): The Colonel's Folly and the President's Distress, American Heritage XV, Oct. 1964, pp. 4–7 and 94–101. Grayson's version is in all essentials concordant with Baker's and, when we remember

Grayson's close relations with the Wilson family, it seems reasonable to assume that this is the "official" version.

Elsewhere in the article Grayson wrote: "The rift between the two men came about primarily because Colonel House was willing to sacrifice, at least temporarily, that which Woodrow Wilson would not compromise (i. e. the inclusion of the league Covenant in the Peace Treaty)" (p. 95).

40. See also Steed's version of the events in the foregoing chapter pp. 143–146.
41. The Times, 14.3.19. The article is dated "Paris, March 13".—In this connexion it is probably worth remembering Steed's close relationship with both House and The Times.
42. Cf. the discussion in the foregoing chapter, and see also Marston, op. cit. pp. 137–150 for further analysis of the problems relating to the preliminary peace. See also below note 63.
43. Auchincloss diary 14.3.19.
44. Auchincloss diary 14.3.19, see also Miller diary I, 14.3.19, pp. 169–170.
45. Baker, Woodrow Wilson and World Settlement, I, p. 311.
46. See R. S. Baker to Wilson. Memorandum, 15.3.19. R. S. Baker papers, Ser. II, Library of Congress.
47. Baker notebook XXIV, 15.3.19. Italics mine.
48. The discussion in the United States in the following period essentially revolved about the question of possible changes in the League Covenant, cf. Current Intelligence Division, American Section, 16.3.19, 17.3.19, 18.3.19 (especially memorandum on the Legaue of Nations), 21.3.19 and 23.3.19. Bullitt papers.
49. Baker notebook 16.3.19.
50. Current Intelligence Summary, France, 14.3.19, 15.3.19 (Bullitt papers), and 17.3.19 (weekly review) (Henry White papers, Library of Congress).
51. Current Intelligence Summary, France, 17.3.19 (White papers), 18.3.19, French Opinion on the League of Nations, 19.3.19, 20.3.19, 24.3.19 (weekly review) (Bullitt papers).—See also Noble, Policies and Opinions at Paris, 1919, pp. 128–133.
52. For Pichon's interview see Baker's notebook 16.3.19, Cecil diary 16.3.19, Auchincloss diary 16.3.19, and Noble, op. cit. pp. 128–129. The British showed much more understanding of Wilson's position: Cecil made a public stand for Wilson on 18.3.19 (Noble op. cit. p. 130, cf. Cecil diary 18.3.19 and Miller diary I, 18.3.19, pp. 176–179 and Great Britain, Daily Report, March 19, 1919 (Bullitt papers); and on March 23, the author of the press reviews wrote: "So far as England is concerned, the President's case for the inclusion of the Covenant in the Peace Treaty may be considered as won" (Bullitt papers).—Lloyd George, however, tried for a while to make use of the situation (cf. Noble, op. cit. p. 130).
53. Auchincloss to Polk 20.3.19, Auchincloss diary 20.3.19.
54. Lansing desk book 21.3.19: "White, Bliss and I conferred. ... Expressed myself strongly that we ought to get on with Peace Treaty regardless of League of Nations. ... Peace is the *first* thing" (Italics Lansing's) and Lansing desk book 22.3.19: "Had talk with White in regard to present situation. We agreed that Prest's insistence on a complete plan of League of Nations, was causing a crisis, that things were going from bad to worse, and that unless something was done promptly the consequences might be terrible..."—See also House diary 24.3.19: cited below p. 184.
55. Marston, op. cit. pp. 156–157.—See also Marston's brilliant discussion of the very tangled problems relating to the concept of the preliminary peace treaty, ibid. pp. 137–165.
56. We also get a glimpse of Wilson's indecision from the following diary entry of House (House diary 16.3.19): "The President gave me a draft of the Military Terms and asked if I would not go over them and indicate which articles we had already agreed upon so that at tomorrows meeting he might confine himself to such articles as had not been acted upon. I pressed this action upon him the other day, when he was in the mood for reopening the terms from start to finish".
57. Auchincloss diary 15.3.19.

58. Quotations from PPC IV, pp. 374–375.—Cf. Marston, op. cit. pp. 154–158.
59. Lansing desk book 17.3.19.—Cf. Miller diary I, 17.3.19, pp. 175–176 and 18.3.19, p. 179, and Scott's and Miller's memorandum 18.3.19, Wilson papers, Ser. 5 A.
60. Thomas W. Gregory, the recently retired Attorney General, had arrived in Europe together with the President.
61. Miller diary I, 19.3.19, p. 192.
62. Cf. Marston, op. cit., p. 152–156.
63. In the article "Woodrow Wilson's plans to enter the League of Nations through an executive agreement" (Western Political Quarterly, XI (1958), pp. 800–812), Kurt Wimer advances—the interesting hypothesis, that Wilson—inspired by the procedure used by Theodore Roosevelt in making a treaty with the Dominican Republic —"contemplated concluding a preliminary peace treaty on his own authority". According to Wimer, he regarded such a preliminary treaty as an "exalted armistice" of only temporary duration. Its conditions would be repeated in the definitive peace treaty, which was to be placed before the Senate. "Presumably such a course of action would have made it difficult for Senators to withhold their consent, but in the event the Senate refused to approve the treaty, the League would have continued to function, provided only that an outright defeat of the treaty in the Senate could have been forestalled". "(T)he President's plan seems to have been to conclude as fast as possible a preliminary treaty with Germany which would contain as its core the military conditions of peace and the Covenant of the League of Nations". Wimer further emphasizes, that "(i)t appears that the key to an understanding of the position of Colonel House lies in his basic disagreement with the President over the manner in which a preliminary peace treaty was to be concluded. ... By ... bringing other than military problems close to a solution, he in practice made Wilson's plan all but impossible ... The President undoubtedly had expected House to carry out presidential policies during his absence and apparently never forgave him for substituting his opinions for those of the President and for allowing Wilson to be confronted with a *fait accompli* upon his return. Differences of such fundamental nature account for Wilson's abrupt withdrawal of his confidence from his most trusted adviser".—Wimer also stresses the close connexion with "the executive-legislative struggle in the United States", and emphasizes Baker's evidence in the matter. However, Wimer leaves several questions unanswered: He is evidently of the opinion that Wilson had planned his tactic *before* the election in November 1918 (p. 802); it is therefore rather remarkable that the initiative for a preliminary peace treaty in some form did not emanate from Wilson (cf. foregoing chapter p. 102). And further: If Wilson really had plans to slip the League of Nations in the back way, why did he then reject a similar initiative from House (cf. the foregoing chapter pp. 137–139)? Furthermore, it seems reasonable to assume that if the President was really following any long range planning in this matter, he would have analyzed the constitutional problems beforehand.
64. Lansing desk book 22.3.19, cf. also note 54.
65. On March 17 he had a personal conversation with the President. The subject matter is not indicated, but the meeting was of extremely short duration: "The President and I got through with our business in short order. We started at twelve and at twenty minutes after had completely finished" (House diary 17.3.19).
66. Cecil diary 16.3.19, Auchincloss diary 16.3.19.
67. Noble, op. cit. p. 132.
68. House himself was evidently relieved: "This has been one of the most fruitful days I have had for a long while. I determined this morning to give the President a talk which would bring some action. ...". House diary 24.3.19.—The following quotation ibid.
69. "... he (Wilson) did do it after a fashion; not as thoroughly as it should be but still ...". House diary 24.3.19. This development was rather the logical conclusion of an evolution House himself had been instrumental in furthering during Wilson's absence and also a justification of the top conferences, which had already become a habit after the return of the President. For the foregoing development, see the

previous chapter, pp. 156–157. See also Hankey, The Supreme Control, pp. 107–112. Hankey makes Lloyd George "the real originator of the plan" (p. 108).

70. Poul Mantoux, Les Délibérations du Conseil des Quatre, I, Éditions du Centre National de la Recherche Scientifique, Paris, 1955, p. 13.—It is naturally also possible that House used an account of the meeting when he dictated the diary entry. But we have no other indication of his knowing anything about the Mantoux minutes, so this hypothesis seems to lack plausibility. (One of the Mantoux minutes, the account of the meeting on April 4, 1919 is to be found in Wilson papers, but this meeting was not typical: Wilson was ill and not present).

71. Ibid. p. 14.

72. Ernest R. May: The World War and American Isolation. 1914–1917. Cambridge, Mass., Harvard University Press, 1959, p. 40. See also House diary 4.12.18.

73. For another interpretation see John M. Blum: Joe Tumulty and the Wilson Era, Boston, Houghton Mifflin, 1951, p. 181: "Wilson harassed at the council tables, intent on rescuing what he could of his grand vision, simply ignored the well-intentioned advice of his secretary, a reflection of American opinion. And trusting his chief to find the best way, Tumulty advised but did not interfere".

74. Just before he left in December Wilson told Tumulty: "I shall rely upon you to keep me in touch with the situation on this side of the water. I know I can trust you to give me an exact size-up of the situation here. Remember, I shall be far away and what I will want is a frank estimate from you of the state of puclic opinion on this side of the water. That is what I will find myself most in need of. When you think I am putting my foot in it, please say so frankly. I am afraid I shall not be able to rely upon much of the advice and suggestions I will get from the other end". Joseph P. Tumulty: Woodrow Wilson as I know him, London, William Heinemann, 1922, p. 341.

75. This correspondence is found in Wilson papers, Ser. 5 A, and part of it is in Tumulty, op. cit. Appendix A, B and C.

76. Tumulty to Wilson 13.3.19, Wilson papers, Ser. 5 A, cf. previous chapter note 385 and above notes 7 and 20.

77. Wilson to Tumulty, received 15.3.19, Tumulty, op. cit., p. 520.

78. Tumulty to Wilson 16.3.19, Wilson papers, Ser. 5 A, Tumulty, p. 520.

79. Wilson to Tumulty c. 17.3.19 (received 18.3.19), Wilson papers Ser. 5 A, Tumulty, p. 534.

80. Tumulty to Wilson 25.3.19, Wilson papers, Ser. 5 A, Tumulty, p. 521.

81. Ammission to Compub 27.3.19, Wilson papers, Ser. 5 A, also in Tumulty, p. 521. On the drawing up of this declaration, see further Baker notebook 27.3.19, Auchincloss diary 27.3.19 and House diary 27.3.19. House attributed the initiative to himself.—Obviously, the declaration was also aimed at the French press campaign, cf. above note 41, but the timing shows that the decisive element was the American situation.

82. Tumulty to Wilson 28.3.19. Wilson papers, Ser. 5 A.

83. Cf. pp. 203–204 and 208 and see also Appendix I.

84. Grayson to Tumulty "(c. April 20, 1919?)", Wilson papers, Ser. 5 A.

85. Wilson to Tumulty, 30.4.19, Wilson papers, Ser. 5 A; Grayson to Tumulty (c. 30.4.19) received 1.5.19, Wilson papers, Ser. 5 A, Tumulty, p. 545.

86. House alone supported Wilson.—On the Shantung decision and House's role see further below pp. 232–234.

87. Cf. previous chapter p. 148.

88. House diary 16.8.1918.

89. House diary 16.8.18 and 8.9.18.—They both joined House in supposing that Wilson was a candidate.

90. In a conversation with Henry Morgenthau on 25.3.19 House said, however, that he was of the opinion, that "W. W. should not run". Morgenthau diary 25.3.19.

91. Wesley M. Bagby: The road to normalcy. The presidential campaign and election of 1920. Baltimore, The Johns Hopkins Press, 1962 (paperback 1968), p. 54.

92. ibid. p. 54,—quotation ibid. p. 55.
93. Current Intelligence Division, American Section, 7.3.19, quoted previous chapter p. 133.
94. The letter is in Baker, Woodrow Wilson and World Settlement III, p. 174 (Document 19). Hitchock's letter was used in the discussions between Wilson, Cecil, House and Miller about the amendments, cf. Miller diary I, 16.3.19, p. 172.
95. Nevins, pp. 397–401.
96. Lamont to Morgan 13.3.19; Morrow to Lamont 14.3.19; Morgan to Lamont 14.3.19; Polk papers.
97. House diary 16.3.19 on the meeting the same day between Wilson, House and Cecil. Cecil also got the impression that Wilson did not want any changes in the Covenant because of the Republican Senators (Cecil diary 16.3.19). Wiseman, in his report to Lord Reading (17.3.19, Wiseman papers), also expressed the opinion that Wilson "has returned entirely confident and wishes to put through present draft without alteration".
98. Miller diary I, 18.3.19, pp. 180–188. House found Wilson "more reasonable than he was the other day", but all "found it nearly impossible to write what the Senate desires into the Covenant, and for reasons which are entirely sufficient. . . ." House diary 18.3.19.
99. Charles Seymour, End of a Friendship, American Heritage, XIV, Aug. 1963, p. 9. —Cf. previous chapter p. 126.—Stephen Bonsal, who was a member of the House entourage in Paris, however, rejected the rumours of an intrigue in a conversation with Lansing in 1921. (See above chapter 2, note 201).
100. House diary 10.3.24; George and George, p. 344.—In 1921 Lansing got the explanation from an "ex-senator and Democrat prominent in National Politics" that "the getting rid of House was all planned and carried through by Baruch, Morgenthau and some others very close to the President". The senator asserted, that he had been in Paris when it happened and had talked to Baruch who "said that House was a bad adviser and they were going to get rid of him". Lansing was very surprised over this version, especially since he himself was selected for the role of chief-adviser after House. However, because of the character of the source. he found no reason to doubt the authenticity. Lansing, Confidential Memorandum, 6.10.21, Lansing papers.
101. On the relation between the two see especially George and George, chapter 10, and Viereck, pp. 241–243 and 247 and 273–277.
102. See W. H. Buckler to G. Buckler 10.6.19. Buckler papers, Yale University Library; Henry Morgenthau diary 11.6.19, 23.6.19 and 25.6.19.
103. Baruch to Grayson 22.10.23; Baruch to Carter Glass 17.3.26, 22.9.26; Glass to Baruch 16.10.26; Baruch papers, Princeton University Library; and Baruch to R. S. Baker 15.10.28, R. S. Baker papers, Ser. I, Library of Congress; R. S. Baker to Baruch 19.10.28, Baruch papers.
104. Polk diary 16.7.19, Polk papers, see also Polk to Lansing 12.8.19, ibid. 78/12, and Lansing to Polk 26.7.19, ibid. copy in Princeton.
105. Cf. pp. 85, 97, 122 and 129.
106. McCormick diary 13.1.19, Cf. p. 85.
107. "Had an interesting talk in afternoon with Gordon Auchincloss. Most amusing to note anxiety of Colonel's outfit over daily meeting of Council of five great powers at which Lansing sits with President. Colonel and Gordon both think things cannot possibly go right without the Colonel's presence and guiding hand. These little human weaknesses make interesting studies during these momentous days. . . ." Mc. Cormick diary 29.1.19.
108. "Rode with Grayson and Buckler—usual nice chat. G. spoke very freely about House—that Auchincloss used to speak of Woody having no batting average this week as House was sick—but he would soon pick up as House was on the job again. Spoke disparagingly of WW even to V. M. (Vance McCormick) whenever things were accomplished he claims credit for House—when they went wrong, he'd ascribe it to House's absence and until W. W. felt that although so he wanted nothing

he was now claiming all the credit ...". Henry Morgenthau diary 25.6.19.—See also ibid. 6.5.19: "Called on V. McCormick in is room—talked 9.30 to 10.45 he told me of House inability to organize—and how they all worked together in 1917 —in London—Auchincloss to blame for House assertiveness here—H. broke up counsel of Ten when W. W. had Lansing at his side—H. uses only people he can order around—wants no strong men in power ... Got impression that V.does not admire House as much as formerly—and resents A. and H. not being quite loyal to W. W.

109. "Memorandum of a conversation with Vance C. McCormick" 15.7.28, R. S. Baker papers, Ser. I, Library of Congress. McCormick also "blamed" House and Auchincloss for the abolishment of the "Big Ten" and the establishment of the 'Big Four", see McCormick's conversation with Lansing 23.5.19 (McCormick diary 23.5. 19.) Lansing here argued that the initiative came from Lloyd George, who wanted to get rid of Lansing, and McCormick commented: "... my own guess is that Colonel House was largely instrumental in breaking up Council of Ten because it left him out and the Colonel could not bear it as he and Gordon have certainly been obsessed to be the whole show".

110. The quotation is taken from the account which Grayson wrote in 1926, (published 1964: American Heritage XV, Oct.) cf. note 39.

111. McCormick diary 16.3.19: "Went to have tea with Mrs. Wilson. President was there and we had a good talk over their American trip and things here in general. President seemed in good shape and ready for coming struggle".

112. McCormick diary 21.3.19: "Auchincloss told me President wanted me to go to Syria for him on errand. Don't believe I can get away just now. Looks to me as though House and Auchincloss fear I am interfering with some of their inside political manipulations. Hoover also probably involved. Don't believe I can get away just now". March 23 McCormick wrote Wilson, that he hoped it would not be necassary to go to Syria, because of his work at the Conference (Wilson papers, Ser. 5 A).

113. McCormick diary 23.3.19.—See also the quotation p. xxx and note 224. And Josephus Daniels diary 7.4.19; Library of Congress. Cronon, p. 385: "Dinner with B. Baruch. The more we saw of GB the more he felt that US was only nation that approached unselfishness and our best hope to protect the Peace of the World was a strong American Navy. Saw Vance McCormick. He and Baruch are doing very important work, and will compromise anything except principle and justice. Others here have compromised and shifted so long think frank statement sensational".—About this, the real cricis of the Conference, see further below.

114. Lansing desk book 23.3.19.

115. See for instance IP IV, p. 409: "The suggestion of an Anglo-American guarantee to France had been made by Lloyd George to House during Wilson's absence. It was repeated at the first meeting of the Premiers with the President on March 14. *House proceeded to define it,* and on March 20 took it to the French Prime Minister" (italics mine); Yates, Louis A. R.: United States and French Security, 1917–1921. Twayne Publishers, New York, 1957, p. 50: "House was *instructed* to devote his attention to working out a presentable idea for a joint guarantee" (italics mine).

116. Birdsall, Versailles ..., pp. 209–210, Yates, op. cit. pp. 53–56 and 74.

117. Land and Power, pp. 228–232, the quotation p. 228, italics mine.—Nelson argues as follows: Lloyd George got Wilson's agreement to the treaty of guarante 14.3., and the same day the plan was laid before Clemenceau, who considered it for three days, and then answered in writing (17.3.). In his reply, Clemenceau accepted the Anglo-American proposition, but demanded further guarantees such as bridgeheads, the establishment of a demilitarized zone, etc. However, although this meant, that France had given up the demand for a separate Rhenish Republic, these new demands were not acceptable to Wilson and Lloyd George, and a new round of negotiations was initiated (pp. 220–222). On March 19 House discussed the question of a treaty of guarantee with his three colleagues, *as if the proposition had*

*come from Clemenceau*. "Was House misleading them or was he himself ill-informed?" asks Nelson (pp. 228–229). In the following days House made several treaty-drafts, which he discussed with Clemenceau, Lloyd George and Balfour, and with his three colleagues. The first three mentioned were very favourably inclined, the last three absolutely negative. On March 20, House received from Tardieu a review of the French demands and on the basis of this David Hunter Miller, William Wiseman and Gordon Auchincloss draw up a memorandum, and after further discussion Auchincloss draw up *a plan, that left out the guarantee-proposal*. This plan got the approval of both Wilson and the three other Commissioners (24.3.). On March 27, however, House learned to his great surprise, that Wilson was, *in addition to this,* prepared to give a treaty of guarantee to France. Nelson therefore concludes, that House in the period between 14.3. and 27.3. did not know that the President had accepted an Anglo-American guarantee of French security (pp. 229–232).

118. Tardieu, La Paix, p. 225.
119. House diary 14.3.19; Auchincloss diary 14.3.19.
120. Auchincloss learned in a conversation with Tardieu on March 16, that "Clemenceau was sending an important document to the President in the morning", and Auchincloss saw to it that House got a copy (Auchincloss diary 16.3.19). Cf. Clemenceau to House 17.3.19. House Coll. 5/4, and "Note sur la Suggestion présentée le 14 Mars", House Coll. 30/168, English translation ibid. See also Clemenceau to Wilson 17.3.19 and "Note sur la Suggestion présentée le 14 Mars", Wilson papers, Ser. 5 A. The note is in Tardieu, La Paix, pp. 197–200. Here we thus have a clear indication that the Wilson–House relationship was broken: House could not be sure that the President would show him the note, and instead got hold of it directly from its author.
121. The English translation runs: "The suggestion presented on March 14th, by the terms of which Great Britain and the United States would bind themselves to bring to France without delay in case of a German aggression, the help of their military forces . . .". (House Coll. 30/168).
122. House diary 12.3.19, cf. previous chapter note 362.
123. House diary 17.3.19.
124. Present were Mr. and Mrs. Wilson and Wilsons two daughters, Robert Cecil, House and Mrs. House, and Dr. Grayson.
125. Cecil diary 18.3.19.
126. See also above about the blocking of the Pichon-interview.
127. Auchincloss diary 19.3.19.
128. Minutes of the Daily Meetings of the Commissioners Plenipotentiary, Thursday, March 20th (Wednesday, March 19th), 1919. PPC XI, pp. 124–125; Lansing desk book 19.3.19; Miller diary I, 19.3.19, pp. 189–190.
129. PPC XI, pp. 124–125. Lansing described it thus: "House came in and said he had just seen Clemenceau who insisted that provision should be made in Covenant to defend France from German attack in future, that Lloyd George had agreed GB would do so, and that he wished US to do the same". (Lansing desk book 19.3.19). Miller illuminates another line of House's argument: ". . . Colonel House had come, and described his interview with Clemenceau, in which Clemenceau said the British were not treating them right, particularly in Syria, and that he wanted some protection from the United States, upon which the French would give up their claims to a buffer state on the left bank of the Rhine. . . .". (Miller diary I, 19.3.19, pp. 189–190).
130. House diary 20.3.19, partly in IP IV, p. 409, italics mine; See also Auchincloss diary 20.3.19. Seymour gives one of the drafts (IP IV, p. 410), see also Auchincloss diary 20.3.19; House diary 20.3.19; House Coll. 30/184 and 2/24, and Wiseman papers and Wilson papers for different drafts. The drafting was preceded by discussions between House, Auchincloss and Miller. (Auchincloss diary 19.3.19 and Miller diary I, 19.3.19, p. 191). Both Miller and Auchincloss were sceptical.
131. Nelson (p. 229) rightly stresses the above quotation as an example of "The compromising nature of Colonel House", but his conclusion: ". . . to reach agreement

on the Rhineland question at any price he was willing in effect partially to mislead Clemenceau", is only half the truth. More to the point is the following remark by House himself: "Tardieu was sent by Clemenceau to find if there was anything new in regard to the security of France which I have undertaken to champion" (House diary 22.3.19).

132. PPCXI, p. 126, see also Lansing desk book 20.3.19: "House sent in proposed declaration of alliance between United States, Great Britain and France for protection of France and Belgium from invasion by Germany. Our opinion is that it would make the League of Nations an almost academic affair. My own view is that France would adhere to League if it got this separate agreement. It is a dangerous document....". The following day, 21.3., the Commissioners rejected the project even more sharply: "They all expressed themselves very strongly against the principle involved in concluding such an agreement, and felt that the whole structure of the League of Nations would be most seriously compromised thereby. ... The Commissioners felt that it was most essential that they should discuss the whole situation with the President in the very near future" (PPC XL, p. 130). The amendment proposed by the Commissioners (20.3.) is found in Tasker H. Bliss Papers, Box 69. It is followed by a handwritten note, in which Bliss states, that neither Lansing, White nor Bliss himself "approve this draft or anything like it. It will surely kill the League of Nations Covenant".

133. Cf. note 120.

134. Memorandum, no name, no date in Wiseman papers, but internal evidence shows that it is set up in connexion with the negotiations related below between Wiseman, Auchincloss and Miller.

135. Tardieu to House 21.3.19. House Coll. 18/34: "Herewith enclosed find a note summing up the different clauses which were proposed during the last days conversations. I have thought that such a memorandum could be of use". Tardieu's memorandum must be the same as "Note for Colonel House" in Wilson papers, Ser. 5 A (provisionally dated "(March 14?)1919)". The note is as follows:

*"Note for Colonel House*

A. Because of the havoc which Germany has brought upon the world by her attack upon France and Belgium in 1914, and in order to prevent as far as possible such another disaster to humanity, we (!) hereby solemnly pledge to one another our immediate military, financial, economic and moral support of and to one another in the event Germany should at any time make a like unprovoked and unwarranted attack against either one or more of the subcribing Powers.

To this effect:

1.—In the zone delimited by a line running 50 kilometers East of the Rhine, Germany will maintain neither military forces nor a military organization; will neither maintain nor construct fortifications; nor will Germany manufacture any war material.

2.—A Franco-Anglo-American Commission shall have the (!) right to verify on the ground that these engagements are fulfilled.

3.—The entry or attempted entry of all or part of the German army in the zone delimited by Article 1, will be considered an act of agression.

4.—If the Commission provided by Article 2. discovers a violation by Germany of the engagements of Article 1, or of the military, aerial and naval Peace clauses, France will have the right to occupy the line of the Rhine with the bridge-heads necessary for the defence of this (!) line.

B. The League of Nations approves the above stated engagement subscribed in the interest of the general Peace, the maintenance of which will be the essential aim of the League.

C. France is entitled to her 1814 frontier, with a right of occupation, without annexation, of that part of the mine basin of the Sarre not included in this frontier. The regime to be established in the occupied zone will be the subject of a special agreement".

Their working basis does not seem to have been the Tardieu-note itself, but a so called "Exhibit A", identical with points 1–4 of the note. It seems reasonable to assume that it was a draft House had received earlier, because there are some—in no way significant differences: See "Clemenceau's proposal to House, March 20", Wiseman papers, and ibid. the same text, but named "A" accompanying a copy of Auchincloss's memorandum (more about this later); and "the paper handed Colonel House by M. Tardieu" marked "Exibit A" in Auchincloss diary 21.3.19 and same in House Coll. 30/184. As a basis of discussion they also used a draft by House of a guarantee similar to point A in Tardieu's note quoted above (cf. Miller diary I, 21.3.19, p. 195; Wiseman papers; Auchincloss diary 21.3.19; House Coll. 30/184).

136. Miller to Lamont 19.3.19, The Drafting of the Covenant I, pp. 300–301. The letter was an answer to a letter from Lamont, giving the views of Senator Elihu Root. See also Auchincloss diary 21., 22. and 27.3.19 and Miller diary I, 21. and 22.3.19, pp. 195–196.

137. Auchincloss diary 21.3.19, cf. Miller diary I, 21.3.19, p. 195.

138. A policy with which Miller himself did not sympathize, cf. the letter to Lamont.

139. Miller's memorandum "The Left Bank of the Rhine" dated 21.3.19 is found in Wiseman papers and in House Coll. 20/48. Auchincloss's memorandum: "The French demand some physical protection..." in Auchincloss diary 21.3.19; Wiseman papers; House Coll. 30/184; and Wilson papers, Ser. 5 A, under the date 23(?).3.19. Tardieu's point 2: the demand for inspection was left out of Millers draft, and only provisionally included in Auchincloss's: "If is thought best this provision can be left out...".

140. "Whether or not it will be acceptable to the French I do not know but the Colonel thought well of it and so did the British representatives to whom he talked. It is not as much as the Colonel has led the French to believe they would get but it may be sufficient" (Auchincloss diary 21.3.19).

141. House diary 24.3.19.—It is not evident from the diary when House brought the matter before the other Commissioners, but we can see that it happened before the conversation with Wilson 24.3., and there are no minutes of meetings of the Commissioners between 22.3. and 27.3.

142. Auchincloss diary 22.3.19, italics mine. Miller wasn't enthusiastic either: "Chatted with Colonel House a moment about the French proposition on the Rhine and told him of my feelings against it, ...". Miller diary I, 22.3.19, p. 196.

143. House diary 22.3.19. The continuation of the quotation shows clearly that House, like all others, was being grasped by the feeling of crisis and frustration over not knowing what happened or, indeed, if anything happened at all: "... Lloyd George never does anything until the crisis is upon him, then he moves swiftly. From the look of the things the crisis will soon be here. I hear rumblings of discontent every day. The people want peace. Bolshevism is gaining ground everywhere. Hungary has just succumbed. We are sitting upon an open powder magazine and some day a spark may ignite it. I feel too that the President's prestige is trembling in the balance and that his future place in history is in jeopardy. He is taking terrible chances... frittering away his time and opportunity. If the world were not in such a fluid state I should not object to matters going as deliberately as they have been going, but under present conditions, I cannot but feel that we are gambling each day with the situation".

144. House diary 24.3.19.

145. Nelson is of the opinion that Wilson "appears to have accepted it" (p. 231), but the diary gives no indication of the President's reaction.

146. Notes of a Conversation between Signor Orlando and Colonel House, at 10 o'clock, Hotel de Crillon, on the morning of the 26th March, 1919. House Coll. 29/31.—About the guarantee: "Colonel House stated that M. Clemenceau no longer insisted that a buffer state should be created on the left bank of the Rhine on condition that a treaty be negotiated between France and the Allies stipulating that the latter should come to France's assistance in case she were (!) invaded.
Signor Orlando's comment was that this would be in contradiction with the League

of Nations. Colonel House quite agreed; they were trying, he said, to find a compromise by which Germany would be prohibited by the Treaty of Peace from either maintaining troops on the Western bank of the Rhine or from sending any troops into that territory; the mere fact of such an introduction of troops to be construed as an act of war".

147. House diary 27.3.19.—The conversation took place on the evening of 26.3. after the meeting in the League of Nations Commission and lasted only a few minutes ("I had a few minutes talk with the President..."). The memorandum referred to is the one Auchincloss quoted (22.3.), cf. IP IV, p. 410). Evidently in the light of his conversation with Orlando, House was now warning Wilson against such a treaty: "I told him among other things that I thought it would be looked upon as a direct below at the League of Nations.... I did not shake him for in a moment of enthusiasm he committed himself to Clemenceau and he does not wish to withdraw his promise, a position which I thoroughly commend (partly in IP IV, p. 410). See also Auchincloss's account (Auchincloss diary 26.3.19): "Tardieu and Clemenceau are very much concerned at the slow progress made in the settlement of the left bank of the Rhine matter. *In the evening the Colonel took this matter up with the President and the President seemed willing to go to the full extent of the Colonel's first suggestion which was a defensive alliance between England, France and the United States against Germany.* I have always felt that this seriously injured the successful working out of the League of Nations. *The President only had a minute with the Colonel on this matter but did not seem to raise any objection to it.* The Colonel told me to see Tardieu in the evening and tell him what progress we had made but as I could not find him I had to defer saying anything about it until tomorrow morning". Italics mine.—Neither House nor Auchincloss apparently knew, then, anything about Wilson's original promise to Clemenceau, and Auchincloss still did not know, he still believed the initiative to be House's.

148. "Proposal. Stipulations to be embodied in the Treaty. 28. Mars. 1919". With the handwritten endorsement "Proposition initiale de Président Wilson", Wilson papers, Ser. 5 A. (French text, Tardieu, La Paix, p. 150). Wilson's guarantee proposal was: "In a separate treaty with the United States:
4. A pledge by the United States; subject to the approval of the executive Council of the League of Nations, to come immediately to the assistance of France so soon as any unprovoked movement of aggression against her is made by Germany,—the pledge to continue until it is agreed by the contracting powers that the League itself affords sufficient protection".
Evidently miles apart from House's "Because of the havoc..."-proposal. Wilson himself, also left out the inspection-paragraph.

149. House diary 24.3.19.

150. Later on, House was evidently willing to accept more exotic tasks: On May 30, he had a conversation with Pessoa, the Brazilian President, and wrote afterwards in his diary: "He bade me goodbye, and gladly accepted my offer to unofficially advise Brazil".

151. House diary 14.3.19: The relationships between House and Steed, and especially between Auchincloss and Steed are treated more thoroughly below.—House was, indeed, showing himself much more in the open, also his treatment of the press. On March 20 he wrote in his diary: "I see the American correspondents every day at six o'clock. I talk freely to them, and they get from me practically all the news of the conference that they get at all. I am sure the President does not approve of my giving our public as much information as I do, but I shall continue until he protests, and then we will have it out together....".

152. House diary 14.5.19.

153. House diary 25.3.19.—For literature on Russia see the previous chapter, note 37. Especially Thompson's detailed discussion (pp. 222–267) has been very useful.

154. House diary 26.3.19.—Cf. "Notes of a Conversation between Signor Orlando and Colonel House". 26.3.19, House Coll. 29/31.

155. Cf. the discussion in the foregoing chapter pp.112–115.

156. Lansing, White and Bliss reacted negatively already on Bullitt's written report (Lansing desk book 19.3.19).

157. Both Gordon Auchincloss and David Hunter Miller, whom House put on the job of working on his plan, were negative towards the project, see Thompson, pp. 234, 236–239.

158. House diary 27.3.19.—The quotation in toto is: "I have taken up actively with the President today the Russian Question. I am trying to think something out that is workable. It is very difficult because no one wanted to deal with such as Lenine and Trotsky. The President suggested that I talk to Hoover and Robinson of the Shipping board and see whether we could get ships and food to Russia in the event we wished to do so. Hoover thought we could, Robinson thought that it would be sixty to ninety days before anything effective could be done".

159. House diary 26.3.19.—Wilson did not want to see Bullitt either, cf. The Bullitt Mission to Russia, pp. 73–74.

160. Cf. note 134.

161. For the fate of this plan, see for instance Thompson, op. cit. pp. 247–267; and Mayer, Politics . . ., pp. 474–487.

162. The Bullitt Mission to Russia, p. 73.

163. For the following discussion see Thompson, pp. 230–233.—McCormick was the leader of the War Trade Board, under which the Russian Bureau belonged, and accordingly he was not a mere Mr. Nobody in Russian matters.

164. "Memorandum for the President", 26.3.19, Wilson papers, Ser. 5 A, Cf. Thompson, p. 232.

165. Thompson, pp. 232–233.

166. Mayer, Politics . . ., p. 474. Mayer's source is the following information given by Hoover (Herbert Hoover: The Ordeal of Woodrow Wilson, New York, McGraw-Hill, 1958, p. 117): "On March 26, after the President's return to Paris, he asked for a memorandum on my information and opinion on the Soviet problem. . . .".

167. Quoted in toto in Mayer, Politics . . ., pp. 474–478.

168. House diary 26.3.19.

169. Thompson gives three possible explanations of the fact that House gave up his original plan on March 27: 1) The opposition from Miller and Auchincloss (Lasch means this is the determining factor, The American Liberals, p. 195); 2) Steed's editorial in the Daily Mail; and 3) "Finally, it is possible that Wilson himself put a damper on House's plans" (p. 238–239). As shown, I am of the opinion that this explanation is the correct one. See also Beatrice Farnsworth, op. cit. p. 51.

170. The House diary mentions conversations with Norman Davis about the reparations negotiations 16.3. and 18.3., with Balfour 16.3. and with Wiseman 17.3. Also Auchincloss had contacts with the economic experts during this period: Cf. Auchincloss diary 14.3., 18.3., 19.3. (Auchincloss to Polk 19.3.19), 22.3.—See too note 191.

171. Both quotations: House diary 24.3.19. House in this connection said only what the experts themselves considered reasonable. Cf. Norman H. Davis, "Peace Conference Notes", 5.7.19, Davis papers, Library of Congress: "Although Mr. Lamont was more optimistic than myself as to Germany's reasonable capacity to pay, he did not feel that she should be called upon to pay over 35 billion dollars as a maximum, and even then that half of this should be paid in German currency at the par of exchange". In the following days, the close contact between House and the economic experts continued: Cf. House diary 25.3.19, 29.3., 1.4., 4.4., and Auchincloss diary 25.3., 26.3., 28.3., 29.3., 4.4.

172. House did not attend the very important conference 1.4. between Wilson, Baruch, Davis, Lamont, McCormick and Dulles about the inclusion of pensions. See "Memorandum of Conference had at President Wilson's Hotel, Paris, April 1, 1919, at 2 pm (by Vance McCormick)", R. S. Baker papers, Ser. I.—Cf. Burnett I, p. 64 and Document 210, 211, pp. 775–777 (the author is given here as Foster Dulles), and see Mc.Cormick diary 1.4.19. On Smuts's role in this matter see George Curry: Woodrow Wilson, Jan Smuts and the Versailles Settlement, AHR, 66, 1961, pp. 968–986, and see "Note on Reparation" by J. C. Smuts, 31.3.19, Wilson papers, Ser. 5 A.

173. Wilson in this matter went straight against the advice of his experts and they were greatly disappointed, cf. Burnett I, p. 64. Burnett (and with him Birdsall (p. 252)) stresses, though, that even if the American experts thought the inclusion of pensions a violation of the spirit of the Pre-Armistice-Agreement, they did not think that the result, in reality, would mean anymore than a changed apportionment among the Allies, because they still took for granted, that there would be a time limit on the reparations payments (pp. 64–65). Cf. Norman H. Davis, "Peace Conference Notes", 5.7.19, Davis Papers. It was only after the giving up also, of the time limit, (5.4.), that the real effect of the inclusion of pensions became evident.—But, in my opinion, it does not alter the fact that Wilson had started down the road of compromise already before the advent of House.

174. For a good summary of the development of the negotiations from Wilson's return to the crisis in April, see Burnett I, pp. 51 77.

175. The French policy was motivated by the wish to weaken Germany, while the English policy was more narrowly determined by the overhasty promises made by Lloyd George during the election campaign. But domestic political pressure was as real on both governments.

176. See for instance Polk to Auchincloss 18.3.19. Polk papers 82/21: "The American people are rather vague on the subject of reparation. They expect Germany to pay but have not thought out the question as to how much or when. There is a strong feeling that we should withdraw from all further foreign contact which may complicate question of compelling Germany to meet her future obligations. The sentiment is generally against putting too heavy a load on Germany". The Americans never accepted the Allied attempts to link the German repations payments to the Allies and the Allied war debts to the United States. (See for instance Davis to Baruch 10.7.1920, Davis papers).—See also Tumulty to Wilson 9.4.19; Wilson papers, Ser. 5 A: "A great number of your friends here fear that the interposition US in matter of indemnity and reparation which is a paramount question with European nations and only of indirect interest of US will solidify the opposition of England, France, Italy and Belgium of a league of nations. Our friends believe that any necessary sacrifice to assure a league of nations should be made. Your supporters would be happy if you could throw upon the other nations the burden of exacting indemnities, and at the same time win their support of a league of nations".

177. "Wilsonians were basically concerned at Paris that, unless the reparation settlement were made in a reasonable enough manner to leave Germany the possibility of economic recovery and to give the international banking community confidence in German bonds, the result would be continued German and European economic dislocation, heightened international tension, and radical social unrest" (Levin, op. cit. p. 141).

178. Baruch to Dr. Simon Baruch 10.3.19. Baruch papers, Princeton University Library. See also Levin, op. cit. pp. 158–159.

179. Cf. note 172. According to the memorandum mentioned there about the meeting 1.4.19, Wilson said inter alios, when the experts referred to the Pre-Armistice Agreement: "The President stated in substance that he did not regard this (the inclusion of pensions) as a matter for decision in accordance with strict legal principles; that it was probable that the question of pensions was not specifically considered in November and that the statement then made was in a very general a loose terminology. He was, however, continuously finding new meanings and the necessity of broad application of principles previously enunciated even though imperfectly, and that he felt that justice would be done by compelling the enemy to make good, if they were able, damage of this category".

180. McCormick diary 31.3.19, italics mine.—Cf. Charles Seymour (IP IV, p. 413): "Unwillingly, President Wilson yielded again and advised the American experts, Mr. Davis, Mr. Lamont, Mr. Baruch, and Mr. McCormick, not to insist upon the statement of a definite sum in the treaty". Seymour gives the information without source. (McCormick diary (copy) arrived to Yale University Library in 1942. Cf. McCormick to Bernard Knollenberg 20.4.1942 in McCormick diary, Yale).—See also Norman H. Davis: "Memorandum for the President" 25.3.19, Wilson papers, Ser.

5 A; Burnett I, Doc. 196, pp. 711–713: (The negotiations about a fixed sum being deadlocked in the second sub-committee of the Reparations Commission, Davis wrote): "... and even if it were possible (an unanimous report), it is, as I understand, your view as well as that of Mr. Lloyd George and Mr. Clemenceau that it would be inadvisable now to have any fixed amount reported by that Sub-Committee even if they could agree upon it". See also Lansing desk book 2.4.19: "White on report of no fixed sum to be demanded of Germany, said Prest. had been won over. Germans will never agree. I am sure as it means slavery. ...".

181. Wilson's choice of House, not Lansing almost provoked the resignation of the Secretary of State: Lansing desk book 4.4.19. See also "Colonel House as the President's substitute on the Council of Four". April 8, 1919, Confidential Memoranda, Lansing papers. Lansing learned of House's appointment through the newspapers.

182. Woodrow Wilson and Colonel House, p. 255; about the scapegoat theory for instance p. 248: "And who was more eligible to serve Wilson as a scapegoat than his alter ego, Colonel House, whose friendship in any event no longer yielded the accustomed gratifications?".

183. See for instance House diary 24.3.19; cited above p. xxx, note 149. On the discontent of the Commissioners, see further Birdsall, pp. 277 and 329–330. As will be seen below, my interpretations of House's relationship with Wilson during this period is somewhat different from Birdsall's.

184. House diary 2.4.9. Auchincloss Diary 3.4.19, cf. below.

185. Baker notebook passim. Cf. Vance McCormick's remark to Henry Morgenthau 6.5. 19: "V.(ance) thinks Baker is nearer to Wilson's thoughts than any one else ...". Morgenthau diary 6.5.19.

186. Woodrow Wilson and World Settlement II, p. 41. Italics mine.

187. Baker notebook 2.4.19. Omissions mine.

188. House diary 2.4.19.

189. ibid. 25.3.19.

190. Cf. above pp.185–186.

191. House diary 27.3.19, cf. above p. 184, and note 147.

192. House diary 27.3.19, cf. above p. 176, and note 81.

193. House diary 28.3.19.

194. House diary 29.3., 30.3., 31.3.19.—March 31 he was present, though, together with Lloyd George and Melville Stone at a lunch which Mr. and Mrs. Wilson gave in honour of Stone, who was leaving Paris. However, House himself arranged the lunch with Mrs. Wilson on March 28.

195. ibid. 1.4.19.—On the expert level, though, House partly on his own initiative, still kept a hand at negotiations: After his conversation with Wilson 24.3. House sent for Sidney Mezes and David Hunter Miller and "asked them to get to work and draft a treaty with the boundary lines that were recommended by our experts". It is not clear if this was arranged with Wilson during the conversation (House diary 24.3.19: "The President again insisted that all the treaties should be made at once, that is the one with Germany, the one with the remains of Austria-Hungary, the one with Bulgaria, and the one with Turkey. *I undertook to get these matters in shape to cause no delay.* It is evident that we know as much about what the proper boundaries should be now as we should in six months hence ...". Italics mine). On 27.3. House discussed the situation relating to the inclusion of the Monroe-Doctrine in the Covenant of the League of Nations: Lloyd George would not accept this "until he had a complete understanding with the President concerning the US naval building program". Wilson wanted House to take the matter up with Lloyd George, but House thought Wilson himself whould do it (House diary 27.3.19). The following day House had a conversation with Admiral Benson—on Benson's initiative—about the current Anglo-American negotiations (House diary 28.3.19. —More about this below). That same day, after the quarrel with Clemenceau about the Saar (cf. below) Wilson agreed to send for Mezes "and ... ask him to do what I (House) have already requested in regard to the boundaries". (House diary 28.3.19,

cf. above 24.3.). The next day Tardieu and Aubert came to see House to discuss the problems relating to the Saar-question and House promised immediately to contact the American experts "and see what could be done to straighten out the situation between the President and Clemenceau". House thereafter sent for Haskins and Mezes, and for the rest of the day he was very actively engaged in the hectic negotiations between the experts (House diary 29.3.19—about these negotiations see below). 30.3. House had a conversation with The Secretary of the Navy, Josephus Daniels, about the Anglo-American negotiations (House diary 30.3.19—more about this later), and the same day he wrote in his diary: "I have seen many of our experts with a view of working out the problems which confront the Congress', The following day the program was the same: "My list today is again a formidable one. The Experts, both financial, economic and geographical were in and out all day. It was Davis, Hoover, Mezes and others. Daniels and Benson came again to consult regarding the British proposals. . . ." (House diary 31.3.19). And again April 1: "I have seen Mezes, Haskins and other of our experts many times during the day trying to work out some solution of the Danzig, the Sarre and the reparation controversies" (House diary 1.4.19).—House, in other words, was very well informed about the negotiations at expert level, but he had no influence on the top level decisions.

196. Cf. pp. 84–85 and 164–175.
197. George and George, op. cit. p. 252.
198. The quotations: Seth P. Tillman: Anglo-American Relations at the Paris Peace Conference of 1919, Princeton, N. J., Princeton University Press, 1961, p. 229.
199. ibid. p.1 176.
200. The Italian question will be treated more fully in another context.
201. House diary 27.3.19: "I had the President also in my room for a few minutes before the meeting. It was to tell him that the draft for the article on the Monroe Doctrine, which Balfour, Cecil and I had agreed upon, was refused by Lloyd George, therefore Cecil asked me to urge him not to present it, or to bring up the matter at last night's meeting. Lloyd George told Cecil that he had no intention of having the Covenant in the Peace Treaty, and that he did not intend to sign any Covenant for a League of Nations until he had had a complete understanding with the President concerning the US Naval building program".
202. Not even the latest discussion—Nelson's very thorough analysis (Land and Power, pp. 249–281)—has an eye for this decisive aspect. R. S. Baker, on the other hand, saw the connection clearly (Woodrow Wilson and World Settlement II, pp. 72–76), and his diary entries about his conversations with Wilson during this period constitute some of the most important sources for the following discussion.—House himself pointed indirectly to the connection between the solution of the Saar conflict and the passing of the Monroe Doctrine amendment: "At the request of the President, I asked Tardieu to call in order to read the riot act to Clemenceau, through him, regarding the left bank of the Rhine and the protection of France. We discussed the Sarre Basin which have now come back to the plan Tardieu and I approved some two weeks ago and which the President rejected, I took occasion to tell Tardieu of the action of Bourgeois and Larnaude concerning the Monroe doctrine" (House diary 12.4.19). Bourgeois and Larnaude were the French representatives on the League Commission. On the related episode see further Birdsall, Versailles . . ., pp. 144–146.
203. House diary 2.4.19: "It could be done so easily that it is maddening to see the days go by and nothing decided". See also Auchincloss diary 2.4.19 about the common impatience and dissatisfaction.
204. House diary 3.4.19. For these negotiations see further below.
205. House diary 3.4.19.
206. House diary 3.4.19.
207. House diary 4.4.19.
208. Auchincloss diary 4.4.19.—Italics mine.
209. House diary 4.4.19.

210. The question of Belgian priority in relation to reparations; a question which, thus, involved the distribution among the Allies themselves.
211. House diary 4.4.19.
212. Which naturally does not preclude that House could be right. Mantoux I, pp. 139–144.
213. Mantoux I, p. 145.—For the state of the Rhine negotiations at this juncture see Nelson, Land and Power, pp. 234–236 and cf. the discussion below.
214. Mantoux I, p. 145.
215. ibid.: "M. Lloyd George.—Qui, à condition que l'inspection ait lieu universellement. Mais il faut convenir qu'une inspection faite par l'étranger dans un seul pays, pendant cinquante ans peut-être, pourrait donner lieu à des difficultés".
216. House diary 4.4.19: "We did not break up until one o'clock. I saw Mrs. Wilson for a moment and she asked me to remain to lunch, but I had an engagement with Frazier".
217. ibid.—The acceptance of the historic boundary, though, were conditioned by Wilson's consent (Mantoux I, p. 149; Auchincloss diary 4.4.19). Mantoux's minutes of this meeting, with a few unessential stilistic differences from the printed version, are found—as the only example of these minutes—in the Wilson papers. About Czekoslovakia see further Nelson, pp. 282–304. Oddly enough Nelson does not mention the House diary in this connection.
218. Auchincloss diary 4.4.19.—Cf. House diary 4.4.19: "George wanted to postpone our next meeting until Sunday, alleging that the President would then be well enough to attend. Clemenceau and I insisted upon having it tomorrow and he finally acquiesced. We also agreed to take up the question of Reparations.

    . . .

    When we went out of the room he (Lloyd George) said he was sorry the subject of reparations was coming up tomorrow when the President was away, for he believed that he and the President were nearer together than he an(d) I. This I answered, might be, nevertheless, I thought there should be no delay in getting at it". See also R. S. Baker notebook 4.4.19: "The Four met today with Col. House taking the President's place. *The Colonel prefers to work with Clemenceau rather than Lloyd George.* He told me to-day that Lloyd George told him: "You and I do not agree as well as the President and I agree". The Colonel is still optimistic!". Italics mine. (Partly in Woodrow Wilson and World Settlement II, pp. 46–47).
219. Mantoux I, p. 150.—Compare this to House's own colourful description in the diary (4.4.19): "I told them (Lloyd George, Clemenceau and Orlando) that in my opinion it was more important to bring about peace quickly than it was to haggle over details. That I would rather see an immediate peace and the world brought to order that I would see a better peace and delay. I jestingly remarked that by tomorrow night we ought to be able to settle all subjects necessary for a peace with Germany and all the differences between us. I told Clemenceau I disliked evading problems which had to be solved. He replied that he was no "dodger". Then, I said, we will come to grips tomorrow". Seymour, and therefore also Burnett and Birdsall wrongly presents these remarks as directed to the economic experts: IP IV, p. 402, Birdsall, Versailles . . ., p. 259, and Burnett I, p. 75 n.
220. Mantoux I, p. 149.
221. House diary 4.4.19: "When I reached the Crillon, I told Lamont, Davis and Mc Cormick, who will be present at the meeting tomorrow, that we must expose the situation and let the French know the story as it was. (Namely the following: "I found in talking with Clemenceau that George or someone had misinformed him as to the American position and that he thought the entire cause of the trouble and and disagreement lay with our experts. Lamont and Davis have done everything possible to save George because of his election promises and in return he uses us to mislead Clemenceau into believing that what we have tried to do to help him was our own idea and not for him" ibid.). Clemenceau, I said, believed that we were the hindrance and we must make it clear in a pleasant, impersonal and cordial way, where the real trouble was. I am looking forward with interest to our meeting".
222. House diary 4.4.19.

223. Baker notebook 4.4.19.—The whole entry bears witness to the desperate mood which seems to have prevailed on the Commission as well as on the Conference as a whole during this period. The above quoted exclamation is also printed by Baker in his Woodrow Wilson and World Settlement (II, p. 47), but there without giving the exact date. Baker also printed a comprehensive excerpt of the diary entry, but he made some changes from the original version, see Mayer, Politics . . ., p. 573 n. In the same place Mayer, too, brings comprehensive excerpts from Baker's diary entries during this period.
224. McCormick diary 4.4.19.
225. Auchincloss diary 4.4.19.—Italics mine.
226. Josephus Daniels diary, 7.4.19. Library of Congress; Cronon, p. 385.
227. Reading to Wiseman 9.4.19, Wiseman papers. A few days later Charles Grasty was able to tell Auchincloss the same thing: ". . . Charley Grasty, who told me that Frank Simonds is spreading it around that the Colonel and the President have fallen out . . ." (Auchincloss diary 15.4.19). While Baker wrote in his notebook on April 19: "The rift between the President and Colonel House seems to be widening. The Colonel compromises everything away—He has gone so far with the Italians that they are now heralding him as the great man of the conference and comparing him unfavorably with the President. The Colonel is still declaring that if he had the peace to make, it could all be done in a day or so.—and it could—by giving away everything we came to fight for".
228. Henry Morgenthau diary 8.6.19, italics mine. See also entries on 11.6. and 25.6. That same day William H. Buckler wrote to his wife: "His (House's) influence with the President has waned in a curious way—presumably owing to his advice beeing found poor . . ." (Buckler papers, House Coll. 51/25).
229. W. H. Buckler to G. Buckler 10.6.19. Buckler papers. Italics mine. For Auchincloss's role see also Henry Morgenthau diary 6.5.19 (conversation with McCormick) and McCormick diary 23.5.19 and 24.6.19, and Morgenthau diary 25.6.19 (conversation with Grayson and Buckler).
230. George and George, p. 246, italics mine, see also Bailey, p. 361 f and cf. the introduction above pp. 12–13.
231. Birdsall, Versailles . . ., p. 277 and the whole of chapter 11 (pp. 264–288). Shotwell, who was a member of the Inquiry, but in this cannot be regarded as a front line witness was of this opinion: James T. Shotwell, At the Paris Peace Conference, New York, The Macmillan Co., 1937, pp. 18–19 and 200–202. Cf. the introduction pp. 12–13 and below pp. 220–224.
232. In Birdsall's argumentation a letter from Henry White to Robert Lansing of 8.11. 19 plays a central role (Birdsall, Versailles . . ., pp. 13 and 288).—For the role of the three Commissioners in the establishment of the House myth see further below.
233. Birdsall, Versailles pp. 15–16.
234. See the following chapter.
235. The French still use the argument that the territorial provisions in the treaty were in agreement with the Fourteeen Points and the Pre-Armistice Agreement—at least in the case of Europe: Pierre Renouvin, Le Traité de Versailles, Paris, Flammarion, 1969, p. 71.
236. Mayer, Wilson versus Lenin, pp. 329–367, cf. appendix I.
237. George and George, p. 263.
238. Levin, op. cit. pp. 154–182, cf. appendix I.
239. "It could be said that the President's reintegrationist approach toward Germany, modified by his punitive orientation, represented not so much a desire to accept the postwar liberalized German state of equality and solidarity, as it represented an effort to curb Allied extremism just enough to permit Germany to be punished and controlled in a manner that would neither encourage Bolshevism nor prevent a lasting peace". (Levin, p. 159).—It is worth mentioning, though, that Levin takes his examples of the "punitive" elements in Wilson's policy from the period after the President's return from the United States, at a time, therefore, when Wilson was on the defensive.
240. ibid. pp. 168–169.

241. Through Thirty Years, II, p. 259.

242. For the relationship between Lloyd George and Northcliffe see History of the Times, 1912–1948, I, passim, and Stanley Morison, Personality and Diplomacy in Anglo-American Relations, 1917, in Essays presented to Sir Lewis Namier, Richard Pares and A. J. P. Taylor (eds.), London, MacMillan and Co., 1956, pp. 431–471. This article gives an account of the Northcliffe-Mission to the United States and the relationship between House and Northcliffe.

243. Cf. the previous chapter pp. 143–144 and notes 285 and 286.—The American Ambassador in Paris gave the following description of the press during this period: "Both the NEW YORK HERALD and the DAILY MAIL (Paris Editions) have contained each morning in their editorial columns the most ungenerous kind of criticism, while not much less severe has been that of several of the French Papers. ... a series of unusually vindictive criticisms on the part of a number of the prominent journals in Paris directed against the work of the Peace Conference. Only the virulence and pourility of some of these criticisms deprive them of the force they might otherwise have. *Those in the DAILY MAIL in particular are so violent in their tone as to, in my judgement, presage a positive reaction.* All this criticism has tended greatly to discredit the Conference in the minds of that class of people who let the newspapers do their thinking for them". (Sharp to SecState, Washington 9.4.19, Wilson papers, Ser. 5 A). Italics mine. See also Baker, Woodrow Wilson and World Settlement II, p. 46: "To make matters still worse—if that were possible —there began a sudden and violent outbreak of criticism of the Conference—and especially of the President—in the Paris (and to some extent in the London) press. It was timed as to make it seem impossible that it was not calculated and directed".—For the attacks from the Northcliffe-Press see also Wiseman to Reading 8.4.19 and 11.4.19, Wiseman papers.

244. Thompson, Russia, Bolshevism, and the Versailles Peace, pp. 242–245, quotations p. 245. A veritable parliamentary revolt was soon threatening Lloyd George: "On April 8 a tory bloc in parliament wired Lloyd George challenging his position on the reparations issue. To meet this parliamentary revolt and to counter Northcliffe's attacks on Russian policy and other issues, Lloyd George returned to London in mid-April" (ibid., p. 245).

245. See for instance the daily review of the British press: "Great Britain, Daily Report—April 1st, 1919. Attack on Wilson and Lloyd George", Bullitt papers. —Morning Post was a Northcliffe-Paper.

246. R. S. Baker notebook 9.4.19. Wilson, himself, seems to have been of the same opinion: He (Wilson) referred also to the attacks in the French press the coincident effort to separate him and Lloyd George. I (Baker) said that Wickham Steed and the Northcliffe press were sharpening their campaign against Lloyd George. "Yes", he said, "the Northcliffe press is like the Hearst press—only a little better" (Baker notebook 2.4.19).

247. Cf. above p. 185.

248. Auchincloss diary 27.3.19, cf. Thompson, pp. 243–244—Auchincloss, it will be remenbered, did not agree with House's favourable opinion of Bullitt's proposal, and he, in this matter, followed a policy that went directly against the intensions of his father-in-law. House, however, could hardly have realized that Auchincloss was deeply involved: "Wiseman was waiting ... to tell me the British news. He and I have been disturbed by the editorials which Steed has been writing on the Russian question in the Mail. Wiseman advised giving Steed the "cold shoulder" for a few days. Instead of that I sent for him and had it out with him. I told him he was not playing the game and he ought not to have written editorials concerning so important a matter without first consulting me. I hoped he would discontinue any mention of the subject until we had worked out a plan. Then he could endorse it or oppose it as he thought best. He promised aquiescence" (House diary 28.3.19). It is probable, though, that Steed went further than Auchincloss had counted, at least, he was not present during this conversation (Auchincloss diary 28.3.19). See Through Thirty Years II, pp. 302–307 for Steed's version of the events.

249. Auchincloss diary 28.3.19. On a conversation with Lord Northcliffe: "We discussed every question under the sun including the reparations matter, the Russian situation, the German territorial situation, and Lloyd George's attitude towards the President's position in the present conferences. Northcliffe was very complimentary to the Colonel and the work that he had done. He gave me a whole lot of clippings from the American papers and he pr'ised to confer with Steed on Sunday as to the best methods to be used to hurry up the decision of the questions now pending before the conference". Auchincloss diary 29.3.19: "I had a long talk with Steed this morning. His (!) is very much exercised over the President's position. In fact we all are. ... Steed is very bitter against George. Steed is such an erratic man that I am afraid before long he will be attacking the President.... I suggested to Steed that he write an editorial in tomorrow morning's paper taking the President up on the mountain tops and showing him the promise(d) land and also depths that might be his if he should stumble. Steed said he would do this and that he would call the editorial Pisgah". See also Steed, Through Thirty Years, II, pp. 307–309. The article was printed in the (Paris) Daily Mail, Sunday, March 30, under the title "Pisgah and Sinai". Steed prints the article p. 308. In the following days Steed followed up the attacks.

250. See the quotations above pp. 194–195.

251. See the quotations above pp. 194–195. See also Polk diary 10.7.19, Polk papers: "Admiral Grayson: Told me of Peace Conference and relations of various members for the conference. Spoke of (the name is left out, but there is hardly any doubt that the person referred to is Steed) articles in the Times and Colonel House's relation to them".

252. Cf. above p. 194.

253. R. S. Baker notebook 17.4.19, italics mine.

254. Many different accounts of this dramatic meeting exist. See, inter alios, Lloyd George's description to House (House diary 28.3.19) and Wilson's to Baker (Baker notebook 28.3.19). Besides Mantoux's minutes of the debate (Les Délibérations... I, pp. 63–75) also Tardieu gives excerpts from the discussion (La Paix, pp. 290–293). They reflect the emotional character of the debate, but, naturally, leave out any trace of the personal clash between Wilson and Clemenceau, which both the involved persons relate, though differently. Tardieu as well as House (who got his information from Lloyd George at a *lunch* the same day) gives the time of the meeting as before noon, while Mantoux places it at 4 pm, which is obviously a mistake. About the relationship between the minutes given by Mantoux and Tardieu respectively, the following information can be given: Mantoux states (p. 67) that Tardieu was present only during the first part of the meeting, when the French demands were presented, but not during the discussion. Tardieu's account, therefore, cannot be based on his own notations. A close analysis shows that Tardieu's account is compiled partly from verbal quotations from Mantoux's minutes, partly from a recasting and condensation of the same: Clemenceau's speech is given almost verbatim (although different sections have been changed about). The quotations are from Baker's notebook.

255. Nelson, pp. 252–253. Cf. Mémoire présenté par la Délégation Française. Tardieu, La Paix, pp. 279–289.

256. Tardieu's memorandum p. 289. Tardieu writes, that his memorandum was "Expliqué et commenté à nos Alliés, dans de nombreuses conversations au cours des mois de janvier et de février... Notre mémoire fut distribué en mars aux chefs des délégations. Le débat, ainsi préparé s'engagea quelques jours après". (ibid. pp. 289–290).

257. Mantoux I, pp. 67–68.

258. ibid. pp. 68, 69 and 72.—Lloyd George, too, declared himself bound by the Pre-Armistice Agreement, but, at the same time, he thought that autonomy would be the solution of the problem: annexation would be avoided. (ibid. pp. 73–74).

259. Ibid. p. 71.

260. ibid. pp. 67 and 73.

261. House diary 9.11.18 and 30.11.18, cf. chapter 2, pp. 73 and 77.

262. The so-called "Black Book", i. e. Inquiry's proposal for a settlement of the territorial problems at the beginning of the Conference ("An Outline of Tentative Recommendations", 21.1.19, Wilson papers, Ser. 5 A; House papers; cf. Gelfand, The Inquiry, p. 182 n), advocated a solution in favour of France against the wish of the local population: "The present desires of these people should not prevent a just disposition of this important coal deposit in favor of a country whose limited coal supplies have been much reduced by unlicensed German exploitations and destruction... in the present war". (Cf. Gelfand, p. 195. Gelfand gives this as an example of an occasion, where the Inquiry recommended a solution running counter to the President's declared principle of national self-determination). The report of February 21, from the Anglo-American group of experts (cf. chapter 3, p. 121) had advocated French ownership and right of exploitation of the coalmines, and one form or another of local self-government under French sovereignty and a tariff union with France. See also Haskins to Wilson 30.3.19, Wilson Papers, Ser. 5 A, where he gives a short outline of his attitude. On the other hand, the Cobb-Lippmann memorandum (cf. chapter 1, p. 48) plainly declared, that the French plans "would be a clear violation of the President's proposal".

263. See foregoing chapter pp. 128–129.

264. See, chapter 2, p. 89.

265. Nelson, pp. 233–234.

266. Birdsall pp. 140–142. See also House diary 27.3.19, cited above note 201.—There were meetings in the League-Commission 22., 24. and 26. March, but thereafter only 10. and 11. April (ibid. p. 137).

267. Birdsall, p. 145.—The amendments Wilson wished were: "exclusion of matters of domestic legislation—i. e. tariff and immigration laws—from the competence of the League; explicit recognition of the Monroe Doctrine in the Covenant; and provision for the withdrawal of any member state from the League of Nations". (ibid. p. 134).

268. Birdsall has suggested, that, "(I)t is possible that the French succeeded in making a definite bargain about the Monroe Doctrine amendment, permitting its adoption only after prior assurance that they might occupy the Rhineland, since only three days elapsed after an adoption of the amendment before they secured concessions in the Rhineland" (Birdsall, p. 213). But Nelson has rightly commented: "The timing of his (Wilson's) statement (the answer to the French note of 2. April), April 12, seems to rule out the suggestion that the French had made a bargain with Wilson in which they exchanged acceptance of his Monroe doctrine amendment to the Covenant for his approval of a Rhineland occupation" (Nelson, pp. 239–240). Neither Birdsall nor Nelson, though, has noticed that the dates on the other hand fits neatly with the Saar-settlement and the adoption of the Monroe-Doctrine amendment: April 10–11. R. S. Baker hints at such a connection (Woodrow Wilson and World Settlement II, p. 75).

269. See "Memorandum to US. Peace Commissioners. Public Opinion and the Present Crisis", 24.3.19 by George Bernard Noble. Henry White papers, Box 66, and Memorandum of a conversation with M. Cachin, Editor of l'Humanité (Commissioners to Wilson 28.3.19, Wilson papers, Ser. 5 A, also in White papers, Box 66: Memorandum to US Peace Commissioners. Cachin interview. (GBN), 28.3.19.: "He (Cachin) says, the remarkable fact during the past two weeks has been the change in popular feeling towards Mr. Wilson.... Mr. Cachin says it is not yet too late, and believes that Mr. Wilson can, through a strong decisive stand, save the day, so that liberalism may come through well-ordered channels rather than through class upheavals".

270. See for instance Tumulty to Wilson 30.3.19. Wilson papers, Ser. 5 A, and Tumulty, p. 523; and Baker notebook 31.3.19 and 2.4.19; Bliss to Newton D. Baker 3.4.19, Bliss papers, and Bliss to Mrs. Bliss 3.4.19 ibid.; and Tumulty to Grayson 5.4.19, Wilson papers, Ser. 5 A and Tumulty, p. 524.

271. Baker notebook 31.3.19, cf. ibid. 2.4.19.

272. After the announcement of the summoning of the GEORGE WASHINGTON (cf. below)—which wasn't the public statement Baker had advocated so warmly, but at

least a clear indication that Wilson had lost patience—the President explained his policy to Baker thus (Baker notebook 7.4.19):

Baker told of the effect of the summoning and Wilson said: "Well the time has come to bring this thing to a head". ... "I. will not discuss anything with them anymore". Baker advocated, as he had done earlier, giving out "a statement" at once, "and with specific applications of his (Wilson's) principles". Wilson, himself, was doubtful regarding "too detailed a statement upon the specific issues". "He said if he had not fallen ill the time for meeting the situation would have been today. He proposed to stand up for his principles".

"Then Italy will not get Fiume".

"Absolutely not—so long as I am here", he said sharply.

"Nor France the Saar".

"No. We agreed among ourselves and we agreed with Germany upon certain general principles. The whole of the conference has been made up of a series of attempts, especially by France, to break over this agreement, to get territory, to impose crushing indemnities. The only real interest of France in Poland is in weakening Germany by giving Poland territory to which she has no right".

He said that a League of Nations founded upon an unjust peace could have no future".

273. House diary 28.3.19.
274. House diary 29.3.19.
275. ibid.—Haskins gave his views in a letter to Wilson 30.3.19. Wilson papers, Ser. 5 A, cf. Nelson, p. 159 and Baker, Woodrow Wilson and World Settlement II, pp. 73–74.
276. Nelson, pp. 260–261.—Italics mine. A special committee was appointed for the study of the economic problems. Members were Headlam-Morley, Haskins and Tardieu (ibid. p. 261).
277. R. S. Baker cites a memorandum by Douglas Johnson of a conversation during the Saar-negotiations between Wilson and three of the territorial experts, where this comes out very clearly: "I am willing to give France any indemnity in kind to which she is entitled", he told them, but added: "I have no right to hand over to her people who do not want to go to her, or to give them a special government, even if it is better for them, if they do not want it". Perceiving how his whole programme of peace terms was at stake, he concluded: "You see, I have to be firm on these points in all places, or I cannot hold out against the exorbitant demands of the Italians" (Woodrow Wilson and World Settlement II, p. 73).
278. Steed, Through Thirty years II, p. 310. House does not mention anything about this initiative in the diary.
279. ibid. pp. 310–311.—Steed was an old friend of Clemenceau.
280. Auchincloss diary 1.4.19.
281. Through Thirty Years II, pp. 310–311.—Steed states that this proposal was "(the) kind of solution which I had more than once discussed with Colonel House".
282. ibid.
283. Steeds proposal is printed in Through Thirty Years II, pp. 311–313. The original, with House's endorsement is in Wilson papers, Ser. 5 A (Steed to Wilson 1.4.19). House wrote "Steed is a very old friend of Clemenceau and it may be well to let him try his hand on this if you consider this valuable". It was Frazier, who placed the letter before the President.
284. Through Thirty Years II, p. 315.—It will be remembered, that Wilson in this matter did not share the opinion of his experts.
285. Haskins to Wilson 1.4.19, Wilson papers, Ser. 5 A. It was about the negotiations with Tardieu and Headlam-Morley. See also Nelson, p. 262: "The striking feature of the Saar formula in Steed's letter was its similarity to Haskins's scheme...". The proposal comprised French occupation and administration of the Saar region on a mandatory basis for 15 years. Thereafter a plebiscite was to be organized by the League either for the region as a whole or by communes. During the mandatory period the Saar-mines were to be exploited as partial reparation, and if it were to turn out that the German damages on the French mines were irreparable, the

mines should stay French permanently. The Saar-region should be demilitarized. In the period during French administration the citizenship of the inhabitants was to be left unchanged, with the exception of those who wished to become French citizens. The local institutions, language and schools should be maintained and the inhabitants exempted from military service. The inhabitants should have no right to representation either in the German or in the French parliament (Wilson papers, Ser. 5 A; Through Thirty Years II, p. 312).

286. For the state of the negotiations at this time see Nelson, p. 234 and Tardieu, pp. 201–205. Steed's proposal "Protection of Eastern France" comprised demilitarization of the whole area up to 50 km east of the Rhine. "Any Allied occupation that may be requisite during the period of reparation shall be undertaken by French or other Allied detachments as mandatories on behalf of the League of Nations. Officers of the Allied and Associated Armies shall be attached to any forces of occupation". Any German attempt at evasion or violation of the terms should result in an immediate reaction by the League "or mandatories that it may appoint *ad hoc*".—Only on April 14, and in quite another phase of the negotiations did Wilson accept stepwise French occupation of the Rhine area (cf. Nelson, p. 240).

287. Through Thirty Years II, p. 313.

288. Morgenthau diary 8.6.19, italics mine. Cf. above p. 195.

289. Cf. note 285.—It is probably worth noting that David Hunter Miller from April 4 was involved in the negotiations of the experts on line with Haskins. Besides his function in the League-committee, which held no meetings for the time being, Miller was also the legal adviser of the American Commission, and there are certain indications that it was in this capacity that he was first connected with the negotiations (Miller diary I, 4.4.19, pp. 222–223, and ibid. 7.4.19, pp. 227–228), but during the critical phase of the discussions Miller's views seem greatly to have influenced Wilson (cf. Nelson, p. 271).

290. For Wilson's views on Steed and the Northcliffe-press see Baker Notebook 2.4.19, cited above, note 246.

291. See House's diary entry about the conversation above p. xxx and note 188. It was during this conversation that Wilson authorized House to negotiate with Tardieu about the Saar and the Rhine, and it was also during this conversation that "(t)he President tried to get me (House) to admit that the solution which our experts have proposed and which Clemenceau might be willing to take as to the Sarre Valley, was inconsistent with the Fourteen Points. I replied that there were many who thought otherwise". (House diary 2.4.19).

292. Printed in Through Thirty Years II, p. 316. The day before Steed had inter alios written to Northcliffe: "... I propose to begin to tell him (Wilson) the truth in public as soon as possible" (ibid. p. 316).

293. See above p. 194.

294. This is as far as I see it the only acceptable interpretation of the above cited quotation from the House diary 4.4.19 (see above p. 194): Wilson became so upset about the course of the negotiations that he, in spite of his illness, demanded one more discussion of the matter with House, and during this it was confirmed that the views he was so much against were not only Tardieu's, but also shared by House: "That Tardieu knew my (House's) views and knowing them had prepared the memorandum". It has not been possible to identify the memorandum. Tardieu mentions French notes on 19., 20., 22., 28., 31. March and 2., *4.*, 5., 15., 16. and 19. April (Tardieu p. 204, italics mine) and House himself writes about the conversation: "Tardieu was another visitor. We discussed the left bank of the Rhine and the Sarre Valley. *It was a continuation of our discussion of the last few days and the memorandum which he brought* on the subject is a part of the record. *We have come closer together*" (House diary 4.4.19, italics mine).
The day before (April 3) House had, at Wilson's request, started negotiations with Tardieu, and during these he had tried—he tells us—to be both firm and flexible: "Tardieu followed Benson. I gave the talk which the President and I agreed upon last night. It had some effect upon him and I hope when it is repeated it

will have some effect on Clemenceau. I put our case as strongly as I could and took occasion to say that as far as I could see, France had not reciprocated in any way. ... *We were demanding nothing, and we were merely trying to hold to the principles upon which the Armistice had been made and to which all the belligerents had agreed.*

The Sarre Valley was injected as an entirely new proposal... a proposal which the Prime Minister himself agreed not to put forth if I thought it unreasonable (cf. chapter 2, pp. 73 and 77). When this proposal was suggested, the only consideration brought forward was the value and necessity for the coal which was to be given France in lieu of the destruction of the coal mines around Lens. *The President had been in sympathy with this request and was willing to give France in fee simple the coal mines, but he was entirely unwilling to place under French sovereignty an absolutely German population. In our opinion, it was not only inconsistent with the Fourteen Points, but it meant trouble in the future for France,* and if we consented, it meant an immediate demand by Italy for Dalmatia and other enemy territory to which she had no just claim.

In reply to this, Tardieu brought attention to the fact that Foch had threatened to resign unless France insisted upon the permanent occupation of the Rhine, although Clemenceau did not go that far. *The upshot of our interview was that Tardieu is to see what practical arrangement can be worked out concerning the use of the mines by France. We will then take the next step,* if indeed, there is to be any next.

*We agreed that in the event the impasse continued we would get together on Sunday and try to work out something between ourselves.* I let him know if these matters were not settled within the next ten days, it was the intention of the President to go home because of the urgent public business requiring his presence in Washington" (House diary 3.4.19, italics mine).

It seems, thus, that House has related Wilson's principle faithfully, but that he at the same time, had taken preliminary steps towards private negotiations. House told Wilson about the conversation (and what he told the President is not necessarily identical with what he wrote about the conversation in his diary), and of Wilson's reaction House only writes: "The President and I had an interesting conversation over the telephone concerning my interview with Tardieu, King Albert and various other matters" (House diary 3.4.19). See further House diary 12.4.19 (italics mine): "At the request of the President, I asked Tardieu to call in order to read the riot act to Clemenceau, through him, regarding the left bank of the Rhine and the protection of France. *We discussed the Sarre Basin which has now come back to the plan Tardieu and I approved some two weeks ago and which the President rejected*".

295. Baker notebook 4.4.19, cf. above pp. 194 and 197–198.

296. Cf. above p. 194.—April 8 House noted with satisfaction about the negotiations discussed here: "We all feel that the big hurdle was gotten over Saturday, Sunday and Monday. Everything now should be comparatively easy sailing" (House diary 8.4.19). As will be remembered (see above, p. 166, and Woodroow Wilson and World Settlement II, p. 380) R. S. Baker stressed the reparations negotiations as one of the points, where House betrayed Wilson, but he did not attribute to it any decisive influence on the break. This is also, in my opinion, impossible.

297. Burnett I, pp. 71–77 and Birdsall, Versailles..., pp. 256–260.—There are four sources relating to the decisive meeting, and only two were known to Burnett and Birdsall, both printed by Burnett (Document 237 and 238): A minute of a meeting by the Council of Four, April 5, at 4 pm which Burnett has taken from the papers of John Foster Dulles and a summary of Hankey's official minutes (IC 170 I) which professor Slosson made for the State Department and which is printed by David Hunter Miller (Miller diary XIX, pp. 300–301). Since then two sets of minutes have been published: Hankey's (PPC V, pp. 31–38) and Mantoux's (Mantoux I, pp. 159–165). From this is evident that Mantoux's minute is almost identical with the minute we know from the Dulles papers. Some passages are divergent, but each time

it is a question of length, not of meaning. It is therefore natural to assume that the minute Burnett prints, was made by either Auchincloss, who was present at the meeting in his capacity as secretary to Colonel House, or by Dulles, who was present in his capacity as secretary to the American economic experts. The latter solution seems the most probable, not only because the minute is found among Dulles's papers, but particularly because the only minute which gives Dulles as one of the speakers is this one. It is also evident that Slosson's extract of Hankey's minute is correct, and we can hereafter eliminate Slosson as an independent source. In my opinion this has the following consequences: During the meeting Clemenceau proposed a formula, which House seized and used as a basis for the compromise. Following Hankey also Norman Davis said, "that it seemed to him to be very similar to the proposal of the United States Delegation", while this remark in the two other versions (Dulles's and Mantoux's)—which following the above discussion are independent—is ascribed to Colonel House. An attribution which gives much more meaning. Cf. also the discussion by Birdsall, p. 327. (We have here, thus, also an occasion where it is possible to compare Mantoux with another independent minute). It is apparently also Dulles's minute that R. S. Baker cites (Woodrow Wilson and World Settlement II, p. 380).

298. See above pp. 187–188. The meetings took place at President Wilson's house (PPC V, pp. 21–23), and House, himself, writes that he kept the President informed during the negotiations (House diary 5.4.19). The following day Wilson gave his definitive acceptance. This took place during a meeting between Wilson —who was still in bed—and all the Commissioners (Auchincloss diary 6.4.19, House diary 6.4.19, see also Auchincloss diary 7.4.19). Both House and Wilson, thus, knew what they were doing, and House himself was perfectly clear that he was acting against the up to then declared policy of the President (Mantoux I, pp. 157–158):
"Le COLONEL HOUSE.—Le Président Wilson à toujours cru que nos évaluations étaient toutes basées sur une période de trente ans.
. . .
LE COLONEL HOUSE.—Peut-être vaut-il mieux ne pas mentionner de période.
. . .
LE COLONEL HOUSE.—Pourquoi, dans ce cas, ne pas dire simplement que l'Allemagne reconnait son obligation de payer les réparations des dommages causés aux propriétés, et aux personnes sans énumerer toutes les catégories qu'on a suggérées et sans indiquer la limite de trente années? Un texte de ce genre peut se rédiger en trois lignes".
House in this matter only followed a policy, which Wilson had already initiated, and this is as far as I see it also an argument—besides those already given (cf. above p. 188)—against the "scape-goat" theory advanced by George and George. That House, nevertheless, *became* a scape-goat was due more to his owner behaviour than to the President's intentions, as we shall see later on!

299. Cf. below p. 210.

300. Baker notebook 7.4.19: "He (House) had actually *not known* until evening that the President had sent for the G. W. Nor did he know that I (R. S. Baker) had seen the President until I told him" (Italics Baker's).

301. Cf. note 296.—It was also during this period that House gave the earlier quoted evaluation of his own role at the Conference: "This conference so far has been run by the President, Lloyd George, Clemenceau, Balfour, Tardieu and myself. Orlando has never been assertive . . ." (House diary 5.4.19).

302. Cf. Baker notebook 6.4.19, and Lansing desk book 3.4., 4.4. and 5.4.19.

303. Auchincloss diary 6.4.19, House diary 6.4.19.

304. Cf. note 298.—Apparently it was also House who brought up the Russian question, which was also discussed at the meeting (House diary 6.4.19).

305. Bliss to Mrs. Bliss 7.4.19, Bliss papers; House diary 6.4.19; Lansing desk book 6.4.19.

306. Baker notebook 2.4.19: On March 31 Wilson had been more hesitant when Baker proposed a public statement. "If I were to do that", he said, "it would immediately

break up the Peace Conference—and we cannot risk it yet". "He is determined to be patient and try to work it through". Also House was now to be found among those pressing for at threat to leave the Conference, but his advice was not whole-hearted: "As a matter of fact, I doubt whether it will ever come to this and I would not advise it except as a last resort" (House diary 5.4.19).

307. Bliss to Newton D. Baker, 3.4.19, Bliss papers. In all probability Wilson in his reflections also used two memoranda by Charles Grasty, sent to Grayson 5.4.19. In his covering letter Grasty wrote inter alios: "Much of it has been said to me in substance by other people, and generally speaking it represents the prevailing American view in Paris". The argumentation is that European, and especially French politics are rotten to the core. Wilson has done his uttermost, but his being present at the private negotiations has no further purpose, he must now stand up and "state the case publicly". And this is to be the prelude to a broad American withdrawal from Europe, political as well as military. "As we turn our faces homeward, a farewell address by President Wilson, enunciating the great principles of World Democracy would form the platform against militarism and Bolshevism". "If the the bright blue banner of Democracy, American Style, were lifted in the hands of President Wilson, the masses of Europe would flock to it". "I believe that the withdrawal of America from field of war in Europe accompanied by a mighty blast on the trumpet would result in putting the real people of Europe in charge..." (Wilson papers, Ser. 5 A).

308. Tumulty to Grayson 5.4.19, Wilson papers, Ser. 5 A; Tumulty, p. 524. In his account R. S. Baker especially emphazises this telgram (II, p. 57). On the other hand he is wrong when he writes (ibid.) that Wilson "reached this resolution (the summoning of the GEORGE WASHINGTON) without consulting anyone, not even those nearest to him". Actually he had asked the Commissioners.

309. R. S. Baker prints the telegram ibid. p. 58. It was sent 7.50 am April 7. About the publication see Baker notebook 7.4.19. It was Admiral Grayson who brought the message to Baker. Due to a mistake the telegram was held up 10$^1/_2$ hours in London: See Carter to Grayson 9.4.19. Carter forwards a telegram from Admiral Benson to Admiral Knapp and Knapp's answer (Wilson papers, Ser. 5 A). On April 7 in the evening Baker had a conversation with the President, and he writes about this inter alia: "He has reached the point when he will go no further. He will win for the principles though he lose the peace and lose his own prestige—and this is what matters" (Baker notebook 7.4.19).

310. The American Ambassador in Paris, Sharp wrote:
"The following is confidential. An interest amounting almost to a sensation was caused by the announcement appearing in all the morning papers that President Wilson had ordered the GEORGE WASHINGTON to proceed to Brest with a view to returning to the United States at the end of another two weeks. ..." (Sharp to SecState, Washington, 9.4.19. no. 8073. Wilson papers, Ser. 5 A). See also Tardieu, La Paix, p. 300: "Le lendemain 7, on répand le bruit que le Président, découragé, a mandé à Brest le George Washington. L'heure est critique". During the evening of April 8 Lord Derby, the British Ambassador, was a guest at a dinner party at which the French Foreign Secretary Pichon and the head of the French Foreign Office Berthelot were also present. Derby thought they were very pessimistic about the course of the Conference, and he wrote further: "They all seemed rather excited too about this statement in the papers that President Wilson has ordered the George Washington to be ready to take him back to America. Nobody seems to know whether it is true and if true whether it is bluff or not". (Derby diary 8.4.19, sent to Balfour 9.5.19.—kindly lent me by Jørgen Sevaldsen). The French Foreign Ministry actually did everything to minimize the episode via the censorship of the French press, see Noble, pp. 322–328.

311. I have earlier (cf. Appendix I) treated this subject from another angle in connection with a discussion of Arno Mayer's thesis. It is my opinion that the threat of revolution did not occupy any prominent position in the President's considerations.

312. Cf. note 308 and cf. also the discussion pp. 175–176 of Tumulty's influence.

Tumulty's telegram was probably due to a request from Grayson 4.4.19.: "... Have you any suggestions as to publicity or otherwise?" (Tumulty, p. 523). See also Grayson to Tumulty 6. or 7.4.19, Wilson papers, Ser. 5 A: "... Have no fear of his taking the bold step if necessary at the psychological moment...", and Grayson to Tumulty 6.4.19, Wilson papers Ser. 5 A, Tumulty, p. 524: "The President says the situation here is extremely complex and intricate but seems to be improving and he expects to have it at hand this week, *but if necessary will act according to your suggestions*. The President is confined to bed but steadily improving. Thanks for your telegram" (italics mine).

313. It would anyway take the GEORGE WASHINGTON a fortnight to reach Brest.
314. See for instance Baker notebook 2.4.19 (cf. note 304); Baker notebook 7.4.19; and Grayson to Tumulty 10.4.19, Wilson papers, Ser. 5 A, partly in Tumulty, p. 526: "The French are the champion time killers of the world".
315. Cf. above p. 194.—It is evident from R. S. Baker's account, that he too, thinks, the Saar is the decisive element in the crisis, see Baker II, pp. 59–83.
316. Baker II, p. 60–61.
317. "The Saar Basin" (Wilson papers, Ser. 5 A, Nat. Arch. R. G. 256. no. 185.1134/16) forwarded 6.4.19. by Auchincloss. A survey of the negotiations is found in the National Archives (185.1134/34). The document is marked in handwriting: "Docket". The author seems to be extremely well informed, is it Haskins? The survey is printed in Appendix IV.
318. Nelson, p. 262.—For further analysis of the proposal see ibid. p. 263.
319. "The Saar Basin", Wilson papers, Ser. 5 A, cf. note 317.
320. Nelson, p. 264.—House's apparently positive reaction was probably more an attempt at procrastination. Cf. Nelson p. 264 n and confer with Mantoux I, p. 182.
321. Nelson, p. 267.
322. Memorandum for Colonel House 8.4.19, by David Hunter Miller, Wilson papers, Ser. 5 A.—House's involvement in this matter seems to have had an entirely practical character, his office was simply functioning as a kind of clearing-office: Haskins delivered the report of the committee to House, and Auchincloss then forwarded it to Close, Wilson's secretary (cf. note 317). And, again, it was from House that Miller got the papers he was to use in the preparation of his draft, and House's comments when he gave the papers to Miller were of a purely practical nature: "Colonel House told me that the President was willing to take this and to agree to it if I possibly could. The President said that there was a great deal in it that was legal and that he wanted me to look it over and see what I thought" (Miller diary I, 7.4.19, pp. 227–228). It was also to House that Miller delivered his memoranda on the morning of April 8, whereafter House forwarded them to Wilson's house (ibid. 8.4.19, pp. 228–229). House did not mention the episode at all in his diary.—The whole procedure probably seems rather elaborate, but it was in no way extraordinary. Thanks to House's maneuvering at the beginning of the Conference, Wilson had neglected the establishment of an adequate secretariat of his own and had instead used the facilities of Colonel House's office. (Cf. above pp. 67–69). When Wilson lost confidence in the Colonel upon his return from the United States, his personal staff was all too small for the enormous task. It comprised only his private Secretary Gilbert Close and his stenographer Charles Swem. Therefore also Admiral Grayson seems to have been involved, and naturally also Mrs. Wilson. But it was not enough. Cf. Henry Morgenthau diary 26.4.19. Library of Congress.
323. Nelson p. 268.
324. "April 7, 1919. Memorandum for the President". Wilson papers, Ser. 5 A. We have here a direct and seemingly unprovoked intervention by Baruch. Already on April 5 he had tried his arguments on House (see Baruch to House 5.4.19, House Coll. 2/29 and Baruch papers, Princeton University Library). But thereafter he chose the road to the President directly. This attitude fits with what we know about Baruch's dissatisfaction with House at this time (see above p. 194, and Lansing, "Confidential Memorandum, The Break between Wilson and House", 6.10.1921,

Lansing papers). For the material at Miller's disposal see Miller diary I, 7.4.19, pp. 227–228. Miller also had verbal discussions with Haskins.—House wrote in his diary 8.4.19: "André Tardieu and Louis Aubert came to discuss the Sarre Basin. We are almost together and if the President will accept my recommendations, there will be but little difference left". House does not seem to have been in touch with Wilson in regard to this matter, though he seems thus to have negotiated on his own account.

325. Mantoux I, pp. 184–193, cf. Fritz Dickmann, Die Kriegsschuldfrage auf der Friedens-konferenz von Paris 1919, R. Oldenbourg Verlag, München, 1964, pp. 38–43; for the background, see ibid. passim. A compromise was reached on April 9 on the basis of a draft by Wilson (ibid. pp. 39–40).

326. House diary 7.4.19 and 8.4.19.

327. For this see further Tillman, p. 187.

328. Cf. above p. 204.

329. Mantoux I, pp. 193–194.

330. Tardieu, La Paix. p. 300. Tardieu prints the French note of April 9 ibid. pp. 301–304, it is also to be found in House Coll. 30/169 and Wilson papers, Ser. 5 A.—Tillman summarizes the situation (pp. 187–188): "Tardieu submitted a note to the Council on the morning of April 9 which rejected the President's proposal of the previous day, insisting on a special political administration under a French mandate but agreeing to a plebiscite in fifteen years. The British presented a draft plan which was in most respects the same as the Tardieu proposal. Lloyd George recommended the Tardieu plan to the President as embodying a great concession and he urged the President to agree now to a special political administration for the Saar" (This happened at the morning-meeting April 9).

331. The following characterization of the situation before the meeting on April 9 is based on Nelson, p. 271.

332. Mantoux I, p. 203.

333. For the negotiations 9.–10.4.19 see Nelson's very penetrating analysis pp. 272–278. Nelson gives the following, very appropriate characterization of Wilson's behaviour during the meeting on April 9: "Throughout the meeting Wilson appeared acutely self-concious, apparantly aware of having been driven from position to position and now anxious to be both conciliatory and firm". (p. 275). During the discussion Wilson returned again and again to the fundamental principles, and especially in the following remark he discloses how far he had actually gone: 'J'ai dit à M. Clemenceau que je suis obligé de rester fidèle à mes quatorze points, mais sans raideur et en allant aussi loin que possible dans le sens de vos désirs légitimes. Nous ne préjugeons pas de la questions de souveraineté, nous la laissons en suspens (Mantoux I, p. 105). Tillman summarizes the plan p. 188.—Lloyd George now swept in behind Wilson.

334. Nelson, p. 277. See also Tillman, pp. 188–189.

335. ibid., The French accept was definitive only from 11.4. (Nelson, p. 279).

336. Birdsall, Versailles . . ., pp. 136–147; see also Baker II, p. 76: ". . . the day following the acceptance of the Saar settlement the revision of the League of Nations was completed by closure of the debate on the Monroe Doctrine amendment, a closure which would have been impossible unless Wilson had had the support of Clemenceau".

337. Cf. also the discussion in Appendix I.

338. Baker notebook 8.4.19.

339. ibid. 11.4.19: "The President is evidently being required to give ground for the political exigencies of Lloyd George and Clemenceau. It is either that or invite at once the explosion of the world. News today indicates that Italy is tottering into the abyss: and word from Germany gives little hope that the Germans will sign the treaty when they really get it".

340. Already on April 10 Grayson forwarded the optimistic version to Joseph Tumulty (see Appendix I for a further discussion of this. Grayson to Tumulty 10.4.19. Wilson papers, Ser. 5 A), and later on Baker "bought" the theory (cf. Appendix I), but

actually he contradicted himself a few pages further ahead (see chapter XXVIII in Woodrow Wilson and World Settlement II, pp. 59–83. There is a constant slip in the argumentation). The optimistic version very quickly found its way to the American press: "Anonymous official adds that only when President ordered George Washington back did, French, British agree to hurry up negotiations and that it cannot be declared too emphatically President will not submit to shameful compromises to secure Peace agreement; says when present negotiations concluded, whether succesful or not, President will make complete report to American people". (Polk to Ammission 29.4.19. Wilson Papers, Ser. 5 A; Nat. Arch. 186.3411/462). Since then also Arno Mayer has taken over the optimistic version from Baker (cf. Appendix I).

341. Cf. the analysis above pp. 205–206.

342. Arno Mayer has stressed—in my opinion—all too much (cf. Appendix I) the influence upon Wilson's thinking caused by fear of the spread of revolution in Europe. But regardless of the evaluation of this phenomenon, I think one must admit, that the danger of revolutions was the same in both situations. The same view must be taken at the argument, which Wilson himself later on seems to have given priority: the preservation of the Alliance. The necessity for this was the same in both situations. Wilson put forward his remarks to Norman Davis shortly after the breakdown of his Italian policy, i. e. after the negative reaction of the Italian people to his statement in the Fiume question, and Davis later told them to Lord Bryce 23.8.1921 ("Copy of Memorandum made by Norman H. Davis of a conversation with Lord Bryce. August 23, 1921. R. S. Baker papers). During the conversation Lord Bryce asked Davis, "why Wilson gave in to Lloyd George and Clemenceau as much as he did in the treaty provisions and what he had in mind when he sent for his ship the George Washington to be in Brest on May 1st, 1919", and Davis answered that Wilson had discussed the matter with him in April (ap parently shortly after the Italian statement). The President had been of the opinion that the Allied prime ministers were neither able nor willing to "make settlements in complete harmony with their moral pledges because they were hampered by the secret treaties". And even if they probably had the will, they would not be able to carry out their plans in front of public opinion in their respective countries, but, "would be supplanted by political leaders even more reactionary and responsive to the then prevailing inflamed public opinion". "He realized with sorrow that with the unfortunate but probably temporary change in public opinion he could not count upon sufficient support to force through just the kind of treaty he wanted. Under such circumstances there were only two courses open to him—either to go home because he couldn't get what he wanted or to remain in Paris and get the best treaty possible". The first solution undoubtedly would be the most popular, the American people would understand a statement, that Europe was still wrapped up in intrigues and selfishness. "This however would be an unwise step and the shirking of responsibility ... Such a course taken by him would throw Europe into still greater turmoil with unforseen consequences". He had therefore chosen the only policy which seemed to him hopeful, "and which certainly was more honourable—namely—to remain in Paris, get the world at peace as soon as possible, get the League of Nations for maintaining peace, get the best treaty possible under the circumstances, and make provisions therein for improving it and adjusting differences growing out of it ...".

343. Tumulty to Grayson 9.4.19. Wilson papers, Ser. 5 A. Tumulty, p. 525. I have earlier (cf. Appendix I) been of the opinion that this telegram had a decisive influence, but it is impossible to determine exactly when it reached the President, therefore, I must confine myself to the statement that the telegram at least cut off any possibility of retreat. The telegram is dated 9.4. but neither the time it was sent nor received is known. If it arrived at April 9 in the morning it could have been decisive or at least it could have contributed to the compliance the President showed during the meeting in the afternoon. But as it now stands, the only thing we know for certain is that the President had seen the telegram on

10.4. at the latest (cf. Grayson to Tumulty 10.4.19, Wilson papers Ser. 5 A; partly in Tumulty, p. 526, cf. Appendix I). In all circumstances, Wilson seems to have decided the retreat already on April 8.

344. Die Kriegsschuldfrage . . ., p. 40.

345. Cf. above p. 202.

346. Cf. above p. 202.

347. Baker notebook 7.4.19; Baker II, p. 60. Also Tardieu writes: "On lance, *malgré M. House,* la nouvelle tendancieuse que le paquebot George-Washington a été d'urgence appelé a Brest" (La Paix, p. 204, italics mine).

348. IP IV, pp. 418–420.—Auchincloss does not mention the episode in his diary either.

349. Cf. above p. 205 and especially note 322.

350. The Times, Monday, April 7, 1919.—Cf. above p. 202 and notes 296 and 301.

351. Sigmund Freud and William C. Bullitt: Thomas Woodrow Wilson. A Psychological Study, pp. 256–258. See also "Memorandum of a talk with Mrs. Woodrow Wilson at 2340 S ST., N. W. Washington, D. C. on December 7, 1925", R. S. Baker papers, and Memoirs of Mrs. Woodrow Wilson, pp. 299–301, and also George and George, op. cit. p. 261, and Viereck, p. 247. For Steed's own version of the episode see above pp.144–145.

352. Auchincloss's judgment (See Auchincloss diary 29.3. and 16.4.19).

353. Auchincloss himself wrote about the article: "I had a raft of people to see me today including . . . Steed, who is in a pretty good humor (He wrote a very complimentary article in the London Times on Monday regarding the Colonel, mentioning him as the man responsible for the general speeding up of the Conference); . . ." (Auchincloss diary 8.4.19). This shows, either that Auchincloss still did not understand the effect this and earlier articles surely must have had, or—what in my opinion is the most likely interpretation—that the whole thing now did not matter.—House himself does not mention the episode.

354. Memorandum of William C. Bullitt: "Conversation with General Bliss, May 19, 1919." Bullitt papers, Yale. The conversation took place on the occasion of Bullitt's resignation in protest of the treaty.

355. Cecil diary 26.3.19; Auchincloss diary 26.3.19; Miller diary I, 26.3.19, pp. 205–206; House diary 27.3.19.

356. Cf. chapter 1, p. 42 and especially note 115.

357. House diary 6.3.19 in connection with the discussion with Lloyd George about an eventual sinking of the German Navy.

358. ibid. 10.3.19. At this also, the remark was occasioned by a discussion of an eventual sinking of the German Navy.

359. Tillman, p. 290. Benson kept House informed about these negotiations.

360. Daniels diary 27.3. and 31.3.19; Cronon, p. 380 and 381.

361. ibid. 31.3.19; Cronon, p. 381.

362. ibid. 31.3.19; Cronon, p. 381.

363. ibid. 1.4.19; Cronon, p. 381.

364. ibid. 1.4., 2.4. and 7.4.19; Cronon, pp. 381–385.

365. ibid. 7.4.19; Cronon, p. 384. Also cited in Daniels memoirs: The Wilson Era. Years of War and After. 1917–1923, Chapel Hill, The University of North Carolina Press, 1946, p. 382.

366. ibid. 7.4.19; Cronon, pp. 384–385.

367. Cecil diary 3.4.19.

368. ibid. 8.4.19. Italics mine.—The choice of House and Cecil for these negotiations seems natural when one remembers the tactical linking of the Monroe-Doctrine amendment and the navy-agreement. The negotiations about the incorporation of the Monroe-Doctrine and the formulation of this had taken place since Wilson's return, and besides House and Cecil also Wiseman, Miller and Balfour had participated at times (see for instance Miller diary I, 18.3.19, pp. 176–179, 180–188; 19.3.19, p. 191; several drafts in Wiseman papers 91/98; draft in Wilson papers, Ser. 5 A, "ca. April 1919", on this is written in House's handwriting: "Balfour and Cecil have

worked this out as a feasible article to cover the point you have in mind—if you approve, please let me know—EMH". The text of the British draft is "Nothing in this Covenant shall be deemed to affect any international engagement or understanding for securing the peace of the world such as treaties of arbitration and the Monroe-Doctrine" (this is almost the final text); Miller diary I, 22.3.19, p. 196; 24.3.19, pp. 199–200; 25.3.19, p. 204; 25.3.19, p. 203: from this entry it is evident that the above cited draft in Wilson papers (and an identical one in Wiseman papers) is of this date; the following day, Lloyd George made it clear that his condition for acceptance of the incorporation was a naval agreement (cf. note 355). When House brought this news to Wilson the President wanted House to discuss the matter with Lloyd George, but House seemingly preferred that Wilson took the negotiations himself (House diary 27.3.19). As late as April 7 House discussed the Monroe-Doctrine with Lloyd George and at this time the British Prime Minister once again mentioned that he would not accept the incorporation before a naval agreement was reached (House to Lloyd George 8.4.19 (not sent), House Coll. 12/32, cf. House diary 8.4.19. The letter is also printed in Miller, The Drafting of the Covenant I, p. 421). This conversation very likely contributed to Lloyd George's wish that Cecil should now engage House in direct negotiations. Cf. also IP IV, pp. 425–447.

369. Cecil to House 8.4.19, printed in Auchincloss diary 9.4.19; Miller, Drafting ... I, pp. 419–420; IP IV, pp. 433–435. Cecil wrote the letter after a conversation with Wiseman (Cecil diary 8.4.19). Seymour writes about the letter—without any reference to his sources—that Cecil wrote the letter "(a)t House's suggestion" (IP IV, p. 433).

370. House to Cecil 9.4.19, printed in Auchincloss diary 9.4.19. The contents of the letter were discussed beforehand with both Thomas W. Gregory (the newly retired Attorney General) and with David Hunter Miller, and the celar-cut precision was the work of Miller. (ibid. 9.4.19, see also Miller diary I, 9.4.19, pp. 229–230 and same, Drafting I, pp. 422–425, and also IP IV, p. 436).
Auchincloss thereafter brought the letter to Wilson, who gave his consent (Auchincloss diary 9.4.19; House to Wilson 9.4.19, House Coll. and IP IV, p. 436 and House diary 9.4.19), and Cecil, too seemed satisfied.—Seymour writes—without any reference to sources—that "(t)his letter (Cecil's) was discussed by the President and House, and it was decided that Wilson should authorize House to reply, agreeing to periodic consultation between the two Governments regarding naval building in the future, but intimating the modification of the naval programme already voted by Congress would not be considered" (IP IV, p. 435). But this must be Seymour's own conclusion based upon the actual course of events, because, actually we do not know anything about with what kind of authority House was negotiating in this matter. It is evident, though, that he did not take any steps without getting the President's acceptance beforehand. About Wilson's acceptance of House's answer to Cecil, he wrote in his diary: "I sent Gordon to the President with the letter. He seemed to think it was a little stiff and that the British would not like it. However, he made no suggestions as to change. . . ." (House diary 9.4.19).

371. House diary 10.4.19; cf. Cecil diary 8.4. (10.4)19; Auchincloss diary 10.4.19; Miller diary I, pp. 234–236.

372. "Memorandum of a Conversation between Colonel House and Lord Robert Cecil", 10.4.19, House Coll. 4/38. The memorandum is printed, with one omission (about the extreme standpoints of the naval people in both countries) in IP IV, pp. 437–438 and Cecil's letter to House of April 10 ibid. Seymour mentions—without any reference to sources—that Cecil drew up the memorandum "at the request of President Wilson" (IP IV, p. 437). But this commentary, too must stand on Seymour's own account. House's own version is this: "Lloyd George, as I anticipated, objected to my letter and wanted it to include ships still not under construction but provided for by law. Cecil had written me a letter covering this which he said he would deliver if I thought worth while, otherwise we could consider that it had never been offered. I declined to accept the letter and he took it back with him.

He then wished to know if I would be willing to have him write a memorandum of our conversation before sending it to the Prime Minister. ..." (House diary 10.4.19).

373. Upon a typed copy of Cecil's handwritten letter, House has written in his own hand (pencil): "I read this letter + memo. to the President tonight and he approved. EMH. April 10/19". House Coll. 4/38. Cf. IP IV, p. 437 n. The day before Wilson gave this approval, he had received a very elaborate memorandum from Admiral Benson, who argued, that "at least two approximately equal naval powers is absolute in order to stabilize the League of Nations. This fact should be recognized, and the United States should give it as a reason for building up and maintaining its Navy" (Benson to Wilson 9.4.19, Wilson papers, Ser. 5 A).

374. "... I did not show him the letters and memoranda which has passed between Cecil and me regarding our naval building program, but I told him of our conversation" (House diary 12.4.19). Daniels writes about this part of the conversation only that they "(t)alked about the naval programme..." (Daniels diary 12.4. 19). Cronon, p. 389. In his memoirs Daniels did not mention this either, but to the contrary he wrote: "The Navy Sea Battle in Paris over Naval strength was a draw. John Bull did not get from Uncle Sam his recognition of Britains primacy or agreement to cease the construction of a navy that would be the equal of the greatest in the world..." (The Wilson Era, p. 383). "... It remained for a future administration to scrap the capital ships Wilson refused to scrap ..." (ibid. p. 382).

375. Arthur J. Marder: From the Dreadnought to Scapa Flow. The Royal Navy in the Fisher Era, 1904–1919, V, London, Oxford University Press, 1970, p. 234. This is not only Marder's own evaluation, it is also the judgment of Warner R. Schilling, whose unpublished book: Admirals and Foreign Policy, 1913–1921 (New York, Columbia University Press, 1971?) Marder cites as "a convincing analysis", and whose views he accepts.

376. Marder, p. 224–238.

377. On April 12 Lloyd George proposed that the Germans should be invited for April 25. Wilson and Clemenceau accepted this proposal while Orlando wanted a solution of the Italian problem before the Germans were called in. And he only accepted after American promises, that the Italian problems would be taken up immediately (The discussions April 12–13, Mantoux I, pp. 231, 237–245). On April 15 Balfour (Lloyd George was temporarily in England) read a rather imposing list of the questions which were to be decided in the following 10 days, and among those were also the problems of the occupation of the left bank of the Rhine and the demilitarization of the right and left banks (Mantoux I, pp. 248–249). It is evident that all four statesmen wanted to demonstrate to their impatient peoples that something was at last happening (see for instance ibid. pp. 242–243).—The term "Alliance" is used in this—as in earlier connections—as a matter of convenience for the common front of Allied and Associated powers. About this element see also note 314.

378. Cf. Nelson, p. 236: "... The Rhineland negotiations simply marked time".—On March 28 Wilson had made the following proposal regarding the Rhine: "Proposal. Stipulations to be embodied in the treaty.

1. No fortifications west of a line drawn fifty kilometers east of the Rhine (as in the military terms already provisionally agreed upon).

2. The maintenance or assembling of armed forces, either permanently or temporarily, forbidden within that area, as well as manoeuvres and the maintenance of facilities *physical* for mobilisation.

3. Violations of these conditions to be regarded as hostile acts against the signatories to bhe (!) treaty and as calculated to disturb the peace of the world.
In a separate treaty with the United States:

4. A pledge by the United States, subject to the approval of the executive council of the League of Nations, to come immediately to the assistance of France so soon as any unprovoked movement of agression against her is made by Germany,—the pledge to continue until it is agreed *by the contracting powers* that the League itself affords sufficient protection".

(Wilson papers, Ser. 5 A). The Document is dated "28 mars (!) 1919", and has the following heading in handwriting: "Proposition initiale de Président Wilson". The same hand has also written the underscored words in the text cited above.— Wilson's standpoint "almost completely coincided with the stand taken by Lloyd George in the Fontainebleau Memorandum of March 25. As on other German territorial questions, at the end of March, Clemenceau faced an almost solid Lloyd George–Wilson front" (Nelson, p. 234).—On April 2 the French forwarded their proposed amendments:

*"Amendments proposed by France.*
1. No fortifications to the West of a line traced East of the Rhine (*in conformity with the annexed map) at a distance very nearly equal to the distance from the Rhine to the Franco-Belgian frontier.*
2. The maintenance and the assembling of armed forces, under permanent or temporary guise, shall be forbidden in this zone as well as any manoeuvres or the maintenance of any means of mobilization, *A force of local gendarmerie of a maximum strength . . . shall alone be authorized.*
3. Any violations of these conditions or of the *military, naval or air clauses* of the treaty of Peace, shall be regarded as an hostile act against the signatories of the treaty and as calculated to disturb the peace of the world.
   *If one of the signatory Powers considers that Germany has violated one of the foregoing clauses it shall have the right to notify the Executive Council of the League which shall proceed immidiately to a verification of the facts as stated. Germany agrees to accept the said verification executed in the interest of peace and to facilitate its execution.*
4. Agreement of the United States (and of Great Britain) subject to the approval of the Executive Council of the League of Nations to come immediately to the help of France the moment that any unprovoked movement of aggression *such as is defined in Article 3.* shall be directed against her by Germany,—this agreement to remain in force until it shall be mutually recognized *by the contracting Powers* that the League itself gives sufficient guarantee.
   . . ."

(House Coll. 26/52 D). The document is dated: "April 2, 1919", and a marginal note (pencil) to point 1 reads: "do not insist", and to points 2 and 3 "indispensible". Italics as in the original, the last omission mine. On April 4 the Rhine problem was discussed in the Council of Four (cf. above p. 193) in connection with the visit of the Belgian King.—The Saar compromise, naturally is part of the Rhine question in a wider sense.

379. The most convenient survey of the negotiations actually is Tardieu, La Paix, pp. 188–215.
380. Baker notebook 2.4.19; 3.4.19; 4.4.19; 7.4.19 and 9.4.19; Woodrow Wilson and World Settlement II, p. 53; Reading to Wiseman 9.4.19 and Wiseman to Reading 11.4.19 both in Wiseman papers); Jules Sauerwein (directeur des Services Étrangers au "Matin") "c. April 7.1919?", and Close to Sauerwein 8.4.19 (both in Wilson papers, ser. 5 A—Close was Wilson's private secretary).—Among other things, it was Lloyd George's remarks to "Le Matin", which had attracted attention. On the evening of April 7 R. S. Baker had a conversation with Wilson, and he wrote: "We had some talk of Lloyd George's position and the clear intimation that he is preparing to throw the blame for delay upon Wilson. "Well", said the President sadly, "I suppose I shall have to stand alone"." (Baker notebook 7.4.19).
381. Nelson, p. 281.
382. J.-B. Duroselle has emphazised that the period following the presentation of the Treaty to the Germans is characterized by the co-operation of Wilson and Clemenceau against the proposed amendments by Lloyd George. See De Wilson à Roosevelt, La Politique Éxtérieure des États-Unis 1913–45, Paris 1960, pp. 114–127, and same 'Wilson et Clemenceau' in Centenaire Woodrow Wilson, Geneve 1956, pp. 75–94.
383. Cf. above pp. 205–208.
384. "Memorandum on the amendments proposed by France to the Agreement suggested

by President regarding the Rhine Frontier", 8.4.19. Wilson papers, Ser. 5 A.—This memorandum, in a somewhat revised version Wilson sent to House 12.4., cf. below.

385. For the text of this see note 378.

386. From the note of March 28 (cf. note 378): The frontier of the German demilitarization east of the Rhine was to be 50 km. Wilson was against the demand for only a maximum force or local gendarmerie, as this would require inspection. He could not accept the inclusion of military-, naval-, and air conditions in point 3 (cf. note 378). He had nothing against the addition of "by the contracting powers" to point 4.

387. Wilson to House 12.4.19, Wilson papers, Ser. 5 A and House Coll. The memorandum Wilson forwarded to House (House Coll.) comprised partly a summary of his note of March 28 and partly his above given memorandum of 8.4.19 (with one exception: the reference to inspection). This definitive memorandum bears the same date as the covering letter: 12.4.19. The French note of April 2 was forwarded with the other papers.—House wrote in his diary: "At the request of the President, I asked Tardieu to call in order to read the riot act to Clemenceau, through him, regarding the left bank of the Rhine and the protection of France . . ." (House diary 12.4.19).

388. House diary 14.4.19, the quotation also in IP IV, p. 422.—Besides the Rhine, Clemenceau also wanted to discuss Syria, because he wanted Wilson to know a few things about the Anglo-French negotiations. Italy was discussed too, and House also got a promise from Clemenceau that he would accept the Hoover-Nansen plan regarding Russia, a promise he had hitherto refused to give. It was probably no accident that Syria was discussed, for already in a conversation with Clemenceau on March 20 House had called attention to the fact that "George did not want to determine the left bank of the Rhine question until the Syrian question was settled . . .". A connection which probably was no surprise to Clemenceau (Auchincloss diary 20.3.19).

389. House diary 15.4.19.

390. ibid. and House to Wilson 16.4.19. Wilson papers, Ser. 5 A and House Coll. At the same time House got Clemenceau's acceptance of the cessation of the French press-attacks upon the President and his acceptance too of realization of the Hoover-Nansen plan regarding Russia (cf. above p. 185).

391. Another series of top-negotiations were required before the definitive drawing-up of the memorandum was effectuated (see Nelson, pp. 240–248).

392. House diary 15.4. and 16.4.19; Auchincloss diary 15.4.19; Miller diary I, 16.4.19, p. 254; Baker notebook 17.4.19; Wiseman to Reading 18.4.19 (Wiseman papers); and McCormick diary 17.4.19.—McCormick remarked in this connection laconically: "Great change in sentiment in French papers towards President and United States. Colonel thinks due to his calling them down but really due to the fact that their people are satisfied with the final terms of treaty".—Together with the letter of 16.4. (cf. note 390) House also forwarded to Wilson a copy of the "Current Intelligence Summary-France" for April 16, 1919 (cf. note 390) with his own underscorings and handwritten commentaries in order to show the effect of his conversation with Clemenceau (Wilson papers, Ser. 5 A).

## Chapter 5

1. Allan Nevins: Thirty Years of American Diplomacy, Harper and Brothers, New York and London, 1930, pp. 475–476. For Birdsall and George cf. the introduction above, and chapter 4, passim, and see further below.

2. Lansing to Polk 1.5.19. Polk papers 78/11, copy in Lansing papers, Princeton.

3. "Conversation with General Bliss, May 19, 1919". Bullitt papers.

4. Nevins, pp. 475–476. The omissions are Nevin's.—The terms "upstairs", "the small upper chamber", "our late colleague" refer, of course, to House and his staff.

5. R. S. Baker notebook 30.4.19 and 1.5.19.
6. Cf. above p. 33.
7. James T. Shotwell's preface in Albrecht-Carrié, p. vi.—Albrecht-Carrié's: Italy at the Paris Peace Conference, from 1938 is still the fundamental account in one of the principal languages. Ivo J. Lederer's: Yugoslavia at the Paris Peace Conference, has, however, added to our knowledge of the diplomatic game, while Arno Mayer's Politics and Diplomacy of Peacemaking illuminates important facets of Italian domestic policy. Nevertheless, an up-to-date analysis of the Italian problem, based on Italian, French, British and American sources is sorely needed. The following is therefore only an outline.—See now also Dragan R. Zivojinović: The Emergence of American Policy in the Adriatic: December 1917–April 1919. East European Quarterly, 1967, pp. 173–215.
8. Nat. Archives, R. G. 256, 186.3411/208, 21.2.19; /220, 26.2.19; /225, Mar. (?) 1919; /226, 1.3.19; /227, Mar. (?) 1919; /232, undated; /234, undated; /263, 9.3.19; 277, 17.3.19; /292, 19.3.19; /297, 20.3.19; /301, 26.3.19; /328, 27.3.19; /355, 4.4.19; /384, 17.4.19; 486, 1.5.19; /530, 8.5.19; /551, 14.5.19; /554, 15.5.19; /561, 17.5.19; /593, 31.5.19; /598, 4.6.19; /634, 19.6.19; /644, 26.6.19; /665, 3.7.19; /42, undated; /44, undated; /48, undated; /49, undated; /51, undated; /52, undated; /54, 1.7.19.—The majority of these memoranda were written by Douglas Johnson.
9. "Black Book I". "Outline of Tentative Report and Recommendations Prepared by the Intelligence Section in accordance with instructions for the President and the Plenipotentiaries. Jan. 21, 1919". House Coll. 29/20; Wilson papers, Ser. 5 A.
10. As introduction to an undated description of "The American Line", we find the almost triumphant: "Delimination of the 'American Line" as furnished to President Wilson in January 1919 by the Chief of the Division of Boundary Geography, American Commission to Negotiate Peace, and as used by the President in all his negotiations with the Italian Delegation ...". National Archives, 186. 3411/143.—The American report has been studied and discussed by Albrecht-Carrié, pp. 90-96.
11. Albrecht-Carrié, p. 94.
12. ibid. p. 127. Wilson had already agreed to the Brenner-frontier (which far exceeded the recommendations of the American experts) during his visit to Italy, either because he felt himself bound by the Cobb-Lippmann memorandum or because of sheer and simple ignorance. Cf. Albrecht-Carrié, pp. 63–66 and Tillman, pp. 317–318.
13. Albrecht-Carrié, pp. 96–103 and Tillman, p. 316.
14. Fiume itself was Italian, but the suburb of Susak and the surrounding country were Yugoslavian. However, economic considerations were probably just as decisive for the attitude of the American experts: Apart from Trieste, Fiume was the only suitable port on the Adriatic coast. If both towns were in Italy's hands (and no one opposed Italy's acquisition of Trieste), the economy, not only of Yugoslavia, but also of the entire inland would be stifled, whereas if Fiume and Trieste were in different hands, healthy competititon would be stimulated. See for example, Memorandum of 18.3.19 to Commissioners from Seymour, Lunt, Day and Johnson, Doc. 28, Albrecht-Carrié, pp. 426–428; and "The Adriatic Negotiations—Another View" by Douglas Johnson, sent to Auchincloss 29.9.21, House Coll. 35/122, which indicates the degree to which Johnson's views were based on political considerations: the fear of Italian political and economic expansion in the Balkans.
15. National Archives, 186.3411/640; Polk papers 74/167. Wilson to Lansing 25.6.19. This reference is a memorandum on the Adriatic policy, which Wilson sent to Lansing before he himself left Europe.
16. The Bissolati-episode, cf. above chapter 2, pp. 91–93.
17. The mediation episode, cf. above, p. 101. The Yugoslavian offer of acceptance of American mediations was sent to the Conference on 11.2.19 and rejected by Italy on 17.2. (Lederer, p. 154).
18. Hoover to Wilson 12.2.19. Wilson papers, Ser. 5 A. See also Hoover to Bliss 19.2.19, Bliss papers.
19. Davis to Wilson 12.2.19, House Co., 29/106 H-2; Wilson papers, Ser. 5 A.
20. Cf. note 19 and Davis and Strauss to Rathbone 13.2.19, House Coll. 29/106 H-2.

21. Wilson to Secretary of the Treasury 19.2.19, Wilson papers, Ser. 5 A.
22. House diary 10.3.19, partly in IP IV, p. 370.—All three participants at the meeting were, incidentally, against giving the Tyrol to Italy, which, thus, clearly indicates that House was not informed of Wilson's dispositions in this matter.
23. "Notes of a Conversation between Colonel House and Signor Orlando. March, 12, 1919, at 10.15 am." House Coll. 31/15.
24. In the diary entry concerning this conversation House wrote: "Orlando called around 10 o'clock to confer upon the various phases of the Italian situation. They seem to look upon me as their "next friend". I foresee trouble for him because Lloyd George and Clemenceau are not sympathetic to their demands as the President and I, and we are nowhere near agreement with them....". House diary 12.3.19, partly in IP IV, p. 370.
25. Albrecht-Carrié, p. 117.
26. Albrecht-Carrié, pp. 117–183; R. S. Baker II, pp. 143–154; Birdsall, pp. 264–288; Gelfand, pp. 325–333.
27. On the contrary, Arno Mayer's attempt to make the conflict a political one, seems to me rather mistaken (Politics and Diplomacy . . ., pp. 695–697: One cannot write, that "significantly, these advisers of the House entourage—especially Miller, Auchincloss and Mezes—energetically opposed any concessions to Lenin at the same time that they advocated an accommodation with Sonnino" (p. 695), without at least reminding the reader that House of all people was the most ardent spokesman in the Delegation for a rapprochement to Lenin, while on the other hand Lansing, White and Bliss were against both a rapprochement to Lenin and a compromise with Italy. The whole affair was not that simple.
28. Birdsall, pp. 264–288.
29. Gelfand, p. 328.
30. Marston, pp. 119–120; Shotwell, pp. 200–202; the quotation is from Marston. For the ealier quarrels within the Inquiry, see above Chapter 2.
31. Miller diary I, 3.2.19, p. 107.—Cf. also the above cited conversation between House and Orlando, 12.3.19, and see Birdsall, pp. 271–272.
32. Miller diary I, 2.3.19, p. 157; Birdsall, p. 271 and p. 273.
33. Regarding the letters to Wilson 4.4.19 and 17.4.19 see further below.
34. Albrecht-Carrié, p. 120.—Mezes recommended, among other things, to give Fiume to the Italians, make the harbour a free port and "cede the islands on the eastern shore of the Adriatic immediately adjoining the territory on the Dalmatian mainland described in the latest Italian proposals ...". Mezes was a member of the Central Committee on Territorial Questions and therefore he was naturally entitled to make these recommendations, but he was probably not very loyal to the other experts when he did not mention that they did not share his opinion, Cf. Shotwell, pp. 200–202.
35. Albrecht-Carrié, p. 120.—The two memoranda is printed ibid. pp. 421–423 and 426–428.
36. Mantoux I, p. 114 and pp. 127–131. House diary 3.4.19: "Lloyd George as usual precipitated something akin to a panic by suggesting that the Adriatic question be taken up". Wilson seems to have been greatly influenced by a report from Fiume by Sherman Miles about the attitude of the inhabitants (cf. the allusion to this in Mantoux I, p. 129). Miles asserted, "that the people in Fiume desire autonomy of a greater or less degree, but that only propagandists who have no local interests desire absolute incorporation into Italy or Jugo-Slavia". "Summary of Report no. 16 by Lt. Col. Sherman Miles on Fiume", forwarded to Commissioners together with the report itself by "Italian Division: Section of Territorial, Political and Economic Itelligence", 26.3.19. Miles's report, which was sent from Fiume with direct courier, is dated 15.3.19. National Archives, 186.3411/301.
37. Mantoux I, pp. 132–138; Orlando to Wilson 3.4.19, Wilson papers, Ser. 5 A. Cf. Albrecht-Carrié, pp. 122–123, and Lederer, pp. 186–187.
38. R. S. Baker notebook 15.3.19.
39. The source (Auchincloss diary 19.3.19) only writes: "Orlando called on the Colonel

at twelve o'clock to tell him some of his troubles about the Dalmatian Coast. The Italians insist on Fiume though they have moderated their demand in some other respects".

40. "Notes of a Conversation between Signor Orlando and Colonel House, at 10 o'clock, Hotel de Crillon, on the morning of the 26th of March, 1919". A pencil note gives A. Hugh Frazier as the author. The conversation, which actually was about everything else than the Adriatic question ended upon this note:
   "Signor Orlando, before taking leave, asked whether he could not see Colonel House before the Adriatic question came up for settlement. Colonel House very readily assented to this. He took the opportunity of informing Signor Orlando that the President had a real affection for him.
   This feeling, Signor Orlando said, was reciprocated". (House Coll. 29/31).

41. Miller diary I, 16.3.19, p. 172; ibid. 22.3.19, p. 198; ibid. 24.3.19, pp. 201–202; ibid. 25.3.19, pp. 202–203.

42. Baker notebook 1.4.19: "He (Wilson) had seen Orlando separately and there had been much discussion of Italian claims".

43. Cf. above p. 189.

44. House diary 2.4.19.

45. Auchincloss diary 2.4.19.

46. Nelson, p. 185.

47. Auchincloss diary 2.4.19.—At the same time, Mezes had also learned that Wilson was willing to accept the Treaty of London line with regard to the Austro-Italian frontier (South Tyrol to Italy), but this in no way indicated that Wilson was willing to support the Italians against the Yugoslavs, to the contrary: "In fact it seems to be indicated that he definitely will not support them (the Italians)". Headlam-Morley to Crowe 3.4.19, Fo. 608/40/323. (Kindly lent me by Jørgen Sevaldsen).

48. The sources are the diaries of House and Auchincloss 3.4.19. Auchincloss writes: "Orlando came around about five-thirty and the Colonel attempted to settle the Fiume question with him on the basis of the principles which are guiding the President respecting Dantzig. Orlando is not at all sympathetic to this and the Colonel made practically no headway", and House himself writes among other things: "I had all the maps out, and Orlando and I went over the lines. He was not happy when he saw that the line ran west of Fiume. He declared Italy could never accept such a settlement. We would have little difficulty if it were not for Fiume. Why they have set their hearts on a little town of 50.000 people, with little more than half of them Italians, is a mystery to me". It also seems evident from what House writes that the two men continued their paying compliments to each other. At least, the Colonel very carefully quoted Orlando for the following remark: "I prefer talking matter over with my dear friend Col. H." (instead of going to the Council of Four to hear Trumbić's exposition of the Yugoslav case).—See also R. S. Baker notebook 3.4.19: "The Colonel had conferences today with Tardieu and Orlando and told them (as he assured me) just what the American position was—Thus, a bright, kindly little man, optimistic in the presence of tragic events!".

49. Albrecht-Carrié, p. 123.

50. Birdsall, p. 274.

51. Lederer, p. 187.

52. The letter is signed "Respectfully submitted", and the names given are Day (Balkan Division), Lunt (Italian Division), Seymour (Austro-Hungarian Division) Johnson (Boundary Geography), Young (Economic Division) and Bowman (Chief Territorial Specialist). Wilson papers Ser. 5 A, Baker III, pp. 278–280, Doc. 36. It is possibly worth noting that something akin to a draft of the letter is found in the House Coll. But it probably has its origin among Seymour's own papers? It is found together with a copy of Wilson's letter of thanks to Bowman of 18.4.19 (House Coll. 31/24). In the House Coll. is also located a "Memorandum for the President", dated 17.4.19, which evidently is a kind of outline of the content of the definitive letter. It bears the handwritten endorsement "Seymour" (House Coll. 31/43). And this memorandum again is almost identical with part of Charles Seymour's letter of

16.4.19 (Seymour, Letters from the Paris Peace Conference, p. 203) from "The claims of the Italians . . ." to ". . . bought at a price".

53. "April 4, 1919. From: Chiefs of the Italian Division, The Balkan Division, The Austro-Hungarian Division, The Division of Boundary Geography, and the Division of Economics. To: President Wilson. Subject: Disposition of Fiume". Wilson papers, Ser. 5 A.

54. R. S. Baker notebook 3.4.19: "Italian friends of mine rushed around this evening with the story that Orlando and the entire delegation were going to leave the Conference if they were not given Fiume. They are all wildly excited in the Italian way . . .".

55. Miller diary I, 5.4.19, pp. 225–226, and 6.4.19, p. 226.

56. Wilson papers, Ser. 5 A.

57. Doc. 33, Baker III, pp. 266–271. Cf. Miller diary I, p. 226; Albrecht-Carrié, on the other hand, has separated the two documents: Doc. 34 and 35, pp. 440–444.

58. National Archives, 186.3411/355.

59. R. S. Baker notebook 19.4.19.

60. Paul Birdsall has given a very penetrating account of this "revolt" by the experts (Birdsall, pp. 273–277). It is my opinion however, that it is possible to introduce a little more light and shade into the picture, and, furthermore, I don't agree with Birdsall's interpretation of the consequences of this episode for the relations between Wilson and House.

61. House diary 7.4.19.

62. House diary 9.4.19.

63. Albrecht-Carrié, pp. 124–125; Lederer, pp. 192–193.

64. Lederer, p. 193; see also Albrecht-Carrié, pp. 126–128.

65. National Archives 186.3411/374: "Report of the Conference between President Wilson and Mr. Ossoinack, Deputy of Fiume to the Hungarian Parliament held in the presence of Signor Orlando, April 14th, 1919, Paris".

66. "Memorandum concerning the Question of Italian Claims on the Adriatic", a pencil note upon ana ttached piece of paper has the text; "memo. sent to Italian Delegation April 14, 1919, made public April 30, 1919", Wilson papers, Ser. 5 A, R. S. Baker III, pp. 274–277, Doc. 35. Albrecht-Carrié, pp. 445 447, Doc. 36.

67. Meeting of the Council of Four 20.4.19, 10.00 am, PPC V, p. 98. The French version reads: "J'ai toujours pensé et j'ai toujours reconnu que l'Italie n'était nullement liée par les Quatorze Points. Mais, pour mois, je ne peux pas faire la paix avec l'Allemagne sur la base d'un principe et la paix avec l'Autriche sur la base d'un autre principe. Nous devons partout nous efforcer de tracer les frontières selon les lignes ethnographiques et nationales". (Mantoux I, pp. 295–296). Cf. Baker II, p. 133. For Italy's oral reservations during the pre-Armistice discussions see chapter 1.

68. House diary 15.4.19, partly in IP IV, p. 457. Auchincloss wrote about the conversation between House and Orlando among other things (diary 15.4.19): "The Fiume question is giving us a good deal of trouble but I think that eventually we will get it straightened out. Orlando is exceedingly popular with the Americans and particularly with our office".

69. Miller diary I, 16.4.19, p. 255. Auchincloss diary 16.4.19.

70. Miller diary I, 16.4.19, p. 255.

71. ". . . and David Miller with whom I conferred respecting the creation of a strange sort of an arrangement giving Fiume to the Italians and then taking it all away from them and putting the administration of the city in the hands of a commission of the League of Nations" (Auchincloss diary 16.4.19).

72. Birdsall, p. 275. Birdsall based his account, inter alios, upon interviews with several of the Experts who took part in the episode.

73. Letter from Charles Seymour 16.4.19, Letters from the Paris Peace Conference, p. 204.

74. Letter from Charles Seymour 19.4.19, ibid. p. 207.

75. Cf. above chapter 4, pp. 179–185.

76. Apparently there are no minutes of this meeting (17.4.), but there is an account of

the events in "Memorandum of Discussion at the Meeting of the Commissioners, April 18, 1919, Regarding Fiume", PPC XI, p. 156.

77. ibid. p. 156.—See also Lansing diary 17.4.19 for a conversation with Auchincloss, partly quoted in Birdsall, p. 275.

78. ibid. p. 156.

79. ibid. pp. 156–157.

80. ibid. p. 157.

81. The minutes themselves read (PPC XI, 154–155): "Colonel House observed that the question of Fiume would shortly come up for consideration by the Council of Four, and asked the other Commissioners' opinion in regard to a certain memorandum on this subject which he had sent down to them on the previous day. The Commissioners discussed at some length the whole question of principle involved in the settlement of the problem of Fiume, and finally came to a decision as to what, in their opinion, the ultimate disposition of this city, together with its immediate hinterland should be".

82. ibid. p. 157.—See also Lansing's account of the meeting, Lansing diary 18.4.19, partly cited in Birdsall, p. 276.

83. House diary 18.4.19, IP IV, p. 459.

84. In 1940 Birdsall had an interview with one of the six experts (the name is not mentioned), and he gave the following account of the House-Wilson conversation: "One of the Commissioners told a member of the expert group, that on the same day, House had put his compromise proposal to President Wilson, alleging that it was supported *by the experts*. Wilson, presumably having had the letter signed by the six experts, asked who "the experts" were, and House replied by naming Mezes, Miller, Beer and Shotwell. President Wilson sent a confidential agent to General Bliss to inquire further into the matter, and Bliss promptly sent for one of the six, who was asked the direct question, "Who are the experts?" The reply which went to Wilson evidently convinced him that an unfortunate ambiguity had confused the real issues, and Colonel House, for his part, abandoned this particular effort at compromise. . . ." (Birdsall, p. 276). It is, however, very difficult to put any confidence in the account, second hand as it is, and given with a delay of 20 years, even more so, as it seems rather unlikely, that House in his very unsafe position should have gone *so* far. (The italics in the quotation are Birdsall's).

85. Baker notebook 18.4.19.

86. Lansing desk book 19.4.19.

87. "Copy of letter signed by the Commissioners and sent to the President", 19.4.19, House Coll. 31/58; Henry White papers, Box 67; Bliss papers; National Archives, 186.3411/397.

88. "Memorandum for the President", 19.4.19, ibid. Cf. House diary 19.4.19 and Lansing desk book 19.4.19.

89. House to Wilson 19.4.19; the original in National Archives 186. 3411/396, copy in House Coll., printed in IP IV, pp. 460–461.

90. "It is a curious situation, for we (the six experts) who are the creation of Colonel House are in this case opposing what I must believe to be his policy. He was not overpleased at the memorandum of the "Lesser Three" (Lansing, White and Bliss) and Auchincloss was furious". Letter from Charles Seymour 20.4.19, Letters from the Paris Peace Conference, p. 208. See also Birdsall, pp. 280–283.

91. House diary 19.4.19.

92. For the several requests for a public statement, see the foregoing chapter, passim.

93. Tasker H. Bliss to Wilson 21.4.19, Wilson papers, Ser. 5 A; Bliss papers. In this personal letter to the President Bliss recommended issuing the statement *before* the break was a fact. At the meeting House had recommended discussing the matter with Clemenceau and Lloyd George "and being governed by their advice" (House diary 21.4.19). House repeated this advice on 23.4. (House diary 23.4.19). Wilson's manifesto is printed in Baker III, pp. 287–290, Doc. 38; and Albrecht-Carrié, pp. 498–500, Doc. 42. A copy, written on the President's own typewriter is in Wilson papers, Ser. 5 A.

94. Norman H. Davis papers; Wilson papers, Ser. 5 A.—See also Norman L 18.4.19, ibid.; Norman Davis to Wilson 23.4.19, Wilson papers, Ser. to Henry M. Robinson (Shipping Board) 28.4.19, ibid.; Norman Davis 29.4.19, ibid.; Wilson to Glass, 30.4.19, ibid.; Miller diary I, 12.5.19, pp. 30C

95. House diary 22.4.19 and 23.4.19.

96. Auchincloss diary 22.4.19; Wiseman to Reading 22.4.19, Wiseman papers.

97. R. S. Baker notebook 20.4.19.

98. Nevins, p. 475; Birdsall, p. 288, cf. above p. xxx.

99. Auchincloss diary 12.5.19; Miller diary I, 12.5.19, p. 301–302; ibid. 13.5.19, pp. 303–306; and Morgenthau diary 8.7.19. See about this discussion further Albrecht-Carrié, pp. 167–183 and Lederer, pp. 208–217. It is about the period 12.–18.5. after the return of the Italians. See also House diary 12.–18.5.19.

100. House diary 15.5.19.

101. Albrecht-Carrié, p. 144.—For the reaction in Italy see ibid., pp. 144–149, and Mayer, Politics and Diplomacy . . ., pp. 701–712.

102. Current Intelligence Summary—France, 24.4.19. Bullitt papers.

103. Great Britain, Daily Summary, 24.4.19, ibid.

104. Tillman, p. 325.

105. Mayer, Politics and Diplomacy . . ., p. 712.

106. About this, see the foregoing chapter, passim.

107. Grayson to Tumulty (c. Apr. 20, 1919?), Wilson papers, Ser. 5 A.

108. Current Intelligence Division, American Section, Weekly Review, 27.4.19, Bullitt papers.

109. Tumulty to Wilson 24.4.19, Wilson papers, Ser. 5 A.

110. Wilson papers, Ser. 5 A, 24.–30.4.19, passim.

111. Frank Polk was very categorical regarding this: "There is no question about it—The President's stand was approved even by the Republicans. The fact that they had to has infuriated them all the more. The only criticism seems to be from Italy . . .". Polk to Lansing 26.4.19, Polk papers, 78/9. See also H. A. Garfield to Wilson 26.4.19, ibid. 82/19 and 74/155; Wilson papers, Ser. 5 A. Reading to Wiseman 26.4.19, Wiseman papers.—Already on April 29, however, Senator Lodge sent an open letter to prominent Italian-Americans in Boston, in which he declared that he was backing the Italian demand on Fiume (Mayer, Politics and Diplomacy . . ., p. 714).

112. Tumulty to Wilson 24.4.19, Wilson papers, Ser. 5 A, also in Tumulty, p. 544. Two days later Tumulty sent one more telegram with a similar content: Tumulty to Wilson 26.4.19, Wilson papers, Ser. 5 A, also in Tumulty, pp. 544–545.

113. "President Wilson, staunchly upheld by all his fellow Commissioners at Paris, except Colonel Edward M. House, and by both his Far Eastern Experts, supported the Shantung position of the Chinese delegation against Japanese, British and French opposition. Moreover, at the council table, he waged a diplomatic offensive against Japan on the issue". Russell H. Fifield: Woodrow Wilson and the Far East. The Diplomacy of the Shantung Question, Archon Books, Hamden, Conn. 1965 (1952), p. xii.—This is the basic account. For shorter versions see for instance Birdsall, pp. 83–115; Roy Watson Curry: Woodrow Wilson and Far Eastern Policy 1913–1921, Bookman Associates, New York 1957, pp. 249–284; Beers, pp. 149–184; Tillman, pp. 333–343.

114. The above given survey is based on Tillman, p. 334.

115. See Orlando's analysis in Orlando to Fifield 25.10.49, quoted in Fifield, p. 295.

116. Fifield, pp. 291–292. Fifield's studies in Japanese archives has clearly shown that the Japanese meant what they said. On April 25 Wilson said to R. S. Baker: "The Japanese question worries him (Wilson). "They are not bluffers", he said, "and they will go home unless we give them what they should not have". "The opinion of the world", I said, "support the Chinese claims". "I know that", he said. "Especially American public opinion", I added. "I know that too", he replied, "but if Italy remains away and Japan goes home, what becomes of the League of Nations?". "He is at Gethsemane". (Baker notebook,

25.4.19). Lansing, on the contrary, thought the Japanese were bluffing. Beers, pp. 163–164.

117. Richard W. Leopold: The Growth of American Foreign Policy, New York, Alfred A. Knopf, 1962, pp. 372–373. Japan kept the promise on 4.2.22.

118. Fifield, p. 267.

119. Cf. note 113.

120. House diary 26.4.19, IP IV, p. 467.

121. Lansing desk book 26.4.19.

122. House diary 28.4.19, partly in IP IV, p. 467.

123. Fifield, p. 268; Curry, pp. 275–276 and 279.

124. Fifield, p. 271. The definitive compromise was reached only on 30.4.19.

125. Lansing memorandum: "Japanese claims and the League of Nations", 28.4.19, Lansing Papers.

126. Bliss diary 29.4.19.—House showed Bliss copies of the correspondence between Balfour and the Japanese delegates, which were the basis of the compromise. However, it is not possible to verify that he had seen the President. On the other hand he had a conversation with Balfour immediately before the Plenary Session, and among other things they also discussed Shantung, it therefore seems likely that he received the documents directly from the British Foreign Secretary (cf. House diary 28.4.19).

127. Bliss diary 29.4.19; Bliss to Mrs. Bliss 1.5.19 (the quotation is taken from this), Bliss papers; see also "Memorandum regarding General Tasker H. Bliss", no date, in R. S. Baker papers, Ser. I. Lansing prints Bliss's letter in the Peace Negotiations, pp. 230–233, it is also found in Wilson papers, Ser. 5 A. For Lansing's view of House see above p. 233, and for White's see above p. 216. Apparently, the Commissioners already at the meeting of April 26 got the impression that Wilson would follow House (Bliss to Mrs. Bliss 1.5.19, Bliss papers).

128. House diary 28.4.19, partly IP IV, p. 467. House to Wilson 29.4.19, IP IV, p. 470.

129. Cf. Baker notebook 30.4.19: "At noon I was able to announce that the Shantung question had been settled by the Big Three, though Colonel House told the correspondents at 6 o'clock that it had not been".

130. R. S. Baker notebook 1.5.19, cf. above note 5.

131. cf. above p. 230.

132. House diary 30.5.19.

133. ibid. 31.5.19.—Hankey began to "cover" the meetings of the Council of Four regularly from April 19, i. e. at a time, when the most important decisions about Germany had been taken. He had participated a few times earlier. We do not know if House has had any knowledge of the minutes taken by Mantoux. As mentioned above, a copy of Mantoux' minutes of the meeting 4.4.19 is found in the Wilson papers.

134. House diary 2.6.19; 4.6.19; 8.6.19; 9.6.19; Auchincloss diary 3.6.19 and 9.6.19.

135. House diary 2.6.19.

136. "Stenographic Report of Meeting Between the President, the Commissioners, and the Technical Advisers of the American Commission to Negotiate Peace, Hotel Crillon, Paris, June 3, 1919, at 11 o'clock am.", PC XI, pp. 197–222, especially p. 222.

137. Auchincloss to Polk 26.7.19, Polk papers 78/4.

138. W. H. Buckler to G. Buckler 10.6.19, Buckler papers; Henry Morgenthau diary 11.6.19 and 23.6.19 and 25.6.19; see also ibid. 6.5.19; 21.5.19; 8.6.19; McCormick diary 6.5.19; 23.5.19; and W. H. Buckler to G. Buckler 8.6.19, Buckler papers.

139. House diary 27.3.19.—House was elected at Wilson's request.

140. House diary 11.4.19, see also ibid. 30.4.19.

141. House diary 30.4.19.

142. House diary 12.4.19; see also ibid. 10.4.19 and 13.4.19.

143. ibid. 4.4.19.

144. ibid. 28.4.19.

145. ibid. 30.4.19; 2.5.19; 3.5.19; 4.5.19; 5.5.19 (IP IV, p. 477); 10.5.19; 25.5.19; 4.6.19; 9.6.19; 10.6.19.

146. Miller diary I, 12.5.19, p. 300.
147. W. H. Buckler to G. Buckler 8.6.19, Buckler papers.
148. Henry Morgenthau diary 25.6.19.
149. Lansing to Polk 4.6.19, Polk papers 78/11, copy in Princeton.
150. House diary 28.7.19.
151. IP IV, pp. 501 and 506.—About these meetings as well as about the mandateproblem as a whole, see Evans, pp. 203–215.
152. House to Wilson 14.7.19, House papers.
153. House diary 24.7.19.
154. Wilson to House 28.8.19, House Coll. 49/20; Polk to Lansing 2.9.19, Polk papers 78/14; House diary 4.9.19.
155. House to Wilson 26.8.19 and 28.8.19, Wilson to House 29.8.19. All House Coll., House diary 4.9.19.
156. House diary 21.9.19; 30.9.19; 21.10.19;—House left Paris 5.10.19.
157. House diary 21.10.19.

## Conclusion

1. Cf. below and Introduction p. 11.
2. Povl Bagge provides us with one of the clearest expressions of this line of thought: »We historians aim at describing and, as far as possible, explaining man's life in society throughout the ages with all the variety, contradiction and coincidence which the net spread out by the other social sciences is too coarsely meshed to catch. ...« Historien og de andre samfundsvidenskaber, Historisk Tidsskrift, 12 rk. bd. III, p. 466).
3. Baker notebook XXV, 23.6.19, cf. above Chapter 1, p. 28.

## Notes to Appendix I:

58. In this context it is interesting to note that exactly the same shift in the problems has been applied in the studies of the British appeasement policy of the 1930s, see Ib Damgaard Petersen: Nogle synspunkter paa aarsagsforløbet ved udbruddet af 2. verdenskrig, Historisk Tidsskrift, 12th ser. Vol. III, pp. 144–150.
59. New Haven 1958.
60. Princeton 1957.
61. The expression is Kennan's. cf. Kennan, cited from p. 93: "I see the most serious fault of our past policy formulation to lie in something I might call the legalistic-moralistic approach to international problems."
62. American Diplomacy during the World War, Baltimore 1934.
63. Mamatey, cited from p. 102. Mamatey's italics.
64. New York and London 1962. Reviewed in Historisk Tidsskrift, 12th ser. Vol. II, pp. 278–279.
65. New Haven 1959. The book has since been published by Meridian Books (Cleveland and New York 1964) under the title, Wilson vs. Lenin. Political Origins of the New Diplomacy, 1917–1918.
66. I have previously discussed this aspect of the book in Historisk Tidsskrift, 12th ser. Vol. III, pp. 122–123 and must refer readers to this, also as regards a detailed discussion of the author's method.
67. Wilson vs. Lenin, p. 139.
68. See below.
69. Wilson vs. Lenin, chapter 9: Wilson issues a counter-manifesto.
70. id. p. 341.
71. id. p. 352.
72. id. p. iv.
73. London 1968. (New York 1967).

74. Politics and Diplomacy . . ., p. vii.
75. As shown by Mayer in his first book (cf. note 66).
76. Politics and Diplomacy . . ., p. 16.
77. id. pp. 20–21. In the article, 'Historical Thought and American Foreign Policy in the Era of the First World War' in Francis L. Loewenheim (ed.): The Historian and the Diplomat. The role of History and Historians in American Foreign Policy, New York 1967, pp. 73–90, Mayer has convincingly deepened this, his Wilsonian interpretation, through an analysis of Wilson as historian. (Wilson had an academic career behind him when he entered politics). The point of this analysis is that Wilson belonged to the "New History" school (p. 73) and therefore: "Had he still been a Rankean, he would have made a fetish of the primacy of foreign policy instead of bowing to it as an unfortunate wartime necessity; he would also have viewed the present struggle as a conventional though geographically inflated struggle between and among monolithic sovereign states. However, as a New Historian turned statesman . . . he could not close his eyes to the fundamental internal social conflicts— . . . "the instinct of the time is social rather than political"—behind this world war. The war was the onrushing tide, and he looked for the silent forces that were lifting it. Presently the onslaught of the Right in America, the revolution in Russia, and the response to that revolution throughout Europe confirmed him in his diagnosis that the external war between the Associated and Central Powers was at the same time an internal struggle the outcome of which would be significantly influenced by the course of the war and the nature of the peace settlement" (pp. 80–81). This passage naturally also covers Mayer's own views, cf. Politics and Diplomacy . . ., pp. 559–565.—The traditional, Keynesian conception of Wilson as the naive idealist in the hands of the European advocates of *Realpolitik* has incidentally been challenged by Jean-Baptiste Duroselle on the basis of more traditional criteria: "Wilson joignait en effet à son ideal un grand réalisme tactique et une belle habilité manoeuvrière" (Pierre Renouvin et Jean-Baptiste Duroselle: Introduction à L'Histoire des Relations Internationales, Paris 1966, p. 301). Duroselle bases his view on an analysis of the negotiations in the Council of Four, as these can be studied in Paul Mantoux's minutes (Pierre Mantoux: Les Delibérations du Conseil des Quatre, I–II, Paris 1955; cf. J.-B. Duroselle: 'Wilson et Clemenceau' in Centenaire Woodrow Wilson, des Etats-Unis 1913–45, Paris 1960, pp. 114–127, especially p. 115).
78. Politics and Diplomacy . . ., p. 21.
79. id. p. 347.
80. id. p. 417.
81. id. p. 29, see also Historical Thought . ., p. 89.
82. The Economic Consequences of the Peace, New York 1920.
83. Peacemaking 1919, London 1933. Most recently published by University Paperbacks, Methuen, London 1964, reviewed in Historisk Tidsskrift, Ser. 12, Vol. II, p. 591.
84. cf. note 31.
85. Baker's correspondence on this can be found partly in Ray Stannard Baker papers, Library of Congress and partly in Frank Polk papers and Edward M. House papers, both Yale University Library.
86. Baker's handwritten diary is in Ray Stannard Baker papers, Library of Congress. Mayer has printed important sections: Politics and Diplomacy . . ., pp. 515, 571–575 and 699–700.
87. Woodrow Wilson and World Settlement, II (cf. note 31), p. 64.
88. cf. Politics and Diplomacy . . ., p. 29.—However, when Baker himself came to write the history of the Peace Conference (Woodrow Wilson and World Settlement I–III, cf. note 31), he partially departed from his thesis because his presentation primarily had a domestic political aim in America: it was intended as a defence of Wilson's policy and especially of the League of Nations.
89. For example, with regard to the interpretation of the appointment of the League of Nations Commission—although without Mayer referring to Baker (Politics and Diplomacy . . ., p. 363). The interpretation is one of the controversial points of Baker's presentation. (For the American debate on the Peace Conference, see Robert

C. Binkley: Ten Years of Peace Conference History, The Journal of Modern History, I, 1929, pp. 607–629, and Paul Birdsall: The Second Decade of Peace Conference History, id. XI, 1939, pp. 362–378). Further, with reference to the interpretation of the effect of Wilson's summoning of the SS. "George Washington" during the crisis in April (Politics and Diplomacy . . ., p. 698), on which more later.

90. Politics and Diplomacy . . ., Part Five, pp. 557–749.

91. The events in Budapest became known in Paris on 22 March.

92. Politics and Diplomacy . . ., pp. 488–520.

93. id., p. 488.

94. id., pp. 492–504.

95. id., p. 504.

96. id., p. 515.

97. id., p. 515.

98. The tense expectations and the subsequent broken illusions are reflected clearly, for example, in the press reaction in the period surrounding and after Wilson's return. (Intelligence Summary, France, Great Britain, United States in William C. Bullitt papers, Yale University Library).

99. Politics and Diplomacy . . ., p. 518, Mayer's italics.

100. id. pp. 519.

101. Politics and Diplomacy, p. 698.

102. Mayer himself refers to Woodrow Wilson and World Settlement, II, p. 57 ff.

103. See Cary Grayson (Wilson's personal physician and confidante) to Joseph Tumulty (Wilson's secretary, Washington) 10. 4. 19: "The French are the champion time killers of the world. The George Washington incident has had a castor oil effect on them all. More progress has been made in the last two days than has been made for the last two weeks." (Wilson papers, Series 5 A, Library of Congress). Grayson's telegram is in reply to Tumulty's sharp reaction, cf. note 111 below.

104. Alexander L. George and Juliette L. George: Woodrow Wilson and Colonel House. A Personality Study, New York 1964 (1956), p. 255, cf. Charles Seymour (ed.): The Intimate Papers of Colonel House, IV, London 1928, p. 419.

105. Woodrow Wilson and World Settlement, II, p. 64. cf. Mayer, Historical Thought . . ., p. 86 n–87 n.

106. cf. note 78.

107. Politics and Diplomacy . . ., p. 168, cf. note 68 above.—See also Historical Thought . . ., p. 81.

108. Politics and Diplomacy . . , chapters 18 and 19, pp. 604–672.

109. I hope later, in another connection, to be able to provide detailed proof of these postulates.

110. I hope later, in another connection, to be able to provide detailed proof for this assertion.—Tumulty-Wilson (Grayson) correspondence is included in Wilson papers, Series 5 A, Library of Congress Part of this has also been printed in Joseph P. Tumulty: Woodrow Wilson as I know him, London 1922, pp. 515–546.

111. Tumulty to Grayson 9. 4. 19. Wilson papers, Series 5 A.—It is, incidentally, noteworthy that Mayer himself in fact cites the above-mentioned telegram (p. 698), but draws no conclusions, merely writing: "In this instance, as in all others, Tumulty was first and foremost attuned to the home reaction to his chief's diplomacy" (p. 699). The crucial point here is, however, not whether Tumulty, but whether *Wilson* was "first and foremost attuned to the home reaction".

112. This is, of course, by no means intended to mean that consideration to the American situation was the only element in Wilson's decision to stay. Many other factors played a part, including especially the fear of leaving Europe to face the danger of revolution alone. What is decisive, however, is the order of priority of these factors.

113. cf. Mayers: Post-War Nationalisms 1918–1919, Past and Present, 34, 1966, p. 114.

114. New York, Oxford University Press, 1968. xii + 340 p.

115. Levin, p. vii.—It is solely foreign policy that interests Levin.

116. id. p. 1.—see also p. 2: "The crucial importance of Wilsonianism then, in the con-

text of twentieth-century American foreign relations, lies in the fact that the Wilson administration first defined the American national interest in Liberal-internationalist terms in response to war and social revolution, the two dominant political factors of our time".—cf. also p. 260.

117. id., p. vii.
118. id., p. 8.
119. Levin himself stresses his debt to Louis Hartz, Arno Mayer and William Appleman Williams.—id., p. vii.
120. "So far our discussion of the Paris Peace Conference has been focused almost entirely on the ideology and politics of the Wilsonian reintegrationist approach to Germany. Historical forces are, however, rarely without their internal contradictions, and if we are really to understand Wilsonian policy at Paris in all its true complexity, we must now complicate the picture by discussing the tension in Wilsonian theory and practice between the desire to reintegrate Germany and the desire to punish and control Germany. Yet even this is not all. We must also come to understand the relationship of this reintegrationist-punitive dialectic, played out in Wilsonian ideology and policy, to the larger Wilsonian program of constructing, under American guidance, a postwar liberal-international order safe from traditional imperialism and socialist revolution" (p. 154), and further: "It will become clear that the Wilsonian vision of a peaceful liberal-capitalist triumph over preliberal reaction, a triumph which was to make revolutionary-socialism unnecessary, was as central to the Administration's approach to the postwar politics of Eastern Europe and Russia as the same missionary vision had been to the determination of America's orientation to the German question at Paris" (p. 183).
121. It is perhaps important to note that, in his description of the "punitive" elements in Wilsonian policy (pp. 156–161), Levin takes almost all his examples solely from the period after Wilson's return, when he was on the defensive.
122. cf. note 78.
123. On the other hand, the authors agree that Wilson's ideal solution was the re-establishment of a Liberal Government à la Kerensky.
124. cf. Mayer, Politics and Diplomacy . . ., pp. 418, 424, 434, 449, 451, 463, 464, 465, 466, 473, 477, 478–479.
125. ". . . At the same time he (Wilson) gave Bullitt the green light to steal away secretly to Russia to sound out Lenin. . . . However, he (Wilson) lacked the courage and insight as well as the political and diplomatic support for a policy of positive accommodation with the Soviets" (id., p. 449).
126. id., p. 466.—Wilson was on his way to the United States.
127. id., p. 468: "Bullitt was no sympathisant or fellow-traveller. He had a reformer's instincts. . . . (He) knew if the direct interventionists had their way with regard to Russia they would also dictate the rest of the peace treaty along Carthaginian lines, with the concomitant result of either enthroning reaction or provoking revolution. On the other hand, a modus vivendi with Lenin was compatible with key tenets of the Wilsonian formula: the Russian people was entitled to choose its own form of government and the minority peoples were entitled to self-determination. Back of this plan was the unspoken assumption that indirect intervention would continue. . . . Whereas Lenin estimated that a truce would facilitate a survival of the Russian Revolution, Bullitt advocated it as an effective instrument of containment."—Note that it is, in fact, not Wilson's, but Bullitt's intentions that the author interprets.
128. id., pp. 478–479.
129. cf. Levin's comprehensive and convincing discussion, pp. 197–220.
130. For the following see Levin's discussion of the Bullitt-mission, pp. 213–220.
131. The result of the so-called Buckler-Litvinov talks in January 1919. It is by comparing the proposal brought by Bullitt with the result of the Buckler-Litvinov talks that Levin has been able to arrive at his new interpretation.
132. "Taken all in all, the evidence suggests that House and Bullitt were probably alone among the American Peace Commissioners in seeking to co-operate with the British in finding a *rapprochement* with the Soviets during February-March 1919,

on the basis of a *de facto* recognition of Lenin's regime in European Russia" (Levin, p. 215).—Mayer lays far less weight on House's role in connection with the Bullitt-plan; he talks only of the Bullitt-Kerr proposal (cf. note 128).

133. "In short, the Bullitt-mission was probably doomed to fail from its inception, because both Bullitt and House had structured the mission around the mistaken assumption that Wilson's intention was to use a Prinkipo conference as a way to recognize a moderate Bolshevik regime in European Russia" (Levin, p. 218).

134. cf. note 119.

135. William A. Williams is a Professor at the University of Wisconsin and at the same time publishes with a number of students—he is one of the founders of "schools" —a journal with the, by American standards, somewhat provocative title: "Studies on the Left". William's best known book is probably: Russian-American Relations, 1781–1947, New York 1952.

136. Cleveland and New York 1959. Just a couple of chapter-headings is sufficient to indicate the direction of the effect on Levin: The Imperialism of Idealism and The Rising Tide of Revolution.

137. The Tragedy of American Diplomacy, p. 67.

138. id., p. 81.

139. id., p. 82.

140. id., p. 75.

141. An Interpretation of American Political Thought Since the Revolution, New York 1955.

142. id., p. 35.

143. id., p. 66.

144. Hartz analyses this problem in chapter 9: Progressives and Socialists.

145. id., pp. 228–237, especially p. 234.

146. On this point, Hartz believes that the American Liberal reform movement (Progressivism) deviates decisively from the corresponding European movements (cf. note 145).

# Sources and Literature

For the account given above I have used both unpublished and published documents, papers and diaries as well as memoirs, biographies and special studies. The literature about the Paris Peace Conference is overwhelming—the last bibliography, Max Gunzenhäuser's mentions over 2000 titles—but all problems have by no means found a solution. The following only gives the titles of works directly used in the account. A short discussion of the unpublished documents, papers and diaries as well as the published source-editions is given below, while other problems relating to these and to the literature as a whole are discussed in the text or notes of the book itself.

## I. Bibliographies and historiographical essays:

Almond, Nina and Ralph H. Lutz: An Introduction to a Bibliography of the Paris Peace Conference; Stanford University Press, 1935.

Baehr, Harry W.: A Cycle of Revisionism between two Wars, i Donald Sheehan and Harold C. Syrett (eds.): Essays in American Historiography, Papers presented in honor of Alan Nevins; New York, Columbia University Press, 1960, pp. 271–286.

Binkley, Robert C.: Ten Years of Peace Conference History; The Journal of Modern History, vol. I, 1929, pp. 607–29.

Birdsall, Paul: The Second Decade of Peace Conference History; The Journal of Modern History, vol. XI, 1939, pp. 362–378.

Cohen, Warren I.: The American Revisionists. The Lessons of Intervention in World War I; Chicago and London, The University of Chicago Press, 1967.

Floto, Inga: Nyere synspunkter på Woodrow Wilsons Udenrigspolitik; Historisk Tidsskrift, 12. rk. bd. 4, (1969), pp. 107–138.

Floto, Inga: Tysk Debat om den Første Verdenskrig; Historisk Tidsskrift, 12. rk. bd. III (1968), pp. 111–128.

Gunzenhäuser, Max: Die Pariserfriedenskonferenz 1919 und die Friedensverträge 1919–1920; Literaturbericht und Bibliographie, Schriften der Bibliothek für Zeitgeschichte. Heft 9, Frankfurt a.M., Bernard und Graefe, 1970.

Leopold, Richard W.: The Problem of American Intervention, 1917: An Historical Retrospect; World Politics II, 1949–50, pp. 405–425.

Smith, Daniel M.: National Interest and American Intervention, 1917: An Historiographical Appraisal; The Journal of American History, LII, No. 1., June 1965, pp. 5–24.

Wüest, Erich: Der Vertrag von Versailles in Licht und Schatten der Kritik. Die Kontroverse um seine Wirtschaftlichen Auswirkungen; Zürich, Europa Verlag, 1962.

## II. Unpublished material:

The Records of the American Commission to Negotiate Peace, Paris, 1918–1919; National Archives of the United States, Record Group 256.

Of this very comprehensive collection I have used the material relating to the ORGANISATION OF THE PEACE CONFERENCE, and parts of the minutes of the daily meetings of the Commissioners which have been left out of the official Foreign Relations edition. I have also used material relating to the SAAR-problem and the ITALIAN question and I have seen the correspondence of WILLIAM C. BULLITT.

Records of the Department of State relating to World War I and its Termination, 1914–29; National Archives Microfilm Publications, Microcopy no. 367, Rolls 383–386. The National Archives of the United States.

Especially material relating to the exchange of notes with Germany.

Newton D. Baker papers; Library of Congress.

I have used the correspondence between Baker and Ralph Hayes, which gives a good view of the problems relating to the organization of the Commission.

Ray Stannard Baker papers; Library of Congress.

The Baker collection contains his diaries (NOTEBOOKS), his correspondence, as well as a great deal of the material he collected for his Wilson-biography, inter alia, memoranda of conversations with important persons. The notebooks are almost invaluable for the understanding of the most critical phase of the Conference.

Tasker H. Bliss papers; Library of Congress.

Bliss's correspondence with Mrs. Bliss, with Secretary of War Newton D. Baker and with the Chief of Staff General March has almost the character of a diary. But also other parts of the papers are of great interest.

Frank I. Cobb papers, AC 6161 in Wilson papers; Library of Congress.

Contain, inter alia, Cobb's diary during the Pre-Armistice negotiations and an interesting correspondence between R. S. Baker and Cobb's widow regarding this.

The diary of Josephus Daniels; Library of Congress.

This has been published in an exemplary way by David Cronon.

Norman H. Davis papers; Library of Congress.

Contain a great deal of material relating to reparations and economic questions, but almost nothing of a more personal character.

Leland Harrison papers; Library of Congress.

Robert Lansing papers; Library of Congress.

Lansing's papers contain his socalled "DESK BOOK", which for the period of the conference is especially valuable, because "the desk book entries assume a diary form, and include more personal matter than usual" (quotation from the catalogue). The papers also include a series of "CONFIDENTIAL MEMORANDA", in which Lansing put down his thoughts about situations and events, probably for personal use, probably with an eye to the future historian. His personal correspondence, which is also included in his papers, is, with a few exceptions, rather disappointing.

Henry Morgenthau (Sr.) diary; Library of Congress.

Contains much important information about House.

Henry White Papers; Library of Congress.

Woodrow Wilson papers; Library of Congress.

Of this important collection I have used the papers relating to the Peace Conference itself, as well as the period directly leading up to it. The collection is invaluable, especially regarding the critical phase of the conference, but personal material is scarce.

Bernard Baruch papers; Princeton University Library.

Contain a lot of material relating to reparations and economic problems. The personal correspondence is very disappointing, almost superhumanly discreet. It is interesting, though, that Baruch among the papers included in the bound volumes called "General Correspondence" also put copies of all the pages in Colonel House's diary where he, Baruch, was mentioned. There is no diary for 1919, and only a few entries for 1918.

Robert Lansing papers; Princeton University Library.

Contain, inter alia, copies of Lansing's letters to personal friends, and material for his book "War Memoirs".

The diary of Gordon Auchincloss; Yale University Library.
House's son-in-law wrote a voluminous and sometimes very personal diary during the Conference. It is important not only because of his own comments and the light he throws on the activities of both himself and his father-in-law, but also because he prints a lot of telegrams which he either sent or received, inter alia, his very important correspondence with Frank Polk. Auchincloss's whole way of writing reminds very much of House's, and his intentions probably were the same.

William H. Buckler papers; Yale University Library.
I have used the correspondence between Buckler and his wife Georgina. This correspondence has almost the character of a diary. Buckler was the half-brother of Henry White, and during the War he worked at the American Embassy in London, from where he sent reports to Colonel House. In January 1919 he held a series of conversations with Litvinov in Stockholm. Later on he was offered the post as America's first ambassador to Poland, but refused.

William C. Bullitt papers; Yale University Library.
Contain a diary (Dec. 1918–Jan. 1919), memoranda and correspondence, and also the daily press reviews for the Commissioners.

The diary and papers of Colonel Edward M. House (House Collection); Yale University Library.
This collection contains both House's voluminous diary, and his no less imposing correspondence (arranged alphabetically), as well as a collection called "PEACE CONFERENCE MATERIAL" which covers everything from private memoranda and drafts to official notes and reports. The diary has been discussed earlier in this book (cf. Introduction). The correspondence is also a valuable source even though the alphabetical organization is not always the most useful. "THE PEACE CONFERENCE MATERIAL" is important for the period ending at the middle of March 1919. Hereafter it clearly reflects the decreasing influence of the Colonel. (This becomes evident, through a comparison with the Wilson papers).

The Diary of Vance C. McCormick; Yale University Library.
In 1942 Yale University Library received a printed copy of the diary. McCormick, who was a personal friend of both House and Wilson made several important observations regarding the behaviour of House and Auchincloss during the Conference.

Frank L. Polk papers; Yale University Library.
During Lansing's stay in Paris, Frank Polk was Acting Secretary of State. His correspondence with Robert Lansing and with Gordon Auchincloss is important. Also the rather brief diary is useful on a few points. Polk and Auchincloss were close friends, but also relations between Polk and Lansing seem to have been very friendly, which at times makes the correspondence doubly revealing.

Sir William Wiseman papers; Yale University Library.
Especially important for the period before the Conference, and the first phase of the Conference itself. The correspondence with Lord Reading gives a good insight into the events on both sides of the Atlantic.

Other.
Regarding a few questions I was able to use material collected in French and British Archives by my two colleagues Karl Christian Lammers and Jørgen Sevaldsen. Further details are given in the notes.

### III. Published material:

#### A. Source-publications

Launay, Jacques de: Secrets Diplomatiques 1914–1918; Bruxelles et Paris, Brepols, 1963.
Contains Louis Loucheur's copy of Paul Mantoux's minutes of the Pre-Armistice negotiations.

Mantoux, Paul: Les Deliberations du Conseil des Quatre, I–II; Paris, Editions du Centre National de la Recherche Scientifique, 1955.
Mantoux was interpreter for the "Big Four", and the volumes contain the unofficial

minutes he made of the discussions in the Council of Four. For several of the most important of these meetings Mantoux is the only source.

Papers Relating to the Foreign Relations of the United States: The Paris Peace Conference 1919, I–XIII; Washington, Government Printing Office, 1942–1947.

> Contain, inter alia, the official minutes of the meetings of the Council of Ten and the Council of Four; the minutes of the meetings of the American Commissioners; as well as important correspondence.

Papers Relating to the Foreign Relations of the United States: Russia, I–III; Washington D. C., Government Printing Office, 1931.

Papers Relating to the Foreign Relations of the United States 1918, Supplement 1, The World War (in two columes) Volume 1; United States Government Printing Office, Washington 1933.

Papers Respecting Negotiations for an Anglo-French Pact; CMD. 2169, London, H. M. Stationary Office, 1924.

Pedroncini, Guy: Les Négociations Secretes pendant la Grande Guerre; Paris, Flammarion, 1969.

> Gives an account of the meetings of the Allied in Paris in the beginning of October, 1918.

Terrail, Gabriel (Mermeix): Les Négociations secretes et les Quatre Armistices, avec Pieces justificatives, Fragments d'Histoire 1914–19, V; Ollendorff, Paris, 1921.

> Contains an unofficial edition of the French version of the official minutes (Hankey's) of the Pre-Armistice negotiations.


B. *Memoirs, Biographies, Diaries, Letters, etc.*

Bagge, Povl: Johan Nicolai Madvig; København, Ejnar Munksgaard, 1955.

Baker, Ray Stannard: What Wilson did at Paris; Doubleday, Page and Company, Garden City, New York, 1919.

Baker, Ray Stannard: Woodrow Wilson and World Settlement I–III; New York, Doubleday, Page and Co., 1923.

Baker, Ray Stannard: Woodrow Wilson, Life and Letters, VII–VIII; New York, Garden City, 1927–29.

Bannister, Robert C.: Ray Stannard Baker. The Mind and Thought of a Progressive; New Haven and London, Yale University Press, 1966.

Baruch, Bernard M.: The Public Years; New York, Holt, Rinehart and Winston, 1960.

Blake, Robert (editor): The Private Papers of Douglas Haig 1914–19; London, Eyre and Spottiswoode, 1952.

Blum, John M.: Joe Tumulty and the Wilson Era; Boston, Houghton Mifflin, 1951.

Bonsal, Stephen: Unfinished Business, London, Michael Joseph, 1944.

Briggs, Mitchell Pirie: George D. Herron and the European Settlement; Stanford University Publications, University Series, History, Economics, and Political Science, Vol. III, no. 2, Stanford University Press, 1932.

Bullitt, William C.: The Bullitt Mission to Russia; Testimony before the Committee on Foreign Relations United States Senate of William C. Bullitt, New York, B. W. Huebsch, 1919.

Callwell, C. E. (ed.): Field-Marshal Sir Henry Wilson, His Life and Diaries, II; London, Cassell, 1927.

Creel, George: Rebel at Large; New York, G. P. Putnam's Sons, 1947.

Cronon, E. David (ed.): The Cabinet Diaries of Josephus Daniels, 1913–1921; Lincoln, University of Nebraska Press, 1963.

Daniels, Josephus: The Wilson Era. Years of War and after, 1917–1932; Chapel Hill, The University of North Carolina Press, 1946.

Fowler, W. B.: British-American Relations, 1917–1918. The Role of Sir William Wiseman; Princeton, Princeton University Press, 1969.

Freud, Sigmund and William C. Bullitt: Thomas Woodrow Wilson. Twenty-Eighth President of the United States. A Psychological Study; Boston, Houghton Mifflin Company, 1967.

Garraty, John A.: Henry Cabot Lodge. A biography; New York, Alfred A. Knopf, 1953.

George, Alexander L. and Juliette L. George: Woodrow Wilson and Colonel House. A Personality Study; John Day Company, New York, 1956.

Grayson, Cary T.: The Colonel's Folly and the President's Distress; American Heritage XV, Oct. 1964, pp. 4–7 and 94–101.

Grew, Joseph C.: Turbulent Era: A Diplomatic Record of Forty Years 1904–1945, ed. Walter Johnson I; Boston, Houghton Mifflin Co., 1952.

Lord Hankey: The Supreme Control at the Paris Peace Conference 1919; London, George Allen and Unwin, 1963.

Holt, Stull W.: What Wilson sent and what House received: Or Scholars need to check carefully; American Historical Review 65 (April 1960), pp. 569–571.

Hoover, Herbert: The Ordeal of Woodrow Wilson; New York, McGraw-Hill, 1958.

Lamont, Thomas W.: Across World Frontiers; New York, Harcourt, Brace and Company, 1951.

Lane, Anne Wintermute and Louise Herrick Wall (eds.): The Letters of Franklin K. Lane. Personal and Political; Boston and New York, Houghton Mifflin Co., 1922.

Lansing, Robert: The Peace Negotiations. A Personal Narrative; London, Constable and Company, 1921.

Lansing, Robert: War Memoirs of Robert Lansing; Indianapolis, Bobbs-Merrill Co., 1935.

Link, Arthur S.: Wilson: Confusions and Crises. 1915–1916; Princeton, Princeton University Press, 1964.

Link, Arthur S.: Wilson: Campaigns for Progressivism and Peace, 1916–1917; Princeton University Press, 1965.

Link, Arthur S.: Wilson the Diplomatist. A Look at his Major Foreign Policies; Baltimore, The Johns Hopkins Press, 1957.

Lloyd George, David: The Truth about the Peace Treaties I–II; London, Victor Gollancz, 1938.

Lloyd George, David: War Memoirs of David Lloyd George, VI; London, Ivor Nicholson and Watson, 1936.

Miller, David Hunter: My Diary at the Peace Conference, I; New York, privately printed, 1928.

Mordacq, General H.: L'Armistice du 11 novembre 1918. Recit d'un temoin; Paris, Librairie Plon, 1937.

Mordacq, General H.: Le Ministère Clemenceau, Journal d'un Temoin, II; Paris, Librairie Plon, 1930.

Murray, Arthur Cecil: At Close Quarters, A Sidelight on Anglo-American Diplomatic Relations; London, Murray, 1946.

Nevins, Allan: Henry White. Thirty years of American Diplomacy; New York and London, Harper and Brothers, 1930.

Nicolson, Harold: Peacemaking 1919; Constable and Co., London 1943 (33).

Palmer, Frederick: Bliss, Peacemaker. The Life and Letters of General Tasker Howard Bliss; New York, Dodd, Mead & Company, 1934.

Richardson, Rupert Norval: Colonel Edward M. House. The Texas Years. 1858–1912; Hardin-Simmons University, Abilene, Texas, 1964.

Roskill, Stephen: Hankey, Man of Secrets, I, 1877–1918; London, Collins, 1970.

Seymour, Charles: End of a Friendship; American Heritage XIV, Aug. 1963, pp. 8–9.

Seymour, Charles (ed.): The Intimate Papers of Colonel House, I–IV; London, Ernest Benn Ltd., 1926–1928.

Seymour, Charles: Letters from the Paris Peace Conference; New Haven and London, Yale University Press, 1965.

Seymour, Charles: The role of Colonel House in Wilson's Diplomacy, in Edw. H. Buehrig (ed.): Wilson's Foreign Policy in Perspective; Bloomington, Indiana University Press, 1957, pp. 11–34.

Shotwell, James T.: At the Paris Peace Conference, New York, The Macmillan Company, 1937.

Steed, Henry Wickham: Through Thirty Years 1892–1922. A Personal Narrative, I–II; London, William Heineman, 1924.

Tardieu, André: La Paix; Paris, Payot, 1921.

Tumulty, Joseph P.: Woodrow Wilson as I know him; Garden City, New York, Doubleday, Page and Co., 1921.

Viereck, George Sylvester: The Strangest Friendship in History. Woodrow Wilson and Colonel House; New York, Liveright Inc., 1932.

Willert, Arthur: The road to safety: A study in Anglo-American relations; London, Verschoyle, 1952.

Wilson, Edith Bolling: My memoir; Indianapolis, Bobbs-Merrill, 1939.

The Times; Marts--April 1919.


*C. Special Studies*

Adler, Selig: The Isolationist Impulse. Its Twentieth-Century Reaction; London and New York, Abelard-Schuman, 1957.

Albrecht-Carrié, René: Italy at the Paris Peace Conference; New York, Colombia University Press, 1938.

Bagby, Wesley M.: The Road to Normalcy. The Presidential Campaign and Election of 1920; The Johns Hopkins University Studies in Historical and Political Science Series LXXX (1962), no. 1., Baltimore, 1962.

Bailey, Thomas A.: Woodrow Wilson and the Lost Peace; New York, Macmillan, 1944.

Beers, Burton F.: Vain Endeavour. Robert Lansing's Attempt to End the American-Japanese Rivalry; Duke University Press, Durham, N. C., 1962.

Binkley, Robert C.: New Light on the Paris Peace Conference, I og II, Political Science Quarterly, XLVI, 1931, pp. 335–361 and 509–547.

Birdsall, Paul: Versailles Twenty Years After; Reynal and Hitchcock, New York, 1941.

Birnbaum, Karl E.: Peace Moves and U-boat warfare; Stockholm Studies in History 2, Stockholm, 1958.

Buehrig, Edward H.: Wilsons neutrality re-examined. World Politics III, (Oct. 1950).

Buehrig, Edw. H.: Woodrow Wilson and the Balance of Power; Indiana University Press, Bloomington, 1955.

Buerig, Edward H.: Woodrow Wilson and Collective Security, in Wilson's Foreign Policy in Perspective; Bloomington, Indiana University Press, 1957.

Buehrig, Edward H. (ed.): Wilson's Foreign Policy in Perspective; Bloomington, Indiana University Press, 1957.

Burnett, Philip Mason: Reparation at the Paris Peace Conference. From the Standpoint of the American Delegation, I–II; New York, Colombia University Press, 1940.

Cox, Frederick J.: The French Peace Plans, 1918–1919: The Germ of the Conflict between Ferdinand Foch and George Clemenceau, in Studies in Modern European History in Honor of Franklin Charles Palm, New York, 1956, pp. 81–104.

Creel, George: The War, the World and Wilson; Harper and Brothers Publishers, New York and London, 1920.

Curry, George M.: Woodrow Wilson, Jan Smuts, and the Versailles Settlement; American Historical Review, LXVI (July 1961), pp. 968–986.

Curry, Roy Watson: Woodrow Wilson and Far Eastern Policy 1913–21; New York, Bookman Associates, 1957.

Davis, George T.: A Navy Second to None. The Development of Modern American Naval Policy; Harcourt, Brace and Company, New York, 1940.

Deist, W.: Die Militärischen Bestimmungen der Pariser Vorortsverträge, in Helmuth Rössler (ed.): Ideologie und Machtpolitik, 1919. Plan und Werk der Pariserfriedens Konferenzen 1919; Göttingen, Musterschmidt Verlag, 1966.

Dickmann, Fritz: Die Kriegsschuldfrage auf der Friedens Konferenz von Paris 1919, München, R. Oldenburg Verlag, 1964.

Duroselle, J.-B.: De Wilson a Roosevelt, La Politique Extérieure des Etats-Unis, 1913–45; Paris, Armand Colin, 1960.

Duroselle, J.-B.: Wilson et Clemenceau, in Centenaire Woodrow Wilson; Genève, Centre Européen de la Dotation Carnegie, 1956, pp. 75–94.

Erdmann, K. D.: Adenauer in der Rheinlandpolitik nach dem Ersten Weltkrieg; Ernst Klett Verlag, Stuttgart, 1966.

Evans, Laurence: United States Policy and the Partition of Turkey, 1914–1924; Baltimore, The Johns Hopkins Press, 1965.

Farnsworth, Beatrice: William C. Bullitt and the Soviet Union; Bloomington and London, Indiana University Press, 1967.

Fifield, Russell H.: Woodrow Wilson and the Far East. The Diplomacy of the Shantung Question; Hamden, Conn., Archon Books, 1965 (1952).

Fleming, Denna Frank: The United States and the League of Nations. 1918–1920; G. P. Putnam's Sons, New York and London, 1932.

Forcey, Charles: The Crossroads of Liberalism. Croly, Weyl, Lippmann, and the Progressive Era, 1900–1925; New York, Oxford University Press, 1961.

Friedensburg, Ferdinand: Die geheimen Abmachungen zwischen Clemenceau und Lloyd George vom Dezember 1918 und ihre Bedeutung für das Zustandekommen des Versailler Vertrages; Berliner Monatshefte 16, 1938, pp. 702–715.

Gelfand, Lawrence E.: The Inquiry, American Preparation for Peace, 1917–1919; New Haven and London, Yale University Press, 1963.

Hankey, Lord: Diplomacy by Conference, Studies in Public Affairs 1920–46; London, Ernest Benn, 1946.

Hartz, Louis: The Liberal Tradition in America. An Interpretation of American Political Thought since the Revolution; New York, Harcourt, Brace and Co., 1955.

Hoffmann, Stanley (ed.): Contemporary Theory in International Relations; Englewood Cliff, N. Y., Prentice Hall, 1960.

(House, Edward M.) Philip Dru: Administrator. A Story of Tomorrow, 1920–1935; New York, B. W. Huebsch, 1912.

Keit, E.: Der Waffenstilstand und die Rheinfrage 1918–19; Bonn, Ludwig Röhrschied Verlag, 1939.

Kennan, George F.: American Diplomacy 1900–1950; Chicago, The University of Chicago Press, 1951.

Kennan, George F.: Russia and the West under Lenin and Stalin; New York and Toronto, Mentor Books, 1960.

Kennan, George F.: The Decision to Intervene; Soviet-American Relations, 1917–1920, II; New York, Atheneum, 1967 (1958).

Keynes, John Maynard: The Economic Consequences of the Peace; New York, Harcourt, Brace and Co., 1920.

King, Jere Clemens: Foch versus Clemenceau: France and German Dismemberment, 1918–19; Cambridge, Mass., Harvard University Press, 1960.

Lasch, Christopher: The American Liberals and the Russian Revolution New York and London, Columbia University Press, 1962.

Lasch, Christopher: The New Radicalism in America. 1889–1963. The Intellectual as a Social Type; Vintage Books, New York, 1967 (1965).

Lederer, Ivo J.: Yugoslavia at the Paris Peace Conference; New Haven and London, Yale University Press, 1963.

Leopold, Richard W.: The Growth of American Foreign Policy. A History; New York, Alfred A. Knopf, 1962.

Levin Jr., N. Gordon: Woodrow Wilson and World Politics. America's Response to War and Revolution; New York, Oxford University Press, 1968.

Link, Arthur S.: Woodrow Wilson and the Progressive Era; New York, Harper and Row, 1954.

Lippmann, Walter: U. S. Foreign Policy; Boston, Little, Brown and Co., 1943.

Livermore, Seward W.: Politics is Adjourned. Woodrow Wilson and the War Congress, 1916–1918; Middletown, Conn., Wesleyan University Press, 1966.

Loewenheim, Francis L. (ed.): The Historian and the Diplomat. The Role of History and Historians in American Foreign Policy; New York, Harper and Row, 1967.

Mamatey, Victor S.: The United States and East Central Europe, 1914–1918; Princeton, Princeton University Press, 1957.

Marder, Arthur J.: From the Dreadnought to Scapa Flow. The Royal Navy in the Fisher Era, V, 1904–1919; London, Oxford University Press, 1970.

Martin, Laurence W.: Peace without Victory. Woodrow Wilson and the British Liberals; New Haven, Yale University Press, 1958.

Marston, F. S.: The Peace Conference of 1919; London, New York, Toronto, Oxford University Press, 1944.

May, Ernest R.: The World War and American Isolation 1914–1917, Harvard Historical Studies vol. 71; Harvard University Press, Cambridge, Mass. 1959.

Mayer, Arno J.: Historical Thought and American Foreign Policy in the Era of the First World War, in Francis L. Loewenheim (ed.): The Historian and the Diplomat. The Role of History and Historians in American Foreign Policy; New York, Harper and Row, 1967.

Mayer, Arno J.: Political Origins of the New Diplomacy, 1917–18; New Haven, Yale University Press, 1959.

Mayer, Arno J.: Politics and Diplomacy of Peacemaking. Containment and Counter Revolution at Versailles, 1918–1919; London, Weidenfeld and Nicolson, 1968.

Mayer, Arno J.: Post-war Nationalisms 1918–1919; Past and Present, 34, 1966, pp. 114–126.

Miller, David Hunter: The Drafting of the Covenant, I–II; G. P. Putnam's Sons, New York-London, 1928.

Morgenthau, Hans J.: In Defence of the National Interest; New York, Alfred A. Knopf, 1951.

Morgenthau, Hans J.: Politics among Nations; New York, Alfred A. Knopf, 1958.

Morison, Stanley: Personality and Diplomacy in Anglo-American Relations, 1917; in Essays presented to Sir Lewis Namier, Richard Pares and A. J. P. Taylor (eds.); London, MacMillan and Co., 1956, pp. 431–474.

Nelson, Harold I.: Land and Power. British and Allied Policy on Germany's Frontiers 1916–19; London, Routledge and Kegan Paul, 1963.

Nevakivi, Jukka: Britain, France and the Arab Middle East 1914–1920; London, The Athlone Press, 1969.

Noble, George Bernard: Policies and Opinions at Paris, 191; New York, The MacMillan Co., 1935.

Osgood, Robert Endicott: Ideals and Self-interest in America's Foreign Relations. The Great Transformation of the Twentieth Century; The Univeristy of Chicago Press, Chicago, 1953.

Pares, Richard and A. J. P. Taylor (eds.): Essays presented to Sir Lewis Namier; London, Macmillan Co., 1956.

Parrini, Carl P.: Heir to Empire: United States Economic Diplomacy, 1916–1923; University of Pittsburgh Press, 1969.

Petersen, Ib Damgaard: Nogle synspunkter på årsagsforløbet ved udbruddet af 2. verdenskrig, Historisk Tidsskrift, 12. rk. bd. III, pp. 144–150.

Petersson, Hans F.: Power and International Order; Lund, Gleerup, 1964.

Renouvin Pierre et Jean-Baptiste Duroselle: Introduction à L'Histoire des Relations Internationales; Paris, Armand Colin, 1966.

Renouvin, Pierre: L'Armistice de Rethondes. 11 Novembre 1918; Paris, Gallimard, 1968.

Renouvin, Pierre: Le Traité de Versailles; Paris, Flammarion, 1969.

Ritter, Gerhard: Staatskunst und Kriegshandwerk, IV; R. Oldenburg Verlag, München, 1968.

Rudin, Harry R.: Armistice, 1918; New Haven, Yale University Press, 1944.

Rössler, Helmuth (ed.): Ideologie und Machtpolitik 1919. Plan und Werk der Pariserfriedenskonferenzen 1919; Göttingen, Musterschmidt Verlag, 1966.

Seymour, Charles: American Diplomacy during the World War; Baltimore, Johns Hopkins University Press, 1934.

Seymour, Charles: The House-Bernstorff Conversations in Perspective, in Sarkissian, A. O. (ed.): Studies in Diplomatic History and Historiography in Honour of G. P. Gooch; London, Longmans, 1961, pp. 90–107.

Sheehan, Donald and Harold C. Syrett (eds.): Essays in American Historiography, Papers presented in Honor of Alan Nevins; New York, Columbia University Press, 1960.

Smith, Daniel M.: The Great Departure. The United States and World War I. 1914–1920; New York, John Wiley and Sons, 1965.

Smith, Daniel M.: Robert Lansing and American Neutrality, 1914–1917; Berkeley and Los Angeles, University of California Publications in History, vol. 59, 1958.

Snell, John L.: Wilson on Germany and the Fourteen Points; Journal of Modern History 26, Chicago 1954, pp. 364–369.

Sprout, Harold and Margaret: Toward a New Order af Sea Power. American Naval Policy and the World Scene, 1918–1922; Princeton, Princeton University Press, 1943.

Stewart, Robert Sussman: Posthumous Analysis, The New York Times Book Review, 29.1.1967, pp. 3 and 42–44.

The History of the Times, 1912–1920, I; London, The Office of the Times, 1952.

Thompson, John M.: Russia, Bolshevism, and the Versailles Peace; Princeton, Princeton University Press, 1966.

Tillman, Seth P.: Anglo-American Relations at the Paris Peace Conference 1919; Princeton, Princeton University Press, 1961.

Trask, David F.: The United States in the Supreme War Council. American War Aims and Interallied Strategy 1917–18; Middletown, Conn., Wesleyan University Press, 1961.

Ullman, Richard H.: Anglo-Soviet Relations, 1917–1921. Britain and the Russian Civil War, November 1918–February 1920; Princeton, Princeton University Press, 1968.

Williams, William Appleman: American–Russian Relations, 1781–1947; New York and Toronto, Rinehart and Co., 1952.

Williams, William Appleman: The Tragedy of American Diplomacy; New York, 1962.

Wimer, Kurt: Woodrow Wilson's Plan to enter the League of Nations through an Executive Agreement, in Western Political Quarterly, XI (1958), pp. 800–812.

Yates, Louis A. R.: United States and French Security, 1917–1921; New York, Twaine Publishers, Inc., 1957.

Zeine N. Zeine: The struggle for Arab independence. Western diplomacy and the rise and fall of Faisal's kingdom in Syria; Beirut, Khayat's, 1960.

## Postscript:

I regret that my manuscript was finished (April 1971) before I was able to make use of Klaus Schwabe: Deutsche Revolution und Wilson-frieden. Die amerikanische und deutsche Friedenstrategie zwischen Ideologie und Machtpolitik 1918/19, Droste Verlag, Düsseldorf, 1971, and Howard Elcock: Portrait of a Decision. The Council of Four and the Treaty of Versailles, Eyre Methuen Ltd., 1972.

# Index of Names

*The names of Woodrow Wilson and Colonel Edward M. House are not referred to in the index. The notes are not indexed.*